Foundations of Biopsychology

Andrew Wickens

An imprint of Pearson Education

Harlow, England · London · New York · Reading, Massachusetts · San Francisco
Toronto · Don Mills, Ontario · Sydney · Tokyo · Singapore · Hong Kong · Seoul
Taipei · Cape Town · Madrid · Mexico City · Amsterdam · Munich · Paris · Milan

Pearson Education Limited
Edinburgh Gate
Harlow
Essex CM20 2JE
England

and Associated Companies throughout the world

Visit us on the World Wide Web at:
http://www.pearsoneduc.com

First published 2000

ISBN 0-13-010913-4

British Library Cataloguing in Publication Data
A catalogue record for this book is available from the British Library

Library of Congress Cataloging-in-Publication Data
A catalog record for this book is available from the Library of Congress

10 9 8 7 6 5 4 3 2
05 04 03 02 01

Typeset in 10 on 12pt Times by Hands Fotoset, Woodthorpe, Nottingham
Printed and bound in Great Britain by Ashford Colour Press, Ashford, Kent

CONTENTS

LIST OF FIGURES

PREFACE

I have long been interested in understanding the reasons why people behave the way they do, and as a young graduate (with a degree in psychology) the subject that I decided offered me the greatest scope in fulfilling my aim was biological psychology. It was, I believe, a wise decision. Nearly two decades on, I remain as convinced as ever that all our thoughts, feelings and behaviour are ultimately explainable in terms of physiological and biochemical events that take place in the grey-pinkish mass which we carry around in our head. The problem, however, is that the human brain also happens to be probably the most complex object in the universe, which makes unlocking its secrets an awesome task. But, there is a great deal to be optimistic about. Biological psychology (and the broader field of neuroscience) is a young discipline and no other area in science has grown as rapidly over the last 20 years. And this growth is set to continue at an even more frantic pace. It is no exaggeration to say that we are at the beginning of a revolution in understanding the brain.

Biological psychology is the study of how the brain produces behaviour. This definition may appear simple, but the content and methods of this endeavour make it one of the most demanding and multidisciplinary subjects of all. The study of biological psychology requires more than a passing understanding of anatomy, physiology, biochemistry, pharmacology, genetics, psychiatry and psychology (to name a few), and one could undoubtedly find a simpler subject to study. But, for someone who is seriously interested in behaviour this is not an option. Indeed, there is no other field in the behavioural sciences that is generating as much excitement, or potential to provide such powerful and insightful explanations of human nature. The Nobel Prize laureate Gerald Edelman has called the subject 'the most important one imaginable' because in his view 'at its end, we shall know how the mind works, what governs our nature and how we know the world' (Edelman 1992). And this is only one side of the coin, because with this knowledge will come the benefit of greater intervention into medical, behavioural and psychological problems. Put simply, the scope and potential for the development of biological psychology is enormous.

My aim in writing this book is primarily to provide an enjoyable introduction to biological psychology for the first-time reader who may not have any previous knowledge of psychology (or biology). A second aim is to make it concise enough so that it can be used to accompany a short semester course of around 10–12 weeks. This task is not without its difficulties. Biological psychology is a wide-ranging subject and one that many students find difficult, especially at outset. Perhaps it is the problem of having to learn new technical or anatomical terms, or the often heavy introductory emphasis on neurophysiology. I have tried to minimise these potential problems by using plain language as far as possible, and covering the topic of neural function in one chapter (the first) while attempting to embed it into a historical and narrative context which I hope makes it more enjoyable. The latter is a novel approach, but one that I feel will make the book much more accessible to the reader who is queasy at the prospect of learning the 'hard stuff' of biology.

But perhaps the feature of the book that will most appeal most to students is the inclusion of multiple choice questions at the end of each chapter. Not only will these provide a unique (and fun) means of monitoring one's progress in the subject, but they are also the types of question that are increasingly being used in many university examinations. There are 20 questions for each chapter, and to get most benefit one should attempt them in one sitting after completing the chapter (there is no time limit). A score of 11 is a pass (roughly equivalent to 40 per cent at first-year university standard); a score of 12–14 is good, and a score of 15 and above is excellent. Hopefully, they will also provide excellent revision, and reassurance that biological psychology is not so difficult after all.

Inevitably, writing a book of this size will reflect the author's interests and biases. There are several areas which merit inclusion, but which have been omitted due to lack of space (this includes, for example, sensory systems other than vision, the topic of pain, and recovery from brain damage). On the other hand, unlike some texts, this book contains a chapter on genetics which introduces some of the exciting new developments that are taking place in molecular biology and which are likely to have a profound effect on biological psychology in the coming years. There is no such thing as a perfect book, nor one that has all the answers and explains everything you want to know. However, this book should hopefully provide an enjoyable introduction to the biological basis of behaviour and a solid foundation for further study. If it whets your appetite to find out more, then it will have done its job.

Hopefully, I have managed to get across in these pages a little of the excitement and wonder that I feel when contemplating the brain and its many remarkable capabilities. Little by little the brain is giving up its secrets, and the one sure thing is that there are many more thrilling discoveries to be made in the future. I like to think that there is someone out there who, after reading this book, will come to the same conclusion as I concerning the 'truth' of human behaviour and seek to pursue it further. If that is your aspiration, then this book is dedicated to you.

Andrew Wickens
August 1999

ACKNOWLEDGEMENTS

The writing of this book has largely been a solitary affair although I would especially like to thank Martina Deery and Andy Hedgecock for their kind help in proofreading some of the chapters. I would also like to thank a number of people at Prentice Hall, both past and present, who have been instrumental in developing this project, particularly Tim Pitts, Jill Birch and Jane Powell. Finally, I would like to apologise to Roxanne for spending too much time at my computer.

1 An introduction to neurons, brains and biological psychology

IN THIS CHAPTER

- Ancient views concerning brain and behaviour
- The contributions of Descartes, Luigi Galvani and Ramon y Cajel
- The key breakthroughs in neuroscience that have taken place in the twentieth century
- The action potential
- How neurons communicate with each other
- An introduction to the brain and its various structures

The brain: first appearances

An isolated human brain is a pinkish-grey mass of tissue which at first sight is not dissimilar in appearance to that of a giant walnut. If held in the palm of one's hand, it is deceptively firm and heavy (an adult brain weighs about three and a half pounds or 1.5 kilograms) and greasy to touch. It may not appear to be the most complex object in the universe, but it probably is. Indeed, when holding a brain in our hands, or viewing it from a distance, it is difficult not to be moved by what we have in our presence. This structure once housed the mind of a human being – memories, thoughts and emotions; wishes, aspirations and disappointments – and the person's capability for consciousness, reflection and free will. Moreover, this organ has enabled the human race to become the most dominant species on Earth with all of its many artistic, scientific, medical and technological achievements. But what exactly is so special about the human brain? Part of the answer is undoubtedly its great complexity. Like any other part of the body, the brain is composed of specialised cells, the most important being **neurons** whose function is simply to communicate with each other (i.e. to receive and send information). It has been estimated that our brain contains in the region of 12 billion neurons – a figure so great that if you took a second to count every single one it would take well over 30,000 years (Gilling and Brightwell 1982). What makes the brain really complex, however, is the way in which its cells or neurons are joined together. Neurons rarely form connections with each other on a one-to-one basis, but rather a single brain neuron may project (or make connections) to over 10,000 other neurons. This means that for 12 billion neurons there may be 100 trillion connections (or synapses) and it is at these sites that much of the information processing of the brain takes place. This figure is truly astronomical – in fact, Richard Thompson (e.g. Thompson 1993) has even gone so far as to say that the number of possible synaptic connections among cells in the human brain is so enormous that it is greater than the number of atomic particles that constitute the entire universe. If you don't fully understand this logic, don't worry, nor does the author of this book – but it is certainly a lot of connections! However, one thing is clear and that is that the brain is so complex that it almost defies comprehension. But not quite. The study of the brain is one of the most rapidly expanding areas in modern science and part of this development is a quest to understand how its physical and chemical make-up can give rise to human behaviour. The brain may be complex but, as this book will show, it is neither unfathomable nor immune to giving up its secrets to modern scientific investigation.

What is biological psychology?

To understand what is meant by biological psychology it is helpful first to put the word 'psychology' under the spotlight. The term derives from the Greek words *psyche* meaning 'mind' and *logos* meaning 'reason'. Thus, 'psychology' means the reasoning (or study) of the mind. However, few psychologists would unreservedly accept this definition today. The study of psychology first emerged in the eighteenth century as a branch of philosophy that was concerned with explaining the processes of thought by using the technique of introspection (i.e. self-reflection). However, the problem with this method is that no matter how skilled its practitioner, it is by its very nature subjective and its findings cannot be verified by others. Because of this, a more experimental approach to psychology began to be developed in the late nineteenth century that focused on behaviour which could be observed and measured (e.g. Watson 1913). This general trend has continued to the present day and it is for this reason that most psychologists would probably define psychology as ***the scientific or experimental study of behaviour***. This does not necessarily mean that psychologists have ceased trying to understand mental or cognitive processes (they haven't), but rather that they generally try to adopt scientific and experimental behavioural techniques wherever possible to infer and measure their existence.

Psychology has now developed into a wide-ranging discipline and is concerned with understanding behaviour and mental processes from a variety of perspectives. As the name suggests, biological psychology is the branch of science which attempts to explain behaviour in terms of biology, and since the most important structure controlling behaviour is the brain, this invariably means that biological psychology is ***the study of the brain and how it causes or relates to behaviour***. Implicit in this definition is the assumption that every thought, feeling and behaviour must have a physical or neural basis in the brain. In fact, this is much the same as saying that the mind is the product of the brain's activity. Although there are some philosophical grounds for criticising this viewpoint (e.g. see Gregory 1981) it must nevertheless be the case that mind and brain are inextricably linked, and this is the main assumption on which biological psychology (and this book) is based.

To link the brain with behaviour, however, is a daunting task. To begin, the situation obviously requires biological understanding of the brain itself, and traditionally the two main areas of biology most relevant to the biological psychologist have been **neuroanatomy** (the study of how parts of the brain are put together) and **neurophysiology** (the study of how neurons 'work'). However, in the last few decades the study of brain function has expanded greatly and has attracted the interest of specialists from other disciplines such as **biochemistry**, **genetics**, **endocrinology**, **pharmacology**, **immunology** and **psychiatry** – to name just a few. Not all scientists working in these fields are necessarily interested in behaviour, although those who are have an important contribution to make to biological psychology. Consequently, over recent years, the researcher interested in the biological basis of behaviour has had to become acquainted with many other areas of biological science that lie outside the traditional domains of anatomy, physiology and psychology.

Largely because of the new influx of ideas and techniques, a number of different terms have arisen to describe the study of brain and behaviour. To the first-time student these terms can appear confusing. For most of this century, researchers interested in understanding brain and behaviour have been called physiological psychologists because they used 'physiological' techniques such as **lesioning** (the removal of parts of the brain) and **stimulation** (both electrical and chemical) as their main experimental tools. This approach was complemented by research on human subjects who had suffered accidental brain damage and the field was generally called **neuropsychology**. These terms are still widely used today although there has been a growing acceptance that they are now too narrow to cover the newer approaches to brain function that are increasingly being utilised. Because of this, others have argued for broader terms such as 'biological psychology' or 'behavioural neuroscience' to describe these areas of research (Davis *et al.* 1988, Dewsbury 1991). Whatever the arguments for and against these terms, they roughly mean the same thing – they are trying to give an appropriate name to the scientific discipline that attempts to relate the biology of the brain with behaviour.

Ancient historical beginnings

Among the first people to realise that the brain was the organ of the mind (and thus behaviour) were the Ancient Greeks. For instance, Plato (429–348 BC) proposed that the brain was the organ of reasoning – although not all agreed, and others (including his pupil Aristotle) believed that the brain merely served to cool the blood that was pumped from the heart! Although the human body was sacred and autopsies prohibited (the first known drawings of the human brain taken from cadavers were made by Andreas Vesalius in 1543), the Greeks were nevertheless aware of the basic shape of the brain (largely through animal dissection) and particularly struck by its **ventricles** – a series of connected fluid-filled cavities that were clearly seen when the brain was sliced open (see Figure 1.1). Because the ventricles stood out as one of the main features of the brain it is perhaps not surprising that they used these structures as a basis to formulate theories about how the brain worked.

One of the first writers to propose a theory of brain function based on the ventricles was Galen (AD 130–200), who is generally regarded as the most important physician of the Roman Empire. Galen believed that the heart was the most important organ of the body because it contained the *vital spirit* that gave the spark of life to the person. However, the vital spirit was also seen as the 'substance' of the mind and was transported to a large group of blood vessels situated at the base of the brain called the *rete mirabile* ('wonderful net'). Here the vital spirit was mixed with air (that had been inhaled through the nose) and transformed into *animated spirit* which was stored in the ventricles. Galen knew that the brain had four main ventricles: the first two are now known as the lateral ventricles which form a symmetrical pair inside the cerebral cortex, and feed into the third ventricle (located in the mid-part of the brain) which, in turn, connects to the fourth ventricle (found near the base of the brain). Using this anatomical knowledge, Galen came to the conclusion that the lateral ventricles were the sites of sensory and mental impressions; the third ventricle the site of reason, thought and judgement; and the fourth ventricle the site of memory. This theory was one of the

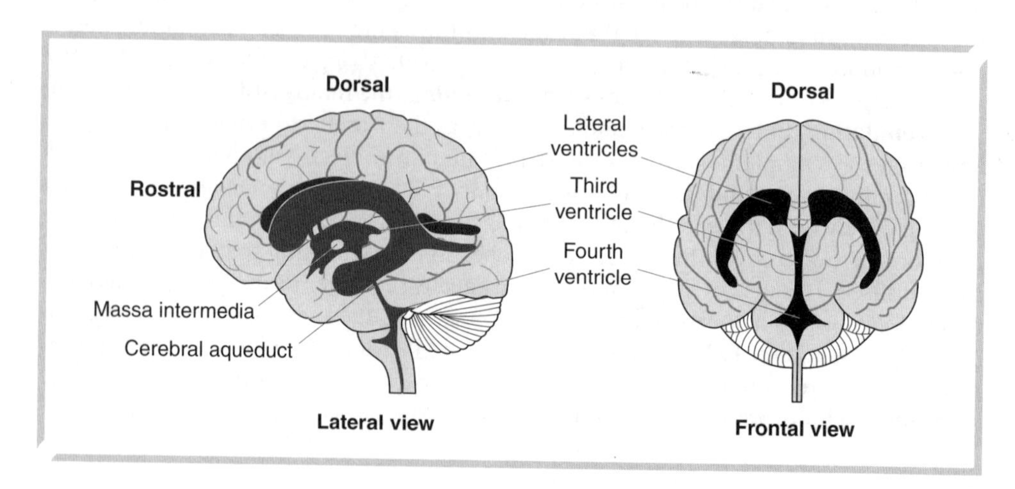

Figure 1.1 Lateral view showing the ventricular system of the brain. (*Source*: From Neil R. Carlson, *Physiology of Behavior*, 6th Edition. Copyright © 1998 by Allyn & Bacon. Reprinted by permission.)

first attempts to localise mental function to particular brain areas and was to remain largely unchallenged for the next 1,500 years (Blakemore 1977).

Rene Descartes

Descartes (1596–1650) was one of the most renowned philosophers of the post-Renaissance period, and well known for his attempt at resolving the mind–body problem. He believed (as did the Ancient Greeks) that mind and body were two entirely different things (this theory is known as dualism), and while the body was made of physical matter, the mind (or what could loosely be called the soul) was non-physical and independent of the material world. Despite this, the mind was clearly connected with the body and the question remained of how this relationship could be explained. In other words, how could the mind, which was non-physical, control the physical workings of the body? In his attempt to provide an answer, Descartes proposed the **pineal gland** as the site where mind and body interacted. His reasoning was simple: since the soul had to be a single indivisible entity it must therefore reside in a single structure of the brain, and one site which fulfilled this requirement was the pineal gland (most other brain structures are bilaterally arranged). Descartes also believed (wrongly) that the pineal gland only existed in the human brain (an observation that was in accordance with his view that animals did not have souls). Thus, it was reasonable for him to believe that the pineal gland was the place where the soul acted upon the body (Mazzolini 1991).

Despite this, Descartes also realised that a great deal of behaviour was mechanical and did not require mental intervention. In fact, it was during a visit to the Royal Gardens in Paris as a young man that Descartes began to develop this idea. The gardens exhibited mechanical statues that moved and danced whenever they were approached (this movement was caused by hydraulic pressure-sensitive plates hidden under the ground) and this experience led Descartes to reason that the human body might also work along similar mechanical principles. From this basis, he developed the concept of the automatic **reflex** which occurs, for example, when a limb is quickly moved away from a hot source such as a fire. To explain this response, Descartes hypothesised that a sensory nerve composed of a hollow tube containing *vital spirit* (this belief had not changed since Greek times) conveyed the message of heat to the ventricles of the brain, which in turn directed animal spirit to flow back through nerves to the muscles of the affected limb thereby causing its withdrawal. The important point was that this behaviour was seen as reflexive: the mind was not involved (although it felt pain and was aware of what had happened) and therefore not a *cause* of behaviour.

Descartes was one of the first to highlight the fact that the body worked according to mechanical principles and this realisation helped to lay the foundations for the later development of physiology and biology. Indeed, Descartes not only argued that functions such as digestion and respiration were reflexive, but he also believed that the same was true for many mental functions, including sensory impressions, emotions and memory. This idea was further supported by his belief that animals (which he accepted *were* capable of sensory processing along with emotion and memory) were simply reflexive machines that belonged to the world of physical phenomena. Despite this,

Descartes was unwilling to fully extend the mechanical theory of behaviour to humans (this was later done in the nineteenth and twentieth centuries). Instead, in accordance with religious teachings at the time, he argued that the mind was immortal and the main agent of thought and free will.

Descartes' theory was to have a lasting impact. Although it continued a dualist theory of the mind that had existed since antiquity, it nevertheless helped to focus attention much more clearly on the problem of how the mind might interact with a structure such as the brain. But, perhaps even more importantly, by regarding the brain as a complex machine, Descartes helped other thinkers to speculate about the inner workings of the brain without fear of contradicting religious dogma. This provided an impetus for experimental research, not least because some of Descartes' ideas could be tested. For example, as we have seen, Descartes believed that the nervous system controlling reflexes was a hydraulic system consisting of hollow tubes through which fluids (or animal spirits) flowed from the ventricles to the muscles. If this idea was correct then it followed that muscles should increase in volume as they 'swelled' with animal spirit during contraction. When investigators tested this theory, however, by flexing a person's arm in a container of water, no increase in its level was found.

The discovery of 'animal' electricity

In 1791, the concept of animal spirit as the cause of nervous activity was challenged by the work of the Italian Luigi Galvani who undertook a series of experiments on amputated frog legs which included the stumps of their severed nerves. Galvani found that he could induce the twitching of a frog's leg in a number of ways – as indeed was shown in one famous case where, during a thunder storm, he connected a nerve stump to a long metallic wire that pointed to the sky and obtained strong muscular contractions in the detached leg. He also found that he could produce twitching when he suspended the frog's leg between two different metals. Although he did not know it at the time, Galvani had shown that when dissimilar metals make contact through a salt solution, an electrical current is produced (this was, in fact, the first demonstration of the battery later formally invented by Volta in 1800). From his research, Galvani correctly reasoned that nerves are capable of conducting electricity and, moreover, the invisible spirit that produced neural activity was electrical in nature. Shortly after Galvani published his work, various ways of measuring electrical currents were discovered and, when these were applied to nervous tissue, electrical currents were indeed observed. Thus, the twitch of Galvani's frogs' legs signalled the end to hydraulic theories of nervous action and the start of a new chapter in understanding how nerve cells work (Piccolino 1997).

The discovery of the nerve cell

Although Galvani had shown that nervous energy was electrical, there was still much to learn about how nerves worked. For example, in the eighteenth century there was no understanding of what nerves looked like (other than they had long thin projections), and there was still a general belief that nerves were joined together in much the same way as blood vessels (i.e. through a system of connecting tubes). These beliefs persisted despite the fact that the microscope had been invented in 1665 by Robert Hooke, and was being used soon after by others such as Anton Von Leeuwenhoek to examine biological tissue. However, early microscopes were primitive and not able to reveal neural structure in any great detail, and it was not until around 1830 when better lenses were finally developed that microscopes were able to provide much stronger and clearer magnification. Even then there was the problem of how to go about preparing the tissue for microscopic work so that nerve cells could be distinguished from other types of tissue. To tackle this problem a number of staining methods were developed in the 1800s that selectively stained nerve cells. Unfortunately, these techniques also tended to stain all neurons indiscriminately, and the only way to visualise a neuron was to try to remove it from the morass in which it was embedded. Not surprisingly, with neurons being too small to be seen with the naked eye, this proved extremely difficult and was only occasionally (partially) successful.

In 1875, however, a major breakthrough occurred when the Italian anatomist Camillo Golgi (1843–1926) discovered a stain that allowed the visualisation of individual nerve cells. By accident, he had exposed his nervous tissue to silver nitrate and found that it stained nerve cells black. The result of this discovery was that cells stood out in bold relief and allowed all parts of the neuron to be clearly seen under a microscope. But, even more important was the fact that Golgi's technique only stained around 2 per cent of the cells in any given piece of nervous tissue. Rather than being a problem, this was a great advantage because instead of ending up with an undifferentiated mass of stained tissue, the technique gave rise to easily observable individual neurons. This method was particularly useful for examining brain cells which up to then had largely resisted visualisation. At last the nerve cell could be clearly seen! And, within a few years of Golgi's discovery the structure of many different neurons in the brain had been described. Indeed, much of the basic terminology which we now use to describe nerve cells (including terms such as neurons, **dendrites** and **axons** – see Figure 1.2) were introduced by anatomists at around this time (*circa* 1880).

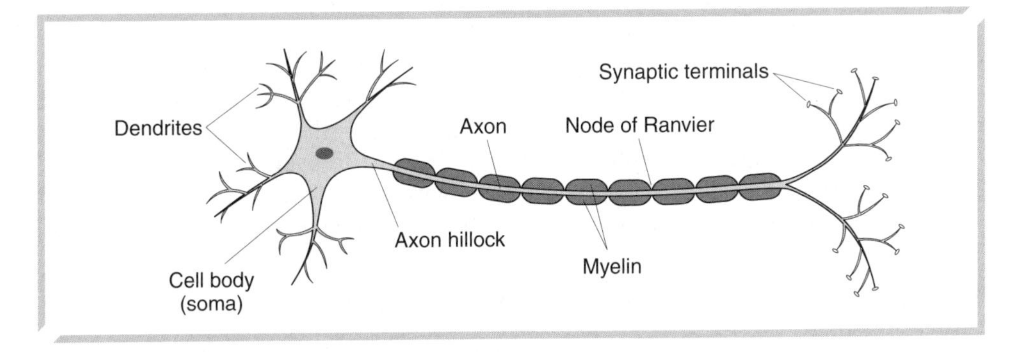

Figure 1.2 The main components of a typical brain neuron.

The person who put the Golgi stain to its greatest use, however, was the Spaniard Ramon y Cajel (1852–1934) who devoted virtually his entire career to studying brain cells stained using this technique and, in doing so, almost single-handedly described the neural structure of almost every part of the brain. For example, he showed that the brain contained a great variety of cells with different characteristics. Although some cells had short axons that projected to cells within the same structure (now known as **interneurons**), others had long axons that often formed bundles (or pathways) that projected to distant brain regions. Furthermore, Ramon y Cajel showed that the brain was not simply a random jumble of nerve cells as had been previously believed, but a highly organised and intricate structure made of different regions and separate nuclei (groups of cell bodies). Indeed, the basic structure of the human brain and its various components was the same for everybody. Ramon y Cajel even helped explain how neurons worked. For example, he realised that neurons received input via their dendrites and, in turn, they projected information along their cable-like pathways called axons (see Figure 1.4 below). Thus, he was one of the first to understand how information might travel throughout the neural circuits of the brain.

Perhaps, Ramon y Cajel's most important contribution to neuroanatomy, however, was his discovery that nerve cells were separate and individual units. Previously, it had been believed that neurons were joined together in a network of tubes which allowed messages to be passed from cell to cell without interruption. In fact, Golgi himself was a strong advocate of this theory. However, Ramon y Cajel proved that nerve cells were not joined in this way. Instead he showed that axon terminals ended very close to the neurons (or dendrites) to which they projected – but did not touch. In other words, each neuron was an individual unit that was physically separated from its neighbour by a very small gap (these gaps were called **synapses** in 1897 by Charles Sherrington). This finding raised several important new questions, including the problem of how neurons could communicate across the synapse, and how this message could generate a new electrical signal in the receiving neuron.

Following Golgi's discovery many other staining techniques were developed which enabled investigators to examine nerve cells in more detail. For example, some stains were able to selectively stain cell bodies (the **soma**), whereas others stained the axons (or rather their **myelin** covering) allowing neural pathways in the brain to be traced. In other instances, staining techniques could be combined with lesioning methods to provide further information (e.g. axonal pathways could be traced by destroying neurons in one part of the brain and staining the degenerative extensions of the same cells that projected elsewhere in the brain). By the turn of the century the study of neuroanatomy had become an established discipline (Shepherd 1991). Moreover, this subject provided one of the pillars on which physiological psychology is based, for without knowledge of brain structure and organisation, very little can be said about how it produces behaviour.

The discovery of chemical transmission

One of the most important questions that followed from Ramon y Cajel's work concerned the nature of the message that flowed across the synapse from the **presynaptic** (projecting) to the **postsynaptic** (recipient) neuron. From the time of Galvani, scientists had known that neurons were electrical in nature, but what about synapses? Did an electrical current jump across the tiny synaptic gap, or was there some other means of communication? As early as 1877 it had been suggested that chemical transmission might be the answer, and in 1905 it was found that the application of adrenaline to nervous tissue produced similar effects to electrical stimulation. However, the crucial experiment that proved the existence of chemical transmission was performed by Otto Loewi in 1921. This experiment has now become part of pharmacological folklore. On the night of Easter Saturday (1921) Loewi awoke from a sleep and wrote down the details of an experiment that he had just dreamed about. He then went back to sleep, but upon waking was unable to decipher the notes he had written. The next night he awoke at 3 o' clock in the morning with the idea back in his mind, and this time he went straight to the laboratory to perform his experiment. Two hours later, the chemical transmission of the nervous impulse had essentially been proved (Finger 1994).

In his experiment, Loewi used frog hearts which are similar to our own in that they are supplied by two different peripheral nerves – the sympathetic nerve that excites the heart and makes it beat more rapidly, and the parasympathetic nerve (sometimes called the vagus nerve) which slows it down. Loewi used two hearts: one with the sympathetic and vagus nerve intact, and one with the nerves removed. He placed the intact heart in a fluid bath and stimulated its vagus nerve causing its beat to slow down. Loewi then collected the fluid surrounding this heart and applied it to the second, and found that this solution also caused its beat to slow down. The results could only mean one thing – the fluid contained a substance (not electricity!) that was secreted by the stimulated heart (Figure 1.3). Later analyses by Sir Henry Dale and his colleagues showed that this substance was acetylcholine, now known to be one of the most important neurotransmitters used by the peripheral and central nervous systems.

It is now well established that neurons do indeed communicate with each other by chemical means, and the series of events that take place to produce this transmission is as follows: (1) the axon terminals of the cell sending the message (the presynaptic neuron) in response to an electrical signal called an **action potential** (see later) secretes a **neurotransmitter** that (2) diffuses across the synaptic gap which then (3) acts on the next nerve cell (or postsynaptic neuron) at special sites called **receptors** (which are sensitive to a particular transmitter). Receptor activation then acts (4) to excite or inhibit the electrical potential of the (postsynaptic) neuron. If this neuron is excited past a certain level, it then (5) generates an electrical signal that is passed down the axon leading to neurotransmitter release, and the whole process begins again.

It has not been an easy task to identify neurotransmitters and, by 1970, only six had been proven beyond doubt to exist in the brain: **noradrenaline**, **dopamine**, **serotonin**, **GABA**, **acetylcholine** and **glutamate** (these will be discussed in much more detail in the later pages of this book). However, the last couple of decades have witnessed the identification of many new neurochemicals, some of which are classical neurotransmitters (as above), and others as **neuromodulators** whose role is to 'modulate' the effect of transmitters. (To make things even more complicated, some neurons may even release gases such as nitric oxide.) There has also been a growing awareness that neurons do not

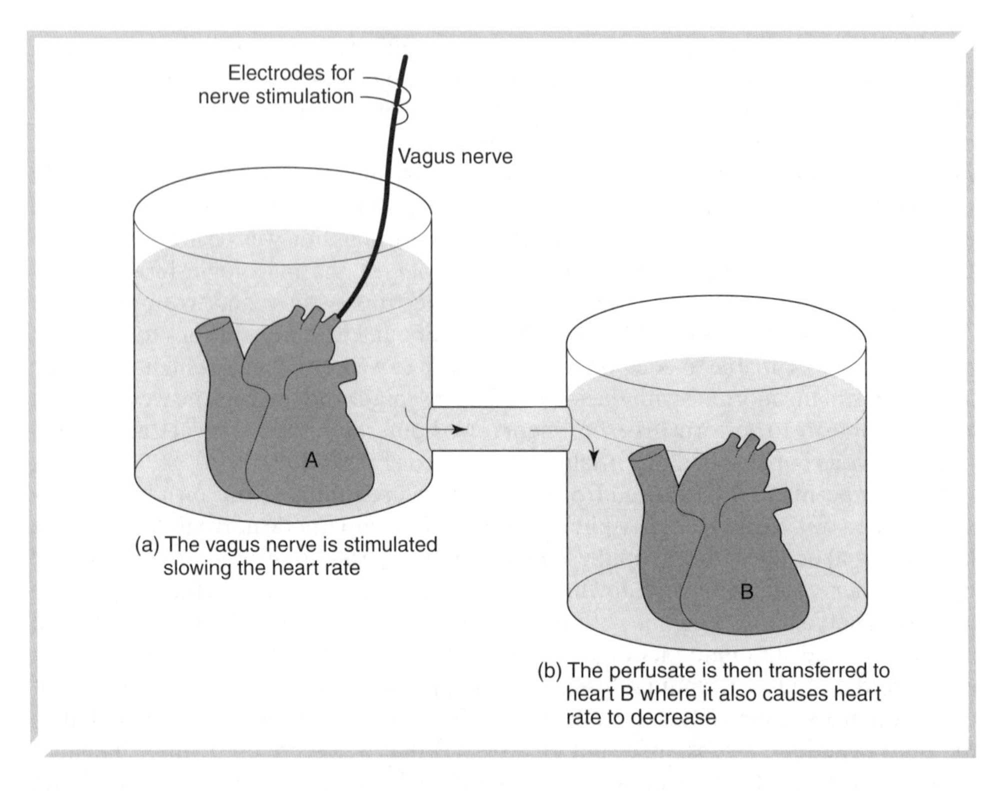

Figure 1.3 Loewi's experimental set-up showing that nerves send messages by releasing chemical substances.

release just one type of neurotransmitter as had been previously thought (this principle was known as Dales Law), but rather they release several different substances in a neurochemical cocktail. Considering that any given neuron may receive input from literally thousands of other neurons releasing a variety of neurotransmitters (this, of course, requires the receiving cell to contain many different types of receptor), it can be seen that the nature of the chemical information crossing the synapse and affecting the postsynaptic neuron is very complex indeed (see Table 1.1).

The discovery of chemical synaptic transmission by Loewi provides one of the pivotal points in the history of biological science. One reason was that it immediately suggested a way of modifying brain function (and behaviour) by the development of drugs that could mimic or block the effects of neurotransmitters on neurons (a drug that mimics the action of a neurotransmitter at its receptor is known as an **agonist**, and one that blocks its action is known as an **antagonist** – see Figure 1.5). Indeed, this possibility has been realised with the development of drugs including those that can be used to treat organic brain disorders such as Parkinson's disease (see Chapter 3) and various types of mental illness such as depression or schizophrenia (see Chapter 10). In addition, more

Table 1.1 Some of the neurotransmitters most commonly found in the central nervous system

Monoamines (each contains a NH_2 group in its chemical structure)
Acetylcholine (ACh)
Adenosine
Catecholamines
Noradrenaline (NA)
Dopamine (DA)
Adrenaline
Histamine
Indolamines
Serotonin (5-HT)

Amino acids
Aspartate
Gamma-aminobutyric acid (GABA)
Glycine
Glutamate

Peptide neurotransmitters (chains of amino acids)
Cholecystokinin
Morphine-like (opioid) substances
Leu-enkephalin
Met-enkephalin
β-endorphin
Neuropeptide Y
Oxytocin
Somatostatin
Substance P
Vasoactive intestinal protein
Vasopressin

recent histochemical advances have made it possible to visualise neurotransmitters in nerve endings, thereby allowing chemical pathways in the brain to be mapped out (see Box 1.2 below).

Neuronal conduction

By the early part of this century biologists knew that neurons were capable of generating electrical currents, but they did not know the finer details of how the impulse was created or conducted. The main stumbling block was the difficulty of recording from the neuron or trying to follow the proposed electrical discharge along the axon. Although biologists had at their disposal recording electrodes with very fine tips, along with oscilloscopes and amplifiers that could greatly magnify minute electrical charges, neurons were simply too small to enable this type of experiment to take place. That was until 1936 when John Z.Young working in Oxford discovered a neuron, located in the body of the squid, that had an axon that was about 1 mm in diameter (this was about 100

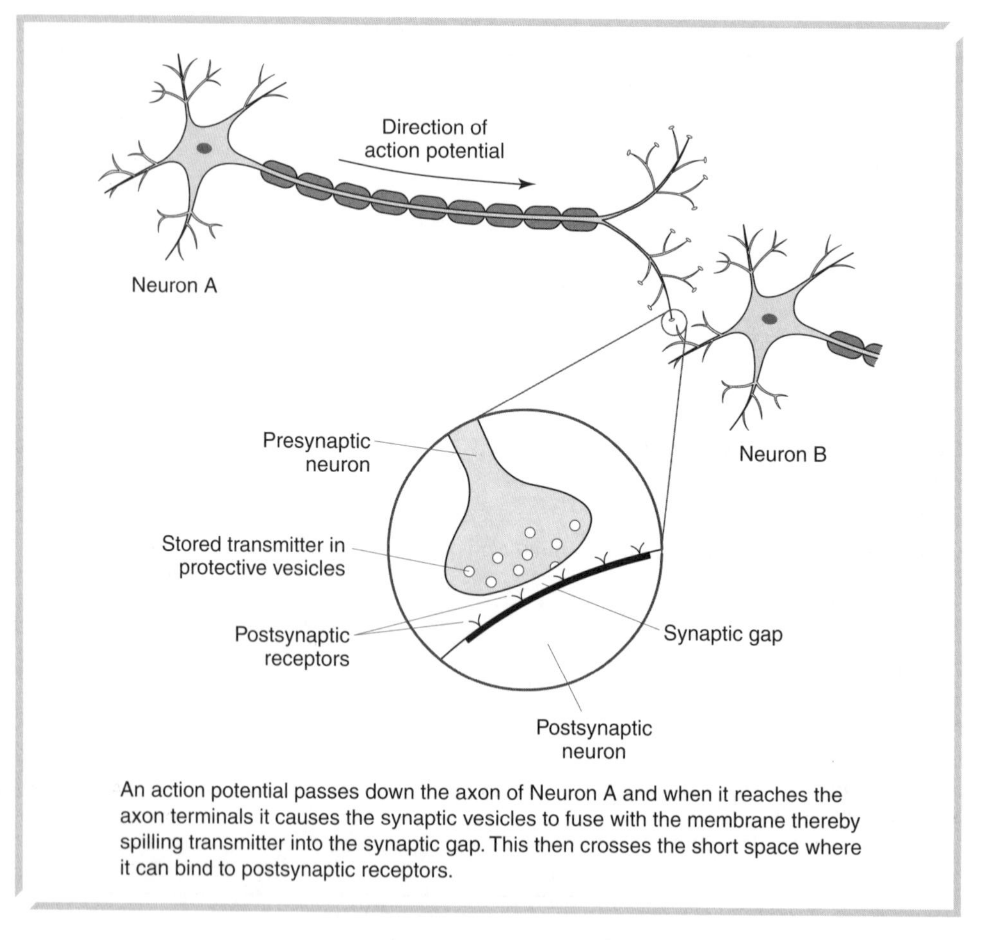

Figure 1.4 Chemical transmission at the synapse.

to 1,000 times larger than a typical mammalian axon). Not only was this axon sufficiently large to allow the insertion of a stimulating or recording electrode, but it could also be removed from the squid's body and kept alive for several hours, thus allowing the neuron's electrical and chemical properties to be examined in detail.

Almost everything we now know about how neurons work (i.e. how they generate electrical impulses and how this current is passed along the axon leading to transmitter release) is derived from work performed on the giant squid axon. Because it is generally accepted that all neurons, no matter what their size or the type of animal they come from, work on the basis of similar principles, the giant squid neuron has thus provided an invaluable means of examining neuronal function. The use of this technique was pioneered by two English researchers, Alan Hodgkin and Andrew Huxley, who published a classic set of papers on their findings in 1952. Not only did these two scientists

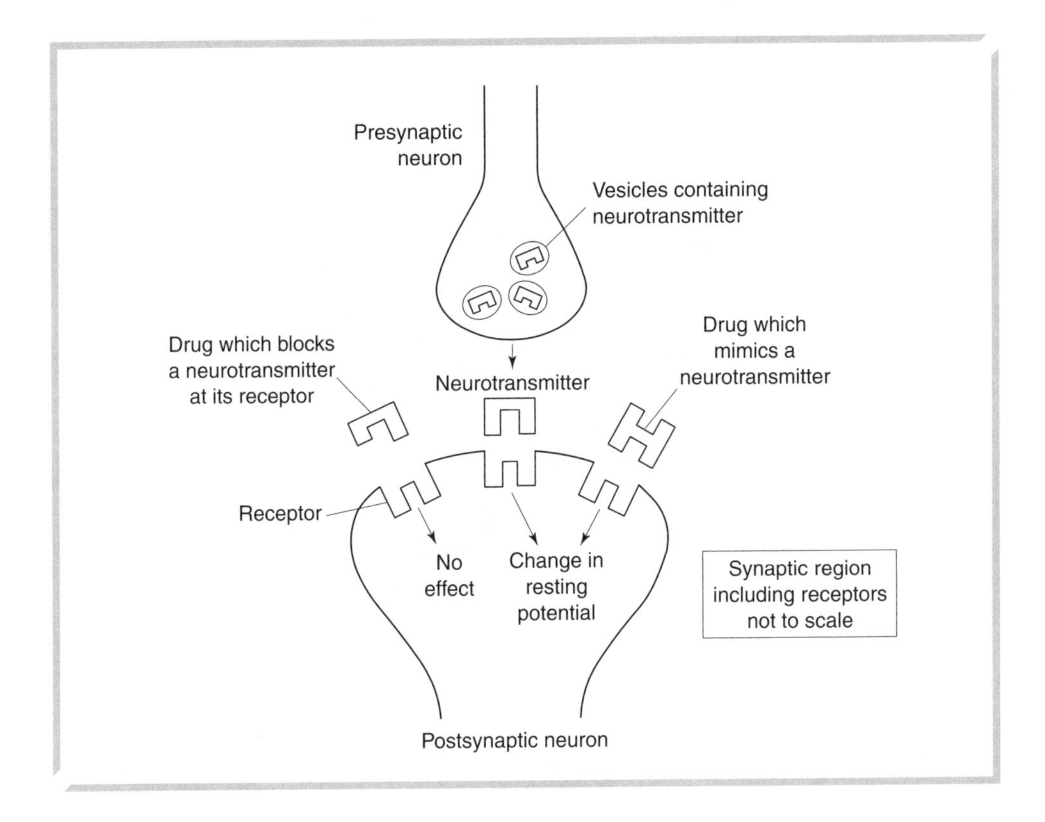

Figure 1.5 Agonist and antagonist effects on receptors.

develop a technique that enabled recording electrodes to be precisely positioned in the neuron without causing it damage, but they were also able to remove cytoplasm from inside the axon thereby permitting examination of its chemical composition. This factor turned out to be crucially important in explaining how neurons produced electrical impulses.

One of the most important features of the giant squid axon is its **resting potential**. If a recording electrode is placed inside the neuron (when it is at rest) and its voltage is compared with an electrode placed just outside, then a small but consistent voltage difference between the two electrodes is found. Importantly, this voltage difference is always found to be around –70 millivolts (mV) with the inside of the cell always negative compared to the outside (this difference is roughly one-tenth of a volt, or about 5 per cent of the energy that exists in a torch battery). This may not appear to be very much, but it is a huge energy difference for such a tiny structure as a neuron to maintain – and it is this voltage differential that holds the key to understanding how the neuron is able to generate action potentials that ultimately cause the release of neurotransmitter from the axon terminals (see Figure 1.6).

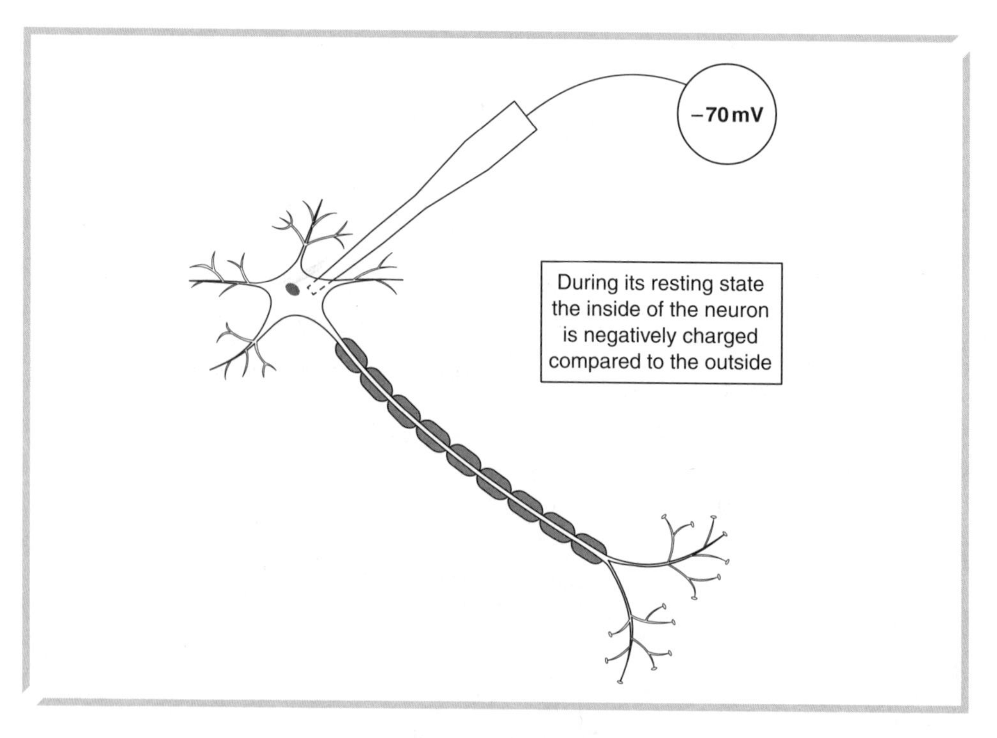

Figure 1.6 Measurement of the resting potential of the nerve fibre using a microelectrode.

To understand why the resting potential of –70 mV occurs, it is necessary to first examine the nature of the chemical environment that exists inside and outside the cell. One of the most important discoveries made by Hodgkin and Huxley was that the intracellular and extracellular environments were very different in terms of their ion concentrations (e.g. see Hodgkin 1958). An ion is simply an electrically charged atom (or particle) that has lost or gained an electron which gives it a positive or negative charge (see Box 1.1). Although there are only a few types of ion in the body, they nevertheless have a crucial role to play in neural function. These ions include sodium (Na^+) and potassium (K^+) which have lost an electron and thus are positively charged; and chloride (Cl^-) and large protein ions called anions (A^-) that have gained an electron and are negatively charged.

As mentioned, Hodgkin and Huxley showed that the concentrations of ions differed significantly between the interior and exterior of the cell when it was in its resting state (Figure 1.8). For example, sodium ions (Na^+) were found to be in a much higher concentration outside the cell than inside it (in a ratio of around 10:1) and a similar situation occurred with negative chloride ions (a ratio of around 14:1). In contrast, potassium ions (K^+) and large negatively charged anions were largely confined to the inside of the cell. (The concentration ratio for potassium is around 40:1, whereas virtually all anions are found inside the neuron.) The distributed net result of all these

Box 1.1 WHAT IS AN ION?

When an atom gains or loses an electron it is called an ion and it becomes positively or negatively charged. To understand why, we first need to look at the structure of an atom. An atom (which is the smallest part of an element) consists of a nucleus (composed of *positively* charged protons and neutrons) surrounded by orbits of *negatively* charged electrons. In its normal state, the

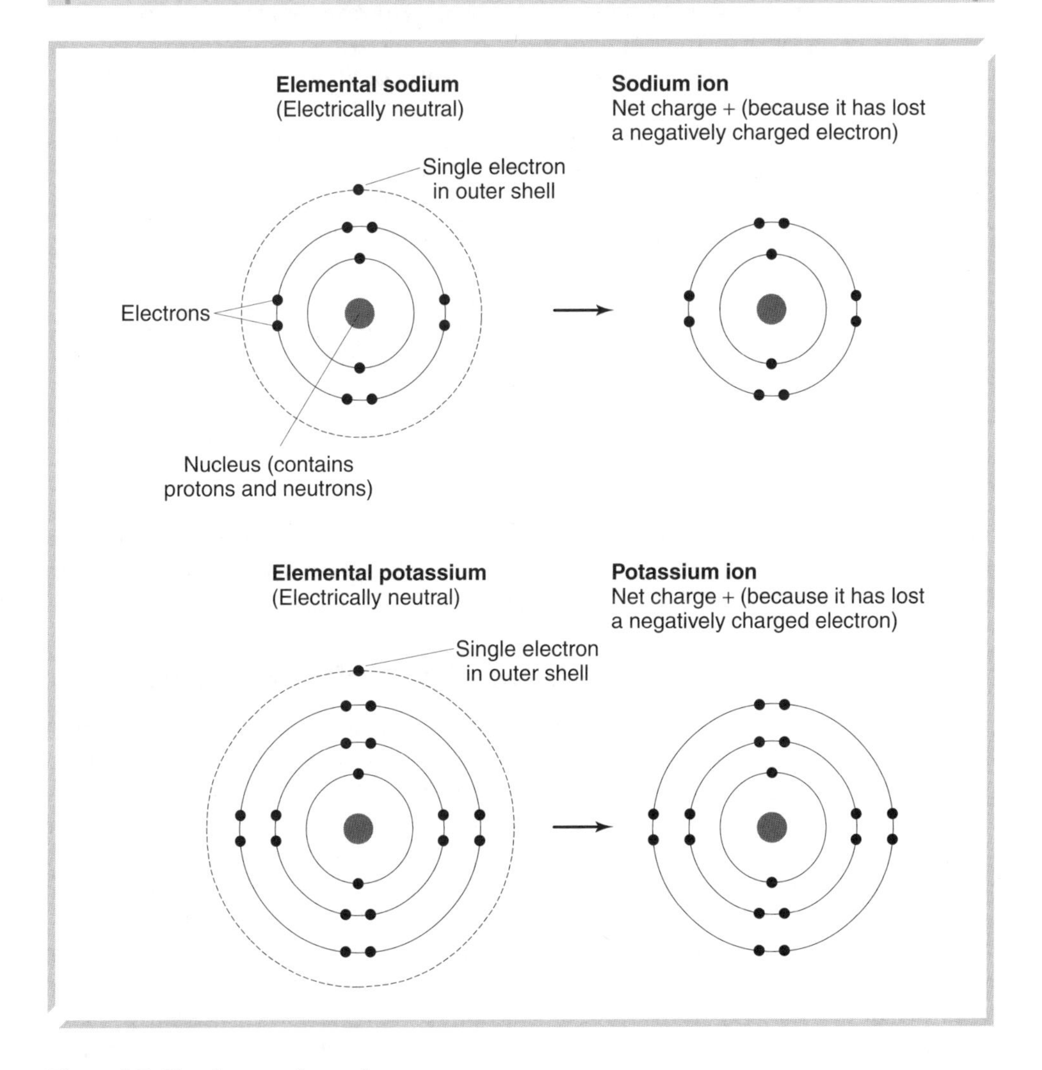

Figure 1.7 How ions are formed.

atom is neutral because the electrical charges of all the protons and electrons cancel each other out. But, of course, if the atom loses (or gains) an electron then this neutrality no longer holds.

Electrons (which move around the nucleus of the atom in an electron shell) hold the key to understanding how ions are formed. The shell nearest the nucleus only holds two electrons and, when this is full, electrons start to fill up the next shell – which may hold up to 8 electrons. In fact, an atom can have up to 7 shells with each shell (other than the first) reaching a stable configuration when it is filled by 8 electrons. However, some atoms only have one electron in their outer shell, and this makes it hard for the atom to hold on to its 'isolated' electron. Two examples of atoms with an isolated electron in their outer shell (see Figure 1.7) are sodium (electron configuration 2,8,1) and potassium (electron configuration 2,8,8,1). Not surprisingly, both these atoms quickly lose their lone electron in chemical reactions, and are turned into ions. Because the loss of an electron means losing a negative charge, the atom now becomes positively charged. And, this is why both sodium and potassium easily become positively charged ions (an atom can also gain an electron which gives it a negative charge). Importantly, flows of ions are able to produce electrical currents, and, as we shall see below, neurons have taken full advantage of this situation by using ion flows to generate their own electrical currents.

ion charges explained why the resting potential inside the neuron was negative (dominated by the electrical charges of the anions and potassium) and the outside was positive (dominated by the electrical charges of sodium and of chloride).

How does the neuron maintain its resting potential?

The fact that there is an uneven distribution of ions in the intracellular and extracellular spaces means that there is a high state of tension or disequilibrium between the inside and outside of the cell. This occurs because positively charged particles are strongly attracted to negative particles and vice versa (this force is called the **electrostatic gradient**); and high concentrations of particles are always attracted to areas of low concentration (this is known as the **diffusion gradient**). Consequently, when there is an unequal distribution of electrical charges and different concentrations of particles between the inside and outside of the cell, then strong electrical and diffusion forces are produced. Thus, in this situation, the extracellular sodium ions will be strongly attracted to the inside of the cell by electrostatic and osmotic forces (i.e. the cell's negative resting potential and its relative lack of sodium ions), whereas the intracellular potassium ions will be forced to the outside of the cell in much the same manner.

	Concentration of ions in axoplasm (mM)	Concentration of ions outside the cell (mM)
Potassium (K^+)	400	10
Sodium (Na^+)	50	450
Chloride (Cl^-)	40	560
Organic anions (A^-)	345	0

Figure 1.8 The concentration of the four important ions inside and outside the axon expressed in millimoles (mM) per litre (l).

If this is the case, then why don't ions travel down their electrostatic and diffusion gradients to correct the ionic imbalance, thus cancelling out the negative resting potential in the neuron? The answer lies with the membrane of the nerve cell. The membrane is the cell's protective semi-permeable outer coating which contains a number of important structures that include **ion channels** – essentially tiny pores through the membrane that allow certain ions to pass in and out (see Keynes 1979). In fact, the membrane is about 100 times more permeable to potassium ions than sodium (largely because it has more channels for potassium than for sodium). This means that while potassium can move into and out of the cell with relative ease, sodium ions are effectively barred entry – despite the fact that strong electrical and diffusion gradients are working to force sodium ions into the neuron. These forces are so great that a few sodium ions actually make it – sneaking into the cell through the potassium channels.

This brings us to another important question: If ions are in constant motion (particularly potassium) how can the resting potential of –70 mV be maintained? Clearly, if physical forces were simply left to predominate, then the flow of potassium to the outside of the cell would reduce the resting potential, and similarly the flow of sodium to the inside, even at a slow rate of infiltration, would also eventually reverse the resting potential. The answer is that the neuron maintains the intracellular and extracellular balance of ions by means of a special **sodium–potassium pump** that forces out approximately three sodium ions for every two potassium ions it takes in. Working at full capacity, it has been estimated that each pump can push out 200 sodium ions for every 130 potassium ions that enter. Not surprisingly, these pumps require considerable energy and it may be that up to 20 per cent of the cell's energy is spent on this process (Dudel 1978). Such is the importance of maintaining the cell's negative resting potential, because without it the neuron would not be able to generate an electrical impulse (action potential).

The action potential

It was known over a century ago that the nerve impulse is a brief pulse of electrical excitation that passes along the nerve fibre. But how does this occur? Hodgkin and Huxley, by using the giant squid axon, showed (as we shall see) that the electrical pulse was, in fact, caused by sudden movements of ions across the neural membrane. And, we now know that the triggering event for this process begins with the chemical messengers that cross the synapse to chemically stimulate the neuron.

The neuron can be compared to a tiny biological battery with the negative pole (–70 mV) inside the cell and the positive pole outside, and it goes to great lengths (e.g. the sodium–potassium pump) to make sure that this polarity is maintained. But, this also creates a very unstable situation, not least because of the sodium ions trying to force their way into the cell. In addition, each neuron is also under constant bombardment from a variety of chemical messengers that further influence its resting potential (by their action on opening ion channels). Indeed, some types of neurotransmitter will produce an excitatory effect on the resting potential (that is, increase the cell's permeability to positive ions making it become more positive), whereas others will have an inhibitory effect (that is, make the inside of the cell more negative or 'hyperpolarised' by increasing the influx of negative ions). It is important to realise that each neuron may have literally thousands of inputs impinging upon it at any given point in time and the net result (or '**summation**') of this stimulation may be a considerable shift in the cell's resting potential. If the neurotransmitter stimulation causes the inside of the cell to become more positive, the change in voltage is known as an **excitatory postsynaptic potential (EPSP)**, and if the cell becomes more negative it is called an **inhibitory postsynaptic potential (IPSP)**.

The change in electrical potential caused by neurotransmitter stimulation normally begins in the dendrites and spreads down into the cell body. But how does the neuron transform these small increments in electrical influx into an action potential? The answer lies with a special part of the neuron called the **axon hillock**, which is situated at the junction between the cell body and axon (see Figure 1.2). Like the rest of the neuron this area normally shows a resting potential of around –70 mV. However, if the summation is sufficient to increase the voltage by about +15 mV (this value is known as the **threshold potential**) then a sudden and rapid sequence of events occurs (lasting no more than 4 milliseconds) that results in the cell becoming depolarised (i.e. the inside of the neuron becomes positively charged) which, in turn, produces an action potential (or nerve impulse).

If a recording electrode is placed into the axon hillock during this event, one will find that the neuron suddenly changes its polarity from about –55 mV (its threshold value) to approximately +30 mV in less than one-thousandth of a second (ms)! This sudden reversal in polarity (from negative to positive) is short lived, however, and the neuron will quickly return to its normal resting potential – although in doing this it will briefly overshoot to –80 mV (this is known as the **refractory period**). In fact, within just 4 or 5 ms, the resting potential at the axon hillock will have returned to –70 mV (see Figure 1.9). But, this is not the end of the electrical flow, which will have begun its journey down the axon to the axon terminals.

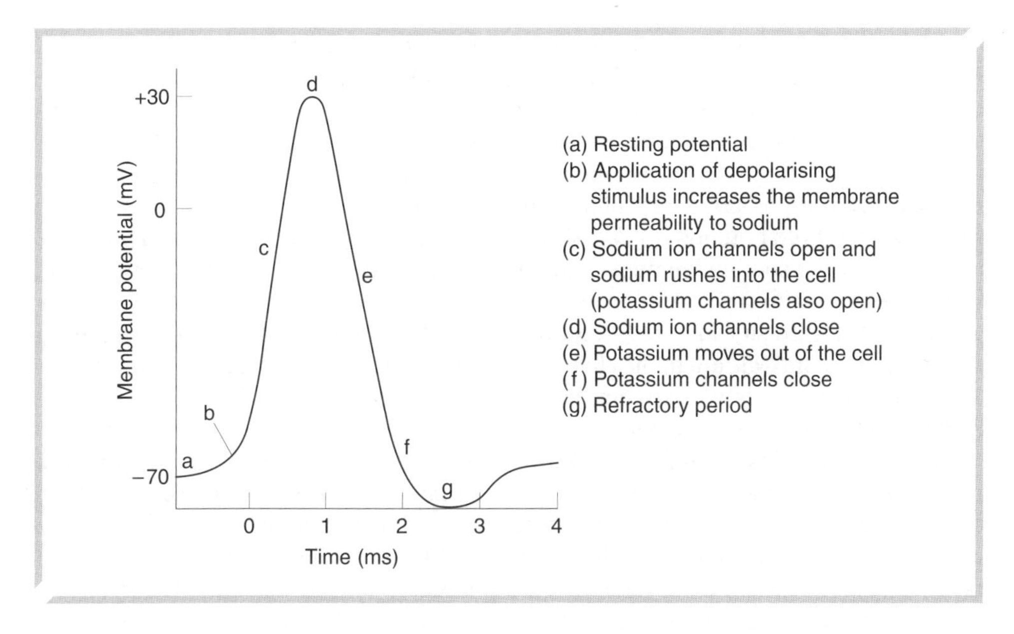

Figure 1.9 Voltage changes and ion movements that accompany the action potential.

Thus, the axon hillock is the region of the neuron where the integration of excitatory and inhibitory postsynaptic potentials takes place, and which 'decides' whether the cell is to fire or not. It can also be seen that the response is 'all-or-nothing'; that is, the neuron either fires or does not (there is no in-between). Once formed, the action potential then has to be transported down the axon. But here lies a problem: axons are long, spindly structures, and if the depolarisation occurring at the axon hillock simply moved passively down the axon's length then it would diminish and decay before moving very far. Thus, the axon must have some means of *actively* moving the action potential from axon hillock to synaptic terminal. The secret of this active transportation lies in the fact that most axons are covered in a fatty sheath called myelin which can be likened to a plastic coating surrounding an electrical cable. However, unlike an electrical cable, the myelin contains short gaps called **nodes of Ranvier**, and it is here that the renewal of the action potential takes place (see also next section). In short, at each node, the action potential is amplified back to its original intensity, and consequently the action potential effectively 'jumps' down the axon. This process is called **saltatory conduction** (from the Latin *saltare* meaning 'to jump') and in this way the action potential can travel large distances without becoming weakened. This process is also remarkably efficient and some mammalian myelinated neurons can move an action potential as fast as 224 miles per hour.

The ionic basis of the action potential

How does the neuron bring about the sudden change in depolarisation to generate an action potential? The answer lies mainly with the sodium and potassium ions. As already mentioned, large numbers of sodium ions are found in the extracellular fluid, and these are attracted to the inside of the cell by both electrical forces (positive ions are attracted to negative ions) and concentration forces (high concentration of sodium ions are attracted to low concentrations). Despite this, the cell's membrane acts as a barrier to sodium, and if any of its ions manage to infiltrate into the cell they are quickly removed by the sodium–potassium pump. However, this situation is changed dramatically when the threshold potential (–55 mV) is reached at the axon hillock. At this point the neuron opens its sodium channels and, almost as if a door is suddenly thrown open, sodium ions rush into the cell, propelled along their electrostatic and concentration gradients. It has been estimated that up to 100,000,000 ions could pass through each channel per second (although the channels only remain open for a fraction of this time). And it is this large flow of sodium current into the cell that transforms its internal negative state into a positive one.

At the peak of this sodium flow (or after 1 or 2 ms of the ion channels opening) the permeability of the membrane changes again. At this point the neuron closes its sodium channels and opens the channels for potassium – causing the propulsion of positive potassium ions from inside the cell. Because the inside of the cell at this point is also positive (due to the influx of sodium), the potassium ions are essentially forced out down their electrostatic gradient. Not only does this ion flow cause the cell's resting potential to return to negative, but it 'overshoots' causing the refractory period, in which the membrane potential falls to around –80 mV. It is only after this hyperpolarisation occurs (that is, some 4–5 ms after the start of the action potential) that the resting potential returns to normal (–70 mV) with the sodium–potassium pump coming back into play to correct the ion balance. This series of events takes place so quickly that most neurons can produce well over 100 action potentials per second.

A similar process of ion influx and efflux also occurs along the axon's length. As we have seen, the axon is covered in myelin, and its underlying membrane is only exposed at gaps in the myelin called the nodes of Ranvier. When the action potential is generated at the axon hillock, the electrical discharge begins to be transmitted passively down the axon, although the impulse would quickly weaken and not travel very far unless it was renewed along the way. This renewal function is provided by the nodes of Ranvier. Although the signal is diminished by the time it reaches the first node, it is still strong enough to open the voltage-controlled sodium channels which, in effect, generate a new full-blown action potential. And, in this way, the action potential is conducted (or 'jumps') down the full length of the axon (Stevens 1979).

Neurotransmitter release

As the action potential reaches the end of the axon, it passes through a large number of axon branches that end in swollen structures called synaptic terminals. Stored within each synaptic terminal are large numbers of **synaptic vesicles**, each holding a few hundred molecules of a specific neurotransmitter. When the action potential arrives at the terminal it stimulates the influx of calcium (*not* sodium) ions which causes **exocytosis** – the process by which synaptic vesicles fuse with the presynaptic membrane thereby spilling their contents into the synaptic gap. In fact, vesicles are continually fusing with the membrane of the axon terminal resulting in the secretion of small amounts of neurotransmitter, but the action potential greatly speeds up this process causing the fusion of many vesicles and enabling a significant amount of neurotransmitter to be released.

The synaptic gap is a tiny fluid-filled space that measures only about 0.00002 mm across. On one side of this gap is the presynaptic neuron (where the axon terminals end) and on the opposite side is the recipient (postsynaptic) neuron. When neurotransmitter is released, it diffuses across the synaptic gap binding to receptors on the postsynaptic neuron (note that the presynaptic neuron may also contain receptors – see Chapter 10). The receptor and its neurotransmitter can be likened to a lock and key – in the same way it takes a specially shaped key to turn a lock, it takes a particular type of transmitter molecule to activate a receptor. Once this occurs, a series of events is set in motion which results in the temporary opening of various ion channels (depending on the type of receptor being stimulated) and a change in the cell's electrical state.

Once the neurotransmitter has bound to its receptor it has to be quickly deactivated, otherwise it would continue to exert an effect and make it impossible for the cell to receive new messages. Because of this, a number of synaptic processes have evolved that either break down the transmitter or help to remove it from the synapse. One such process involves the enzyme **monoamine oxidase**, which is found in both the axon terminals and synapse, and whose function is to break down excess neurotransmitter (some antidepressant drugs work by inhibiting this enzyme – see Chapter 10). Another way of limiting the action of a neurotransmitter is to remove it from the synaptic gap. Indeed, some presynaptic neurons have a **re-uptake pump** that is able to take (i.e. recapture) the neurotransmitter back into its axon terminals, so that it only has a brief time to exist in the synaptic gap. Neurons that release noradrenaline and serotonin have this type of re-uptake mechanism. Indeed, drugs that block re-uptake for either noradrenaline (e.g. imipramine) or serotonin (e.g. prozac) have been used successfully to treat depression (Snyder 1986).

Chemical events in the postsynaptic cell

As we have seen, neurotransmitters bind to receptors which induces a change in the permeability of the neural membrane to various ions, thus producing a change in its resting potential. But how exactly does the neurotransmitter attaching itself to the receptor lead to the opening of ion channels? The answer is that there are two different types of mechanism: one involving direct activation of the ion channel and the other using an indirect process that requires the interaction of intracellular chemicals known as **second messengers**. In the first example, the receptor and ion channel form part of the same unit so that occupancy of the receptor causes a direct change in the shape of the ion channel (sometimes called a ligand-activated channel). An example of this type of ion channel complex is the GABA-A receptor (sensitive to the neurotransmitter GABA) which consists of five elongated protein molecules arranged in the shape of a cylinder that passes through the membrane. Normally these proteins are tightly held shut together, but if GABA binds to receptor sites on the surface of this complex, then the proteins change their shape forming a channel that allows the passage of ions (in this case negative chloride ions) to flow briefly into the cell (see Figure 1.10). Another example of a ligand-gated channel complex is the cholinergic nicotinic receptor found at the neuromuscular junction (see Chapter 3).

However, not all receptors are located on their respective ion channels. In fact, the receptor may be some distance from its ion channel, or it may be able to open many ion channels at once. In this case, activity at the receptor causes the opening of ion channels through a sequence of chemical reactions that occur between the two (separate) sites. This process normally begins with the activated receptor altering the configuration of a G-protein to which it is attached on the inside of the cell. In turn, this produces a series of chemical events, one of which can be the increased production of an enzyme called **adenylate cyclase** which converts ATP (a substance that the cell uses to provide energy) into **cyclic AMP (cAMP)**. Cyclic AMP is called a second messenger (the first messenger in this case being the neurotransmitter) because it sets into motion a series of chemical reactions inside the neuron that results in the 'opening' of the proteins that form the ion channels (this process is called **protein phosphorylation** – see Figure 1.11). In addition, there are other types of second messenger system although their details need not concern us here.

Second messenger systems may appear at first sight to be a complex way of opening ion channels (and thereby changing the neuron's permeability to ions), but this process

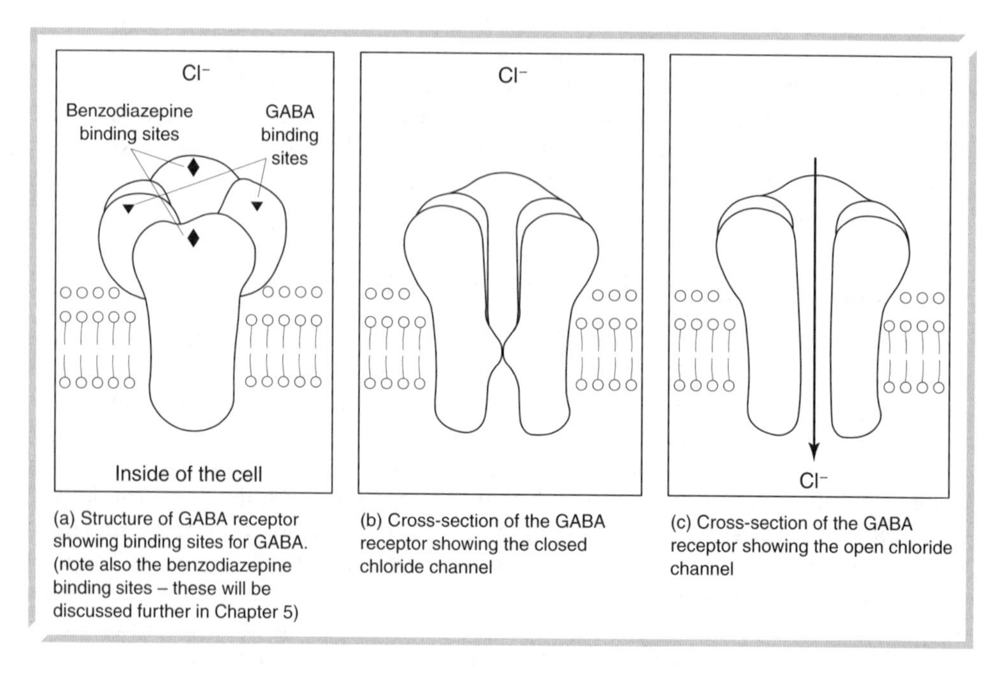

(a) Structure of GABA receptor showing binding sites for GABA. (note also the benzodiazepine binding sites – these will be discussed further in Chapter 5)

(b) Cross-section of the GABA receptor showing the closed chloride channel

(c) Cross-section of the GABA receptor showing the open chloride channel

Figure 1.10 The GABA receptor.

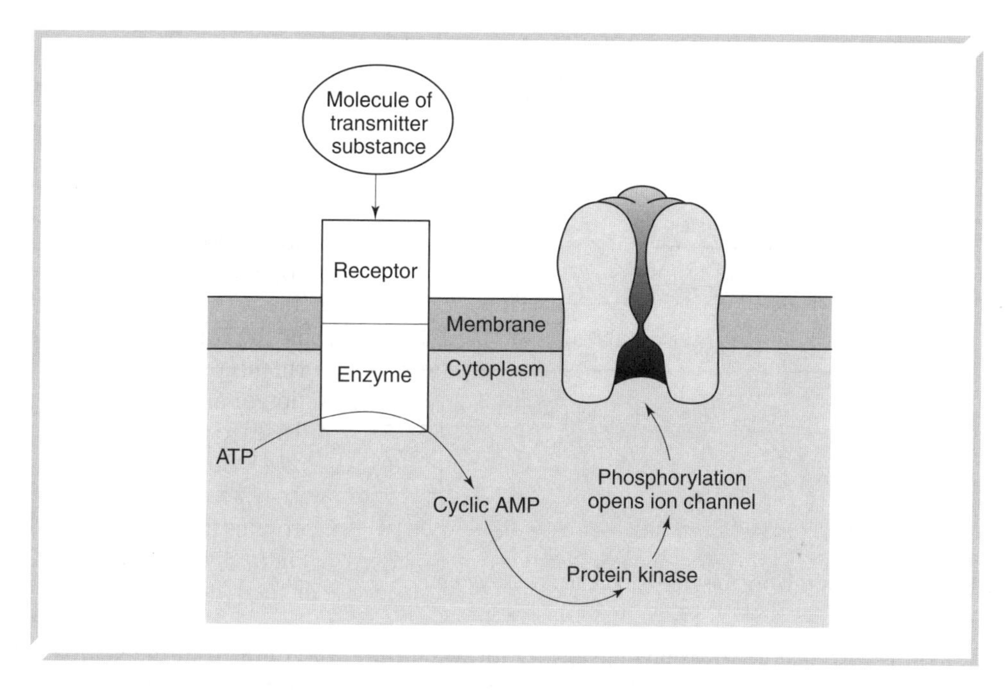

Figure 1.11 Diagram showing the main steps in the cAMP second messenger system.

actually gives the cell far greater adaptability and flexibility. For example, activation of ion channels directly (as with the GABA receptor) may result in the rapid depolarisation of the cell in as little as 2 to 10 ms (which may be ideally suited for a rapid response such as a muscle contraction or encoding of a pain response) but it shows little variation. In contrast, the slower action of second messenger systems may take from 20 ms to over 10 s and involve a multitude of different types of ion channel. This type of response may be particularly useful when the neuron needs to adapt to new events, and it should come as no surprise to discover that changes in second messenger systems have been implicated in the cellular basis of learning and memory (see Chapter 8).

An introduction to the nervous system

The complete network of all nerve cells in the human body is divided into two systems (see Figure 1.12): the **central nervous system (CNS)** and the **peripheral nervous system**. The central nervous system is composed of the spinal cord and the brain, and its main function is to act as a control centre for receiving and interpreting sensory information, making decisions (both unconscious and conscious), and for directing movement (both involuntary and voluntary). The peripheral nervous system on the other hand contains the input (sensory) neurons and output (motor) neurons of the body (most of which feed in and out of the CNS) and is composed of two main divisions: the **somatic nervous system** and the **autonomic nervous system**. The somatic nervous

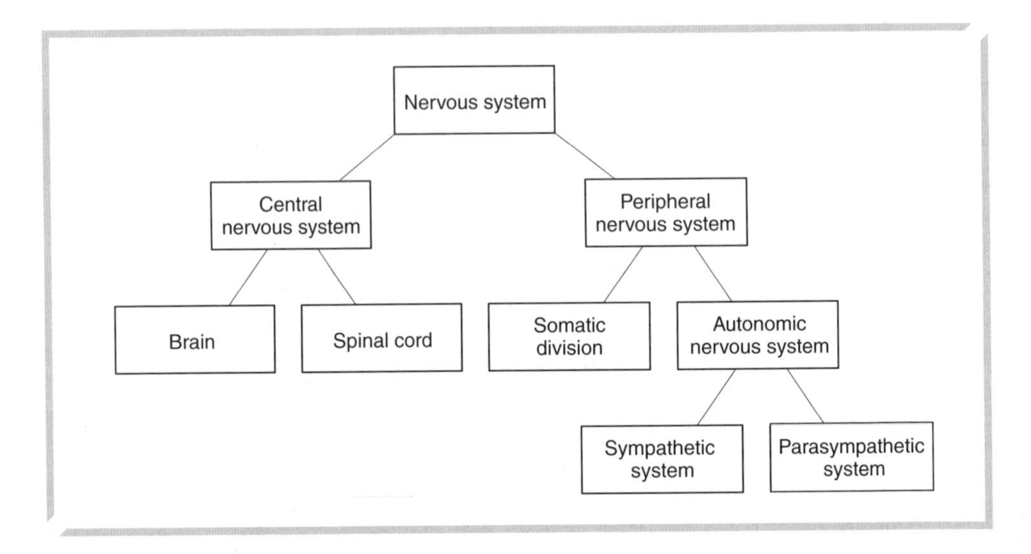

Figure 1.12 Overall organisation of the nervous system.

system is responsible for relaying sensory information to the CNS from the skin and musculature, as well as providing the output to the skeletal muscles necessary for voluntary movement. We shall discuss the role of this system in more detail when we come to examine motor behaviour in Chapter 3.

In contrast, the autonomic nervous system consists of motor nerve fibres that regulate the activity of involuntary muscle (and certain endocrine glands) controlling vital bodily functions such as heart rate, blood pressure, kidney function, breathing, etc. The autonomic nervous system is further composed of two subdivisions – the **sympathetic nervous system** (**SNS**) and the **parasympathetic nervous system (PNS)** – which tend to have opposite functions. For example, the sympathetic system prepares the organism for a **flight or fight response** by increasing the output of the heart, opening the airways to the lungs, allowing more light to enter the eye, inhibiting digestion, and by diverting blood from the skin to the skeletal muscles (this is why the skin often goes white after a sudden fright). In addition, it also activates the adrenal gland to stimulate the release of adrenaline and noradrenaline. In other words, this system helps prepare the body to cope with an actual (or potential) emergency or stressful situation. In contrast, the parasympathetic system reverses or normalises the effects of sympathetic activity, and acts to conserve energy or maintain resting body function. As we shall see later, the autonomic nervous system plays a particularly important role in emotion (Chapter 5) as well as other behaviours such as feeding (Chapter 4) and sex (Chapter 6).

The endocrine system

The endocrine system provides another essential communication system in the body and is also an important determinant of behaviour. The endocrine system consists of a number of glands scattered throughout the body that secrete chemicals called **hormones** (from the Greek *hormon* meaning 'to excite') which are released into the blood where they are transported to various parts of the body (see Table 1.2). More than 50 different hormones may be circulating through the body at any one time and each has its own special function. In humans more than a dozen organs secrete hormones, the most important being the thyroid (situated in the neck), the thymus (placed in the upper chest), the adrenal glands (located just above the kidneys), and the gonads including the testes and the ovaries. All of these structures come under the control of a single master gland situated on the underside of the brain and attached to the **hypothalamus**. This all-important grape-sized master gland, known as the **pituitary gland**, releases a number of trophic hormones whose role is to regulate the other endocrine glands of the body (see Figure 1.13). The pituitary actually consists of two glands: the anterior pituitary (connected to the hypothalamus via a complex series of blood vessels) and the posterior pituitary (which has neural connections with the hypothalamus).

The control of hormonal release by the pituitary gland generally works on the basis of **negative feedback**; that is, when hormone levels begin to increase, the pituitary gland will detect this change and respond by decreasing the output of its controlling hormone. In practice things are not quite so simple because the brain will also be receiving feedback about hormone levels and the effects they are having on various organs of

Table 1.2 Summary of the main hormone systems in the human body

Endocrine gland	Hormone(s)	Main actions
Adrenal cortex	Glucocorticoids (including cortisol and cortisone)	Adapts the body to long-term stress
Adrenal medulla	Adrenaline (Epinephrine)	Increases sympathetic arousal and stimulates the breakdown of glycogen
Ovaries	Estrogen and Progesterone	Female sexual development and control of the menstrual cycle
Pancreas gland	Insulin and Glucagon	Involved in regulation of blood sugar
Pineal gland	Melatonin	Control of circadian rhythms
Pituitary gland (anterior part)	Vasopressin and Oxytocin	Control of water balance and female sexual behaviour
Pituitary gland (posterior part)	Master control of other endocrine glands. Also produces growth hormone and prolactin	Wide range of functions. Growth and protein synthesis. Milk production
Testes	Testosterone	Male sexual development and behaviour
Thyroid gland	Thyroxine and Triiodothyronine	Increases metabolic rate

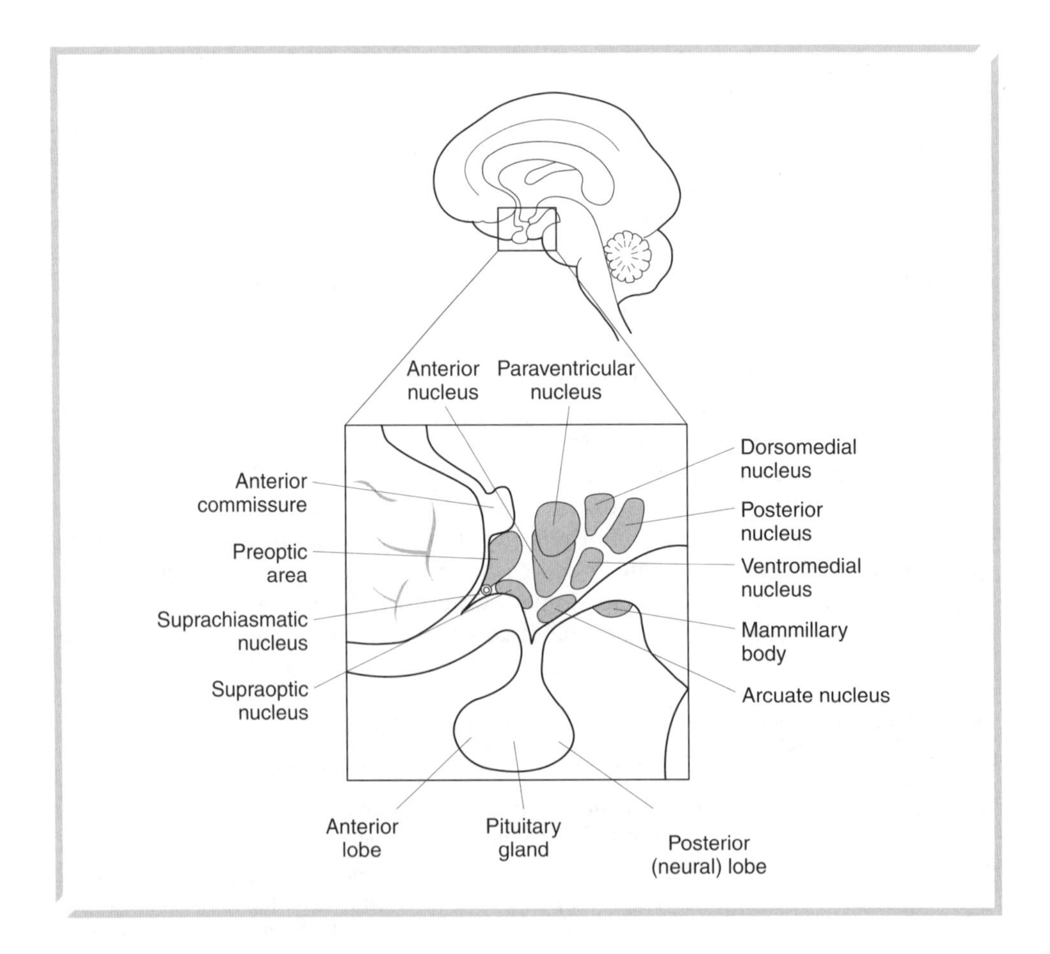

Figure 1.13 The hypothalamus and pituitary gland.

the body – and consequently the brain (via the hypothalamus) will also regulate the pituitary gland's response. Nevertheless, the principle remains the same: negative feedback occurs when the hormone (or its biological response) feeds back onto a control centre to turn the system off. Thus, the combination of the hypothalamus and the pituitary gland working together means that the control exerted over hormone secretion is complex and finely tuned.

Both the endocrine and nervous systems provide an important means of communication in the body. The nervous system allows for very rapid responses that require immediate action, whereas the endocrine system responds more slowly (in fact, hormones may take minutes or even hours to reach their target) and they typically have a much longer duration of action. Despite this, both systems work towards integrated functioning in many types of behaviour, and we shall see several examples of this relationship throughout the book.

The central nervous system

The central nervous system is the main control centre of the body. It exerts executive control over the peripheral nervous system and endocrine system, and is also the instrument of behaviour, emotion, memory and consciousness. In other words, it is the nervous system with which biological psychology is mainly concerned. However, trying to visualise how the central nervous system is organised can be a daunting challenge for the student. One problem is the terminology. Greek, Latin and English words are used to describe parts of the central nervous system (in addition, some structures are named after people such as Broca and Wernicke), and trying to visualise where they are situated and how they are interconnected presents a real challenge.

The evolution of the human brain has also added to its complexity, and, as it has developed, newer structures have taken over the roles of older ones. (This, however, does not mean that these regions have become redundant as they are still incorporated into the neural circuits of the brain and have vital roles to play.) One feature of this evolutionary development is **cephalisation**, that is, the massive increase in size of the brain in relation to the rest of the body. This development is particularly noticeable in the forebrain, which in mammals has become folded to increase its surface area. This area has reached its greatest size and complexity in humans and serves an enormous range of functions.

To complete this chapter we shall describe the various regions and structures of the central nervous system. Many of these areas will be discussed again in the following chapters of this book, and it might prove helpful advice not to try to remember all the new terms at the first reading, but rather to return to these pages when encountering their names later. It is probably more important to learn the behavioural relevance of these structures than simply remembering their names.

The spinal cord

The spinal cord is actually an extension of the brain that forms a cylinder of nervous tissue that runs down the back. Its main function is to distribute and relay motor neurons to their targets (e.g. muscles and glands), and to return internal and external sensory information to the brain. Furthermore, the spinal cord is also capable of producing certain types of behaviour by itself, including simple spinal reflexes (such as the knee-jerk response) or more complex patterns of rhythmical activity (the postural components of walking).

When examined visually, the most striking feature of the spinal cord is its grey and white nervous matter. The grey tissue forms a butterfly shape in the centre of the spinal cord (surrounding the central canal) and is made up of nerve cell bodies, synapses and dendrites. This region of the spinal cord contains the cell bodies of (a) motor neurons that send their axons out to innervate the muscles of the body, and (b) neurons that receive information from the sensory axons that return to the spinal cord. The grey matter also contains a large number of interneurons between input and output that allow complex reflexes to take place (see Chapter 3). In contrast, the white matter (lying

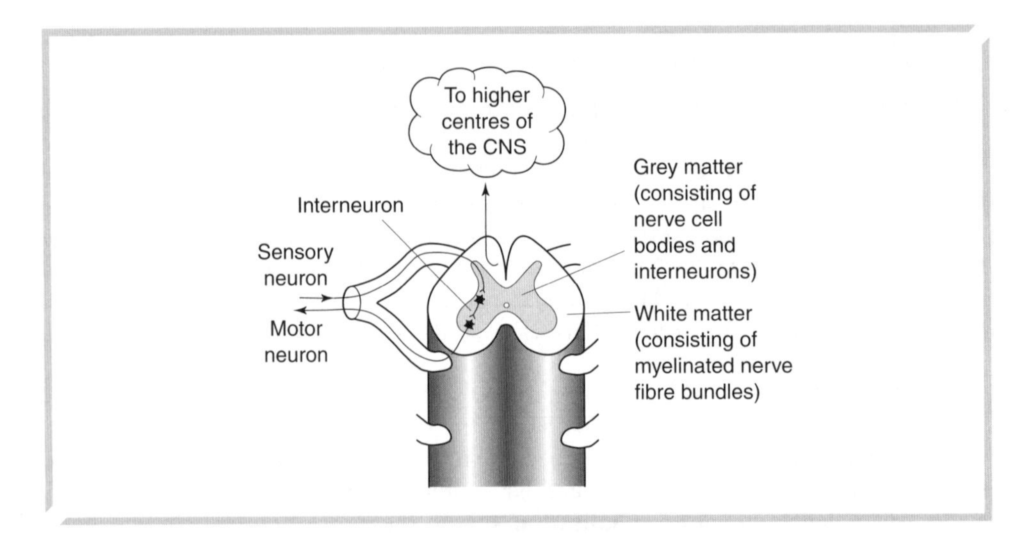

Figure 1.14 Section of spinal cord (from the front) with spinal nerves attached.

on the outside of the grey matter) is composed mainly of fatty 'whitish' myelinated axon fibres that form ascending and descending pathways that send information up and down the spinal cord (see Figure 1.14).

Axons enter and leave the spinal cord via spinal nerves that contain thousands of fibres. There are 31 pairs of spinal nerves (right and left) along the length of the spinal cord with each nerve serving one side of the body. Each spinal nerve is also made up of two branches (called roots) which enter and leave the grey matter of the spinal cord at different places. The dorsal (back) root of each spinal nerve provides the sensory (input) pathway from the body to the spinal cord, whereas the ventral (front) root consists of motor (output) pathways from the spinal cord to the muscles (this also include the fibres of the autonomic nervous system). The spinal cord also has a central canal containing cerebrospinal fluid which is connected with the brain's ventricles. Samples of this spinal fluid can be a very useful diagnostic tool in determining various brain disorders.

The brainstem

As the spinal cord enters the brain it enlarges and forms the **brainstem** (Figure 1.15), which is the oldest and most primitive part of the brain. The first part of the brainstem to follow on from the spinal cord is the **medulla** ('long marrow') which contains various nuclei, most of which serve vital functions essential for life, including those controlling cardiac function and respiration, as well as a profusion of ascending and descending nerve pathways. If the brain is cut above the medulla, basic heart rate and breathing can be maintained, but damage to the medulla is inevitably fatal. The next region to be found is the **pons** (from the Latin for 'bridge') which appears as a significant enlarge-

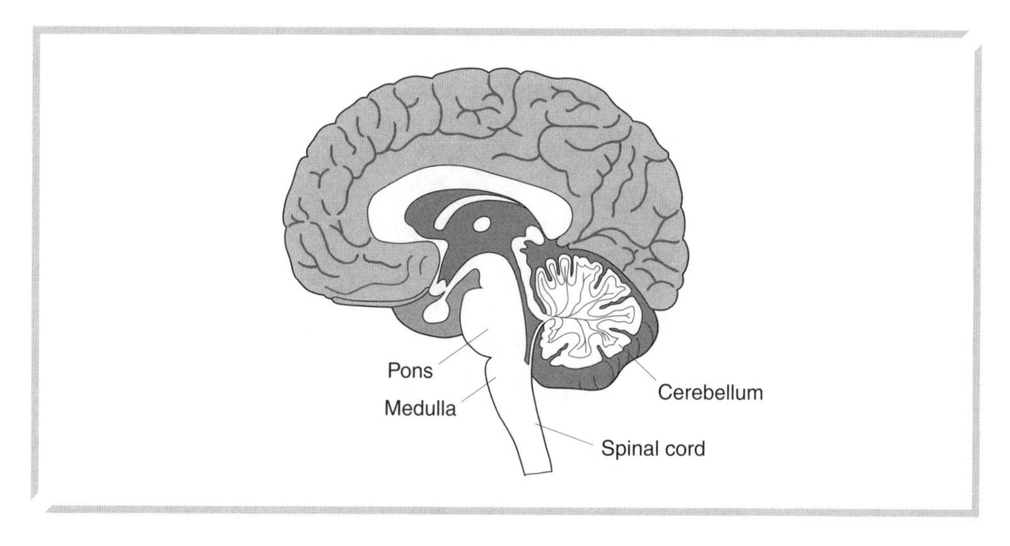

Figure 1.15 Brainstem structures (and spinal cord) of the human CNS.

ment of the medulla. This area also contains many nuclei, although its increased size is largely due to the many ascending and descending fibre tracts that cross from one side of the brain to the other at this point. The pons is also the main junction between the **cerebellum** ('little brain'), spinal cord, and the rest of the brain. The cerebellum with its distinctive wrinkled appearance is located at the back of the brain and is involved in co-ordinating muscular activity (especially that required for balance) and providing smooth automated movement. For example, people with cerebellar damage are at first not able to walk, but can learn to do so, although walking remains awkward as it is no longer 'automatically' controlled (see Chapter 3). The cerebellum is also involved in some types of simple learning including classical conditioning.

The midbrain (the mesencephalon)

The midbrain is the name given to the region that lies immediately on top of the brainstem and is divided into two areas: the **tectum** ('roof') and the **tegmentum** ('covering'). The tectum contains two pairs of nuclei, called colliculi (derived from Latin, meaning 'small hills'), which protrude from its upper surface. The **superior colliculi** are involved in visual processing and control reflexes such as blinking and orientation (see Chapter 2), and the **inferior colliculi** serve a similar function for auditory processing. The tegmentum is less easy to define as it consists of several important nuclei (including the **red nucleus** and **substantia nigra**) as well as more diffuse areas including the **ventral tegmental area** (discussed in more detail in Chapters 10 and 11), and the upper portions of the **periaqueductal grey area** (which contains opiate receptors and is involved in pain processing) – see Figure 1.16.

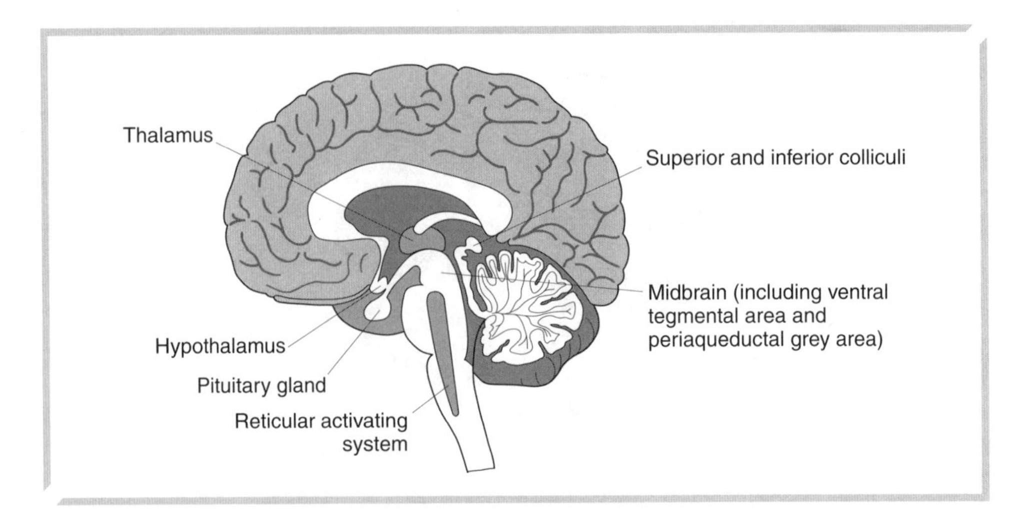

Figure 1.16 Midbrain (mesencephalon) structures of the human CNS (including the hypothalamus and the thalamus of the diencephalon).

Also coursing through the centre of the brainstem and the midbrain is the **reticular activating system**, a large net-like structure consisting of a diffuse interconnected mass of neurons in which over 90 nuclear groups are embedded, including the **locus coeruleus** and the **raphe nuclei**. The reticular activating system serves many essential functions although one of its most important roles is to control the level of arousal in the cerebral cortex. For example, stimulation of the reticular formation arouses a resting animal and makes an awake one more alert. In contrast, destruction of reticular structures results in coma. It should be no surprise, therefore, to find that the reticular system is involved in sleep (Chapter 6).

The forebrain (the diencephalon)

Up to this point, the brain can be compared to a neural tube that has evolved and enlarged from the spinal cord. However, with the development of the forebrain, we now see the brain 'mushrooming out' so that it not only covers and surrounds much of the older 'tubular' brain, but also grows outwards, increasing in size and complexity with the addition of many new structures. And, with this development, comes much more complex or higher function behaviours.

The forebrain has two main regions. The central area is sometimes called the diencephalon (or 'interbrain') and consists of two structures, the **thalamus** and the hypothalamus. The thalamus (from Greek, meaning 'interchamber') is a large central structure containing many different nuclei, most of which act as relay stations between the cerebral cortex and the rest of the brain. Indeed, most of the neural input that the cerebral cortex receives is obtained from the thalamus. For example, the thalamus contains the **lateral geniculate bodies** which pass on visual information to the **visual cortex**, and the **medial geniculate nuclei** which pass on input to the **auditory cortex**. The pineal gland (which Descartes believed was the site of the soul) is also attached to part of the thalamus.

Located just underneath (and in front of) the thalamus is the hypothalamus (*hypo* meaning 'under') which also contains a large number of cell groups. As we shall see, the hypothalamus has been implicated in a wide range of behaviours including eating and hunger (Chapter 4), emotion (Chapter 5), biological rhythms (Chapter 6), sexual behaviour (Chapter 7) and reward (Chapter 11). It is also the main co-ordinating centre for the autonomic nervous system as well as exerting executive control over the pituitary gland (see Figure 1.13).

The forebrain (the telencephalon)

The remainder of the forebrain is called the telencephalon ('endbrain') and by far its most striking feature are the two symmetrical wrinkled cerebral hemispheres that make up the **cerebral cortex**. The cerebral cortex has a deceptive appearance. It is only 2–3 mm thick in humans, although it is also highly folded (not unlike a piece of paper that has been crumpled) which greatly helps to increase its surface area (in fact, if the cerebral cortex was flattened out its total surface area would be about 2.5 ft square). Because of this, about two-thirds of the cortex is actually hidden from view in fissures (the gaps between the cerebral ridges or gyri). The cerebral cortex serves a wide range of functions. It contains sensory projection areas for vision, audition and touch, and is also the site of the motor cortex which controls movement. Furthermore, the cerebral cortex is crucially involved in learning, memory and language, which underpins our ability to plan and see the consequences of our actions and to engage in various forms of abstract thought. It is also the site of consciousness and our sense of self. In other words, it is the one structure in the brain, more than any other, that makes us uniquely human. The cerebral cortex is traditionally composed of four lobes (frontal, temporal, parietal and occipital) and the two hemispheres are joined together by a huge fibre bundle called the **corpus callosum** (see Chapter 9).

Hidden from view underneath the cerebral cortex are also two other important brain systems called the **limbic system** and the **basal ganglia**. Although the limbic system and basal ganglia both receive input from the cerebral cortex, they are nevertheless separate (and more primitive) brain systems that have relatively little interaction with each other. The most important structures of the limbic system are composed of evolutionary 'old' cortex and include the **cingulate gyrus**, **hippocampus** and **amygdala** – areas that are known to be involved in emotional behaviour and memory consolidation (see Chapters 5 and 8). The basal ganglia are made up of the **striatum**, **globus pallidus** and **substantia nigra** (although the latter structure is technically part of the midbrain). Like the limbic system, the basal ganglia are also involved in a wide range of behaviours although their main function would appear to be in the control of movement. (For example, **Parkinson's disease** is due to the degeneration of a pathway from the substantia nigra to the striatum that uses the neurotransmitter dopamine (see Chapter 3).)

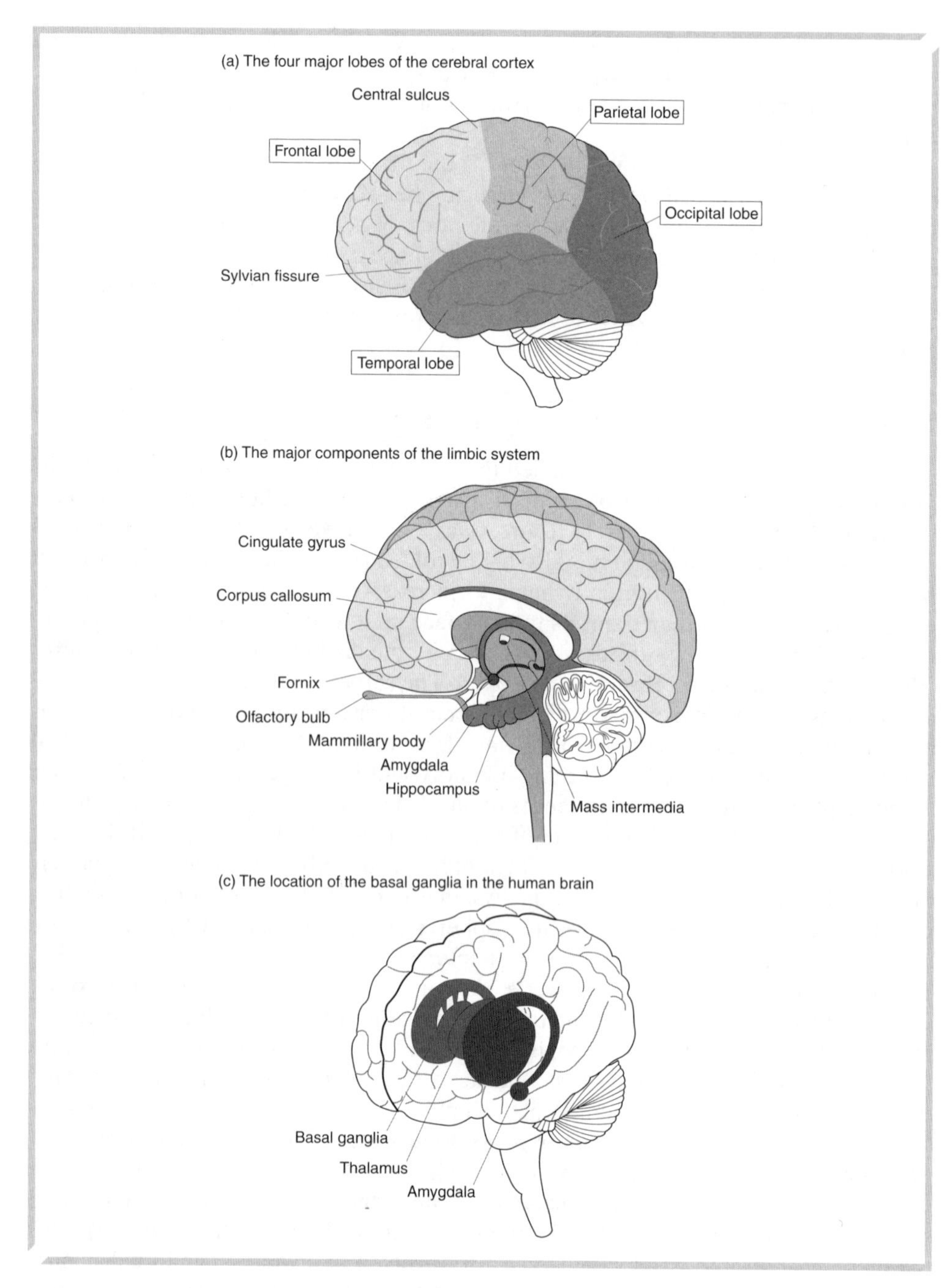

Figure 1.17 Forebrain (telencephalon) structures of the human CNS. (*Source*: Figures b and c from Neil R. Carlson, *Physiology of Behavior*, 6th edition. Copyright © 1998 by Allyn & Bacon. Reprinted by permission.)

Box 1.2: MONOAMINE PATHWAYS IN THE BRAIN

In the early 1950s it was found that if the cells of the adrenal gland were treated with formalin and exposed to ultraviolet light they would fluoresce. This occurred because the cells contained monoamines (primarily adrenaline) which reacted with the formalin to produce fluorescent chemicals. This simple discovery was to have an important effect on understanding the brain, because it also contains monoamines (now known to function as neurotransmitters) and this technique provided a means of identifying their location. The first successful application of this method to the brain was undertaken by Dahlstrom and Fuxe in 1964 who found that they could distinguish between noradrenaline and dopamine (which both fluoresced as green) and serotonin (which fluoresced as yellow). Later research was able to map the location of these neurotransmitters with great precision. This work showed that noradrenaline-, dopamine- and serotonin-containing neurons all originated from small and clearly defined areas of the upper brainstem or midbrain, and, in turn, formed large diffuse pathways that projected to many regions of the forebrain (see Figure 1.18).

The origin of most noradrenergic neurons in the forebrain is a tiny structure in the upper pontine region of the brainstem called the locus coeruleus. Remarkably, in humans, this structure is only composed of about 12,000 large neurons on each side of the upper brainstem, yet they project with their multiple axon branches to literally millions of cells throughout the brain, particularly the cerebral cortex, limbic system and thalamus. In fact, no other brain nucleus has such widespread projections (Foote 1987). The function of this system is not fully understood although it is probably linked to attention and arousal. The raphe nuclei (also situated in the pontine region) provide a serotonergic counterpart to the locus coeruleus. There are two main raphe nuclei with ascending projections – the dorsal and the median – and between them they account for about 80 per cent of forebrain serotonergic fibres. Like the locus coeruleus, the raphe nuclei are relatively small (e.g. in humans the dorsal raphe contains around 24,000 cells) and they have long axons with many branches. In many places in the brain, the projections of serotonergic fibres overlap with noradrenergic fibres (particularly in the limbic system), although there are some places (notably the basal ganglia) where serotonergic input predominates. Like the locus coeruleus, it is difficult to ascribe a precise function to the serotonergic system, although it has been shown to be involved in sleep, arousal, mood and emotion.

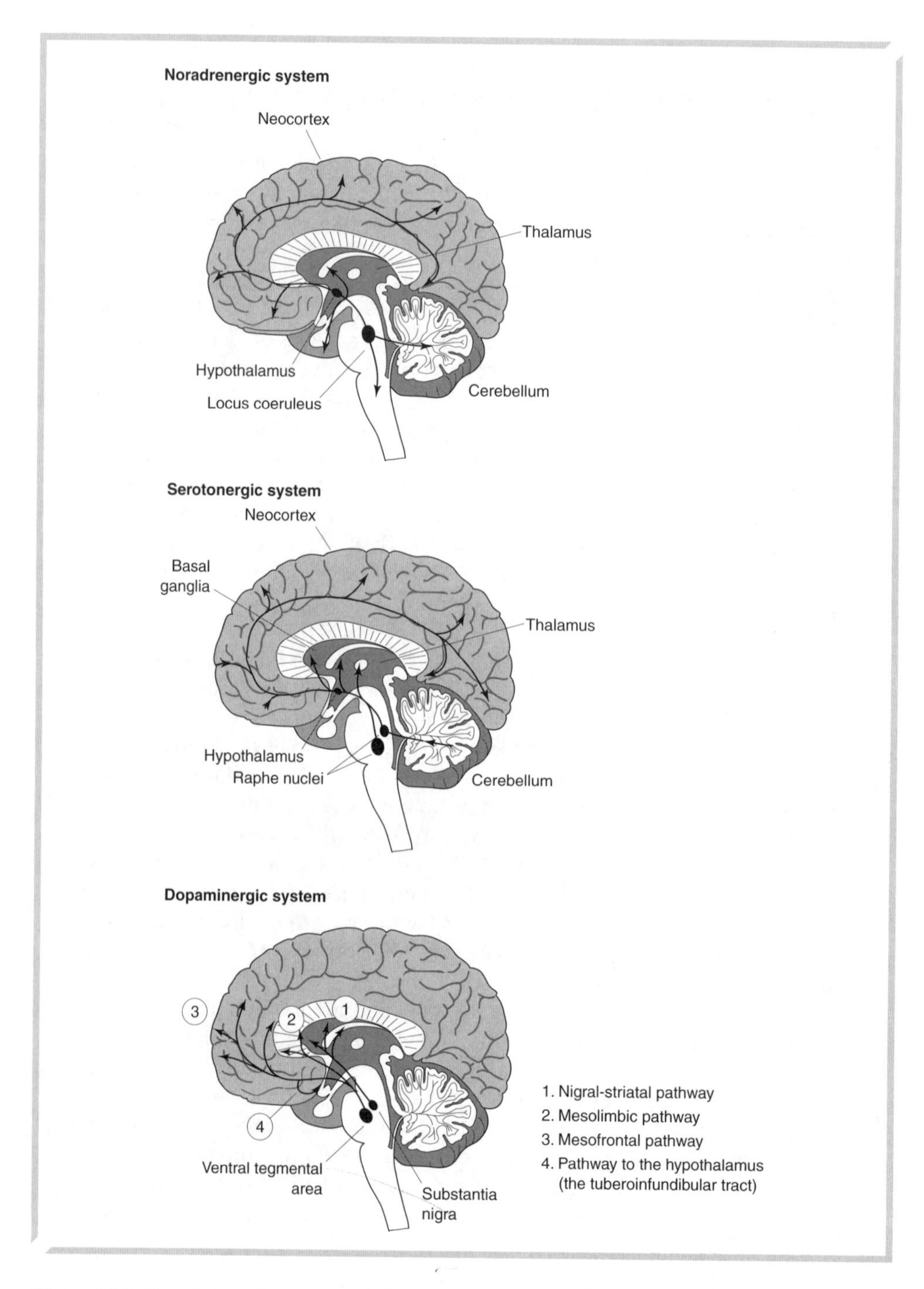

Figure 1.18 Noradrenergic, serotonergic and dopaminergic pathways in the brain.

The central dopaminergic pathways are considerably more complex than the above two systems. Not only are there significantly more dopamine containing neurons in the brain than for noradrenaline and serotonin (e.g. there are about 40,000 dopaminergic cells in total), but they appear to form at least four distinct pathways that terminate in different regions of the brain. The pathway which has attracted the most attention (largely because of its involvement in Parkinson's disease) is the nigral-striatal pathway which projects from the substantia nigra to the **striatum** (see Chapter 3). The substantia nigra is embedded in a region of the midbrain called the ventral tegmental area which is the origin of the three remaining dopaminergic pathways. Two of these pathways – the mesocortical and mesolimbic – have long axons which project to the frontal cortex and limbic system respectively (these pathways have been implicated in schizophrenia and reward – see Chapters 10 and 12). The fourth pathway projects to the hypothalamus and is known to control the release of the hormone prolactin.

Self-test questions

1. What is biological psychology?
2. How many ventricles are there in the brain?
3. How did Descartes try to resolve the mind–brain problem?
4. What contribution did Luigi Galvani make to understanding neural communication?
5. How did Ramon y Cajel use the Golgi technique to describe the brain?
6. Draw a picture of a typical brain neuron and label its various parts.
7. What is the gap between neurons called?
8. How did Otto Loewi prove the chemical nature of neurotransmission?
9. What is the difference between a drug with agonist actions and one that has an antagonistic effect?
10. Why was the discovery of the giant squid neuron important?
11. What is an ion?
12. Describe the differences in ion concentration that exist in and outside the cell when it is at rest.
13. Describe how an action potential is created and propagated along the axon.
14. Explain what is meant by presynaptic and postsynaptic neurons.
15. Explain what is meant by the terms *receptor*, *second messenger* and *ion channel*.
16. What is the master gland of the endocrine system called, and how is it controlled?
17. Briefly describe the main divisions of the nervous system.
18. How are monoamine neurons organised in the brain?
19. What types of neurotransmitters are found in neurons deriving from the locus coeruleus and the raphe nuclei?

Key terms

Acetylcholine (p.9)
Action potential (p.9)
Adenylate cyclase (p.22)
Agonist (p.10)
Amygdala (p.31)
Antagonist (p.10)
Auditory cortex (p.31)
Autonomic nervous system (p.23)
Axon (p.7)
Axon hillock (p.18)
Basal ganglia (p.31)
Biochemistry (p.3)
Brainstem (p.28)
Central nervous system (p.23)
Cephalisation (p.27)
Cerebellum (p.29)
Cerebral cortex (p.31)
Cingulate gyrus (p.31)
Corpus callosum (p.31)
Cyclic AMP (p.22)
Dendrite (p.7)
Diffusion gradient (p.16)
Dopamine (p.9)
Electrostatic gradient (p.16)
Endocrinology (p.3)
Excitatory postsynaptic potential (p.18)
Exocytosis (p.20)
Flight or fight response (p.24)
GABA (p.9)
Genetics (p.3)
Globus pallidus (p.31)
Glutamate (p.9)
Hippocampus (p.31)
Hormone (p.25)
Hypothalamus (p.25)
Immunology (p.3)
Inferior colliculi (p.29)
Inhibitory postsynaptic potential (p.18)
Interneuron (p.8)
Ion channel (p.17)
Lateral geniculate bodies (p.31)
Lesioning (p.3)
Limbic system (p.31)
Locus coeruleus (p.30)
Medial geniculate nuclei (p.31)
Medulla (p.28)
Monoamine oxidase (p.21)
Myelin (p.8)
Negative feedback (p.25)
Neuroanatomy (p.3)
Neuromodulator (p.9)
Neuron (p.2)
Neurophysiology (p.3)
Neuropsychology (p.3)
Neurotransmitter (p.9)
Nodes of Ranvier (p.19)
Noradrenaline (p.9)
Parasympathetic nervous system (p.24)
Parkinson's disease (p.31)
Periaqueductal grey area (p.29)
Peripheral nervous system (p.23)
Pharmacology (p.3)
Pineal gland (p.5)
Pituitary gland (p.25)
Pons (p.28)
Postsynaptic (p.9)
Presynaptic (p.8)
Protein phosphorylation (p.22)
Psychiatry (p.3)
Raphe nuclei (p.30)
Receptor (p.9)
Red nucleus (p.29)
Reflex (p.5)
Refractory period (p.18)
Resting potential (p.13)
Reticular activating system (p.30)
Re-uptake pump (p.21)
Saltatory conduction (p.19)
Second messenger (p.21)
Serotonin (p.9)
Sodium–potassium pump (p.17)
Soma (p.8)
Somatic nervous system (p.23)
Stimulation (p.3)

References

Blakemore, C. B. (1977) *Mechanisms of Mind*. Cambridge: Cambridge University Press.

Davis, H. P. *et al.* (1988) Biological psychology's relationships to psychology and neuroscience. *American Psychologist*, **43**, 359–71.

Dewsbury, D. A. (1991) 'Psychobiology'. *American Psychologist*, **46**, 198–205.

Dudel, J. (1978) Excitation of nerve and muscle. In R. F. Schmidt (ed.) *Fundamentals of Neurophysiology*. New York: Springer-Verlag.

Finger, S. (1994) *Origins of Neuroscience*. New York: Oxford University Press.

Foote, S. L. (1987) Locus ceruleus. In Adelman, G. (ed.) *Encyclopedia of Neuroscience*. Boston: Birkhauser.

Gilling, D. and Brightwell, R. (1982) *The Human Brain*. London: Orbis.

Gregory, R. L. (1981) *Mind in Science*. London: Penguin.

Hodgkin, A. L. (1958) The Croonian Lecture: Ionic movements and electrical activity in giant nerve fibres. *Proceedings of the Royal Society of London, B*, **148**, 1–37.

Keynes, R. D. (1979) Ion channels in the nerve-cell membrane. *Scientific American*, **240**, 126–35.

Mazzolini, R. G. (1991) In Corsi, P. (ed.) *The Enchanted Loom: Chapters in the History of Neuroscience*. New York: Oxford University Press.

Piccolino, M. (1997) Luigi Galvani and animal electricity: two centuries after the foundation of electrophysiology. *Trends in Neuroscience*, **20**, 443–8.

Sheperd, G. M. (1991) *Foundations of the Neuron Doctrine*. New York: Oxford University Press.

Snyder, S. H. (1986) *Drugs and the Brain*. New York: Scientific American Library.

Stevens, C. F. (1979) The neuron. In *The Brain*. New York: Scientific American Books.

Thompson, R. F. (1993) *The Brain: A Neuroscience Primer*. New York: Freeman.

Watson, J. B. (1913) Psychology as the behaviorist views it. *Psychological Review*, **20**, 158–77.

FURTHER READING

Brodal, P. (1998) *The Central Nervous System: Structure and Function*. Oxford: Oxford University Press.

Guyton, A. C. (1991) *Basic Neuroscience: Anatomy and Physiology*. Philadelphia: Saunders.

Levitan, I. B. and Kaczmarek, L. K. (1991) *The Neuron*. Oxford: Oxford University Press.

Kandel, E. R. *et al.* (1991) *Principles of Neural Science*. New York: Prentice Hall.

Kiernan, J. A. (1998) *Barr's The Human Nervous System*. Philadelphia: Lippincott-Raven.
Nicholls, J. G. *et al.* (1992) *From Neuron to Brain* (3rd edn). Sunderland, MA: Sinauer.
Smith, A. (1984) *The Mind*. London: Hodder & Stoughton.

Multiple choice questions

For each chapter:

11 correct = pass
12–14 correct = good
15+ correct = excellent

1. If you took a second to count every neuron in the brain it would take over:

(a) 100 years
(b) 1,000 years
(c) 10,000 years
(d) 30,000 years

2. The connected series of fluid-filled cavities that occur throughout the brain are known as the:

(a) rete mirabile
(b) vesicles
(c) subarachnoid spaces
(d) ventricles

3. According to Descartes, the site at which the mind and body interacted was the:

(a) hypothalamus
(b) pineal gland
(c) lateral ventricles
(d) pituitary gland

4. The discovery of the Golgi technique was important because:

(a) it was the first stain that 'worked' on brain neurons
(b) it only stained a small number of brain cells in any piece of tissue
(c) it caused brain cells to fluoresce
(d) it only stained axons enabling the brain's pathways to be mapped out

5. The __________ is the main part of the neuron that receives incoming messages, and the _________ is the main conductor of information along the neuron's length.

(a) axon, dendrites
(b) nucleus, axon
(c) dendrites, axon
(d) nodes of Ranvier, dendrites

6. The person who discovered the chemical basis of neurotransmission was:

(a) Otto Loewi
(b) Charles Sherrington
(c) Ramon y Cajel
(d) Luigi Galvani

7. In response to an action potential, the presynaptic neuron releases a chemical called a ________________ which diffuses across the ____________ to activate ____________ on the postsynaptic cell.

(a) neuromodulator, synaptic gap, end plate
(b) neurotransmitter, synaptic gap, calcium channels
(c) catecholamine, myelin, receptors
(d) neurotransmitter, synaptic gap, receptors

8. During its resting state, the electrical charge inside the neuron is ___________ compared to the outside.

(a) positive (+70 mV)
(b) negative (–70 mV)
(c) neutral (0 mV)
(d) it differs greatly depending upon what part of the neuron is examined

9. During the neuron's resting state, large amounts of positive __________ions are found in the extracellular fluid, whereas relatively more positive ______________ ions are found inside the cell.

(a) chloride, anions
(b) sodium, potassium
(c) potassium, chloride
(d) sodium, calcium

10. The site where the threshold potential (–55 mV) has to occur in order to produce an axon potential is the:

(a) axon
(b) axon hillock
(c) dendritic spines
(d) soma

11. The reason why there is a sudden shift in the electrical potential of the neuron (from about –70 mV to about +50 mV) during an action potential is largely due to the sudden influx of ____________ ions.

(a) calcium
(b) chloride

(c) potassium
(d) sodium

12. When the action potential reaches the axon terminal it stimulates the release of neurotransmitter by causing ________________ to fuse with the presynaptic membrane.

(a) sodium ions
(b) calcium ions
(c) cyclic AMP
(d) synaptic vesicles

13. Monoamine oxidase is an enzyme which is involved in:

(a) synthesising catecholamines
(b) breaking down excess neurotransmitter
(c) the working of the re-uptake pump
(d) removing sodium from the intracellular compartment

14. A second messenger is:

(a) a neuromodulator that is released along with a neurotransmitter
(b) a neurotransmitter that binds with more than one type of receptor
(c) a chemical in the postsynaptic cell that causes the opening of ion channels
(d) a chemical that enhances the effects of neurotransmitter at the receptor

15. The central nervous system consists of the:

(a) brain and the spinal cord
(b) brain and the autonomic nervous system
(c) brain and the somatic nervous system
(d) brain only

16. What is the 'master gland' of the hormone system?

(a) the pineal gland
(b) the thalamus
(c) the thyroid gland
(d) the pituitary gland

17. Grey matter is composed of _____________ while white matter is composed of __________________.

(a) cell bodies, myelinated axons
(b) sensory neurons, motor neurons
(c) interneurons, sensory and motor neurons
(d) myelinated axons, cell bodies

18. As the spinal cord enters the brain it develops into the:

(a) cerebellum
(b) brainstem
(c) pons
(d) hippocampus

19. The two main structures of the diencephalon are the:

(a) hypothalamus and thalamus
(b) lateral and medial geniculate bodies
(c) locus coeruleus and raphe
(d) none of the above

20. Which of the following structures is not an area of the forebrain?

(a) cerebral cortex
(b) basal ganglia
(c) the limbic system
(d) substantia nigra

2 The visual system

IN THIS CHAPTER

- The structure of the eye and the retina
- Visual pathways from the retina to the visual cortex
- The concept of receptive fields
- How the visual cortex processes orientation, form and depth
- The role of visual association cortex
- Theories of colour vision
- Subcortical structures involved in vision including the superior colliculus
- Blindsight

Introduction

Most people would agree that our ability to detect changes in light (vision) provides us with our most important sense. Human beings have a highly sophisticated visual system and it provides us with detailed information about the form and pattern of the world around us. For example, we are able to detect shapes, follow movement, differentiate colours and judge distances. Furthermore, we can focus on nearby objects one second and see far into the distance the next; and if an object should unexpectedly appear in the corner of our eye, then we are likely to reflexively turn our gaze to it in a fraction of a second. Indeed, it would be remarkable enough if our vision was simply like a cine camera that faithfully recorded our visual world for us, but even this does our visual system an injustice because what we perceive is often different to what the eyes 'see'. In

Figure 2.1 A jumble of lines – until you realise that there is a picture there! (See answer at foot of page.)

other words, vision is a creative process (see Figure 2.1). Clearly, our ability to process visual information is extremely complex and about one-third of the human brain is devoted to visual analysis and perception. As might be expected, the visual system is the most extensively studied of all our senses and we probably know more about the mechanisms underlying vision than any other aspect of brain function. Because of this, the study of vision provides one of the most important and instructive topics in biological psychology.

What is light?

The stimulus for activating the visual system is **light**, which is a form of electromagnetic radiation generated by the oscillation of electrically charged particles called photons. There are many forms of electromagnetic radiation (such as gamma rays, ultraviolet light and radio waves) and all move at the same speed: 186,000 miles per second (one might wonder why something travelling this fast does not hurt us!). What differentiates each form of electromagnetic radiation is its wavelength (see Figure 2.2) and light is no exception. In fact, light is simply a narrow band of the electromagnetic spectrum that has a wavelength ranging from about 380 to 760 nanometres (a nanometre, shortened to 'nm', is one-billionth of a metre). In other words, our visual system is designed to detect only a very small portion of the electromagnetic spectrum that surrounds us.

The two most important qualities that we *perceive* from light are its colour and brightness. Colour is produced by the length of the light's wavelength. For example, the shortest wavelength detectable by the human eye occurs at about 380 nm and this produces the sensation of violet. And, as the length of the light waves increases so the sensation of colour changes (e.g. approximating to violet, blue, green, yellow and, finally, red). The brightness of a colour, however, is not related to its wavelength, but

Answer: Back view of a washer-woman kneeling down with her bucket!

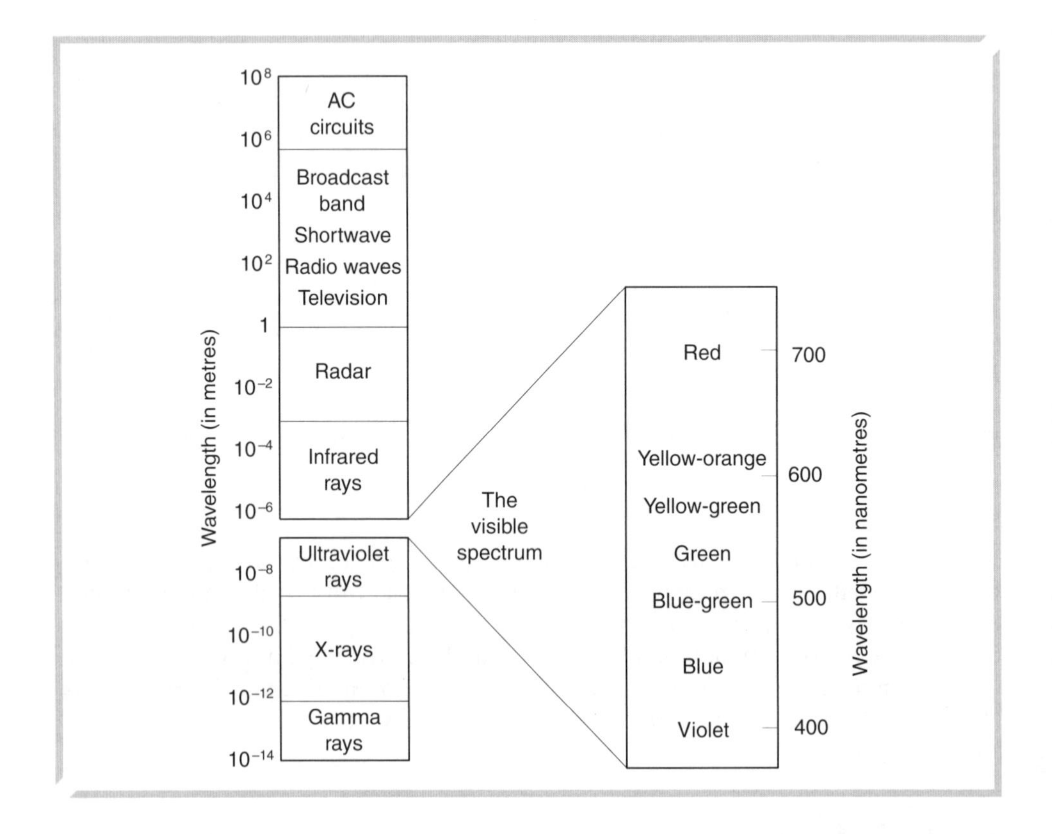

Figure 2.2 The total electromagnetic spectrum.

rather to the amplitude (or height) of its oscillation, and this is directly proportional to the density (energy) of photons in the wave. In other words, the more photons per unit area in the wave, the brighter the light will appear to be.

Of course, we rarely see just pure shades of light and most of our visual world is made up of objects that reflect a wide range of different wavelengths. In fact, we can only see an object if light striking its surface is partially absorbed (if an object was to absorb all light hitting its surface then it would appear to us as pitch black, and if the same object reflected all light, then we would only see a mirror surface of the light source). Thus, it is the patterns of reflection and absorption (along with the many wavelengths they create) that allow us to see the shapes and surfaces of objects.

The structure of the eye

The eye is the sensory organ for sight and its main function is to detect changes in light intensity and to transmit this information via the optic nerves to the brain. The human eye can be compared to a camera: both are basically darkened chambers with a small aperture at the front (to let in light); a focusing mechanism; and a plate to receive the projected image at the back (see Figure 2.3). In the case of a camera it is the photographic film which records the image, and in the eye it is the photoreceptors located on the retina that perform the same role. Unlike the camera, however, the eye's photoreceptors have to translate light into continuous neural information in order to send it to the brain.

If we were to remove an eye from its socket we would find that it has a spherical shape, and, for the most part (except for the front), is covered in a tough white tissue called the **sclera** (which we normally see as the 'white of the eye'). The front of the eye, however, is transparent and its surface is called the **cornea**, which is the round window where light first enters the eye. The cornea gives the eye most of its focusing power, and once light has passed through this transparent layer it travels through the **aqueous humour** and reaches the **pupil**. This is simply an aperture (gap) that controls the amount of light entering the next chamber of the eye, and is controlled by a ring of muscles called the **iris** which gives the eye its colour. The iris contains two bands of muscles: the dilator (whose contraction enlarges the pupil), and the sphincter (whose contraction reduces it). Situated just behind the pupil is the **lens** whose function is to help bring visual images into sharp focus by acting as a 'fine adjustment' to the cornea. The shape of the lens is under the control of the **ciliary muscles** which can either contract to make the lens 'bend' (to enable vision of nearby objects) or relax to make it 'flat' (to allow distance vision). Behind the lens lies the **vitreous humour**, a clear gelatinous substance which helps maintain the shape of the eye. After passing through the vitreous humour, light falls on the **retina**.

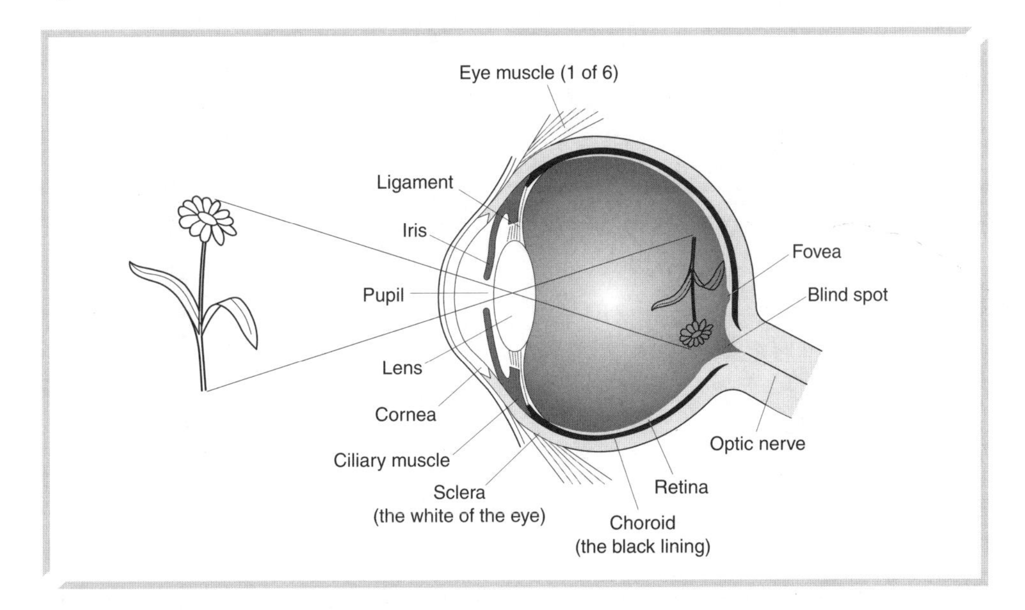

Figure 2.3 The structure of the human eye. (*Source*: From John P. J. Pinel, *Biopsychology*, 3rd edition. Copyright © 1997 by Allyn & Bacon. Reprinted by permission.)

The structure of the retina

The neural processing of visual information begins with the photoreceptors located at the back of the retina, of which there are two types: **rods** and **cones**. There are approximately 120 million rods and 6 million cones in each retina, and they are also differently distributed with the rods being mainly found on the periphery and the cones located in the centre (or **fovea**). Moreover, the rods and cones are also specialised to deal with different types of light. The rods allow us to see in dim lighting conditions (although they are poor at seeing visual detail), whereas the cones function best in bright light, as well as enabling us to see fine detail (i.e. they provide vision of the greatest sharpness) and colour (i.e. they are able to discriminate different wavelengths of light). Thus, although the cones are heavily outnumbered by rods, they nevertheless provide us with our most detailed visual information.

The retina is only about 250 micrometres thick (about the same size as the edge of a razor blade) but contains several layers of other cells (Figure 2.4). The rods and cones

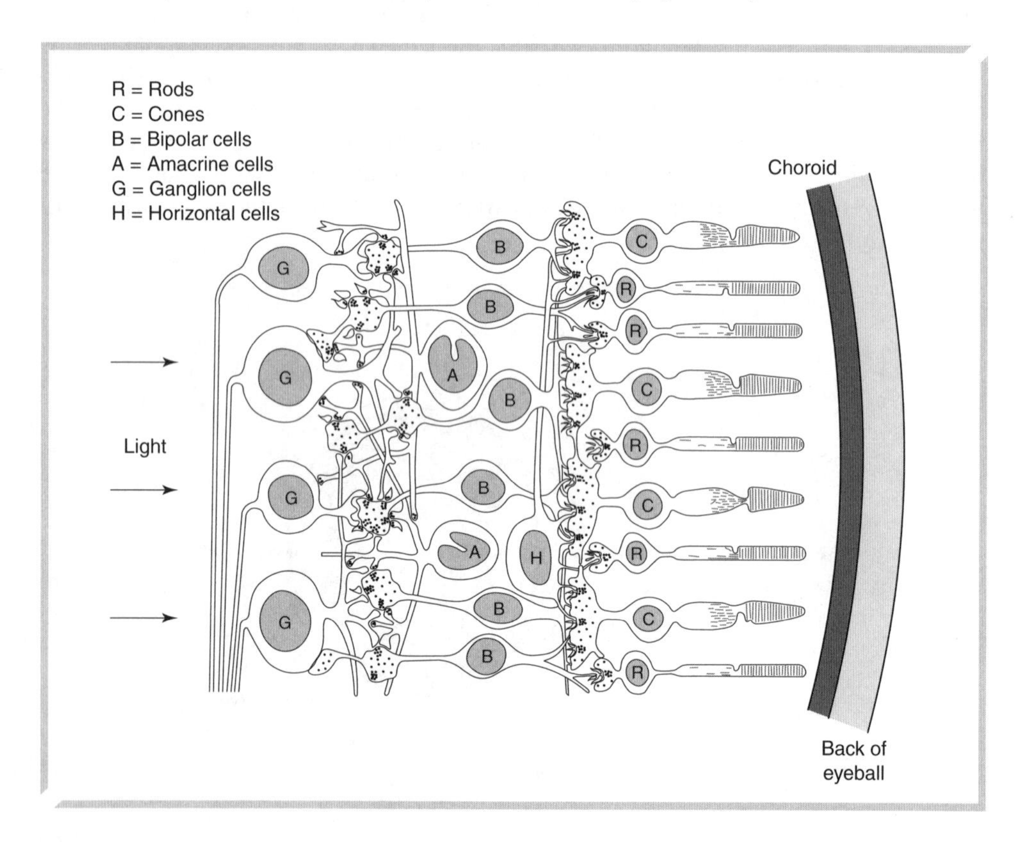

Figure 2.4 The neural structure of the human retina. (*Source*: Redrawn from J. E. Dowling and B. B. Boycott, *Proceedings of the Royal Society of London* (1966), **166**, 80–111. Reprinted by permission.)

are located on the back surface of the retina and, oddly, light has to pass through the overlying cell layers to reach them. This would appear to be an unusual way of 'designing' the retina, particularly as one would expect the overlying cells to interfere with the projection of the visual input, but it seems that little visual disturbance occurs. One function of both the rods and cones is to transduce light into neural information which they pass on to the next layer of cells, known as the **bipolar cells**. In turn, the bipolar cells project to the **ganglion cells** whose cell bodies are situated in the outer layer of the retina and whose axons travel on its surface, to form the optic nerve that carries visual information to the brain. The retina also contains **horizontal cells** (which project laterally and interconnect the photoreceptors) and **amacrine cells** (that link the bipolar and ganglion cells in much the same way). Although the function of these cells is not fully understood, it is known that they transmit and modify signals travelling through the retina. Thus, a considerable amount of neural processing takes place at the retina before visual information reaches the optic nerve (e.g. see Michael 1969).

There are approximately 800,000 axons in each optic nerve and, as we have seen, over 120 million photoreceptors in the retina. This means that a considerable convergence of neural input must take place by the time information has been transferred from the rods and cones to each ganglion cell. In fact, the degree of convergence depends largely upon the location of the photoreceptor in the retina. In the periphery, several hundred photoreceptors may converge onto a single ganglion cell. But this figure gets less towards the centre of the retina, and in the fovea there is a much closer correspondence between photoreceptor and ganglion cell (i.e. it may receive input from just a few cones). This relationship helps to explain the better acuity of foveal vision compared to peripheral (or rod) vision. In contrast, because large numbers of rods send information to individual ganglion cells, this 'extra' stimulation means that it is more likely to fire, which helps to explain why rods are better at detecting changes in dim light (see Figure 2.5).

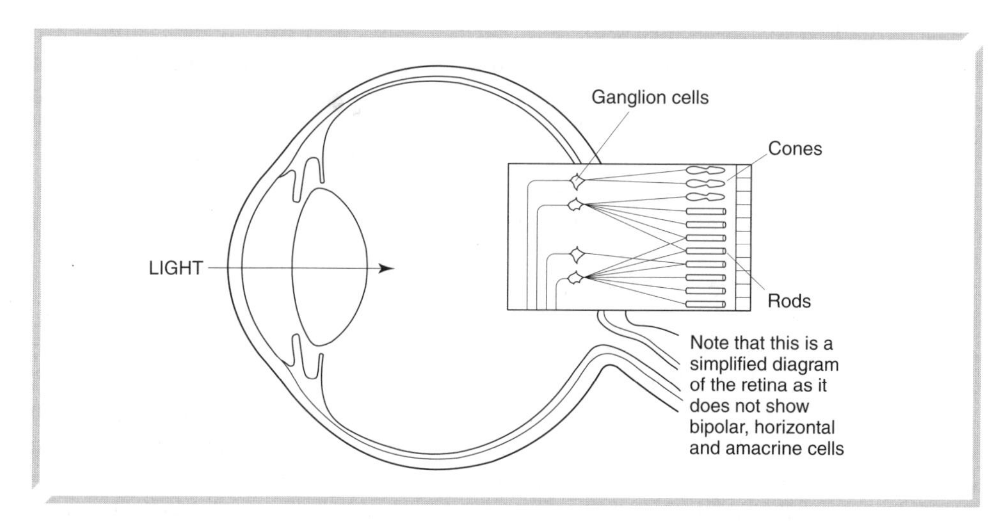

Figure 2.5 The convergence of input from cones and rods onto retinal ganglion cells.

The visual pathways to the brain

The axons of the ganglion cells join together to form the optic nerve, which leaves the retina (at the 'blind spot') and travels along the lower surface of the brain until it reaches the front of the pituitary stalk. At this point, the two optic nerves converge and form the **optic chiasm**. The optic chiasm is a 'crossing-over' point where some (but not all) of the optic nerve axons cross to the opposite side of the brain. This occurs in the following way: the axons extending from the nasal side of the retina (which includes most of the fovea) cross to the opposite (contralateral) side of the brain; while the fibres from the rest of the retina continue on the same (ipsilateral) side. Although no synapses occur in the optic chiasm (i.e. the axons pass straight through), the fibres that leave the optic chiasm are sometimes referred to as the optic tract. Each tract then enters the brain where the majority of axons (about 80 per cent) will terminate in the **dorsal lateral geniculate nucleus** (located in the thalamus). The remainder of the optic tract branches away and projects instead to a number of subcortical structures including the **superior colliculus** and **tectum**.

There are two lateral geniculate nuclei (one on each side of the brain) and each contains six layers of cells. Although each nucleus receives information from both eyes, at this point the input is still segregated since each cell layer receives input from only one eye (see later). In turn, the axons from the various geniculate layers form a pathway (called the **optic radiations**) which projects ipsilaterally to the **primary visual cortex**. This region is situated in the **occipital lobe** (the most posterior part of the cerebral cortex) and is often referred to as the **striate cortex** because of its striped appearance. In the human brain the visual cortex is about 1.5 mm in thickness and, like the rest of the cortex, is composed of six distinct layers (the axons from the lateral geniculate nucleus terminate in the fourth layer). It is also the first structure where input from both the eyes converges enabling binocular processing to take place.

The visual cortex is organised topographically – that is, if two adjacent points are stimulated on the retina (resulting in two different ganglion cells firing) then adjacent areas in the visual cortex will also be activated. In other words, there is a direct correspondence (or 'mapping') between the layout of the photoreceptors in the retina and layout of neurons in the visual cortex (see Figure 2.6). Despite this, the topographic organisation of the visual cortex is heavily biased to processing foveal information. Although the fovea forms only a small part of the retina (less than half a millimetre in diameter), about 25 per cent of the visual cortex is devoted to analysing its input. It can also be seen from Figure 2.6 that because the axons from the nasal halves of the retina cross to the other side of the brain, each hemisphere thus receives information from the opposite side of the visual scene. In other words, if a person looks straight ahead, the left hemisphere will receive information from the right half of the overall visual field, and the right hemisphere will obtain visual input from the left – that is, although each visual cortex receives input from *both* eyes, the right visual cortex only processes information from the left side of its world and the left visual cortex only processes information from the right side of its world. (You will need to study Figure 2.6 carefully to understand this point!)

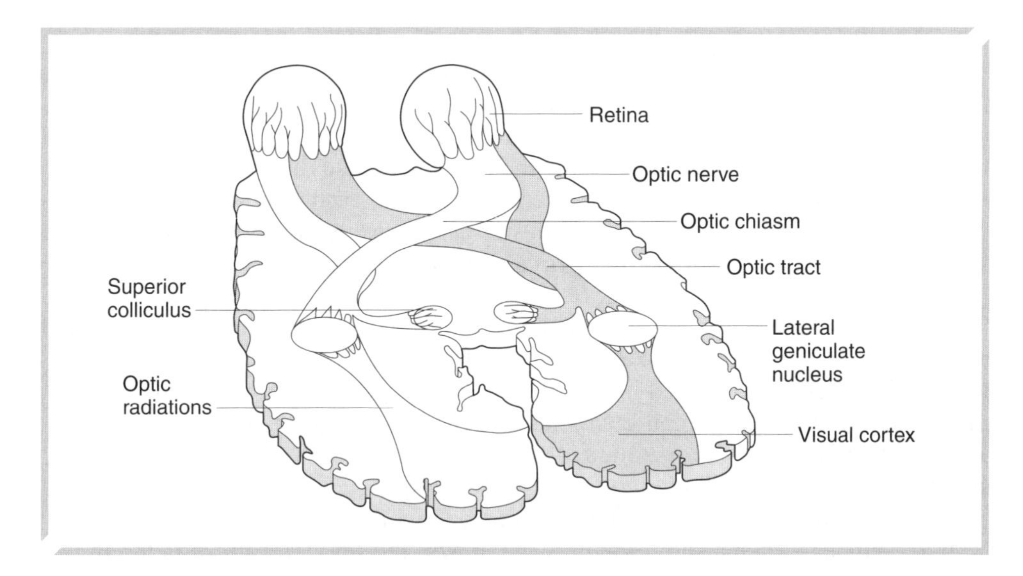

Figure 2.6 The primary visual pathways from retina to cortex. (*Source*: Reproduced by permission of the Open University from Course SD286, Module C7.)

Once information has been processed by the visual cortex it is then passed to the adjacent **prestriate cortex** at which point it can take a number of routes through the brain. In fact, there are at least 30 other areas of the cortex that are known to have at least some involvement in further visual processing, which gives some idea of how complex the processing of vision really is.

The receptive fields of retinal ganglion cells

A single retinal ganglion cell (whose axon travels through the optic nerve) receives information from a population of receptor cells (rods and cones) located at the back of the retina. The surface area covered by these photoreceptors – or, more accurately, all the retinal receptors that contribute to the ganglion cell's neural activity – is called its **receptive field** and, as we shall see, the mapping of these fields has provided researchers with a very powerful means of understanding how the visual system encodes information. To identify a ganglion receptive field, however, is no easy task. First, a microelectrode has to be inserted into the retina or optic nerve of an anaesthetised animal, following which the eye is presented with a series of stimuli (projected directly onto the retina or onto a white screen the animal is facing) until the microelectrode picks up the electrical activity of the visual input. This search may take hours, but once identified the characteristics of the receptive field can then be mapped in fine detail.

Much of what we know about the receptive fields of mammalian retinal ganglion cells we owe to the work of Stephen Kuffler who first pioneered this type of research in the 1950s working with cats (e.g. Kuffler 1953). One of Kuffler's first discoveries was that ganglion cells were never 'silent'; in fact, they were continually generating action potentials – with diffuse light and darkness sufficient to produce a background spontaneous firing rate of approximately 5 impulses per second. But Kuffler was much more interested in discovering how ganglion cells responded to different types of stimuli, and to examine this problem he began to map their receptive fields using a fine spot of light. Using this technique, he found that the receptive field of each ganglion cell was always circular in shape, and that they varied in size across the retina with foveal receptive fields being small, and those on the periphery being much larger.

There was, however, a much more important characteristic of ganglion receptive fields: they contained two zones – a circular central area and a surrounding ring-shaped outer zone. Moreover, these zones produced different types of neural activity in response to visual stimulation. For example, in some ganglion cells, a spot of light shone directly into the central region greatly increased its rate of firing (an 'on' response), whereas light falling on the surround inhibited it (an 'off' response). In other cells, the situation was reversed: illumination of the centre producing an 'off' response and stimulation of the surround an 'on' response (see Figure 2.7).

What happens when a spot of light is shone over the whole receptive field? In this case Kuffler found that the 'on' and 'off' responses tended to cancel each other out. Furthermore, the extent of this antagonistic effect depended on the relative proportions of the on–off regions that were stimulated. For example, if a spot of light was progressively made larger at the centre of an on-centre cell, Kuffler found that the firing rate of this cell increased until the centre was completely filled – at which point the response began to decline as the light encroached into the off-surround. As the surround became filled, however, it cancelled out the cell's on-response, returning it to

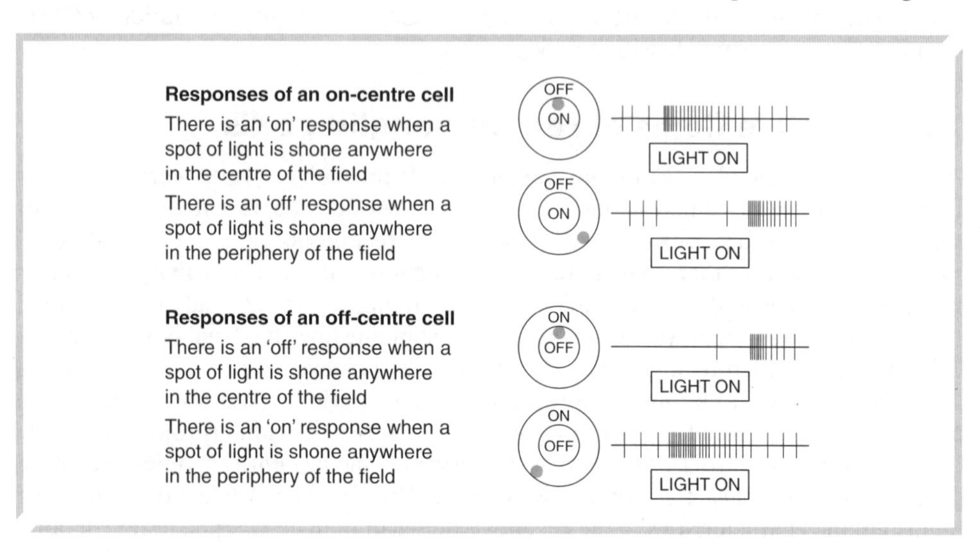

Figure 2.7 The receptive fields of an on-centre and off-centre ganglion cell. (*Source*: From John P. J. Pinel, *Biopsychology*, 3rd edition. Copyright © 1997 by Allyn & Bacon. Reprinted by permission.)

its baseline level of firing. In other words, the ganglion cell shows a graded response to a light stimulus projecting on its receptive field.

Receptive fields in the visual cortex

In the late 1950s and early 1960s, David Hubel and Tortsten Wiesel extended Kuffler's work by examining the receptive fields of neurons located in the lateral geniculate nucleus and visual cortex (Hubel and Wiesel 1959, 1963a). Their approach was similar to Kuffler's – they presented anaesthetised cats (who wore special contact lenses) with various types of visual stimuli and recorded the resulting activity of single neurons in the brain. Because the lateral geniculate nucleus and visual cortex both contain several layers of very small cells, it took Hubel and Wiesel several years before they perfected the technique of being able to visually stimulate groups of retinal cells while simultaneously recording from individual neurons in the brain. Nevertheless, their work was worth the effort as it has provided many crucial insights into the cortical processing of vision, and was to win them the Nobel Prize for Physiology and Medicine in 1981 (see Jasper and Sourkes 1983).

Hubel and Wiesel first examined the receptive fields of neurons located in the lateral geniculate nucleus which forms the main relay station between the retina and the visual cortex (i.e. geniculate neurons receive input from the retinal ganglion cells and, in turn, send their axons onwards to the visual cortex). When Hubel and Wiesel did this, they found that the geniculate receptive fields had essentially the same characteristics as those obtained from retinal ganglion cells. In other words, the receptive field of all the neurons in the visual pathway from retina to visual cortex showed the same basic type of concentric on–off response as described by Kuffler.

However, when Hubel and Wiesel recorded from cells in the visual cortex, they found that their receptive fields were considerably different to those in the retina and lateral geniculate nucleus. Like other areas of the cerebral cortex, the visual cortex contains six layers of cells and, counting down from the surface, it is the fourth layer that receives the incoming axon fibres from the lateral geniculate nucleus. When recording from single cells at this level, it was found that the maximal stimulus was not a single spot of light, but a series of spots arranged in a straight line. Thus, before a cell in this layer of the visual cortex could have any significant increase in its firing, the stimulus that was presented to its receptive field (at the retina) had to be a straight line. These cells were also found to show antagonistic on–off regions (like the receptive fields of ganglion cells) except that they were now oblong in shape rather than round. Also, as might be expected, these brain cells tended to fire maximally when the line was located in a very specific orientation on the retina that corresponded to the 'on' region of the receptive field (e.g. see Hubel and Wiesel 1977a). Hubel and Wiesel named these cells in the visual cortex **simple cells** (see Figure 2.8).

How does a concentric receptive field of the ganglion cell become oblong in the cortical simple cell? The answer lies with the way simple cells receive input from the lateral geniculate nucleus. In short, it appears that each simple cell receives converging input from an array of lateral geniculate neurons, and the connections are 'wired' in

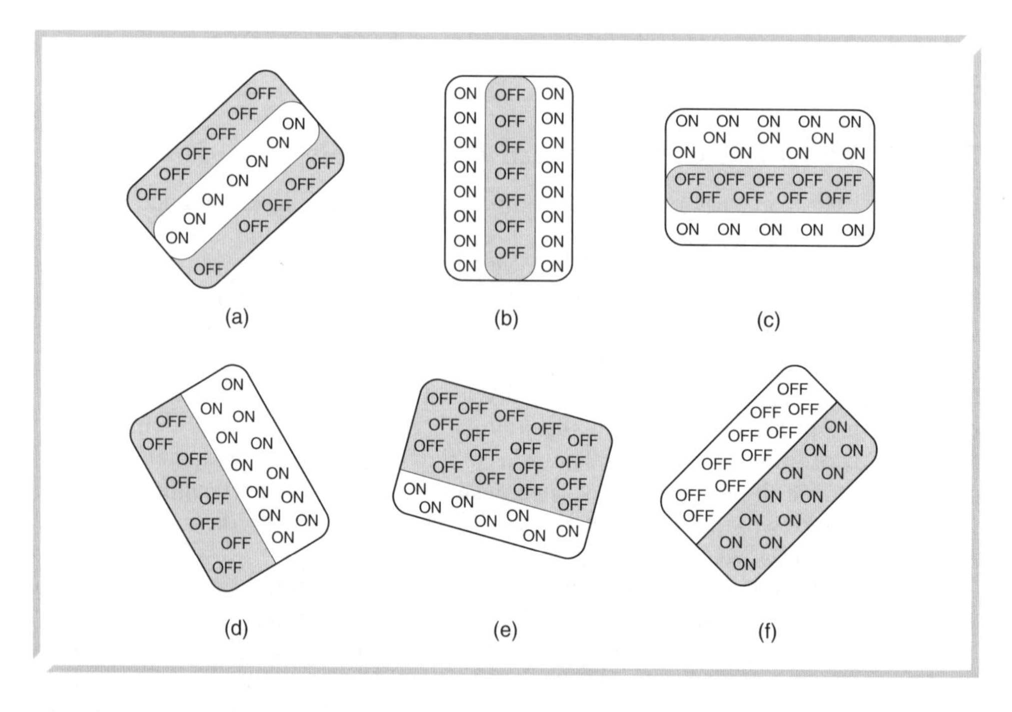

Figure 2.8 Examples of simple cortical cell visual fields. (*Source*: From John P. J. Pinel, *Biopsychology*, 3rd edition. Copyright © 1997 by Allyn & Bacon. Reprinted by permission.)

such a way that a straight line that stimulates many receptors on the retina has an effect on only a single cell in the cortex. In other words, there is convergence of input from arrays of cells feeding into 'higher' individual cells (see Figure 2.9). Not only is this type of hierarchical wiring pattern found throughout the visual system, but it also appears to be a general feature of the brain.

Complex and hypercomplex cells

Simple cells were not the only type of cell to be found in the visual cortex. When Hubel and Wiesel moved their recording electrodes from layer IV (where simple cells were located) through the other layers of the visual cortex, they discovered two other types of cell which they called **complex** and **hypercomplex**. Complex cells (which are, in fact, the most common type of cell in the visual cortex) are similar to simple cells, except that they respond maximally when a line is anywhere in their oblong receptive field providing it is in the correct orientation. In other words, the line stimulus does not have to be precisely located in the centre of the receptive field as long as it is parallel with it. Complex cells also appear to be much more sensitive to movement than simple cells since they often fire maximally when a stimulus (usually a line) is moved into the appropriate region of a receptive field from a particular direction (Hubel and Wiesel 1977b).

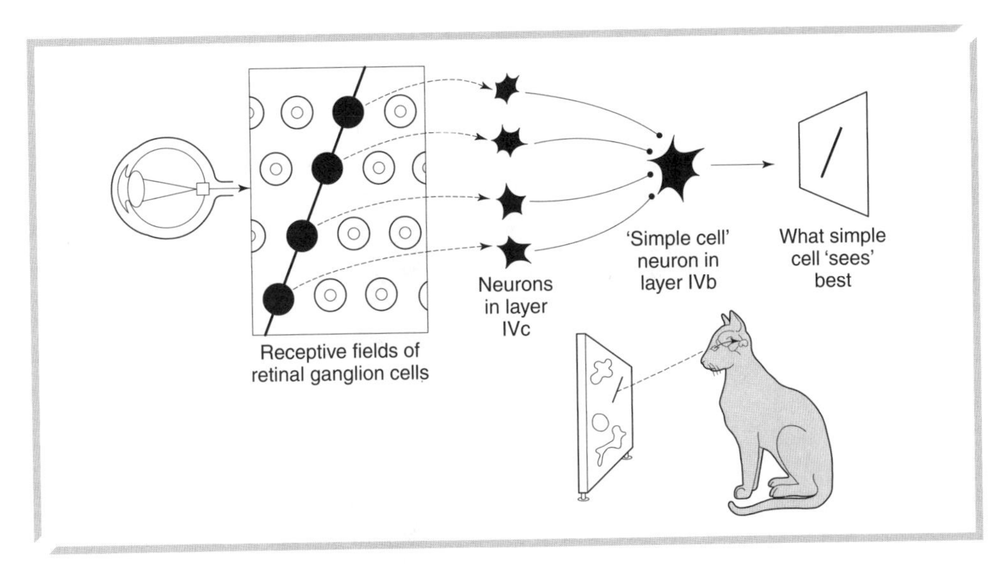

Figure 2.9 An illustration of how simple cells may be 'wired' from geniculate neurons. (*Source*: From A. M. Schneider and B. Tarshis, *Elements of Physiological Psychology*. Copyright © 1995 by McGraw-Hill. Reprinted by permission.)

Hypercomplex cells are similar to complex cells, except that they appear to have an extra inhibitory area at the ends of their receptive field. This means that they respond best when the line is not only in a specific orientation, but also of a certain length. In fact, if the line is too long and extends into the inhibitory part of the receptive field (or out of the receptive field completely) then the firing rate of the cell declines. Some hypercomplex cells also appear to respond maximally to two line segments meeting at a particular point, suggesting that they may also act as angle detectors.

The arrangement of cells in the primary visual cortex

Hubel and Wiesel also discovered that the visual cortex comprises columns in which all the cells share similar properties. For example, if a microelectrode is lowered into the cortex, perpendicular to its surface, not only will simple, complex and hypercomplex cells be found, but the centres of their respective receptive fields will also be approximately the same. In other words, all neurons in a particular column respond maximally to the same stimulus orientation within their receptive field. Thus, if a simple cell is found to respond best to a vertical line, the complex and hypercomplex cells in the same column will also respond preferentially to vertical lines.

As the recording electrode is moved from one column to the next, however, another interesting feature of the visual cortex is observed. In short, the preferred axis of orientation of the lines rotates in a clockwise manner with each 0.05 mm of lateral movement producing a corresponding rotation of 10° (see Figure 2.10). In other words, if the cells

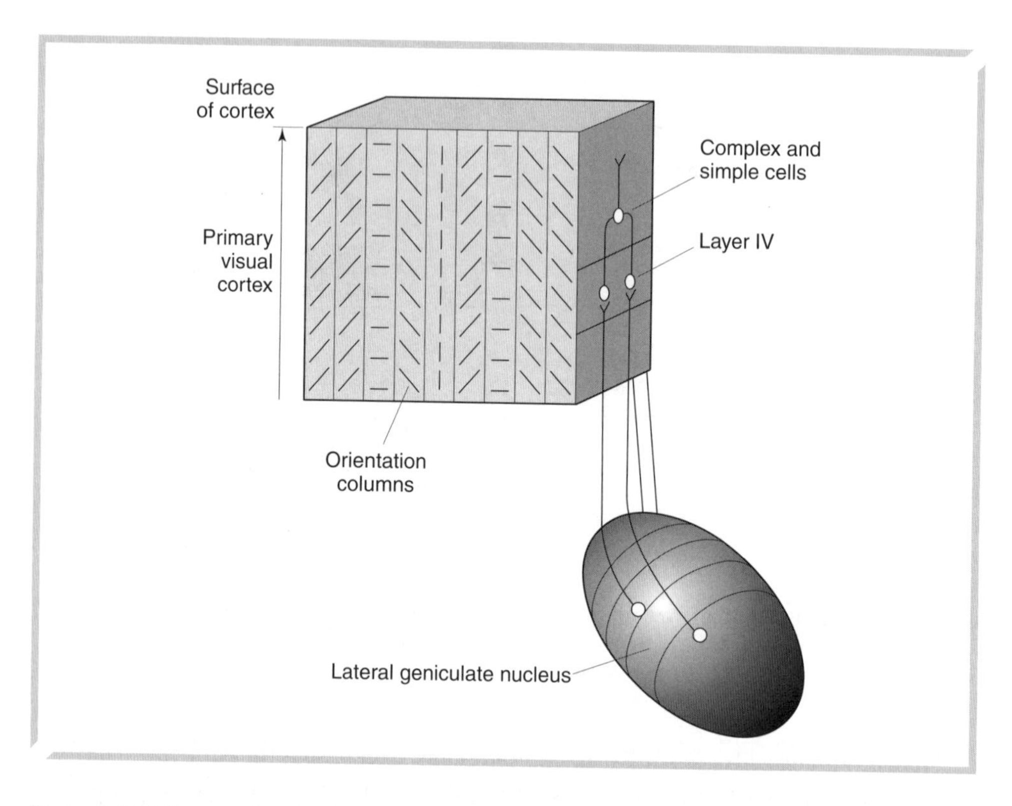

Figure 2.10 Diagram showing how the orientation sensitivity of neurons in the visual cortex rotates when a recording electrode is moved across its surface. (*Source*: From A. M. Schneider and B. Tarshis, *Elements of Physiological Psychology*. Copyright © 1995 by McGraw-Hill. Reprinted by permission.)

in one column are all 'tuned' to vertical stimuli, the cells in the next column will respond best to lines 10° from vertical, and so on. In fact, there are enough columns in a 2 mm length of cortex to detect every possible line orientation across 360°. Furthermore, although the cells in each unit have many different preferred receptor field orientations, they all derive from the same part of the retina, showing that each block of orientation cells is involved with processing visual information from the same part of the world (Hubel 1988).

In addition, the columns of the visual cortex are also organised on the basis of ocular dominance. Although we have two eyes, we only see one visual world, indicating that convergence of visual input takes place somewhere in the brain – and the first place where this occurs is the visual cortex. Indeed, it has been found that many cells in the visual cortex have binocular receptive fields (i.e. they respond to information from both eyes), although most show a marked preference for one of the eyes – that is, they will fire more strongly when the 'favoured' eye is stimulated. Moreover, the organisation of ocular dominance in the visual cortex follows a pattern similar to that found for

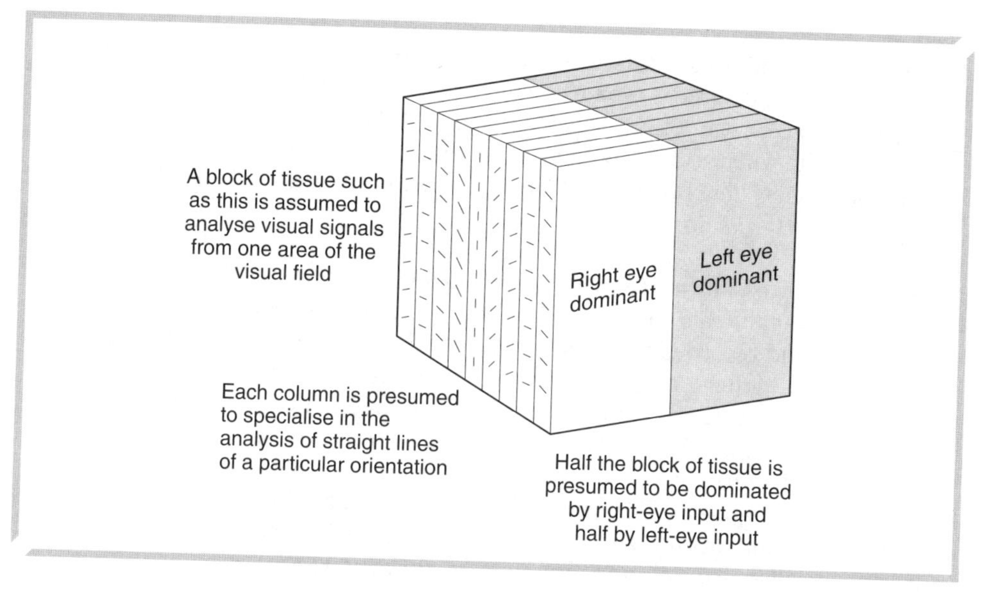

Figure 2.11 An example of a hypercolumn (including ocular dominance and orientation columns).

orientation. In other words, if an electrode is lowered perpendicularly into a column, all of its cells (e.g. simple, complex or hypercomplex) will show a preference for the same eye. As the electrode is moved laterally, however, it is found that right-eye and left-eye preference alternates – with each band alternating every millimetre or so. In fact, as can be seen in Figure 2.11, the orientation and ocular columns are arranged together in functional units, and the term **hypercolumn** has been used to describe this 'unit' of the visual cortex (Mecacci 1991).

Box 2.1 THE EFFECTS OF EARLY VISUAL DEPRIVATION

We may be born with the basic neural architecture of our visual system in place, but this does not mean that in a functional sense our visual system is fully developed. In fact, the visual system is surprisingly malleable – particularly early in life – and early experience can have a considerable bearing on the development of the visual system. This fact has been known since the 19th century when the surgical removal of cataracts became commonplace. For example, when cataracts were removed that had developed in later life, it was found that this procedure quickly reinstated full vision. However, when congenital cataracts were removed from children, full vision was typically not restored – even when an artificial lens was used to produce a good image on the retina. This indicated that there was a sensitive period early in life when visual experience was crucial for the proper development of the visual system to occur, and once this period had passed then vision was permanently impaired.

This idea was shown to be correct by Hubel and Wiesel in the 1960s who reared animals (cats and monkeys) with one eye closed. When they opened that eye and recorded from the visual cortex they found that nearly all the cells were dominated by the eye that had remained open. In fact, very few cells were activated by stimuli that were presented to the eye that had been closed (Hubel and Wiesel 1963b). It was further shown that young animals with restricted visual experience also developed visual cortex cells with abnormal properties. For example, if a kitten is reared in an environment that only contains horizontal lines, almost all of its simple and complex cortical cells will develop a preference for horizontal lines – so much so, that when the cat is later exposed to a normal environment it virtually ignores vertical lines and objects (Hirsch and Spineli 1970).

Similar types of visual deficit also occur with humans. For example, some children are born with a **strabismus** (or 'squint') so that their eyes never look in the same direction at the same time. If this condition is not corrected by the age of 5 or 6, then these children typically develop one good eye with normal vision and one permanently 'lazy' eye with poor acuity. Moreover, if the strabismus is the result of an asymmetric curvature of the cornea, then **astigmatism** may result – that is, a blurring of vision for either horizontal or vertical lines. Like the kittens described earlier, if this is not corrected in early life, then the person's ability to see these lines may become permanently impaired.

Introduction to colour vision

The processing of colour information takes the same anatomical route to the visual cortex as that for pattern vision, and the process starts with the cones in the retina that are specialised to respond to certain wavelengths of light. Our ability to detect colour begins with light wavelengths of around 400 nm which produce the sensation of blue – and this changes to blue–green at around 500 nm; red at around 600 nm; and finally reddish purple as the wavelengths get longer. Obviously, we detect all these different wavelengths because they are transduced by our cones into neural impulses. But this raises an interesting question: How is it we can see so many different colours when we only appear to have one type of photoreceptor for colour (i.e. the cone)?

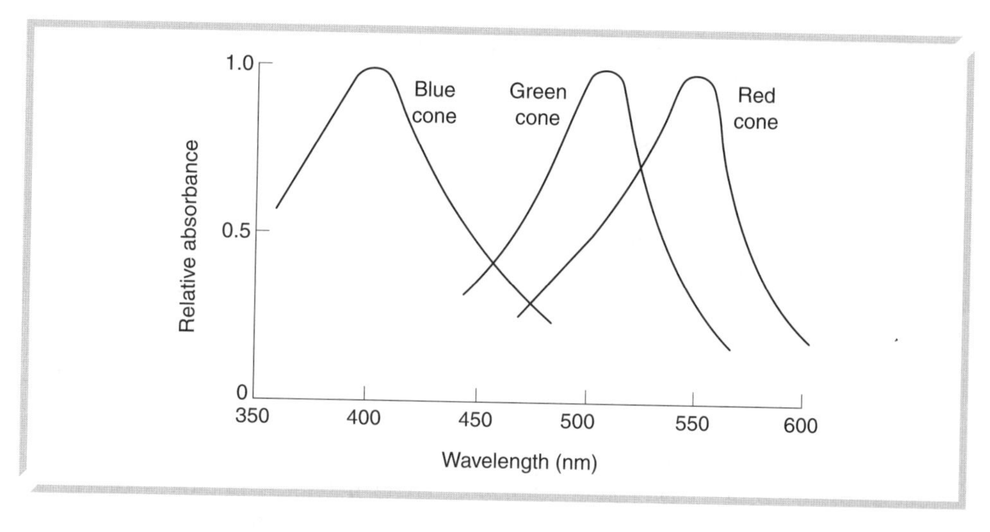

Figure 2.12 The absorbance of light by rods and the three types of cone ('blue', 'green' and 'red') in the human retina.

The answer is that there are three different types of cone: one which absorbs the most light at around 445 nm (blue-sensitive); one which absorbs light at around 535 nm (green-sensitive); and one which absorbs light at around 570 nm (called red-sensitive). These cones, however, also show considerable overlap in their detection of wavelengths (Figure 2.12). For example, light peaking at 600 nm will evoke the greatest response from the red cones, but it will also produce a weaker response from the green cones. Thus, the red-sensitive cones do not respond only to long (red) wavelengths of light, they just respond better – and the same principle also holds for the other two cones (Baylor 1987).

Theories of colour vision

The idea that our eyes must also contain receptors for these three wavelengths of light was first predicted by the British physicist Thomas Young in 1802, long before cones were actually discovered. He made his claim on the basis that any colour of light could be produced (including white) by mixing three different types of wavelength in the right proportion – providing the wavelengths were far enough apart from each other. Because of this, Young proposed that the retina must also contain three different receptors for colour, and that their probable sensitivities were for blue, green and red. This theory was further supported by Hermann von Helmholtz in the 1850s, and it consequently became known as the Young–Helmholtz or **trichromatic theory** of colour vision.

However, one problem with the trichromatic theory was that it could not adequately explain the effect of negative after-images. For example, if you stare at a red square against a white background for some time, then suddenly remove the square, you will see a green after-image of the square. Alternatively, staring at a black square produces white, and staring at blue produces a yellow after-image. Moreover, a not dissimilar type of colour relationship also appears to hold for colour blindness. For example, the most common form of colour blindness is for the colours red–green; followed by the much rarer blue–yellow forms (note that there is no such thing as red–blue blindness). Thus, the colours red–green, and blue–yellow appeared to be linked in a way that was not explained by the trichromatic theory.

In 1870, the German physiologist Ewald Hering proposed an alternative explanation of colour vision. In agreement with Young and Helmholtz, he believed that there were only a few primary colours, and that the whole of the colour spectrum could be produced by mixing these. But, Hering did not accept that yellow was derived from a mixture of red and green (as the trichromatic theory held), but that it was a primary colour along with red, green and blue. With four primary colours (instead of three) Hering proposed that the visual system only needed to contain two types of colour detector – with one type of detector responding to red or green, and the other to blue or yellow. In other words, Hering believed that each type of detector could respond in two different ways to produce two different colour sensations, and because the colours acted to oppose each other (red versus green; yellow versus blue; as well as black versus white) the theory was called the **opponent theory** of colour vision.

What theory is correct?

As we have seen, there is strong evidence to support the trichromatic theory – namely, the fact that there are three types of cone in the retina that respond to different wavelengths of light. In fact, it is now known that each cone contains a different type of pigment (a protein called opsin) that has different light-absorbing properties (corresponding to blue, green and red) which are, of course, the three primary colours predicted by the trichromatic theory (e.g. see MacNicol 1964).

Although this evidence appears to disprove the opponent-process theory, there is also considerable evidence to show otherwise. For example, retinal ganglion cells have been found that increase their activity in response to one colour, but decrease their activity to another (i.e. 'opponent neurons'). In fact, there are two types of opponent neuron: those that produce opposite responses to red and green; and those that produce opposite responses to blue and yellow. For example, one type of cell is excited by the colour of red and inhibited by green (R^+, G^-) or vice versa (R^-, G^+). And the other type of cell is excited by the colour of blue and inhibited by yellow (B^+, Y^-) or vice versa (B^-, Y^+). Thus, the optic nerve leading from the retina to the lateral geniculate nucleus contains exactly the type of cells predicted by the opponent-process theory (De Valois and De Valois 1988).

In fact, things are a little bit more complex than described above, because most of the opponent cells also have concentric receptive fields as first described by Kuffler – except, in this case, the centres and surrounds are colour sensitive, but the principle remains the same. For example, a ganglion cell might be excited by green and inhibited by red in the centre of its receptive field, while showing the opposite response in the surrounding ring. Similarly, a ganglion cell may show the same response to blue and yellow. (There is also a third type of ganglion cell which does not respond to colour in this way, but instead responds to differences in brightness.)

Thus, both the trichromatic and opponent theories appear to be correct. If this is the case then the fundamental problem is: How do the three types of cone located in the retina (red, green and blue) combine to form the two main types of opponent cell (corresponding to red–green and blue–yellow) in the optic ganglia? Or, put simply: Where does yellow come from?

The answer to this problem must lie with the type of neural 'wiring' that takes place between the cones and the ganglion cells. Indeed, assuming that this is the case, then the red–green opponent cell is relatively easy to explain as it presumably receives input from both the red and the green cones. For example, if the input from the red cones was excitatory, and if the input from the green cones was inhibitory, then this would explain the R^+, G^- opponent cell. Similarly, a reversed 'wiring system' could account for the R^-, G^+ opponent cell. But, using the same logic, how can the blue–yellow opponent cell be explained when there is no cone specific for yellow?

The answer seems to be that the blue–yellow opponent cell receives neural input from three sources: in this case from the blue, green and red receptors. In this scheme, the input to the blue 'part' of the opponent cell is similar to that occurring with the red–green cell (i.e. there is a cone for blue). But in the case of yellow it is assumed that the opponent cell encoding this colour combines the input from both red and green receptors (see Figure 2.13). In other words, we see yellow not because we have a specific photoreceptor for yellow, but because it is 'made up' (or combined) from the inputs deriving from the red and green cones. We can put this another way: when we detect the

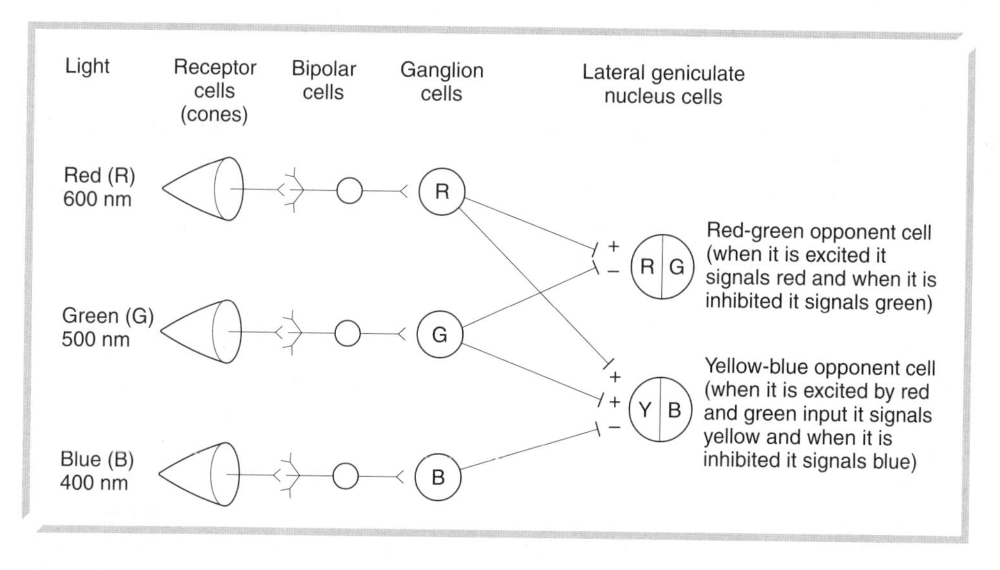

Figure 2.13 Colour coding in the retina as predicted by the opponent-process theory of colour vision.

wavelength of light corresponding to yellow (which falls between the red and green bands) this wavelength stimulates both red and green cones equally – and this 'dual stimulation' then feeds into the yellow part of the yellow–blue ganglion cell to produce its excitation (or inhibition).

In order for ganglion cells to show opponent red–green and blue–yellow responses, it is clear that the 'wiring' of the neural pathways linking the cones with opponent ganglion neurons must take place in the retina. It is believed that this function is served either by the retinal horizontal cells which link the cones with the bipolar cells, or by the multi-branched connections of the bipolar cells that synapse with the ganglion cells.

A closer look at the lateral geniculate nucleus

In the human brain, the lateral geniculate nucleus (the word *geniculate* means 'bent like a knee') consists of six layers of cells that can be distinguished both in terms of their neural input and by their shape. For example, each layer receives input from one eye only – with layers 1, 4 and 6 receiving input from the nasal part of the contralateral (opposite) eye, and layers 2, 3 and 5 receiving input from the peripheral part of the ipsilateral (same-sided) eye. Although it is difficult to visualise (see Figure 2.4), this means that each lateral geniculate nucleus receives information from the opposite side of the visual world. In addition, the upper four layers of the lateral geniculate nucleus contain small neurons (called **parvocellular cells**) which are sensitive to colour (in fact they show the same type of opponent red–green and blue–yellow responses as found with the ganglion cells); whereas the lower two layers contain larger neurons (called **magnocellular cells**) that respond equally to light of any wavelength (i.e. they do not respond specifically to colour). There are also other important differences between these two types of cell. For example, the parvocellular neurons have small receptive fields which indicate that they are involved in the detection of fine visual details, whereas the magnocellular neurons have much larger receptive fields suggesting that they are better at detecting the broader outline of shapes. In addition, parvocellular cells tend to give a sustained response to an unchanging stimulus, whereas magnocellular neurons respond rapidly but briefly to a constant stimulus. These findings suggest that parvocellular cells are better suited to analysing stationary objects, whereas magnocellular neurons respond best to movement.

These ideas have been largely confirmed by examining the visual capabilities of monkeys after selective lesioning of the lateral geniculate nucleus. For example, damage to the magnocellular layers have little effect on visual acuity or colour vision, but impairs the monkey's ability to see quickly moving stimuli. In contrast, damage to the parvocellular layers has little effect on motion perception, but reduces fine pattern vision and abolishes colour perception. These findings show that parvocellular cells are essential for high-resolution vision which enables the detailed analysis of shape, size and colour of objects to take place, whereas the magnocellular cells process information that is vital for analysing the movement of objects in space (Livingstone and Hubel 1988).

Surprisingly, the retina only provides about 20 per cent of the total input to the lateral geniculate nucleus, and the rest derives mainly from the visual cortex and, to a lesser extent, from the brainstem. Even more puzzling is the fact that this input does not appear to significantly alter the nature of the visual responses recorded from the lateral geniculate nucleus. Clearly, there is still much to learn about the role of the lateral geniculate nucleus in visual processing.

Colour processing in the cortex

It is only within the last 20 years or so that brain researchers have begun to understand how cells in the visual cortex process colour information. Before then, colour-sensitive cells in the visual cortex had been detected, but since they appeared to occur at random this made it difficult to study them in any systematic way. However, in 1978, a means of identifying colour-processing cells became possible when it was unexpectedly found that if the visual cortex was stained with a mitochondrial enzyme called cytochrome oxidase (**mitochondria** are small structures inside cells that produce energy) then unusual-looking clusters of cells called **cytochrome blobs** were produced. Not only were these peg-like columns scattered throughout the visual cortex, but when David Hubel and Margaret Livingstone recorded from cells located in them, they found that they lacked orientation specificity (i.e. they did not respond to lines) but were instead sensitive to colour. Moreover, their colour responses were very similar to those obtained from the parvocellular cells of the lateral geniculate nucleus (i.e. they had concentric receptive fields which responded to red–green and blue–yellow).

It might be expected from this finding that parvocellular cells projecting to the visual cortex will only terminate on neurons located in the blobs. However, this is not entirely the case. Although most of the parvocellular axons entering the visual cortex (in layer IV) pass into the blob regions, the remainder project to areas between the blobs (called appropriately enough interblobs). The magnocellular cells (which are colour blind) also surprisingly send some of their axons into the blobs, perhaps to provide information concerning brightness or contrast.

The modular structure of the visual cortex

The discovery of cytochrome blobs has also led to a revision of ideas concerning the structure of the visual cortex. As we have already seen (e.g. Figure 2.11), the visual cortex is organised into hypercolumns with blocks of orientation columns (made up of simple, complex and hypercomplex cells) and ocular dominance columns (made up of neurons that have a preference for input from one of the eyes). Into this columnar unit we now have to place the colour-processing blobs, and one term that has been used to describe this new complex is the **cortical module**.

It is now known (see Figure 2.14) that a cortical module consists of two ocular dominance units (one for each eye) with each unit containing a peg-like blob that passes through all its layers with the exception of layer IV (this gives the appearance of there being four blobs in each complete module). In addition, each module also contains the full range (in fact twice over) of orientation columns that cover every orientation across 180°. Thus, it can be inferred that each cortical module has several important functions

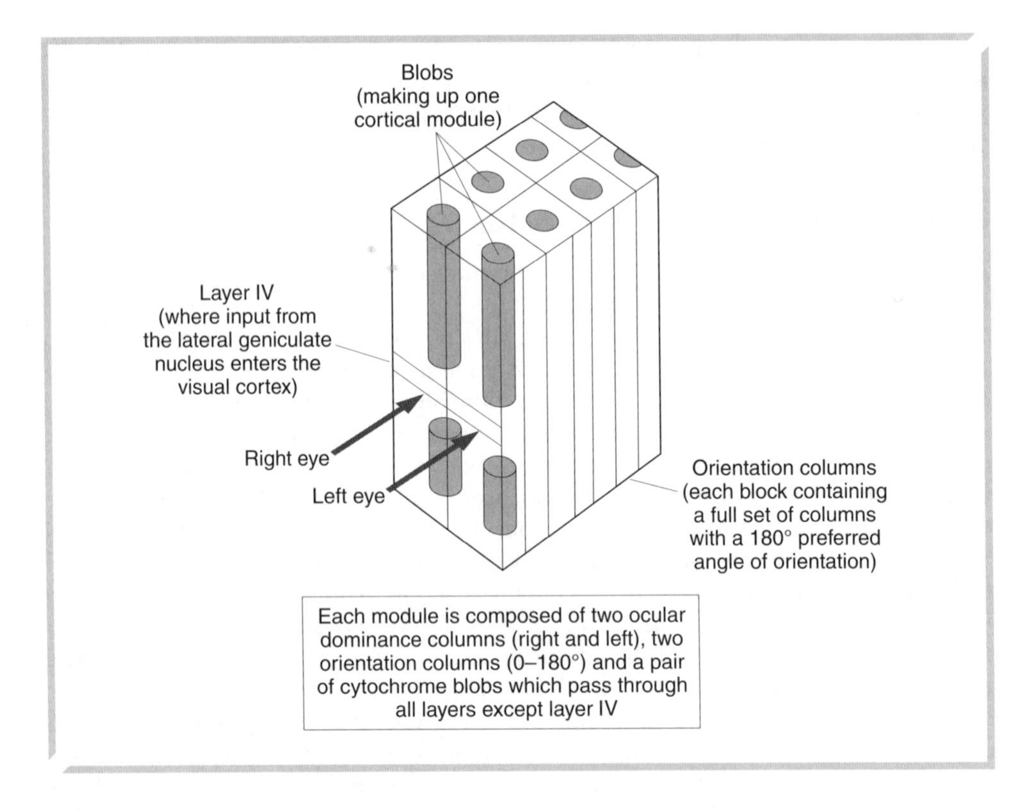

Figure 2.14 Hubel and Livingstone's proposed model of the modular structure of the visual cortex.

including the analysis of pattern, wavelength, luminance, movement and depth. In other words, it is a complete processing unit for incoming visual input.

It has been estimated that the visual cortex contains around 2,500 cortical modules, with each one containing in the region of 150,000 neurons and measuring approximately 1 × 1 × 2 mm. Moreover, each module is responsible for analysing only a small region of the visual scene from a tiny part of the retina (this is shown by the fact that the removal of a cortical module leads to a blind spot on the retina). To analyse the visual world in this way, it has also been estimated that each module receives in the region of 10,000 neural inputs, as well as sending out a staggering 50,000 outputs to other cortical structures (and subcortical areas) to enable further visual processing. Thus, visual processing appears to get even more complex the further we go into the system!

Visual processing at higher levels

The modules of the visual cortex provide the first stage of visual processing following the relay of information from the lateral geniculate nucleus. Despite this, it is almost certain that our perception of the visual world does not take place at this point. Each module of the visual cortex only sees what is happening in its own small part of the visual field and, therefore, if we are to perceive the totality of our visual world, it must be that information from the cortical modules is integrated elsewhere in the brain. The most likely sites for this integration are the adjacent areas of visual association cortex and/or the areas that span out from these extrastriate regions into the temporal and parietal lobes.

Because the visual (striate) cortex is the first region to receive information from the visual pathways it is sometimes called visual area 1 (V_1). The next stage in visual processing takes place in the adjacent prestriate region (V_2) which forms a band of tissue (some 6 to 8 mm wide) surrounding the V_1 cortex. When the prestriate cortex is stained it reveals three types of parallel stripe – thick, thin and pale – and these have been found to contain cells that receive different types of input from the V_1 area. In short, the thick stripes receive information about depth perception; the thin stripes receive information from the blobs (i.e. they are concerned with colour processing); and the pale stripes obtain input from the extrablob areas that are involved with orientation, form and motion vision. In other words, the prestriate cortex maintains the segregation of visual input that occurs in the striate (V_1) cortex.

However, at this point these streams of visual information diverge and travel into different areas of the brain. There are numerous cortical areas involved in visual function (Van Essen *et al.* 1992), which makes it difficult to follow the pathways with any precision. However, it does appear that one major route turns upward into the posterior parietal lobe, while the other turns downward and passes through the temporal cortex. As might be expected, these pathways are also involved in different types of visual processing (see Figure 2.15).

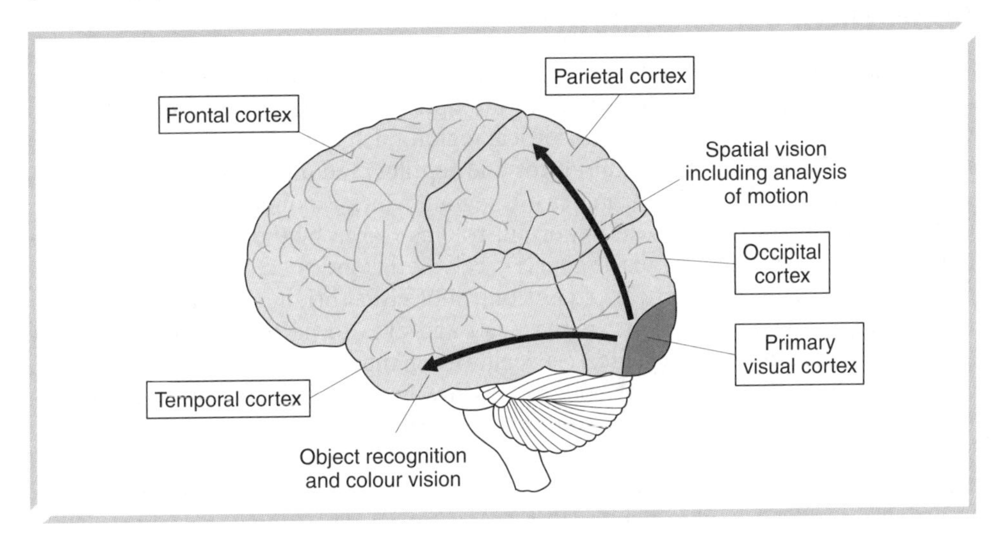

Figure 2.15 Diagram showing the spatial-visual (dorsal stream) and object recognition (ventral stream) pathways in the brain.

The parietal route has been shown to be involved in spatial aspects of vision, including the analysis of motion and determining the positional relationships of objects in the visual world. This is seen, for example, in the case of **Balint's syndrome** where people suffer bilateral damage to the region bordering the occipital and parietal lobes. Although individuals with this syndrome can perceive and recognise objects, they will often show misdirected movement when they try to grasp them (**optic ataxia**). In addition, they will often have difficulty fixing their gaze on objects or following their movement (**ocular apraxia**). Interestingly, individuals with Balint's syndrome may also demonstrate **simultanagnosia** – an inability to see two objects at once (e.g. if presented with a pen and a toothbrush they may be able to see one object at a time, but not both together).

In contrast, the pathway that projects into the temporal lobe has been shown to be involved in high-resolution pattern vision, object recognition and colour processing. This route is sometimes called the object recognition pathway and one consequence of its damage can be visual **agnosia** – an inability to recognise (or sometimes even perceive) a stimulus or object visually, despite being able to recognise it through other sensory modalities. There are many different types of agnosia (including those for objects and colour) but one of the most interesting is an inability to recognise faces (**prosopagnosia**). For example, Damasio *et al.* (1990) reported the case of a 60-year-old woman (with normal intelligence and visual acuity) who suffered a bilateral stroke to the border of the occipital and temporal lobes and became unable to recognise the faces of her husband or daughter – despite being able to identify them by other means such as their voice. Curiously, people with prosopagnosia are often able to recognise the age and gender of the face, and even its emotional expression, despite not being able to recognise the person to whom it belongs (Tranel *et al.* 1988).

Subcortical visual systems

The geniculate–striate–cortex pathway is not the only visual system in the brain. A number of axon fibres branch away from the optic nerve before reaching the lateral geniculate nucleus and project to subcortical regions including the midbrain tectum. In many species (e.g. fish, amphibians, birds and reptiles) the midbrain tectum provides the main visual system, and in primates this region (which is dominated by the superior colliculus) also clearly serves an important role as shown by the fact that it receives approximately 10 per cent of all the ganglion cells in the optic nerve. The main function of the superior colliculus appears to be control of visual orientation. For example, it enables appropriate movements of the head and eyes to be made towards sensory stimuli (visual, auditory, touch, etc.) especially when they occur unexpectedly (Gordon 1972). In addition, the superior colliculus is involved in co-ordinating **saccadic eye movements** – sudden rapid movements of the eyes that we are not aware of making, but which enable us to explore changing visual scenes and to continually bring new visual targets onto the fovea. Although we do not appear to consciously 'see' the world with our superior colliculus (although see Box 2.2), it is nevertheless an important structure for reflexive eye (and head) movements to which we generally give no thought when we look at the world.

Box 2.2 BLINDSIGHT

Neurologists have long known that damage to the pathways from retina to visual cortex (and beyond) produces blindness in the visual field opposite to the side in which the damage has occurred. However, in 1974, Larry Weiskrantz and his colleagues (Weiskrantz *et al.* 1974) obtained a surprising result with a patient called DB who had undergone surgery to have most of his right striate cortex removed. Following surgery, as expected, DB was almost totally blind in his left visual field, although over the next three years he was to regain much of his sight, leaving only the lower left quadrant of his visual field without vision. Although he was 'blind' in this remaining part of the visual field, it was found that DB could nevertheless use it to point to the position of markers on a wall; decide whether a stick was horizontal or vertical; and distinguish between the letters 'X' and 'O'. In fact, DB performed with a very high level of accuracy which included reaching towards the objects, despite protesting that he could not see or understand what he was doing! Thus, DB apparently had a residual form of vision that was independent of awareness which the investigators called **blindsight.**

How then can we explain this form of vision? Most researchers believe that blindsight depends on the superior colliculus, which then sends its input via a pathway that projects to the secondary visual cortex, but bypasses the primary visual cortex. However, not all researchers agree. For example, Campion *et al.* (1983) have proposed that blindsight could be an artefact of stray light – i.e. light presented to the blind visual field could stray into the sighted field thereby giving a clue to the target's location. Whatever view is correct, it is clear that the two visual systems (e.g. the geniculate-striate and superior-collicular) have evolved to serve different functions. Indeed, this was shown by Schneider (1967) who found that lesions of the striate cortex in hamsters impaired the performance of simple visual discrimination tasks whereas lesions of the superior colliculus produced an inability to localise the spatial location of objects (e.g. these animals could not locate a nearby sunflower seed unless it touched their whiskers). This has led to the theory that the striate system is primarily concerned with 'what things are' whereas the superior colliculi system is more concerned with 'where things are' (Schneider 1969).

Another important subcortical brain structure is the pretectum, which controls a variety of pupil reflexes. For example, if bright light is suddenly shone into the eye, a pupillary light reflex will occur (i.e. the pupil will constrict). This occurs because the light from the eye causes neurons in the pretectum to fire, which then activates a small structure called the **Edinger–Westphal nucleus** that, in turn, causes the parasympathetic arm of the autonomic nervous system to induce contraction of the pupil. A further subcortical structure that also receives visual input is the **suprachiasmatic nucleus** located in the hypothalamus. This tiny structure is involved in generating (and synchronising) circadian rhythms and will be discussed in more detail in Chapter 6.

Self-test questions

1. Draw a picture of the eye and label its various parts.
2. How are the cells of the retina organised?
3. Describe the visual pathway from retina to visual cortex.
4. What is meant by the terms contralateral and ipsilateral?
5. Each lateral geniculate nucleus receives information from the contralateral visual field. What is meant by this statement?
6. What is the difference between an on-centre and off-centre ganglion cell?
7. Describe the main characteristics of simple, complex and hypercomplex cells.
8. What layer of the visual cortex receives input from the lateral geniculate nucleus?
9. Compare the trichromatic and opponent-process theories of colour vision.
10. Why are cytochrome oxidase blobs important?
11. Describe how a cortical module is organised.
12. What areas of the brain are involved in spatial processing and object recognition?
13. What is the role of the superior colliculus?
14. What theories have been proposed to explain blindsight?

Key terms

Agnosia (p.64)
Amacrine cells (p.47)
Aqueous humour (p.45)
Astigmatism (p.56)
Balint's syndrome (p.64)
Bipolar cells (p.47)
Blindsight (p.65)
Ciliary muscles (p.45)
Complex cells (p.52)
Cones (p.46)
Cornea (p.45)
Cortical module (p.61)
Cytochrome blobs (p.61)
Dorsal lateral geniculate nucleus (p.48)
Edinger–Westphal nucleus (p.66)
Fovea (p.46)
Ganglion cells (p.47)
Horizontal cells (p.47)
Hypercolumn (p.55)
Hypercomplex cells (p.52)

Iris (p.45)
Lens (p.45)
Light (p.43)
Magnocellular cells (p.60)
Mitochondria (p.61)
Occipital lobe (p.48)
Ocular apraxia (p.64)
Opponent theory (p.58)
Optic ataxia (p.64)
Optic chiasm (p.48)
Optic radiations (p.48)
Parvocellular cells (p.60)
Prestriate cortex (p.49)
Primary visual cortex (p.48)
Prosopagnosia (p.64)
Pupil (p.45)
Receptive field (p.49)
Retina (p.45)
Rods (p.46)
Saccadic eye movements (p.64)
Sclera (p.45)
Simple cells (p.51)
Simultanagnosia (p.64)
Strabismus (p.56)
Striate cortex (p.48)
Superior colliculus (p.48)
Suprachiasmatic nucleus (p.66)
Tectum (p.48)
Trichromatic theory (p.57)
Vitreous humour (p.45)

References

Baylor, D. A. (1987) Photoreceptor signals and vision: Proctor Lecture. *Investigations in Ophthalmology and Visual Science*, **28**, 34–49.

Campion, J. *et al.* (1983) Is blindsight an effect of scattered light, sparred cortex and near threshold vision? *Behavioral and Brain Sciences*, **6**, 423–86.

Damasio, A. R. *et al.* (1990) Face agnosia and the neural substrates of memory. *Annual Review of Neuroscience*, **13**, 89–109.

De Valois, R. L. and De Valois, K. K. (1988) *Spatial Vision*. New York: Oxford University Press.

Gordon, B. (1972) The superior colliculus of the brain. *Scientific American*, 72–82.

Hirsch, H. V. B. and Spineli, D. N. (1970) Visual experience modifies distribution of horizontally and vertically oriented receptive fields in cats. *Science*, **168**, 869–71.

Hubel, D. H. (1982) Cortical neurobiology: A slanted historical perspective. *Annual Review of Neuroscience*, **5**, 363–70.

Hubel, D. H. (1988) *Eye, Brain and Vision*. New York: Scientific American Library.

Hubel, D. H. and Wiesel, T. N. (1959) Receptive fields of single neurones in the cat's striate cortex. *Journal of Physiology*, **148**, 574–91.

Hubel, D. H. and Wiesel, T. N. (1963a) Shape and arrangement of columns in the cat's striate cortex. *Journal of Physiology*, **165**, 559–68.

Hubel, D. H. and Wiesel, T. N. (1963b) Receptive fields of cells in the striate cortex of very young, visually impaired inexperienced kittens. *Journal of Neurophysiology*, **26**, 994–1002.

Hubel, D. H. and Wiesel, T. N. (1977a) Ferrier Lecture. Functional architecture of macaque monkey visual cortex. *Proceedings of the Royal Society of London, B*, **198**, 1–59.

Hubel, D. H. and Wiesel, T. N. (1977b) Brain mechanisms of vision. *Scientific American*, **241**, 150–63.
Jasper, H. H. and Sourkes, T. L. (1983) Nobel Laureates in neuroscience: 1904–1981. *Annual Review of Neuroscience*, **6**, 1–42.
Kuffler, S. W. (1953) Discharge patterns and functional organization of the mammalian retina. *Journal of Neurophysiology*, **16**, 37–68.
Livingstone, M. S. and Hubel, D. S. (1988) Segregation of form, colour, movement and depth: Anatomy, physiology and perception. *Science*, **240**, 740–9.
MacNicol, E. F. (1964) Three-pigment color vision. *Scientific American*, **211** (6), 48–56.
Mecacci, L. (1991) Pathways of perception. In Corsi, P. (ed.) *The Enchanted Loom: Chapters in the History of Neuroscience*. New York: Oxford University Press.
Michael, C. R. (1969) Retinal processing of visual images. *Scientific American*, **220**, 104–14.
Schneider, G. E. (1967) Contrasting visuomotor functions of tectum and cortex in the golden hamster. *Psychologische Forschung*, **31**, 52–62.
Schneider, G. E. (1969) Two visual systems. *Science*, **163**, 895–902.
Tranel, D. *et al.* (1988) Intact recognition of facial expression, gender, and age in patients with impaired recognition of face identity. *Neurology*, **38**, 690–6.
Van Essen, D. C. *et al.* (1992) Information processing in the primate visual system: An integrated systems perspective. *Science*, **255**, 419–23.
Weiskrantz, L. *et al.* (1974) Visual capacity in the hemianoptic field following a restricted occipital ablation. *Brain*, **97**, 709–28.

FURTHER READING

Bruce, V. *et al.* (1996) *Visual Perception: Physiology, Psychology and Ecology* (3rd edn). Hove: Psychology Press.
Hubel, D. H. (1982) Exploration of the primary visual cortex. *Nature*, **299**, 515–24.
Valberg, A. and Lee, B. B. (1991) *From Pigments to Perception*. New York: Plenum Press.
Zeki, S. (1993) *A Vision of the Brain*. London: Blackwell.

Multiple choice questions

1. The aperture controlling the amount of light entering the eye is called:

(a) the lens
(b) the cornea
(c) the pupil
(d) ciliary muscles

2. The fovea is the part of the retina that contains:

(a) rods
(b) cones
(c) amacrine cells
(d) ganglion cells

3. The rods and the cones synapse directly on to:

(a) bipolar and horizontal cells
(b) horizontal cells only
(c) amacrine cells
(d) ganglion cells

4. Axons extending from the nasal part of the retina project to the _______________ side of the brain, whereas axons from the remainder of the retina project to the _______________ part of the brain

(a) opposite (contralateral), same side (ipsilateral)
(b) same side (ipsilateral), opposite (contralateral)
(c) dorsal, ventral
(d) medial, lateral

5. The first structure which the majority of retinal ganglion cells project to, and synapse with, in the brain is the:

(a) optic chiasm
(b) lateral geniculate nucleus
(c) superior colliculus
(d) visual cortex

6. Axons from the lateral geniculate nuclei project to the:

(a) primary visual cortex
(b) striate cortex
(c) occipital lobe
(d) all of the above (they are different names for the same part of the brain)

7. Stephen Kuffler found that retinal ganglion cells:

(a) respond best (with tonic firing) to brief flashes of light
(b) respond best to highly specific wavelengths of light
(c) have elongated receptive fields which preferentially respond to moving lines
(d) have concentric receptive fields with on and off components

8. A simple cell in the visual cortex has a receptive field (at the retina) that is:

(a) concentric with on and off components (responding best to a stationary spot of light)
(b) concentric with phasic and tonic components (responding best to a moving spot of light)
(c) elongated with on and off components (responding best to a stationary line)
(d) dependent upon which layer of the visual cortex one examines!

9. A complex cell in the visual cortex:

(a) responds best to angles
(b) responds best to lines, but requires visual input from both eyes
(c) responds maximally when a line is anywhere in its receptive field providing it is in the correct orientation
(d) responds best to moving lines of any orientation

10. A cortical hypercolumn:

(a) consists of an individual column that contains simple, complex and hypercomplex cells
(b) is made up of seven different types of ocular dominance cells
(c) is made up of (a) and (b) above
(d) consists of a number of columns containing simple, complex and hypercomplex cells that detect every line orientation over 360°

11. When Hubel and Wiesel reared kittens in an environment consisting of horizontal lines they found that the same cats as adults:

(a) had simple and complex cells that showed a preference for horizontal lines
(b) had simple and complex cells that responded to lines of all orientations but located in the wrong part of the visual cortex
(c) could not judge distances properly
(d) there was no deficit in seeing vertical lines showing that the visual system is 'hard-wired' and not susceptible to the effects of early experience

12. How many types of cone are found in the fovea of the retina?

(a) one
(b) two
(c) three
(d) none (there are no cones in the fovea – only rods)

13. How many types of opponent cell are found in the optic nerve and lateral geniculate nuclei?

(a) one (black–white)
(b) two (red–green, blue–yellow)
(c) three (red–green, blue–yellow, red–blue)
(d) four (red–green, blue–yellow, red–blue, green–yellow)

14. The parvocellular and magnocellular cells are found in the:

(a) retina
(b) lateral geniculate nucleus
(c) striate cortex
(d) prestriate cortex

15. Neurons that are stained by cytochrome oxidase in the visual cortex are sensitive to:

(a) the orientation of lines
(b) moving stimuli
(c) depth cues
(d) colour

16. Cortical modules contain:

(a) orientation columns
(b) ocular dominance columns
(c) cytochrome oxidase blobs
(d) all of the above

17. From the visual cortex information passes to the adjacent:

(a) prestriate cortex
(b) parietal cortex
(c) temporal cortex
(d) somatosensory cortex

18. The largest subcortical structure involved in visual processing (receiving approximately 10 per cent of all ganglion cells) is the:

(a) suprachiasmatic nucleus
(b) pretectum
(c) superior colliculus
(d) reticular activating system

19. The visual system structure involved in the regulation of circadian rhythms is the:

(a) suprachiasmatic nucleus
(b) pretectum
(c) superior colliculus
(d) Edinger–Westphal nucleus

20. The patient DB who demonstrated blindsight had damage to the:

(a) right visual (striate) cortex
(b) lateral geniculate nuclei
(c) right superior colliculi
(d) optic chiasm

3 The control of movement

IN THIS CHAPTER

- The structure of muscles and the neuromuscular junction
- Monosynaptic and polysynaptic spinal reflexes
- Pyramidal and extrapyramidal systems of the brain
- The functions of motor cortex, cerebellum and basal ganglia
- Parkinson's disease and the development of L-dopa therapy
- Huntington's chorea

Introduction

The human brain is able to process an enormous amount of information from the body's senses – gathering and analysing input from the external environment and receiving feedback from the internal state of its own body. But, no matter how much information is analysed, it is of little use unless it can be acted upon. Indeed, one characteristic of all animals, from the simplest to the most complex, is the ability to produce movement – whether it is to control and maintain the automated functions of the body (such as respiration, heart rate, digestion, etc.) or to carry out more complex and purposeful behaviour. Thus, one of the most crucial functions of the central nervous system is to control movement or, more precisely, to control the action of muscles that enable movement to take place. Trying to understand the neural basis of movement, however, presents a considerable challenge. As the central nervous system has evolved, movement has become hierarchically organised with increasing levels of complexity, from simple reflexes in the spinal cord to extremely complex patterns of behaviour produced by higher brain areas. This not only makes the study of movement a challenging one, but also an important one in psychology because in attempting to explain how the brain produces movement we are getting to the heart of what causes behaviour itself. In addition, a number of crippling brain disorders (such as Parkinson's disease and Huntington's chorea) also affect the motor systems of the brain, which makes it imperative that we understand their causes, and neural basis, so that more effective treatments can be developed.

Muscles

All movement involves the contraction of muscles. The body contains three different types of muscle: skeletal (muscle that is attached to the bones and which moves parts of the skeleton); smooth (muscle that is located in the walls of hollow internal structures such as blood vessels); and cardiac (muscle forming the bulk of the heart). In this chapter we shall be mainly concerned with skeletal muscle (also known as **striated muscle** because of its striped appearance) that is under the control of the **somatic nervous system** (see Chapter 1). There are over 600 striated muscles in the human body (making up about 50 per cent of body weight) and these are mainly responsible for voluntary movement and posture. In contrast, the other muscles of the body (i.e. the smooth and cardiac muscles) come under the control of the **autonomic nervous system** (and certain hormones) which govern the involuntary functioning of the body's organs. Although smooth and cardiac muscle will function in the absence of neural input (e.g. the heart has its own pacemaker cells which produce contractions), skeletal muscles do not work (i.e. contract) without some form of neural innervation.

One of the most important functions of skeletal muscles is to produce movement of the skeletal joints thereby allowing the various limbs to move, and in order to do this, a given muscle has to be attached (via tendons) to pairs of bones. Despite the complexity of movement, muscles only work in one way – by contraction (e.g. pulling on a joint). Because of this, joints have to be controlled by at least two sets of muscles whose effects oppose or antagonise each other. For example, the arm is composed of the upper bone (the humerus) and the lower bones (ulna and radius) which are joined at the elbow joint. The biceps (the flexor muscles) connect the upper and lower bones at the *front* of the joint and their contraction causes the elbow joint to bend, whereas the triceps (the extensor muscles) run along the *back* of the upper and lower arm bones, and their contraction causes the limb to straighten (see Figure 3.1). In practice, the flexor and extensor muscles have to be finely co-ordinated with the contraction of one muscle being counter-balanced by the relaxation of the other. Thus, even the simple movement of the elbow requires the integrated action of different muscles, and this principle also holds true for all other types of freely moving joint and movement.

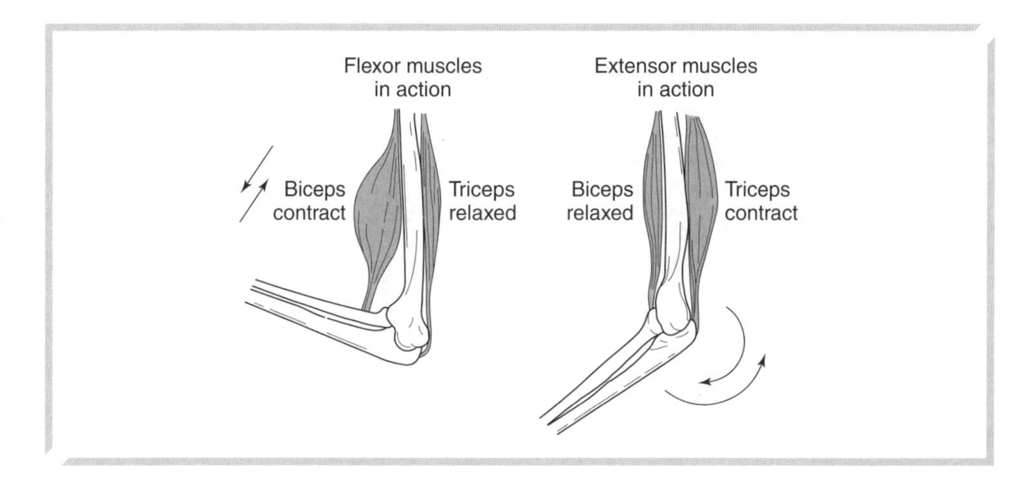

Figure 3.1 The flexion and extension muscles of the upper arm.

The fine structure of muscle

If a skeletal muscle is examined microscopically it will be found to consist of a large mass of long thin cells called **muscle fibres**, each containing several nuclei and is enclosed by its own outer membrane (called the **sarcolemma**). Packed tightly within each individual muscle fibre are hundreds (sometimes thousands) of long cylindrical structures called **myofibrils** that run the entire length of the cell (see Figure 3.2). These make up about 80 per cent of the muscle cell's volume and are the components that allow it to contract in response to an action potential (that sweeps down the sarcolemma). In turn, the myofibrils are made up of repeated short segments called **sarcomeres** which contain very fine filaments made from either **actin** or **myosin** that are anchored at one end to inflexible disk-like protein sheets called Z lines (which give the muscle its striated appearance). It is the movement of the actin and myosin filaments relative to each other that causes the myofibril to contract.

How then do the actin and myosin filaments interact together to produce movement? The simple answer is that they are made to slide over each other – which, in turn, pulls the anchoring Z sheets inwards. The secret of this movement lies with two main essential features of the sarcomere: (1) the myosin and actin lie sandwiched between each other, and (2) they have different (movable) shapes – the myosin filaments being thick and having protruding hooks (called cross-bridges), and the actin filaments being thin with a twisted knobbly appearance. In short, when an action potential arrives at the muscle fibre, it causes a rotation in the shape of the myosin's hook-like protuberances which, in turn, catches on the actin filaments and forces them to slide along its surface. This contracts the sarcomere(s), thereby shortening the myofibril(s), and causing the contraction of the muscle fibre. The combined activity of large numbers of muscle fibres then results in the contraction of the body's skeletal muscle.

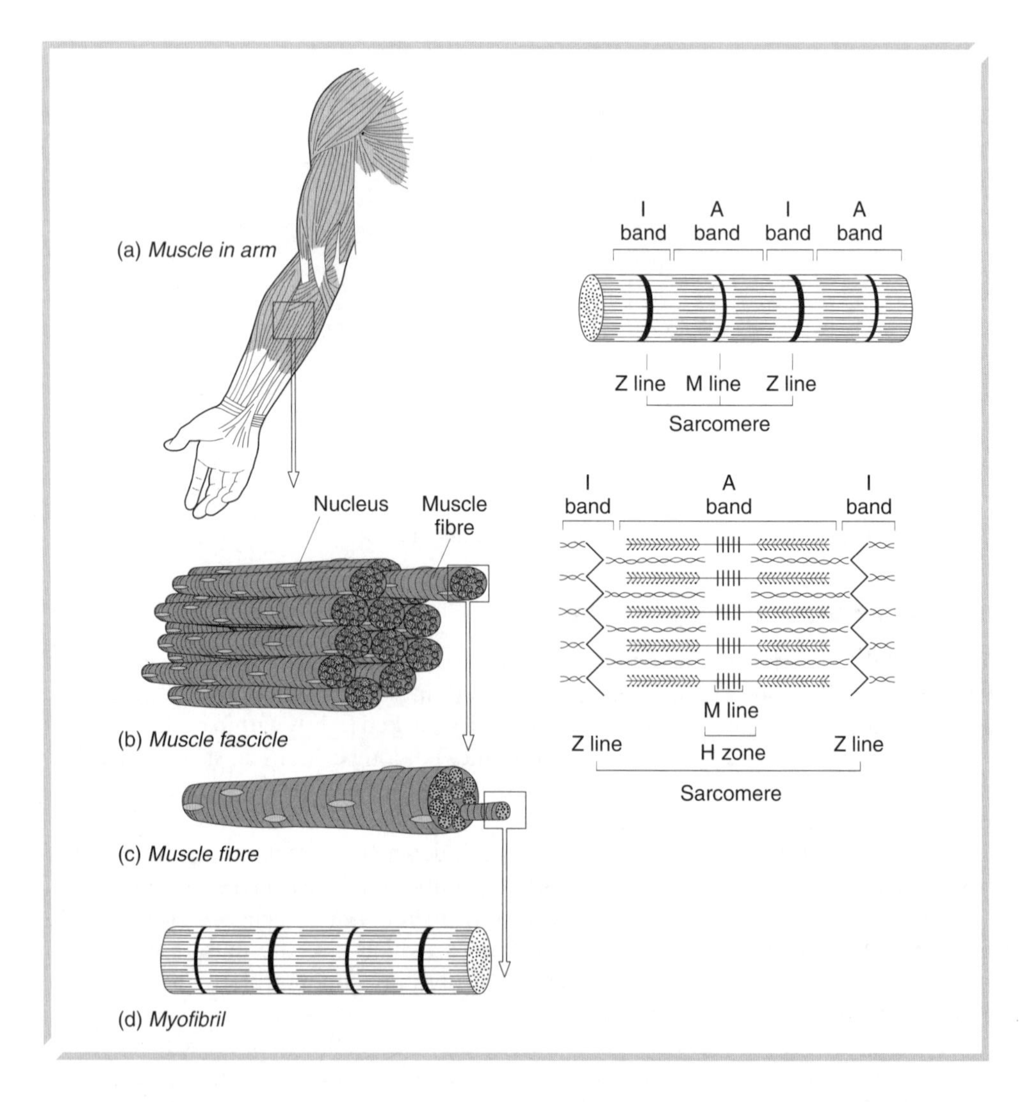

Figure 3.2 The anatomy of a skeletal muscle. (*Source*: From R. Carola, J. P. Harley and C. R. Noback, *Human Anatomy and Physiology*. Copyright © 1990 by McGraw-Hill. Reprinted by permission.)

The neural innervation of muscle

All skeletal movement is produced by the action of muscular contraction in response to neural input derived from the spinal cord and brain. In fact, this information is delivered to the muscle by a special type of neuron called the **alpha motor neuron**, which arises from cell bodies located in the ventral horn of the spinal cord. Each individual muscle is served by at least one motor neuron which typically gives rise to hundreds of multi-branching axonal endings allowing it to innervate a large number of muscle fibres over a large surface area. Consequently, when the motor neuron fires, it causes all of its target muscle fibres to contract at the same time. The number of muscle fibres innervated by a single axon depends on the type of muscle. For example, the ocular muscles of the eye receive approximately one motor axon for every 10 muscle fibres; some muscles of the hand may receive a motor neuron for every 100 muscle cells; and this figure may increase to 2,000 for certain large muscles of the trunk and leg. In general, muscles with low ratios tend to be involved in fine and dextrous movement, while those with high ratios tend to be involved in crude and less flexible responses.

The synapse that lies between the axon endings of the alpha motor neuron and the muscle cell is called the **neuromuscular junction,** and the neurotransmitter used at this site is **acetylcholine**. When acetylcholine crosses the synapse, it comes into contact with a highly specialised part of the muscle fibre called the **motor endplate**. Not only is this form of synaptic transmission fast, but it is also very reliable since the release of acetylcholine by the motor neuron nearly always causes an action potential in its recipient muscle fibre (it is interesting to compare this with a brain cell which typically requires the summation of many inputs for it to produce an action potential). The reliability of the muscle cell to respond to synaptic transmission is largely due to the large surface area of the motor endplate (which is made larger by folding) and which is also packed full with cholinergic receptors. Because neuromuscular junctions are larger and more accessible than synapses in the central nervous system, much of what we know about synaptic transmission has actually been derived from research involving this type of synapse. Moreover, an understanding of this site also has a much broader significance. For example, certain diseases are known to have a specific effect on the neuromuscular junction (see box) and a number of deadly poisons such as curare and bungarotoxin (found in the venom of various snakes such as cobras) also exert their main effect at this synapse (e.g. by blocking nicotinic cholinergic receptors).

Box 3.1 MYASTHENIA GRAVIS

Myasthenia gravis is an auto-immune disorder in which antibodies attack and destroy the body's own acetylcholine receptors at the neuromuscular junction. Although new receptors are made to replace the loss, they are unable to fully correct the damage and, consequently, when acetylcholine is released onto the motor endplate, fewer receptors exist to translate the message into a muscle contraction, and this results in muscle weakness and fatigue. The course of the illness is highly variable and is fatal in about 10 per cent of cases. It normally begins with weakness of the facial muscles, including the eyes (which causes drooping of the eyelids) as well as throat and tongue (causing difficulty in chewing and swallowing food). As the disorder progresses it may also affect the limbs (making it impossible to engage in, or sustain, muscular exertion) and impair breathing. Muscle wasting may also occur in the later stages of the disease.

The prevalence of myasthenia gravis is about 1 in 25,000 and it is twice as common in females than in males. It tends to first manifest itself in early adulthood although there is a second smaller peak of incidence around the age of 60 which appears to affect males and females equally. The reason why the disorder occurs in the first place is not known, although dysfunction of the thymus gland (an immune structure located just below the neck in the chest) has long been suspected. Indeed, thymic abnormalities have been noted in about 75 per cent of myasthenia patients and removal of the thymus gland has been shown to be a successful treatment for the disorder in about 30 per cent of cases.

One of the main forms of treatment for myasthenia gravis is the use of anticholinesterase drugs, which include physostigmine and neostigmine. These are drugs that inhibit the action of an enzyme called **acetylcholinesterase (AChE)** which normally acts to break down excess acetylcholine in the synapse. Thus, these drugs extend the lifetime of acetylcholine at the neuromuscular junction by preventing its destruction, thereby effectively increasing the stimulation of the remaining receptors. Unfortunately, these compounds have no effect on the progression of the underlying disease and for this reason this treatment is likely to be supplemented by the use of immunosuppressive drugs (such as corticosteroids).

Muscle spindles

Deep within the layers of most skeletal muscles (squashed between the muscle cells) are long, thin, fibrous capsules called **muscle spindles**. Although each muscle spindle receives a specialised motor neuron (called **gamma motor neuron**) that causes it to contract, this has a negligible effect on the main contraction of the muscle. Instead, the main function of the muscle spindle is to provide sensory information to neurons in the spinal cord concerning the stretch of the muscle and, for this reason, they are sometimes called stretch receptors.

The importance of stretch receptors can be seen when a heavy weight is placed in a person's hand. At first the arm will begin to drop and the bicep muscles (controlling the elbow) will be forced to stretch. However, as the muscle stretches, the muscle spindles in the biceps become extended, and this causes their associated sensory neurons to fire, sending information into the spinal cord. This input then activates the alpha motor neurons projecting back to the muscle fibres, to cause their contraction and to resist the stretch. In this way the muscle is able to make a reflexive movement to the force of the weight as well as helping to avoid injury to the muscle. In fact, a basic prerequisite

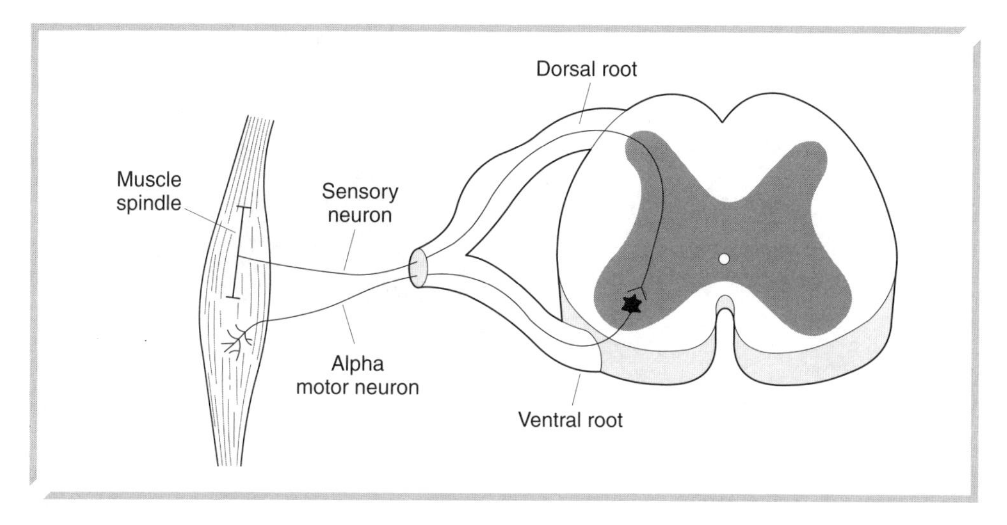

Figure 3.3 The spinal monosynaptic reflex.

for smooth movement throughout the body is the capacity to adjust muscle tone very quickly to sudden shifts in weight. The stretch reflex is particularly important in this respect and is essential for maintaining muscle tone and posture. In addition, it also has to take place very rapidly, which explains why the stretch reflex is controlled automatically at the level of the spinal cord, and not by the brain.

The best-known example of the stretch reflex is the **patellar tendon reflex** (knee jerk) which is commonly used by doctors to assess the condition of the nervous system. When the doctor strikes the tendon of the patient's knee, this causes the extensor muscle running along the thigh (called the quadriceps) to be stretched. The sudden stretching of this muscle causes its muscle spindle to fire, thereby exciting the motor neurons in the spinal cord, which responds by sending out action potentials back to the stretched muscle. The result is a compensatory muscle contraction and sudden leg extension. This reflex is also called a **monosynaptic stretch reflex** because only one synapse (located in the spinal cord) is encountered along the route from receptor (muscle spindle) to effector (leg muscle). In other words, the sensory neuron from the muscle spindle directly synapses with the motor neuron controlling the movement (see Figure 3.3).

The polysynaptic reflex

Most spinal reflexes are much more complex than those involving a single synapse between a sensory and motor neuron. In fact, most are polysynaptic (involving more than one synapse) and one example is the withdrawal or **flexion reflex** which occurs if one painfully stubs one's big toe. In this reflex, receptors in the toe send pain information to the spinal cord via a sensory neuron that synapses with several **interneurons** confined to the grey matter of the spinal cord. At this point (e.g. see Figure 3.4) the input takes several routes through the spinal cord, and the end result is a more complex

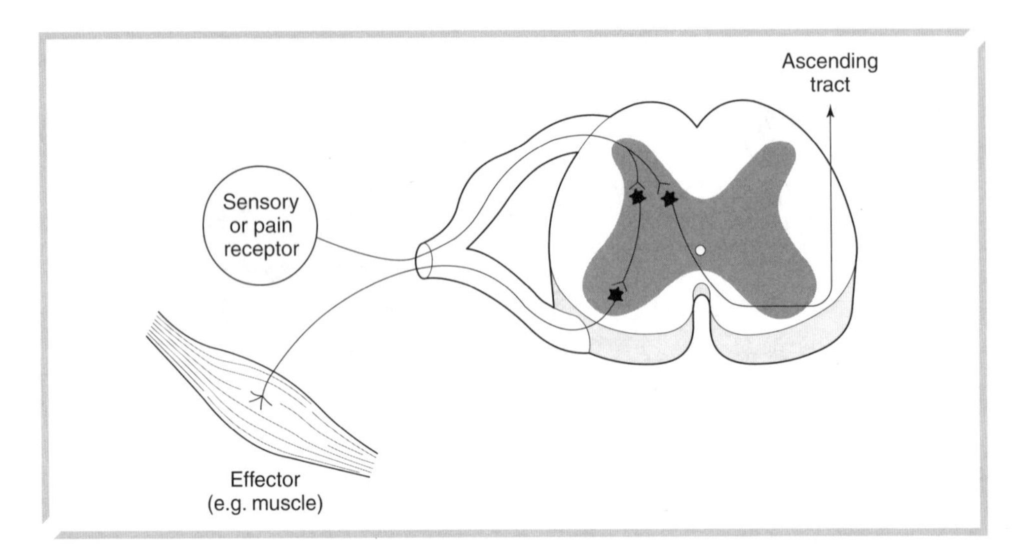

Figure 3.4 The spinal polysynaptic reflex.

and co-ordinated response involving several muscles. This reflex is slower than the monosynaptic reflex, however, because the involvement of an interneuron means that at least two synapses will have to be crossed before the motor neuron is activated.

Most of the information that passes to the alpha motor neurons controlling our skeletal muscle is, in actual fact, derived from interneurons in the spinal cord. Moreover, not only do these interneurons receive input from sensory neurons (including those from muscle spindles and pain receptors), but they also receive information from other segments of the spinal cord and the brain – indicating that they serve a wide range of functions in the co-ordination of movement and execution of motor programmes. Indeed, interneurons are involved in a wide variety of reflexive movements. For example, if you step on something sharp, not only will your leg be withdrawn from the painful stimulus, but your opposite leg will also support the weight suddenly shifted on to it. This is known as the **crossed extensor reflex** and is particularly important in maintaining balance. Polysynaptic reflexes can also produce rhythmical movement of the limbs. For example, the vigorous scratching movements produced by a dog in response to a flea are caused by circuits of interneurons (called central pattern generators) located in the spinal cord that generate rhythmical movement of the legs. In fact, similar spinal mechanisms (under the executive control of the brain) are also believed to underlie much of our own 'automated' locomotion, including walking, running and swimming (Grillner 1996).

The control of movement by the brain

The most important structure for controlling movement is the brain. A number of areas throughout the brain are involved in regulating and producing movement, although four main regions can be identified that are particularly important. These are the **brainstem**, the **cerebellum**, the **basal ganglia** (a collection of nuclei which include the **substantia nigra**, **caudate nucleus** and **putamen**) and the **motor cortex**.

All regions of the brain concerned with movement are connected to the motor neurons of the spinal cord via two major pathway systems called the **pyramidal system** and the **extrapyramidal system** (see Figures 3.5 (a) and (b)). The pyramidal system originates in the cerebral cortex (mainly from the motor cortex and surrounding areas) and forms the **corticospinal tract** – a massive bundle of fibres containing around one

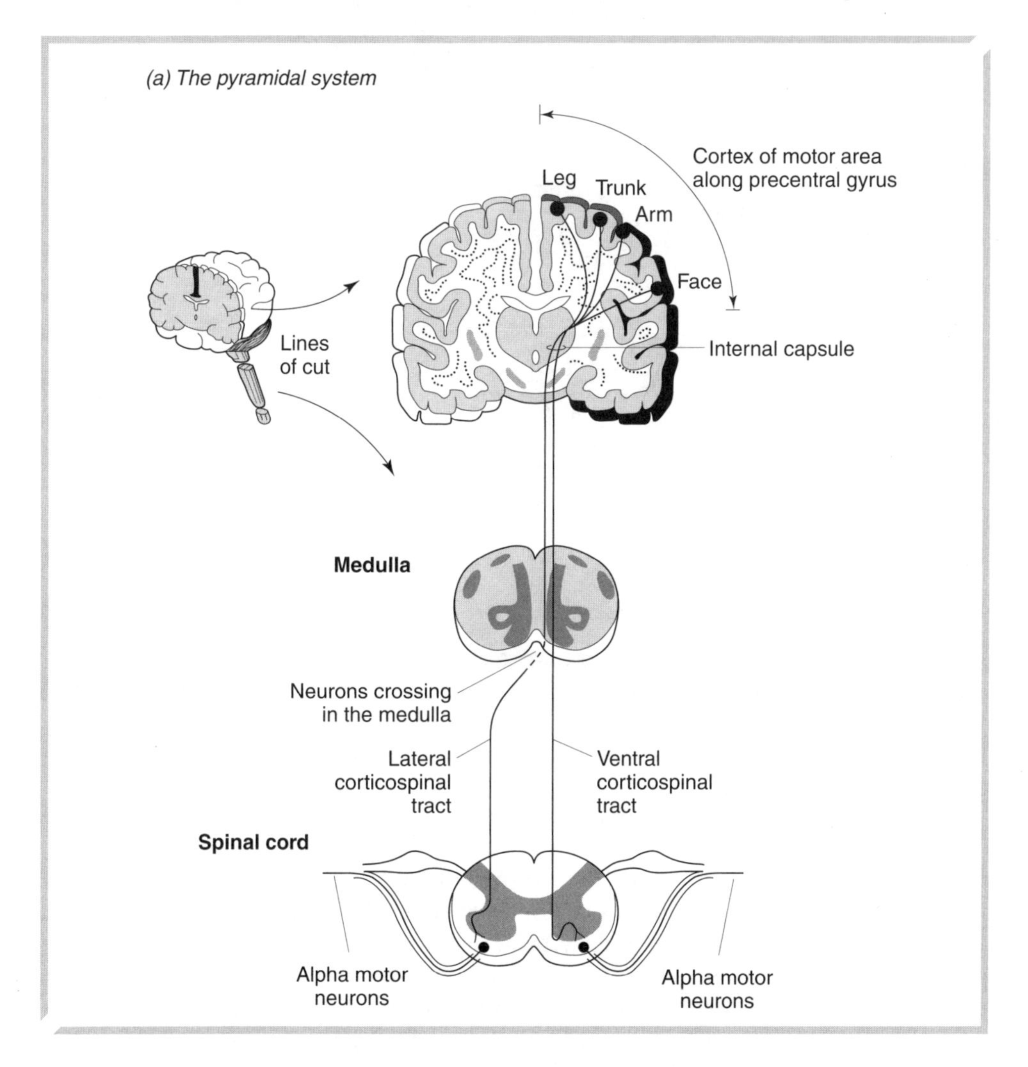

Figure 3.5 (a) The pyramidal neural system of the brain and spinal cord. (*Source*: From A. M. Schneider and B. Tarshis, *Elements of Physiological Psychology*. Copyright © 1995 by McGraw-Hill. Reprinted by permission.)

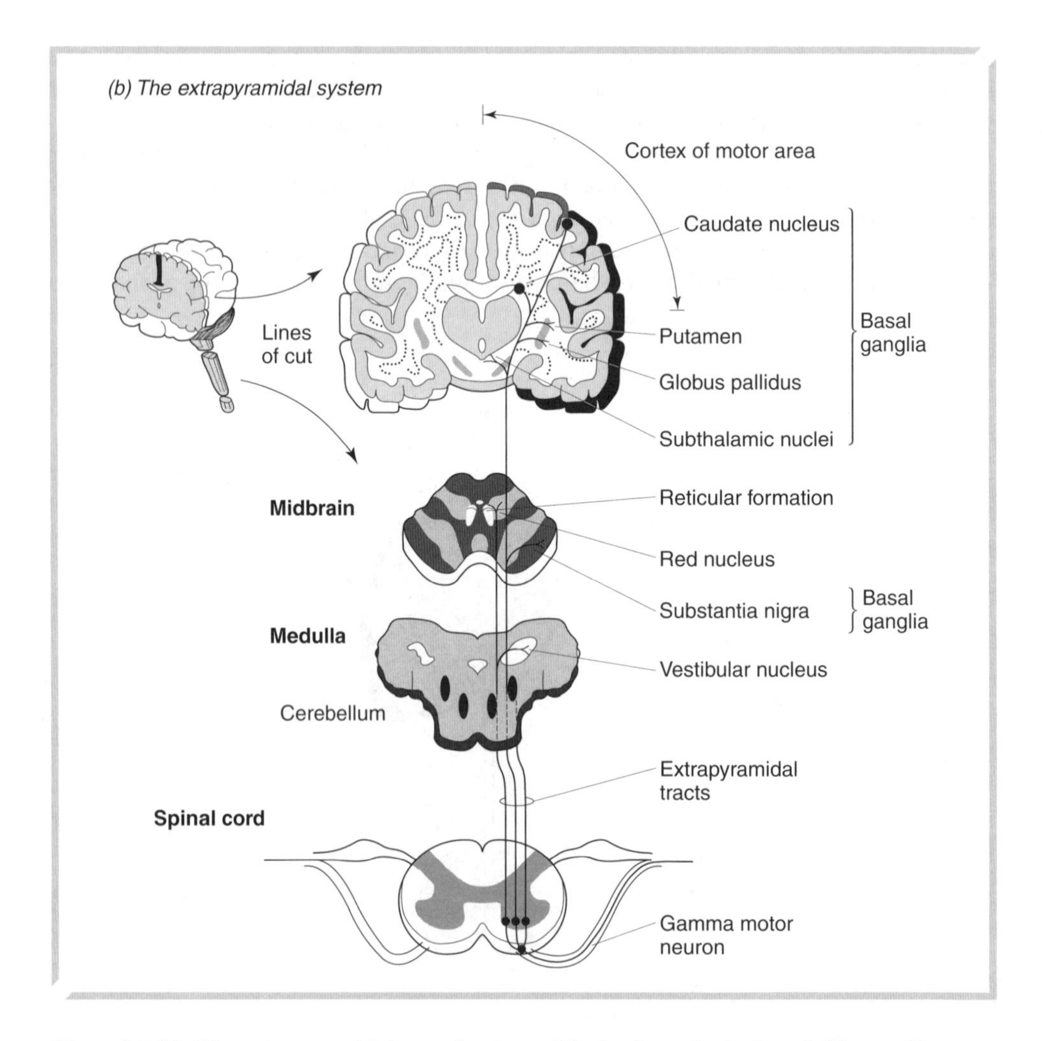

Figure 3.5 (b) The extrapyramidal neural system of the brain and spinal cord. (*Source*: From A. M. Schneider and B. Tarshis, *Elements of Physiological Psychology*. Copyright © 1995 by McGraw-Hill. Reprinted by permission.)

million axons that projects directly down into the spinal cord. On route, the majority of these fibres (about 80 per cent) cross to the contralateral (opposite) side of the brain in a region of the upper brainstem called the pyramidal decussation (from which the pyramidal system gets its name). The remainder of the fibres continue their journey down into the spinal cord where they finally cross to the contralateral side in the spinal segment where they terminate. Thus, the pyramidal system is completely contralateral – the right cortex controlling movement on the left side of the body and the left cortex governing movement on the right, although there are two routes by which this is achieved.

In contrast, the extrapyramidal system is a term widely used to describe all the motor regions and pathways of the brain whose output does not contribute to the pyramidal system. It is also made distinct from the pyramidal system because its output pathways do not cross over to the opposite side of the spinal cord, but pass down on the same side. One of the most important sites for the output of extrapyramidal information is the brainstem, which is the origin of a number of descending tracts that travel to the spinal cord including the **reticulospinal tract** (originating from a number of reticular nuclei), the **rubrospinal tract** (originating from the red nucleus) and the **vestibulospinal tract** (originating from the vestibular nuclei). The first two of these tracts are also influenced by pathways from the cerebral cortex, which suggests that higher order or conscious information may also have access to basic reflexes. But undoubtedly the two main structures of the extrapyramidal system that have attracted the most attention are the basal ganglia and cerebellum. These large structures form complex and multisynaptic pathways, which, although having no direct link with the spinal cord, are nevertheless well integrated with other extrapyramidal areas including the reticular formation, thalamus and motor portions of the cerebral cortex.

Traditionally, the extrapyramidal system has been linked with postural, reflexive and stereotypical forms of movement, and the pyramidal system connected with voluntary movement – although most researchers now believe that this division is much too simple, and misleading. Moreover, the divisions between the pyramidal and extrapyramidal systems are to some extent more imaginary than real. For example, many fibres from the extrapyramidal system go to the thalamus and from there go on to influence the pyramidal regions of the motor cortex. In turn, the motor cortex innervates many regions of the extrapyramidal system (such as the striatum) and some of its fibres even project into the descending tracts used by the extrapyramidal system to pass information to the spinal cord. Thus, both systems are richly interconnected and contribute to each other's functions.

The brainstem

The brainstem is involved in a wide range of automated motor functions including respiration and cardiovascular function, eye movements, postural adjustment and a multitude of reflex reactions (including complex patterns of species-typical behaviour). However, by itself, the brainstem is unable to attach meaning to any given motor act. For example, as Leonard (1998, page 34) has pointed out, an animal with an intact brainstem, but which has been severed from the rest of the brain, will be able to walk perfectly well and apparently show no deficit in locomotion until it encounters an obstacle such as a wall, at which point it will bump against the obstacle and continue to produce stereotypical walking movements despite having its path blocked. In other words, without the rest of the brain to guide behaviour, the brainstem's walking reflex becomes a purposeless act.

Despite this, the brainstem is an absolutely vital area for the control and production of movement, particularly as much of our own motor behaviour is undertaken without conscious intervention. For example, the brainstem includes vestibular nuclei which are of vital importance for balance, head control and eye movements, along with the red nucleus which exerts control over the large postural muscles of the body (especially those of the abdomen, neck and back). And, there are also numerous other structures and neural networks within the brainstem that contribute to reflexive movement (via direct pathways to the spinal cord). Furthermore, the brainstem receives 'higher-order' projections from many other brain areas including the cerebellum, basal ganglia and cerebral cortex. Thus, although the brainstem can be regarded as an autonomous unit for motor behaviour (among its many functions), in practice it is perhaps more realistic to view it as being closely integrated with other systems of the brain.

The cerebellum

The cerebellum (Figure 3.6) is one of the oldest and most intricate structures in the brain. Although it makes up only about 10 per cent of the human brain's mass, the cerebellum contains more than 50 per cent of its neurons. The surface of the cerebellum also contains many small fissures and ridges, similar to the cerebral cortex, which provide it with a much larger surface area than would otherwise be the case (e.g. an 'unfolded' human cerebellum measures about 120 cm by 17 cm). Indeed, it is believed by some researchers that the neural complexity of the cerebellum is such that its capacity for information processing is comparable to that of the cerebral cortex.

Despite containing large numbers of neurons, the structure of the cerebellum is highly organised and consists of an outer surface of highly packed grey cell bodies (the cerebellar cortex) that project inwards (forming white matter) to a group of three structures enclosed within the cerebellum called the **deep cerebellar nuclei** (the fastigal, interposed and dentate). In turn, these nuclei provide the main output pathways of

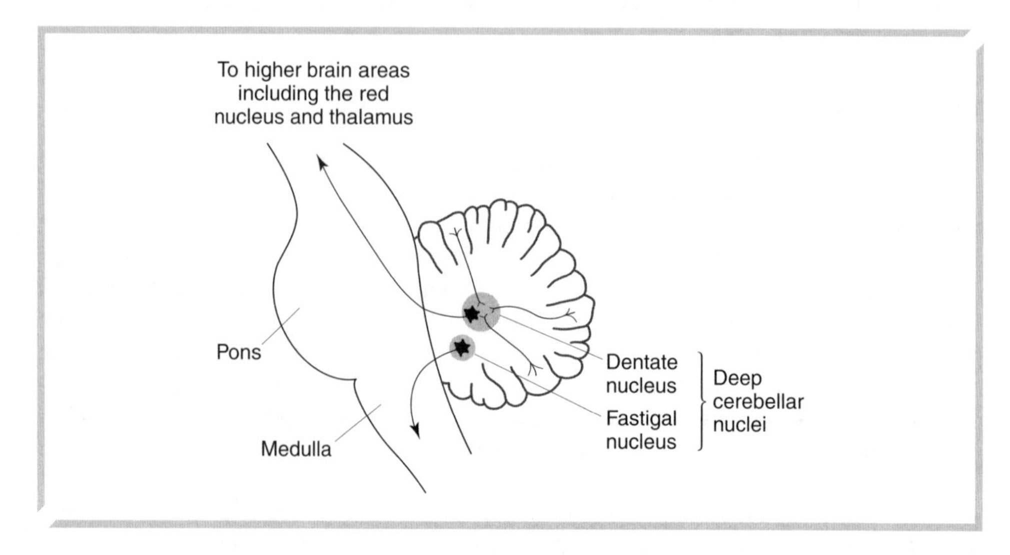

Figure 3.6 Lateral section through the cerebellum and lower brainstem.

the cerebellum which allow it to influence other areas of the extrapyramidal system including, most importantly, the motor regions of the cerebral cortex (via the thalamus) and certain reticular nuclei (including the vestibular system and red nucleus).

The cerebellum also receives a wide range of movement-related information. For example, it receives information from the spinal cord (which enables it to keep track of the position of the limbs), from the vestibular system (which provides information about balance) and from the cerebral cortex which relays motor and sensory information (also backed up by direct information from the senses via cranial nerves). In fact, the cortical input (which derives mainly from the motor cortex, its adjacent areas and the somatosensory cortex) in humans provides a massive input to the cerebellum and contains about 20 million axons – which is about 20 times more than the number of axons making up the pyramidal tracts. This is called the corticopontocerebellar pathway as it first projects to the **pontine nuclei** before being passed on to the cerebellum.

The functions of the cerebellum

One way of understanding the functions of the cerebellum is to consider the effect of its damage. In humans, damage to the cerebellum reduces the fluidity of voluntary movement and makes it mechanical and robot-like. This is particularly noticeable in tasks which require a series of rapid movements, as occurs during dancing, playing sports, writing or playing a musical instrument. Although a person with cerebellar damage may be able to make individual movements, he or she will probably not be able to link them together into a continuous smooth sequence. For example, imagine you are to throw a baseball with your right hand: if you act out this movement the chances are that you will shift your body weight to the right, stretch out your left arm for balance, and move your head towards the throwing arm. However, a person with cerebellar damage will tend to throw the ball without making the necessary adjustments to his or her body. Furthermore, this action is likely to be jerky and the arm may even show an 'intentional' tremor that disappears once the movement has ceased (this is different to the 'resting tremor' seen in Parkinson's disease which tends to disappear during movement).

Thus, the cerebellum regulates the fluidity of movement enabling it to be smooth, quick and free of tremor. It is believed that the cerebellum does this by assessing the rate of movement required for a particular action and then calculating the amount of time necessary for the body or limb to reach its intended position. In short, the cerebellum is involved in the timing and feedback correction of voluntary movement (Leonard 1998). Following its calculations, the cerebellum makes sure that this information is co-ordinated with the motor instructions being issued from the cerebral cortex (or basal ganglia). It is important to note that the cerebellum is also involved in other motor functions. For example, damage to the cerebellum impairs the regulation of saccadic eye movements (see previous chapter) and also causes **dysarthria** – an inability to make fine articulatory movements of the vocal system resulting in slurred speech. In addition, there is substantial evidence that the cerebellum is also involved in motor learning (e.g. the acquisition of classical conditioning) and a variety of cognitive tasks (e.g. including certain spatial and language tasks).

The basal ganglia

The basal ganglia (Figure 3.7) is the name given to a group of interconnected subcortical nuclei and pathways that lie buried underneath the folds of the cerebral hemispheres on each side of the brain. The structures include the caudate nucleus and putamen (together these are known as the **striatum**), the **globus pallidus**, the **subthalamus** and the substantia nigra (located in the midbrain).

To understand the anatomy of the basal ganglia it is perhaps best to view it as part of a circuit that is connected with the cerebral cortex. Most regions of the cerebral cortex (including those without an obvious involvement in movement) project to the striatum (particularly the putamen) and, in turn, the striatum sends its main output to the globus pallidus, which then passes much of the information back to the motor regions of the

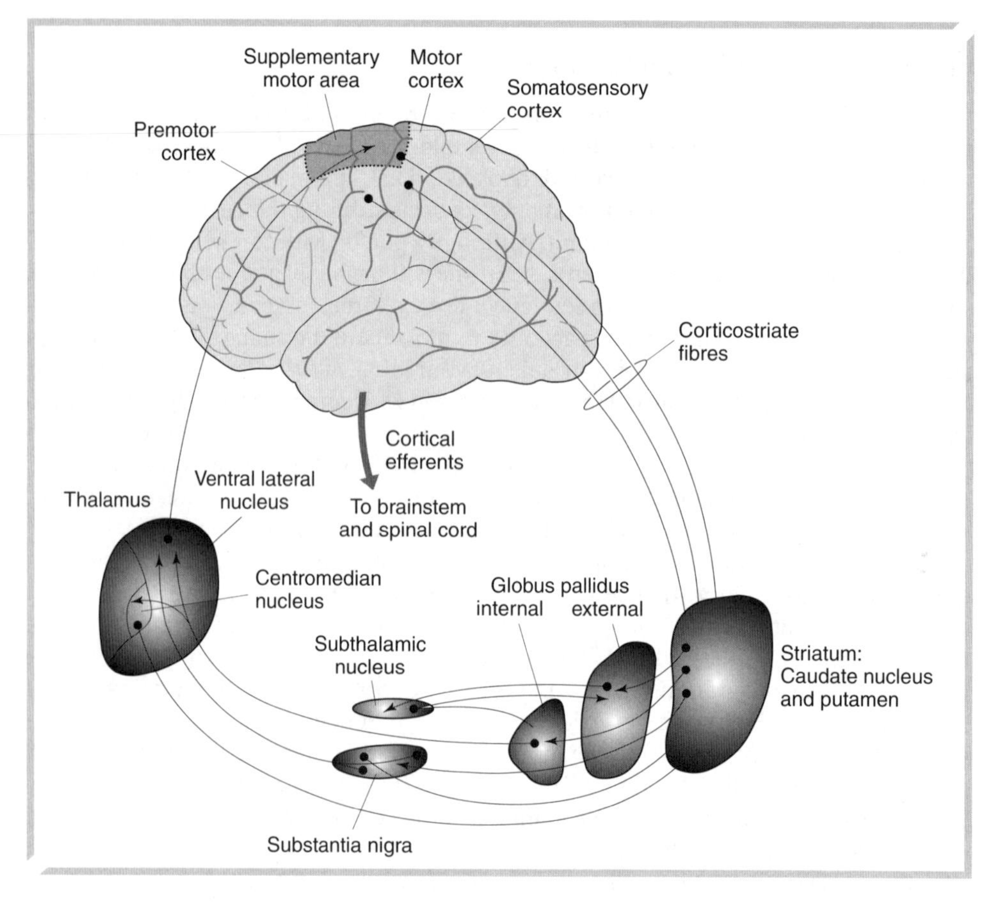

Figure 3.7 The anatomical structures and connectivity of the basal ganglia. (*Source*: From A. M. Schneider and B. Tarshis, *Elements of Physiological Psychology*. Copyright © 1995 by McGraw-Hill. Reprinted by permission.)

cerebral cortex (via the motor nuclei of the thalamus). In other words, the striatum and cerebral cortex form part of a large multisynaptic loop that connects two major brain regions. Other pathways that feed into the striatum include those from the thalamus (which includes input from the cerebellum) and substantia nigra (see Figure 3.7). In turn, the striatum also projects directly back to the substantia nigra (this also provides a route for striatal information to gain access to the brainstem) and subthalamus (via the globus pallidus).

The functions of the basal ganglia

The basal ganglia forms one of the most enigmatic of all brain structures and its function continues to perplex researchers. One possibility is that the basal ganglia is a system that is involved in making postural adjustments to the body that supports the motor cortex in its ability to produce voluntary and precise movement. That is, the basal ganglia is responsible for making gross body movements, whereas the cerebral cortex is necessary for the performance of more precise movements such as those of the fingers, hands and face. Indeed, in support of this idea is the fact that people with basal ganglia damage (e.g. Parkinson's disease) often show gross postural dysfunction and have great difficulty producing purposeful movement (see below). Moreover, it has been shown experimentally that the basal ganglia plays a particularly critical role in the control of slow, smooth movements (e.g. see Kornhuber 1974). For example, when monkeys move their arms slowly, neural activity increases in the putamen, but this does not occur when they move their arms quickly (De Long 1974).

Evidence from cellular recording also demonstrates that striatal neurons generally do not fire or modulate their activity until *after* a movement has started (Beckstead 1996). Thus, it may be that the basal ganglia does not initiate movement (this is left to the cerebral cortex), but rather, once the motor act has begun, it backs up the motor plan of the cerebral cortex with automatic adjustments. It has also been suggested that the basal ganglia performs a particularly important role in the execution of movements influenced by learning or cognitive processing (Marsden 1982, Evarts *et al.* 1984) – a hypothesis that makes sense considering that all regions of the cerebral cortex (and not just its motor areas) project to the striatum.

Parkinson's disease

In 1817, a London doctor called James Parkinson first described the condition which he called shaking palsy (shaking paralysis) and today bears his name. Parkinson's disease is now known to be a degenerative disorder of later life, and by far the most common disease involving the basal ganglia (afflicting around one in every 200 people over the age of 50). The main symptoms are slowness of movement (**bradykinesia**), difficulty in initiating movement (**akinesia**) and increased muscle tone (**rigidity**). In addition, there tends to be a persistent resting tremor of the hands, and a loss of facial muscle tone which gives the face a blank mask-like appearance. As the disorder progresses there is gradual deterioration of gait and posture so that those afflicted may be unable to walk, move their arms, or even hold up their head – and, if left untreated, the disease will often lead to general invalidity within 15 to 20 years. Also in the later stages of the disease there are often signs of dementia, or a general impairment of intellectual and cognitive functioning.

The underlying cause of Parkinson's disease was first identified by Ehringer and Hornykiewicz in 1960. In short, it is due to a loss of neurons occurring in the substantia nigra which, in turn, results in the degeneration of nigral axons that form the pathway projecting to the striatum (the **nigral–striatal pathway**). This pathway was also found to have another important characteristic – it used the neurotransmitter **dopamine**, and thus accompanying the neural degeneration is also a severe loss of dopamine in the striatum. In fact, the symptoms of Parkinson's disease typically do not begin to manifest themselves until dopamine levels in the striatum have fallen by about 90 per cent – and, in the long term, levels are likely to fall even further, becoming almost non-existent in the later stages of the disease.

Levodopa (L-dopa)

The discovery that Parkinson's disease was linked to dopamine deficiency had very important implications: if the disease was due to lack of dopamine, then it followed that if a way could be found of replenishing it in the brain, then a treatment for the disorder might be achieved. Unfortunately, injections of dopamine were of little use since it was unable to cross the blood–brain barrier. However, in 1967 it was discovered that large oral doses of the dopamine precursor **L-dopa** (in doses that were some thousand times greater than had previously been used) had dramatic effects on relieving Parkinson's symptoms (Cotzias *et al.* 1967). Not only was this substance able to pass into the brain, but it appeared that the remaining neurons in the substantia nigra could take it into their axon terminals to make more dopamine. The impact of this discovery was to provide a dramatic turning point in the management of Parkinson's disease.

It has been found that the vast majority of patients (around 75 per cent) with Parkinson's disease will show improvement with L-dopa treatment, and that in many cases the effects are immediate and sometimes dramatic. Indeed, the response is usually so good as to be widely regarded as diagnostic for the disease. Slowness of movement and rigidity are usually the first symptoms to respond, with tremor often improving with continued treatment (Bradley 1989). Although postural instability often remains a problem, there is little doubt that L-dopa enables many Parkinson patients to enjoy a much improved quality of life that they would otherwise not have experienced.

Unfortunately, L-dopa treatment is not a cure for Parkinson's disease. It does not stop the underlying degeneration of the substantia nigra, and there comes a point when there are not enough dopamine-containing neurons to take up the L-dopa to make it effective. In addition, there are other problems associated with the use of L-dopa. For example, after about two years of treatment it is not unusual for the effectiveness of L-dopa to become highly variable with the Parkinson symptoms fluctuating 'on and off' several times a day. There is no satisfactory explanation for this effect and it is not clear whether it is due to the L-dopa or to the underlying progression of the disease. Another serious side effect of long-term treatment is **dyskinesia**, that is, involuntary movements of the hands, limbs and face. Although dyskinesia can be treated by reducing the dosage of L-dopa, this in turn often causes the symptoms of Parkinson's disease to reappear. This problem also makes it very difficult for the physician to find the right dose to treat the disorder, and for this reason some doctors recommend taking 'L-dopa holidays' in the hope that this will minimise the long-term chances of side effects.

The causes of Parkinson's disease

The reason why substantia nigra degeneration occurs in Parkinson's disease is still not fully understood. Parkinson's disease does not appear to be inherited and this is supported by evidence showing that it is rare for identical twins to both develop the disorder (Johnson *et al.* 1990). Although this finding need not necessarily rule out the possibility of genetic influences (e.g. see Golbe *et al.* 1990) it nevertheless remains that most researchers have sought to find environmental causes for the disease. Some of the earliest evidence implicated viral infections. For example, a severe parkinsonism syndrome occurred in many patients who survived the epidemic of **encephalitis lethargica** that occurred throughout the world in the years 1915 to 1926. At first this illness resembled influenza, but in many cases it led to its victims falling into a prolonged stupor with paralysis, which came to be known as 'sleeping sickness'. The illness claimed many lives (the mortality rate was about 40 per cent) and even then recovery was not complete as over half of the people who survived developed parkinsonism. Moreover, later post-mortem examination of these patients confirmed that degeneration of the substantia nigra had occurred. Interestingly, a few patients who had spent over 30 years in a state of somnolence caused by the sickness were given L-dopa treatment in the 1960s, and many 'awoke' from their plight, albeit for a short period of time (this story is told in the film 'Awakenings' which is based on the book of the same name by Oliver Sacks). These types of finding have raised suspicions that Parkinson's disease may have a similar cause (e.g. a virus). Despite this, it must be said that there is no good evidence, experimental or otherwise, to show that Parkinson's disease is caused in this way.

More recently attention has focused on environmental toxins as the causal factor in Parkinson's disease. In 1982, several young people in Northern California developed severe Parkinson-like symptoms after using an illegal drug that was designed to resemble heroin. This drug was produced and supplied by the same dealer, and on closer examination was found to contain a chemical called MPTP, which also happened to be a highly selective neurotoxin for the substantia nigra. In fact, it provided brain researchers with a very powerful research tool by which to mimic the effects of Parkinson's disease in laboratory animals. For example, injections of MPTP in monkeys cause slow movement, rigidity, tremor and impaired posture, along with a marked loss of dopaminergic neurons in the substantia nigra. Interestingly, these types of motor deficit do not occur in rodents whose substantia nigra neurons, unlike those in humans and primates, are not heavily pigmented (or contain melanin). This has led to the suspicion that the pigments contained in the cells of the substantia nigra may somehow be an important contributing factor to the development of the disease.

How then does MPTP cause the degeneration of the substantia nigra? The answer is that it bonds to an enzyme called monoamine oxidase B (MAO-B) found in glial cells near the substantia nigra which, in turn, converts it into the highly toxic **free radical** MPP^+. Free radicals are chemicals that have lost an electron and are normally formed from the breakdown of oxygen. Although they only exist for a few millionths of a second, they can nevertheless do considerable damage to biological tissue. Moreover, it appears that MPP^+ in the substantia nigra has a particular affinity for melanin, thereby causing it damage and harming the cell (Youdin and Riederer 1997).

Does this finding, therefore, have any relevance for understanding the cause of Parkinson's disease? Many researchers believe that the answer may be 'Yes'. The substantia nigra produces a number of free radicals (as a result of metabolism and during the breakdown of dopamine) and, although it also contains special enzymes to protect itself against these chemicals, it may be that these are deficient in people with Parkinson's disease. Alternatively, there may be chemicals in the environment that resemble MPP^+ and contribute directly to substantia nigra degeneration. Indeed, substances related to MPTP are present in many foods (Singer and Ramsey 1990); and the chemical structure of MPP^+ has been shown to be very similar to the pesticide paraquat (see Snyder and D'Amato 1986).

The research on MPTP has also led to the development of new treatments for Parkinson's disease. As mentioned above, MPTP is harmless by itself, but becomes extremely toxic when it is converted into MPP^+ by monoamine oxidase. Thus, drugs that inhibit monoamine oxidase should help prevent the damage caused by MPTP. Indeed, this type of protective effect on substantia nigra neurons has been shown to occur in monkeys treated with high amounts of MPTP (Langston *et al.* 1984a, b). But even more importantly, these findings also appear to have relevance for humans. For example, the MAO-B inhibitor selegrine (deprenyl) has been shown to delay the need for L-dopa therapy in Parkinson patients (Shoulson *et al.* 1989) as well as producing a marked improvement in symptoms (Terud and Langston 1989). Thus, deprenyl is probably the first treatment that actually slows down the progression of Parkinson's disease, and for this reason it is now becoming standard therapy for patients along with L-dopa. Moreover, because deprenyl inhibits MAO from breaking down dopamine, it has the extra benefit of allowing this neurotransmitter to stay in the synapse for longer, thus assisting the action of L-dopa.

Box 3.2 ADRENAL AND FOETAL TRANSPLANTATION

In recent years there has been considerable interest in the possibility of treating Parkinson's disease by the transplantation of tissue into the brain that is able to replace the 'lost' dopamine. The issue of brain transplantation actually has a long history. One of the first attempts was undertaken in 1890 by W. Gilman Thompson who transplanted cerebral cortex tissue from cats into dogs. Although no neurons survived this operation, a later attempt by Elizabeth Dunn in 1903 used small bits of tissue taken from the cerebral cortex of newly born rats. After 3 months she examined the transplanted tissue and found that in about 10 per cent of cases the brain grafts had survived. Thus, the key to successful grafting appeared to be the use of immature (or foetal) tissue, along with the development of a rich blood supply to nourish the implant.

Despite this, many investigators remained sceptical about these early findings. However, in the early 1970s, researchers showed beyond doubt that immature neurons could survive when transplanted into recipient brains. In fact, such cells matured, formed new connections, and presumably became fully functional. Moreover, the brain appeared to be an 'immunologically privileged' site and the rejection of tissue rarely occurred – even when the donor and host were different animals. In theory, this suggested that the grafting of brain tissue (say into humans) could be undertaken with (foetal) tissue taken from other animals.

But could transplanted neural tissue restore the behaviour of brain-damaged animals? If it could, then this would open up the possibility of treating Parkinson's disease (and other neurodegenerative disorders) by means of neural transplantation. The first study to examine this question was undertaken by Perlow *et al.* (1979) who made unilateral lesions to the substantia nigra in rats (which caused movement abnormalities limited to one side of the body). Following this, the investigators transplanted the substantia nigra from rat foetal tissue to sites where its cells would normally make synapses in the adult rat brain. The results showed that the grafts survived in 29 out of the 30 rats. More importantly, within four weeks the majority of the recipients had recovered most of their movement. Similar results have also been obtained with monkeys (e.g. Ridley and Baker 1991).

By the early 1980s research had shown that foetal transplantation into human patients was a feasible idea. However, because of anticipated social and legal problems, the first attempts at brain transplants in humans were undertaken with tissue taken from the adrenal glands. Although the main substance secreted by the adrenal glands is adrenaline, it also releases small amounts of dopamine. Consequently, researchers (Backlund 1985; Lindvall *et al.* 1987) implanted small bits of adrenal tissue into the striatum to function as 'mini-pumps' for dopamine. Although there were no serious side effects from this transplantation, the results from these initial studies showed that the improvements were modest and generally did not last longer than six months. However, there have been claims of much more lasting benefits from the procedure (e.g. Madrazo *et al.* 1987; Goetz *et al.* 1989) and, because of this, the value of adrenal transplantation in Parkinson's disease remains highly controversial. However, it is probably fair to say that, at present, the results of this procedure are far too unpredictable, and its benefits too short-lasting, for it to be used in clinical practice.

In 1986 the Swedish Society of Medicine issued ethical guidelines for human embryonic tissue grafting and this quickly paved the way for the first foetal substantia nigra (dopamine cell) transplants in human patients. The first operation of this type was performed by Lindvall *et al.* (1988) on two female patients aged 48 and 55 using foetal tissue that had been obtained from consenting women who had undergone terminations at Lund University. Soon after, this operation started to be performed by other investigators worldwide and, by the early 1990s, around 100 Parkinson patients had received transplants of foetal brain tissue. The results of this procedure have shown that some 'mild to moderate' relief from Parkinson's disease is obtained from the transplant, but in no case has it provided a full reversal of symptoms (Lindvall 1991). Again, it is unlikely to provide a treatment for Parkinson's disease, at least in the foreseeable future. Despite this, the subject of neural transplantation remains a very exciting area of neuroscience and one with many potential clinical applications (e.g. see *Trends in Neuroscience* (1991), vol. 14, pp. 319–88).

Huntington's chorea

Another degenerative brain disease that is associated with cell loss to the basal ganglia is **Huntington's chorea**, first described by George Huntington in 1872 (the word *chorea* means 'dance' and refers to the complex twisting and involuntary tic-like movements shown by people with the disease). Huntington's chorea is an inherited condition and the result of a single mutated gene (now known to be located on chromosome 4) which follows an autosomal mode of inheritance – that is, if one parent has the disorder then there will be a 50 per cent chance that each offspring will also carry the gene and develop the condition (see also Chapter 12). Despite being a genetic disease, Huntington's chorea is also a disorder of later life which doesn't normally manifest itself clearly until after the age of 40. Unfortunately, by this time, a Huntington's carrier (not knowing whether the mutated gene is carried or not) is likely to have had children, thereby also putting them at great risk of inheriting the condition. Until recently there has been no way of knowing if one was a carrier, although new developments in genetic testing have now enabled the Huntington's gene to be identified with a high degree of accuracy from a simple blood test. However, whether prospective carriers want to find out if they have an incurable, fatal and extremely unpleasant disorder is another matter, and it appears that only a small percentage of people (12–15 per cent) take up the offer of the test (Harper 1991).

Huntington's chorea is a rare disorder that affects about 1 person in every 20,000, although, because of its genetic nature, there can be pockets of high prevalence in certain places. The initial symptoms often include facial twitching and excessive fidgeting. But as the disorder progresses these symptoms develop into rapid and complex flailing movements of the arms and upper parts of the body. As Hopkins (1993) has pointed out, the chorea movements are difficult to describe, but once seen are seldom forgotten. The body writhes and jerks incessantly, making purposeful behaviour such as walking or holding an object almost impossible. Muscle tone may also be difficult to maintain, occasionally resulting in collapse. Other features accompanying the disorder, especially in its later stages, include changes in personality, a decline of intellectual function leading to dementia and psychosis, and blurred speech. Ultimately, the person becomes bedridden with death occurring on average some 10 to 20 years after the onset of the disorder. One well-known person to die from the disease was the American folk singer Woody Guthrie.

Brain changes in Huntington's chorea

The most conspicuous pathological characteristic of Huntington's chorea is cell death in the caudate nucleus and putamen, although by the later stages of the disorder there may also be generalised shrinkage of the brain itself (which can be up to 20 per cent in severe cases). However, the caudate nucleus and putamen are the first regions to show neural degeneration, and the loss of cells continues throughout the disease so that up to 95 per cent of neurons may be destroyed by the time of death. Moreover, as the striatum degenerates, so cell loss in other areas of the brain may also become apparent – particularly in associated pathways and structures of the basal ganglia, including the globus pallidus, cerebellum and cerebral cortex.

Unfortunately, the neurochemical deficit seen in Huntington's chorea is not as straightforward as that occurring with Parkinson's disease. The most important neurochemical change appears to occur with the inhibitory neurotransmitter **GABA** (and its synthesising enzymes) whose levels in the striatum may be reduced by up to 80 per cent. This is followed by levels of acetylcholine which may be reduced by 50 per cent. In contrast, the nigral–striatal pathway tends to be preserved in Huntington's chorea and levels of dopamine in the striatum may even be increased by up to 70 per cent (Martin and Gusella 1986).

In fact, the increase in dopaminergic activity is probably caused by the loss of GABA-containing cells in the striatum, as some of these neurons form pathways that project back to the substantia nigra where they normally act to inhibit the dopamine neurons. With the loss of this inhibitory control, the cells of the substantia nigra become excited and release dopamine into the striatum, which may then contribute to the abnormal movements that characterise Huntington's chorea. Evidence for this idea comes from pharmacological work showing that drugs which increase dopamine (such as L-dopa) exacerbate the symptoms of Huntington's disease, whereas drugs that block or reduce dopaminergic activity (such as chlorpromazine or haloperidol) may help to reduce the symptoms.

How does the gene cause Huntington's disease?

A central (and as yet unanswered) question concerns the function of the gene that causes Huntington's chorea. In short, what is the normal role of this gene, and how does it result in the cascade of degenerative changes that take place in the brain of those with the disorder? Because all genes produce proteins (which serve a huge range of biological roles – see Chapter 12), Huntington's disease must be the result of a faulty protein appearing in the brain. But what this protein does is not clear. Perhaps, for example, the gene produces a toxic substance that directly destroys neurons; or it may be that it normally protects brain cells from other toxic chemicals. Alternatively, the protein could play a vital role in the metabolism of the cell.

One chemical that has been implicated in the pathology of Huntington's disease is the neurotransmitter **glutamate**. Glutamate is an excitatory transmitter that is contained in fibres projecting from the cortex to the striatum, and is known to have the potential to cause neural degeneration if released in abnormally high amounts. For example, when quinolinic acid – which directly stimulates glutamate receptors – is injected into the striatum of experimental animals, it produces a very similar type of neural degeneration to that found in Huntington's chorea (Beal *et al.* 1986). The possibility exists, therefore, that the Huntington's gene might somehow act on glutamate functioning (perhaps by increasing its release or changing the sensitivity of its receptors) to set into motion the process of neural degeneration. And, in accordance with this theory, there is evidence to show that certain types of glutamate receptor (particularly NMDA receptors) are significantly reduced in number (by 93 per cent) in the striatum of people with Huntington's chorea (Young *et al.* 1988). Because of this, attempts are presently under way to develop drugs that can block glutamate receptors to determine if they can retard the progression of the disease.

The motor areas of the cerebral cortex

In 1870 Gustav Fritsch and Eduard Hitzig were the first to show that electrical stimulation of certain regions of the cerebral cortex in dogs was able to produce a wide range of movement on the opposite side of the body. In fact, what they had discovered was the **primary motor cortex** (the main site that contributes to the pyramidal tract). Later work by Wilder Penfield in the 1950s mapped this region in awake humans using electrical stimulation (which was being used to identify epileptic tissue in patients prior to its removal) and found that the body's representation in the motor cortex was topographically organised (i.e. the layout of the motor cortex contained a point-to-point map of the body). For example, if the motor cortex was stimulated along its length, from top to bottom, it produced movement of the feet, legs, body, arms and head (see Figure 3.8). Moreover, the amount of motor cortex given over to each part of the body was related

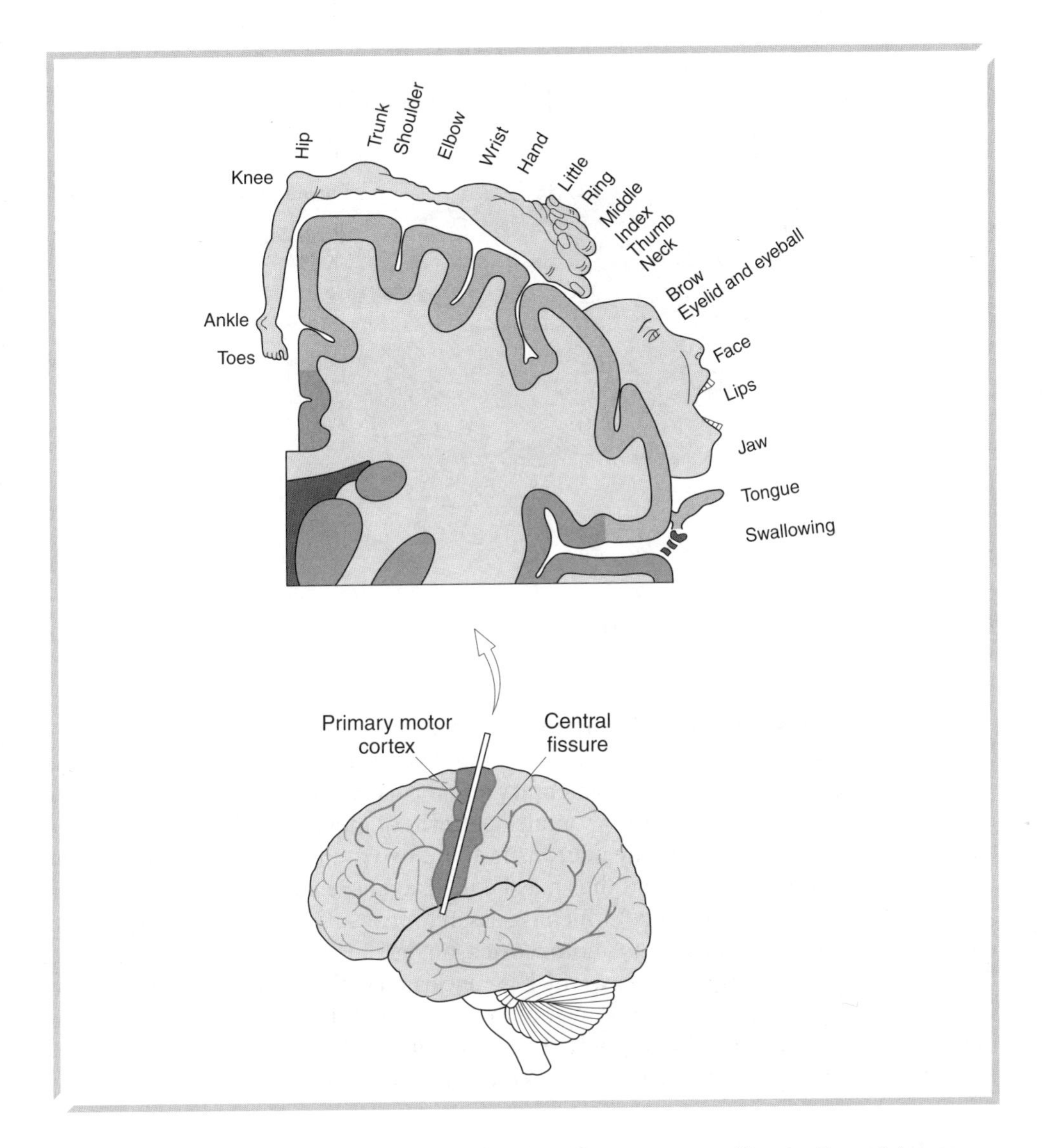

Figure 3.8 Topographic representation of the human motor cortex. (*Source*: From John P. J. Pinel, *Biopsychology*, 3rd edition. Copyright © 1997 by Allyn & Bacon. Reprinted by permission.)

to the precision of its movement. For example, the motor cortex devotes much of its tissue to controlling the small muscles of the face (particularly the mouth region), and the hands (particularly fingers and thumb), but relatively little to the trunk and legs. Interestingly, Penfield also showed that his subjects were unaware of the movements produced by the electrical stimulation and that they had no memory of them afterwards (Penfield and Rasmussen 1950).

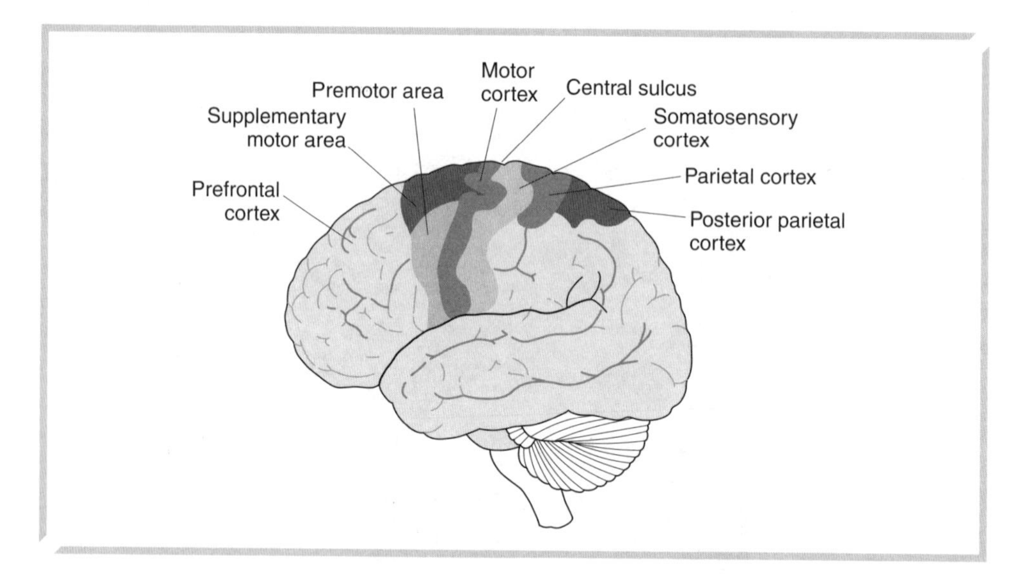

Figure 3.9 Motor areas of the cerebral cortex.

Further work has shown that the motor cortex is surrounded by other areas that also have a bearing on its function. For example, immediately anterior to the motor cortex is the **premotor cortex** and the **supplementary motor cortex** (Brodmann's area 6) which appear to contain neural circuits for complex patterns of movement. In fact, recording studies have also found that many neurons in these two areas are active just prior to actual movement of the body, and thus may be involved in selecting the correct motor response (or pattern of responses) which is passed for execution to the primary motor cortex. Just posterior to the primary motor cortex, on the other side of the central sulcus, is the **primary somatosensory cortex**, which is concerned with receiving somatosensory input (touch, temperature and body position) from the body (see Figure 3.9). This area of the brain is also arranged in a topographical fashion (similar to the motor cortex) and is probably important for movement which requires sensory feedback.

The functions of the motor cortex

What then is the function of the primary motor cortex? The answer from a number of sources suggests that its main role is as an executive for voluntary movement – especially for responses that require very fine movement of the limbs. For example, the function of the human motor cortex has been examined by the Danish neurologist Per Roland and his colleagues who used **positron emission tomography** (see Chapter 9) to measure the blood flow through this region during the performance of various movement tasks (this technique works on the assumption that the more active a brain area is, the more blood it will require to provide oxygen and nutrients). When Roland asked his subjects to perform a simple task, such as keeping a spring compressed between two fingers, it was found that blood flow increased markedly in the hand area of the contralateral motor cortex and in the adjacent somatosensory cortex. Moreover, when the complexity of the task was increased (a series of finger movements from memory) the area of blood flow extended anteriorly into the supplementary motor cortex, and posteriorly into the somatosensory cortex and parietal cortex. Interestingly, when subjects were simply asked to rehearse the complex movement in their mind, the increase in blood flow was found to be confined to the supplementary motor cortex (Roland *et al.* 1980; Roland 1984).

Further clues to the role of cerebral cortex in movement has come from clinical cases in which people have incurred damage to the motor cortex (or pyramidal system) through an accident such as a stroke. This type of injury often produces a condition known as **hemiplegia** which is characterised by flaccid muscle paralysis that is confined to the opposite side of the body from the damage. Despite this, there is often considerable recovery with reflexes and voluntary movement returning, although the control of fine movement is rarely regained. In addition, many patients often report a 'weakness' in the affected muscles, which makes them 'disinclined' to use the affected limb.

One problem with human brain injuries is that the site of damage is rarely localised to just one area. Because of this problem, neuroscientists have undertaken animal studies where precise damage to the motor cortex can be produced. Surprisingly, this work has shown that lesions of the motor cortex rarely produce paralysis, even if lesions are made to both hemispheres. For example, six weeks after bilateral lesioning of the pyramidal pathways, monkeys can run, climb and reach for food. In fact, the only persistent deficit appears to be an ability to make fine movements of the fingers, and slower-than-normal movements which become easily fatigued (e.g. see Lawrence and Kuypers 1968). Similar findings have also been found by Edward Evarts who trained monkeys to make specific movements (such as reaching towards a target) while recording from neurons in the motor cortex. The results showed that cells in the motor cortex often fired whenever a fine hand movement was made, but not when there were gross movements of a limb (Evarts *et al.* 1985).

These findings may at first appear surprising since they show that the motor cortex is not involved in the initiation of movement, but rather it enhances the accuracy (or fineness) of motor control. Where, then, does the initiation of movement come from? This question has no simple answer. For example, a number of cortical areas contribute to movement including the prefrontal cortex, premotor area, supplementary motor cortex, primary and secondary somatosensory areas and posterior parietal cortex. It may be that all these regions are able to initiate movement independently or jointly, depending on the circumstances. Furthermore, not only do most of these cortical areas have access to the primary motor cortex and/or the corticospinal tract, but they also project into extrapyramidal movement systems. In short, voluntary movement probably springs from no single cortical site, and nor is it dependent upon any single pathway.

Self-test questions

1. What are the three main types of muscle found in the human body?
2. Briefly explain the difference between muscle fibres, myofibrils and myofilaments.
3. What is the main function of muscle spindles?
4. Give an example of a monosynaptic *and* a polysynaptic reflex.
5. Why are the pyramidal and extrapyramidal systems so named? What brain structures contribute to these systems?
6. What are the main functions of the cerebellum?
7. Draw a diagram showing the structures and pathways of the basal ganglia.
8. What brain structure is known to degenerate in Parkinson's disease?
9. How does L-dopa therapy work?
10. What is MPTP and why is it important in the understanding of Parkinson's disease?
11. What causes Huntington's chorea?
12. Describe the neurochemical changes that take place in the brains of people with Huntington's chorea. Why is glutamate particularly important?
13. Describe how the motor areas of the cerebral cortex are organised.
14. What are the effects of damage to the motor cortex?

Key terms

Acetylcholine (p.77)
Acetylcholinesterase (AChE) (p.78)
Actin (p.75)
Akinesia (p.87)
Alpha motor neuron (p.76)
Autonomic nervous system (p.74)
Basal ganglia (p.81)
Bradykinesia (p.87)
Brainstem (p.81)
Caudate nucleus (p.81)
Cerebellum (p.81)
Corticospinal tract (p.81)
Crossed extensor reflex (p.80)
Deep cerebellar nuclei (p.84)
Dopamine (p.88)
Dysarthria (p.85)
Dyskinesia (p.89)
Encephalitis lethargica (p.89)
Extrapyramidal system (p.81)
Flexion reflex (p.79)
Free radical (p.90)
GABA (p.93)
Gamma motor neuron (p.78)
Globus pallidus (p.86)
Glutamate (p.94)
Hemiplegia (p.97)
Huntington's chorea (p.92)
Interneurons (p.79)
L-dopa (p.88)
Monosynaptic stretch reflex (p.79)
Motor cortex (p.81)
Motor endplate (p.77)
Muscle fibres (p.75)
Muscle spindles (p.78)
Myofibrils (p.75)
Myosin (p.75)
Neuromuscular junction (p.77)
Nigral–striatal pathway (p.88)
Patellar tendon reflex (p.79)
Pontine nuclei (p.85)
Positron emission tomography (p.96)
Premotor cortex (p.96)
Primary motor cortex (p.94)
Primary somatosensory cortex (p.96)

References

Backlund, E. O. (1985) Transplantation of adrenal medulary tissue to striatum in Parkinsonism. In Bjorklund, A. and Stenevi, U. (eds) *Neural Grafting in the Mammallian CNS*. Amsterdam: Elsevier.

Beal, M. F. *et al.* (1986) Replication of neurochemical characteristics of Huntington's disease by quinolinic acid. *Nature*, **321**, 168–71.

Beckstead, R. M. (1996) *A Survey of Medical Neuroscience*. New York: Springer-Verlag.

Bradley, P. B. (1989) *Introduction to Neuropharmacology*. London: Wright.

Cotzias, G. C. *et al.* (1967) Aromatic acid amino acids and modication of Parkinsonism. *New England Journal of Medicine*, **276**, 374–9.

De Long, M. R. (1974) Motor functions of the basal ganglia: Single unit activity during movement. In Schmitt, F. O. and Worden, F. G. (eds) *The Neurosciences: Third Study Program.* Cambridge, MA: MIT Press.

Evarts, E. V. *et al.* (1984) *Neurophysiological Approaches to Higher Brain Functions*. New York: Wiley.

Evarts, E. V. *et al.* (1985) *The Motor System in Neurobiology*. New York: Elsevier.

Goetz, C. G. *et al.* (1989) Multicentre study of autologous adrenal medullary transplantation to the corpus striatum in patients with advanced Parkinson's disease. *New England Journal of Medicine*, **320**, 337–41.

Golbe, L. I. *et al.* (1990) A large kindred with autosomal dominant Parkinson's disease. *Annals of Neurology*, **27**, 276–82.

Grillner, S. (1996) Neural networks for vertebrate locomotion. *Scientific American*, **271**, 48–53.

Harper, P. S. (ed.) (1991) *Huntington's Disease*. London: Saunders.

Hopkins, A. (1993) *Clinical Neurology*. Oxford: Oxford University Press.

Johnson, W. G. *et al.* (1990) Twin studies and the genetics of Parkinson's disease: A reappraisal. *Movement Disorders*, **5**, 187–94.

Kornhuber, H. H. (1974) Cerebral cortex, cerebellum and basal ganglia: An introduction to their motor functions. In Schmitt, F. O. and Worden, F. G. (eds) *The Neurosciences: Third Study Program.* Cambridge MA: MIT Press.

Langston, J. W. *et al.* (1984a) Selective nigral toxicity after systemic administration of MPTP in the squirrel monkey. *Brain Research*, **292**, 390–4.

Langston, J. W. *et al.* (1984b) Pargyline prevents MPTP-induced Parkinsonism in primates. *Science*, **225**, 1480–8.

Lawrence, D. and Kuypers, H. (1968) The functional organisation of the motor system in the monkey. *Brain*, **91**, 1–36.

Leonard, C. T. (1998) *The Neuroscience of Human Movement*. St Louis: Mosby.
Lindvall, O. (1991) Prospects of transplantation in human neurodegenerative diseases. *Trends in Neuroscience*, **14**, 376–84.
Lindvall, O. *et al.* (1987) Transplantation in Parkinson's disease: Two cases of adrenal medullary grafts to the putamen. *Annals of Neurology*, **22**, 457–68.
Lindvall, O. *et al.* (1988) Fetal dopamine-rich mesencephalic grafts in Parkinson's disease. *Lancet*, **ii**, 1483–4.
Madrazo, I. *et al.* (1987) Open microsurgical autograft of adrenal medulla to the right caudate nucleus in two patients with intractible Parkinson's disease. *New England Journal of Medicine*, **316**, 831–4.
Marsden, C. D. (1982) The mysterious motor function of the basal ganglia: The Robert Wartenberg Lecture. *Neurology*, **32**, 514–39.
Martin, J. B. and Gusella, J. F. (1986) Huntington's disease: Pathogenesis and management. *New England Journal of Medicine*, **315**, 1267–76.
Penfield, W. and Rasmussen, T. (1950) *The Cerebral Cortex of Man*. New York: Macmillan.
Perlow, M. J. *et al.* (1979) Brain grafts reduce motor abnormalities produced by destruction of nigrostriatal dopamine system. *Science*, **204**, 643–7.
Ridley, R. M. and Baker, H. F. (1991) Can fetal transplants restore function in monkeys with lesion-induced behavioral deficits? *Trends in Neuroscience*, **14**, 366–70.
Roland, P. E. *et al.* (1980) Supplementary motor area and other cortical areas in the organisation of voluntary movements in man. *Neurophysiology*, **43**, 118–36.
Roland, P. E. (1984) Organisation of motor control by the normal human brain. *Human Neurobiology*, **2**, 205–16.
Shoulson, E. *et al.* (1989) Effect of deprenyl on the progression of disability in early Parkinson's disease. *New England Journal of Medicine*, **321**, 1364–71.
Singer, T. P. and Ramsey, R. R. (1990) Mechanism of neurotoxicity of MPTP. *FEBS Letters*, **274**, 1–8.
Snyder, S. H. and D'Amato, R. J. (1986) MPTP: A neurotoxin relevant to the pathophysiology of Parkinson's disease. *Neurology*, **36**, 250–8.
Terud, J. W. and Langston, J. W. (1989) The effect of deprenyl (selegrine) on the natural history of Parkinson's disease. *Science*, **245**, 519–22.
Youdin, M. B. H. and Riederer, P. (1997) Understanding Parkinson's disease. *Scientific American*, Jan., 38–45.
Young, A. B. *et al.* (1988) NMDA receptor losses in putamen from patients with Huntington's disease. *Science*, **241**, 981–3.

FURTHER READING

Brooks, V. B. (1986) *The Neural Basis of Motor Control*. Oxford: Oxford University Press.
Lindvall, O. *et al.* (1990) Grafts of fetal dopamine neurons survive and improve motor function in Parkinson's disease. *Science*, **247**, 574–7.
Quinn, N. P. and Jenner, P. G. (1989) *Disorders of Movement*. San Diego: Academic Press.
Rosenbaum, J. (1991) *Human Motor Control*. San Diego: Academic Press.

Multiple choice questions

1. Striated or skeletal muscle is under the control of the:

(a) sympathetic nervous system
(b) parasympathetic nervous system
(c) somatic nervous system
(d) all of the above

2. Muscle fibres (or cells) are composed of:

(a) sarcolemma
(b) myofibrils
(c) myofilaments
(d) all of the above

3. Myofilaments are composed of:

(a) actin filaments
(b) myosin filaments
(c) a series of disk-like protein sheets called Z lines
(d) all of the above

4. The number of muscle cells innervated by an alpha motor neuron is:

(a) always one
(b) always two (one at each end of the muscle)
(c) dependent upon the type of muscle being innervated
(d) none of the above (muscle cells are innervated by beta motor neurons!)

5. The neurotransmitter always used at the neuromuscular junction is:

(a) acetylcholine
(b) noradrenaline
(c) dopamine
(d) dependent upon the type of muscle being innervated

6. The main function of muscle spindles is to act as:

(a) stretch receptors
(b) structural support for the muscles
(c) compartments to hold together the myofilaments
(d) fast-twitch fatiguable fibres

7. The patellar tendon reflex (knee jerk) is an example of a __________________ stretch reflex, whereas the flexion reflex is an example of a __________________ stretch reflex.

(a) monosynaptic, polysynaptic
(b) polysynaptic, monosynaptic
(c) monosynaptic, central nervous system mediated
(d) alpha motor neuron mediated, gamma motor neuron mediated

8. In what region of the brain is the motor cortex found?

(a) temporal cortex
(b) parietal cortex
(c) posterior part of the frontal cortex
(d) cingulate cortex

9. Which of the following structures is not part of the basal ganglia?

(a) caudate nucleus
(b) putamen
(c) substantia nigra
(d) hypothalamus

10. The motor cortex sends most of its output fibres into the ________________ whereas the basal ganglia sends most of its output into the ________________.

(a) extrapyramidal system, pyramidal system
(b) pyramidal system, extrapyramidal system
(c) cerebellum, substantia nigra
(d) somatosensory cortex, cerebellum

11. Just anterior to the motor cortex in the frontal cortex lies the:

(a) premotor area
(b) supplementary motor cortex
(c) (a) and (b) above
(d) primary somatosensory cortex

12. The somatosensory cortex receives sensory information from:

(a) touch
(b) temperature
(c) body position
(d) all of the above

13. Lesions to the motor cortex in animals typically produce:

(a) total loss of voluntary movement
(b) flaccid muscle paralysis

(c) loss of fine but not gross movements
(d) (a) and (b) above

14. In humans damage to the cerebellum typically produces:

(a) total loss of voluntary control
(b) resting tremor
(c) flaccid muscle paralysis
(d) movements that are slow and robot-like

15. Parkinson's disease is primarily due to degeneration of the:

(a) globus pallidus
(b) substantia nigra
(c) cerebellum
(d) subthalamus

16. The main neurotransmitter used by the nigral–striatal pathway is:

(a) acetylcholine
(b) noradrenaline
(c) dopamine
(d) GABA

17. Some patients suffering from sleeping sickness (encephalitis lethargica) were 'awakened' with the drug:

(a) dopamine
(b) L-dopa
(c) MPTP
(d) dopamine combined with adrenaline

18. MPTP is a highly selective neurotoxin for the:

(a) cerebellum
(b) globus pallidus
(c) pyramidal system
(d) none of the above

19. If one parent carries the gene for Huntington's chorea then each of their offspring will have a ______ chance of developing the disease:

(a) 100 per cent
(b) 50 per cent
(c) 0 per cent (both parents have to carry the gene)
(d) it depends on the sex of the child

20. The main neurochemical that is depleted in the striatum of victims of Huntington's disease appears to be:

(a) dopamine
(b) acetylcholine
(c) GABA
(d) glutamate

4 Hunger and eating behaviour

IN THIS CHAPTER

- The concept of homeostasis
- The different bodily states of absorption and fasting
- The glucostatic theory of hunger
- The dual set-point model of hunger and eating
- The effects of hypothalamic lesions on feeding behaviour
- The effects of learning and cognitive factors on eating
- The causes of obesity
- Anorexia nervosa and bulimia

Introduction

In the previous two chapters we have examined the remarkable ability of the human brain to provide us with vision and movement. However, both these abilities would be of little use if the body was unable to keep itself alive. The maintenance of life has many vital requirements and requires the support of a huge number of finely tuned control systems throughout the body. And, the main control centres responsible for governing these processes are to be found in the oldest parts of the brain (particularly the brainstem) that are beyond conscious control. But one essential behaviour that we are all fully aware of is eating. We constantly have to eat to provide the energy and nutrients which enable us to grow and sustain our bodies, and it is also clear that hunger is an important determinant of behaviour. But is hunger really a problem for brain researchers? After all, on first sight, hunger appears to be a simple physiological response with important roles for the stomach and peripheral mechanisms (i.e. it is easy to imagine that we eat when levels of nutrients become low and we stop when our stomach becomes full). On closer inspection, however, it can be seen that eating is much more complex than this. In fact, hunger and eating behaviour are the end points of a hugely complex biological system that involves all levels of the brain, and doesn't appear to be linked to simple physiological responses in any direct way (this can readily be seen by the fact that we typically eat not in response to hunger, but in *anticipation* of it). Thus, higher brain processes clearly have an important bearing on eating behaviour and, as we shall see, this also extends to several eating disorders, including obesity and anorexia nervosa.

Homeostasis

Traditionally, eating behaviour has been viewed as a homeostatic process. To understand the concept of **homeostasis** it is important to realise that, in order to survive, all animals have to maintain the chemical balance of their bodies within very fine limits, even when they are subjected to fluctuating change from the outside world. For example, human beings are warm-blooded and have to keep their body temperature at about 37°C regardless of whether they live in the Antarctic or in the tropics. A change in core body temperature of just a few degrees either side of 37°C will seriously interfere with the chemical reactions taking place in our cells, and ultimately cause organ failure and death. Thus, it is essential that the body is able to regulate its temperature within a narrow margin (i.e. homeostasis). To manage this, the body must not only be able to detect temperature change, but must also be able to initiate adaptive responses (such as increased perspiration or shivering) to correct body temperature should it deviate too far from normal.

This simple example helps illustrate several important features about homeostatic systems: first, there must be a set-point or some optimal level that the system tries to maintain; secondly, there must be receptors (in this case thermoreceptors) in the body that detect the changes taking place; and, thirdly, there must be a control centre which is informed of the body state and decides on what action to be taken. Furthermore, most homeostatic systems, particularly those involving hormone release, work by a process of negative feedback, which means that they *switch off* their response when the correct level of variable has been achieved. Not dissimilar principles apply to a number of systems including thermostats used to maintain a constant temperature in buildings.

It is easy to imagine that eating behaviour must also be a homeostatic process (similar to the thermostatic model described above). For example, it is self-evident that nutrition is one of the main requirements of all living things, and that the intake of energy must be closely related to energy expenditure. Thus, it makes sense to suppose that hunger occurs in response to an energy deficit, and that eating is simply the means by which energy levels are restored to their set-point value. Similarly, a case can be made for levels of nutrients (e.g. carbohydrates, fats, proteins, etc.) to be controlled in

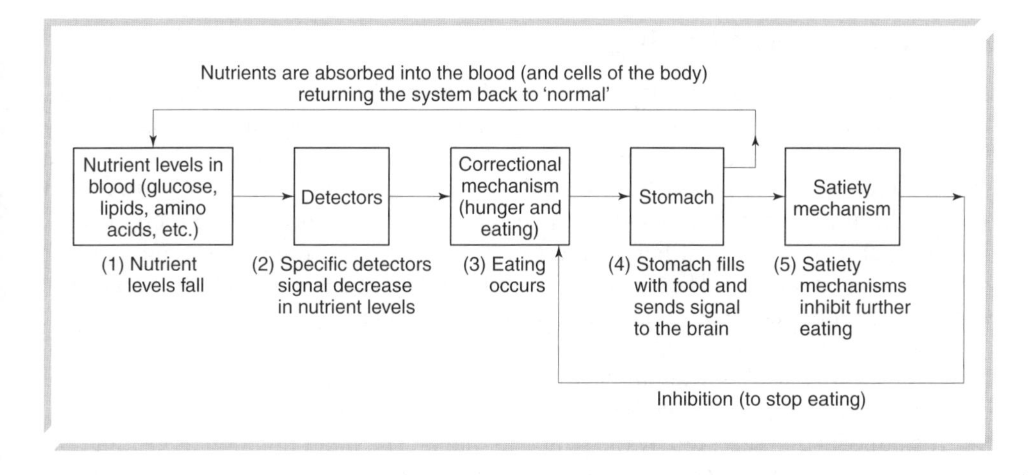

Figure 4.1 A hypothetical outline of a homeostatic system that controls eating.

much the same way. However, as we shall see, eating behaviour does not appear to fit easily into this type of simple energy- or nutrient-deficient model. This is not to say that there are no homeostatic mechanisms at work in the underlying biology of eating, but rather, in the final analysis, they do not appear to be particularly important determinants of our eating behaviour (or even that of other species).

The process of digestion

No matter what its taste or appearance may be, food is no more than a collection of proteins, fats and carbohydrates (along with a small amount of essential vitamins and minerals). Digestion is the process of breaking these foodstuffs down into simple molecules so that they can be absorbed into the blood and used by the body. The process of digestion begins in the mouth where food is broken up and mixed with saliva enabling starch-like substances to be turned into sugars. The food is then swallowed and passed to the stomach where it is mixed with gastric juices (containing hydrochloric acid and pepsin) that break it down further into a semifluid mixture called chyme. This is then emptied into the small intestine where absorption takes place. The upper part of the small intestine (called the **duodenum**) is particularly important as it contains a duct from the **pancreas gland** which secretes pancreatic juice (containing a number of enzymes that also help to break down food), as well as two hormones that play a vital role in the digestive process: **insulin** and **glucagon** (see later). The remainder of the small intestine (which is about 600 cm in length) absorbs the chyme's nutrients. From here, emulsified fats are absorbed into lymphatic vessels (from where they will eventually reach the blood) and the other nutrients (mainly glucose) are absorbed into veins which travel directly to the liver via the hepatic portal system. These nutrients can be stored in the liver (as **glycogen**) or pass into the general circulation.

Absorption and fasting

The intake of food must be sufficient to supply the metabolic needs of the body. But, here lies a problem. A large meal contains much more energy than is immediately needed to serve the body and, if it was made available all at once, the sudden increase in blood glucose would probably have fatal consequences. Thus, for the body to obtain any worthwhile benefit from a meal, it needs to be able to quickly store the nutrients following absorption, whilst being able to gradually release them in the intervening periods between feeding. These two bodily states are known respectively as the **absorptive** and the **post-absorptive phases** and are controlled by different physiological processes (see Figure 4.2).

The absorptive phase of metabolism occurs soon after a meal. But how does the body control the flood of glucose that is beginning to occur in the blood? The answer lies with the hormone insulin secreted by the pancreas gland. The main function of insulin is to enable glucose to enter the cells of the body (the exception are brain cells which do not require insulin) where it can be used to produce energy. In this way, the cells can utilise the body's newly acquired blood glucose for their own immediate energy needs. In addition, insulin has three other important ways of controlling the level of blood glucose during absorption: (1) it helps convert excess blood glucose into glycogen which is stored by the liver and the muscles; (2) it facilitates the transport of amino acids into cells allowing protein synthesis to occur; and (3) it facilitates the transport of fats into adipose cells thus enabling fat storage. In other words, insulin enables excess nutrient levels in the blood to become quickly stored in the tissues of the body.

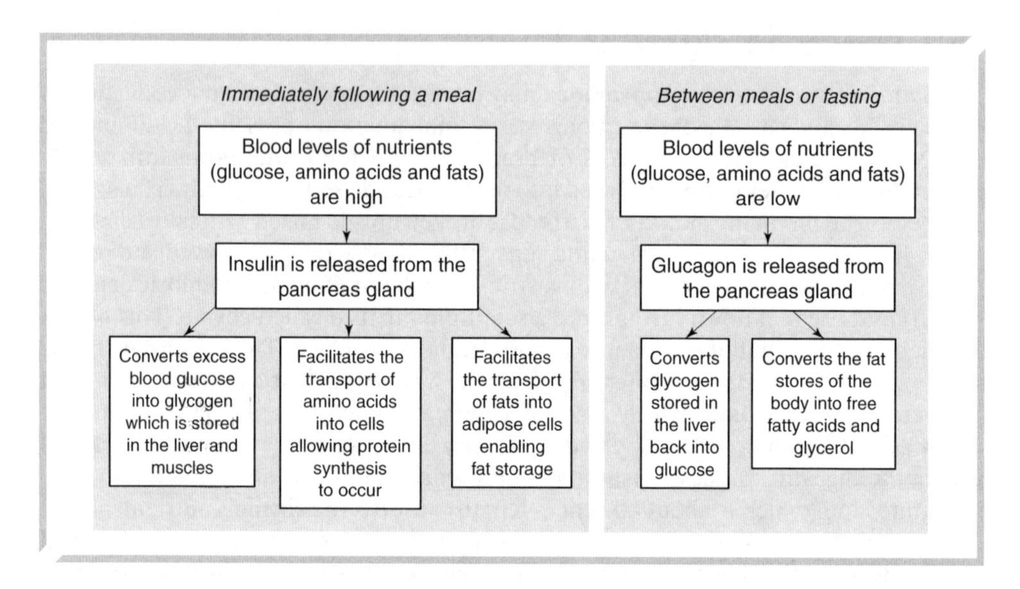

Figure 4.2 Flow chart of metabolic events that take place following absorption (immediately following a meal) and post-absorption (between meals).

Once the nutrients have been absorbed into the blood the post-absorptive phase of metabolism takes over. The main signal for this phase to begin is a drop in blood glucose which is detected by cells in the brain. This results in increased sympathetic stimulation of the pancreas gland which halts insulin secretion, and instead causes glucagon to be released. This effect of glucagon is opposite to insulin as – in the short term – it causes the liver to convert its glycogen back into glucose. However, if the fasting period is prolonged (e.g. more than a few hours), glucagon will also begin to break down the body's fat stores into fatty acids (which can also be used by body cells for energy) and glycerol (which can be converted into glucose by the liver). This later process is particularly important for the brain as it cannot utilise fatty acids for energy (unlike other cells), and thus during the post-absorptive phase has to rely on glucose provided by the liver.

What causes hunger?

Hunger is a powerful drive that motivates us to find food. But what causes hunger in the first place? Since there is no motivation to eat once we have just finished a large meal it seems clear that whatever the causes are, they must work in the post-absorptive state. One of the oldest theories of hunger is that it is due to the movements of the stomach. For example, we tend to feel 'full' when the stomach is distended, and we often attribute 'hunger pangs' to the contractions produced by an empty stomach. The first experimental test of this hypothesis was undertaken by W.B. Cannon in 1912 who persuaded his research student A. L. Washburn to swallow a balloon that was inflated in his stomach. The balloon was then connected by a tube to a water-filled glass U-tube so that whenever any stomach contractions occurred, they produced an increase in the level of the water at the other end of the U-tube, resulting in an upward mark on a moving piece of paper (see Figure 4.3). The results showed that Washburn's reported hunger pangs were nearly always accompanied by contraction of the stomach. In other words, hunger (and satiety) appeared to have a peripheral cause and was little to do with the brain (Cannon and Washburn 1912).

These findings were also confirmed by a study of a patient who had accidentally swallowed acid that had caused his oesophagus to fuse shut. This person could only be fed by passing wet food through a tube that had been surgically implanted into his stomach. However, this tube also enabled researchers to observe the internal activity of the stomach directly and, again, the findings showed that when the stomach was empty, large contractions occurred which were associated with feelings of hunger (Carlson 1912).

Despite this, it soon become clear that the gastric theory of hunger was far too simple as an explanation of hunger. For example, although the first bite of food was often found to stop stomach contractions, it did not immediately stop appetite. Moreover, it was found that humans who had their stomachs removed (often due to cancer), and whose oesophagus had been connected directly to the duodenum, reported normal sensations of hunger. And, although these patients tended to eat smaller meals they nevertheless showed proper regulation of food intake (Wangensteen and Carlson 1931).

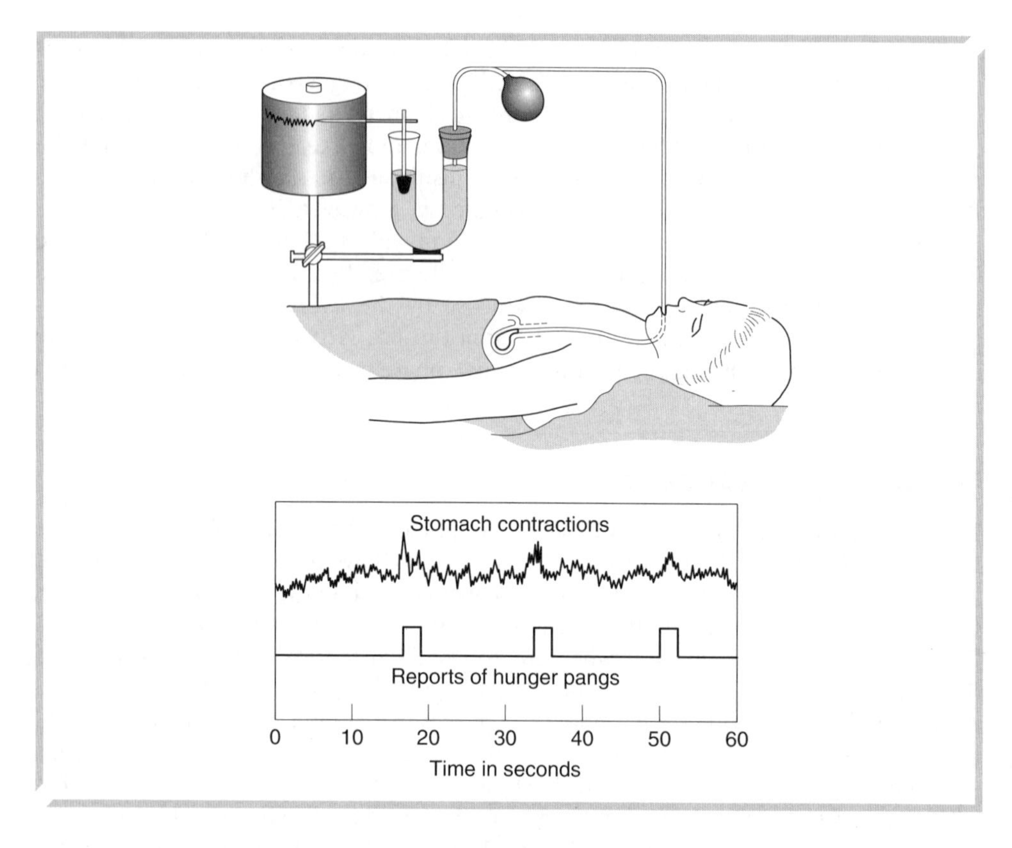

Figure 4.3 The type of experimental set-up used by Cannon and Washburn (1912). (*Source*: From John P. J. Pinel, *Biopsychology*, 3rd edition. Copyright © 1997 by Allyn & Bacon. Reprinted by permission.)

These findings were also backed up by animal studies that looked at the effects of severing the neural connections between stomach and brain and found that this operation had little effect on food intake (Morgan and Morgan 1940).

The chemical signals of hunger

In attempting to discover the nature of the feedback signals from the body that the brain may use to produce hunger, many investigators have focused not on organs (such as the stomach) but on chemical messengers carried in the blood. As we have seen above, a number of substances are released into the blood during the absorptive and fasting stages of metabolism, and it would be surprising if some of these were not linked to satiety and hunger.

Some of the strongest evidence that blood-borne chemicals are able to signal satiety has come from a study where hungry and food-deprived rats were given blood transfusions from satiated, well-fed rats (Davis *et al.* 1969). Clearly, if the blood contains a substance that signals whether an animal has eaten, then the transfusion of blood from well-fed animals should stop hunger in food-deprived animals. And this is exactly what Davis and his colleagues found. For example, when the hungry rats were given blood transfusions from satiated animals and presented with food, they ate very little. Moreover, this effect could not be explained by the transfusion itself, because it was found that hunger was only suppressed when well-fed rats donated the blood. In fact, to be most effective, the blood had to be taken from the donor animals 45 minutes after their meal, which is about the time it takes for the blood to start accumulating appreciable amounts of nutrients and hormones following eating.

But what is it in the blood that influences eating behaviour? There is no shortage of ideas. Many theorists have argued that blood glucose is the main agent, although others have proposed a similar role for fats or amino acids. More recently, there has been a growing awareness of the importance of certain hormones (such as cholecystokinin) in the regulation of hunger. Despite this, it is probably the case that no one single messenger is responsible. Nonetheless, if there is one substance that is more important than the rest it is probably glucose. For this reason we will concentrate on glucose although it is probable that the principles underlying its role in hunger and satiety will also apply to other essential blood-borne factors.

The glucostatic theory of hunger

The basic idea behind the **glucostatic theory** of hunger is simple: if there is a drop in blood glucose reaching the cells of the body the individual gets hungry; and if there is an increase in glucose the individual becomes satiated. However, there is also a fundamental problem with this theory – at least in its simplest version. Not only does the level of glucose in the blood vary little in normal circumstances (and this is particularly true for the brain), but, even more importantly, people with **diabetes** (who are unable to produce insulin) typically have very high levels of blood glucose (as it cannot enter their cells), yet they are often ravenously hungry. To get around this problem, Jean Mayer in 1955 proposed that the brain contained special cells (called 'glucostats') that monitored glucose, and they did this not by measuring its level in the blood, but by measuring the rate at which it was being used up to provide energy. One predictor of hunger, therefore, according to Mayer, was not the actual level of glucose in the blood, but the difference between levels of arterial blood glucose entering the brain and the venous blood leaving it. In short, if there was a large difference between the two values, this provided an indicator that sugar was being quickly removed from the blood as it passed through the brain.

Soon after Mayer proposed the idea of glucoreceptors in the brain, his theory received convincing support (Mayer and Marshall 1956). Mayer reasoned that if glucoreceptors really existed, then they should be able to be identified by injecting mice with a compound called gold thioglucose. Gold is a heavy metal which is toxic to living cells, and it can also be combined with glucose to make a substance which 'acts' like glucose (i.e. it is taken up into cells) but is neurotoxic. Mayer reasoned that this form of glucose should attach itself to the glucoreceptors (wherever they may be) and then cause the death of the cells that contained them. Indeed, soon after injecting his mice with gold thioglucose, Mayer found that they began to eat huge quantities of food and quickly become obese – a finding that was consistent with the idea that something was wrong with the feeding systems of the brain. Moreover, when histological examination was undertaken, the results showed that neural damage had taken place to a small region of the brain called the **ventromedial hypothalamus**. Thus, this region appeared to contain the all-important glucostats.

Do glucoreceptors control feeding?

Although it has been shown that the ventromedial hypothalamus contains cells that detect glucose, their role in eating behaviour remains controversial. For example, if they are involved in controlling food intake, then infusions of glucose into the ventromedial hypothalamus would obviously be expected to reduce food intake in hungry animals – but, surprisingly, this does not occur (Lytle 1977). Moreover, the electrical response of ventromedial hypothalamic neurons to glucose is very brief (although enhanced in the presence of insulin) which again is not consistent with a role in suppressing hunger. Thus, the hypothalamic glucose receptors do not appear to be directly involved with the feeding process.

More recently, researchers have focused on the liver as the most important site for the location of glucoreceptors. The liver is the first organ of the body that receives nutrients from the small intestine and obviously it is in an ideal position to monitor food intake. In addition, it is known that cutting the part of the **vagus nerve** that sends information from the liver to the brain reduces eating in hungry animals. But, what is the liver telling the brain? Evidence relating to this question was provided by Maurio Russek and his colleagues who injected glucose into different areas of the body (Russek 1971). When they injected glucose into the jugular vein (which made glucose circulate through the body before it reached the liver) they found that it had little effect on eating behaviour. However, when it was injected into the hepatic portal vein (the blood vessel connected to the liver), hungry animals immediately stopped eating. Thus, the liver appeared to be telling the brain about levels of glucose it was receiving in the blood.

Further evidence linking the liver with glucose detection has been provided by Stricker *et al.* (1977) who made rats hungry by injecting them with insulin that lowered their blood glucose. Following this insulin administration, the rats were given the sugar fructose. Although this type of sugar can be metabolised by the liver, it cannot be used (or detected) by the brain as it is too large to cross the **blood–brain barrier**. Thus, these animals should have relatively low glucose levels in the brain, but a satiated liver. Clearly, if glucose receptors in the brain were having an important role in causing hunger then the insulin-treated fructose-fed animals should have eaten when presented with food. However, this did not happen, indicating again that the liver was providing the most important satiety signal.

Not surprisingly, perhaps, it has been found that one brain structure in receipt of glucose information from the liver is the hypothalamus. For example, it has been shown that the vast majority (67 per cent) of hypothalamic cells that contain glucose receptors, also decrease their firing rate in response to glucose injected in the hepatic portal vein (Shimizu *et al.* 1983). Thus, it appears that the hypothalamus obtains much of its information regarding glucose levels from the liver.

Does this mean therefore that it is the liver that provides the most important signal that controls feeding behaviour? Unfortunately, things are not so simple. For example, if the vagus nerve is cut (severing input from the liver to the brain) eating behaviour is disrupted with loss of food intake, but only in the short term. In fact, vagotomised animals eventually resume normal eating patterns, indicating that other mechanisms must compensate for the loss of the liver. Thus, we can conclude that the liver is either not the only site monitoring glucose levels, or that the brain uses other types of nutrient information to control hunger and satiety.

Other chemical messengers

Although changes in the level of glucose (or its utilisation) may be one of the most important physiological signals used to induce hunger and satiety, it is certainly not the only one. Our bodies use a range of nutrients and it is probably the case that our brain integrates many different signals, rather than relying exclusively on any one signal, to determine hunger and satiety. Indeed, during the fasting phase (when hunger actually occurs) the majority of cells in the body do not use glucose as their main source of energy – rather they derive energy from glycerol and free fatty acids that are broken down from fat. Thus, one might predict that lipids are also likely to play a vital role in hunger. Indeed, this hypothesis has been supported by Friedman *et al.* (1986) who injected rats with either a drug (methyl palmoxirate) that interfered with the metabolism of fatty acids into energy, or one that interfered with the cell's utilisation of glucose (2-deoxyglucose). The results showed that when either drug was given alone, there was little effect on the animal's food intake. However, when both were given together, eating was significantly increased. Thus, signals conveying information about the availability of both glucose and lipids appear to be important in the control of hunger (see also the discussion of leptin later in the chapter).

Hormones that flow into the bloodstream and pass to receptors in the brain may also play a crucial role in providing the brain with information concerning the nutrient status of the body. Perhaps the most obvious hormone that we might expect to have in this type of role is insulin. In fact, insulin receptors are found in the brain (including the hypothalamus), although their function is not fully understood and their involvement in appetite is far from certain.

Another hormone that has been strongly implicated in feeding is **cholecystokinin (CCK)** which is released by cells of the duodenum in the presence of fat. This hormone gets its name because it acts on the gallbladder (the *cholecyst*) to cause it to secrete bile into the duodenum which helps to break down fats into small particles. In addition, cholecystokinin also acts on the stomach to control the rate at which it empties its contents into the duodenum. Because levels of cholecystokinin increase immediately after a meal, they could (in theory) provide the brain with a very useful signal of satiety (especially concerning the level of fat passing through the duodenum). Indeed, in accordance with this idea, a number of studies have found that injections of cholecystokinin in hungry animals quickly stop them eating. Moreover, this effect does not occur if the vagus nerve is cut – indicating that the cholecystokinin message is sent to the brain via a neural pathway (this also makes sense because cholecystokinin does not appear to cross the blood–brain barrier).

Despite this, the role of cholecystokinin in feeding behaviour remains controversial because it is also known to produce nausea in humans, and it is not clear whether this effect might account for its actions on feeding behaviour in animals (Chen *et al.* 1993). The situation is further complicated by the fact that cholecystokinin is found in neurons throughout the brain, especially in the cerebral cortex and the limbic system (where it tends to be co-localised in nerve endings with several 'traditional' transmitters including dopamine). Moreover, in some species, injections of cholecystokinin into the brain has been shown to suppress feeding, which suggests that its neurons may also have a role to play in feeding behaviour. (This finding has also raised suspicions that cholecystokinin may be able to cross into the brain after all.) Thus, it is fair to say that a great deal of uncertainty remains concerning the role of cholecystokinin and its role in feeding behaviour.

It is worth pointing out that many other chemical substances are involved in digestion (e.g. somatostatin, vasoactive intestinal polypeptide, gastric inhibitory peptide to name a few) and some could, in theory at least, play a similar 'signalling' role in feeding behaviour. Indeed, the brain probably uses a complex array of signals (both neural and hormonal) to keep itself informed of the digestive and nutrient status of the body.

Box 4.1 WHAT IS A CALORIE?

Although we all use the term **calorie** in everyday language, few of us have a clear idea of what the term means. Put simply, a calorie is the quantity of heat required to raise the temperature of 1 gram of water by 1°C (although confusingly in everyday usage we tend to talk of 'Calories' – note the capital 'C' – which is a unit of 1,000 calories). This may at first appear to be a very strange definition, but it begins to make sense when one considers that heat is basically the same as energy. Energy is not an easy concept to understand because it can only be inferred when some type of change is occurring. Thus, energy is not a 'thing' but the capacity to do work, or a force that puts matter into motion. In living organisms, energy is stored in cells as chemical bonds that hold atoms and molecules together, and it is released when chemical reactions (which also require heat to take place) transfer energy from one molecule to the next. Thus, a calorie is essentially a unit of energy (or heat) that enables biological work (the moving of molecules) to be undertaken.

The original energy source for the body is the food we eat, which is broken down into smaller molecules (such as glucose, fatty acids and amino acids). These molecules are then transported to the many billions of cells that make up the body. However, even in this form they are only a potential energy source because our cells have to break them down further. Where in the cell, therefore, does the breakdown of these nutrient substances into energy take place? The main site are tiny intracellular structures called **mitochondria** which, through a series of complex chemical steps (requiring the presence of oxygen), form a substance called **adenosine triphosphate (ATP)**. This molecule can be likened to a tightly coiled spring which, when released (in chemical reactions), is able to generate considerable energy (and heat) and is the substance that almost every cell in the body uses to drive its chemical reactions. Next time you enjoy a large meal (with lots of calories) it might be interesting to bear in mind that much of it will be ending up as this very simple molecule!

Where are the control centres for feeding behaviour?

So far, we have looked at some of the feedback signals that the brain might use to regulate hunger. But, of course, these signals would have little effect on behaviour unless there are control centres in the brain that are able to co-ordinate this information. Thus, another very important question concerns the location of areas in the brain that regulate feeding and satiety.

For over a hundred years, the hypothalamus has been recognised as one of the most important sites for controlling feeding behaviour, particularly as damage to this structure in humans (or to the nearby pituitary gland) was known to cause obesity. Research by Hetherington and Ranson during the late 1930s confirmed this finding by showing that lesions of the ventromedial hypothalamus in rats caused excessive eating (**hyperphagia**) and weight gain. Furthermore, as we have already seen, Jean Mayer in the 1950s also implicated this part of the hypothalamus in feeding by showing that it contained glucoreceptors. But, the ventromedial hypothalamus was not the only area to be linked with feeding behaviour. In 1951, Anand and Brobeck made the dramatic discovery that lesions to the **lateral hypothalamus** caused profound **aphagia** where the animal completely stopped eating (and drinking). In fact, such animals would die of starvation (unless force-fed) even though food and water were freely available.

The importance of the hypothalamus in feeding was also confirmed by studies using electrical stimulation. For example, stimulation of the lateral hypothalamus produced voracious eating in animals that had been previously satiated, whereas stimulation of the ventromedial hypothalamus inhibited eating in otherwise hungry animals. These findings (along with the lesion data mentioned above) strongly suggested that the hypothalamus was involved in the initiation and termination of feeding. In 1954, a

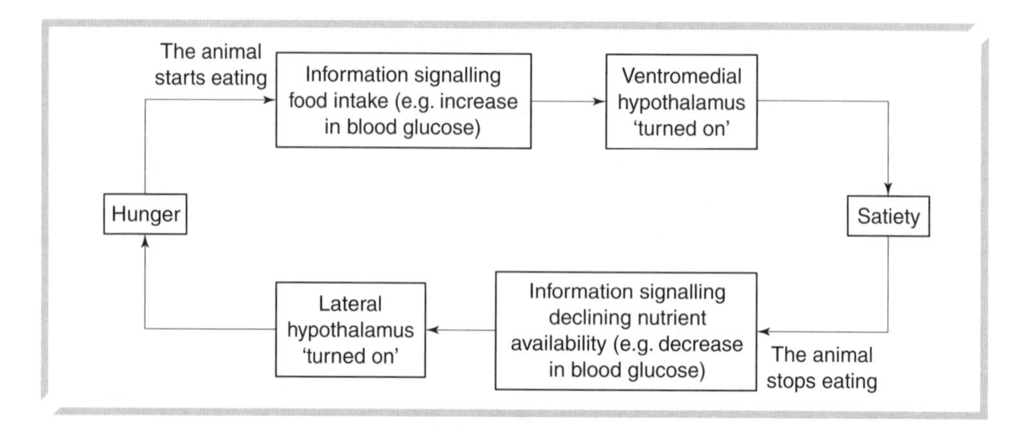

Figure 4.4 The dual-centre set-point model of feeding.

theory based on this notion was formally proposed by Eliot Stellar who argued that the ventromedial hypothalamus acted as the brain's satiety centre, and the lateral hypothalamus as its hunger centre (Stellar 1954).

This theory became known as the **dual-centre set-point theory** (Figure 4.4), and it was to dominate thinking into the causes of feeding behaviour over the next two decades. Put simply, the theory held that when the ventromedial hypothalamus (VMH) was 'turned on' (that is, by neural or hormonal information signalling food intake) the lateral hypothalamus (LH) became 'turned off' and satiation was the result. In contrast, when the ventromedial hypothalamus was 'turned off' (e.g. by signals specifying declining nutrient availability), the lateral hypothalamus was released from its inhibition, thus causing hunger. Not only was this theory simple to understand, but it also fitted nicely into a homeostatic framework of feeding that researchers assumed must exist. The only problem (it seemed at the time) was to identify the signals and the receptors that initiated hunger and satiety, and to determine how these were integrated in the hypothalamus. Not surprisingly, the attempts to do this resulted in an enormous amount of research.

A closer look at ventromedial hypothalamic lesions

Damage to the ventromedial hypothalamus causes an animal to becomes ravenously hungry and/or unable to stop feeding, indicating that this brain area (when intact) inhibits eating (i.e. acts as a satiety centre). However, on closer examination the evidence supporting this idea is not as convincing as it first seems. In the immediate post-lesioning period (sometimes called the dynamic phase) the animal does indeed become a voracious eater and quickly gains weight, often doubling its weight within a few weeks. However, this period of rapid weight gain does not last, and after about 3 or 4 weeks the food intake drops off with the animal returning to relatively normal feeding (this is called the static phase). Although the animal remains obese and does not go back to its old weight, it nevertheless appears to show normal satiety in response to food intake (see Figure 4.5). In terms of the dual-centre set-point model this finding does not make a great deal of sense because these animals are able to become satiated despite having no ventromedial hypothalamus.

Rather than being impaired in the processing of satiety messages, there is evidence that the ventromedial hypothalamus lesion might instead be causing the animal to adopt a new 'set point' for its body weight. For example, if an obese rat in the static phase is force-fed, its weight can be made to increase even further. However, if this animal is returned to normal feeding, it is found that its weight will also quickly readjust back to that which existed in the static phase. Similarly, after a lesioned (obese) rat has been made to lose weight by being starved, and then given free access to food, it will soon regain its static phase weight. Thus, animals without a ventromedial hypothalamus appear to be regulating their body weight at a new higher level.

Does this mean that the ventromedial hypothalamus is the site where the set point for body weight is located? Unfortunately, even this hypothesis appears to be too simple to explain all the research findings obtained with ventromedial hypothalamus lesions. For example, animals in the static phase are very finicky and much prefer to eat palatable food (e.g. food with extra fat or sugar) rather than their normal 'dry' diet of

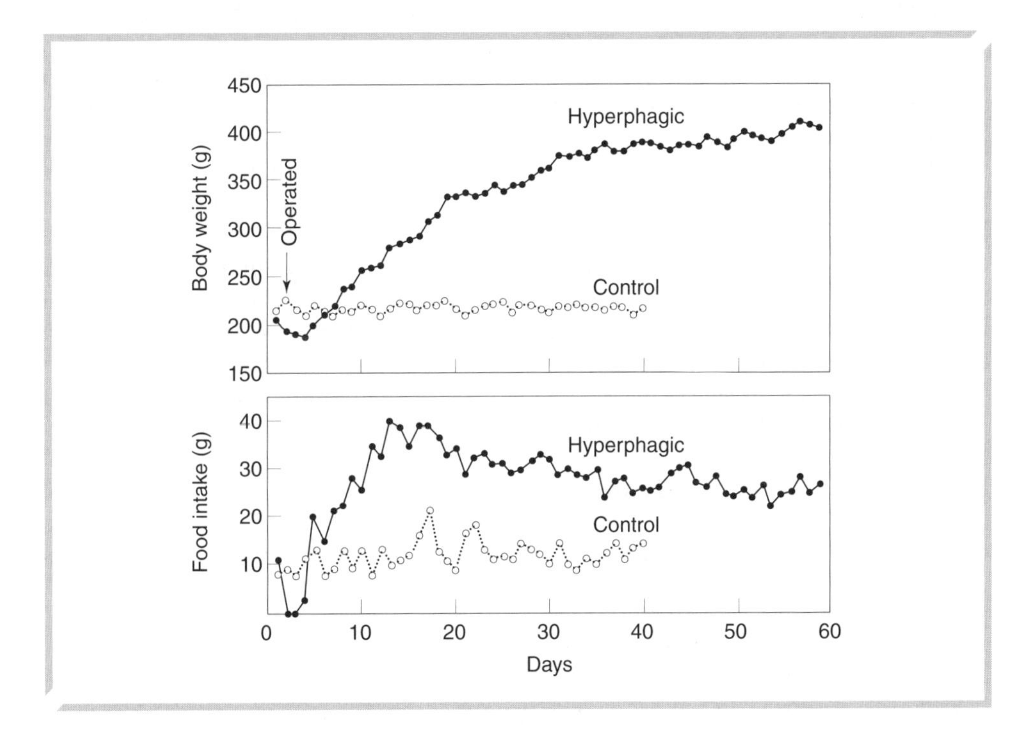

Figure 4.5 The effects of ventromedial hypothalamic lesions on body weight and food intake. (*Source*: Adapted from P. Teitelbaum, *Journal of Comparative and Physiological Psychology* (1955), **48**, 156–63.)

laboratory chow. Moreover, if animals are given food that is slightly stale, or made to taste bitter by the addition of quinine, they actually eat less than control animals! Furthermore, lesioned animals do not like to work to obtain food, and will often starve if it is made contingent on the performance of some task (such as pressing a lever in an operant box). Thus, it could be said that these animals are finicky, lazy and show exaggerated reactions to palatability. Clearly, these findings do not square very well with the theory that the ventromedial hypothalamus is the brain's satiety centre – or even one that views it as providing the set point for body weight.

A closer look at lateral hypothalamic lesions

Lesions of the lateral hypothalamus produce a severe loss of feeding behaviour with animals refusing to eat or drink. Not surprisingly, this was initially taken as evidence that it was the controlling centre for the initiation of eating (i.e. when the lateral hypothalamus was lesioned this function was lost). However, this theory soon ran into a number of difficulties. For one thing, despite their profound initial aphagia, it was found that if lesioned animals were given proper care and attention, then they were often able to recover and return to normal feeding behaviour. Thus, the aphagia produced by lateral hypothalamic damage is not permanent – an awkward finding for the 'feeding centre' hypothesis.

It has also become increasingly clear that lesions of the lateral hypothalamus lead to a wide range of other impairments. For example, lesioned animals show marked sensory deficits and generally do not respond to touch, or visual stimuli, suggesting that they might not be feeding because of a sensory difficulty. In addition, these animals show little movement and do not right themselves when turned on their side. In fact, these animals give the impression of being grossly under-aroused, and this idea was supported when it was found that a mild pinch to the tail (causing arousal) could induce lesioned animals to start eating (Antelman *et al.* 1975). Thus, the aphagia that followed lateral hypothalamic damage appeared to be part of a much larger deficit than that simply associated with feeding behaviour.

Why, then, does damage to one small region of the brain cause such a wide variety of impairments? One reason lies with the fact that the lateral hypothalamus also contains many 'fibres of passage' – axons from other brain areas that pass through the lateral hypothalamus *en route* to somewhere else. One such pathway is the dopaminergic **nigral–striatal pathway** linking the substantia nigra with the striatum (see previous chapter). In fact, it is now established that damage to the nigral–striatal pathway in rats also causes significant sensory and motor deficits as well as aphagia and weight loss – a pattern very similar to lateral hypothalamic damage (Ungerstedt 1971).

These findings motivated researchers to look for alternative ways of destroying the cell bodies in the lateral hypothalamus without damaging its fibres of passage. During the 1970s this became possible when it was found that certain drugs which (over)-stimulated glutamate receptors (such as kainic acid or ibotenic acid) were able to destroy cell bodies while sparing the axons that passed through from other areas. When these compounds were injected into the lateral hypothalamus it was found that they still produced a long-lasting decrease in food intake and body weight, but they did not produce the deficit in motor or sensory function (Winn *et al.* 1984). In short, this latter deficit appeared to be largely due to the nigral–striatal pathway.

Thus, the lateral hypothalamus does indeed appear to play an important role in feeding behaviour. Despite this, its exact function still remains obscure. For example, if it is a feeding centre then it is clearly not the only one, as animals with lateral hypothalamic lesions show recovery of function. Indeed, it is now known that a number of other regions are involved in feeding including the temporal lobe, orbitofrontal cortex and striatum (Rolls 1985). Moreover, because damage to the dopaminergic fibres of the nigral–striatal pathway causes aphagia, and since neurons of the lateral hypothalamus also project down into this pathway (see Chapter 11), then it can be assumed that they are both separate components of a common feeding system. To make things even more complex, the lateral hypothalamus has also been shown to be involved in a wide range of motivational behaviour including aggression, sexual behaviour and reinforcement. Thus, it is clearly an oversimplification to describe the lateral hypothalamus as the feeding centre.

Non-homeostatic mechanisms of eating

Do we really eat, or become hungry, because of a decline in blood glucose (or some other nutrient variable) that acts on the hypothalamus? In fact, we do not have to look far to see that eating behaviour is not as homeostatically controlled as traditional physiological psychologists would like us to believe. For example, one of the most important factors that determines whether we feel hungry, is not blood sugar level, stomach rumblings, or something happening in the hypothalamus. It is our wristwatch! (Bolles 1990, p. 8). This is shown by the fact that we tend to eat at fixed times of the day and will often become hungry in anticipation of the meal that we know is about to take place. Furthermore, this is as true for other animals as it is for us. For example, as early as 1927, Richter showed that rats given one meal a day, quickly began to anticipate their feeding time with increased running in their activity wheels. Thus, learning is a very important component of feeding behaviour, and this was also neatly demonstrated in an experiment by Harvey Weingarten who presented a paired light and tone to rats every time they were given a meal of evaporated milk. Weingarten fed his animals six times every day over a period of 11 days and, following this 'learning' phase, the rats were allowed free access to liquid food. Despite being fed well, these animals always began to eat whenever the light and tone were presented. Thus, these rats were not eating to restore an energy deficit, they were eating because they had been conditioned to do so. Quite clearly, the same type of situation also occurs with humans (Weingarten 1983).

The effects of learning can also be seen at work in the choice of foods we eat. There is little doubt that few of us would find squid cooked in its own ink, fried grasshoppers or sheep eyes very appetising – yet, these are delicacies that are enjoyed in other parts of the world. Thus, we learn *what we like to eat* and this has also been shown in animal studies. For example, if a rat comes across a new food, it tends very cautiously to eat just a small amount, and only on further encounters will it consume more. However, should the new food cause illness, then the rat will avoid eating that food again. In this case, the animal will have formed a conditioned taste aversion to the food, and this type of learning can occur even if the delay between eating and the onset of illness is 24 hours or more (this is sometimes known as the **Garcia effect**). Alternatively, if the food does not cause any adverse reaction then it is likely to become part of the dietary regime of the animal.

Another crucial factor in feeding behaviour is the *anticipated pleasurable* effect of eating. For example, hunger can often be elicited by a highly palatable food such as a dessert – even after the person has eaten several courses of a large meal. This example shows that it is the incentive value of the food, and not its nutrient value, that causes hunger. Again, this can also be shown to occur in animals. For example, the addition of a small amount of sugar to standard laboratory rat food tends to produce a large increase in its consumption and a marked increase in the animal's body weight. Alternatively, the addition of bitter-tasting quinine has the opposite effect.

It should come as no surprise, therefore, to find that another way of increasing food intake in laboratory animals is to feed them a highly varied or 'cafeteria' diet. For example, Peter Rogers and John Blundell working at the University of Leeds have found that rats given bread and chocolate along with their normal diet increased their food intake by 60 per cent, and this resulted in a 49 per cent increase in weight gain after only 120 days of feeding. This effect is probably caused by what is known as **sensory-specific satiety** – that is, the tendency to get bored eating a particular food if one consumes it over a long enough period of time. Laboratory rats are particularly susceptible to this type of effect because they are normally only given a 'boring' diet of dry chow and water. Thus, the introduction of new food into their cages is likely to significantly increase the rat's 'pleasure' of eating. The same principle also applies to humans. For example, Barbara Rolls has found that if subjects are given a free meal of a particular food (e.g. cheese and crackers) and then unexpectedly given a second course of something different (e.g. bananas) they will eat much more of the new food compared to a second helping of the first (Rolls *et al.* 1981). In other words, the second portion of food now becomes much more appetising than the first.

All this evidence shows that a wide variety of factors play an important role in determining feeding behaviour, and while it may be tempting to explain hunger in terms of homeostatic mechanisms, it appears that behaviour is far too complex for such explanations to offer more than just a partial account of hunger and satiety. Indeed, learning, anticipation, attitudes, social factors and a host of other psychological variables appear to be a much better predictor of feeding behaviour than physiological factors such as blood glucose levels or stomach contractions. Perhaps this should not surprise us. As the brain has evolved so has the complexity of the behaviour it produces, and there is no reason to believe that feeding behaviour should be any different.

Eating disorders

Most of us take eating so much for granted, that we do not generally consider feeding as a behaviour that can go wrong; but evidence shows otherwise. Obesity, anorexia nervosa and bulimia, for example, are three disorders where abnormal feeding behaviour occurs with serious repercussions for health and psychological well-being. Increasingly, attempts are being made to understand these conditions, and to find successful treatments for them, with the biological psychologist playing a central role in this endeavour.

Obesity

Obesity is defined as body weight that is 10 to 20 per cent above 'normal' due to the excessive accumulation of fat. Approximately 2–5 per cent of children in Western society are obese, and this figure increases with age so that, by 50, about 20 per cent of the population will suffer from obesity. This is also associated with a wide range of health problems including heart disease, stroke, certain cancers and diabetes (to name a few) and, if this wasn't enough, obese people often pay higher medical insurance as well as suffering other types of discrimination. Indeed the obese person is often perceived as gluttonous, lazy or simply lacking in will power. In fact, in the vast majority of cases, none of these attributes is true.

A body cell that stores fat is called an **adipocyte**. An average person has around 25 billion adipocytes and their numbers appear to be relatively stable by early adulthood. Thus, we normally put on weight not because we produce new adipocytes, but because our adipocytes get larger. In the case of obesity it appears that people fall into two broad groups: those with predominantly enlarged fat cells (hypertropic obesity) and those with increased numbers of fat cells (hyperplastic obesity). Unfortunately, these two forms of obesity are not easy to distinguish, and although there may well be a different set of factors associated with each, they nevertheless tend to get combined together and studied as one (Bouchard 1989). In short, obesity is not a single disorder and it certainly does not have any simple cause or explanation.

There are many potential reasons why people are (or become) obese, but the evidence indicates that the most important single factor of all is genetic inheritance. For example, if body weight is genetically controlled then one would expect identical twins (who have identical genes) to show a much greater similarity in body weight across their life span than fraternal twins (who share 50 per cent of their genes). Indeed, this has been shown to be the case. For example, in one report that compared thousands of twin pairs, it was found that identical twins were much closer in terms of weight, body mass and skin fold thickness than fraternal twins (Grilo and Pogue-Geile 1991). In fact, the results of this and other studies have shown a concordance (heritability) rate of about 60–70 per cent for identical twins and 30–40 per cent for non-identical twins (Plomin *et al.* 1997). Remarkably, identical twins usually maintain their weight levels within 1 kg of each other throughout life – and 2.5 kg if their lifestyles become markedly different.

Despite this, we should not discount the importance of lifestyle factors in the development of obesity. Childhood is a particularly important time in setting body weight since it appears that new fat cells may be able to be formed in this period, and once formed we do not lose them. Thus, over-eating in childhood may lead to a pre-disposition towards obesity later in life. In addition, cultural mores may also play a role in the development of obesity. For example, one of the biggest factors contributing to obesity could be the widespread belief that healthy eating requires three large meals a day. In fact, it has been shown that after the age of 30 years, the human body reduces its energy expenditure by about 12 calories per year, and since a decline in the efficiency of metabolism also occurs with ageing, this makes it likely that weight gain will occur unless we reduce our meal intake. But, because most of us find eating such a pleasurable experience, this is easier said than done. Other factors such as high-fat diets and low levels of physical activity are also likely to compound the problem (Hill and Peters 1988).

How do genes influence obesity?

It has long been known that genes are able to have an important bearing on body weight. For example, in 1950, a genetic mutation was found in a certain strain of mice (these are now known as *ob/ob* mice since they have to carry two mutant copies of the *ob* gene) that made them extremely obese and twice the weight of normal mice. Since this discovery, a number of other genetic strains (with different gene mutations) have been found that also produce grossly overweight animals. Moreover, these obese strains tend to share a number of features in common, including hyperphagia, increased levels of insulin and decreased heat production in response to food, that could account (at least in part) for the obesity. The difficult question, however, was explaining how genetic mutations could set in motion the biological events that caused these changes.

One of the most fascinating findings concerning the *ob/ob* mice was the discovery made by Douglas Coleman in 1973 that when the circulatory systems of these mice were joined with normal mice (in what is known as a parabiotic preparation) the *ob/ob* mice lost weight. This strongly suggested that the normal mice were producing a substance that was acting on their obese counterparts to make them less fat (or put another way, the *ob/ob* mice were missing this factor which made them gain weight). But what could this substance be? The crucial breakthrough in answering this question came in 1994 when the gene that was known to be mutated in *ob/ob* mice was cloned (Zhang *et al.* 1994). The sequencing of this gene showed that it produced a protein called **leptin** (from the Greek *leptos* meaning 'thin') and, moreover, when this substance was injected into *ob/ob* mice it was found that food intake and body weight dramatically decreased (in fact, a daily injection of leptin over the course of just two weeks caused the mice to lose 30 per cent of their body weight – Halaas *et al.* 1995). In other words, the *ob/ob* mice apparently over-eat and are obese because they did not produce the leptin protein.

It is now known that leptin is not only found in mice, but it is also produced by humans (and other animals). In fact, it is a hormone that is secreted into the blood by fat cells in amounts directly proportional to the level of body adipose mass. In other words, the more fat that the body stores, the greater the level of leptin that is produced and released into the circulation. Thus, people (and animals) who are obese may have higher levels of leptin compared to those who are not overweight (although paradoxically the *ob/ob* mice are an exception to this general rule).

The main function of leptin, therefore, appears to be as a feedback signal which informs the brain and, in particular, the hypothalamus about the stores of fat in the body. However, this is not the only role played by leptin since it also controls the level of a hypothalamic neurotransmitter substance called **neuropeptide Y**, known to be involved in appetite regulation. For example, when neuropeptide Y is infused into the hypothalamus, satiated and very well-fed rats will start eating again (in fact, if these injections are maintained over several days, animals eat voraciously and quickly become overweight). Thus, increased levels of neuropeptide Y are a very powerful stimulator of hunger. Importantly, low levels of leptin also cause neuropeptide Y levels to be increased, which presumably increases hunger and motivates the animal to find food in order to replenish 'lost' fat stores.

The discovery of leptin has raised the possibility that human obesity may also be linked to this 'fat hormone' in some way. Perhaps obese people do not produce sufficient levels of leptin (thus stimulating hunger), or maybe the hypothalamic receptors are not sensitive to leptin's effects. In fact, there are many possible theories, although as yet none has been adequately tested or proved to be correct. Nevertheless, these are exciting times in obesity research and many more breakthroughs are likely in the near future.

Anorexia nervosa and bulimia

The term **anorexia** (meaning loss of appetite) was first used by the English physician Sir William Gull in 1873. Although the term has remained, it is not an accurate description of the disorder since anorexics still experience hunger. However, anorexics are so obsessed with being thin and keeping their weight low that they ignore their hunger and eat a bare minimum. Even then, they might purge themselves, take laxatives, or drink large amounts of water to suppress appetite. This eating regime may be so successful that the anorexic's weight may drop to 60–70 per cent of what is considered 'normal' for their height and age. In addition, there is often an intense preoccupation with body size and a distorted perception of body image so that these individuals believe themselves to be fat when they are emaciated. Not surprisingly, the disorder is associated with a number of health problems such as loss of the menstrual cycle, lowered blood pressure, sleep disturbances, and metabolic abnormalities including excess secretion of cortisol from the adrenal glands and decreased thyroid function. Moreover, starvation, or complications arising from these problems can be so severe that 2–5 per cent of anorexics will die from their illness (a famous example being Karen Carpenter in 1983).

Anorexia nervosa is mainly (although not exclusively) a disorder of young adult women. Approximately 95 per cent of anorexics are women and it is rare for the illness to occur for the first time in someone who is over 25. There is also evidence that anorexia is now occurring more frequently than it did in the past (it was almost unheard of 40 years ago) and is largely confined to women in developed countries. Indeed, anorexia now affects approximately one teenager in every 200, reaching a peak incidence of one in 100 among adolescents between 16 and 18 (Abraham and Llewellyn-Jones 1987).

A variety of explanations have been proposed to explain anorexia nervosa. For example, anorexics are sometimes viewed as people who use their disorder as a means of gaining attention, or as a misconceived attempt to achieve some degree of control in their lives (early evidence suggested that anorexics often came from middle-class backgrounds where there were high parental expectations). Others have pointed out that cultural influences may also play a role, not least because thinness is generally considered to be highly attractive (and constantly featured in advertising and glamour magazines). However, biological causes may also be important. For example, some researchers have argued that menstruation stops sooner in anorexics than would be expected on the basis of their weight loss which might indicate an underlying hormonal abnormality. Others have shown that thyroid abnormalities can often remain in anorexics after they have returned to a normal body weight. If these observations are true, this would implicate the hypothalamus since this structure exercises important control over the pituitary gland and hormonal release. Indeed, a number of researchers (e.g. see Anderson and Kennedy 1992) have speculated that neurotransmitter abnormalities in the hypothalamus may cause anorexia, although this idea has been difficult to test directly (but see below).

Bulimia is different to anorexia nervosa because individuals usually do not starve themselves for long periods of time, but engage in bouts of binge eating where they consume large amounts of food in a short space of time. Indeed, they may gorge themselves with many thousands of calories (especially if they have access to highly palatable sweet and carbohydrate-rich food) in bouts lasting an hour or so. Following a binge, however, they will often induce vomiting, or use laxatives to purge themselves of the food they have just eaten. Despite this, bulimia and anorexia have several features in common. For example, individuals with bulimia are usually adolescent females with menstrual problems and a distorted body image of themselves. Furthermore, both disorders are often seen together. For example, about 40 per cent of anorexics show binge eating, although many people with bulimia do not necessarily develop anorexia. Thus, bulimia qualifies as an eating disorder in its own right.

Like anorexia, there are undoubtedly many reasons why bulimia occurs. However, it is interesting to point out that some bulimic patients with a history of binge eating show reduced levels of the serotonergic metabolite 5-HIAA, and the dopaminergic metabolite HVA, in their cerebrospinal fluid. Both metabolites are likely to be breakdown products derived from the brain and thus reflect central serotonergic and dopaminergic dysfunction. Moreover, it has also been speculated that reduced serotonergic function might contribute to the blunted satiety responses in bulimic patients, while low levels of dopamine might play a role in their addiction-like craving for food (Jimerson *et al.* 1992). Thus abnormal brain chemistry may have an important role to play in the development of eating disorders.

Box 4.2 CAN FOOD ADDITIVES CAUSE HYPERACTIVITY?

Attention-deficit hyperactivity disorder (ADHD) is the name given to the syndrome where children suffer from a set of behavioural problems characterised by inattention, impulsivity and overactivity. Children with this disorder are often constantly 'on the go' – running, climbing and being disruptive. In addition, they tend to be inattentive and easily distracted, which makes them difficult to educate in a normal school setting. It has been estimated that 3–5 per cent of children suffer from ADHD (which makes it by far the most common behavioural problem in childhood) and it is 4–6 times more common in males. Moreover, some estimates show that as many as a third of children with ADHD grow up with a lifetime set of problems ranging from conduct disorders to increased anxiety and depression.

What causes hyperactivity? One controversial theory is that the disorder can be caused by food additives. This idea was first proposed by Dr Benjamin Feingold in 1975 who claimed that diet was the critical factor in around 50 per cent of cases. Feingold first got his idea when he discovered that some of his patients showed an allergic reaction to a class of chemicals called salicylates (found in aspirin and a wide range of foodstuffs) that also resulted in hyperactivity. Following this, Feingold placed a group of hyperactive children on a diet free of salicylates and found that nearly 50 per cent showed a significant improvement. On this basis Feingold concluded that hyperactive children should be placed on a diet free of salicylates, including artificial food colourings, flavourings and preservatives.

There is little doubt that Feingold's advice has become popular and that many children with ADHD have been placed on additive-free diets by their parents. Despite this, most scientists remain sceptical about the practice – particularly as most studies have not been able to show any clear-cut benefit of additive-free diets (e.g. see Connors 1980). Nevertheless, there seems to be little harm in following this type of dietary regime, and in 1980 the National Institute of Health advised that parents should feel free to try this approach if they so wished, although this advice has not been well received in all quarters (e.g. see Logue 1986, p. 142). What, then, are the alternatives? Paradoxically, one of the best pharmacological treatments for the disorder (although again highly controversial) is the stimulant Ritalin (an amphetamine), which has been shown to reduce hyperactivity and increase attention. Although it is not clear how Ritalin exerts its calming effect in hyperactive children, it nevertheless implicates the neurotransmitter dopamine in the disorder.

Self-test questions

1. What is meant by homeostasis? What is negative feedback?
2. Describe the process of digestion.
3. What body organ is the first to receive nutrients from the small intestine?
4. What are the functions of insulin, glucagon and glycogen?
5. Where are glucoreceptors found?
6. Describe the main features of the dual set-point model of hunger.
7. What are the main effects of ventromedial hypothalamic lesions?
8. Why are lesions to the lateral hypothalamus very difficult to interpret?
9. What neurotoxin can be used to destroy dopaminergic neurons selectively?
10. Briefly discuss some of the ways learning has been implicated in eating behaviour.
11. What is sensory-specific satiety?
12. What is an adipocyte?
13. What evidence suggests that obesity has a genetic basis?
14. Describe the main differences between anorexia and bulimia.

Key terms

Absorptive phase (p.108)
Adenosine triphosphate (ATP) (p.115)
Adipocyte (p.121)
Anorexia (p.123)
Aphagia (p.115)
Attention-deficit hyperactivity disorder (p.125)
Blood–brain barrier (p.112)
Bulimia (p.124)
Calorie (p.114)
Cholecystokinin (CCK) (p.113)
Diabetes (p.111)
Dual-centre set-point theory (p.116)
Duodenum (p.107)
Garcia effect (p.120)
Glucagon (p.107)
Glucostatic theory (p.111)
Glycogen (p.107)
Homeostasis (p.106)
Hyperphagia (p.115)
Insulin (p.107)
Lateral hypothalamus (p.115)
Leptin (p.122)
Mitochondria (p.115)
Neuropeptide Y (p.123)
Nigral–striatal pathway (p.118)
Pancreas gland (p.107)
Post-absorptive phase (p.108)
Sensory-specific satiety (p.120)
Vagus nerve (p.112)
Ventromedial hypothalamus (p.112)

References

Abraham, S. and Llewellyn-Jones, D. (1987) *Eating Disorders: The Facts*. Oxford: Oxford University Press.

Anand, B. K. and Brobeck, J. R. (1951) Hypothalamic control of food intake. *Yale Journal of Biological Medicine*, **24**, 123–40.

Anderson, G. H. and Kennedy, S. H. (1992) *The Biology of Feast and Famine: Relevance to Eating Disorders*. San Diego: Academic Press.

Antelman, S. M. *et al.* (1975) Tail pinch-induced eating, gnawing and licking behaviour in rats: Dependence on the nigrostriatal dopamine system. *Brain Research*, **99**, 319–37.

Bolles, R. C. (1990) A functionalist approach to feeding. In Capaldi, E. and Powley, T. L. (eds) *Taste, Experience and Feeding*. Washington: American Psychological Association.

Bouchard, C. (1989) Genetic factors in obesity. *Medical Clinics of North America*, **73**, 67–81.

Cannon, W. B. and Washburn, A. L. (1912) An explanation of hunger. *American Journal of Physiology*, **29**, 441–54.

Carlson, A. J. (1912) The relation between the contractions of the empty stomach and the sensation of hunger. *American Journal of Physiology*, **31**, 175–92.

Chen, D. Y. *et al.* (1993) The induction and suppression of c-fos expression in the rat brain by cholecystokin and its antagonist L364,718. *Neuroscience Letters*, **149**, 91–4.

Connors, C. K. (1980) *Food Additives and Hyperactive Children*. New York: Plenum Press.

Davis, J. D. *et al.* (1969) Inhibition of food intake by a humoral factor. *Journal of Comparative and Physiological Psychology*, **67**, 407–14.

Friedman, M. I. *et al.* (1986) Integrated metabolic control of food intake. *Brain Research Bulletin*, **17**, 855–9.

Grilo, C. M. and Pogue-Geile, M. F. (1991) The nature of the environmental influences on weight and obesity: A behavioral genetic analysis. *Psychological Bulletin*, **10**, 520–37.

Halaas, J. L. *et al.* (1995) Weight-reducing effects of the plasma protein encoded by the obese gene. *Science*, **269**, 543–6.

Hill, J. O. and Peters, J. C. (1988) Environmental contributions to the obesity epidemic. *Science*, **280**, 1371–4.

Jimerson, D. C. *et al.* (1992) Low serotonin and dopamine metabolite concentrations in CSF from bulimic patients with frequent binge episodes. *Archives of General Psychiatry*, **49**, 132–8.

Logue, A. W. (1986) *The Psychology of Eating and Drinking*. New York: Freeman.

Mayer, J. and Marshall, N. B. (1956) Specificity of gold thioglucose for ventromedial hypothalamic lesions and hyperphagia. *Nature*, **178**, 1399–400.

Morgan, C. T. and Morgan, J. D. (1940) Studies in hunger: The relation of gastric denervation and dietary sugar to the effect of insulin upon food intake. *Journal of General Psychology*, **57**, 153–63.

Plomin, R. *et al.* (1997) *Behavioral Genetics*. New York: Freeman.

Rolls, B. J. *et al.* (1981) Sensory specific satiety in man. *Physiology and Behavior*, **27**, 137–42.

Rolls, E. T. (1985) The neurophysiology of food intake. In Sandler, M. and Silverstone, T. (eds) *Psychopharmacology and Food*. Oxford: Oxford University Press.

Russek, M. (1971) Hepatic receptors and the neurophysiological mechanisms controlling feeding behaviour. In Ehrenpreis, S. (ed.) *Neurosciences Research*, vol. 4. New York: Academic Press.

Shimizu, N. *et al.* (1983) Functional correlations between lateral hypothalamic glucose-sensitive neurons and hepatic portal glucose-sensitive units in the rat. *Brain Research*, **265**, 49–54.
Stellar, E. (1954) The physiology of motivation. *Psychological Review*, **61**, 5–22.
Stricker, E. M. *et al.* (1977) Homeostasis during hypoglycemia: Central control of adrenal secretion and peripheral control of feeding. *Science*, **196**, 79–81.
Ungerstedt, U. (1971) Adipsia and aphagia after 6-hydroxydopamine induced degeneration of the nigrostriatal dopamine system. *Acta Physiologia Scandinavica*, **367**, 95–122.
Wangensteen, O. H. and Carlson, H. A. (1931) Hunger sensations in a patient after total gastrectomy. *Proceedings of the Society of Experiential and Biological Medicine*, **28**, 545–7.
Weingarten, H. P. (1983) Conditioned cues elicit feeding in sated rats: A role for learning in meal initiation. *Science*, **220**, 431–3.
Winn, P. *et al.* (1984) Ibotenic acid lesions of the lateral hypothalamus: Comparison with the electrolytic lesion syndrome. *Neuroscience*, **12**, 225–40.
Zhang, Y. *et al.* (1994) Positional cloning of the mouse gene and its human homologue. *Nature*, **372**, 425–32.

FURTHER READING

Capaldi, E. D. and Powley, T. L. (1990) *Taste, Experience and Feeding*. Washington: American Psychological Association.
Le Magnen, J. (1985) *Hunger*. Cambridge: Cambridge University Press.
Lytle, L. D. (1977) Control of eating behavior. In Wurtman, R. J. and Wurtman, J. J. (eds) *Nutrition and the Brain*, vol. 2. New York: Raven Press.
Smith, G. P. (ed.) (1998) *Satiation: From Gut to Brain*. Oxford: Oxford University Press.

Multiple choice questions

1. The pancreas gland has a duct which opens into the:

(a) stomach
(b) duodenum
(c) small intestine
(d) large intestine

2. Which of the following substances are released by the pancreas gland?

(a) insulin
(b) glucagon
(c) (a) and (b) above
(d) pepsin

3. The main function of insulin is to:

(a) speed up the contractions of the stomach
(b) allow the absorption of nutrients through the small intestine
(c) break down protein
(d) enable glucose to enter body cells

4. During the post-absorptive phase __________ helps to break down the liver's stores of ____________.

(a) glucagon, glycogen
(b) glycogen, glucagon
(c) insulin, glycogen
(d) insulin, glucose

5. Patients who have had their stomachs removed:

(a) find it difficult to regulate their feeding behaviour
(b) require regular injections of insulin
(c) require special dialysis treatment
(d) report normal sensations of hunger

6. Davis *et al.* (1969) found that when hungry animals were given blood transfusions from satiated (well-fed) animals they:

(a) stopped eating or ate very little
(b) continued to eat normally
(c) ate only palatable food
(d) showed an aversion to salt

7. Which of the substances below may provide blood-borne signals in the regulation of hunger and eating?

(a) glucose
(b) fats
(c) amino acids
(d) all of the above

8. People with diabetes have low levels of:

(a) blood glucose
(b) glucagon
(c) insulin
(d) all of the above

9. Mayer and Marshall (1956) by using gold thioglucose found glucoreceptors in the:

(a) ventromedial hypothalamus
(b) liver
(c) stomach wall
(d) all of the above

10. When Maurio Russek injected glucose into the ____________ (but not the ____________) he found that this quickly stopped eating in hungry animals.

(a) jugular vein, hepatic portal vein
(b) hepatic portal vein, jugular vein
(c) stomach, hepatic portal vein
(d) ventromedial hypothalamus, jugular vein

11. The dual-centre set-point model of eating proposes that the ______________ acts as the brain's satiety centre and that the ______________ acts as its feeding centre.

(a) ventral hypothalamus, medial hypothalamus
(b) lateral hypothalamus, ventromedial hypothalamus
(c) medial hypothalamus, basal forebrain
(d) ventromedial hypothalamus, lateral hypothalamus

12. Animals with ventromedial hypothalamic lesions:

(a) lose weight and will die unless force-fed
(b) will work extremely hard to obtain food
(c) are very finicky and much prefer to eat palatable food
(d) causes excessive eating and weight gain

13. Following lesions of the lateral hypothalamus, animals do not:

(a) eat or drink (and have to be force-fed to survive)
(b) respond to touch or sensory stimulation
(c) right themselves when turned on their side
(d) all of the above

14. Neurotoxins such as kainic acid and ibotenic acid selectively destroy:

(a) glucoreceptors
(b) cell bodies (leaving fibres of passage spared)
(c) axons
(d) both cell bodies and axons

15. Part of the reason why lesions of the lateral hypothalamus have such deleterious behavioural effects is because the lesion also causes damage to the:

(a) nigral–striatal pathway

(b) ventromedial hypothalamus
(c) vagus nerve
(d) pituitary gland

16. Harvey Weingarten showed that rats can be made to eat as a result of:

(a) stress (caused by a tail pinch)
(b) an energy deficit involving glucose
(c) being introduced into a new environment
(d) conditioning involving a light and tone

17. Sensory-specific satiety occurs when:

(a) an animal (or person) gets 'bored' eating the same food over a long period of time
(b) the eating of a particular food causes illness
(c) a person is 'fooled' into thinking that he or she has eaten a big meal
(d) an unpleasant smell accompanies a meal

18. According to Grilo and Pogue-Geile (1991) 40–60 per cent of the variability in body fat between individuals is due to:

(a) environmental influences (especially adult eating habits)
(b) differences in the level of insulin release
(c) early upbringing
(d) genetic influences

19. Which of the following statements is *not true* regarding anorexia nervosa?

(a) people with anorexia typically have a distorted body image of themselves
(b) anorexia mainly occurs in young women
(c) people with anorexia do not feel hungry
(d) approximately 2–5 per cent of anorexics will eventually die from their illness

20. Bulimia:

(a) occurs when people engage in bouts of binge eating followed by purging
(b) always accompanies anorexia nervosa
(c) is only found in young women
(d) all of the above

5 Emotional states

IN THIS CHAPTER

- The autonomic nervous system
- The James–Lange and Cannon–Bard theories of emotion
- Cognitive factors and emotion
- The limbic system with particular reference to the hypothalamus and the amygdala
- The neural basis of fear
- The role of the orbitofrontal cortex
- Psychosurgery
- Anxiety and the use of benzodiazepines

Introduction

The word emotion is derived from the Latin *emovere* meaning 'to move' or 'to disturb'. Although the roots of this word may at first come as a surprise, there is little doubt that its meaning is highly appropriate. Emotions move us into action and signal that something significant is happening to us. They also create a feeling – love, elation, happiness, fear, anger, joy, surprise, and irritation, to name just a few – and they colour our perception and add richness to our personal world. Emotions are so much part of human life that it is hard to imagine the dull and grey world that would exist without them. Despite this, we should not forget that emotions do not solely belong to humans, and, as Charles Darwin pointed out over 100 years ago, many of our emotions can also be recognised in other animals.

Thus, emotions have evolved to serve many important functions as well as being an integral part of all higher behaviour. Although the study of emotions in psychology is plagued with a number of conceptual difficulties (not least because psychologists are even unable to agree on a definition of the term), most would nonetheless accept that an emotion is composed of at least four components: (1) a cognitive appraisal of the event; (2) physiological changes in the **viscera** (or main organs of the body); (3) an increased readiness to act; and (4) a subjective sense of feeling. Further consideration of these responses shows that the brain is crucially involved in all of them – in fact, there could be no emotion (or indeed any component of an emotion) without a brain. The challenge for biological psychologists, therefore, is to explain how (and why) the brain produces all these changes.

The autonomic nervous system and emotion

The term autonomic means 'self governing' and this succinctly describes the autonomic nervous system which operates for the most part beyond the reaches of voluntary or conscious control (see also Chapter 1). The autonomic nervous system consists of motor nerve fibres that control the activity of the internal organs of the body, as well as certain hormonal glands (particularly, the adrenal glands which release **adrenaline**) – and comprises two main divisions: the **sympathetic nervous system** and the **parasympathetic nervous system** (see Figure 5.1). The first of these acts mainly to mobilise the body's resources in response to emergency or stressful situations. The noted physiologist Walter Cannon in the 1920s called the pattern of responses produced by the sympathetic nervous system the **'flight or fight' response** because they prepare us for danger should it occur. For example, it increases heart rate and blood pressure, and acts to shunt blood away from the skin to the muscles where it may be needed for vigorous exercise (this is the reason why skin may go pale after a shock). In addition, it promotes deeper and faster breathing, while inhibiting digestion and increasing perspiration (among its many other responses). In short, these are adaptive reactions that help prepare the body for sudden energy output.

In contrast, the parasympathetic system promotes relaxation and is most active during normal and non-stressful conditions. In other words, this system operates when the body is at rest, during which time it is mainly concerned with control of the digestive system and conserving body energy. Although the sympathetic and parasympathetic systems innervate the same body organs and are often seen as acting in an opposite (or antagonistic) manner (i.e. as one increases its activity, the other decreases), in practice these two systems often work together to finely control the function of a given organ.

What has this to do with emotion? The simple answer is that when we experience a significant emotional reaction, a number of bodily changes typically take place that involve the autonomic nervous system. For example, if we are suddenly frightened we may experience a rapid heartbeat, increased respiration, tense muscles, trembling, a dry mouth, sweaty hands, and a sinking feeling in the stomach. These sensations are part of the flight–fight response due to the activation of the sympathetic nervous system.

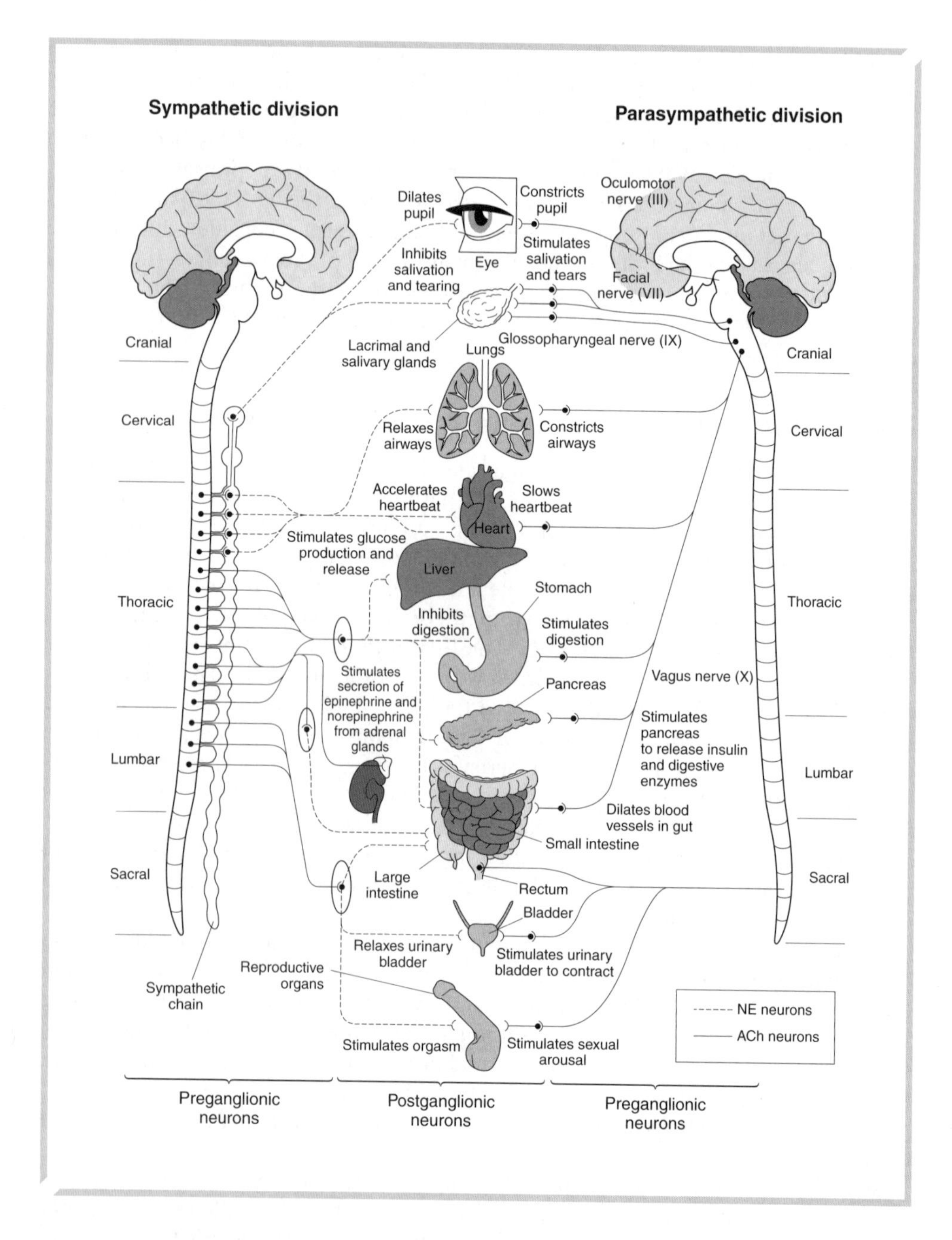

Figure 5.1 Sympathetic and parasympathetic divisions of the autonomic nervous system and the organs they innervate. (*Source*: From M. F. Bear, B. W. Connors and M. A. Paradiso, *Neuroscience: Exploring the Brain*. Copyright © 1996 by Lippincott Williams & Wilkins. Reprinted by permission.)

Although not all emotions necessarily produce these effects, it is generally the case that arousal produced by the autonomic nervous system is a very important component of *most* emotional states. Thus, it is fair to say that the autonomic nervous system underpins both the expression and experience of emotion. However, as we shall see below, there may be much more to this relationship than first meets the eye.

The James–Lange theory of emotion

At first sight, identifying the cause of a particular emotion appears to be straightforward. We see a snarling, barking dog run aggressively towards us and we prepare to flee; or we are threatened by a mugger who demands our wallet and we defend ourselves. In both cases the cause of the bodily changes producing the emotion appear to be obvious: we first perceive the event, and it is the appraisal of this situation that results in an autonomic response and subsequent emotion. However, around the turn of the century the American philosopher William James and the Danish physiologist Carl Lange suggested an alternative theory. Rather than accepting that we run because we are afraid (as the above examples suggest), they proposed instead that we are afraid because we run. In other words it is the action (or emotional response) that comes before the sensation (or perception) of emotion. Or, put another way, the conscious state that we experience as an emotion only occurs once we have received information about the changes taking place in our body.

This theory is known as the James–Lange theory of emotion (Figure 5.2) and it can be briefly summarised as follows: a stimulus is processed by the appropriate part of the brain (such as the visual or auditory cortex) which then assesses its relevance. If the stimulus is emotionally significant, then information is passed to the autonomic nervous system (ANS) which immediately produces the appropriate bodily changes and arousal. The changes produced by the aroused body state, in turn, feed back to the conscious part of the brain which then interprets the nature of the emotional state it is experiencing. In fact, taking this reasoning to its logical conclusion it can be seen that since

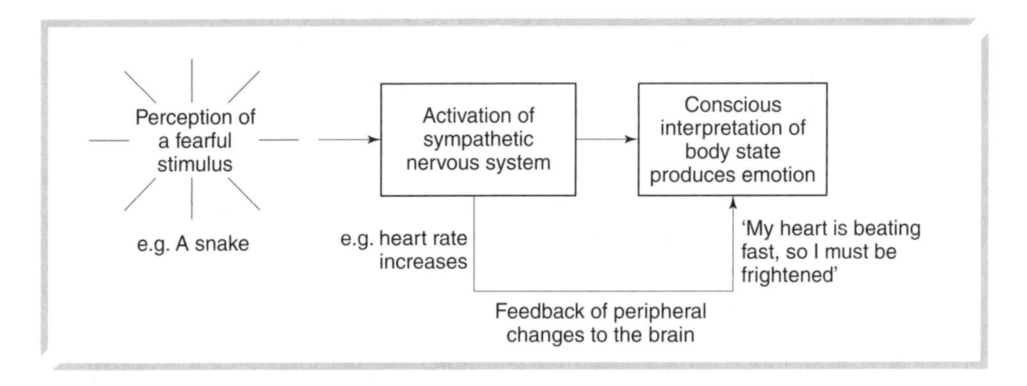

Figure 5.2 The James–Lange theory of emotion.

emotion only becomes a cognitive (or conscious) response once it has been produced in the periphery, and because different emotions 'feel' different, the implication must be that each emotion has its own unique set of physiological changes that accompany it. In other words, it is the pattern of peripheral body changes that tells the brain what emotion it is experiencing.

At the time of its formulation there was little experimental evidence to support this idea, although James did strongly argue that it was impossible to feel an emotion without, at the same time, experiencing the body symptoms that accompany it. In addition, he also noted that sometimes people can feel anxious, angry or depressed without knowing why – showing that bodily states may sometimes be independent from cognitive or conscious analysis.

The Cannon–Bard theory of emotion

The James–Lange theory dominated thinking on emotion until the late 1920s when Walter Cannon compiled an impressive body of experimental evidence against it. For example, Cannon managed to surgically remove (from cats) the whole sympathetic division of the autonomic nervous system and found that this abolished their ability to exhibit arousal – yet, these animals still showed emotional reactions such as anger, fear and pleasure. Moreover, Cannon also noted that the same was equally true of animals that had undergone transection of the spinal cord which stopped all visceral input travelling to, and from, the brain. Clearly, both these findings provided strong evidence against the James–Lange theory. In addition, Cannon's work also indicated that emotions were 'experienced' before many parts of the body (such as smooth muscle) had time to react. In other words, we are capable of feeling emotion before the accompanying bodily changes take place. And, even allowing for this difficulty, Cannon believed that visceral feedback was neither variable nor sensitive enough to provide a basis for each of the wide range of emotions that humans are able to experience (Cannon 1927).

Further evidence against the James–Lange theory also came from studies in which human subjects were injected with adrenaline that produced body reactions resembling excitement and strong fear (i.e. heart palpitations, trembling, tightness in the throat and drying of the mouth). Despite these changes, the injection procedure did not cause the subjects to experience fear, or any other strong emotion. In fact, subjects were able to interpret their bodily reactions without perceiving them as emotional – a finding that was also against the predictions of the James–Lange theory.

To provide an alternative to the James–Lange theory, Cannon proposed that emotional events have two separate effects on the brain: they stimulate the autonomic nervous system to produce arousal and (just as important) at the same time produce the sensation of emotion in the cortex. Thus, the state of autonomic arousal and the cognitive interpretation of the emotional event were seen as occurring together (see Figure 5.3). Cannon also believed that emotional events affected the sympathetic system indiscriminately by causing general arousal. In other words, he did not accept that each emotion had its own individual pattern of body activity (as the James–Lange

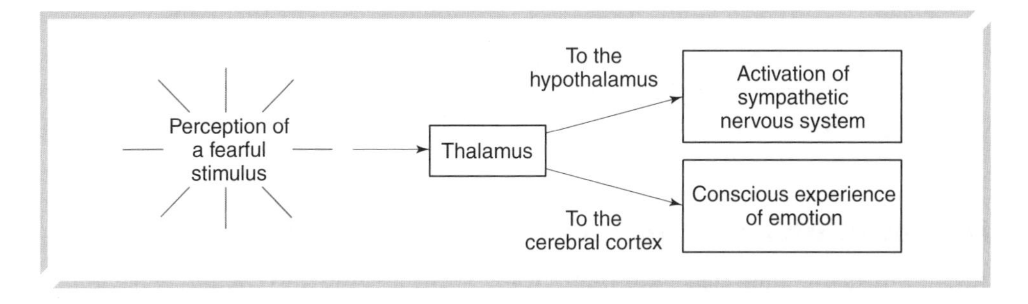

Figure 5.3 The Cannon–Bard theory of emotion.

theory maintained) but rather that the autonomic nervous system responded in exactly the same way to all types of emotion (Cannon 1927).

Cannon's theory was developed by the work of Philip Bard, in the 1930s, who set about trying to identify the brain areas responsible for producing emotion. One structure that had been implicated in emotional behaviour was the **cerebral cortex**. However, when Bard removed the cortex of cats, he found that not only were these animals capable of emotional (aggressive) behaviour, but they were highly emotional and responded with pronounced responses (e.g. arching their backs, hissing, snarling, etc.) to the slightest provocation. Moreover, this behaviour showed all the usual autonomic features associated with emotion (e.g. increased heart rate, blood pressure, etc.). Despite this, the emotional response was not entirely normal since it was never directed towards the threatening stimulus and it quickly stopped when the threat was removed (this suggested that one function of the cortex was to direct the emotional behaviour to the appropriate situation). For this reason, Bard called the aggressive behaviour 'sham rage'.

Bard's discovery was important because it indicated that the cerebral cortex acted to inhibit emotion and aggression. Indeed, this accorded with several other observations. For example, surgeons and dentists had long known that some patients show a strong emotional response – crying, laughter and aggression – during the early stages of anaesthesia when the cortex is beginning to become inhibited. Furthermore, it had been shown in some cases of **hemiplegia** (i.e. paralysis of one side of the body due to cortical damage) that although the muscles of the face might be paralysed, patients sometimes produced an involuntary reaction (i.e. a smile) in response to an emotion (i.e. happiness). This indicated that the brain had other mechanisms, below the level of the cortex, that could initiate emotional behaviour.

Further work by Bard showed that sham rage could be elicited by brain lesions all the way down to the level of the **hypothalamus**. However, if the hypothalamus was removed then the rage did not occur (although some unco-ordinated components of the behaviour could still be observed). Thus, the hypothalamus appeared to be the critical pivotal structure associated with emotional behaviour. On this evidence, Bard concluded that the control of rage behaviour lay in the antagonistic relationship between the cortex and the hypothalamus. In short, although an intact cerebral cortex was important for receiving sensory stimulation – as well as being necessary to direct the emotional response properly – the co-ordinated pattern of emotional behaviour (including reflex movements and visceral responses) depended on the integrity of the hypothalamus.

Hypothalamic stimulation and aggression

Around the same time that Philip Bard was performing his work on the behavioural effects of decortication, Walter Hess (working in Switzerland) was pioneering the technique of electrical brain stimulation in freely moving animals (he examined the functions of many brain regions using his method and won a Nobel prize for this work in 1949). One of the first areas that Hess stimulated was the hypothalamus, and he discovered that it produced marked changes in the autonomic nervous system (e.g. stimulation of the posterior nuclei causing marked sympathetic activation, and stimulation of the anterior regions causing parasympathetic activity). In addition, Hess also found that stimulation of the **medial hypothalamus** could elicit a full-blown rage (with sympathetic arousal) in which the cat arched its back, hissed, and raised its fur (piloerection). Not only this, but it would strike out aggressively towards a threatening object with its unsheathed claws. Thus, unlike the rage produced by decortication, Hess showed that hypothalamic stimulation could actually elicit an aggressive and directed attack *towards* a threatening stimulus.

These findings lent further support to the Cannon–Bard theory of emotion. Despite its small size, the hypothalamus was obviously involved in the expression of the autonomic nervous system which, as we have seen above, is also responsible for producing the body state associated with emotion. Moreover, it was also clear that stimulation of the hypothalamus caused certain types of (species-specific) emotional behaviour to be elicited. Thus, in terms of the Cannon–Bard model, it made sense to view the hypothalamus as an 'emotional' centre that received input from the sensory areas of the cerebral cortex and translated this into behavioural output. Cannon also believed that the hypothalamus had a pathway that went back to the cerebral cortex, which informed the conscious part of the brain about the emotion it was experiencing.

The cognitive-arousal theory

An experiment which cast doubt on certain aspects of the Cannon–Bard theory was undertaken by Stanley Schachter and his colleague Jerome Singer in 1962. They injected subjects with adrenaline which mimics the effects of sympathetic stimulation and causes physiological arousal. In one condition, the subjects were given accurate information about the physiological effects of the injection, but in the other group, subjects were not told of the drug's action. Subjects from both groups were then put into a room which, unknown to them, contained an actor (employed by the experimenters) who had been instructed to behave either in a happy and euphoric way, or in an irritated and surly manner. Later, the subjects were questioned about their own emotional states. The

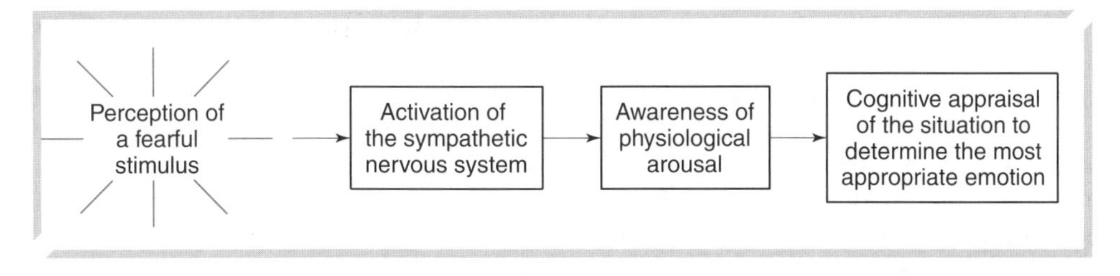

Figure 5.4 The Schachter–Singer theory of emotion.

findings showed that the informed group experienced little emotional change in response to the situation – but, in contrast, the uninformed subjects reported strong feelings (euphoria or anger) which closely matched the 'emotion' of the confederate (Schachter and Singer 1962).

What does this study tell us about emotion? Firstly, it confirms the idea that the same type of physiological arousal may underlie different emotions, as originally proposed by Cannon and Bard. But, in contrast to the Cannon–Bard theory, Schachter and Singer's results show that physiological arousal provides important feedback which enables individuals to interpret what is happening to themselves. In other words, a bodily sensation – a rapid heartbeat for instance – serves as a signal to trigger emotion, although it is up to the person (e.g. the cognitive analysis provided by the cerebral cortex) to decide what emotion he or she is experiencing. Schachter and Singer's experiment also lends some degree of support to the James–Lange theory which viewed visceral (or body) responses as being the important determinant of emotion. But, their theory is only partially supported because Schachter and Singer also show that only one type of physiological arousal is needed to produce different types of emotion. In other words, the key to understanding different emotions lies with cognitive interpretation of the event, which includes analysis of both the internal body state and the external situation (see Figure 5.4).

There is, however, one small difficulty with this theory, and that is: What causes the body to produce an emotional physiological reaction in the first place? A consideration of this matter leads to the conclusion that since the 'emotional' body changes must have been set in motion by the brain, it therefore must have at least analysed (or appraised) the situation on an unconscious level. Thus, the conscious interpretation of an emotion (as shown by Schachter and Singer) is only the final stage of the appraisal, and presumably a great deal of emotional processing precedes this stage below the level of conscious awareness.

Does the same pattern of arousal underlie all emotions?

One of the main tenets of the Cannon–Bard theory of emotion, and also indirectly supported by the findings of Schachter and Singer, is that there is one basic state of physiological arousal which underpins all emotion. However, the evidence regarding this issue is not as clear-cut as it may seem. For example, in an often quoted study, Ax (1953) measured 14 different physiological responses in an elaborate experimental situation that was designed to realistically invoke fear and anger. Subjects were led to believe that they were participating in a study looking at hypertension, and, while doing this, they were either confronted with an inept laboratory technician, whose incompetence 'made real' the possibility that they could receive an electric shock from faulty equipment (to elicit fear), or confronted with an abusive person (to invoke anger). Although self-reports obtained from the subjects after the study confirmed that it had been convincing, and the appropriate emotions produced by the situation, Ax nevertheless found that seven of the physiological measures were significantly different between the two emotional states (e.g. he found that the increases in pulse rate and blood pressure were much greater when invoked by fear than by anger). In a somewhat similar vein, Funkenstein (1955) showed that while the adrenal glands respond to fear by releasing adrenaline, they react to anger by secreting noradrenaline.

More recently, Paul Ekman and his colleagues have provided evidence that different patterns of autonomic activity may accompany different emotions (Ekman *et al.* 1983). These investigators asked subjects to make a facial expression for each of six emotions (anger, fear, sadness, happiness, surprise and disgust), or to imagine re-enacting a past emotional experience, during which time a number of physiological variables were recorded. The results showed that a different pattern of autonomic arousal accompanied each emotion. For example, increased heart rate was found in response to anger and fear, but increased body temperature only occurred with anger. Interestingly, a similar pattern of responses was also obtained from members of the Minangkabau tribe of Western Sumatra, showing that these physiological changes may be universal (Levenson *et al.* 1992).

Unfortunately, this area of research remains fraught with problems of interpretation, not least because of the difficulty in knowing whether the physiological differences are due to the nature of the emotion itself, or due to its severity (i.e. in this case anger may have produced a more severe emotion than imagined fear). Nevertheless, on balance, it is probably the case that not all emotions are associated with the same type of autonomic arousal (e.g. as the Cannon–Bard theory maintains), although this does not necessarily mean that each emotion has its own individual pattern of autonomic activity (as the James–Lange theory maintains). In short, even if autonomic activity helps to differentiate some emotions, it is unlikely that it differentiates *all* emotions.

The facial feedback hypothesis

To complicate matters ever further it is probably the case that feedback from other parts of the body not controlled by the autonomic nervous system, such as the skeletal muscles, may also contribute to the sensation of emotion. For example, there is evidence that our facial expression may also be an important determinant of how we feel. One way this can be tested is to ask subjects to perform movements of the face that correspond to a particular emotion, without letting the subjects know what emotion they are being asked to mimic. For instance, subjects may be asked to follow a set of instructions such as 'pull your eyebrows down and together, raise your upper eyelids and tighten your lower eyelids, narrow your lips and press them together' (Ekman and Friesen 1978). In this case, the facial expression will resemble one of anger although this is not necessarily obvious to the subject. Alternatively, researchers may get subjects to perform a task such as clenching a pen between their teeth to mimic a smile, or holding a pen between the lips to simulate a frown.

Experiments using these types of procedure have found that the acted facial expression can influence the subject's emotion. For example, when subjects were asked to judge a series of cartoons, the ones who had been biting a pen between their teeth (i.e. 'smiling') rated them as funnier compared to those who were 'frowning' (Strack *et al.* 1988). Alternatively, when subjects performed either happy, angry or neutral movements of the face while watching neutral or emotionally charged slides, it was found that subjects reported feeling happier when making a happy face, and angrier when making an angry expression (Rutlidge and Hupka 1985)

Perhaps these findings should not surprise us. The brain is an extremely complex organ which uses all of the information at its disposal to interpret what is happening to it. Thus, it is probably the case that the experience of emotion can occur as a result of cognitive appraisal (and unconscious processing) in the absence of visceral feedback. Nonetheless, it may be that bodily feedback, whether from the autonomic nervous system or from the skeletal muscles, is helpful in enabling the brain to produce a more appropriate and subtle emotional response. Indeed, such feedback may be an important factor in 'colouring' our emotional state and creating a 'harmony' between our conscious and unconscious states.

Introduction to the limbic system

We have already identified the hypothalamus as an important structure in the production of emotions, but this structure is actually part of a much larger brain region called the **limbic system**. The existence of the limbic system was first recognised by Paul Broca in 1878 who identified a group of interconnected structures lying just below the medial surface of the cerebral cortex. These structures appeared to form a border between the cortex and the upper brainstem and, for this reason, Broca called the area the limbic lobe (from the Latin word *limbus* meaning 'border'). This region contained a number of structures including the **cingulate cortex**, the **hippocampus**, the **amygdala** and the **septum**. Although Broca hypothesised about the possible functions of the limbic lobe he appeared to give little thought to its possible role in emotion. Instead, he and other researchers tended to emphasise its possible importance in olfaction – and it became widely known as the rhinencephalon ('nose brain').

In 1937, the neurologist James Papcz began to recognise the importance of the limbic system in emotion. His ideas were largely based on the work of Cannon and Bard who had made the distinction between the behavioural expression of emotion (requiring the hypothalamus), and the subjective 'feeling' of emotion (that was believed to occur in the cortex). In agreement with the Cannon–Bard theory, Papez viewed the hypothalamus as being responsible for the expression of emotion via its control of the sympathetic nervous system. However, he believed that the circuit for the 'feeling' of emotion was more complex. Papez believed that the neural basis for experiencing emotion began in the hypothalamus, but then followed a circular route through the limbic system, passing upwards to the **anterior thalamus** (via the mammillary bodies) and then on to the cingulate cortex. At this point, the pathway was seen as splitting into two: one route going to the **frontal cortex** (for conscious emotional experience), and the other being diverted to the hippocampus and then back to the hypothalamus via a long arching pathway called the **fornix** (see Figure 5.5). Thus, in this scheme, the hypothalamus and cerebral cortex were seen as being part of a much larger neural circuit whose function was to link the behavioural expression of emotion with its subjective feeling.

The concept of an integrated limbic system was further popularised by the work of Paul MacLean (1952) who proposed that the limbic system formed one of the three major divisions of the brain. The three divisions in MacLean's scheme were the reptilian brain corresponding to the brainstem (involved in vital life functions and stereotyped behaviour); the old mammalian or 'limbic' brain (involved in emotional behaviour), and the new mammalian brain or neocortex (involved in higher cognition). MacLean also saw the limbic system and cerebral cortex as interacting together, with the former being responsible for what we 'feel' and the latter being responsible for what we 'know'. Again, this view fitted in well with the prevailing James–Lange theory of emotion.

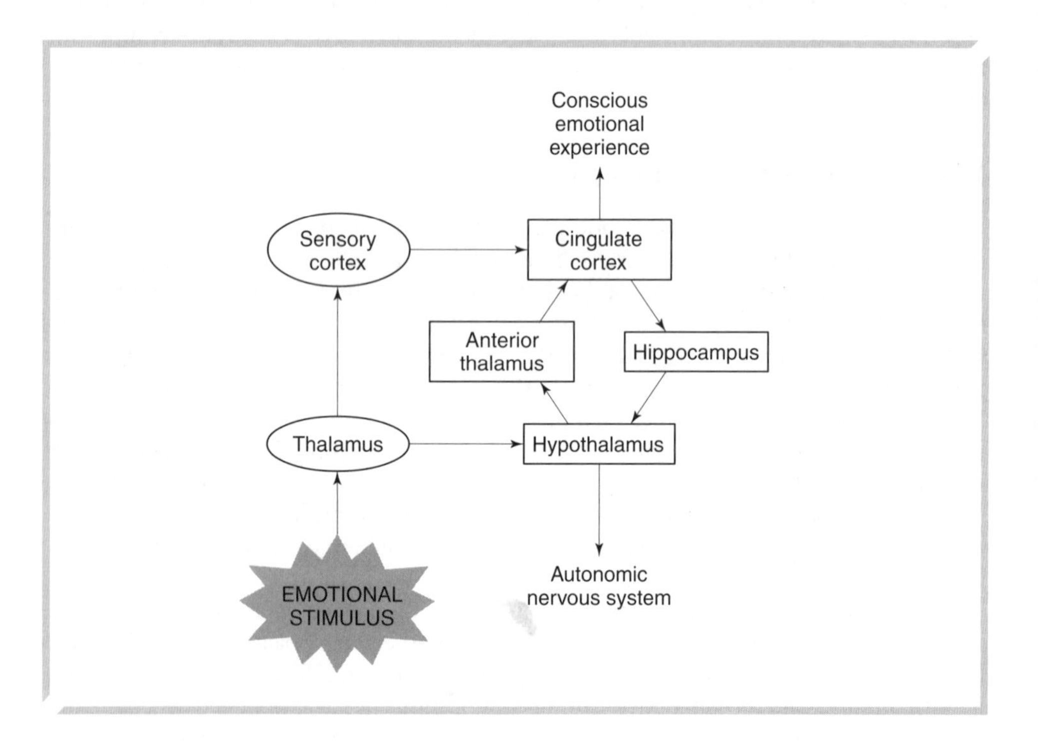

Figure 5.5 The main structures of the **Papez circuit**.

The Kluver–Bucy syndrome

Some of the most striking evidence for the involvement of the limbic system in emotional behaviour came in the late 1930s when Heinrich Kluver and Paul Bucy found that bilateral removal of the temporal lobes (which included the amygdala and parts of the hippocampus) had a dramatic effect on reducing fear in rhesus monkeys. Normally these animals are highly aggressive and dangerous, but Kluver and Bucy found that they became extremely docile and showed no signs of fear or rage following lesioning. Further, these monkeys also exhibited a number of bizarre behaviours. For example, they were hypersexual, as shown by continual masturbation and indiscriminate attempts to mate with other male and female monkeys. These animals were also obsessed with touching everything they came across, partly because they did not appear to recognise objects unless they could pick them up and put them in their mouths (Kluver and Bucy called this phenomenon 'psychic blindness').

One problem with Kluver and Bucy's work was that their lesion had destroyed a large brain region (the temporal lobes) which included both cerebral cortex and parts of the limbic system. Consequently, they set about trying to identify the most important part of the temporal lobe that contributed to the taming effect they had observed. One structure, in particular, appeared to be particularly important – the amygdala.

The amygdala (which is derived from the Latin for *almond*) is located in the anterior tip of the temporal lobe and contains two main groups of nuclei – the **corticomedial** and **basolateral nuclei**. Both of these groups receive extensive input from various regions of the cerebral cortex, including areas involved in sensory and memory processing. In turn, the phylogenetically 'older' corticomedial amygdala projects directly to the hypothalamus, whereas the 'newer' basolateral nuclei have a more extensive and diffuse set of projections (these pass first to the **central nucleus of the amygdala** which, in turn, sends fibres to many regions of the brain, including an important pathway to the frontal cortex). Thus, the anatomical site of the amygdala clearly indicates that it has a pivotal link in the circuitry of neural pathways involved in emotion (Figure 5.6).

Despite this, not all researchers have managed to replicate Kluver and Bucy's findings. For example, Bard and Mountcastle (1948) surprisingly found that removal of the amygdala produced animals that exhibited *increased* rage and emotion, and this has also been confirmed on occasion by others. Why these behavioural differences should occur has never been fully resolved, although the amygdala is a very complex structure (it contains 22 separate nuclei) and it may be that different researchers have produced different patterns of damage. Part of the problem may also lie with the fact that the amygdala has both excitatory and inhibitory effects on emotion (and aggression) and that the regions responsible for these effects lie in close proximity. Alternatively, it might be that the animal's previous learning might have a bearing on how the amygdala lesion manifests itself. For example, Rosvold *et al.* (1954) made an amygdala lesion in the most dominant and aggressive monkey of a group of eight, and found that this monkey quickly fell to the bottom of the dominance hierarchy. However, when a similar lesion was made in the third most dominant monkey, it did not show a decline in aggressive behaviour or status. A possible explanation is that the effects of the amygdala lesion are dependent

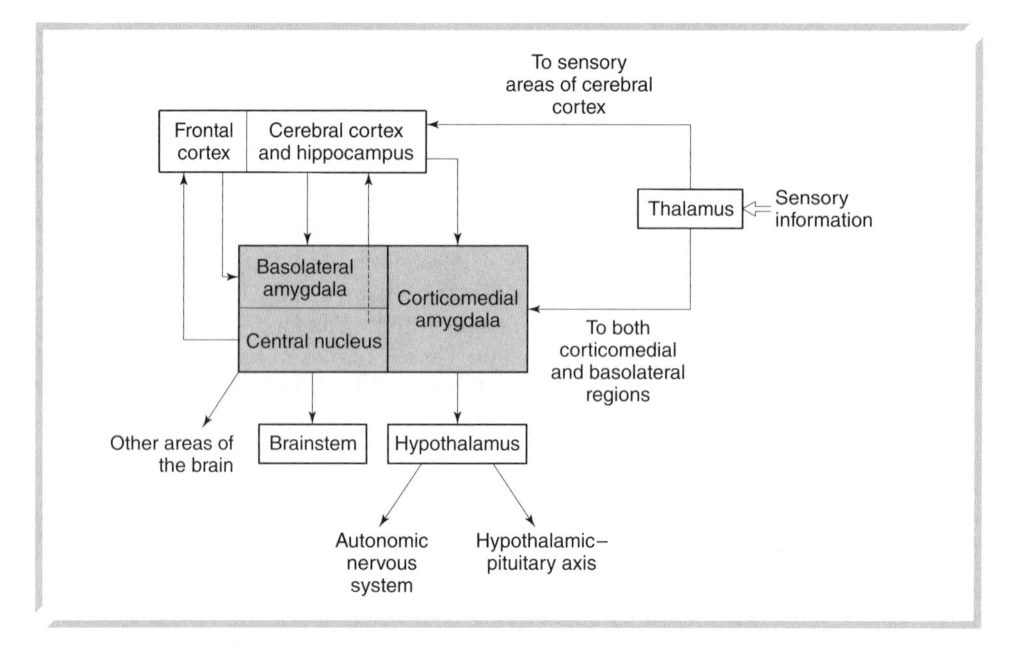

Figure 5.6 The main anatomical connections of the amygdala.

upon the monkey's previous experience, or the type of social environment into which the monkey is returned (e.g. the return of the previously most dominant monkey back into its group might mean that this animal is attacked more fiercely by competitors).

The amygdala and fear

All higher animals show fear in response to threatening situations, and this can also be demonstrated in a laboratory situation. For example, one way to examine this is through **classical conditioning** in which an animal (typically a rat) is presented with a neutral stimulus (such as a light and a tone) that is followed by an electric shock. After a few paired trials, the animal will typically begin to exhibit fear in response to the neutral stimulus (e.g. it will freeze, show increased blood pressure and heart rate, and will startle easily). In other words, the animal will show a conditioned emotional response which can be quantified using either behavioural or physiological measurements.

This type of fear conditioning has also been used to examine the functional role of the amygdala. For example, Bruce Kapp and his colleagues performed an experiment where they presented rabbits with two tones: one tone was always followed by an electric shock and the other had no punishing consequence. During the conditioning, Kapp also recorded the electrical activity from cells in the central nucleus of the amygdala. The results showed that although prior to training the neurons in the amygdala failed to respond to the tones, after learning the cells fired to the shock-related tone, but not to the harmless stimulus. In addition, Kapp found that the rabbit's heart rate developed a 'fearful' anticipatory response to the tone that was associated with shock, but not to the one that was neutral. However, this autonomic response was abolished by lesions of the central nucleus of the amygdala, indicating that this structure was a crucial part of the system in which fear is expressed by the sympathetic nervous system (Kapp *et al.* 1979, 1984).

This conclusion is also supported by experiments that have examined the amygdala through the use of electrical stimulation. As might be expected this procedure often produces behaviours associated with fear. For example, stimulation of the amygdala in animals may cause a sharp increase in respiration, heart rate and vigilance. Moreover, certain amygdala sites also elicit 'fearful' escape behaviour or aggression. Indeed, in the few cases where the amygdala has been electrically stimulated in humans (generally in order to identify epileptic tissue prior to surgery), patients not only show changes in autonomic activity but also frequently report feeling fear and anxiety. In some instances this feeling may be so intense that the patient lets out a terrifying scream and acts as if he or she is in the grips of the most extreme terror (Gloor *et al.* 1982).

Neural circuits for learned fear

The classical conditioning technique can also be used to examine the neural pathways that connect the amygdala with other brain structures involved in producing fear. On first sight, it might be expected that the amygdala would receive its main sensory input from the cerebral cortex. Indeed, it is known that auditory information (e.g. a tone signalling an electric shock) goes first to the **auditory cortex** which, in turn, has neural connections with the amygdala. Thus, this route might appear to be the most obvious way for auditory information to influence the amygdala. However, research by Joseph Le Doux and his colleagues in New York has shown that this is not the case. They lesioned the auditory cortex and found that animals were still able to learn a conditioned emotional (fear) response involving tone stimuli. However, lesions made to subcortical structures involved in the precortical stages of auditory processing (e.g. the **inferior colliculi** and **auditory thalamus**) eliminated conditioned fear responding. Thus, these findings show that auditory information does not have to attain the higher reaches of the auditory cortex before it is passed to the amygdala. Instead, there appears to be a more important subcortical route. These two routes to the amygdala have been called the 'low' and 'high' roads (Le Doux 1998).

This finding should not surprise us. Both animals and humans require a quick alarm mechanism to respond to a potentially dangerous stimulus, and this is what subcortical input to the amygdala allows. In fact, it appears that the thalamus activates the amygdala at around the same time as it activates the cortex – an arrangement that probably enables fear responses to begin in the amygdala before we are completely aware of what is happening to us. Indeed, failing to respond to danger for most animals is likely to prove fatal and it is thus better to be safe than sorry. Thus, the subcortical route to the amygdala allows for this quick 'react first–think later' response to take place (Le Doux 1994).

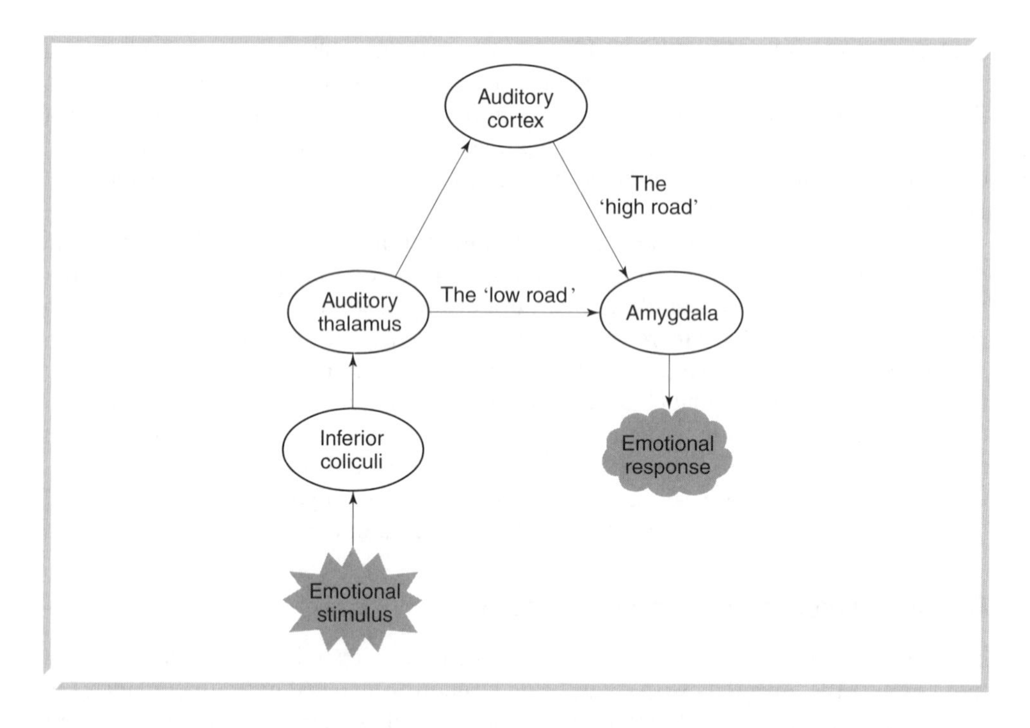

Figure 5.7 The 'low' and 'high' roads to the amygdala.

Nevertheless, the cortical route to the amygdala is also important because it enables us to form a much more accurate representation of the fear-provoking stimulus. Moreover, cortical analysis allows us to consciously interpret what is happening to us, and to make decisions based on knowledge and previous experience. Interestingly, the amygdala also receives input from the nearby hippocampus which appears to inform the amygdala about dangerous environments. For example, Philips and Le Doux (1992) found that lesions to the hippocampus had no effect on a rat's ability to learn a conditioned emotional response to a tone. But, when these animals were later placed in the apparatus in which they had been conditioned, they showed no fearful responses (unlike intact animals). This example shows that frightening events are often complex and require simultaneous analysis of many different aspects of the situation.

Research by Le Doux and his colleagues has also examined the output pathways from the amygdala involved in producing fearful responses. To do this they lesioned various structures 'downstream' from the central nucleus of the amygdala (which, as we have seen above, is crucially involved in control over the autonomic nervous system), and determined the extent to which these lesions interfered with the behavioural expression of a conditioned emotional response. The results showed that two pathways had important roles to play in this respect, with lesions of the **lateral hypothalamus** interfering with conditioned changes in blood pressure, and lesions of

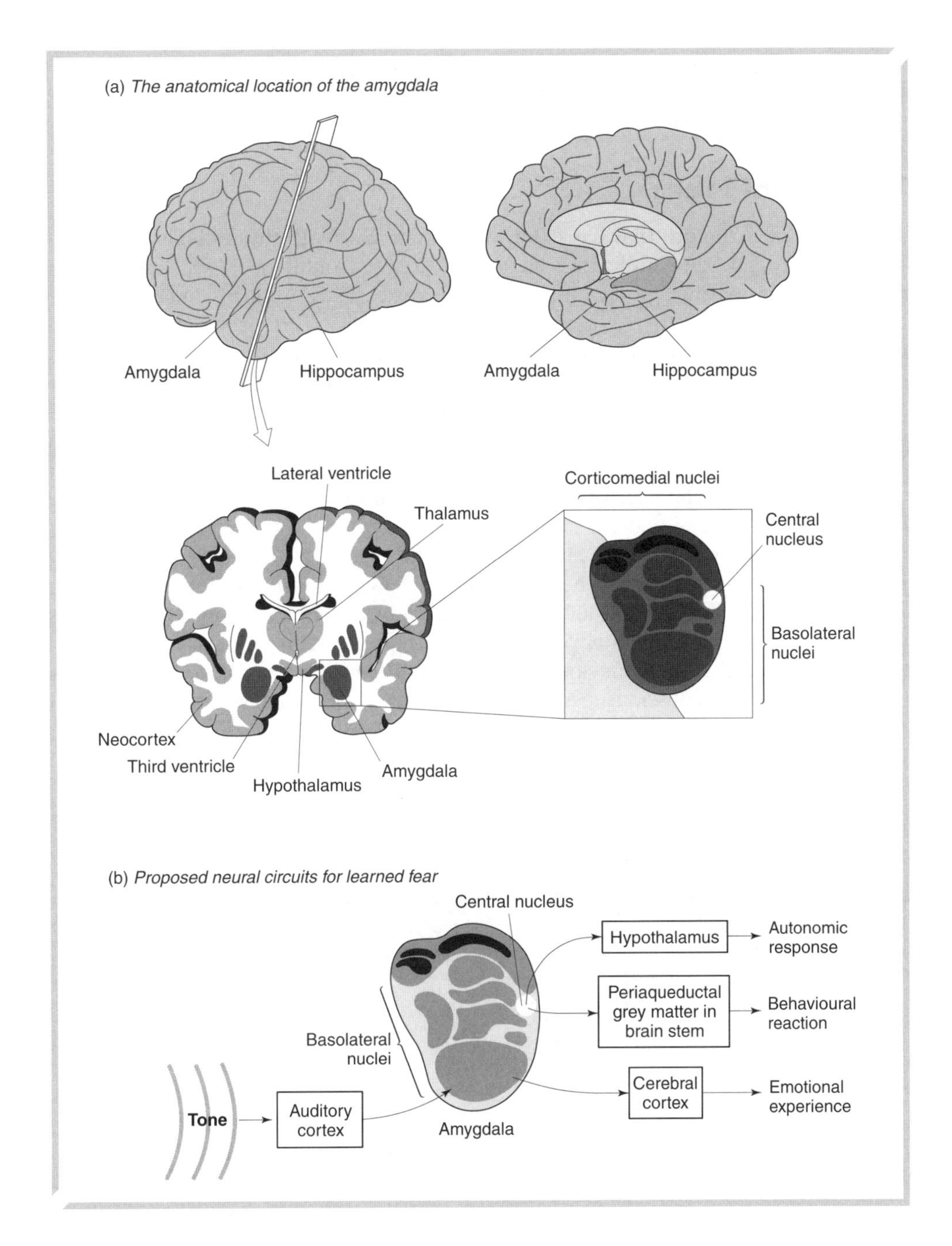

Figure 5.8 The different outputs of the amygdala for the behavioural expression of fear. (*Source*: From M. F. Bear, B. W. Connors and M. A. Paradiso, *Neuroscience: Exploring the Brain*. Copyright © 1996 by Lippincott Williams & Wilkins. Reprinted by permission.)

the **periaqueductal grey matter** interfering with the expression of the freezing response. In addition, other pathways from the amygdala are known to be involved in producing startle responses and mediating the control of hormones (Figure 5.8).

The frontal lobes

Another brain structure that has extensive connections with the limbic system, and which has strongly been implicated in emotion, are the frontal lobes, which in humans make up about one-third of the entire cerebral cortex. The anterior (front) part of the lobe is often referred to as the **prefrontal cortex** and is further subdivided into a **dorsolateral area** and an **orbitofrontal region** (Figure 5.9). Of particular interest is the orbitofrontal region which lies at the base of the frontal lobes and gets its name because it is the part of the brain that lies just above the orbits (the bones that form the eye sockets). This region receives input from the amygdala (via the **dorsolateral thalamus**) and, in turn, projects to several regions of the limbic system including the cingulate cortex, hippocampus, lateral hypothalamus and the amygdala – all areas that play a role in emotion.

Some of the earliest evidence linking the frontal lobes with emotion was reported by Harlow in 1868 who described the case of Phineas Gage, a railroad foreman who, in 1848, suffered a horrifying accident in which an explosion shot an iron rod (measuring approximately 100 cm long and 2.5 cm in diameter, and weighing almost 6 kg) through his cheek and out the top of his skull (landing some 30 metres away!). Remarkably, not only did Gage regain consciousness seconds after the accident (and was able to talk with

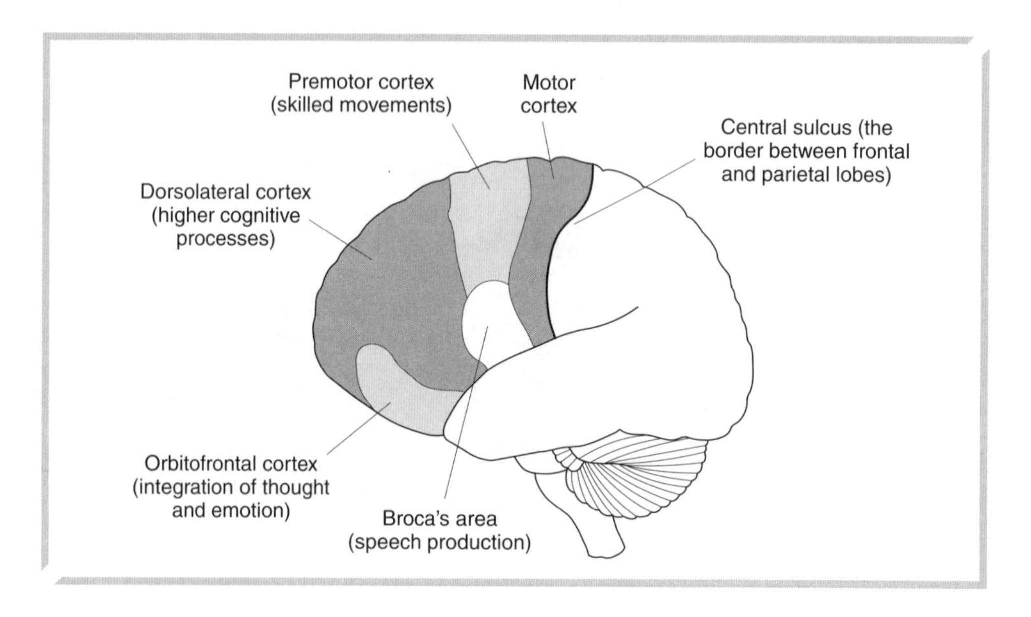

Figure 5.9 The main regions of the frontal cortex.

his companions who led him away from the scene for medical assistance) but, on first sight at least, the injury appeared to have little effect on his behaviour.

In the weeks and months following the accident, however, Gage began to show marked changes in his personality. Gage had been described as 'the most efficient and capable' employee in the company, but after the injury he started to lose interest in work. He became rude and disrespectful to fellow workers, and paid little attention to advice from others, particularly if it interfered with his own wishes or desires. He also experienced great difficulty in planning an action and carrying it through to its conclusion, making him unable to carry out successfully any task that demanded responsibility. However, this seemed not to bother him and he apparently became emotionally apathetic and childish. Phineas Gage was fired from his position as foreman and never again regained full employment, although he was to find various types of temporary work until his death from a severe epileptic fit some 11 years later (Macmillan 1996).

Unfortunately, it is not known for certain what parts of his brain were damaged by the accident because no autopsy was performed at the time of Gage's death. However, John Harlow (the physician who first reported Gage's accident) was permitted to exhume the body several years after death and he estimated from the skull that damage had occurred mainly to the left anterior part of the frontal cortex including the orbitofrontal cortex. The skull was in fact preserved in a museum at Harvard Medical School and has recently been re-examined using neuro-imaging techniques involving computer simulation (Damasio *et al.* 1994). This new analysis has indicated that the rod severely damaged tissue in the frontal lobes of both hemispheres, with damage being especially marked in the left orbitofrontal cortex (Figure 5.10).

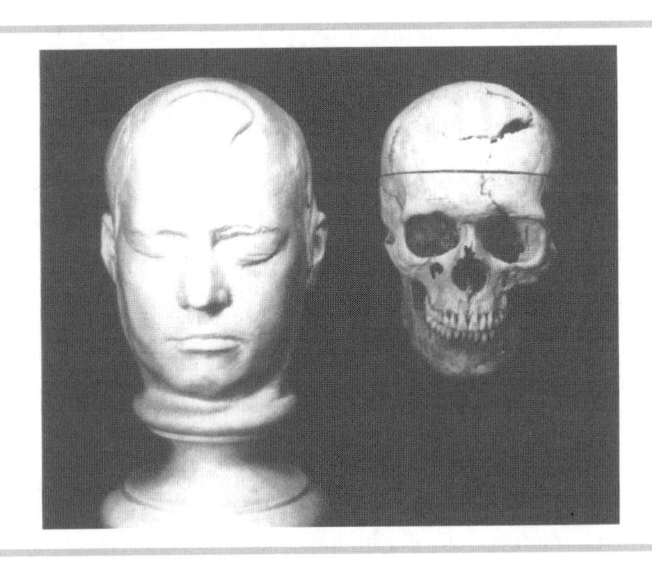

Figure 5.10 Death mask and skull (showing exterior damage) of Phineas Gage. (*Source*: From the Warren Anatomical Museum, Harvard Medical School. Reprinted by permission.)

Frontal lobe surgery

In the years following Gage's accident a number of other clinical cases were reported that also linked the frontal cortex with behavioural and personality change. However, there seemed to be a general reluctance to view the frontal cortex as being involved in emotion until 1935, when John Fulton and Carlyle Jacobsen accidentally found that frontal lobe lesions had a calming effect on chimpanzees. This finding was to have far-reaching consequences. On hearing about this work, the Portuguese neurologist Egas Moniz had the idea that similar lesions might also be used to treat emotionally disturbed patients. And, within a few months, Moniz had persuaded neurosurgeon Almeider Lima to help him perform the operation on one of his patients, thus producing the first prefrontal lobotomy. The operation – which involved severing the main connections between the frontal lobes and the rest of the brain with cutting devices called leucotomes – was so successful that it quickly became widespread and, in 1949, Moniz won a Nobel Prize in Medicine for his work (although, tragically, this was not before Moniz had been shot and made paraplegic by one of his lobotomised patients).

A number of surgical operations involving different brain areas soon evolved from Moniz's work. One procedure, called transorbital lobotomy, could even be performed in the physician's surgery without hospitalisation. This involved a leucotome that was positioned beneath the upper eyelid and driven through the bottom of the cranium into the brain by a mallet! This instrument was then swept back and forth so that it severed the white matter connecting the orbitofrontal cortex with subcortical structures (see Figure 5.11). This technique (which became known as 'ice-pick' **psychosurgery**) was performed on thousands of patients in the United States in the 1940s. In fact, one of its advantages, and no doubt one reason for its popularity, was that it left no obvious scar. However, many other types of lesioning procedure were also developed around this time (i.e. before the advent of modern drug therapy) and it has been estimated that as many as 50,000 patients received psychosurgery during the 1940s and 1950s in the USA alone (Culliton 1976).

Psychosurgery, that is, the use of brain lesions to treat psychiatric illness in the absence of any identifiable brain damage, is rarely performed today. In fact, in the UK, fewer than 100 such operations are carried out each year (Lader and Herrington 1990). Despite this, it nevertheless remains that, in many cases, lobotomy was successfully found to reduce the patient's emotional suffering (particularly in cases of depression, anxiety, obsessions and compulsions). Unfortunately, such operations were also found to produce a variety of other problems that significantly undermined the psychological well-being of the person. For example, lobotomised patients were often found to have difficulty solving problems and following instructions. Emotions tended to be dampened indiscriminately and often led to such people having no social inhibitions, doing what they want without concern for the consequences. Thus, in some respects, they resembled the behavioural characteristics of Phineas Gage. Despite this, psychosurgery still retains its advocates (Culliton 1976; Ballantine *et al.* 1987) and it may be that, in some cases, the benefits of surgery are preferable to its disadvantages (however, see Breggin 1993 for an alternative viewpoint).

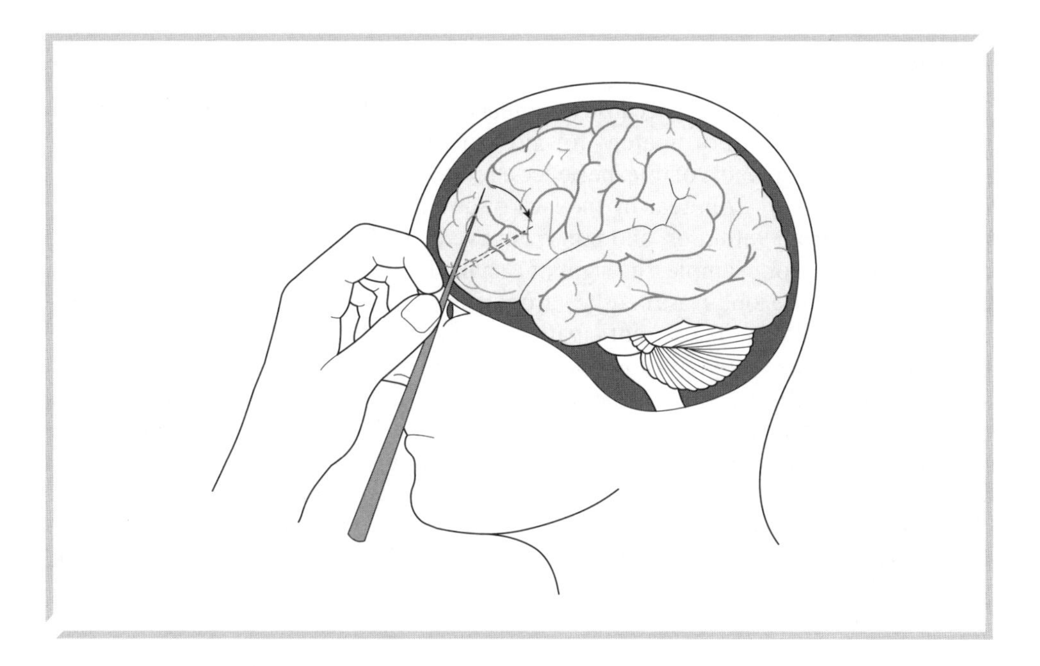

Figure 5.11 'Ice-pick' surgery. (*Source*: From Neil R. Carlson, *Physiology of Behavior*, 6th edition. Copyright © 1998 by Allyn & Bacon. Reprinted by permission.)

What, then, is the role of the orbitofrontal cortex in emotional behaviour? One of the most interesting studies bearing on this question was undertaken by Eslinger and Damasio (1985) who reported on a 35-year-old man (known simply by the initials EVR) who had extensive bilateral damage to the orbitofrontal cortex caused by a tumour (which was successfully removed). Following the operation, Eslinger and Damasio had tested EVR and found that he had superior intelligence on IQ tests and showed above normal comprehension of complex social and political issues. Furthermore, he was capable of sound social judgement when given hypothetical 'moral dilemma' situations that required him to make a decision about whether a certain behaviour in a given situation was right or wrong. Indeed, he provided convincing and sensible answers to these types of problem and justified them with reasoned logic. However, his own behaviour did not follow the same rules and when confronted with real-life problems he often acted with disastrous consequences, both at work and in his personal relationships. In fact, he was described by acquaintances as being irresponsible, disorganised, obsessive and lazy. Moreover, he was extremely detached and showed very little emotion (e.g. see Damasio 1994, p. 45). Thus, it appears that the orbitofrontal cortex is not necessarily involved in making judgements about situational events, but it is involved in translating these judgements into appropriate feelings and behaviours in the real world.

Anxiety

Fear is an important reaction because it protects us from dangerous and potentially life-threatening situations. Fortunately, for most of us, fear tends not to be an everyday occurrence, although most of us experience a related emotion called **anxiety**. Anxiety is usually distinguished from fear by the lack of an immediate external threat – that is, anxiety comes from within us, and fear from events taking place in the outside world (Le Doux 1998). For example, the sight of a snake in long grass may elicit fear, but the anticipation that the long grass may be harbouring a snake causes anxiety. Thus, anxiety can also be described as fearful anticipation (Lickey and Gordon 1991) which typically occurs in situations that are not necessarily dangerous. Both anxiety and fear share a similar biological basis, with increased activation of the sympathetic nervous system, although in anxiety the autonomic arousal tends to be far less intense but much more prolonged. For most of us, this is no bad thing as anxiety helps to increase apprehension and caution while acting as a brake against excessive or careless behaviour. Thus, anxiety is a useful, albeit unpleasant, necessity of life. Unfortunately, for others, anxiety can be so intense that it loses its adaptive function and causes mental dysfunction and general ill health.

Anxiety becomes a clinical disorder when it occurs for no good reason, or is more intense than is justified by the perceived threat. In clinical practice, anxiety disorders are surprisingly common and it has been estimated that around 15 per cent of the population will suffer from an anxiety disorder at some time in their lives. Such disorders can take many forms. Phobias (irrational fears) are the most common type of anxiety problem (with a prevalence of about 13.5 per cent in the population) followed by obsessive–compulsive disorder (2.5 per cent) and panic disorders (2.5 per cent) (Holmes 1991). However, these figures probably represent just the tip of the iceberg as many of us also suffer anxiety from the 'normal' pressures of modern life. In fact, it has been suggested that as many as 30 per cent of patients seen in general practice have problems that are due in some way to anxiety (Beaumont 1990). Thus, not only are we all susceptible to the effects of anxiety, but it is also a major problem for our general practitioners.

Box 5.1 OBSESSIVE–COMPULSIVE DISORDER

Obsessive–compulsive disorder (OCD) is an anxiety disorder characterised by the intrusion of thoughts (obsessions) that produce patterns of strange and ritualistic behaviours (compulsions). By far the most common form of compulsion involves hand washing – accompanied by obsessive thoughts about dirt and contamination. For example, people with OCD may be compelled to wash their hands over a hundred times a day, and to use paper towels whenever they touch objects. Checking compulsions accompanied by fears of future harm if they are resisted provides another relatively common form of OCD. Indeed, such individuals may check lights, doors, locks or electric switches for hours before leaving their house. In other cases, OCD may take the form of strange doorway rituals. For example, Rapoport (1990) reports the case of a person called Paul who had to take 74 steps in a specific zigzag pattern (that had to be performed perfectly) before he could enter his front door. And, there are yet others who have to engage in rituals that involve rolling about on the grass and touching various trees before entering houses. This behaviour is not only extremely embarrassing for the individual concerned, but the obsessive thoughts are often repugnant as well. Yet, despite this, they remain overwhelmingly persistent and difficult to control, and the individual is compelled to perform them at whatever cost. Indeed, OCD is classified as an anxiety disorder because of the acute anxiety the person 'feels' if the intrusive thoughts are not acted upon or obeyed.

Until relatively recently, OCD was treated with behavioural therapy (and in resistant and severe cases by psychosurgery). However, in the early 1980s, reports began to appear showing the effectiveness of a **serotonin uptake blocker** called **clomipramine** in the treatment of OCD (Marks *et al.* 1980; Thoren *et al.* 1980). Not only did this drug provide a means of treating the disorder, but it also indicated for the first time that OCD might have a serotonergic basis. Indeed, further support for this idea came from the finding that people with OCD had higher levels of the serotonergic metabolite **5-HIAA** in their cerebrospinal fluid, which indicated overactivity of serotonergic CNS function. Moreover, treatment with clomipramine was shown to normalise 5-HIAA levels in OCD, which further supported this hypothesis (Thoren *et al.* 1980).

Where in the brain, therefore, does increased serotonin function occur? At present much of the evidence, although indirect, implicates the basal ganglia and frontal cortex. For example, damage to the striatum and frontal cortex is often associated with obsessive and compulsive symptoms (Laplane *et al.* 1989). Moreover, ritualistic behaviour is very common in Sydenham's chorea, which is known to be a childhood autoimmune disorder which attacks the cells of the caudate nucleus (Swerdo *et al.* 1989). Further support has also come from the use of PET scans. For example, Baxter *et al.* (1987) examined 10 OCD patients with PET scans and found increased metabolic activity in the striatum and throughout the cerebral cortex, particularly the orbital frontal cortex which receives input from the striatum. As we saw in the previous chapter, the striatum has long been implicated in movement, and the frontal cortex in emotion and planning. Thus, the involvement (and dysfunction) of these two brain regions in OCD makes a great deal of sense – especially as they both receive serotonergic innervation from the raphe nuclei.

Anxiolytic drugs

Humans have always turned to drugs to help them cope with the stresses of life. Alcohol, opium and barbiturates are just some of the substances that have been used in the past to sedate and reduce anxiety. However, in the early 1960s a new class of drug was developed which had the ability to reduce anxiety without producing sedation. These drugs were the **benzodiazepines**, which included diazepam (Valium) and chlordiazepoxide (Librium), and within a decade of being introduced into clinical practice they had become the most heavily prescribed drugs in the world. The extent of their popularity can be gauged by the number of annual prescriptions in the United Kingdom, which had risen to 18 million in 1972 and was over 30 million by 1979 (Beaumont 1990). Although there has recently been a decline in their use, it has nevertheless been estimated that there are 1.2 million long-term benzodiazepine users in the UK and several million worldwide (Ashton 1992). Indeed, they remain a commonly prescribed drug for anxiety, and are also widely used as hypnotics (sleeping tablets).

Not only do benzodiazepines reduce anxiety in people, but they also appear to have similar effects in animals. One way this can be tested is to examine the effects of benzodiazepines in a conflict test (Gellar 1962). In this situation, a rat is first trained to press a lever in an operant box for food reward. Following conditioning, a hungry rat is put back into the box, but this time whenever a tone is presented, a lever press delivers food accompanied by a mild electric shock. Drug-free rats quickly become very 'nervous' during the tone presentation and, despite their hunger, typically stop responding to the lever. However, if these animals are treated with a benzodiazepine they generally continue to press the lever as before (see Figure 5.12). It has been shown that benzodiazepines neither increase hunger nor suppress pain – consequently, they appear to be acting on the conflict itself, apparently making the animal less anxious about pressing the lever and being punished. Similar results can also be obtained with barbiturates and alcohol, except in this case they generally cause sedation and a depression of responding in both unpunished (tone off) and punished (tone on) conditions. This does not occur with benzodiazepines (except at very high doses), indicating that they exert a genuine anxiolytic effect.

The neurochemical basis of anxiety

How do benzodiazepines work? Until relatively recently, the mechanism of their action was not understood. However, in 1977 a breakthrough occurred when it was discovered that benzodiazepines had their own specific receptor (Squires and Braestrup 1977). In other words, certain neurons in the brain contained receptors that were highly selective for benzodiazepines. In fact, the benzodiazepine receptor turned out to be a component of the much larger **GABA-A receptor** found on postsynaptic neurons in the vicinity of chloride ion channels (see also Chapter 1). This site of this large receptor also provides an important clue to how it 'works'. In short, when the GABA receptor is activated, it causes a configurational change in the proteins forming the ion channel, thus enabling

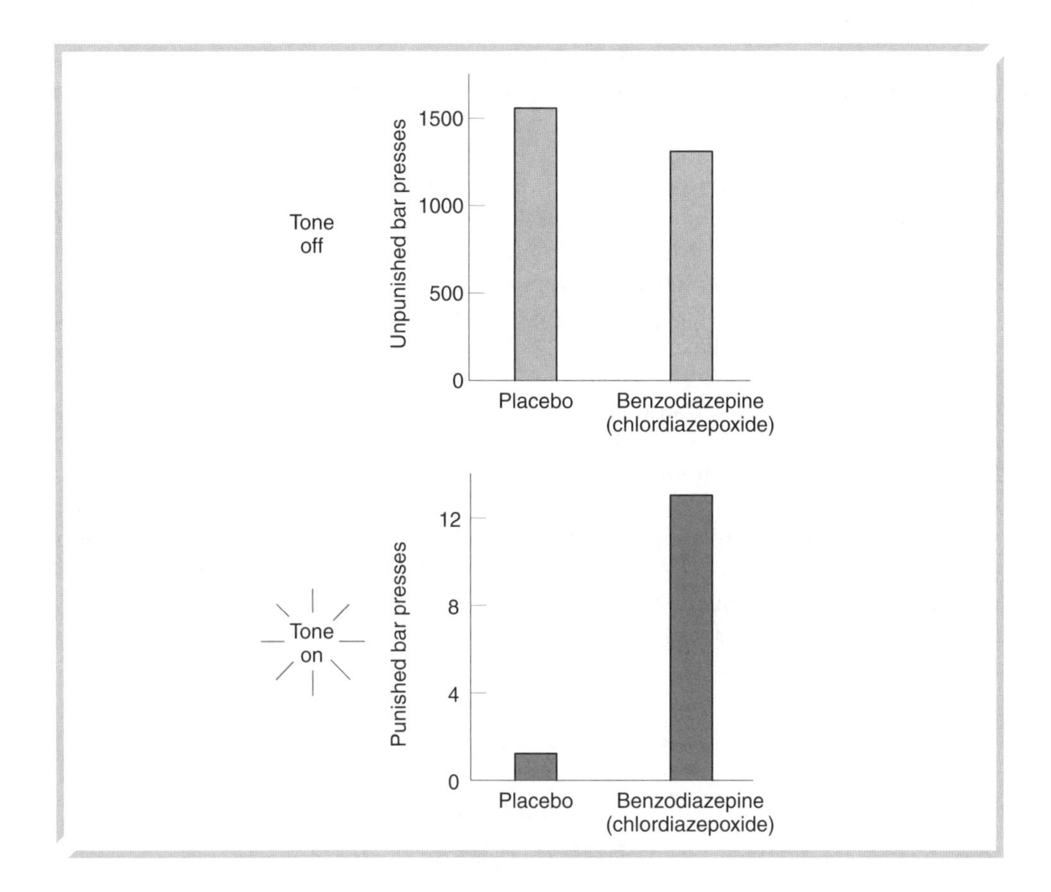

Figure 5.12 The effects that benzodiazepines have on punished responding (as recorded by the number of bar presses) in the Gellar conflict test.

negative chloride ions to flow into the neuron where they produce inhibition of the neuron's resting potential.

It might be expected, therefore, that benzodiazepine receptors act in a similar fashion – that is, by opening the chloride channels. In fact, strictly speaking this is not quite true, as benzodiazepines do not appear to open the channel by themselves. Rather, they produce their effect by facilitating the effects of GABA. In other words, if the benzodiazepine receptor is stimulated along with the adjacent GABA receptor, there is greater neural inhibition (i.e. the chloride ion channel remains open for a longer period) than if GABA receptor is stimulated by itself (this facilitatory action is known as 'alloseric modulation'). Both alcohol and barbiturates have a similar effect on GABA receptors through a similar alloseric mechanism.

Benzodiazepine (along with GABA) receptors are found throughout the brain, although the highest numbers are located in the basal ganglia and cerebellum, the cerebral cortex, and the limbic system (including the amygdala) – a distribution that helps to explain the muscle relaxant, cognitive and emotional effects of the benzodiazepines respectively. But why should the brain have receptors for benzodiazepines in the first place? The obvious answer is that the brain presumably makes its own substances that act on the receptor. Interestingly, a number of substances have been found in the brain that may fulfil this function, including the β-carbolines, and a peptide called diazepam-binding inhibitor – except that these substances increase anxiety rather than reduce it! In other words, the natural (endogenous) substances appear to exert effects opposite to that of the benzodiazepines.

The action of the benzodiazepine receptor has turned out to be rather complex. While benzodiazepines such as diazepam have been shown to facilitate GABA transmission, other substances (such as RO 19-4603) have been found to act on the same receptor but produce the opposite effect and decrease GABA transmission (a substance with this effect is known as an **inverse agonist**). In fact, the benzodiazepine receptors were the first type of receptor to be found in the CNS where this type of bidirectional effect was shown to be possible. To make matters even more complex there are yet other substances (e.g. flumazenil) that are true antagonists at the benzodiazepine receptor (i.e. they block the effects of both agonists and inverse agonists). All of this shows that, in theory, the role of endogenous 'benzodiazepines' in the brain may be potentially very complex, with some substances having anxiogenic (anxiety-inducing) effects and others having anxiolytic properties.

Box 5.2 ARE BENZODIAZEPINES REALLY ADDICTIVE?

One of the biggest controversies concerning the use of benzodiazepines is their potential to cause addiction. When benzodiazepines were first marketed in the early 1960s they were widely regarded as being 'addictive-free'. Addiction is a notoriously difficult concept to define, but one measure of a drug's potential to cause addiction is the likelihood of it being able to cause physical dependence (see also Chapter 11). This form of dependence can be illustrated with the example of alcohol. For example, in the later stages of alcoholism, a person who stops drinking may suffer withdrawal symptoms including anxiety, tremors, delirium tremors and even seizures. Thus, to function 'normally' the chronic alcoholic has to continue drinking to keep the withdrawal symptoms at bay. Other drugs with the potential to cause physical dependence are the barbiturates and opiates (including morphine and heroin). However, the benzodiazepines were not believed to cause this type of dependence, although withdrawal symptoms (mainly agitation and insomnia) had occasionally been noted when extremely high doses had been used in psychiatric patients. Indeed, in 1978 it was claimed that only 24 cases of dependence had been reported in the UK since the introduction of benzodiazepines in 1960 and that the evidence for dependence worldwide was fewer than 500 cases (Marks 1978).

However, beginning in the 1980s this view began to change with the publication of findings showing that physical dependence to benzodiazepines was much higher than previously suspected. For example, some studies showed that withdrawal symptoms occurred in around 40 per cent of patients who had been taking benzodiazepines for more than a year – and in some cases these symptoms could be observed after just 4 weeks. Although there is a great deal of controversy concerning these figures, there does seem to be general agreement that long-term benzodiazepine usage (i.e. a year or more) can lead to dependence (along with withdrawal problems) in a large proportion of users. Since it has been estimated that 1.25 million people in the UK may have taken a benzodiazepine regularly for a year or more (Silverstone and Turner 1988) this represents a sizeable number of people who may have had problems trying to give up benzodiazepine medication.

Because of this, there has been an attempt by doctors in recent years to reduce the use of benzodiazepines; to limit prescriptions in many patients for 4–6 weeks; and to inform patients of the risks of dependence. In addition to physical dependence there is also a phenomenon known as psychological dependence – a craving and a compulsion that is psychologically based, which is arguably a much more important cause of drug addiction. This provides yet another reason why long-term benzodiazepine usage should not be encouraged. Despite these limitations in prescription, the use of benzodiazepines remains controversial. For example, some medical practitioners (e.g. Snaith 1984) believe that benzodiazepines no longer have a place in clinical practice, whereas others (e.g. Oswald 1986) argue that they are so safe that they should be available without a prescription!

New developments

Because of the addictive potential and side effects associated with the use of benzodiazepines, there have been a number of attempts in recent years to develop alternative substances by which to treat anxiety. One such substance is **buspirone** (BuSpar), first introduced into clinical practice in 1986. This drug has been shown to be as effective as diazepam in the treatment of anxiety, yet have fewer side effects. For example, buspirone does not cause sedation or muscle relaxation, and does not interact with alcohol. Perhaps even more important, it does not lead to dependence or cause withdrawal symptoms. For example, in one study, patients underwent benzodiazepine or buspirone treatment for 6 months, after which they were suddenly switched to placebo. The results showed that 80 per cent of the benzodiazepine group suffered side effects (e.g. rebound anxiety or recurrence of symptoms) which required them to resort to 'reserve' medication, while none of the patients taking buspirone reported withdrawal symptoms or a need for extra drug treatment (Rickels *et al.* 1988).

Although it has a proven anxiolytic effect, buspirone is structurally unrelated to the benzodiazepines, and does not bind to benzodiazepine or GABA receptors. Instead, buspirone has a complex pharmacological mode of action that involves it being able to bind antagonistically to dopamine D-2, as well as to noradrenergic alpha-2 receptors (see Chapter 11). However, buspirone is believed to produce its main anxiolytic effect by acting on serotonergic receptors (particularly 5-HT_{1A} **autoreceptors**) that are found in several brain regions including the limbic system and **dorsal raphe**. In fact, buspirone is known to inhibit dorsal raphe neurons, and to significantly reduce serotonin release in the hippocampus (and to a lesser extent the cortex), but interestingly not in the striatum (Leonard 1992). Thus, buspirone appears to produce its main anxiolytic effect by acting on the limbic system.

Unfortunately, clinical trials of buspirone have shown it to have a slower onset of action than the benzodiazepines (e.g. it may take up to two weeks before it exerts an anxiolytic effect) which limits its usefulness in treating sudden (or short-term) anxiety. This problem is confounded by the fact that buspirone is not effective in alleviating anxiety associated with benzodiazepine withdrawal. Despite these drawbacks, the discovery of buspirone along with the realisation that there are now at least seven different types of serotonin receptor (Feldman *et al.* 1997) has led to considerable optimism that more efficient anxiolytic serotonergic drugs can be developed. Indeed, as well as 5-HT_{1A} agents, drugs which antagonise 5-HT_{1C}, 5-HT_2 and 5-HT_3 receptors have also been shown to have anxiolytic effects and are currently under development for this purpose.

Self-test questions

1. Briefly describe the functions of the sympathetic and parasympathetic nervous systems.
2. What is the unusual feature of the James–Lange theory of emotion?
3. What criticisms did Cannon make of the James–Lange theory?
4. In what ways did the work of Philip Bard extend Cannon's theory of emotions?
5. What role does the hypothalamus play in the expression of emotion?
6. In what ways did Schachter and Singer contribute to our understanding of emotion?
7. Outline the various brain structures that make up the Papez circuit.
8. Describe the main features of the Kluver–Bucy syndrome.
9. In what ways has the amygdala been implicated in fear?
10. Who was Phineas Gage?
11. How do the frontal lobes contribute to emotional behaviour?
12. What is psychosurgery? Why is it rarely performed today?

13. Explain how benzodiazepines affect GABA receptor activity.
14. How have benzodiazepine receptors been linked to emotional behaviour?

Key terms

Adrenaline (p.133)
Amygdala (p.141)
Anterior thalamus (p.142)
Anxiety (p.152)
Auditory cortex (p.145)
Auditory thalamus (p.145)
Autoreceptors (p.158)
Basolateral nuclei of the amygdala (p.143)
Benzodiazepines (p.154)
Buspirone (p.157)
Cannon–Bard theory (p.136)
Central nucleus of the amygdala (p.143)
Cerebral cortex (p.137)
Cingulate cortex (p.141)
Classical conditioning (p.144)
Clomipramine (p.153)
Cognitive-arousal theory (p.138)
Corticomedial nuclei of the amygdala (p.143)
Dorsal raphe (p.158)
Dorsolateral area (p.148)
Dorsolateral thalamus (p.148)
Facial feedback hypothesis (p.140)
5-HIAA (p.153)
'Flight or fight' response (p.133)
Fornix (p.142)
Frontal cortex (p.142)
GABA-A receptor (p.154)
Hemiplegia (p.137)
Hippocampus (p.141)
Hypothalamus (p.137)
Inferior colliculi (p.145)
Inverse agonist (p.156)
James–Lange theory (p.135)
Lateral hypothalamus (p.146)
Limbic system (p.141)
Medial hypothalamus (p.138)
Obsessive–compulsive disorder (p.152)
Orbitofrontal region (p.148)
Papez circuit (p.142)
Parasympathetic nervous system (p.133)
Periaqueductal grey matter (p.148)
Prefrontal cortex (p.148)
Psychosurgery (p.150)
Septum (p.141)
Serotonin uptake blocker (p.153)
Sympathetic nervous system (p.133)
Viscera (p.133)

References

Ashton, H. (1992) *Brain Function and Psychotropic Drugs*. Oxford: Oxford University Press.

Ax, A. (1953) The physiological differentiation between fear and anger in humans. *Psychomatic Medicine*, **15**, 433–42.

Ballantine, H. T. *et al.* (1987) Treatment of psychiatric illness by stereotactic cingulotomy. *Biological Psychiatry*, **22**, 807–19.

Bard, P. and Mountcastle, V. B. (1948) Some forebrain mechanisms involved in the expression of rage with special reference to suppression of angry behaviour. *Association of Research into Nervous and Mental Disorders*, **27**, 362–404.

Baxter, L. R. *et al.* (1987) Local cerebral glucose metabolic rates in obsessive-compulsive disorder: A comparison with rates in unipolar depression and in normal controls. *Archives of General Psychiatry*, **44**, 211–18.

Beaumont, G. (1990) The use of benzodiazepines in general practice. In Hindmarch, I. *et al.* (eds) *Benzodiazepines: Current Concepts*. Chichester: Wiley.
Breggin, P. (1993) *Toxic Psychiatry*. London: HarperCollins.
Cannon, W. B. (1927) The James–Lange theory of emotions: A critical examination and an alternative theory. *American Journal of Psychology*, **39**, 106–24.
Culliton, B. J. (1976) Psychosurgery: National commission issues surprisingly favorable report. *Science*, **194**, 299–301.
Damasio, A. R. (1994) *Descartes' Error*. New York: Picador.
Damasio, H. *et al.* (1994) The return of Phineas Gage: Clues about the brain from the skull of a famous person. *Science*, **264**, 1102–5.
Ekman, P. and Friesen, W. V. (1978) *The Facial Action Coding System*. Palo Alto: Consulting Psychologists Press.
Ekman, P. *et al.* (1983) Autonomic nervous system activity distinguishes among emotions. *Science*, **221**, 1208–10.
Eslinger, P. J. and Damasio, A. R. (1985) Severe disturbance of higher cognitive function after bilateral frontal lobe ablation: Patient EVR. *Neurology*, **35**, 1731–41.
Feldman, R. S. *et al.* (1997) *Principles of Neuropsychopharmacology*. Sunderland, MA: Sinauer.
Funkenstein, D. (1955) The physiology of fear and anger. *Scientific American*, **192**, 74–80.
Gellar, I. (1962) Use of approach avoidance behavior (conflict) for evaluating depressant drugs. In Nodine, J. H. and Moyer, J. H. (eds) *Psychosomatic Medicine*. Philadelphia: Lea & Febiger.
Gloor, P. *et al.* (1982) The role of the limbic system in experimental phenomena of temporal lobe epilepsy. *Annals of Neurology*, **12**, 129–44.
Holmes, D. (1991) *Abnormal Psychology*. New York: HarperCollins.
Kapp, B. S. *et al.* (1979) Amygdala central nucleus lesions: Effects on heart rate conditioning in the rabbit. *Physiology and Behaviour*, **23**, 1109–17.
Kapp, B. S. *et al.* (1984) The amygdala: A neuroanatomical systems approach to its contributions to aversive conditioning. In Butters, N. and Squire, L. R. (eds) *The Neuropsychology of Memory*. New York: Guilford Press.
Lader, M. and Herrington, R. (1990) *Biological Treatments in Psychiatry*. Oxford: Oxford University Press.
Laplane, D. *et al.* (1989) Obsessive compulsive and other behavioral changes with bilateral basal ganglia lesions. *Brain*, **112**, 699–725.
Le Doux, J. E. (1994) Emotion, memory and the brain. *Scientific American*, June, 32–9.
Le Doux, J. E. (1998) *The Emotional Brain*. London: Weidenfeld & Nicolson.
Leonard, B. E. (1992) *Fundamentals of Psychopharmacology*. Chichester: Wiley.
Levenson, R. W. *et al.* (1992) Emotion and autonomic nervous system activity in an Indonesian culture. *Journal of Personality and Social Psychology*, **62**, 972–88.
Lickey, M. E. and Gordon, B. (1991) *Medicine and Mental Illness*. New York: Freeman.

MacLean, P. D. (1955) The limbic system ('visceral brain') and emotional behaviour. *Archives of Neurology and Psychiatry*, **73**, 130–4.
Macmillan, M. (1996) Phineas Gage: A case for all reasons. In Code, C. *et al.* (eds) *Classic Cases in Neuropsychology*. Hove: Psychology Press.
Oswald, I. (1986) Drugs for poor sleepers? *British Medical Journal*, **292**, 715.
Philips, R. G. and Le Doux, J. E. (1992) Differential contribution of amygdala and hippocampus to cued and contextual fear conditioning. *Behavioural Neuroscience*, **106**, 274–85.
Rapoport, J. (1989) *The Boy Who Couldn't Stop Washing*. London: Fontana.
Rickels, K. *et al.* (1988) Long term treatment of anxiety and risk of withdrawal. *Archives of General Psychiatry*, **45**, 444–50.
Rosvold, H. E. *et al.* (1954) Influence of amygdalectomy on social behaviour in monkeys. *Journal of Comparative and Physiological Psychology*, **47**, 173–8.
Rutlidge, L. L. and Hupka, R. B. (1985) The facial feedback hypothesis: Methodological concerns and new supporting evidence. *Motivation and Emotion*, **9**, 219–40.
Schachter, S. and Singer, J. E. (1962) Cognitive, social and physiological determinants of emotional state. *Psychological Review*, **69**, 379–99.
Silverstone, T. and Turner, P. (1988) *Drug Treatment in Psychiatry*. London: Routledge.
Snaith, R. P. (1984) Benzodiazepines on trial. *British Medical Journal*, **288**, 1379.
Squires, R. F. and Braestrup, C. (1977) Benzodiazepine receptors in the rat brain. *Nature*, **266**, 732–4.
Strack, F. *et al.* (1988) Inhibiting and facilitating conditions of the human smile: A non-obtrusive test of the facial feedback hypothesis. *Journal of Personality and Social Psychology*, **54**, 768–77.
Swerdo, S. E. *et al.* (1989) Cerebral glucose metabolism in childhood-onset obsessive–compulsive disorder. *Archives of General Psychiatry*, **46**, 518–23.
Thoren, P. *et al.* (1980) Clomipramine treatment of obsessive–compulsive disorder. *Archives of General Psychiatry*, **37**, 1281–5.

FURTHER READING

Bard, P. (1934) On emotional expression after decortication with some remarks on certain theoretical views. *Psychological Review*, **41**, 309–29.
Damasio, A. R. (1994) *Descartes' Error: Emotion, Reason and the Human Brain*. Putnam and Sons: New York.
Marks, I. M. *et al.* (1980) Clomipramine and exposure for obsessive compulsive rituals: 1. *British Journal of Psychiatry*, **136**, 1–25.
Marks, J. (1978) *The Benzodiazepines: Use, Overuse, Misuse, Abuse*. Lancaster: MTP Press.
McNaughton, N. (1989) *Biology and Emotion*. Cambridge: Cambridge University Press.
Panksepp, J. (1998) *Affective Neuroscience: The Foundation of Human and Animal Emotions*. Oxford: Oxford University Press.
Plutchik, R. (1994) *The Psychology and Biology of Emotion*. New York: Harper & Row.
Stein, N. L., Leventhal, B. and Trabasso, T. (eds) (1990) *Psychological and Biological Approaches to Emotion*. Hillsdale, NJ: Lawrence Erlbaum.

 Multiple choice questions

1. The sympathetic nervous system is primarily concerned with ________________ whereas the parasympathetic system is primarily concerned with ____________________.

(a) mobilising the body in response to stress, maintaining the body at rest
(b) the release of adrenaline, the release of glucocorticoids
(c) activation of skeletal muscle, activation of smooth muscle
(d) all of the above

2. According to the James–Lange theory it is the ________________________ that tells the conscious brain it is experiencing emotion.

(a) visual sensation of the emotional stimulus
(b) hypothalamus
(c) neural feedback from the pattern of body changes
(d) amygdala

3. According to Walter Cannon:

(a) animals without a sympathetic nervous system can still experience emotion
(b) animals with complete transection of the spinal cord can still experience emotion
(c) emotions can be 'experienced' before the body has time to react
(d) all of the above

4. According to the Cannon–Bard theory of emotion:

(a) the autonomic nervous system responds in exactly the same way to all types of emotion
(b) there is a different pattern of body activity for each emotion
(c) cognitive appraisal of the emotional situation has to take place *before* activation of the sympathetic nervous system can occur
(d) the autonomic nervous system has no role to play in emotion

5. Philip Bard found that lesions of the cerebral cortex:

(a) abolished aggression
(b) abolished the behavioural manifestations of emotion
(c) produced highly emotional and aggressive animals
(d) had no effect on aggression and emotion (providing the hypothalamus was intact)

6. Walter Hess found that electrical stimulation of the ________________ produced sympathetic arousal and aggressive attack.

(a) lateral hypothalamus
(b) frontal cortex
(c) amygdala
(d) medial hypothalamus

7. When subjects were unknowingly injected with adrenaline and then placed into a room with an 'angry' confederate (Schachter and Singer 1962) they:

(a) also tended to become angry
(b) showed little emotional change
(c) experienced palpitations and fear
(d) scored higher marks on an aggression questionnaire

8. According to the facial feedback hypothesis:

(a) people tend to judge emotions in others by their facial expression
(b) emotion has evolved in order to facilitate social expression
(c) simulated facial expressions can influence a person's emotion
(d) emotion is primarily the result of feedback from facial expression and has little to do with the hypothalamus (at least in humans)

9. Which of the following structures *does not* belong to the limbic system?

(a) hypothalamus
(b) hippocampus
(c) amygdala
(d) striatum

10. In the Papez circuit, the ________________ projects to the hypothalamus via a long arcing pathway called the fornix

(a) amygdala
(b) hippocampus
(c) frontal cortex
(d) cingulate cortex

11. The main symptoms of the Kluver–Bucy syndrome are:

(a) markedly decreased aggression and docility
(b) psychic blindness
(c) bizarre sexual behaviour
(d) all of the above

12. The amygdala contains the:

(a) corticomedial nuclei
(b) basolateral nuclei
(c) central nucleus
(d) all of the above

13. Rosvold *et al.* (1954) found that when they made an amygdala lesion in a male monkey that was ranked third in the dominance status of its group:

(a) it quickly dropped to near the bottom of the dominance hierarchy
(b) it had no effect on its dominance ranking
(c) it surprisingly moved to the top of the dominance hierarchy
(d) it was attacked by both males and females and was forced out of the troupe

14. Bruce Kapp has shown that neurons in the amygdala fire in response to:

(a) aggressive encounters
(b) unconditioned (innate) sensory stimuli
(c) conditioned (learnt) fearful stimuli
(d) sympathetic stimulation

15. Joseph Le Doux found that lesions to the _______________ completely eliminated conditioned emotional responding to a tone stimulus.

(a) auditory cortex
(b) subcortical auditory structures (auditory thalamus and inferior colliculi)
(c) hippocampus
(d) hypothalamus

16. What part of the brain lies at the base of the frontal lobe just above the bones that form the eye sockets?

(a) prefrontal cortex
(b) dorsolateral area
(c) orbitofrontal region
(d) subiculum

17. The first person to undertake psychosurgery using a leucotome was:

(a) Walter Cannon
(b) John Fulton and Carlyle Jacobsen
(c) Egas Moniz
(d) Phineas Gage

18. Which is by far the most common type of clinical anxiety disorder?

(a) obsessive–compulsive disorder
(b) panic disorder
(c) post-traumatic stress
(d) phobia

19. Benzodiazepines exert their effect in the brain by altering activity at the __________ receptor.

(a) cholinergic
(b) dopaminergic
(c) serotonergic
(d) GABAergic

20. Which of the following substances does not act on the benzodiazepine receptor?

(a) diazepam (valium)
(b) chlordiazepoxide (librium)
(c) buspirone
(d) β-carbolines

6 Sleep and circadian rhythms

IN THIS CHAPTER

- EEG brain waves associated with waking and sleep states
- The characteristics of slow wave and REM sleep
- The functions of sleep
- The effects of sleep deprivation
- The neurological basis of sleep
- Circadian rhythms
- The role of the suprachiasmatic nucleus
- The pineal gland and melatonin

Introduction

The urge to sleep is an extremely powerful one. We spend approximately one-third of our lives asleep – that is, roughly 25 years of an average life in a state of inertia where normal consciousness is suspended. Sleep occurs in all mammals (and probably all vertebrates as well) which indicates that whatever sleep does, it presumably must serve a very important purpose. Indeed, the instinct to sleep is never far away. We crave sleep if we are deprived of it, and animal studies have shown that sleep deprivation, if prolonged, has fatal consequences. Thus, sleep is an essential behaviour. But, why do we sleep? On first sight, the likeliest answer appears to be that it is a form of rest or recuperation. But, on closer inspection, it is clear that sleep is more than just the brain (or body) 'resting'. In fact, as we shall see, sleep is an integrated neural state consisting of several distinct stages that are under the control of various brainstem nuclei. In other words, sleep is not simply a passive winding down in response to tiredness, but a series of different arousal states that are actively produced by the brain. However, why the brain should go to the bother of producing sleep is an enigma. Indeed, one leading sleep researcher has even gone as far as to say that, after 50 years of research, all we can conclude about the function of sleep is that it overcomes sleepiness! (Horne 1988, p. 1). Clearly, there is much more to sleep than this, although proving the point is far from easy. We also have the tantalising puzzle of dreaming which accompanies certain stages of sleep to add further spice and interest to the mystery.

What is sleep?

It is tempting to think of sleep as a resting state that is the opposite of being awake. In fact, until the 1950s most researchers believed that this was indeed the case. However, in 1953 this view changed with the work of Nathaniel Kleitman and Eugene Aserinsky who were the first to examine sleep in humans using the **electroencephalogram (EEG)**. This technique, first invented by the German psychiatrist Hans Berger in 1929, records electrical brain activity by means of electrodes placed on the scalp. The electrodes detect the very small voltages of neurons firing beneath the skull and the brain's protective meninges, and this activity is then fed into an amplifier which increases the electrical signal many thousands of times. The results of this recording are then displayed on a polygraph consisting of a moving strip of paper and marker pens for each electrode placement.

It might be expected that this procedure, with each electrode recording from many tens of thousands (if not millions) of neurons, would produce a random and disorganised mess of neural activity. However, Berger found that this was not the case. In fact, he showed that the electrical activity of the brain was highly regular and wave-like, which indicated that large numbers of neurons (in the cerebral cortex at least) were firing in a synchronised pattern 'in beat' together. Moreover, Berger identified two different types of firing pattern that occurred during waking, which he called **alpha** and **beta waves** (Figure 6.1). Beta waves were the most common and characterised by low-amplitude and very irregular (desynchronised) waves that varied between 13 and 30 cycles (Hz) or 'beats' per second. This pattern occurred when subjects were wide awake, aroused, or typically engaged in some mental activity. During periods of rest and relaxation, however, the brain waves slowed down (8–12 Hz) resulting in a more synchronised 'high-amplitude' pattern of activity called alpha waves.

When Kleitman and Aserinsky began to examine brain activity during sleep, however, they discovered other types of EEG activity that did not occur during waking. In fact, they showed for the first time that sleep contained two distinct types of EEG pattern that were associated with very different forms of sleep – **slow-wave sleep (SWS)** and **rapid eye movement sleep (REM)**. Slow-wave sleep was identified by EEG activity whose 'beat' was much slower than that normally found during the awake state and, furthermore, it could also be divided into four distinct stages (stages 1–4). In contrast, rapid eye movement sleep was characterised by EEG activity that resembled more

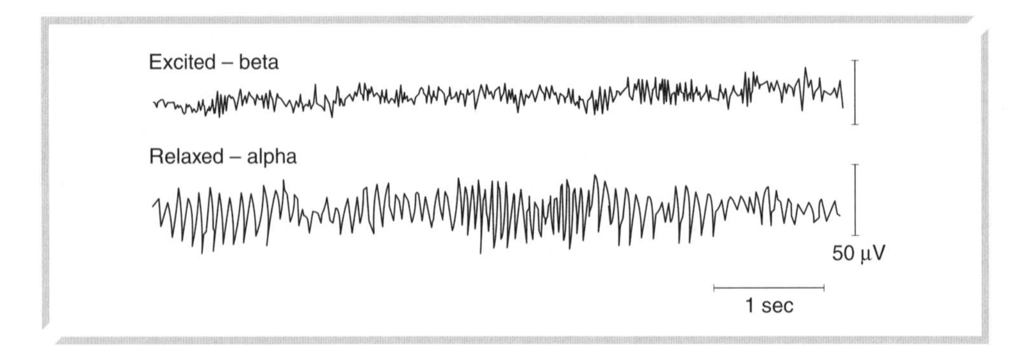

Figure 6.1 Alpha and beta EEG waves.

closely the type of brain waves found during waking. As its name suggests, this type of sleep was also accompanied by eye movements that darted about (under the eyelids), not unlike the eye movements that occur when we are awake.

The characteristics of slow-wave sleep

As mentioned, slow-wave sleep is defined by the presence of slower brain waves than those typically found in waking. The onset of sleep (stage 1 sleep) is characterised by **theta waves** that are slightly slower (4–7 Hz) than the alpha waves (8–12 Hz) that occur when we are relaxed but awake. Although the first signs of theta waves normally signify the transition between waking and sleeping, if the person is wakened during this stage he or she typically reports being drowsy rather than asleep. As sleep becomes deeper, however, stage 2 sleep is reached in which the person is now 'properly' asleep. This stage is again characterised by theta activity, except this time it is frequently interrupted with brief (0.5 second) bursts of 12–15 Hz activity called sleep spindles. In stage 3 sleep, the frequency of sleep spindles declines and the EEG begins to show the first signs of very slow (1–4 Hz) high-amplitude waves called **delta waves**. Finally, stage 4 is reached which is the deepest sleep state and the most difficult to be wakened from. This stage is similar to the previous stage, except now delta waves predominate and make up at least 50 per cent of the brain waves (see Figure 6.2).

There are also other important changes that take place in the brain (and body) during slow-wave sleep. For example, the energy consumption of the brain as measured by cerebral blood flow gradually declines over the stages, falling to about 25 per cent of its waking value by the fourth stage of sleep. Thus, the brain appears to be slowing down and becoming more 'restful'. Similarly, the body also shows signs of resting – muscle tone is reduced and the sleeping person is generally inactive (perhaps only changing his or her body position every 10 or 20 minutes). In addition, the parasympathetic nervous system becomes more active resulting in decreases in heart rate, blood pressure, respiration and body temperature (although activity of the gastrointestinal system increases). In short, slow-wave sleep seems to produce a state of relaxation.

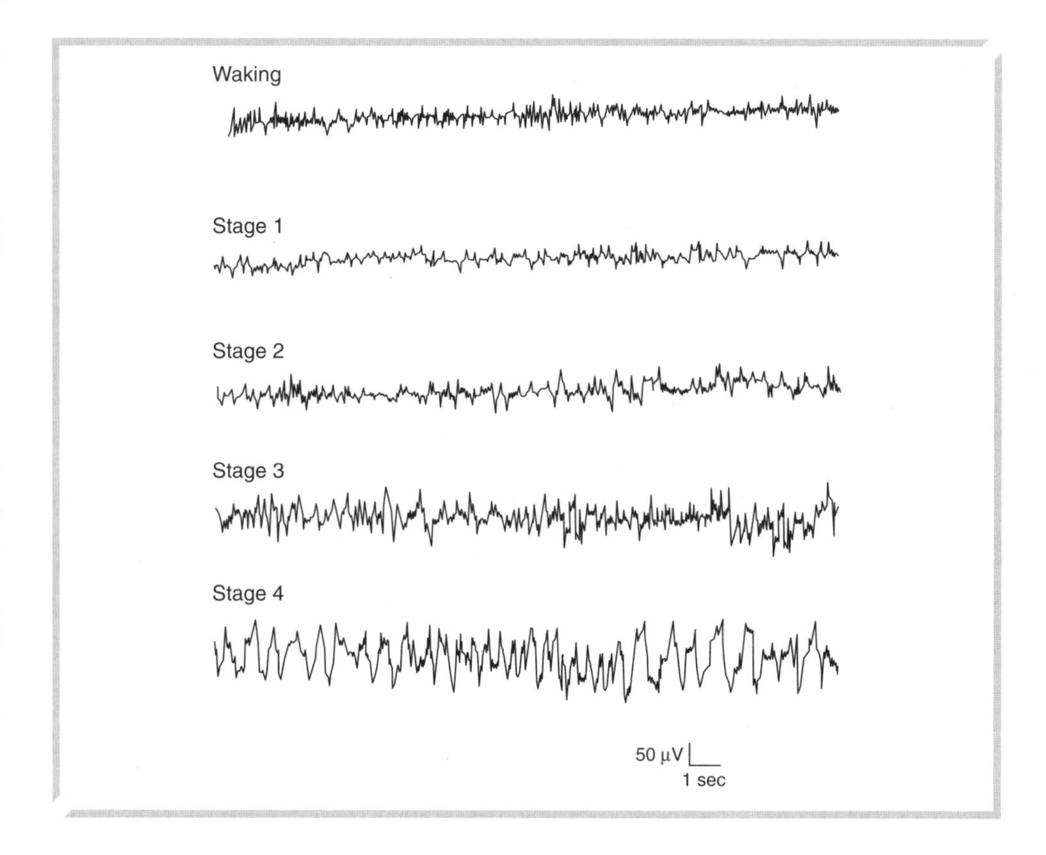

Figure 6.2 The stages of sleep as recorded from the EEG.

The characteristics of REM sleep

After about 90 minutes of slow-wave sleep, an abrupt and dramatic change takes place in the brain's electrical activity. The EEG pattern suddenly enters a highly desynchronised state in which the brain waves are faster and smaller (e.g. they have less amplitude) than before. Moreover, these waves appear to be very similar to the desynchronised beta-wave patterns that occur during arousal and waking. Indeed, if oxygen consumption and blood flow are measured in the cerebral cortex at this point they are found to be close to levels found in waking. This is REM sleep, and it appears that the brain has now decided to leave its slow-wave resting state behind.

Changes also take place in the body. For example, there is a general loss of muscle tone with the body becoming effectively paralysed, apart from odd 'twitches' involving facial and eye muscles, and those of the fingers and toes. Indeed, because the activity of the body and brain are so different (i.e. the brain appears to be awake but the body is unresponsive) this form of sleep has been called 'paradoxical'. Unfortunately, this term is somewhat misleading because the lack of muscle tone probably acts as an important safety device to stop the dreamers acting out their dreams (see next paragraph). REM sleep also causes increased activation of the sympathetic nervous system (e.g. there are periods of cardiac acceleration and increased blood pressure with irregular changes in breathing). Furthermore, in males there is often penile erections and, in females, increased vaginal blood flow. Obviously, with the exception of the reduced muscle tone, it can hardly be said that the body is in a restful state during this phase of sleep.

There is also another very important characteristic of REM sleep – it is the main stage of sleep in which we dream. For example, Dement and Kleitman (1957) found that when people were wakened during REM sleep, 80 per cent of them reported that they had been dreaming, although this figure fell to just 20 per cent when subjects were wakened from slow-wave sleep. The two types of dream also tend to be different with REM dreams typically following a narrative (or story line) with vivid or intense situations that on waking often appear bizarre or illogical, whereas slow-wave dreams often involve repetition of ideas that do not progress (Hobson 1989). In fact, night terrors in children, and nightmares where the person feels 'trapped', are more likely to occur in slow-wave sleep. Despite this, dreams are often quickly forgotten and subjects who are wakened only minutes after the end of a REM period rarely remember dreaming. It is probably the case that all people dream, but as the dreams are quickly forgotten this may explain why some people claim that they never dream.

The sleep cycle

What normally happens after we have undergone a period of REM sleep? The simple answer is that we fall back into slow-wave sleep (unless we wake up!). Thus, slow-wave sleep and REM sleep occur in repeating cycles that follow a regular pattern throughout the night (see Figure 6.3). As we have seen, the first cycle of slow-wave sleep normally lasts for about 90 minutes, and this is followed by a period of REM sleep. The four stages of slow-wave sleep and the subsequent REM stage are called a **sleep cycle** and because, on average, people sleep for around 6–8 hours per night, this means that most people will undergo four or five sleep cycles during a normal sleep. In fact, it appears that all mammals show this cycle (although the length of the cycle varies considerably between species) with slow-wave sleep taking up a far larger proportion of the cycle than REM (this is also true for humans who spend around 80 per cent of sleeping time in slow-wave sleep and the remainder in REM sleep).

Despite this, in humans, the relative proportions of slow-wave sleep and REM in each cycle change as the sleep progresses. For example, although the REM periods will generally occur at regular 90-minute intervals, the actual amount of time spent in REM sleep will tend to increase – from about 20 minutes during the first REM period to around 40 minutes in the last. This means that as sleep continues the time spent in slow-wave sleep gradually gets less and less. In fact, things are even more complex than this because slow-wave sleep also gets shallower, with stages 3 and 4 dropping out of the cycle. Thus, by the time the last sleep cycle occurs (just before waking), it may consist entirely of stage 2 slow-wave sleep (stage 1 is a transitional stage that only occurs when the person first falls asleep).

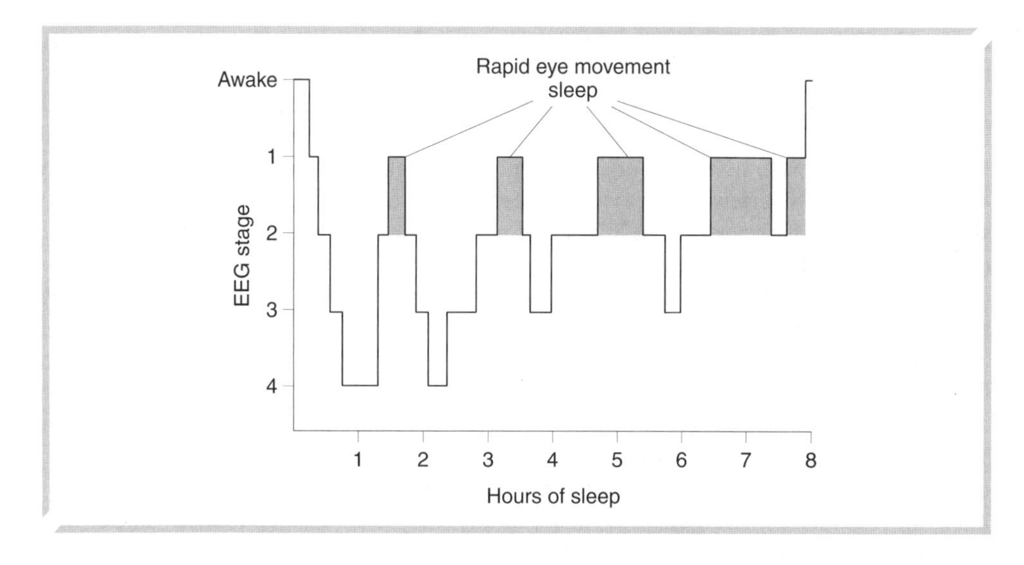

Figure 6.3 The sequence of EEG stages during an average night's sleep.

Why do we sleep?

As far as we know, all vertebrates (mammals, birds and reptiles) sleep, although only mammals (and some birds) apparently show REM activity. However, even the simplest creatures have a rest–activity cycle that, in most instances, like sleep, follows a **circadian rhythm** (from the Latin words *circa* meaning 'about' and *dies* for 'day'). Thus, cycles of rest and activity appear to be an essential feature of life, and it would appear that sleep is a variation on this basic requirement. But why have cycles of rest and activity – or sleep?

From an evolutionary perspective it is hard to avoid the conclusion that sleep must have bestowed some advantage to the animals that indulged in it, otherwise it would never have evolved. Indeed, it seems clear that, for whatever reason, each species has evolved its own characteristic pattern of sleep. For example, giant sloths sleep for about 20 hours each day; cats for about 14 hours; humans around 8 hours; and horses around 3 hours. But why have animals developed these different sleep characteristics? And, what is it telling us about the functions of sleep? Surprisingly, there is no satisfactory answer to these questions.

Most theories that attempt to explain the reasons for sleep fall into one of two categories: those that highlight the importance of body restoration, and those that emphasise evolutionary adaptation. The first theory suggests that the body needs regular periods in which to rest and recuperate. The implication is that being awake impairs the functioning of the body in some way, and that sleep is needed to return it back to its optimal state. This theory makes intuitive sense, not least because the body does appear to be in a more restful state when it is in slow-wave sleep. But, if sleep is restorative, what exactly is it restoring? Sadly, this theory flounders on the simple fact that no one has yet clearly identified a specific physiological process that is restored by sleep. For example, if the function of sleep was to repair the daily effects of wear and tear, then one might predict that heavy exercise would increase the duration of sleep. However, in general, this seems not to be the case. A number of studies have examined this issue and, in a review of the evidence, Horne has concluded that subjects typically show little increase in sleep following increased mental activity or heavy exercise (Horne 1988). But, maybe we only need to look at the animal world to see problems with this theory. For example, the giant sloth sleeps around 20 hours a day, yet is clearly not the most active of animals!

Adaptive theories of sleep function come in many forms, but they all share the fundamental idea that sleep has evolved to enhance the survival of the species. For example, it is possible that predatory animals (such as lions) have evolved a rest pattern that allows them to sleep for long uninterrupted periods because there is little danger from other predators. However, smaller animals or grazing animals (such as zebras) need to be much more vigilant and, consequently, they tend to sleep for shorter periods of time (e.g. a zebra sleeps only about 2 or 3 hours a day). There are probably many other types of evolutionary explanation: for example, in some species, sleep may have evolved as an adaptive response to conserve energy rather than to avoid unnecessary danger; or perhaps the pattern of sleep is determined by the amount of time the animal has to spend searching for food and eating. Indeed, it would be surprising if sleep has not been modified by evolutionary pressures in this way. However, there is one major problem with adaptation theories and that is: animals simply have to sleep! Perhaps this can best be illustrated by the case of the Bottlenose dolphin which must continually break the surface of the water to breathe. Remarkably, these animals 'sleep' with one hemisphere at a time – that is, the two sides of the brain take turns to sleep and one hemisphere always remains awake to guide behaviour. Thus, it is difficult not to agree that sleep must provide some vital need and, consequently, restoration (or something similar) must presumably take place.

Evidence supporting the restorative hypothesis has come from the finding that, in humans, a huge increase in **growth hormone** release occurs during the first few hours of sleep. In fact, this surge of growth hormone appears to be directly linked to the onset of sleep since it does not occur during periods of sleep deprivation. The main role of this hormone in children is to promote growth, and in adults it also stimulates the growth of cells and increases protein metabolism – exactly the type of effect one would expect if it was providing a restorative function. Despite this, the restorative role of growth hormone in sleep remains unproved. For example, it has been pointed out that protein synthesis requires both a steady release of amino acids into the blood, and insulin to allow them to be taken up into cells. Yet, neither of these two things apparently occurs at night (e.g. night-time levels of insulin and amino acids are low). In fact, it has been suggested that the surge in growth hormone may occur simply to spare the use of protein as an energy source thus stimulating the breakdown of fat instead (Horne 1988). In other words, the release of growth hormone may have nothing to do with reconstitution! However, there is still considerable room for doubt over this conclusion (e.g. see Adam and Oswald 1977; Hodgson 1991), and this is particularly the case regarding the repair of brain tissue (Dorociak 1990).

Sleep across the life span

Another way to consider the possible functions of sleep is to examine how sleep patterns change across the life span (see Figure 6.4). It is well known that newborn infants sleep a great deal (e.g. they generally sleep for around 16 to 17 hours a day), but what is less widely known is that much of this is REM sleep. In fact, about 50 per cent of a newborn infant's sleep is made up of REM, and this proportion is even greater in premature infants (e.g. a baby born after 30 weeks of gestation will spend about 80 per cent of its sleep in the REM state). However, although the very young infant shows rapid eye movements there is no motor paralysis at this early stage. Instead there are spasmodic movements of the hands, feet and facial muscles, and occasionally the movements include the facial expressions associated with crying, anger and rejection (the first smile that the infant makes is normally made during REM sleep). As the infant develops through the first year, however, the percentage of time spent in REM decreases, falling from 50 per cent at 3 months, to 33 per cent at 8 months, and stabilising at about 25 per cent at one year of age (which is roughly the same proportion of REM found in young adults).

There are also other differences between a young infant's sleep and that of an adult. For example, an infant's sleep cycles are considerably faster, with each cycle taking around 60 minutes, compared to 90 in the adult. Moreover, there is a tendency for babies to enter their first REM state immediately upon falling asleep, unlike adults where this occurs at about 90 minutes after sleep onset. It is also interesting to note that after the first 8 months of life the child sleeps for around 14–15 hours a day (i.e. the child

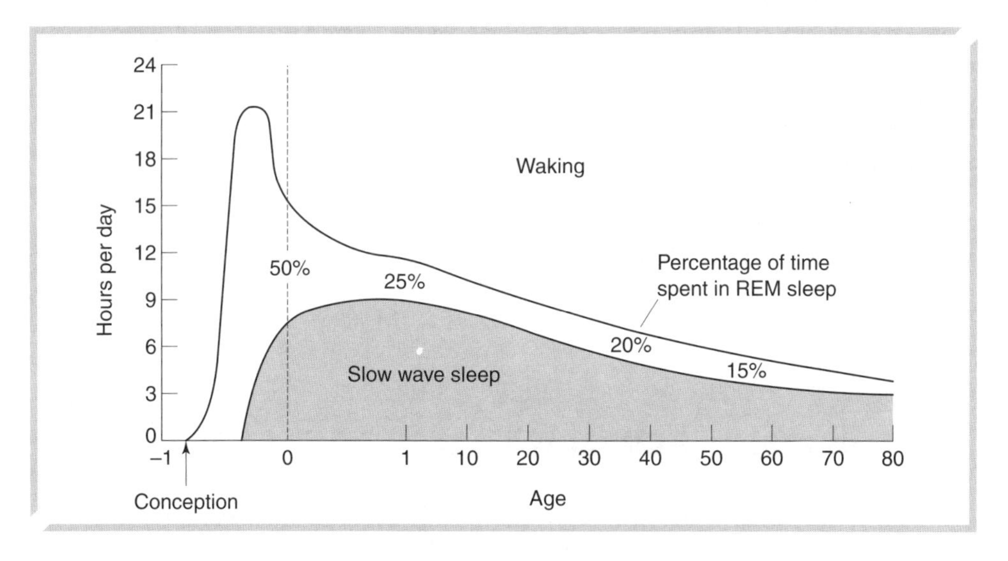

Figure 6.4 The duration and pattern of sleep as a function of age.

is awake for an extra 3 hours each day), and that the 'lost' 3 hours of sleep is made up almost entirely of REM sleep (Hobson 1989).

The fact that there is a high amount of REM sleep in the first year of life (and during foetal development) has led some researchers to argue that this form of sleep has a particularly important role in neural development and the maturation of the central nervous system. For example, Roffwarg *et al.* (1966) proposed that REM sleep plays a role in the development of the nervous system which is not unlike that of physical exercise in the development of muscles. Just as muscles require motor activity to develop properly, so Roffwarg and colleagues argued that the nervous system appears to require exposure to sensory stimulation at certain critical stages of development (e.g. kittens reared in total darkness from birth show impaired vision and degeneration of cells in the visual cortex). Thus, REM sleep may serve a similar role by ensuring that the cerebral cortex receives the 'sensory stimulation' that is crucial to the development of nerve cells during a critical period. In support of this theory, it has been shown that REM deprivation in rats, starting some 11 or 12 days after birth, is associated with a reduction in size of the cerebral cortex (Mirmiran 1986). The problem with this theory, however, is that it does not explain why REM sleep (and dreaming) continues after the brain has fully developed. An alternative theory is that REM is necessary for the storage of information in the brain to allow learning and memory to take place. Indeed, it is generally accepted that we learn more during our first year of life than at any other time in our life span, and perhaps this is reflected in the time we spend in REM sleep.

The maturation of the sleep cycle normally occurs by early adolescence, at which point the young adult will probably sleep between 6 and 8 hours each night, with about a quarter of this time spent in REM. However, as ageing takes place, the characteristics of sleep change yet further. The most striking change is the decline in the amount of time spent sleeping, which falls to approximately 4–6 hours by the age of 50. But, even more dramatic is the decline in slow-wave sleep, particularly stages 3 and 4, which by the age of 60 years is typically only 50 per cent of what it was at the age of 20 years. This decline appears to start relatively early (perhaps even in the late 20s) and its continual loss means that, by the age of 90, stages 3 and 4 slow-wave sleep have virtually disappeared (humans are not alone in this as a similar loss also occurs in other mammals). No one knows for certain why this decline occurs, although it may be related to diminished cognitive abilities that can accompany ageing. Support for this theory comes from evidence showing that there is an especially marked reduction of slow-wave sleep in people with Alzheimer's disease. In contrast to the decline of slow-wave sleep, however, it appears that the relative amounts of REM sleep are well maintained until extreme old age.

Box 6.1 HOW MUCH SLEEP DO WE NEED?

'Early to bed, early to rise, makes a man healthy, wealthy and wise' is a saying that many people would agree with. But is it really true? In fact, there are many notable individuals whose sleeping habits do not (or did not) follow this advice. For example, Napoleon needed little sleep. Apparently, he went to bed about midnight and slept for about 2 hours, at which point he got up and worked until 5 a.m., and then went back to bed for another 2 hours. In fact, Napoleon is even quoted as saying that 5 hours' sleep is enough for a man, 6 for a woman and 7 for a fool. Few would agree with Napoleon today – but, nevertheless, there is little doubt that Napoleon was not alone in his sleep habits. For example, Winston Churchill worked until 3 or 4 a.m. and was up again by 8 a.m. (although he generally took a 2-hour nap in the afternoon), and it is well known that Margaret Thatcher only needed a few hours' sleep each night. On the other hand, there are others who needed much longer. For example, Albert Einstein apparently enjoyed spending 10 hours a night in bed where apparently he 'discovered' crucial aspects of his relativity theory (Borbely 1986).

What then are the norms for patterns of sleeping in 'normal' individuals? According to Empson (1993), surveys have shown that adults sleep on average for 7½ hours with a standard deviation of about 1 hour. This means that about two-thirds of the population can be expected to sleep between 6½ and 8½ hours per night – and that another 16 per cent regularly sleep over 8½ hours with a further 16 per cent sleeping under 6½ hours. However, healthy individuals who regularly sleep less than 5 hours (and in some cases as little as 2 hours each night) represent a sizeable minority. For example, Jones and Oswald (1968) verified in a sleep laboratory the cases of two middle-aged Australian men who claimed that they only needed 2–3 hours' sleep per night. Interestingly, not only did their sleep contain relatively more deep sleep (stages 3 and 4) but it was also made up of increased amounts of REM which occurred soon after the onset of sleep. Perhaps the shortest 'healthy' sleeper examined by sleep researchers is the case of Miss M, a 70-year-old retired nurse who only slept for about an hour each day (Meddis 1977). Although this lack of sleep is unusual there are nevertheless other individuals where similar sleep patterns have been reported.

Despite this, it is probably the case that all people sleep. There have been some claims to the contrary, but these have rarely stood up to closer scrutiny. For example, Oswald and Adam (1980) reported the case of a man who claimed that he had not slept for 10 years following a car accident. When examined for several nights in a sleep laboratory it was found that he remained awake for the first few nights. However, by the fifth day he became sleepy and fell asleep and snored loudly until his wife woke him 2½ hours later! According to Oswald this was a clear case of a short sleeper who attempted to make some profit out of his alleged disability (he had been awarded £12,000 at the insurance company's expense). It is perhaps fair to say that on the basis of this, and other reports, no healthy person has yet been found who does not require at least a small amount of sleep.

The effects of sleep deprivation

Another way in which investigators have attempted to understand the function of sleep is to look at the effects of sleep deprivation. The reasoning behind this procedure is simple: a change in behaviour or decrement in performance caused by keeping an individual (or animal) awake can thus be attributed to the lack of sleep. Unfortunately, sleep deprivation in humans has not been so easy to interpret, because in most cases but not all, it appears to have relatively little consistent effect other than to make the person feel very sleepy! A famous example of the adverse effects of sleep deprivation is the case of Peter Tripp, a disc jockey who attempted to stay awake for 200 hours as a publicity stunt to raise money for charity. He made radio broadcasts from a glass booth in New York's Times Square (in full view of the public) and was constantly attended (in order to prevent sleeping). At first he suffered no problems and it was only during the last days of his deprivation that Tripp began to experience difficulties. The first signs were slurred speech followed by night-time auditory hallucinations and paranoia. Indeed, by the end of his ordeal he believed that he was being drugged and refused to co-operate with his helpers (Dement 1976). It had taken about a week's sleep deprivation to produce these effects and if there was an implication, it was that prolonged sleep deprivation might have adverse effects on mental health.

However, this interpretation was put into considerable doubt by the case of a 17-year-old college student from San Diego called Randy Gardner who, in 1965, challenged the sleep deprivation record of 260 hours (10 days and 20 hours) that was, at the time, given as the world record in the *Guinness Book of Records*. Gardner was constantly under the scrutiny of two schoolmates and, for the last 5 days, he was closely followed by William Dement and George Gulevich from Stanford University. During his attempt, Gardner experienced a number of difficulties including fatigue, irritability and memory problems, and by the seventh day his EEG no longer showed the normal patterns of alpha waves associated with being awake. Despite this, his symptoms showed considerable fluctuation, and on the last night he went to an amusement arcade for several hours where he played William Dement at a penny basketball game and won every single game! Furthermore, after breaking the record, he gave a coherent and impeccable account of himself at a national press conference. He then slept for 15 hours (followed by another night's sleep of 10½ hours) after which he appeared to show no adverse effects from the ordeal.

The cases of Peter Tripp and Randy Gardner have not provided a great deal of illuminating evidence concerning the functions of sleep, and other deprivation studies have arguably not done much better. For example, Horne (1978) has reviewed over 50 studies in which humans have been deprived of sleep for varying lengths of time, and found that the main effect appears to be on the performance of complex mental or physiological tasks requiring a steady degree of concentration. Changes in personality, such as those experienced by Peter Tripp (i.e. confusion and suspicion), are also sometimes found, although they are not inevitable. Nevertheless, all things considered, the results from these studies do not provide convincing evidence that sleep is an absolutely vital process. This conclusion has also been supported from other lines of evidence. For example, Lavie *et al.* (1984) first reported the case of a 33-year-old man

(YH) who, as a young man in the Israeli army, suffered a shrapnel injury to the brain which resulted in his having almost no REM sleep. In fact, on 3 out of 8 nights in which he was tested in a sleep laboratory, it was found that he engaged in no REM whatsoever, and on the remaining 5 nights the average time spent in REM was 6 minutes. Moreover, this REM deficit did not seem to produce any ill-effects since after the injury YH had completed high school, was accepted at law school, successfully graduated, and went on to become a successful lawyer (Lavie 1996).

With this case study in mind, it might come as a surprise, therefore, to find out that following periods of sleep deprivation, the brain attempts to make up for lost sleep. For example, a person who is deprived of sleep for 24 hours will usually make up 100 per cent of the 'sleep debt' in a day or two (although the recovery of sleep may not be complete if sleep deprivation is more prolonged). Moreover, the brain appears particularly intent on recovering its REM sleep. For example, if subjects are deprived of REM (by being wakened every time they enter this phase of sleep) they normally show a 'rebound' of REM in their next main sleep period that is about 50 per cent above normal. In fact, if subjects are deprived of REM sleep for several days, the rebound effect may be as high as 90 per cent on their first night of sleeping, with increased REM recovery also continuing for several days. Clearly, this appears to be a perplexing finding when considering the case study of YH discussed above.

Sleep deprivation in animals

Although sleep deprivation in humans does not appear to produce any obvious life-threatening effects, the same cannot be said of other animals. One way of producing sleep deprivation in rodents is to use a carousel apparatus, which consists of two chambers in a Plexiglas cylinder that share a rotating turntable as a floor (Figure 6.5). A rat is placed in each chamber (with food and water) and implanted with electrodes that record sleep EEG and body temperature. One rat is designated as the sleep-deprived animal and the other its control. When EEG recordings show that the deprived rat is beginning to sleep, the floor automatically begins to rotate, thus forcing the 'sleeping' rat to fall into a shallow pool of water, or to walk backwards. But, of course, during the period while the deprived rat is awake (and the floor is motionless) the control animal can snatch periods of sleep. In this way the control animal gets exactly the same amount of exercise as the deprived rat, but gains more sleep.

In terms of producing sleep deprivation this procedure is very successful. For example, in one study it was found to reduce the amount of sleep by 87 per cent in the deprived condition and by 31 per cent in the control. But, most striking were the consequences of the forced deprivation. Although no effects were observed in the first 7 to 10 days (which interestingly is the limit in most human experiments), after this period the deprived rat began to show marked deterioration. For example, the rats began to look sick and they stopped grooming themselves. In addition, they started to lose weight (despite eating significantly more) and their body temperature declined. And, with continued sleep deprivation, these animals typically died within 2 to 3 weeks of their ordeal (Rechtschaffen *et al.* 1983).

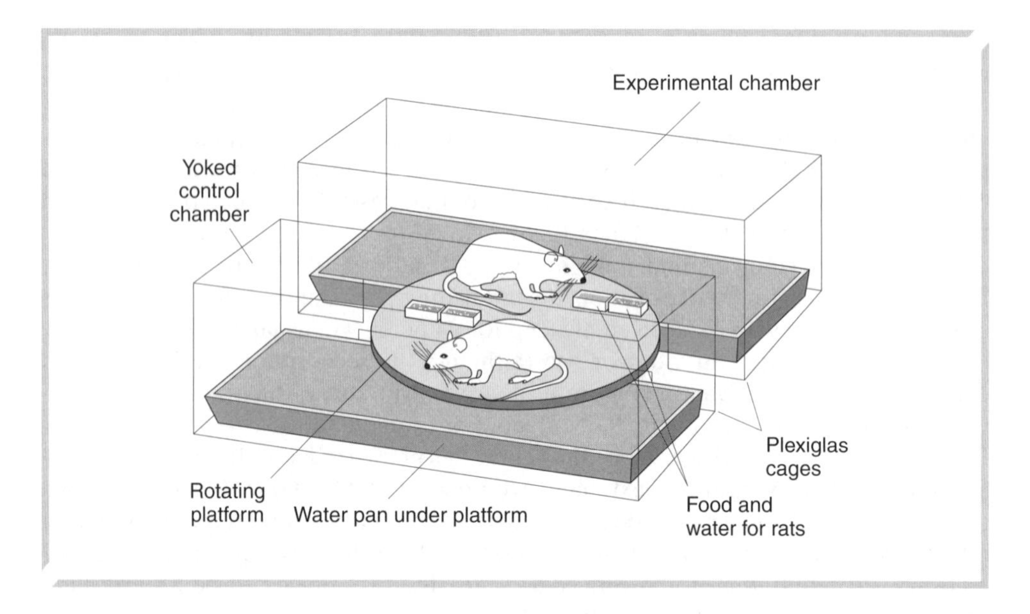

Figure 6.5 The sleep carousel apparatus as used by Rechtschaffen. (*Source*: From Neil R. Carlson, *Physiology of Behavior*, 6th edition. Copyright © 1998 by Allyn & Bacon. Reprinted by permission.)

What was the cause of death in these animals? Surprisingly, there is no clear-cut answer to this question. For example, when various body organs (such as brain, liver, spleen, stomach, thyroid and thymus) were examined no difference was found between the sleep-deprived and control animals. There was, however, an increase in the size of the adrenal glands and the release of cortisol in the sleep-deprived rats in the final few days before their death. Also there was a marked drop in body temperature at this time. Indeed, it was initially hypothesised that the sleep-deprived animals were dying because they could not maintain their body temperature. However, when the deprived rats were kept warm with increased external heating they still died. Thus, the cause of death is not known, although it is probably linked to some form of metabolic malfunction in which the brain can no longer adequately control the metabolism (or chemical reactions) of the body. Interestingly, if the animals were removed from the apparatus when near death and allowed to sleep, they quickly recovered and showed huge rebounds in REM sleep, which was sometimes 10 times greater than normal.

Despite these dramatic findings, it is not clear how far they can be extrapolated to human behaviour. For example, a human in a sleep deprivation study knows that they are being observed and that they can terminate the proceedings at any time. In contrast, the rat has no control over the situation and no way of 'knowing' if the situation is going to end. Thus, the stress placed on the animal is much more severe, and this may also be an important factor in producing the deleterious effects of sleep deprivation.

Brain mechanisms of sleep

Until the late 1930s it was widely believed that sleep was a passive process that simply occurred in response to sensory deprivation. In short, the idea was simple: deprive the brain of sensory input and the animal will fall asleep. One of the first to test this idea was Frederic Bremer (1937) who made a complete cut in the upper brainstem of cats (called a **cerveau isolé preparation**) which eliminated most of the sensory input reaching to the higher reaches of the brain (Figure 6.6). If the passive theory was correct then this operation should produce sleep. Indeed, this appeared to be the case, for when Bremer recorded EEG activity from the cerebral cortex of these animals he found that they showed almost continuous slow-wave sleep.

However, Bremer soon discovered a problem with his theory. When he made another cut – this time at the base of the brainstem where it joined the spinal cord (called **encéphale isolé**), which also severed sensory input – a different result occurred. This time, to his surprise, he found that the normal cycle of sleep and waking was not affected by this type of lesion (see Figure 6.7). Despite this, Bremer remained strongly convinced of the passive theory and he continued to explain his findings in terms of sensory stimulation. However, there was a much simpler explanation: sleep was an active process, and the mechanism for producing sleep and wakefulness was located somewhere between the two transections in the brainstem. In fact, this theory turned out to be the correct one.

The brainstem is a long tubular structure that enters the brain from the spinal cord, and the inner core of this structure, called the **reticular formation**, is now known to be

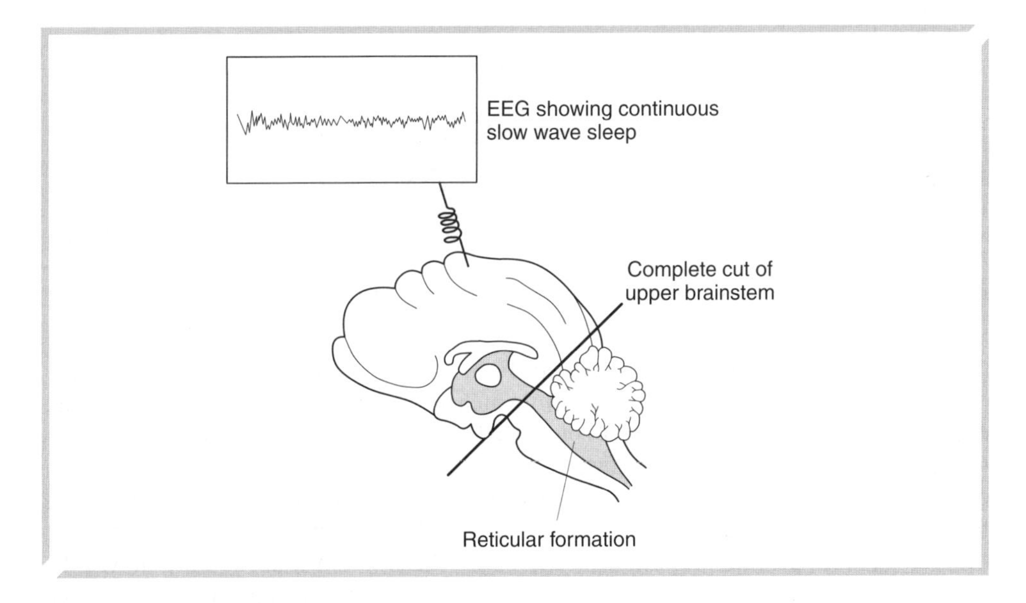

Figure 6.6 The cerveau isolé preparation.

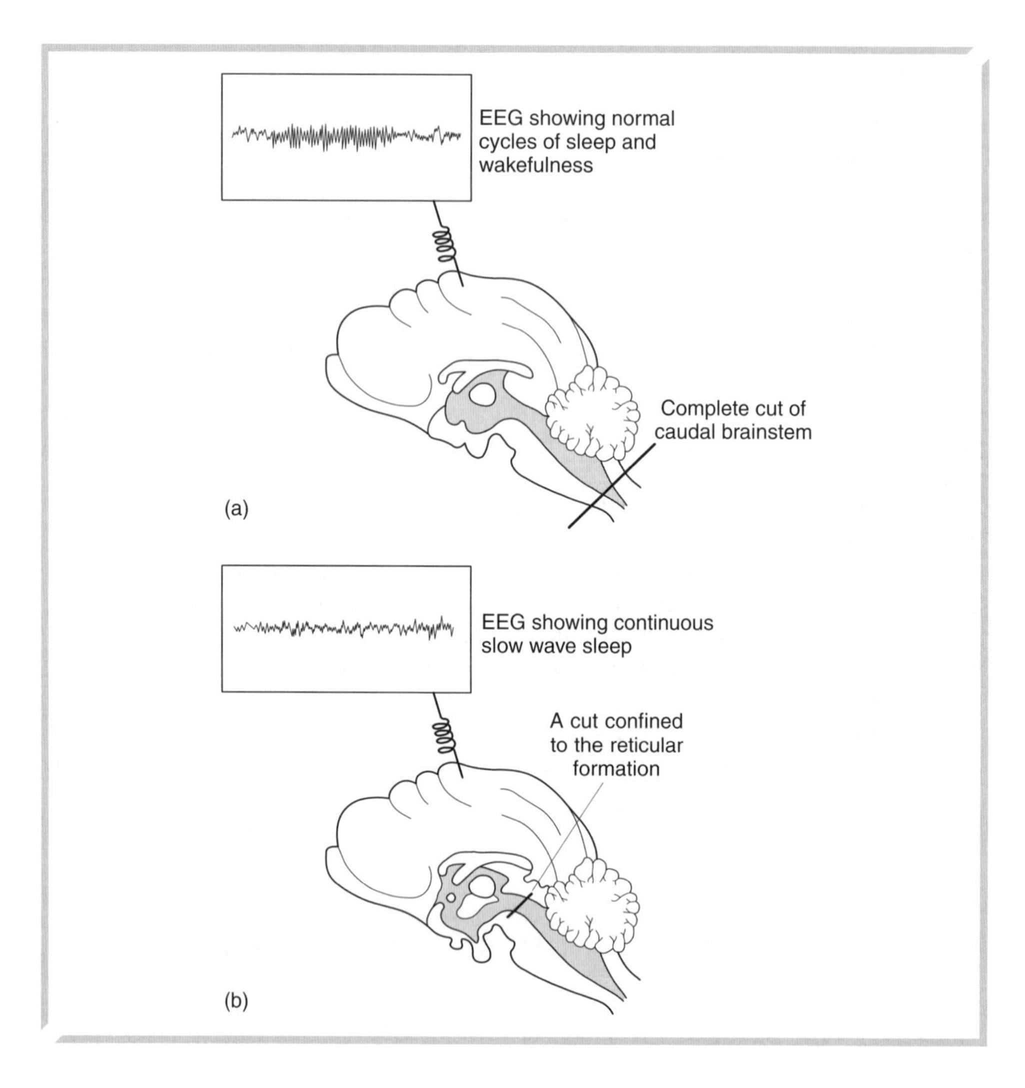

Figure 6.7 Two other types of brainstem lesion and their effect on sleep.

the crucial site involved in causing sleep. For example, lesions restricted to just the upper part of the reticular formation, but which spared the nearby ascending sensory pathways to the cortex, were found to produce EEG activity characteristic of deep sleep (Lindsley *et al.* 1949). In other words, lack of sensory input to the cortex could not explain this effect. Moreover, electrical stimulation of the reticular formation was found to cause exactly the type of desynchronised EEG patterns that were characteristic of waking (Moruzzi and Magoun 1949). In short, these findings showed that it was the brainstem, or rather the inner part of it called the reticular formation, that was the critical factor in the control of sleep and wakefulness (see also Figure 6.7).

The reticular activating system

The reticular formation (*reticulum* means 'net') is made up of a diffuse group of neurons (mainly interneurons) whose axons criss-cross through the medial part of the brainstem from the spinal cord up to the thalamus. It was once thought that the reticular formation was simply a random mass of neurons without structure or organisation, but this view is incorrect as it is now known to contain large numbers of different centres and pathways. Indeed (as we have seen in previous chapters), the reticular formation is involved in a wide range of functions (including autonomic activity, motor reflexes and sensory analysis) and it also receives input from widespread regions of the brain. Certain parts of the reticular formation also have another very important characteristic: they are capable of generating their own rhythms of electrical activity. Moreover, many of these regions send their axons out into a diffuse pathway that projects extensively to the thalamus and cerebral cortex (called the **ascending reticular activating system**). In fact, it is this system which is largely responsible for causing the wave-like patterns of neural activity in the cerebral cortex (as measured by the EEG) that accompany sleep and wakefulness (see Figure 6.8).

But what areas of the reticular formation are involved in the production of sleep? In the 1950s it was found that injections of anaesthetic into certain areas of the posterior reticular formation awakened sleeping cats and caused a desynchronised EEG that was characteristic of waking (Magni *et al.* 1957). This indicated there were specific areas in the brainstem where neural activity was actually needed (rather than its inhibition) to produce sleep. In other words, the reticular formation apparently contained sleep centres, which, if activated, caused sleep. The next important question was: Where were these sites located?

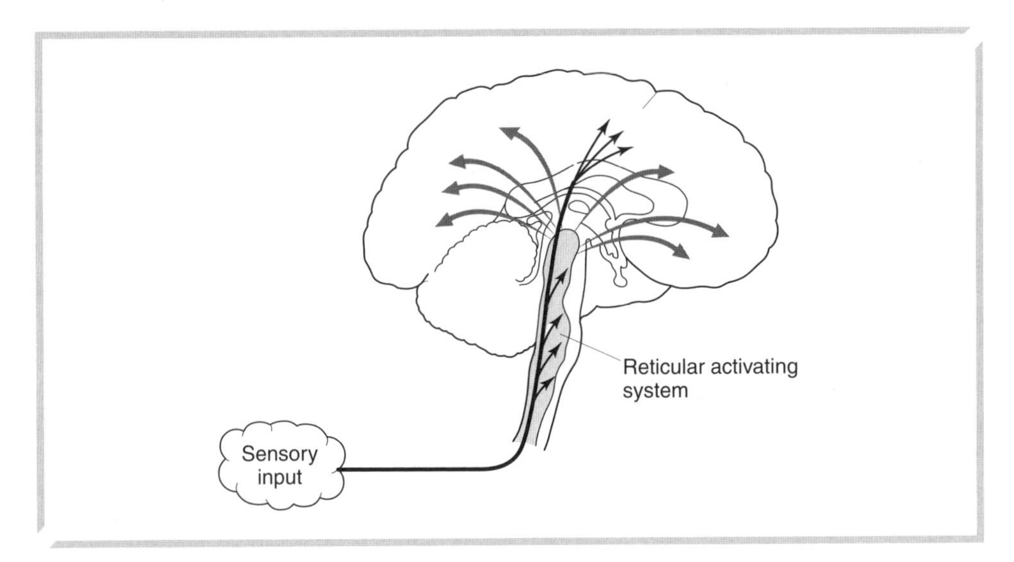

Figure 6.8 The ascending reticular system.

What areas of the brainstem are involved in sleep?

The first attempts to identify specific regions of the reticular formation that were involved in sleep took place in the early 1960s. This search was assisted by the development of new histofluorescent techniques that allowed the visualisation of certain neurotransmitters in the brain along with their pathways. Two neurotransmitters that were mapped-out in this way were **noradrenaline** and **serotonin**. Although neuron fibres containing these neurochemicals were found to innervate large areas of the brain (including the cerebral cortex) their site of origin was traced back to small structures in the reticular formation. In short, the site of noradrenaline fibres was found to be the **locus coeruleus** and the site of serotonin fibres were the **raphe nuclei** (see Chapter 1). Moreover, both were located close to each other in the **pons region** of the brainstem that had also been implicated in the production of sleep.

These new histological techniques also enabled the raphe and locus coeruleus to be lesioned with a reasonable degree of precision. In 1966, the French researcher Michel Jouvet destroyed the raphe (and parts of the adjacent reticular formation) in cats, and found that this abolished slow-wave sleep and resulted in total insomnia for some 3–4 days after the operation. Although there was some partial recovery of sleep after this period, it never exceeded 2½ hours each day (cats normally sleep about 14 hours). Further evidence linking the raphe with sleep also came from studies that used drugs (such as p-chlorphenylalanine) to block the synthesis of serotonin. These drugs also caused marked insomnia for a few days and the recovery of sleeping that followed such treatment was found to correlate with the recovery in serotonin levels that took place in the brain (Jouvet 1972). Thus, this evidence appeared to support the idea that the raphe was a sleep-promoting area, responsible for the initiation of slow-wave sleep.

Another area that was implicated in sleep by Jouvet was the part of the reticular formation that included the locus coeruleus. Damage to this area had a very different effect on sleep. Unlike raphe lesions, damage to the locus coeruleus had little influence on slow-wave sleep, but it abolished REM sleep. Furthermore, electrical stimulation of the locus coeruleus was found to produce an EEG pattern that closely resembled the brain waves found in REM sleep, as well as resulting in decreased muscle tone (which, of course, is another important characteristic of REM sleep). Thus, evidence pointed to the locus coeruleus as being the main site for the production of REM sleep.

The proposed involvement of these two brain structures in sleep led Jouvet in 1967 to propose a theory that linked these two regions together. Jouvet hypothesised that the raphe produced slow-wave sleep by inhibiting cortical arousal through its influence over the reticular formation, including the locus coeruleus. However, while the raphe was exerting this effect, the locus coeruleus was building up its own activity which, upon reaching a certain point, acted to turn off the raphe, thereby causing cortical arousal and REM sleep. However, this inhibition was only temporary and consequently the raphe would regain its control over reticular neurons. In this way, the two systems would alternate back and forth throughout the night to produce slow-wave and REM sleep (Jouvet 1967).

Problems with the dual process view

Although the idea of two brainstem areas interacting together to produce slow-wave and REM sleep is attractive, there is now strong evidence to suggest that if such areas do exist, they are not the raphe and locus coeruleus. For example, if the raphe is a sleep-promoting centre then it follows that electrical stimulation of this region should produce sleep – but this does not occur (Kostowski *et al.* 1969). Furthermore, studies that have recorded activity from single neurons in both the raphe and locus coeruleus have produced results that are at odds with Jouvet's theory. For example, contrary to what might be expected, neural activity in both the raphe and locus coeruleus is at its highest during waking, becomes depressed during slow-wave sleep, and is almost non-existent during REM (Hobson *et al.* 1975; Trulson and Jacobs 1979). Clearly, this is not the pattern of activity one would predict from Jouvet's theory.

In fact, several other brain areas have now been identified which also have an effect on slow-wave sleep (see Figure 6.9). For example, a structure that lies just below the raphe, called the **nucleus of the solitary tract**, has been implicated since stimulation of this region produces a synchronising effect on EEG similar to that found in slow-wave sleep (although paradoxically lesions to this region do not seem to disrupt sleep). Interestingly, this area receives information from the stomach, liver, duodenum and tongue, and this may help to explain why a large meal often facilitates sleep. Another structure linked to slow-wave sleep (this time outside the reticular formation) is the **preoptic-basal forebrain region** that lies close to the hypothalamus. Lesions to this area produce marked insomnia in cats while electrical stimulation causes drowsiness and sleep-like synchrony of the EEG. This region is also sensitive to the effects of temperature with neurons being more active when the body is warm (this might explain why we feel more sleepy when warm and comfortable).

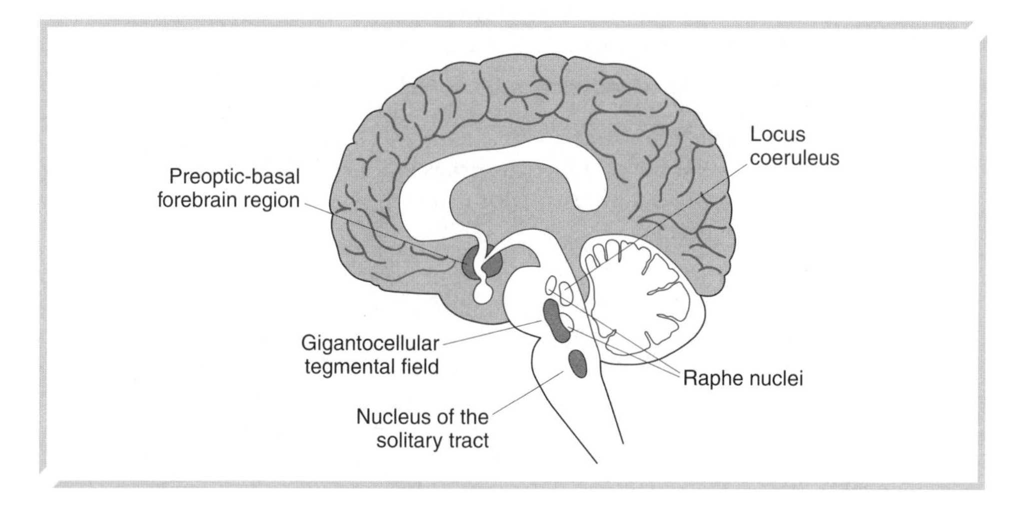

Figure 6.9 Some of the most important brainstem regions involved in sleep.

It also now appears that it is not the locus coeruleus which is involved in the initiation of REM sleep, but rather a nearby area of the brainstem called the **gigantocellular tegmental field (GTF)** which receives input from both the locus coeruleus and raphe. Indeed, lesions of the GTF disrupt REM sleep while leaving slow-wave sleep intact (Hobson 1988). Further support for the involvement of GTF neurons in REM sleep has come from the finding that these cells show a phasic burst of firing which precedes rapid eye movements by about 250 milliseconds, and that they are the origin of pontine-geniculato-occipital waves which are distinctive EEG waves that occur at the onset of (and during) REM sleep. Despite this, lesions of the gigantocellular tegmental field do not abolish the REM state completely, which indicates that other areas of the brain must also be involved in producing REM sleep.

The neural control of sleep thus appears to be extremely complex and many researchers have now come to the conclusion that it is a pointless exercise looking for 'executive centres' for either slow-wave or REM sleep. Indeed, it is much more likely that both of these sleep states will be found to be the result of several interacting brain areas. Moreover, the problem is not so much identifying these regions, but trying to understand how they all work together. With so many areas involved with sleep (some of which lie outside the reticular formation, such as the basal forebrain) this makes developing a coherent model explaining their function all the more difficult.

Box 6.2 SLEEP DISORDERS

Sleep disorders are extremely common. Surveys have shown that approximately one-third of the population will suffer from a sleep disturbance and, in about a third of cases, the problem may require medical intervention. Furthermore, the problems associated with sleep disturbances (which also are more prevalent in women and increase in severity and frequency with age) should not be underestimated. For example, about 50 per cent of people complaining of insomnia will also suffer from poor physical health, depression and anxiety. In addition, unsatisfactory sleep is a major cause of accidents, comparable to the effects of drugs and alcohol. In other words, sleep disturbances are a serious health problem which greatly affect the well-being of the individual.

The most common sleep problem is insomnia, which occurs when the individual has difficulty initiating or maintaining sleep to such an extent that it affects daytime behaviour. In about 85 per cent of cases, insomnia is related to psychological problems. For example, anxious individuals normally have great difficulty in getting to sleep, and people who are depressed often experience early morning awakenings. In addition, the use of alcohol may provide another cause of insomnia (e.g. alcohol usually enhances the onset of sleep but causes wakefulness later on). Although there can be physiological causes of insomnia (e.g. muscle spasms) these are relatively rare. The main treatment for insomnia is sleeping tablets, the most common form of which are **benzodiazepines** and, in particular, flurazepam. Another condition where insomnia occurs is **sleep apnoea** which generally starts shortly after the onset of sleep and is where the person suddenly stops breathing and is forced to gasp for air. Most attacks are mild and the person does not actually wake up, but in some cases individuals suffering from this condition may wake up over 500 times a night and experience extreme sleep loss. Sleep apnoea has also been controversially implicated in the sudden-infant-death syndrome.

In contrast to the above, there are also conditions of excessive sleep. The most common of these is **narcolepsy**, characterised by sudden attacks of sleep (or extreme sleepiness) during the day. Narcoleptic attacks (which usually last from 5 to 30 minutes) tend to occur first in adolescence (it rarely develops after the age of 30) and continue through life. Although it only occurs in about one person in 1,000, it nevertheless presents a serious problem (attacks are most common after meals, in monotonous situations or as the day progresses). Narcoleptics often have two other symptoms: sleep paralysis where they suddenly realise that they can't move (this normally occurs just before sleep), and extremely vivid dreams (known as hypnagogic hallucinations). Narcolepsy can also be accompanied by **cataplexy** – an abrupt loss of muscle tone causing the affected limbs to become flaccid (if the legs are affected this means that the person will fall to the ground). Cataleptic attacks are normally triggered by strong emotion, with laughter surprisingly being the most common cause (Kales and Kales 1974). Interestingly, the cause of narcolepsy appears to be due to the sudden intrusion of REM sleep intruding or 'spilling over' into wakefulness (with the cataplexy resulting from the inhibition of the motor system that normally occurs in the REM state). Indeed, some of the most effective forms of treatment for narcolepsy are the stimulants (such as amphetamine or Ritalin) which are known to suppress REM sleep.

Other types of sleep problem are more prevalent in young children. For example, night terrors (characterised by intense anxiety and extremely high autonomic arousal, but fortunately with little recall of the dream afterwards) are known to occur in stage 4 of slow-wave sleep. These awakenings are much more intense and terrifying than nightmares (which normally occur in REM sleep and across all ages). Another problem that occurs in stage 4 of slow-wave sleep is somnambulism (sleepwalking) where the person gets out of bed and walks around. It is particularly common in young children (estimates put its prevalence at around 1–6 per cent and it is more frequent in males). But the most common childhood problem of all is enuresis (bed-wetting). Approximately 10–15 per cent of all children between 4 and 5 years wet the bed, although in the majority of cases this problem is overcome by the age of 7 (Kales and Kales 1974).

Circadian rhythms

Almost without exception, all land animals co-ordinate their behaviour with the daily (circadian) cycles of light and dark that dominate living on Earth. Indeed, the most conspicuous daily body rhythm of all (and perhaps the most important) is the sleep–wake cycle. It hardly needs to be said that we are more inclined to be awake during the day and to sleep at night, but less obvious is the fact that nearly every physiological and biochemical function in the body also follows its own unique circadian rhythm. For example, body temperature fluctuates by about 3°F during the 24-hour day, reaching its peak in the late afternoon and dropping to its lowest value in the early hours of the morning. Hormones also follow clear circadian release patterns. For example, peak levels of **melatonin** are released late in the evening, and growth hormone is released in the early part of the night. In contrast, most **cortisol** and **testosterone** is released in the morning (around waking) and **adrenaline** in late afternoon. Even birth and death appear to follow their own circadian rhythms – for example, approximately one-third of natural births occur at around 3 a.m. in the morning, whereas death is more likely at 5 a.m. (Groves and Rebec 1992).

On first sight the existence of circadian body rhythms may not appear to be too surprising. After all, it is easy to imagine that they are caused, in some way, by the world around us – presumably by the alternating periods of light and dark, which, in turn, affect the biological processes of the body. However, things are more complex than this. In fact, rather than being passive responders to events around us, we actually have our own internal clocks that time and control the body's rhythms. And, we are not alone since nearly every form of life has its own time-keeping mechanisms. For example, in 1729, the French astronomer DeMarian became intrigued when he noted that his heliotrope plant opened its leaves during the day and shut them at night. To examine this further, he shut his plant away in a dark cupboard. None the less, the plant continued to open and shut its leaves in time with the light and dark cycles outside. In short, the rhythms of the plant were controlled by its own innate mechanism. Similar types of finding have also been found with creatures as simple as single-celled algae (Palmer 1975).

In 1832, the Swiss botanist de Candolle performed a similar experiment to the one undertaken by DeMarian, except this time he noted a new finding: when placed in the dark, his plant opened and shut its leaves not every 24 hours as expected, but every 22 hours. In other words, the plant appeared to have an internal clock that did not have a very accurate timing mechanism. In fact, what de Candolle had shown was the first example of a 'free-running' rhythm – that is, a rhythm which was running at a speed that didn't quite match the outside world. To entrain itself to the rhythms of the outside world, the plant was apparently 'resetting' its clock by using external time cues such as periods of light and dark, temperature or humidity, etc. These types of cue are now known to be important regulators of circadian rhythms and are collectively known as **zeitgebers** (from the German for 'time-givers').

Free-running rhythms in humans

What evidence is there that humans have internal biological clocks with their own time-keeping mechanism? In fact, to show that such clocks exist it is necessary to prove that circadian rhythms still operate in the absence of time cues. However, the problem with human subjects is that it is extremely difficult to keep them separated from this type of information. Even in the confines of a laboratory, there are many subtle time cues such as the sound of the outside world, or people coming and going, that provide information about the time of day. How then does one cut off all time cues from a human subject? One of the most ideal (isolated) environments for this type of study are deep caves and, indeed, these have on occasion become useful 'laboratories' by which to examine free-running circadian rhythms in humans.

One of the most famous isolation experiments was performed on the French geologist Michel Siffre who, in 1972, agreed to live for 6 months in a carefully prepared cave, 100 feet below the ground in Texas (see Siffre 1975). During this time he was cut off from all sources of time information from the outside world (even the temperature of the cave was constant at 70°F) and although he was linked to the surface by a telephone (which was manned at all times) his conversations were kept to a bare minimum. He had a stockpile of food (the same type as used on the Apollo 16 space mission), and water (780 one-gallon jugs), and he phoned to the surface whenever he wanted to sleep so that the support team could turn off the lights. When Siffre went to bed he also attached himself to equipment that enabled his sleep cycles to be recorded, as well as his heart rate, blood pressure and muscle activity. He also saved his beard cuttings, recorded his temperature several times a day and sent his urine samples to the surface for analysis.

Not surprisingly, the experience took its toll on Siffre who by the 80th day of his isolation was experiencing severe depression and failing memory (at this point the experiment was to continue for another 100 days). Moreover, long after the confinement had ended, Siffre complained of 'psychological wounds' from the ordeal that he did not 'understand'. But, from the scientific point of view the study was a success. One of its main findings was that the body appeared to have (at least) two internal clocks that ran at different speeds. For example, Siffre's sleep–wake cycle tended to free-run between 25 and 32 hours, which meant that he went to sleep at later times each day (or, put another way, his 'days' were much longer than normal). In fact, Siffre was on his 151st sleep–wake cycle by the last (179th) day of the experiment, so that he had psychologically 'lost' 28 days. However, Siffre's temperature rhythm was more stable and it ran consistently on a 25-hour cycle with little fluctuation. This meant in effect that his temperature cycle went in-and-out of synchronisation with the sleep–wake cycle, an unusual situation since we normally go to sleep when our body temperature is dropping. Thus, there appeared to be at least two oscillators controlling circadian rhythms: one which was relatively stable that controlled temperature (this has sometimes been called the X pacemaker), and one that was more variable (sometimes called the Y pacemaker).

The neural basis of circadian rhythms

If the sleep–wake cycle is under the control of a circadian pacemaker, then the question arises: Where in the body does this clock exist? One of the first investigators to address this question was Carl Richter who (beginning in the 1950s) began his search by focusing on the endocrine glands of the body. However, removal of the endocrine glands had little effect on altering the circadian rhythms of laboratory animals, and thus Richter turned his attention to the brain. He made lesions to many different sites in the brain and found only one which disrupted circadian behaviour – the ventral hypothalamus. But, partly because this region was small (and anatomically complex) he went no further with his exploration.

However, in 1972, two separate teams of researchers (Stephan and Zucker 1972; Moore and Eichler 1972) identified a small cluster of neurons in the front part of the ventral hypothalamus, called the **suprachiasmatic nucleus (SCN)**, whose damage resulted in the disruption of circadian rhythms (including corticosteroid release, drinking and locomotor activity). Further research showed that this lesion also disrupted a number of other rhythms including the sleep–wake cycle. Although it did not alter the length of time spent sleeping, or the relative proportions of slow-wave and REM sleep, the SCN lesion did alter the pattern of sleep so that it occurred randomly during the 24-hour cycle of day and night. In other words, lesions of the suprachiasmatic nucleus abolish the circadian rhythmicity of sleep.

Why did it take so long to discover the suprachiasmatic nucleus? One reason is that it is extremely small. In humans, each of the nuclei (there are two – one on each side of the brain) comprises approximately 10,000 neurons that are confined in a space of about 0.05 mm. And, of course, in rodent brains the nuclei are even smaller. It is hardly surprising, therefore, that Richter with his relatively crude lesioning techniques was unable to narrow his search down to this tiny structure.

Evidence linking the suprachiasmatic nucleus with circadian rhythms

If a region of the brain is to qualify as a circadian pacemaker then it must have three properties: (1) it receives information from the senses (particularly helpful in this respect would be visual information concerning day and night) to account for the fact that circadian rhythms can be reset by zeitgebers; (2) it has an intrinsic rhythm of its own to account for the fact that circadian rhythms can be free-running; and (3) it has output to other regions of the brain that are involved in circadian types of behaviour such as the sleep–wake cycle. In fact, the suprachiasmatic nucleus fulfils all these criteria thus confirming its role as a circadian pacemaker.

To begin with, the anatomical location of the suprachiasmatic nucleus strongly supports its involvement in visual processing. For example, these nuclei lie just above the **optic chiasm** (*supra* means 'above') where the nerve fibres from each eye cross to the contralateral side of the brain. And, branching off from the optic nerve, near the chiasm is a pathway (known as the retinohypothalamic tract) that projects to the suprachiasmatic nucleus. When this pathway is lesioned, it is found that light and dark cues that normally are able to reset the circadian 'clock' become inoperative, although animals still maintain their ability to see (Rusak 1977). Thus, the suprachiasmatic nucleus is in an ideal position to receive rudimentary visual information that can be used as a zeitgeber to reset its rhythms.

It has also been shown that the suprachiasmatic nucleus is able to generate its own rhythmical activity. For example, it is possible to keep slices of brain tissue that contain the suprachiasmatic nucleus alive in a culture medium, and then to make electrical recordings from its neurons. This type of work has shown that the suprachiasmatic neurons show discharge rates of electrical activity that are synchronised to the light–dark cycle that the animal previously experienced when alive (Bos and Mirmiran 1990). Similar types of neural activity have also been demonstrated in the intact animal. For example, Schwartz and Gainer (1977) injected rats with **2-deoxyglucose** (a radioactive form of glucose) that is taken up and accumulates into neurons, but unlike normal glucose cannot be used as energy. Because the most active neurons in the brain are the ones that will take up most 2-deoxyglucose, this substance thus provides a way of measuring regional differences in brain activity. Using this technique it was found that the suprachiasmatic nucleus took up significantly more 2-deoxyglucose (i.e. was more active) during the day than at night – again supporting its role in circadian rhythmicity.

But how does the suprachiasmatic nucleus produce the circadian changes that take place in the rest of the body? The answer partly lies with the fact that the projections of the suprachiasmatic nucleus innervate a large number of brain structures – including other regions of the hypothalamus (and pituitary gland) along with various brainstem nuclei. But, the most important projection is to the **pineal gland**. This structure (which functions as a 'third eye' in some reptiles and birds) has long intrigued researchers (see Chapter 1) although it was not until the early 1960s that it was identified as an endocrine gland which releases the hormone melatonin into the blood. Moreover, in most animals, the secretion of melatonin is directly under the control of light (i.e. light suppresses melatonin release whereas darkness is stimulatory) and is controlled through a pathway (called the **superior cervical ganglion**) that projects to the pineal gland from the suprachiasmatic nucleus. In short, darkness causes the superior cervical ganglion to release noradrenaline onto pineal cells which then transforms serotonin (through an enzyme called *N*-acetyltransferase) into melatonin. Most animals are very sensitive to light's effects on melatonin secretion (e.g. in rats the light from a candle flame is sufficient to inhibit its release), although it takes much higher intensities of light to suppress melatonin in humans. Despite this, humans show a circadian pattern of melatonin release with most being secreted during the late part of the evening and negligible amounts during the day (Lewy 1980).

The functions of melatonin

In animals, melatonin has been shown to be involved in a wide range of functions including the synchronisation of circadian rhythms and seasonal patterns behaviour.

For example, melatonin has been shown to affect the circadian function of most other endocrine organs in the body as well as influencing the daily activity of brain neurotransmitter metabolism, thermoregulation, locomotor activity, feeding behaviour and sleepiness (Reiter 1987). In addition, melatonin has shown to produce seasonal changes in body weight, coat colour and reproductive behaviour. Thus, in many animals, melatonin regulates the changing response of the body to light over the course of the year, as well as serving a circadian function. In humans, seasonal changes in behaviour are less clear cut, although there is little doubt that melatonin has an important effect on circadian rhythms. For example, melatonin administration makes people feel drowsy and prepares them for sleep. In addition, there is evidence showing that melatonin helps orchestrate the activity of other hormone systems in the body, enabling them to synchronise their activity with the sleep–wake cycle (e.g. administration of melatonin has been shown to cause significant increases in the release of growth hormone). Thus, melatonin may be involved in making sure that a wide range of other circadian rhythms are 'in tune' with sleeping and waking.

Interestingly, melatonin has also begun to be used in preparations to help overcome jet-lag where the body's circadian rhythms fall out of step with the zeitgebers of the new time zone. By taking melatonin during the early evening at one's arrival destination (and in some cases in the days before the journey), it is possible to effectively shift the body's circadian rhythm into phase with the new prevailing time conditions (Arendt *et al.* 1987).

Self-test questions

1. What does the EEG measure?
2. Briefly describe the sleep cycle and how it typically progresses throughout the night.
3. What are the main features of slow-wave sleep?
4. What is 'paradoxical' about REM sleep?
5. How does sleep change across the life span?
6. What two main theories have been proposed to explain sleep?
7. What hormone is released in large amounts in the early part of sleep?
8. What are the effects of sleep deprivation in animals?
9. Describe how the work of Bremer had an important impact on sleep research.
10. Whereabouts in the brain is the reticular formation situated?
11. In what ways have the locus coeruleus and raphe been implicated in sleep?
12. What are circadian rhythms?
13. In what ways has Michel Siffre contributed to our understanding of circadian rhythms?
14. What evidence indicates that the suprachiasmatic nucleus is a pacemaker that controls circadian rhythms?
15. What hormone does the pineal gland secrete?

Key terms

Adrenaline (p.186)
Alpha waves (p.167)
Ascending reticular activating system (p.181)
Benzodiazepines (p.185)
Beta waves (p.167)
Cataplexy (p.185)
Cerveau isolé preparation (p.179)
Circadian rhythm (p.171)
Cortisol (p.186)
Delta waves (p.168)
Electroencephalogram (EEG) (p.167)
Encéphale isolé preparation (p.179)
Gigantocellular tegmental field (GTF) (p.184)
Growth hormone (p.172)
Locus coeruleus (p.182)
Melatonin (p.186)
Narcolepsy (p.185)
Noradrenaline (p.182)
Nucleus of the solitary tract (p.183)
Optic chiasm (p.188)
Pineal gland (p.189)
Pons region (p.182)
Preoptic-basal forebrain region (p.183)
Raphe nuclei (p.182)
Rapid eye movement sleep (REM) (p.167)
Reticular formation (p.179)
Serotonin (p.182)
Sleep apnoea (p.185)
Sleep cycle (p.170)
Slow-wave sleep (SWS) (p.167)
Superior cervical ganglion (p.189)
Suprachiasmatic nucleus (SCN) (p.188)
Testosterone (p.186)
Theta waves (p.168)
2-deoxyglucose (p.189)
Zeitgebers (p.186)

References

Adam, K. and Oswald, I. (1977) Sleep for tissue restoration. *Journal of the Royal College of Physicians*, **11**, 376–88.

Arendt, J. *et al.* (1987) Some effects of jet-lag and their alleviation by melatonin. *Ergonomics*, **30**, 1379–93.

Bremer, G. (1937) L'activité cérébrale au cours du sommeil et de la narcose. *Bulletin de l'Académie Royale de Belgique*, **4**, 68–86.

Borbely, A. (1986) *Secrets of Sleep*. London: Penguin.

Bos, N. P. A. and Mirmiran, M. (1990) Circadian rhythms in spontaneous neuronal discharges of the cultured suprachiasmatic nucleus. *Brain Research*, **511**, 158–62.

Dement, W. C. (1976) *Some Must Watch While Some Must Sleep*. San Francisco: Freeman.

Dement, W. and Kleitman, N. (1957) Cyclic variations in EEG during sleep and their relation to eye movements, body motility and dreaming. *Electroencephalography and Clinical Neuropsychology*, **9**, 673–90.

Dorociak, Y. (1990) Aspects of sleep. *Nursing Times*, **86**, 38–40.

Empson, J. (1993) *Sleep and Dreaming*. New York: Harvester Wheatsheaf.

Groves, P. M. and Rebec, G. V. (1992) *Biological Psychology*. Dubuque: William Brown.

Hobson, J. A. (1988) *The Dreaming Brain*. London: Penguin.

Hobson, J. A. (1989) *Sleep*. New York: Scientific American Library.
Hobson, J. A. *et al.* (1975) Sleep cycle oscillation: Reciprocal discharge by two brainstem neuronal groups. *Science*, **189**, 55–8.
Hodgson, L. (1991) Why do we need sleep? Relating theory to nursing practice. *Journal of Advanced Nursing*, **16**, 1503–10.
Horne, J. (1978) A review of the biological effects of total sleep deprivation in man. *Biological Psychology*, **7**, 55–102.
Horne, J. (1988) *Why We Sleep*. Oxford: Oxford University Press.
Jones, H. S. and Oswald, I. (1968) Two cases of health insomnia. *Electroencephalography and Clinical Neurophysiology*, **24**, 378–80.
Jouvet, M. (1967) Neurophysiology and the states of sleep. *Science*, **163**, 32–41.
Jouvet, M. (1972) The role of monoamines and acetylcholine containing neurons in the regulation of the sleep–waking cycle. *Ergebnisse Physiology*, **64**, 166–307.
Kales, A. and Kales, J. D. (1974) Sleep disorders. *New England Journal of Medicine*, Feb., 487–99.
Kostowski, W. *et al.* (1969) Electrical stimulation of the midbrain raphe. Biochemical, behavioral and bioelectrical effects. *European Journal of Pharmacology*, **7**, 170–5.
Lavie, P. (1996) *The Enchanted World of Sleep*. New Haven: Yale University Press.
Lavie, P. *et al.* (1984) Localised pontine lesion: Nearly total absence of REM sleep. *Neurology*, **34**, 118–20.
Lewy, A. J. (1980) Light suppresses melatonin secretion in humans. *Science*, **210**, 1267–9.
Lindsley, D. B. *et al.* (1949) Effect upon the EEG of acute injury to the brainstem activating system. *Clinical Neurophysiology*, **1**, 475–86.
Magni, F. *et al.* (1957) EEG arousal following inactivation of the lower brain stem by selective injection of barbiturate into the ventribal circulation. *Archives Italiennes de Biologie*, **95**, 33–46.
Meddis, R. (1977) *The Sleep Instinct*. London: Routledge.
Mirmiran, M. (1986) The importance of fetal/neonatal REM sleep. *European Journal of Obstetrics, Gynecology and Reproductive Biology*, **21**, 283–91.
Moore, R. Y. and Eichler, V. B. (1972) Loss of circadian adrenal corticosterone rhythm following suprachiasmatic lesions in the rat. *Brain Research*, **42**, 201–6.
Moruzzi, G. and Magoun, H. W. (1949) Brain stem reticular formation and activation in the EEG. *Electroencephalography and Clinical Neurophysiology*, **1**, 455–73.
Oswald, I. and Adam, K. (1980) The man who had not slept for 10 years. *British Medical Journal*, **2**, 1684–5.
Palmer, J. D. (1975) Biological clocks of the tidal zone. *Scientific American*, **232**, 70–9.
Rechtschaffen, A. *et al.* (1983) Physiological correlates of prolonged sleep deprivation in rats. *Science*, **221**, 182–4.
Reiter, R. J. (1987) Pineal rhythmicity: Neural, behavioral and endocrine consequences. In Shafi, M. and Shafi, S. L. (eds) *Biological Rhythms. Mood Disorders, Light Therapy, and the Pineal Gland*. Washington: American Psychiatric Association.
Roffwarg, H. P. *et al.* (1966) Ontogenetic development of the human sleep–dream cycle. *Science*, **152**, 604–19.

Rusak, B. (1977) Involvement of the primary optic tracts in mediation of light efferents on hamster circadian rhythms. *Journal of Comparative Physiology*, **118**, 165–72.
Schwartz, W. J. and Gainer, H. (1977) Suprachiasmatic nucleus: use of 14-C labelled deoxyglucose uptake as a functional marker. *Science*, **197**, 1089–91.
Siffre, M. (1975) Six months alone in a cave. *National Geographic*, **147**, 426–35.
Stephan, F. K. and Zucker, I. (1972) Circadian rhythms in drinking behaviour and locomotor activity of rats are eliminated by hypothalamic lesions. *Proceedings of the National Academy of Science* (USA), **60**, 1583–6.
Trulson, M. E. and Jacobs, B. L. (1979) Raphe unit activity in freely moving cats: Correlation with level of behavioural arousal. *Brain Research*, **163**, 135–50.

FURTHER READING

Aserinsky, E. and Kleitman, N. (1953) Two types of ocular motility occuring in sleep. *Journal of Applied Physiology*, **8**, 1–10.
Aserinsky, E. and Kleitman, N. (1955) Regular occuring periods of eye motility and concomitant phenomena during sleep. *Science*, **118**, 273–4.
Carkadon, M. A. (ed.) (1993) *Encyclopaedia of Sleep and Dreaming*. New York: Macmillan.
Cooper, R. (ed.) (1994) *Sleep.* New York: Chapman & Hall.

Multiple choice questions

1. When we are awake the EEG normally shows:

(a) alpha waves
(b) beta waves
(c) (a) and (b) above
(d) theta waves

2. Which of the following is not a characteristic of slow wave sleep?

(a) reduced blood flow to the cerebral cortex
(b) increased parasympathetic activity
(c) rapid eye movements
(d) reduced (but not total loss of) muscle tone

3. Dement and Kleitman (1957) found that when most subjects were awakened during REM sleep they:

(a) could not remember anything
(b) reported dreaming
(c) claimed that they had not been sleeping
(d) were very 'sleepy' and disinclined to answer the experimenter's questions

4. As sleep cycles progress over the course of an average night, the amount of time spent in REM sleep:

(a) decreases
(b) doesn't change much
(c) increases
(d) becomes zero (i.e. REM eventually drops out of the sleep cycle)

5. According to James Horne, strenuous exercise appears to:

(a) increase the total duration of sleep
(b) have little effect on the duration of sleep
(c) decrease SWS but increase the duration of REM sleep
(d) increase the length of the sleep cycle

6. What is unusual about the bottlenose dolphin?

(a) it doesn't sleep
(b) it can sleep with its eyes open
(c) it has a sleep cycle like a human being
(d) one cerebral hemisphere sleeps at a time

7. Within the first three hours of sleep there is a huge surge in the release of:

(a) growth hormone
(b) melatonin
(c) testosterone
(d) thyroxin

8. Over the life span the greatest proportion of REM sleep occurs:

(a) in the newborn
(b) after about one year of life
(c) in the onset of adolescence and early adulthood
(d) in old age

9. It has been shown that REM sleep deprivation in infant rats is associated with:

(a) reduced immune function
(b) a decreased body size
(c) a reduction in the size of the cerebral cortex
(d) all of the above

10. If there is any consistent effect of sleep deprivation on humans it is on:

(a) mood
(b) paranoia

(c) tasks involving co-ordinated movement
(d) the performance of complex mental tasks that require concentration

11. Rechtschaffen has shown that sleep deprivation in animals:

(a) generally causes death in 2–3 weeks
(b) decreases body temperature
(c) causes a loss of body weight (despite the animal eating more)
(d) all of the above

12. The inner core of the brainstem is known as the:

(a) medulla oblongata
(b) pons
(c) mesencephalon
(d) reticular formation

13. When Frederic Bremer (1937) lesioned the base of the brainstem in cats (where it joined the spinal cord) and then recorded electrical activity from the cortex he found that this operation:

(a) abolished all EEG activity
(b) had no effect on cycles of sleep and waking
(c) produced continuous slow-wave sleep
(d) produced desynchronised EEG patterns

14. The locus coeruleus contains neurons that release the neurotransmitter ________________ whereas the raphe contains neurons that release ________________.

(a) noradrenaline, serotonin
(b) serotonin, noradrenaline
(c) dopamine, serotonin
(d) acetylcholine, noradrenaline

15. Early research by Jouvet indicated that damage to the locus coeruleus:

(a) abolished slow-wave sleep
(b) produced marked insomnia
(c) had no effect on sleep
(d) abolished REM sleep

16. Microelectrode recording from the locus coeruleus and raphe have tended to show that neural activity in these structures is highest during:

(a) REM sleep
(b) slow-wave sleep

(c) waking
(d) (a) and (b) above

17. When Michel Siffre lived alone in a cave for 6 months isolated from all outside cues it was found that:

(a) his free-running sleep–wake cycle was around 25–32 hours
(b) his free-running temperature rhythm was constantly about 25 hours
(c) (a) and (b) above
(d) his free-running sleep–wake and temperature cycles were both about 22–24 hours

18. The part of the brain that has been shown to function like a 'biological clock' is the:

(a) optic chiasm
(b) gigantocellular tegmental field
(c) nucleus of the solitary tract
(d) none of the above

19. The suprachiasmatic nucleus influences the release of melatonin by its effect on the ____________.

(a) pituitary gland
(b) pineal gland
(c) thyroid gland
(d) hypothalamus

20. In humans a surge of melatonin release occurs:

(a) during the morning
(b) during late afternoon
(c) during the evening
(d) during the night

Sexual behaviour

IN THIS CHAPTER

- The importance of hormones for sexual development
- Sex-related hormone developmental disorders and genetic syndromes
- The organisational and activational effects of sex hormones
- Sexual differentiation of the central nervous system
- The menstrual cycle
- Brain areas and sexual behaviour
- The biological basis of homosexuality

Introduction

Although sexual behaviour satisfies no vital tissue need, nor is it needed for individual survival, from an evolutionary perspective it is one of the most important activities we engage in, for without it we would not be able to produce offspring or continue the survival of the species. It is hardly surprising, therefore, that the drive to engage in sexual activity is very powerful. It is also a behaviour with many manifestations. Not only has evolution gone to the great trouble of developing two different sexes, but it also requires that they come together in the process of courtship to engage in sexual intercourse. In addition to this, most higher animals will engage in some kind of parental assistance to ensure that their offspring can reach a stage where they can look after themselves. It is easy to take this species-specific behaviour for granted, but it must nevertheless be the case that it is largely programmed into the brain. Understanding how the brain controls sexual behaviour presents a major challenge in biological psychology, especially when it comes to trying to understand human sexuality, which goes far beyond the act of procreation. Indeed, it has been said that the well-being of individuals, couples, families and even entire societies can depend on matters that are fundamentally sexual (Haas and Haas 1993). Despite this, sexual behaviour is a biological phenomenon that largely depends on genetic, hormonal and neural functioning, which makes it explainable in terms of biological psychology.

Why have sex?

The obvious answer to this question is that it is enjoyable! But, as true as this answer is, we must ask why sexual behaviour has evolved in the first place. On first sight the answer appears to be straightforward: sexual behaviour is necessary for the continuation of the species. But, this is not an entirely satisfactory answer for the simple reason that reproduction without sex (asexual reproduction) is also possible. Indeed, many plants produce seeds that are clones of themselves (e.g. dandelions), and most single-celled organisms (e.g. bacteria) replicate by dividing into two. Some other creatures also reproduce asexually. For example, female greenfly give birth to 'virgin' young for several generations, and there are even some vertebrates that reproduce without sex (e.g. the Whiptail lizard and a type of fish called the Amazon Molly are all-female). Since these forms of life can reproduce successfully, why go to the bother of inventing sexual reproduction? Sex is all the more puzzling when one considers that it is not without its risks (e.g. it can cause harmful mutations, result in sexually transmitted diseases and prove extremely hazardous during courtship and copulation). Yet sexual behaviour is the norm in nature. Why?

The main reason for the evolutionary development of sex probably lies with the great variety of gene combinations it is able to produce compared to asexual reproduction. With sexual reproduction, each parent passes on a unique set of genes to each of its progeny, thereby creating a 'new' mixture which guarantees that the offspring will be different to either of its parents (and to its brothers and sisters, with the exception of identical twins). In theory, therefore, a single couple can produce an almost infinite number of genetically different offspring. This constant shuffling of genes, and the large number of different individuals it creates, produces 'variation' which is of great evolutionary advantage to the species. For example, if we were all genetically identical, or even close to being the same, then we would be equally vulnerable to the same diseases, environmental changes and other threats to our survival. However, a species with many genetically different individuals is much more likely to survive these types of catastrophe. Furthermore, variability between individuals also means that some will become better suited to their environments than others, and these will be the ones more likely to survive to pass on their genes. In this way, the survival of the 'fittest' ensures that the species is able to adapt optimally to its own ecological niche. Thus, it can also be seen that sexual reproduction greatly assists the process of evolution.

Sexual development and differentiation

Nearly every cell in the human body contains 23 pairs of **chromosomes** that carry the 100,000 or so **genes** that we inherited from our parents at the moment of our conception. One type of cell which is an exception to this rule, however, are the **gametes** (sperm and ova) which contain only 23 single chromosomes. In fact, it is only when the sperm and ova come together during fertilisation that the 23 chromosomes become paired together and a totally new genetic cell is created. Remarkably, we all start life as this single cell. But, perhaps even more astonishing, encoded in our first set of chromosomes are the genetic instructions that will ultimately build us into an adult human being containing more than 100 million million cells. Another surprising fact is that males and females only differ genetically in terms of one single chromosome! All genetically normal humans, regardless of their sex, share 22 pairs of chromosomes and only differ in terms of just one pair, called the sex chromosomes, which come in one of two forms: X and Y. Put simply, females inherit two X chromosomes (XX), and males inherit an X and a Y chromosome (XY). Because only males can supply both types of chromosome, it must follow, therefore, that the father determines the genetic sex of the fertilised egg.

Although the egg receives its full complement of chromosomes at conception, it takes another 6 weeks of foetal development for the first overt sex differences to emerge. Up to this point, males and females are identical and have the potential to develop into either sex as they both contain the precursor tissue for making either male or female **gonads** (testes or ovaries). This tissue is connected to two tubular structures: the **Wolffian duct** that has the capacity to develop into the male reproductive system, and the **Müllerian duct** that has the capacity to turn into the female reproductive system. However, only one of these ducts will develop to determine the sex of the foetus. The event that initiates this change occurs in the sixth week of gestation when a gene on the (male) Y chromosome produces an enzyme (called **testis-determining factor**) that causes the foetal gonadal tissue to develop into **testes**. There is no female equivalent of this substance and in its absence the gonadal tissue (carrying XX chromosomes) will remain undeveloped until it starts to develop into **ovaries** at about 12 weeks of gestation.

The differentiation of gonadal tissue into testes or ovaries is the first stage of sexual development where a difference between the sexes can be observed. Moreover, it also marks the point where the genetic influence on sexual differentiation effectively ends, and hormonal influence takes over (see Figure 7.1). The importance of the testes and the ovaries at this stage lies in the fact that they produce male or female sex hormones which, in turn, set in motion the changes that ultimately result in the birth of a male or female. In the case of a male, the testes start to produce two hormones: **testosterone** and **Müllerian duct-inhibiting substance**. The first (testosterone) masculinises the sex organs by promoting the growth and development of the Wolffian duct system (which will turn into the internal male sex organs including epididymis, vas deferens, seminal vesicles and prostate), while the second prevents the (female) Müllerian system from

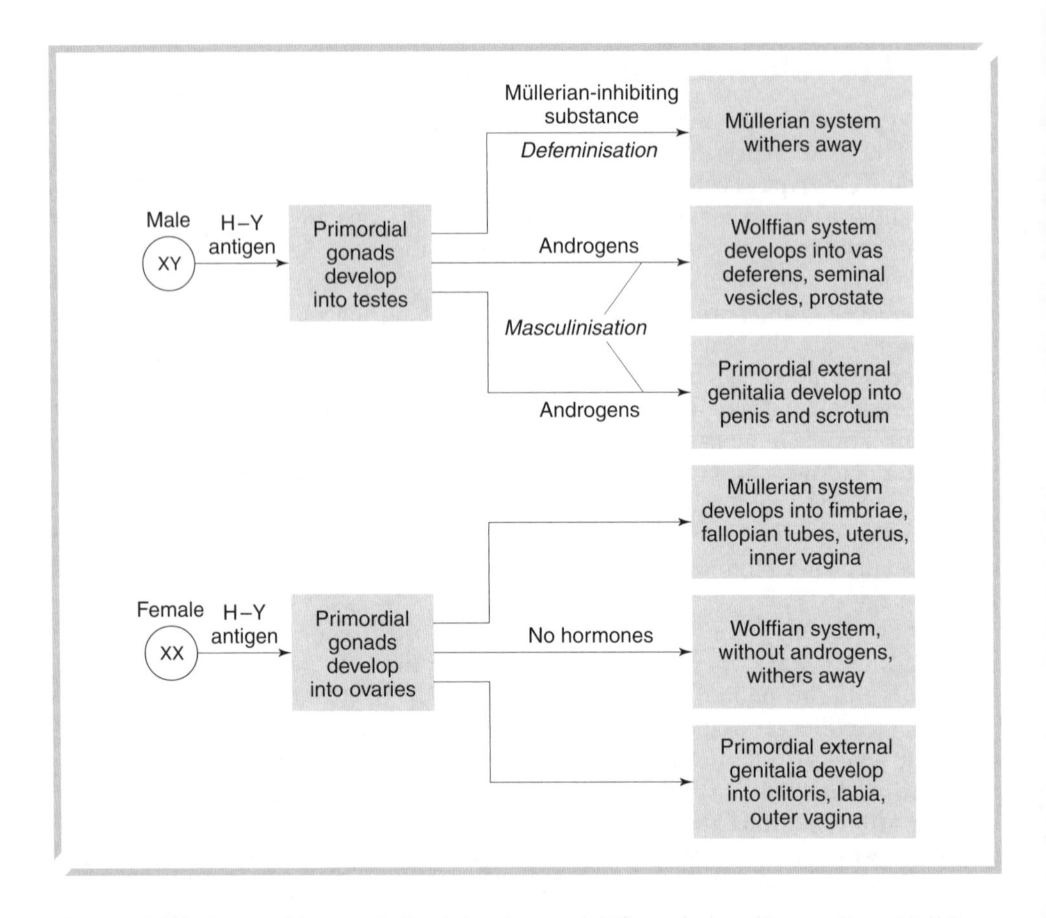

Figure 7.1 The hormonal control of embryonic sexual differentiation. (*Source*: From Neil R. Carlson, *Physiology of Behavior*, 6th edition. Copyright © 1998 by Allyn & Bacon. Reprinted by permission.)

developing. In contrast, the female ovaries do not secrete any specific sex hormones at this early stage (e.g. 6–12 weeks). Nevertheless, the lack of hormonal stimulation still exerts an important effect on the foetus as it causes the Wolffian system to degenerate and the Müllerian system to develop into the internal sex organs of the female (including the uterus and fallopian tubes).

The external genital anatomy (penis and vagina) start to appear at about 8–12 weeks of gestation – and again, the same principles of hormonal organisation hold as for internal development. In other words, the release of testosterone by the testes causes the male sex organs to be formed, and the absence of this hormone results in the development of the female sex organs. With this differentiation of the external genitalia the final step in the development of sexual morphology has taken place – the foetus is now a boy or a girl.

The andrenogenital syndrome

As we have seen, the normal sexual development of the foetus depends on the differentiation of the gonads into testes or ovaries to provide the correct hormonal environment for the internal and external sex organs to develop. But, what if something goes wrong? What happens, for example, if the female foetus is exposed to high levels of testosterone (say, around the sixth week of gestation) when sexual differentiation of the sex organs is normally taking place? In fact, this type of event occurs in a condition known as congenital **adrenal hyperplasia** in which the foetal adrenal glands (which normally produce insignificant amounts of male steroids or **androgens**) secrete excessive amounts of these hormones. A similar situation can also occur when the mother uses androgenic drugs (such as **anabolic steroids**) during the early stages of pregnancy. In both cases, the consequence of high androgen exposure is the masculinisation of the female genitalia.

The effects of androgens on early female development were first shown by researchers in the 1940s, who injected pregnant monkeys with testosterone and found that their female offspring were born with well-formed scrota and a small penis. In other words, the treatment produced a **pseudo-hermaphrodite** (an animal born with gonads that match their sex chromosomes, but with a genital appearance of the opposite sex). An analogous situation can also occur with humans. For example, newborn females with congenital adrenal hyperplasia often have an enlarged clitoris and partially fused labia (although in most cases the internal sexual organs are normal because the adrenal androgens are released too late in development to stimulate the development of the Wolffian system). If identified at birth, the external genitals can be surgically corrected and drug therapy used to reduce the levels of androgens. However, in some cases, the genitals may be so masculinised that the sex of the newborn child is misidentified. Contrary to what might be predicted, these children are often happily reared as boys, with problems of sexual development and identification only emerging during adolescence.

It also appears to be the case that females who have experienced prenatal adrenal hyperplasia have a greater tendency to show masculine characteristics. For example, young female monkeys exposed to prenatal androgens are more aggressive, and as adults tend to exhibit male sexual behaviour. Similarly, in humans there is evidence that young girls with andrenogenital syndrome have a high rate of tomboyishness, and as adults are more likely to be bisexual or lesbian (see below).

Testicular feminisation syndrome

Although increased levels of androgens in foetal development have little effect on changing the sexual appearance of males, there is nevertheless a condition that can result in male pseudo-hermaphroditism called **testicular feminisation syndrome**. This occurs when testosterone (and other androgens) have no biological effect on body tissues. In this instance, the foetus has normal levels of male sex hormones (produced by the testes), but the androgen receptors in the tissues they stimulate are not sensitive to its effects. The consequence is that the male develops external female genitalia (e.g. labia and clitoris) and the infant appears to be female at birth. However, because the testes still continue to produce Müllerian duct-inhibiting substance (which causes the internal female sexual organs to degenerate) the foetus does not develop a uterus or fallopian tubes.

A newborn baby with testicular feminisation syndrome looks like a normal baby girl and will often be mistaken for one (unless the testes have descended into the labia). Consequently, these children are normally raised as females and their condition is not recognised until puberty when the lack of menstruation is identified as abnormal. In fact, during adolescence the individual develops feminine breasts because some of their circulating testosterone is metabolised into oestrogen. Thus, these 'genetic males' have a feminine appearance and their sexual behaviour also typically matches that of a female (although, of course, conception is not possible). In fact, in cases of complete testicular feminisation, physicians recommend that the child should be raised as a girl, since neither surgery nor hormonal treatment can create a functioning penis or alter the feminine appearance of the body (Masters *et al.* 1995). This does not generally present a problem, however, as these individuals typically regard themselves as female.

Genetic syndromes

We normally inherit 23 pairs of chromosomes including a pair of sex chromosomes (XX or XY). But there can be occasions when this type of inheritance does not occur. One such condition is **Turner's syndrome** (occurring in about one in 2,500 live births) in which the egg is fertilised by a sperm that has lost its sex chromosome. This means that the individual only inherits one X chromosome (X0). Because the Y chromosome is missing, the gonads do not differentiate into testes and the male sexual organs do not develop. Instead, there are poorly developed ovaries and this causes a female to be produced. At birth these infants have normal external genitalia and they develop normally as females until puberty. However, at this point, because of their non-functional ovaries, they do not undergo the adolescent growth spurt, begin menstruation or develop breasts. In addition, there can be webbing of the neck and heart problems. Interestingly, the male version of Turner's syndrome (Y0) does not exist, since embryos with this combination do not survive.

There are also genetic conditions where females inherit extra copies of the X chromosome including triple (XXX), tetra (XXXX) and even penta (XXXXX) inheritance. The triple X female appears 'normal' but, as an adult, is normally beset with menstrual cycle irregularities and a premature menopause. Despite this, they are fertile and give birth to normal offspring. In cases where tetra and penta inheritance occurs there is a much greater likelihood of problems with sexual development, and a chance of mental retardation.

Another sex-related genetic condition is **Klinefelter's syndrome** where males inherit an extra (female) X chromosome (XXY). As might be expected, this disorder (which occurs in about one in every 500 live births) increases the feminine characteristics of the person although this is not usually noticed until adulthood. The main problem with the extra X chromosome is that it leads to abnormal development of the testes with reduced release of androgens. This results in adult males tending to be very tall with poor muscular development and enlarged breasts. In addition, they are often infertile with low sexual desire or impotence, and there can also be mild mental retardation, or lack of drive and ambition.

Males can also be born with an extra copy of the Y chromosome (XYY). This is one of the most controversial of all genetic syndromes because it appears to be linked with mental retardation, criminal behaviour and violent tendencies. Furthermore, these males tend to be very tall and have low IQs. Although XYY inheritance only occurs in about one in 1,000 births, some surveys have shown that these individuals may make up 2–3 per cent of the inmates of mental or penal institutions (Emery and Mueller 1992). However, because this genetic abnormality normally only comes to light when individuals are institutionalised, it has been pointed out that the incidence of XYY inheritance could be much higher in the general population than estimates currently show. Indeed, in support of this, it is known that some XYY individuals are neither delinquent nor mentally retarded (i.e. this condition is not inevitably linked with behavioural problems) and, thus, there may be many other cases where the genetic abnormality has not been detected.

The organisational effects of hormones on behaviour

Prenatal androgen secretion has an effect not only on the development of the internal and external reproductive organs, but also on the brain – that is, to organise (or prime) the nervous system so that it will later function or 'behave' as a male or female. This was shown in an experiment by Phoenix *et al.* (1959) which examined female sexual behaviour in guinea pigs that had been exposed to increased levels of testosterone during foetal development. As an adult, the female guinea pig will normally show **lordosis** (a behaviour that includes the raising of the hind quarters to signal sexual receptivity) around the time of ovulation in response to interested males. Lordosis can also be induced in guinea pigs by mimicking the hormonal state of the body that occurs just before and during ovulation – that is, by giving the female oestrogen for a few days followed by an injection of progesterone. However, when Phoenix *et al.* (1959) attempted to induce sexual receptivity this way in females that had been exposed to high levels of testosterone during foetal development, they found that lordosis was not produced. In other words, the early exposure to testosterone had influenced later sexual behaviour.

This example shows that prenatal sex hormones not only determine the sexual (male or female) characteristics of the individual, but they also have an important bearing on adult behaviour. In other words, sex hormones have an **organisational effect** on the developing central nervous system, which influences the type of sexual behaviour that is expressed at a later stage. Whether a hormone is able or unable to exert an **activational effect** on behaviour (such as lordosis) is largely dependent on the way the brain has been 'organised' during development.

What is the situation regarding males? As might be expected, male rats do not normally show lordosis when given injections of oestrogen and progesterone. But, if rats are castrated at birth (in rats this is the sensitive period where sex hormones have a particularly important effect on development) they do show lordosis in response to female sex hormones. Furthermore, if these rats are castrated at birth, they also show reduced levels of male-related sexual behaviour as adults, even if they are given injections of testosterone. Thus, the neural circuits governing sexual responses are organised early in development (during the first few weeks of life in male rats) although the sexual behaviour is not produced until later.

Because of the clear influence of androgens on the sexual behaviour of rodents, there have been attempts to discover if early exposure to high levels of these hormones in humans, or primates, also produces similar effects. Although the behaviour of higher animals is much more complex than that of rodents, it nevertheless appears that a hormonal influence is at work. For example, Goy *et al.* (1988) examined the behaviour of prenatally androgenised female monkeys and found that they engaged in much more rough-and-tumble play than normal. A similar finding was also found by Money and Ehrhardt (1996) in human females that had been subjected to high levels of male sex hormones due to adrenogenital syndrome (see above). In addition, these girls also show a strong tendency to play with toys that are normally preferred by boys, such as trucks rather than dolls.

But what about sexual behaviour as adults? Interestingly, Money *et al.* (1984) questioned 30 young adult women who had a history of adrenogenital syndrome. When asked to describe their sexual orientation, 37 per cent described themselves as bisexual or homosexual; 40 per cent said they were exclusively heterosexual; and 23 per cent refused to disclose their sexuality. In short, these findings indicate that high prenatal androgen levels in females may bias the person towards bisexuality or homosexuality, although it must be stressed that this is far from inevitable (indeed, as far as can be established, the majority of the sample were heterosexual).

Sexual differentiation of the nervous system

It is only relatively recently that structural differences between male and female brains have been found that occur as a result of hormonal secretion during early development. One of the first studies to show that there were important sex differences in brain structure came from Raisman and Field (1973) who examined the **preoptic area** of the hypothalamus – an area that had also been implicated in the sexual behaviour of male and female rats (see below). These researchers found that the female preoptic area contained significantly more synapses than in the male. However, when males were castrated soon after birth the number of synapses increased to female levels. Alternatively, testosterone given to young females resulted in a decrease of synapses to male levels. Thus, this was evidence that early androgen exposure could at least alter the neural structure of certain hypothalamic areas.

Following this research, another important discovery was made; a small nucleus was found embedded in the preoptic area of rats that was some 3 to 5 times larger in males than in females (Gorski *et al.* 1978). This nucleus was called the **sexually dimorphic nucleus** (see Figure 7.2) and its size was shown to be directly linked with androgen

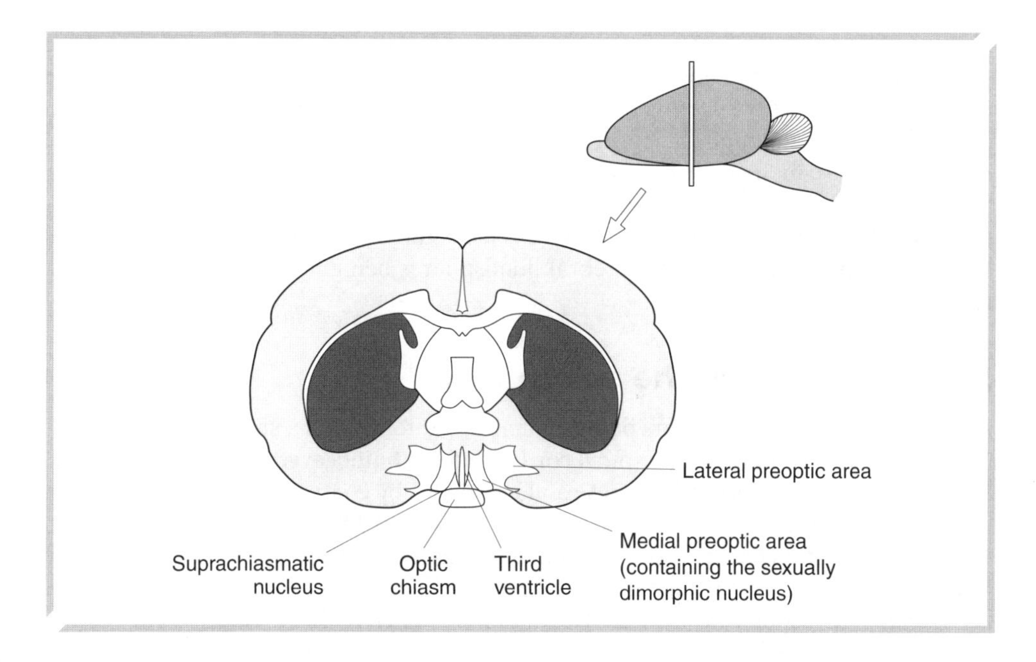

Figure 7.2 The location of the sexually dimorphic nucleus in the rat brain.

stimulation. For example, males castrated at birth (but not later in life) had much smaller dimorphic nuclei, whereas females given androgens at birth (but not as adults) had much larger dimorphic nuclei. Furthermore, the size of the sexually dimorphic nuclei could only be changed in this way during a critical stage corresponding to the first 10 days after birth. After this period, androgen stimulation had no effect upon the size of this nucleus in either males or females.

What about the humans? The preoptic area of the hypothalamus is much more complex in the human brain and, instead of having just one dimorphic nucleus, we actually have four! For example, Allen *et al.* (1989) examined the preoptic area in 22 individuals at post-mortem and located these nuclei, which they called the **interstitial nuclei of the anterior hypothalamus** (INAH 1–4). Perhaps, more importantly, while the INAH-1 and INAH-4 did not show any size difference between the sexes, the remaining two nuclei (particularly INAH-3) were found to be much larger in males (although this did not hold for homosexual men – see below). The functions of the INAH nuclei are not known, although presumably they are somehow involved in sexual behaviour.

Another area where differences have been found between males and females is the **corpus callosum**, which is the huge bundle of white matter (axons) that connect the two cerebral hemispheres (see also Chapter 9). In 1982 it was reported that the posterior part of the corpus callosum (called the **splenium**) which joins the occipital and parietal regions, was significantly larger in females than in males (Lacoste-Utamsing and Holloway 1982). Unfortunately, subsequent research has provided a more confused picture with one study confirming these results (Clarke 1990), one showing increased splenium size in right-handed, but not left-handed women (Witelson 1989), and one reporting no sex differences whatsoever (Byne *et al.* 1988). Despite this, it has been pointed out that although the corpus callosum is roughly the same size in males and females, because men on average have brains that are approximately 15 per cent bigger than females, this essentially means that women have relatively bigger corpus callosums (LeVay 1993). Thus, it appears that there is a sex difference in the size of the corpus callosum after all, with the two cerebral hemispheres being more richly connected in females.

Sex differences in the spinal cord

Another structure which differs between males and females is a small group of motor neurons in the lower half of the spinal cord called the **bulbocavernosus nucleus** which, in males, plays an important role in sexual behaviour by controlling the reflexes of the penis during copulation. This structure shows a marked difference between the sexes, with adult male rats having around 200 neurons in their nucleus and females typically having less than 70 (these neurons are also significantly larger in the male). Although this nucleus is present in both sexes, it atrophies early in female development due to the lack of androgen stimulation. Indeed, females given testosterone during a critical period of development will show an increased number of bulbocavernosus neurons in adulthood. In contrast males deprived of testosterone early in life will develop a nucleus that resembles the one found in females.

Humans also have bulbocavernous motor neurons although they are found in a spinal structure called **Onuf's nucleus**. Again, there is a difference between the sexes with males having a much bigger nucleus than females. It is also known that this difference occurs around the 26th week of gestation when the male foetus produces high amounts of androgens (Forger and Breedlove 1986). Interestingly, in men these motor neurons are partly under voluntary control and can be used to urinate, whereas in women, the muscles innervated by these neurons surround the opening of the vagina.

Adult sexual development

At birth, human males and females (apart from the obvious differences in sexual anatomy) are physically similar, and remain so until puberty. However, with the onset of puberty, secondary sexual characteristics occur which transform the youngster into an adult capable of reproduction. One of the most striking changes that takes place during this period is the adolescent growth spurt, which results in both sexes growing taller. In males, this is mainly caused by the development of the testes (and subsequent testosterone production) which increases skeletal and muscle growth, along with the formation of body and pubic hair, a deepening of the voice, and the ability to ejaculate. In females, the release of sex hormones helps promote a fuller figure along with enlarged breasts and wider hips. And, approximately 2 years after the start of puberty in the female the first signs of menstruation occur, which marks the point where pregnancy (in theory) becomes possible, although in practice it normally takes another year before the release of mature ova finally occurs.

Thus, the onset of puberty is put into motion by the release of sex hormones from the gonads. As we have seen, these are the testes (which produce testosterone) and the ovaries (which produce oestrogen and progesterone) and, at this point, both come under the direct control of the **hypothalamus** and the adjoining **pituitary gland** (see Figure 7.3). In fact, the release of sex hormones begins with the hypothalamus, which secretes a substance called **gonadotropin-releasing hormone (GnRH)** that controls the secretion of two hormones from the anterior pituitary gland called **luteinising hormone (LH)** and **follicle-stimulating hormone (FSH)** . These two hormones are released into the bloodstream where they are transported to the gonads. They also have different functions. In males, the release of luteinising hormone stimulates the **Leydig cells** in the testes to manufacture testosterone, whereas in the female the same hormone serves as a trigger for ovulation (see next section). In contrast, follicle-stimulating hormone in males stimulates the production of sperm, while in females it prepares the ovary for ovulation. Although both LH and FSH play an important role in the development of puberty, they also continue to influence gonadal functioning throughout much of life.

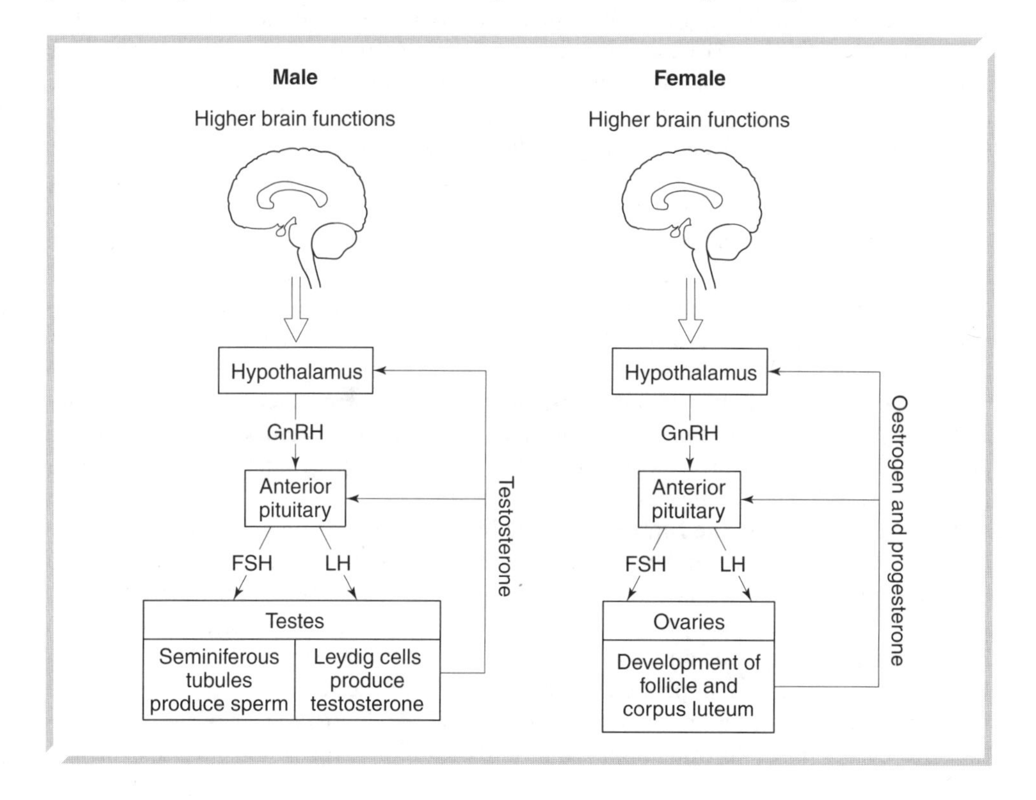

Figure 7.3 Flowchart showing how the hypothalamic-pituitary system influences activity of the testes and ovaries.

The menstrual cycle

For most species, the female is sexually receptive and only able to conceive during a specific period known as **oestrus** (when ovulation usually occurs). However, human females (along with certain other primates) are an exception to this rule because they can be sexually receptive at any point in their reproductive cycle, and not just when ovulation occurs. The human reproductive cycle is called a **menstrual cycle** (from *mensis* meaning 'month') and it also differs from the oestrus cycle because of menstruation – the process by which the lining of the uterus is discarded at the end of the cycle. Despite this, oestrus and menstrual cycles show some similarities, and both are under the control of hormones released by the pituitary gland.

The menstrual cycle has three main phases, known as follicular, ovulatory and luteal. By convention, the first day of the menstrual cycle begins with menstruation (which usually lasts for a few days) and this also marks the start of the follicular phase. During this period, the hypothalamus begins to secrete GnRH (see above) which causes the pituitary gland to release follicle-stimulating hormone (FSH) and luteinising hormone (LH). The former has the most important role at this stage because it stimulates the development of a follicle in the ovary (the follicle is a protective sac that surrounds the ovum or unfertilised egg) which, in turn, releases oestrogen. Indeed, as the follicle develops (as many as 20 follicles may begin to develop at each cycle although only one usually reaches maturity) it secretes increasing amounts of oestrogen until a level is reached (usually around the 12th day of the cycle) which is sufficient to turn off the pituitary gland's release of FSH. At this point, the pituitary begins to secrete large amounts of luteinising hormone instead.

By this stage of the cycle, the follicle has grown large enough to form a large bulge in the lining of the ovary, and the sudden surge in LH causes the walls of the follicle (and ovary) to rupture, releasing the mature egg into the upper fallopian tubes – a process known as **ovulation**. At this point the egg can be fertilised by a male sperm. However, the time frame for this event is relatively short – the egg is only viable for about 12–24 hours – and most sperm can only exist in the female reproductive tract for about 24 hours (although some 'super' sperm may survive up to 72 hours). Thus, there is a period of around three days in every menstrual cycle when pregnancy can take place as the egg moves down the fallopian tubes into the uterus.

Following ovulation, the ruptured follicle in the ovary forms a yellow mass of tissue (called the corpus luteum) and begins to secrete large amounts of progesterone (and to a lesser extent oestrogen), thus initiating the luteal phase of the menstrual cycle. The main function of progesterone ('pro-gestation') is to build up the lining of the uterus with blood and nourishing substances for the implantation of the egg should it be fertilised. In addition, the increase in progesterone also turns off the release of GnRH from the hypothalamus, producing a rapid decline in LH and FSH. If fertilisation of the egg occurs then the level of progesterone remains high and the lining of the womb develops further. However, if fertilisation does not take place, the corpus luteum will begin to shrink and reduce its secretion of hormones. Because the lining of the uterus cannot be maintained without progesterone it will thus fall away causing menstruation (Figure 7.4).

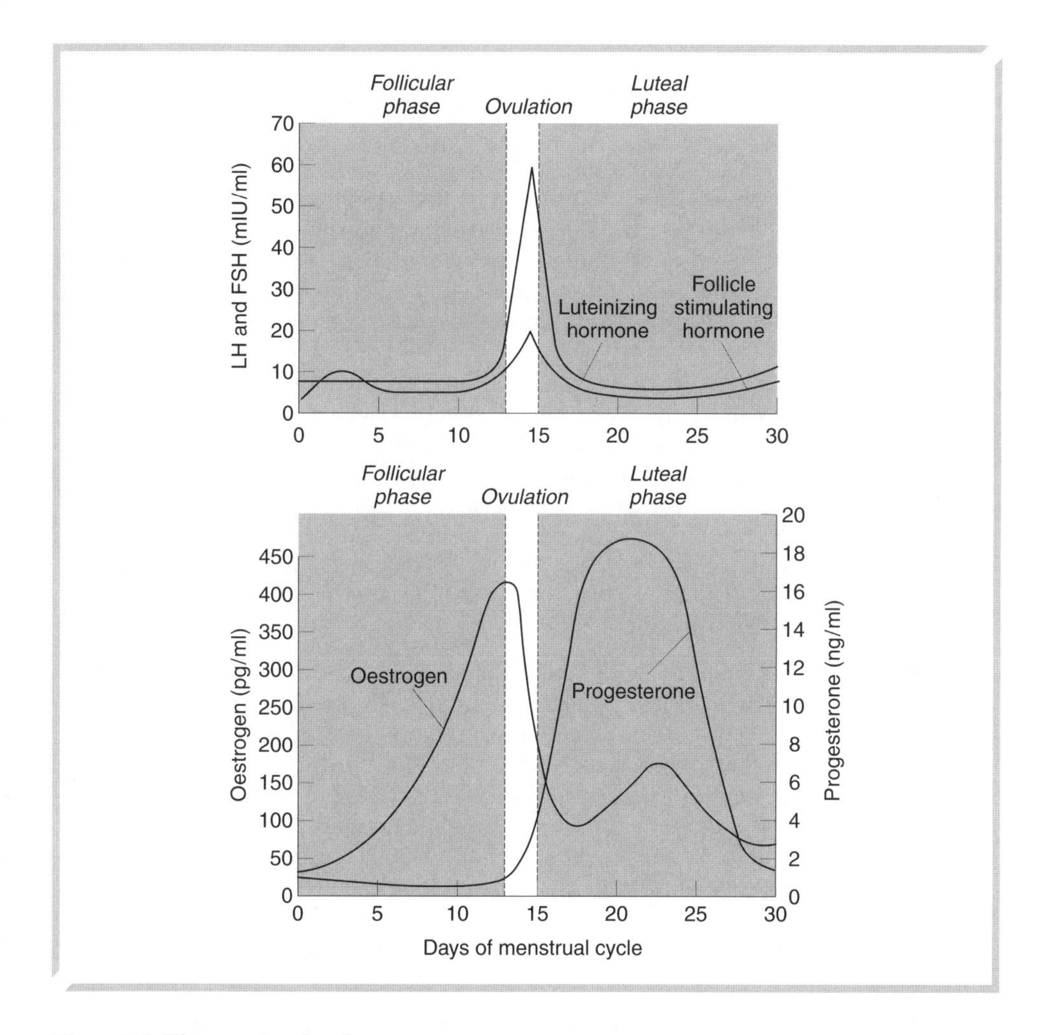

Figure 7.4 The menstrual cycle.

The total amount of blood lost is usually around 30 millilitres (or around a twentieth of a pint).

On average, most women have menstrual cycles that last 28 days (although they can range from 20 to 40 days) and they continue until the menopause (thus a non-child-bearing female can expect to undergo around 400 menstrual cycles in her life). It is also of interest to note that birth-control pills prevent pregnancy by interfering with the normal development of the menstrual cycle. The most widely used contraceptive pill (e.g. the combination pill) contains oestrogen and progesterone and works in two ways: the increased level of oestrogen suppresses the release of FSH thereby blocking the development of the follicle, while the increased level of progesterone inhibits the secretion of LH thus making sure that ova will not be released by the ovary.

Box 7.1 THE WORK OF MASTERS AND JOHNSON

William Masters (a gynaecologist) and Virginia Johnson (a psychologist) became world-renowned almost overnight with the publication of their book *Human Sexual Response*, in 1966. The reason was simple: Masters and Johnson went beyond questioning people about their sexual habits, and instead directly observed and measured their sexual behaviour in the laboratory under controlled conditions. In short, they described in great detail (on the basis of direct observation of more than 10,000 male and female orgasms) how the various parts of the body (including penis, vagina, labia, clitoris, etc.) responded to erotic stimulation during masturbation and sexual intercourse. Moreover, on the basis of this work they provided an authoritative and objective account of the human sexual cycle from the first thoughts of sexual desire through to orgasm and relaxation. This in itself was a considerable feat, but Masters and Johnson did more than just record sexual behaviour, they were also therapists and their work contributed greatly to the understanding, treatment and greater awareness of sexual dysfunction and inadequacy.

Masters first began his research looking at sexual function in 1954 when he interviewed 118 female and 27 male prostitutes. Eight of the women and three of the men then participated in a laboratory investigation with physiological and film recording. However, one objection made by critics was that prostitutes were not necessarily typical of 'normal' people, and consequently Masters began to recruit people from the local academic community (it was also around this time that he recruited Virginia Johnson). The news of their research spread and by the time of their book they had examined 382 women (ranging in age from 18 to 78) and 312 men (from 21 to 89). The work had taken 11 years to complete and research into sexual behaviour was never the same again.

Masters and Johnson made a number of important discoveries, but one of their main findings was that both sexes underwent a four-stage cycle of sexual arousal, consisting of excitement, plateau, orgasmic and resolution phases. Thus, males and females were surprisingly similar in their general sexual responses. Despite this, Masters and Johnson also showed that there were interesting differences, particularly the discovery that there is normally only one pattern of sexual response cycle for the male, but three different types of cycle for the female (see Figure 7.5). In addition, Masters and Johnson also helped to dispel a myth that had originated with the work of Freud that held there was a difference between clitoral and vaginal orgasms. Instead, they showed that both types of orgasm were, in fact, physiologically identical and characterised by rhythmical muscular contractions of the outer third of the vagina and uterus (see Masters *et al.* 1995).

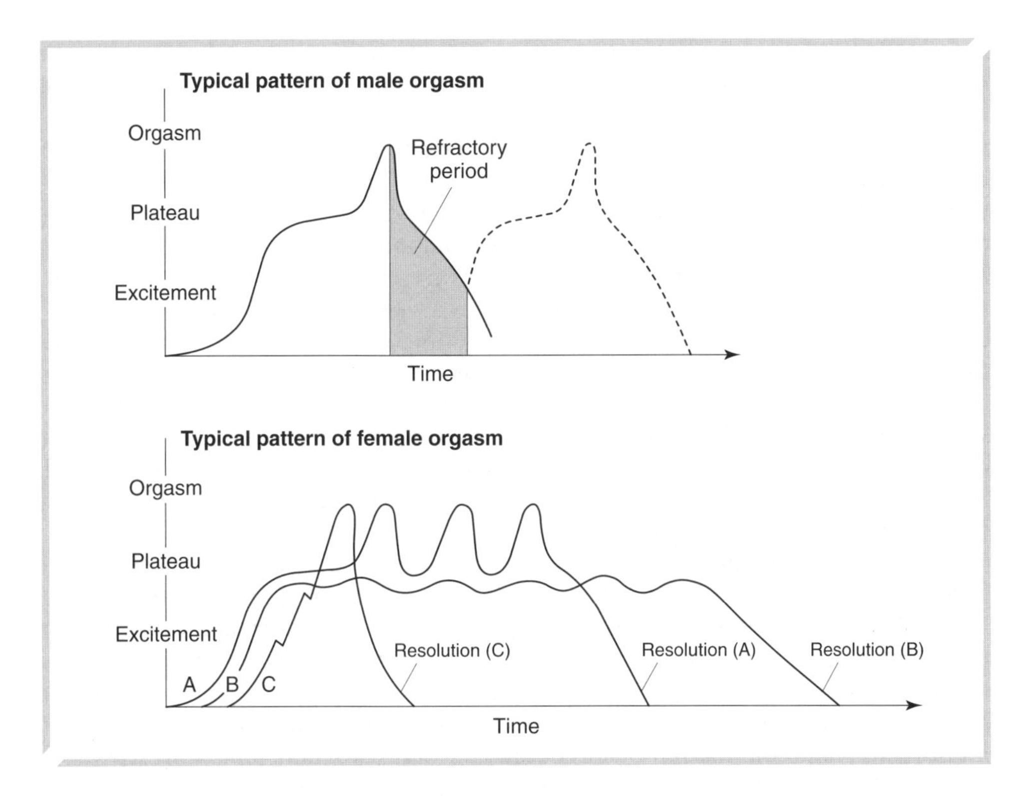

Figure 7.5 The four stages of sexual arousal (the sexual response cycle). (*Source*: Adapted from W. H. Masters, V. E. Johnson and R. C. Kolodny, *Human Sexuality* (1995). HarperCollins.)

The activational effects of hormones on sexual behaviour

Up to this point, we have looked at some of the ways that sex hormones influence development, both at the foetal stage and later at puberty. But, long after these hormones have shaped sexual differentiation and produced secondary sex characteristics, they still continue to exert an important effect on adult behaviour. We have already seen (above), how hormones activate lordosis behaviour in female guinea pigs, but a similar relationship also appears to hold true for sexual behaviour in general. That is, adult sexual activity is dependent not only on the organisation of the nervous system, but also on the levels of certain hormones circulating in the body. For example, if an adult male rat is castrated (causing it to have low levels of testosterone) it will quickly stop mating and show little interest in a sexually receptive female. Similarly, an adult female rat who has her ovaries removed will not go into oestrus or exhibit sexually receptive behaviour. Despite this, in both cases, sexual behaviour is quickly restored by the appropriate hormonal treatment (Davidson 1969). In fact, for the male of many lower species, it appears that there is a direct relationship between testosterone and the activation of sexual behaviour – with increased levels of testosterone producing increased sexual motivation and behaviour (Becker *et al.* 1993).

But what about humans? In fact, for higher animals, the relationship between testosterone and sexual activity is not so clear-cut. For example, male primates are typically able to maintain sexual behaviour for some years after castration, although it does eventually produce a decrease in activity and interest. In humans, the situation appears to be even more complex with castration first resulting in the loss of ejaculation, then the ability to achieve an erection, and finally a waning of sexual motivation (interestingly, these findings suggest that the relative importance of testosterone in these three functions is different). However, there is also great variability between individuals in response to castration. For example, Money and Ehrhardt (1972) report that, for some men, the loss of erectile potency (impotence) may occur within weeks of castration, whereas in others it may take years to manifest itself. Despite this, it is clear that human sexual activity is far less dependent on circulating levels of sex hormones than it is in many other animals.

Nevertheless it is also apparent that testosterone does exert some activational influence on human male sexual behaviour. For example, a certain level of testosterone is needed, at least in the long term, for normal sexual behaviour, and castration (if untreated) will eventually result in impotence. Despite this, it must be emphasised that low testosterone is not the only cause of impotence. In fact, most men who are impotent have normal levels of testosterone and providing them with extra testosterone does not improve the condition (this is probably because most cases of impotence have a psychological rather than a hormonal cause). These findings again show that there is more to male sexual behaviour than simply the effects of hormones.

The activational effects of gonadal hormones on the sexual behaviour of humans females is even less marked. As already mentioned, female rodents only show sexual interest during oestrus, and this behaviour can be abolished by removal of the ovaries. In marked contrast, however, it appears that ovariectomy in the human female has little effect on sexual activity. In fact, evidence suggests that sexual behaviour in women may be more under the control of male hormones (small amounts are secreted by the adrenal glands) than those produced by the ovary. For example, women who receive injections of testosterone generally report a heightened sexual desire, whereas removal of the adrenal glands has the opposite effect (Michael 1980). Despite this, women normally have testosterone levels that are one-tenth that of males, and it is probably the case that their sexual behaviour is even less influenced by these hormones than for men.

The effects of testosterone on aggressive behaviour

Male sex hormones also have an important effect on aggressive behaviour (in the animal kingdom this is normally linked to sexual behaviour in some way, e.g. the establishment of territory or the procurement of a mate). For example, most animals that show seasonal aggression tend to fight when their testosterone levels are highest. This relationship was also shown by Beeman (1947) who found that castration of male mice reduced their aggressive behaviour, and that administration of testosterone restored it. However, similar to other sex-related behaviours, the 'activational' effects of testosterone on aggression are also dependent on the earlier 'organisation' of the nervous system: if the animal is castrated early in life and given testosterone as an adult, there is usually little effect on aggression.

Even allowing for this, however, the link between testosterone and aggression is not straightforward. For example, in species where members live in social groups with dominance hierarchies, the males with the higher ranks tend to have the higher levels of testosterone – and this has been shown in a number of species, including chickens and monkeys (Allee *et al.* 1939; Rose *et al.* 1971). At first sight this suggests that the most dominant males are also the ones who are the most aggressive as a result of their (high) testosterone levels, but research has shown that this need not be the case. For example, Rose *et al.* (1975) found that a monkey's testosterone level *prior* to being put into a social group did not correlate with the rank he would later attain in the group. However, once social groups were established and dominance ranking stabilised, a significant rise in testosterone (as much as tenfold) could often be found in the dominant male. This finding indicates that it is the success or failure in achieving dominance (presumably through aggressive encounters) that determines the testosterone levels, with victory increasing levels of testosterone and defeat reducing them.

This hypothesis has also been tested in a study where young male monkeys were introduced to a new unfamiliar group. If the monkey was attacked and defeated it was then removed from the group and its level of testosterone measured. The results showed that in defeated animals, testosterone levels fell by about 10–15 per cent within 24 hours, and remained depressed for several weeks. However, males who successfully defended themselves, showed elevated testosterone levels (Monaghan and Glickman 1993). In other words, although testosterone is clearly linked to aggression, the levels of this hormone in monkeys are also dependent upon the experience of the animal.

But what about human behaviour? In fact, it appears that a similar process may be at work. For example, it has been shown that watching an erotic film increases the levels of testosterone in young men (Hellhammer *et al.* 1985), and even the anticipated expectation of sexual activity may have the same effect (Anonymous 1970). In addition, competition can also have a significant effect on testosterone release, particularly in sporting contests where levels of this hormone have been shown to increase prior to competition, and remain high in the victors compared to the losers (Archer 1994). However, the reason for this effect is controversial because some research indicates that high testosterone may correlate better with the improved mood and performance satisfaction than with aggression (McCaul *et al.* 1992). Whatever the correct explanation, this work, nevertheless, shows that cognitive appraisal of the event has an important bearing on testosterone release.

There is also evidence of a relationship between levels of testosterone and aggression in humans. For example, throughout the world, males become engaged in more violent behaviour than females, and this is most marked in young men who have the highest amounts of testosterone in their blood. Despite this, the association between testosterone and aggression is not as significant as most people imagine. For example, studies that have compared testosterone in groups of men that have been designated as aggressive or non-aggressive have tended to find a positive correlation (generally in the range of 0.24 to 0.62), but one which is far from perfect (1.00). One of the most comprehensive studies in this area was undertaken by Dabbs and Morris (1990) who examined 4,462 US military veterans and found that those with the highest testosterone levels were also the ones who had previously shown greater amounts of antisocial behaviour, including assault. Although this relationship was significant, it was relatively small, and was more pronounced for men from lower socio-economic groups. Thus, as with sexual behaviour, it appears that sexual hormones do have an effect on aggressive behaviour, but in higher species (such as ourselves) the relationship is complex and influenced by a great many other variables.

Box 7.2 THE ACTIONS OF SEX HORMONES AND ANABOLIC STEROIDS

The sex hormones (which include testosterone, oestrogen and progesterone) are all steroids derived from cholesterol. They are also lipid (fat) soluble, and instead of binding to receptors on the cell surface (like neurotransmitters), they diffuse into the cell where they become attached to special proteins in the cytoplasm and nucleus. Furthermore, once inside the cell, they may be converted into other compounds that have greater or lesser androgen activity. For example, in many tissues (including the brain), testosterone may be converted into dehydrotestosterone by the enzyme 5α-reductase (and then dehydrotestosterone may be converted to estradiol). This makes understanding how sex hormones act on neural function difficult to establish, although they are known to have two general effects: firstly, they can influence the neuron 'directly' by acting on neurotransmitter function (e.g. altering synthesis, release, re-uptake or receptor sensitivity); and, secondly, they may affect the cell by attaching themselves to the DNA (located in the nucleus) and increasing protein synthesis. This type of action is known as 'indirect' as this process may take minutes or even hours to take effect.

Testosterone was first synthesised in 1935 and became the forerunner of many other androgen substances known as anabolic steroids. The term 'anabolic' refers to the ability to promote tissue growth (particularly of muscle) and, because of this property, steroids were soon used by athletes to enhance performance (in fact, it was not until 1976 that the International Olympic Committee banned their use). Surprisingly, whether anabolic steroids actually increase strength or speed still remains scientifically unclear (Wilson 1988), but nevertheless they are used on a large scale and this is probable testimony to their effectiveness. What is more certain, however, is that there is a wide range of possible harmful side effects associated with the use of anabolic steroids. In women, the most visible effect is growth of body hair (sometimes accompanied by baldness), along with menstrual irregularities and masculinisation of the sex organs. In men, the use of steroids can cause shrinkage of the testes and sterility (because steroids reduce the normal production of testosterone), and enlargement of the breasts (because high doses of androgens may be converted into oestrogen). Furthermore, many males using high doses of steroids eventually develop low levels of sexual desire and erectile dysfunction. In both sexes there is also a serious risk of liver dysfunction and increased heart disease – the latter caused partly by high levels of cholesterol.

Psychological effects can also occur after anabolic steroid usage, including increased aggression and rage. Rapid mood swings are also common, and one study (Pope and Katz 1988) found that 12 per cent of steroid users regularly suffered from psychotic symptoms. There is also some evidence that long-term (or high) use of anabolic steroids can lead to dependence. For example, Brower *et al.* (1991) surveyed 49 male weightlifters and found that they suffered a number of withdrawal symptoms following regular steroid use which included: craving (52 per cent), fatigue (43 per cent), depression (41 per cent), restlessness (29 per cent), anorexia (24 per cent), insomnia (20 per cent), decreased libido (20 per cent) and headaches (20 per cent). Thus, athletes who take high doses of anabolic steroids may be paying a high price for their enhanced performance.

The neural control of sexual behaviour

As animals become more advanced, they become less dependent on their sex hormones to control sexual behaviour, and this is particularly true for humans who show the most complex and varied sexual behaviour of all. This is undoubtedly due to our more complex brains (especially our cerebral cortex), which means that our sexual behaviour becomes less instinctual and more influenced by cognition and experience. Despite this, we still share much of the neural circuitry underlying sexual behaviour with other animals. For example, sexual performance and arousal requires the participation of the autonomic nervous system – particularly the parasympathetic division for increasing blood flow to the erectile tissue of the penis and clitoris, and the sympathetic division for ejaculation and contraction of the vaginal muscles.

In fact, many of the basic reflexes that are an integral part of our sexual behaviour are controlled by the spinal cord, and not the brain. For example, stimulation of the genitals in animals is able to elicit sexual responses (penile erections, pelvic thrusting and ejaculations) even when the brain is severed from the spinal cord (Hart 1967), and similar responses have also been observed in men made paraplegic by damage or transections of the spinal cord. For instance, Money (1960) in a study of males with broken spinal cords (which severed communication between the brain and sex organs) found that 65 per cent of the sample were able to achieve complete erection; 20 per cent managed partial erections; and 20 per cent were still able to engage in coitus. Furthermore, many of these paraplegic men managed to achieve ejaculation (although they did not 'sense' the event mentally). Thus, even in a species as advanced as ourselves, erection and ejaculation can take place without a brain!

Despite this, the brain remains the most important structure by far that exerts control over sexual behaviour, and the region that has received most attention in this respect is the hypothalamus. The hypothalamus not only influences the release of hormones from the pituitary gland (which in turn controls the secretion of the sex hormones from the gonads), but it also exerts important control over the autonomic nervous system. Moreover, some regions of the hypothalamus appear to be more important than others in their control of sexual behaviour. One such area in the male is the **medial preoptic area**. For example, lesions of the preoptic area have been shown to eliminate copulatory behaviour in male rats, an impairment that is not corrected with testosterone treatment (Heimir and Larsson 1967). In contrast, electrical or androgen stimulation of the same region facilitates sexual behaviour in male rats, even if they have been castrated (Davidson 1980). As might be expected, this region of the brain contains a high concentration of androgen receptors – more than five times the amount found in female brains. And, as mentioned above, the preoptic area is also the site of the sexually dimorphic nucleus which is much bigger in male brains, and whose size is also dependent on circulating androgen levels (Gorski *et al.* 1978).

The area of the brain that has been most implicated in female sexual behaviour is the **ventromedial hypothalamus**. For example, female rats with lesions of this structure will not show lordosis even when injected with oestrogen and progesterone – while direct implants of oestrogens into the ventromedial hypothalamus produce this behaviour, even in animals that have been ovarectomised. Thus, similar to the preoptic area in males, the ventromedial hypothalamus in females appears to be an important mediator of the behavioural response to gonadal sex hormones, and contains high numbers of oestrogen and progesterone receptors (Pfaff and Modianos 1985).

The hypothalamus is not the only brain region involved in the control of sexual behaviour. For example, the temporal lobes (particularly the amygdala) may help to direct attention towards an appropriate sex object. Indeed, lesions of this brain region have been shown to produce hypersexuality in monkeys and a tendency to mate with almost any object in their environment (see discussion of the Kluver–Bucy syndrome in Chapter 5). In addition, damage to several regions in the limbic system, including the dorsal hippocampus, septal region and pyriform cortex, has also been shown to impair sexual functioning in laboratory animals.

Another area of the brain that has been shown to have an important role in sexual behaviour is the cerebral cortex (this is probably the most important region of all for human beings). For example, Beach (1940) found a decrease in male copulatory behaviour in rats following cortical lesions, with lesions involving 60 per cent of the cortex abolishing copulatory behaviour completely. However, similar cortical damage did not have any effect on female sexual activity! Although at first sight this seems to indicate a different role for the cerebral cortex in sexual behaviour between the sexes, the reason for this difference probably lies more with the act of copulation than with motivation. For example, a receptive female can simply prepare for sexual intercourse by raising her hindquarters, whereas males have to overcome a greater challenge that involves approaching the female, mounting, and finally a large degree of motor co-ordination. Thus, the male's sexual behaviour, because of its greater complexity, may depend on more neural circuits (particularly in motor areas of the cortex) than the female's sexual response.

The biological basis of homosexuality

There is perhaps no other topic associated with as many controversies and prejudices as that of homosexuality. And, the question of homosexuality is also one that greatly interests the biological psychologist. At the heart of the debate is a simple question: Are some people biologically predisposed to become homosexuals, or is their sexual orientation a learned behaviour influenced by such factors as childhood experiences, parental relationships or adolescent sexual encounters? In fact, this question is relevant not only to homosexuality, but for understanding the development of sexual orientation in all of us.

One thing that is reasonably clear at the outset is that heterosexuals and homosexuals do not show any significant differences in levels of their circulating hormones. Moreover, altering the levels of sex hormones has no change in homosexual sexual preference. For example, castration reduces the sexual behaviour of both heterosexual and homosexual men, but does not change sexual orientation. Similarly, injections of testosterone can help increase sexual desire in both sexes, but it does not change their sexual preference (Money and Ehrhardt 1996).

The question of whether there is hormone influence at work during foetal development, however, is less easy to answer. For example, some researchers (e.g. Ellis and Ames 1987) believe that male homosexuality is, in part, due to decreased levels of testosterone occurring prenatally (or, to be more exact, from the middle of the second month of pregnancy to the end of the fifth month) which alters the development of the hypothalamus (or possibly some other brain structure), thus predisposing the person towards becoming homosexual. Although this theory is difficult to test in humans, it nevertheless appears to be the case that male laboratory animals, exposed to low levels of testosterone early in life, show a greater sexual preference for their own sex as adults (Adkins-Regan 1988). Indeed, as mentioned above, the high percentage of homosexuals in women with adrenogenital syndrome also appears to be in accordance with the idea that early hormonal exposure may have a bearing on later sexual preference. Note, however, that this is not the same as saying that all homosexuals are 'made' this way, or that low levels of testosterone occurring prenatally inevitably produce an adult male with a same-sex preference.

Another way of examining whether a biological factor is involved in the causation of homosexuality is to determine the extent to which genetic factors play a role in shaping this type of behaviour. One way of doing this is to compare rates of homosexuality in identical twins (who share the same genes) and fraternal twins (who share 50 per cent of their genes). One study which examined this issue was undertaken by Bailey and Pillard (1991) who studied a group of male homosexuals who had twin brothers and found a concordance rate of 52 per cent for identical twins and 22 per cent for non-identical twins. Similar results (48 per cent compared to 16 per cent) have also been found for a group of female homosexuals (Bailey *et al.* 1993). These results suggest that homosexuality may have a genetic component, but it is certainly not marked, and environmental factors may be just as important. Indeed, supporting this view is the fact that there are many cases of identical twins where one of the twins is homosexual and the other is heterosexual (Byne 1994).

Brain structure and homosexuality

If there is a biological basis to homosexuality then one would expect to find a biological difference, somewhere in the brain, between heterosexuals and homosexuals. Indeed, in the early 1990s a difference of this type was discovered by Simon LeVay who examined the interstitial nuclei of the anterior hypothalamus. As mentioned previously, there are four of these nuclei (called INAH 1–4) located in the medial preoptic area of the hypothalamus, with INAH-2 and INAH-3 being much larger in the male. Simon LeVay confirmed these findings, but he also looked at these nuclei in homosexual men and found that one of them (INAH-3) was more than twice as large in heterosexuals than in homosexuals (Figure 7.6). In fact, the size of INAH-3 in homosexual men was very similar to that found in heterosexual women. This finding led LeVay to suggest that homosexuality may, in part, be due to the 'feminisation' of the INAH-3 nucleus (LeVay 1993).

Despite the plausibility of this idea, the significance of LeVay's work remains unclear. For example, although LeVay examined a relatively large sample of homosexual men at post-mortem ($N=19$), all had died from AIDS, which raised the possibility that the decreased size of INAH-3 was in some way due to this illness (although it is relevant to note that he still found a large INAH-3 in a sample of six heterosexual men who had also died of AIDS). However, even if these criticisms are not justified, and even if LeVay's findings are found to be reliable (and most researchers believe they are), they still leave many questions unanswered. For example, are the changes in the size of INAH-3 due to genetic or environmental causes? Also, if there is a hormonal involvement, does this act prenatally or postnatally? In short, researchers are still a long way from knowing whether a small INAH-3 is a potential 'cause' of homosexuality, or whether it is simply a consequence of this type of behaviour. Nevertheless, LeVay's discovery offers the exciting prospect of these questions being examined more closely and the possibility of finding out more about the biological basis of sexual orientation.

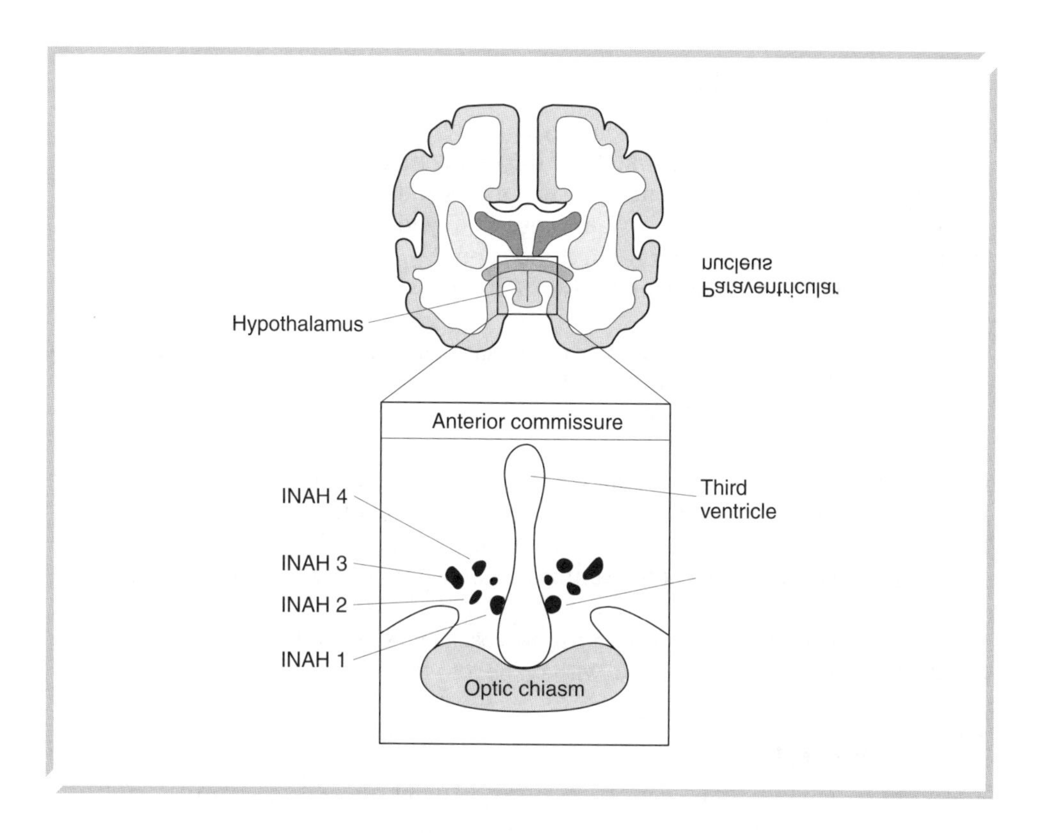

Figure 7.6 (a) The size of INAH-3 in heterosexual men and women, and in homosexual men.

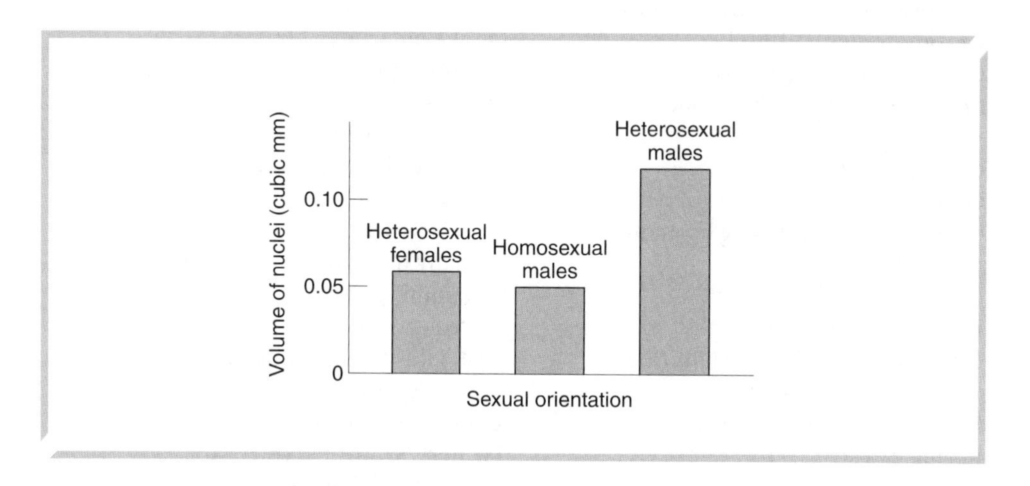

Figure 7.6 (b) Diagram showing location of INAH nuclei in the human brain.

Self-test questions

1. What are the evolutionary advantages of sex?
2. When does sexual differentiation of the foetus first begin?
3. What is the genetic difference between males and females?
4. What are the consequences of adrenogenital syndrome?
5. How does testicular feminisation come about?
6. Describe the causes and symptoms of Turner's syndrome and Klinefelter's syndrome.
7. What is the difference between an organisational and activational hormonal effect?
8. Where is the bulbocavernosus nucleus?
9. Where is the sexually dimorphic nucleus found? What is unique about this area of the brain in humans?
10. Briefly describe the main hormonal features of the menstrual cycle.
11. Does increased testosterone lead to increased aggression?
12. What brain areas underlie sexual behaviour in the male?
13. What effects do lesions of the ventromedial hypothalamus have on female behaviour?
14. Is there a genetic predisposition for homosexual behaviour?
15. What has Simon LeVay shown with respect to the brains of homosexual men?

Key terms

Activational effect (p.203)
Adrenal hyperplasia (p.201)
Anabolic steroid (p.201)
Androgen (p.201)
Bulbocavernosus nucleus (p.206)
Chromosomes (p.199)
Corpus callosum (p.205)
Follicle-stimulating hormone (FSH) (p.207)
Gametes (p.199)
Genes (p.199)
Gonadotropin-releasing hormone (GnRH) (p.207)
Gonads (p.199)
Hypothalamus (p.207)
Interstitial nuclei of the anterior hypothalamus (p.205)
Klinefelter's syndrome (p.202)
Leydig cells (p.207)
Lordosis (p.203)
Luteinising hormones (LH) (p.207)
Medial preoptic area (p.216)
Menstrual cycle (p.208)
Müllerian duct (p.199)
Müllerian duct-inhibiting substance (p.199)
Oestrus (p.208)
Onuf's nucleus (p.206)
Organisational effect (p.203)
Ovaries (p.199)
Ovulation (p.208)
Pituitary gland (p.207)
Preoptic area (p.204)
Pseudo-hermaphrodite (p.201)
Sexually dimorphic nucleus (p.204)
Splenium (p.205)
Testes (p.199)
Testicular feminisation syndrome (p.201)
Testis-determining factor (p.199)
Testosterone (p.199)
Turner's syndrome (p.202)
Ventromedial hypothalamus (p.216)
Wolffian duct (p.199)

References

Adkins-Regan, E. (1989) Sex hormones and sexual orientation in animals. *Psychobiology*, **16**, 335–47.

Allee, W. C. *et al.* (1939) Modification of the social order in flocks of hens by the injection of testosterone propionate. *Physiological Zoology*, **12**, 412–40.

Allen, L. S. *et al.* (1988) Two sexually dimorphic cell groups in the human brain. *Journal of Neuroscience*, **9**, 497–506.

Anonymous (1970) Effects of sexual activity on beard growth in man. *Nature*, **226**, 869–70.

Archer, J. (1994) Testosterone and aggression. *Journal of Offender Rehabilitation*, **21**, 3–26.

Bailey, J. M. and Pillard, R. C. (1991) A genetic study of male sexual orientation. *Archives of General Psychiatry*, **48**, 1089–96.

Bailey, J. M. *et al.* (1993) Heritable factors influencing sexual orientation in women. *Archives of General Psychiatry*, **50**, 217–23.

Beach, F. A. (1940) Effects of cortical lesions upon the copulatory behavior of male rats. *Journal of Comparative Psychology*, **29**, 193–239.

Becker, J. B. *et al.* (1993) *Behavioral Endocrinology*. Cambridge, MA: MIT Press.

Beeman, E. A. (1947) The effect of male hormone on aggressive behavior in mice. *Physiological Zoology*, **20**, 373–405.

Brower, K. J. *et al.* (1991) *British Journal of Addiction*, **86**, 759–68.

Byne, W. (1994) The biological evidence challenged. *Scientific American*, May, 26–31.

Byne, W. *et al.* (1988) Variations in human corpus callosum do not predict gender: A study using magnetic resonance imaging. *Behavioral Neuroscience*, **102**, 222–7.

Clarke, J. (1990) Interhemispheric function in humans: Relationships between anatomical measures of the corpus callosum, behavioral laterality effects and cognitive profiles. Unpublished doctoral dissertation, University of California, Los Angeles.

Dabbs, J. M. and Morris, R. (1990) Testosterone, social class, and antisocial behavior in a sample of 4,462 men. *Psychological Science*, **1**, 209–11.

Davidson, J. M. (1969) Effect of estrogen on the sexual behavior of male rats. *Endocrinology*, **84**, 1365–72.

Davidson, J. M. (1980) The psychobiology of sexual experience. In Davidson, J. M. and Davidson, R. J. (eds) *The Psychobiology of Consciousness*. New York: Plenum Press.

Ellis, H. H. and Ames, M. A. (1987) Neurohormonal functioning and sexual orientation: A theory of homosexuality–heterosexuality. *Psychological Bulletin*, **101**, 233–58.

Emery, A. E. H. and Mueller, R. F. (1992) *Elements of Medical Genetics*. Edinburgh: Churchill Livingstone.

Forger, N. G. and Breedlove, S. M. (1986) Sexual dimorphism in human and canine spinal cord: Role of early androgen. *Proceedings of the National Academy of Sciences (USA)*, **83**, 7257–31.

Gorski, R. A. *et al.* (1978) Evidence for a morphological sex difference within the medial preoptic area of the rat brain. *Brain Research*, **148**, 333–46.

Goy, R. W. *et al.* (1988) Behavioral masculinisation is independent of genital masculinisation in prenatally androgenised female rhesus monkeys. *Hormones and Behavior*, **22**, 552–71.
Haas, K. and Haas, A. (1993) *Understanding Sexuality*. St Louis: Mosby.
Hart, B. L. (1967) Testosterone regulation of sexual reflexes in spinal male rats. *Science*, **155**, 1283–4.
Heimer, L. and Larsson, K. (1967) Impairment of mating behavior in male rats following lesions in the preoptic-anterior hypothalamic continuum. *Brain Research*, **3**, 248–63.
Hellhammer, D. H. *et al.* (1985) Changes in saliva testosterone after psychological stimulation in men. *Psychoneuroendocrinology*, **10**, 77–81.
Lacoste-Utamsing, M. C. and Holloway, R. L. (1982) Sexual dimorphism in the human corpus callosum. *Science*, **216**, 1431–2.
LeVay, S. (1993) *The Sexual Brain*. Cambridge, MA: MIT Press.
Masters, W. H. and Johnson, V. E. (1966) *Human Sexual Response*. Boston: Little Brown.
Masters, W. H. *et al.* (1995) *Human Sexuality*, 5th edn. New York: HarperCollins.
McCaul, K. D. *et al.* (1992) Winning, losing, mood and testosterone. *Hormones and Behavior*, **26**, 486–504.
Michael, R. P. (1980) Hormones and sexual behaviour in the female. In Krieger, D. T. and Hughes, J. C. (eds) *Neuroendocrinology*. Sunderland, MA: Sinauer.
Monaghan, E. P. and Glickman, S. E. (1992) Hormones and aggressive behavior. In Becker, J. B. *et al. Behavioral Endicrinology*. Cambridge, MA: MIT Press.
Money, J. (1960) Phantom orgasm in the dreams of paraplegic men and women. *Archives of General Psychiatry*, **3**, 373–82.
Money, J. and Ehrhardt, A. E. (1996) *Man and Woman, Boy and Girl.* Northvale: Aronson.
Money, J. *et al.* (1984) Adult erotosexual status and fetal hormonal masculinization and demasculinization. *Psychoendocrinology*, **9**, 405–14.
Pfaff, D. and Modianos, D. (1985) Neural mechanisms of female reproductive behavior. In Adler, N. *et al.* (eds) *Handbook of Behavioral Neurobiology*, vol. 7. New York: Plenum Press.
Phoenix, C. H. *et al.* (1959) Organising action of prenatally administered testosterone propionate on the tissues mediating mating behaviour in the female guinea pig. *Endocrinology*, **65**, 269–382.
Pope, H. G. and Katz, D. L. (1988) Affective and psychotic symptoms associated with anabolic steroid use. *American Journal of Psychiatry*, **145**, 487–90.
Raisman, G. and Field, P. M. (1973) Sexual dimorphism in the neuropil of the preoptic area of the rat and its dependence on neonatal androgen. *Brain Research*, **54**, 1–29.
Rose, R. M. *et al.* (1971) Plasma testosterone, dominance rank and aggressive behaviour in a group of male rhesus monkeys. *Nature*, **231**, 366–8.
Rose, R. M. *et al.* (1975) Consequences of social conflict on plasma testosterone levels in rhesus monkeys. *Psychomatic Medicine*, **37**, 50–62.
Wilson, J. D. (1988) Androgen abuse by athletes. *Endocrine Reviews*, **9**, 181–99.
Witelson, E. E. (1989) Hand and sex differences in the isthmus and genu of the human corpus callosum. *Brain*, **112**, 799–846.

FURTHER READING

Bullough, V. L. (1994) *Science in the Bedroom: A History of Sex Research*. New York: Basic Books.

Fausto-Sterling, A. (1992) *Myths of Gender: Biological Theories about Women and Men*. New York: Basic Books.

Multiple choice questions

1. The sex chromosomes of females are _______ and the sex chromosomes of males are ______.

(a) XY, XX
(b) YY, XX
(c) XX, YY
(d) XX, XY

2. During early foetal development, the ______________ has the capacity to develop into the male reproductive system and the ____________ has the capacity to develop into the female reproductive system.

(a) Wolffian duct, Müllerian duct
(b) testes, ovaries
(c) Müllerian duct, Wolffian duct
(d) prostate gland, corpus luteum

3. Females with congenital adrenal hyperplasia:

(a) are often brought up as boys
(b) show masculinisation of their external genitalia
(c) are often pseudo-hermaphrodites
(d) are all of the above

4. The testicular feminisation syndrome occurs when:

(a) testosterone has no effect on the developing (male) body tissues
(b) males produce excess amounts of oestrogen
(c) females produce excess amounts of androgens leading to masculine genitalia
(d) Müllerian duct-inhibiting substance is not produced by the male foetus

5. ________________ occurs when the individual inherits only one (female) X chromosome.

(a) Klinefelter's syndrome
(b) congenital adrenal hyperplasia
(c) testicular feminisation syndrome
(d) Turner's syndrome

6. Which of the following is not an activational effect of a sex hormone?

(a) the development (organisation) of the nervous system
(b) the production of sperm
(c) lordosis behaviour
(d) ovulation

7. When John Money (1984) questioned 30 young women who had a history of adrenogenital syndrome, the majority (40 per cent) described themselves as:

(a) bisexual
(b) homosexual
(c) heterosexual
(d) they refused to say

8. Raisman and Field (1973) found that the ________________ had more synapses in female rats than in males.

(a) mammillary bodies
(b) preoptic area
(c) ventral hypothalamus
(d) paraventricular nucleus

9. The sexually dimorphic nucleus is:

(a) normally larger in males than in females
(b) smaller in males (compared to other males) that are castrated at birth
(c) larger in females given androgens at birth
(d) all of the above

10. In humans, the sexually dimorphic nuclei are otherwise known as the:

(a) habenular nuclei
(b) mammillary bodies
(c) interstitial nuclei of the anterior hypothalamus
(d) none of the above

11. According to LeVay (1993), in relative terms women have a bigger ________________ than men.

(a) hypothalamus
(b) right hemisphere
(c) corpus callosum
(d) preoptic area

12. The bulbocavernosus nucleus is found in the:

(a) brainstem

(b) hypothalamus (adjacent to the sexually dimorphic nuclei)
(c) splenium
(d) spinal cord

13. In males, the release of luteinising hormone (by the anterior pituitary gland) stimulates the Leydig cells to produce:

(a) small amounts of oestrogen
(b) sperm
(c) testosterone
(d) androstenone

14. In females, the release of luteinising hormone causes:

(a) ovulation
(b) the ovaries to produce oestrogen
(c) the adrenal cortex to produce testosterone
(d) menstruation

15. During the menstrual cycle, progesterone levels are at their highest during:

(a) the luteal phase
(b) ovulation
(c) the follicular phase
(d) menstruation

16. The main cause of impotence in men is a result of:

(a) low levels of testosterone
(b) increased levels of oestrogen
(c) anxiety and psychological factors
(d) reduced androgenic stimulation of the bulbocavernosus nucleus

17. Rose *et al.* (1975) have found that a monkey's testosterone level prior to being put into a social group:

(a) directly correlated with the dominance rank it would later attain
(b) directly correlated with the level of aggression it would later show
(c) both (a) and (b) above
(d) did not correlate with later dominance ranking or aggressive behaviour

18. Males who have been paraplegic by transection of the spinal cord:

(a) can never achieve an erection
(b) can never achieve ejaculation
(c) can never 'experience' the feedback from an orgasm
(d) all of the above

19. The ________________ has been shown to be important for male sexual behaviour and the ____________________ for female sexual behaviour.

(a) anterior hypothalamus, paraventricular hypothalamus
(b) medial preoptic area, ventromedial hypothalamus
(c) hippocampus, amygdala
(d) lateral hypothalamus, medial preoptic area

20. Simon LeVay makes the controversial claim that:

(a) homosexuality is genetic
(b) homosexuality is a result of early upbringing
(c) there are differences in brain structure between heterosexual and homosexual men
(d) homosexuality is abnormal

8 Learning and memory

IN THIS CHAPTER

- The search for the location of memory (the engram) in the brain
- The effects of experience on the physiology of the brain
- The synaptic basis of learning and memory
- Long-term potentiation
- The role of the medial temporal lobes in human memory
- Diencephalic amnesia including Korsakoff's disease
- Working memory and cognitive mapping in rats
- The use of primates in memory research

Introduction

Learning and memory go hand in hand. Learning can be defined as the acquisition of new information, while memory is the capacity for storing and retrieving this material. Clearly, there can be no evidence of learning without memory, although there are certain types of memory that are not learned (e.g. instincts and reflexive behaviour). But for all intents and purposes, our memory is derived exclusively from learning experiences. We tend to take learning and memory for granted, although without them we would not be able to recognise our friends, our home, our possessions or even ourselves. We would not be able to think or use language, and it is even doubtful whether we would be conscious or be able to perceive the world around us. In other words, without learning and memory we would be psychologically dead. Indeed, our great capacity for learning (linked to the evolution of our cerebral hemispheres) is one of the things that makes us uniquely human. Yet, the ability to learn is not a unique human skill since we also share this same basic capacity with probably every other living creature on Earth (including single-celled organisms). This is of particular interest to the biological psychologist, for if we can understand how learning and memory occur in simpler creatures, we may also gain important insights into our own remarkable ability.

The scope of the problem

Learning and memory must involve some relatively permanent change in the structure of the nervous system. But how are memories stored? Although this question probably has no simple answer, part of the explanation must lie with changes taking place in neurons. There are a number of possible ways this could occur. For example, perhaps memory results in changes taking place in the neuron's structure (including the creation of new synapses or dendrites); or maybe it involves altering the release of certain neurotransmitters (or the receptor's sensitivity to them). Alternatively, learning and memory may set up changes in the pattern of electrical activity that takes place in circuits of many thousands, if not millions, of neurons. Indeed, as we shall see below, all these forms of neuronal change (or 'plasticity') have provided plausible explanations of how the brain is able to encode and memorise new information.

Although the types of change taking place in an individual neuron may be relatively simple, the sheer number of cells that are involved in human learning and memory makes any simple account of this phenomenon practically impossible. The human brain contains around 12 billion neurons, with their axon terminals perhaps making over 10 trillion synaptic connections (see Chapter 1). But it is this point of contact between neurons that is probably the most important site where the structural, chemical or electrical changes underlying learning and memory take place. Unfortunately, the extremely small size of synapses (they can only be seen with an electron microscope), along with their incredible abundance in the brain (especially in the cerebral cortex), means that even simply identifying where memory occurs is fraught with great difficulty – let alone identifying the neurochemical and physiological changes that take place.

The work of Karl Lashley

Karl Lashley was one of the first scientists to examine the question of where in the brain memory is located, and he spent most of his research career (which spanned over 30 years) trying to discover the anatomical site of the memory trace, or what he called the **engram**. When Lashley first began his research (in the 1920s), psychologists were strongly influenced by the work of the Russian physiologist Ivan Pavlov who believed that learning took place through the process of conditioning. In short, Pavlov argued that learning was a reflex which resulted from the animal linking specific stimuli (or events) with particular responses. For example, Pavlov showed that the presentation of food to a hungry dog always elicited salivation (an unconditioned or 'unlearnt' response). But, if he paired a tone with the presentation of the food a number of times, then the tone alone would begin to elicit salivation (i.e. the response had now become conditioned or 'learnt'). This form of learning is known as **classical conditioning** (see Figure 8.1). Moreover, in anatomical terms, Pavlov's notions of stimulus and response also appeared to correspond with the sensory and movement areas of the cerebral cortex. Thus, Pavlov proposed that the neural basis of learning involved the growth of new connections or pathways that linked the sensory (stimulus) regions of the cerebral cortex with its motor (response) areas.

It was in this intellectual climate that Lashley set about trying to discover the engram. Lashley reasoned that if learning took place in the cerebral cortex, and was the result of new connections being formed between sensory and motor areas, then making a knife cut between these two brain areas following conditioning should impair the memory of the learned response. To test this hypothesis, Lashley trained rats on a variety of maze tasks to a high level of performance, and then made knife cuts to the cerebral cortex, after which he tested the animals again. For each rat, Lashley made a cut in a different

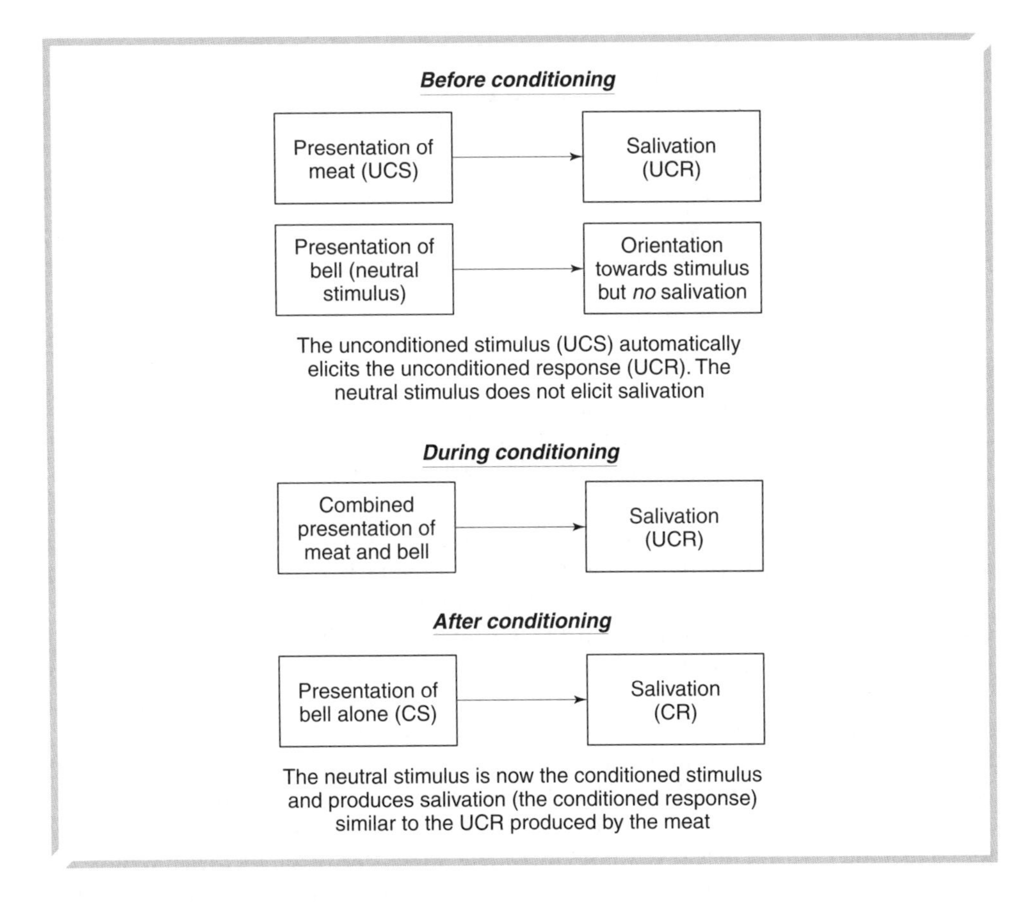

Figure 8.1 An illustration of how classical conditioning occurs.

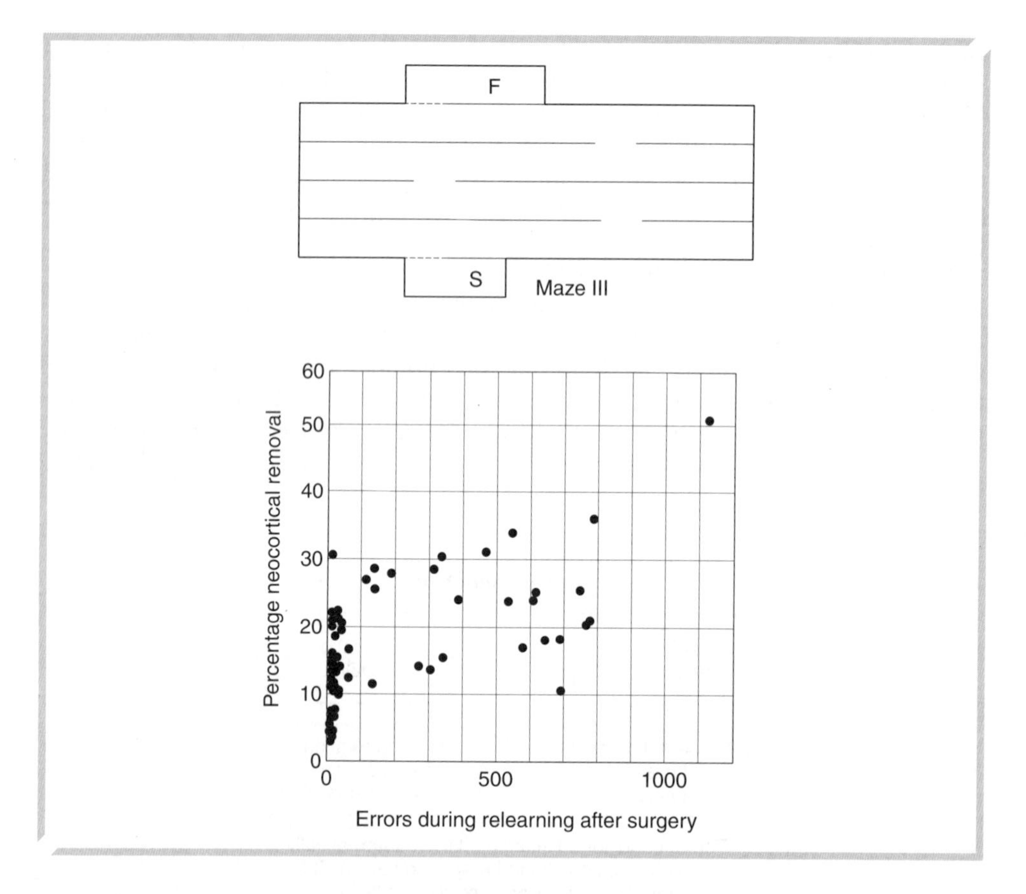

Figure 8.2 The maze used by Lashley along with a graph of his findings showing relearning performance as a function of cortex removal. (*Source*: From K. S. Lashley, *Brain Mechanisms and Intelligence*. Copyright © 1963 by Dover Publications. Reprinted by permission.)

location. However, to his surprise, he found that no cut (or combination of cuts) appeared to interfere with the animal's memory of the task. In other words, the site of the knife cut had no effect on the rat's memory of how to run through the maze. This finding appeared to be at odds with the Pavlovian idea that learning required the formation of new connections in the cerebral cortex.

In a further set of experiments, instead of using knife cuts, Lashley removed (lesioned) parts of the cerebral cortex. This time Lashley did find a deficit when lesioned animals were placed back in the maze. In fact, he found that the deficit in relearning the task was proportional to the amount of cerebral cortex he removed. For example, if a small amount of cortex (around 5 or 10 per cent) was destroyed, Lashley found that the performance loss was scarcely detectable. However, if large amounts (50 per cent) were removed, then the memory appeared to be destroyed, and retraining back to previous levels of performance took a large number of trials (see Figure 8.2).

But, again, as with his previous work, the actual site of damage did not appear to be important. Moreover, cortical lesions of equal size produced similar effects regardless of where they were placed. It was as if memory was stored everywhere – or at no site in particular.

On the basis of these findings Lashley concluded that memories for maze tasks were stored diffusely throughout the cerebral cortex (which he called the principle of **Mass Action**) and that all parts of the association cortex played an equal role in their storage (the principle of **equipotentiality**). Although Lashley found that some areas of the cerebral cortex were more important than others in the storage of certain memories (e.g. the visual cortex was particularly important in tasks requiring the discrimination of visual patterns), he nevertheless found that no structure was absolutely crucial. No matter what area of the cortex was removed the animal could eventually relearn the task he gave it.

Was Lashley correct?

Lashley was probably correct in his belief that memories are distributed throughout the brain and not localised in one place. Despite this, his conclusion that all parts of the cerebral cortex play an equal role in learning and memory is not widely accepted today. To the contrary, it is clear that certain areas of the cerebral cortex in humans have specialised and localised functions. For example, as we shall see in the next chapter, there is strong evidence that the two cerebral hemispheres have different functions, and within each hemisphere there are also clearly different localised areas for different types of specialisation such as language and movement. This also suggests that memory is not distributed homogeneously throughout the cortex.

Why did Lashley therefore probably overstate his case? One reason was his choice of task (maze learning). It is now accepted that this particular task was inappropriate for studying localisation of function. Indeed, rather than requiring the involvement of just one area of the cerebral cortex, it is almost certainly the case that the maze task requires the formation of many 'engrams' spread throughout the cerebral cortex. For example, as the rat runs through the maze, it may be combining many different types of sensory information (e.g. vision, olfaction, proprioception, etc.) to guide itself. Thus, although the individual engrams may be localised, the maze task may be so complex and draws upon so many different types of learning, that the total memory is, in effect, stored throughout the cortex. Moreover, because no one area is absolutely crucial, this explains why an animal can relearn the maze task following the removal of large parts of the cortex (e.g. other parts of the brain can compensate for the lost tissue).

Another criticism of Lashley is his assumption that the cerebral cortex is the only site of learning and memory. Although to some extent this bias was due to the initial influence of Pavlov, and the difficulties in accurately performing lesions to subcortical structures of the brain, it is nevertheless now clear that a large number of subcortical structures also have a role to play in learning and memory. In fact, as we shall see later, some subcortical areas (particularly the limbic system) have a vital role in learning and the retrieval of memory.

The contribution of Donald Hebb

Donald Hebb (who obtained his PhD at Harvard University under Lashley's guidance in 1936) was interested in how neurons might encode memory, and he set about trying to explain how this might occur. To begin, Hebb was aware that neurons formed huge amounts of connections with each other, and on this basis he hypothesised that memory must involve large circuits of neurons distributed throughout the brain. But how could circuits of neurons encode memory? To provide an answer, Hebb reasoned that circuits (or what he called cell assemblies), once activated by a learning experience, began to reverberate with electrical activity for some time after the event. In effect, this activity could 'hold' the memory for a short period and therefore provide an explanation for short-term memory.

But, of course, it was unrealistic to believe that such reverberatory circuits were active over long periods of time. Thus, to explain permanent memory, Hebb took his idea one step further. In short, he proposed that if reverberatory circuits maintained their activity long enough, then this would cause a structural change (e.g. a growth process or metabolic change) in the neurons making up the cell assembly. And, the likeliest site for this change according to Hebb was the synapse (in fact, a synapse that is 'strengthened' as a result of learning is now called a **Hebbian synapse**). In other words, as reverberation produced structural change in cell assemblies, the consolidation of memory would occur (see Figure 8.3). Hebb's theory was intuitively appealing since it was compatible with the idea that memory was distributed throughout the brain, yet it also explained how neurons might encode and store memory. Although Hebb had no practical way of testing his theory, recent research has lent considerable support to his ideas.

The effects of experience on the brain

Psychologists have long known that the effects of early experience and rearing can have a profound effect on later development. Indeed, Donald Hebb in 1949 also noted that the same principle applied to rats. In particular, he was struck by the observation that his own pet rats (that had been raised at home) were superior to laboratory rats when it came to learning to run through a maze. This implied that an enriched environment had produced a 'brighter' animal. But could such a rat be distinguished from a less intelligent one on the basis of brain structure? This was the question that Mark Rosenzweig set out to examine in the mid-1950s. The likelihood of finding any difference using the relatively crude histological and neuroanatomical techniques of the time appeared to be improbable – but his findings soon proved otherwise.

In one study, Rosenzweig reared rats for various lengths of time in impoverished or enriched environments. In the impoverished condition, the animal lived alone in a small cage, located in a quiet room, with as little stimulation as possible. In the enriched condition, groups of 12 rats lived together in a large cage furnished with a variety of toys, runways and objects. Moreover, a new object was also placed in the cage each day to add further novelty and stimulation. At the end of a given period – between 30 days and

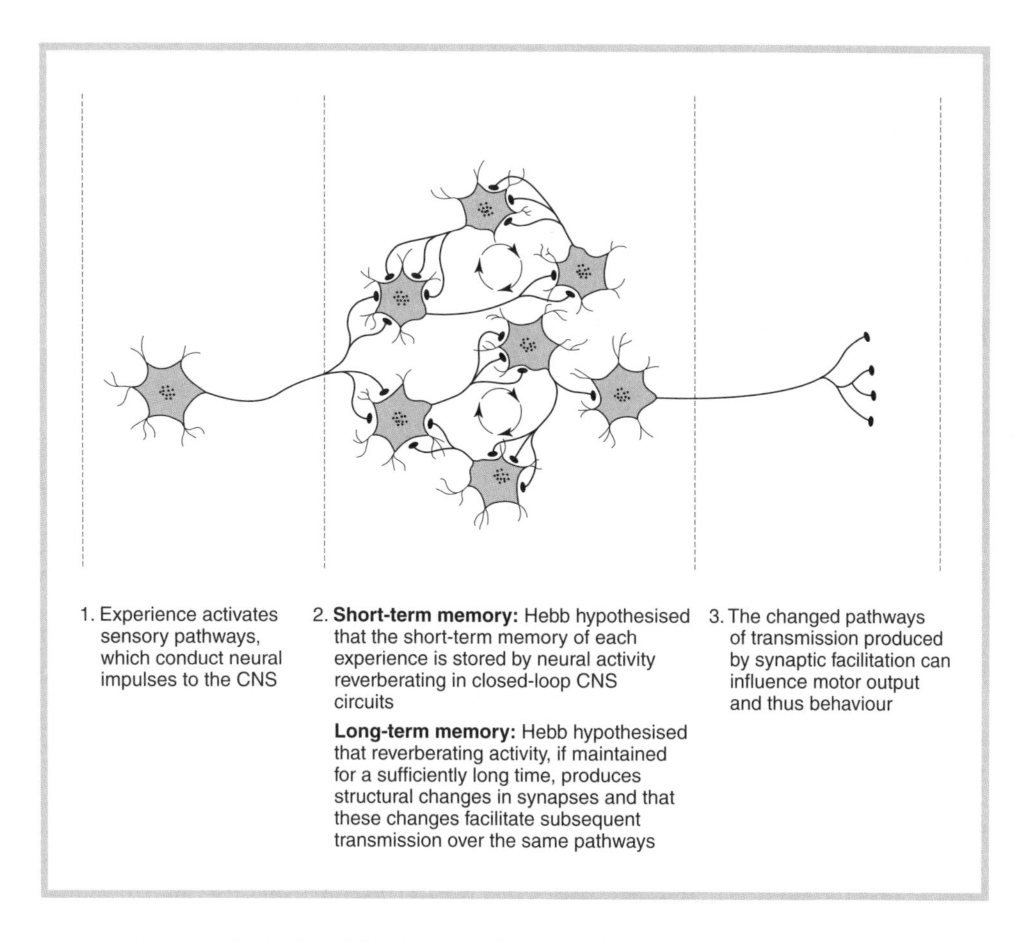

Figure 8.3 A hypothetical model of how reverberatory circuits may be set up in neural networks. (*Source*: From John P. J. Pinel, *Biopsychology*, 3rd edition. Copyright © 1997 by Allyn & Bacon. Reprinted by permission.)

several months – the rats were sacrificed and their brains examined to detect whether any neural changes had taken place.

The results showed that the animals reared in the enriched conditions differed in a number of important respects to control rats. For example, the enriched rats had a thicker cerebral cortex which was also significantly heavier than that of the impoverished animals (this increase in size was especially marked for the occipital area). Rosenzweig also found that the enriched animals had greater levels of the enzyme **acetylcholinesterase (AChE)** in their cortex (this enzyme breaks down **acetylcholine**, thus helping to enhance neurotransmission). But, the most striking discovery of all was the difference in the shape of the neurons taken from this part of the brain. In particular, animals reared in the enriched environment were found to have more spines on their dendrites, and because it was known that spines normally contain large numbers of synapses, this indicated that the number of synapses may also be increased as a result of experience. This prediction, along with evidence showing that dendritic synapses were much larger in the enriched animals, was later confirmed by electron microscopy (Turner and Greenough 1983, 1985). In fact, the enriched rats were shown to have about 9,400 synapses per neuron (taken from the occipital cortex) compared to about 7,600 for the deprived animals – an increase of more than 20 per cent. Thus, experience clearly has a marked effect on the structure of the brain.

Learning and memory in *Aplysia*

It is one thing showing that the structure of dendrites and synapses change with experience, but quite another to prove convincingly that these types of alteration are the underlying basis of learning and memory. Although the rat has long been a favoured subject in psychological research, it has limited usefulness when it comes to showing how engrams (memory traces) may occur. For this reason, researchers have looked for organisms with simpler nervous systems in an attempt to discover how engrams are formed. The animal that has taken pride of place in this quest in recent years is perhaps a surprising one: it is a large marine snail (related to the common slug) found off the coast of California and northern Mexico called ***Aplysia***. The use of *Aplysia* has been pioneered by Eric Kandel and his colleagues, and there is little doubt that this work has enabled the synaptic and neural basis of learning and memory to be studied in considerable detail (Hawkins *et al.* 1987).

Aplysia has a number of advantages for the researcher interested in understanding how neural systems can learn. Firstly, it has a relatively simple nervous system containing approximately 20,000 neurons grouped together in several ganglia (this is significantly less than any vertebrate). Secondly, the number of neurons and their location are the same for all individuals. Thirdly, *Aplysia*'s neurons are relatively large and can be studied much more easily than vertebrate neurons. Finally, and perhaps most important, *Aplysia* is capable of several types of learning, including habituation, sensitisation and classical conditioning. We shall only examine habituation here to illustrate some of the ways a simple nervous system can learn (the reader interested in other forms of learning shown by *Aplysia* is referred to Kandel *et al.* 1995).

Habituation simply refers to a decrease in behavioural response when a stimulus is repeatedly presented to the organism. When a stimulus is novel or unexpected, animals often respond with a defensive or startled reflex. But if the stimulus is harmless it will quickly be ignored and habituation occurs. Humans also demonstrate habituation. For example, the ticking of a clock which fades away as we try to sleep, or an unusual smell which we initially experience when entering a friend's house, are two examples. Simple as it may seem, this form of learning must nevertheless entail information being stored somewhere in the nervous system. In the case of *Aplysia*, the question is how and where?

Kandel examined the process of habituation in *Aplysia* by measuring its **gill-withdrawal reflex**. *Aplysia* has a large gill (situated on its back) that extracts oxygen from water (similar to a fish) which, in turn, is adjoined to a siphon which expels the sea water

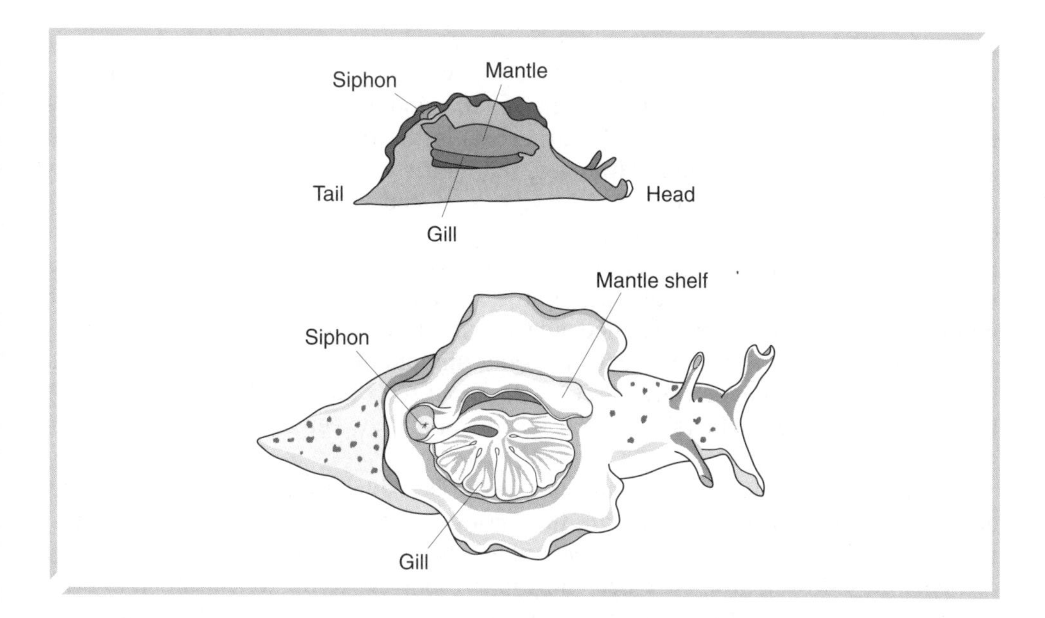

Figure 8.4 An *Aplysia*.

and waste (see Figure 8.4). Both the gill and siphon are delicate organs and, if touched, *Aplysia* responds by vigorously retracting them into its protective cavity, which is then covered with a large fleshy pad called the mantle shelf. However, if a weak stimulus (Kandel used a calibrated jet of water) is applied repeatedly to the siphon, then *Aplysia*'s withdrawal response habituates – that is, it becomes less and less pronounced until it doesn't occur at all. This response may last several minutes following a single training session of 10 stimuli (short-term habituation), or over three weeks following four training sessions spaced over a number of days (long-term habituation).

The neural basis of short-term habituation in *Aplysia*

To understand how short-term habituation occurs in *Aplysia* it is necessary to identify the neural circuitry that is responsible for producing the gill-withdrawal reflex. The first stage of this reflex involves the siphon, which contains 24 sensory neurons, that respond to tactile information (i.e. the water jet). In turn, the axons of the siphon's neurons project to just six motor neurons that control the retraction of the gill (several groups of excitatory and inhibitory interneurons also lie between the sensory and motor neurons, although we need not discuss these here). Thus, somewhere in this neural circuit of sensory and motor neurons, learning (habituation) is taking place. The question is: Where?

To answer this question, Kandel and his colleagues first placed electrodes into the sensory and motor neurons and measured the number of neural impulses that accompanied the habituation of the gill-withdrawal reflex. It was found that the sensory neurons leading from the siphon did not show any decline in activity despite repeated stimulation by the jet of water (i.e. whenever the siphon was stimulated the sensory neurons fired). Thus, changes (or lack thereof) in the firing of the sensory neurons could not explain the learning. However, the motor neurons did show a decline in neural activity (i.e. fewer nerve impulses were produced with each siphon stimulation) which also correlated with the decline of the gill-withdrawal reflex. There were two possible explanations: either the motor neuron was becoming less able to invoke a response, or changes were taking place at the synapses between sensory and motor neurons. The first possibility was ruled out when it was found that electrical stimulation of the motor neurons always produced the same amount of muscle contraction (i.e. the motor neuron was not getting 'tired' with repetitive firing). Thus, the cause of habituation appeared to be taking place at some point between the sensory and motor neurons (i.e. the synapse).

At the synapse, there were again two possible explanations: changes could be occurring presynaptically (i.e. perhaps the sensory neurons were releasing less neurotransmitter with each stimulation); or postsynaptically (i.e. perhaps the receptors on the postsynaptic motor neuron were becoming less responsive to the transmitter). In fact, the changes were found to be occurring presynaptically. In short, it was shown that fewer molecules of transmitter (believed to be glutamate) were being released from the siphon's sensory neurons with each action potential (Castellucci and Kandel 1974). In turn, the reduced amount of neurotransmitter release into the synapse caused less stimulation of the motor neurons innervating the gill, thus producing a decline in the behavioural response (habituation).

But what causes the reduction in the release of neurotransmitter? The answer, it appears, is partly due to the decreased number of calcium ions that enter the presynaptic terminal. For example, in response to an action potential reaching the axon terminal, the influx of calcium ions normally act to fuse (or propel) the **synaptic vesicles** (containing neurotransmitter) into the presynaptic membrane, thus spilling the neurotransmitter into the synaptic cleft (see Chapter 1). However, with repeated stimulation of the neuron, it appears that there is a reduced influx of calcium into the synaptic terminal, which is responsible for causing less neurotransmitter release (see Figure 8.5). Thus, reduced to its most basic explanation, habituation of the gill-withdrawal reflex can be blamed on calcium ions!

These findings show that learning can take place by modifying the effectiveness of synaptic transmission, even though the anatomy of the neural circuit is fixed. However, this is not the only way in which habituation can take place. For example, Baily and Chen (1983) have examined the terminals of the sensory neurons in long-term habituated *Aplysia* (long-term habituation is where the animal has been trained to exhibit learning that lasts several weeks) and found that they had fewer and smaller synapses. In other words, the sensory neurons showed structural alterations, which indicates that biochemical processes other than those involving calcium had taken place. As we have already seen, changes in the number (and structure) of synapses have also been found in rats reared in enriched conditions. Thus, these types of synaptic

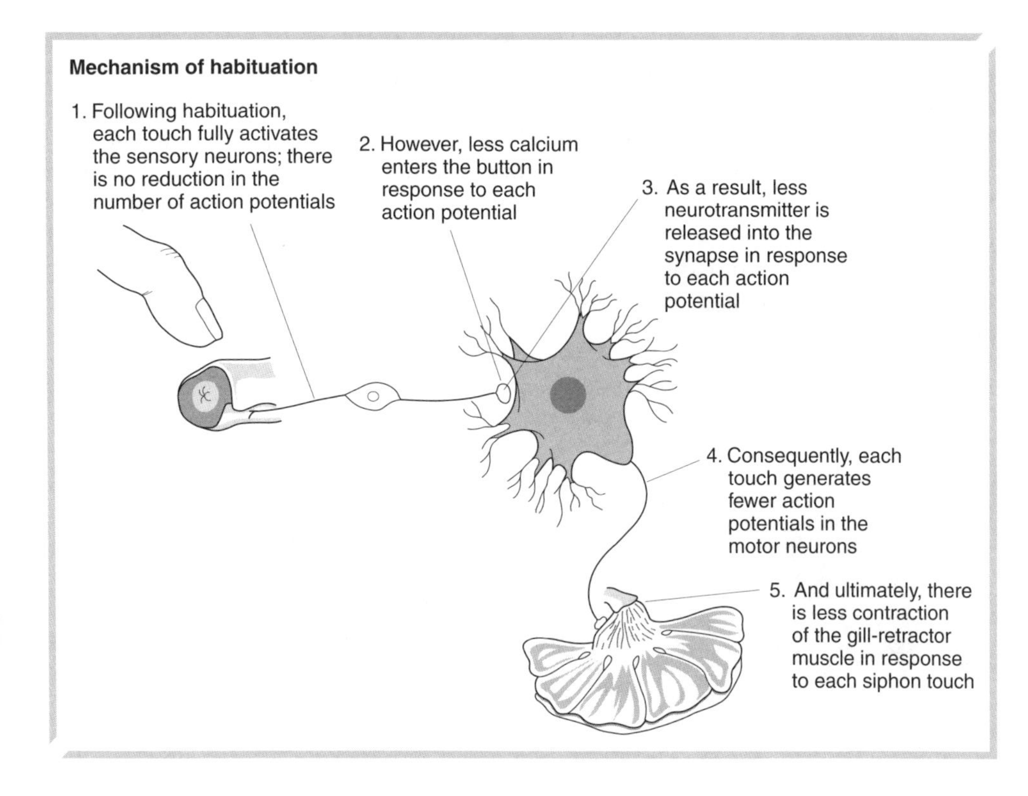

Figure 8.5 The neural and biochemical stages underlying habituation of the gill-withdrawal reflex in *Aplysia*. (*Source*: From John P. J. Pinel, *Biopsychology*, 3rd edition. Copyright © 1997 by Allyn & Bacon. Reprinted by permission.)

change may be a common form of information storage for a wide range of different species.

Brain structures involved in human memory

So far, we have looked at learning in individual (or small systems of) neurons, but of course, our brains contain many billions of neurons arranged in various structures and pathways. Moreover, some of these structures are likely to be more important than others in learning and memory. But what are the structures that have this type of role? One site we have already mentioned (in conjunction with Lashley's work) is the cerebral cortex. Indeed, across species, learning ability is roughly correlated with the size and complexity of the cerebral cortex and, of course, this structure is the most highly evolved in humans. Moreover, examination of people with accidental brain damage (such as stroke, injury and disease) has also shown that the cerebral cortex is crucially involved in cognition and many specialised forms of learning and memory (see next chapter).

Despite this, the brain region that has arguably attracted the most attention in memory research is not part of the cerebral cortex, but is an 'old' (sub)cortical structure that in evolutionary terms preceded its development – the **hippocampus** (see Figure 8.6).

The hippocampus was first identified as having an important role in human memory when a Canadian patient who had this part of the brain removed in a surgical operation became severely amnesic. This person is simply known by his initials HM and he has probably had more written about him than any other clinical case in the history of psychology. He has also participated in many hundreds of hours of research. Despite this, only a few researchers know his real name and no pictures of him have ever been published.

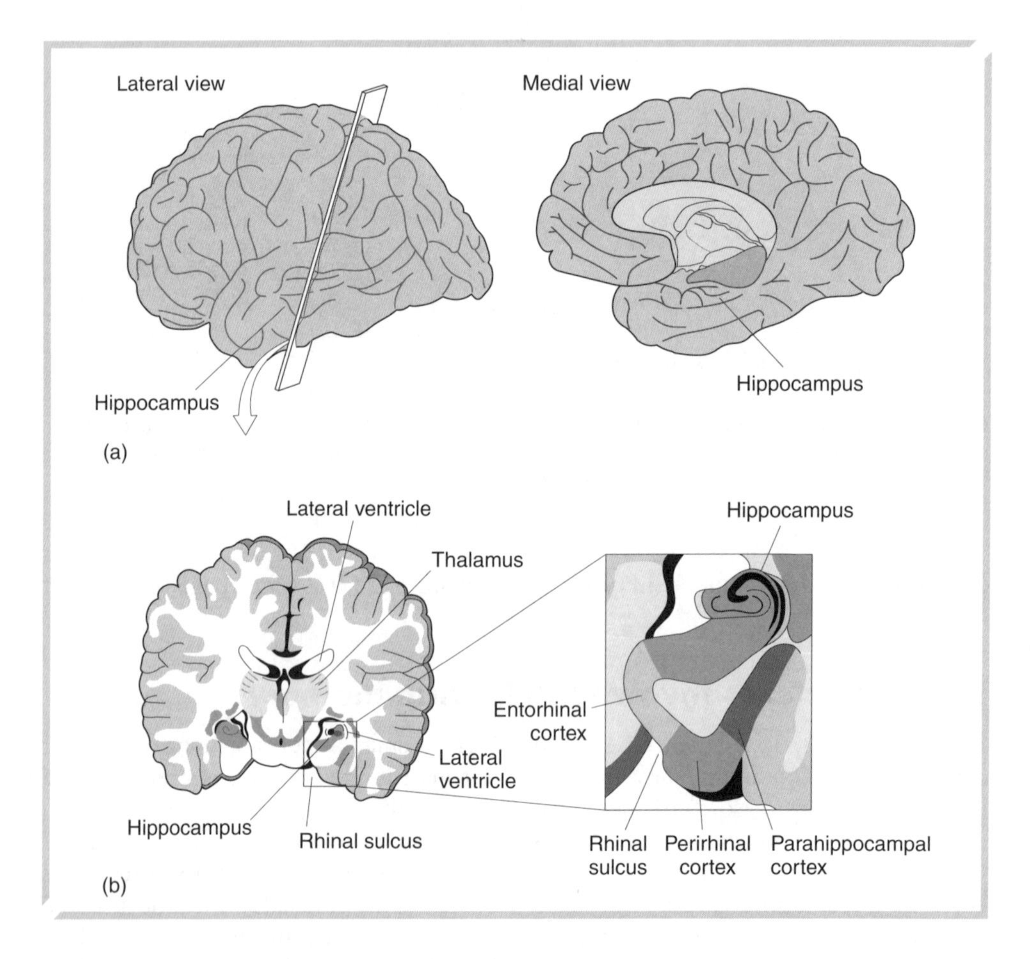

Figure 8.6 The hippocampus. (*Source*: From M. F. Bear, B. W. Connors and M. A. Paradiso, *Neuroscience: Exploring the Brain*. Copyright © 1996 by Lippincott Williams & Wilkins. Reprinted by permission.)

HM was born in 1926 and had a 'normal' childhood until the age of 9 when he was knocked down by a bicycle and lost consciousness for several minutes. Soon after this accident, HM began to suffer from seizures which developed in severity to grand mal epilepsy by the time he was 16. His fits continued throughout early adulthood and, by the time he was 27, they were so severe (and frequent) that he could not work (despite taking near-toxic levels of medication). At this point (in 1953), the neurologist William Scoville identified the **medial temporal lobes** (including the hippocampus and amygdala) as being the origin of his seizure activity, and he decided to bilaterally remove these areas in an attempt to control the epilepsy. Similar operations had been performed before and, although smaller amounts of tissue had been removed, there was little to suggest that the operation was going to have a seriously debilitating effect. In fact, in terms of reducing the seizures, the operation was a great success. Unfortunately, the operation left HM with a profound loss of memory (**amnesia**), the severity of which had never been seen before.

The characteristics of HM

The main consequence of HM's operation was a severe **anterograde amnesia** (*antero* means 'in front') that caused him to forget the episodes of his daily life almost as soon as they occurred. For example, if HM meets someone new, he quickly forgets them once they leave his presence, and does not recognise them again if he re-meets them (this includes researchers such as Dr Brenda Milner who have worked with HM for over 40 years). Similarly, if asked to remember something (say, a number), he will not only forget it (especially if distracted from his task) but also that he had been asked to perform the task in the first place. He also cannot find his way around his own neighbourhood (his family moved to a new house after his operation), always underestimates his age, and is unable to recognise a current picture of himself. In short, with only few exceptions (see below), HM has been unable to remember anything since his operation. This also includes the death of his parents. For example, his father died in 1967 and HM lived with his mother until she died at the age of 94 in 1981, but when asked whether his father was alive (several years after his death) HM replied that he wasn't sure, and in 1986 when asked where he lived, HM answered that he lived in a house with his mother.

Despite this, in most other respects, HM appears to be normal. For example, he has a good vocabulary, normal language skills and an IQ which is above average (Corkin 1984). Moreover, HM shows excellent retention of older memories, particularly if they occurred before the age of 16, although there is some memory loss (i.e. evidence of **retrograde amnesia**) for the year or two preceding his operation. HM also has a normal short-term memory and can repeat a string of seven numbers forward and five numbers backward, repeat sentences and perform mental arithmetic. Indeed, he can rehearse a piece of information in his mind for a considerable time if left to concentrate on the task, but if distracted for just a moment then it is forgotten. Poignantly, HM is vaguely aware of his condition and very apologetic to others about his memory loss:

> *'Right now I am wondering. Have I done or said anything amiss? You see, at this moment everything looks clear to me, but what happened just before? That's what worries me. It's like waking from a dream. I just don't remember.'*
>
> (Milner 1970)

Despite this, HM sometimes has 'islands' of memory. For example, he has shown some recall of the space shuttle disaster (several years after the event) and on occasion remembers that his parents are dead. When asked where he is, he sometimes correctly guesses the Massachusetts Institute of Technology (the place where he has been regularly tested over the last 40 years). Nevertheless such memories are fragmented and unpredictable. Although HM requires constant supervision and now lives in a nursing home (at the age of 72), he remains a great favourite with researchers and clinical staff alike – in no small part 'because of his endearing nature, his sense of humour and his willingness to be helpful' (see Ogden and Corkin 1991).

Tasks that HM can perform

Although HM has a very severe anterograde amnesia, there are nevertheless some tasks where he demonstrates learning. For example, in 1965, Brenda Milner presented HM with a mirror-drawing task which required him to trace around the outline of a complex geometric figure that was hidden from direct view, and which could only be observed by using a mirror. At first, most subjects find the task difficult (and very frustrating) but within a few trials they become reasonably proficient at it. And, this is also true of HM. For example, when given 10 trials each day, for three days, HM became more efficient at drawing around the shape and made fewer errors with repeated trials over the first session. Furthermore, this learning was maintained over the next two days of testing (despite the fact that HM claimed not to recognise the apparatus or know what to do!).

It might be thought that HM's ability to perform mirror drawing is in some way linked to the motor (drawing) requirements of the task, but there is more to his abilities than this. For example, HM has shown learning in a priming task where he is given a 'prompt' to help him recall past information. One example of this is the recognition of incomplete pictures task (Milner *et al.* 1968). In this test, subjects are presented with fragmented and incomplete drawings, one at a time, and in progressively more detail, until they can recognise the picture. When most subjects are shown the incomplete pictures again (after a given delay) they normally recognise the pictures more quickly. And, this type of recognition also occurs with HM. For example, when he is given a series of incomplete pictures, and then tested one hour later, he shows a significant improvement on his initial performance. A similar effect also occurs with verbal material. For example, when HM was shown a word such as 'Define', and then later given the prompt 'Def' and asked what word came to mind, he typically gave the correct word (Ogden and Corkin 1990).

These tasks show that HM can retain certain types of information over a period of several hours (or days). Despite this, there are some circumstances in which HM appears to forget information very quickly. For example, Prisko (1963) presented HM with pairs of tones, coloured lights or patterns of clicks, and found that he had considerable difficulty judging whether the two stimuli were the same or not. A similar example of this was also shown by Sidman *et al.* (1968), who asked HM to indicate which of eight ellipses matched a sample ellipse that had been presented a few seconds earlier. It was found that HM was unable to perform this task if a short delay was interposed between the stimuli. However, when HM was presented with verbal stimuli (three consonants) he had no difficulty identifying the matching stimulus even after a 40-second delay. Thus, these results show that HM has a relatively intact ability to store short-term verbal information, which does not extend to non-verbal information.

The fact that HM is able to use verbal information (even if only for a short period of time) has enabled him to perform some quite complex tasks. For example, Cohen and Corkin (1981) taught HM a puzzle called the Tower of Hanoi which (in its simplest version) consists of three wooden spindles, with the left-sided spindle holding three disks arranged on top of each other in descending size. The objective is to move the disks, one disk at a time, from the left on to the right-sided spindle, without placing a large disk on top of a smaller one. Moreover, the task has to be learnt through trial and error with the quickest solution for a three-disk puzzle being 7 moves. Remarkably, HM managed to learn a five-disk version of this puzzle (which requires a minimum of 31 moves) in only 32 moves.

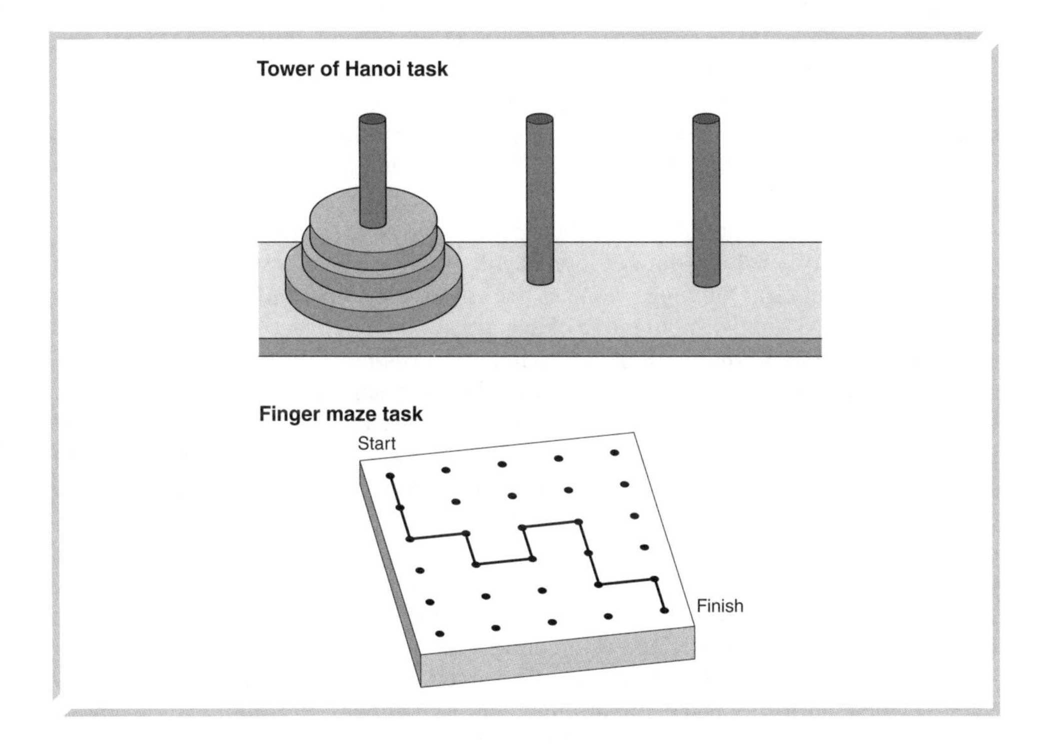

Figure 8.7 The Tower of Hanoi task and 'stepping stone' finger maze.

Despite this, HM cannot perform the stepping-stone maze which requires a set pathway to be learnt through a 10 × 10 maze (this maze is constructed from metal bolts screwed into wood and the subject has to touch the bolts to illustrate the route). Although most subjects find this task relatively easy, HM was unable to learn the task even when given 125 trials. When HM was given a simple 4 × 4 version of the maze he eventually learnt the task – but he took 155 trials! What, then, is the difference between the Tower of Hanoi and the stepping-stone tasks? The answer appears to be that the former can be performed on the basis of learning simple rules, whereas the latter requires the subject to learn an arbitrary pattern of movements, which probably cannot be rehearsed in short-term memory (see Figure 8.7).

Theories of medial temporal lobe function

The fact that HM can retain certain types of information over the long term shows that his amnesia is not complete and that the brain must also contain memory systems that are not dependent on the hippocampus (or medial temporal lobes). Nonetheless, the hippocampus clearly has a special role to play in higher forms of learning and memory. But what sort of role? Firstly, it seems certain that this region is not the site of memory storage because HM retains intact memories of his early life. It is more likely, therefore, that the hippocampus is involved in the formation (or consolidation) of new memories. In terms of Hebbian terminology, this could mean that the hippocampus (and adjacent areas) is responsible for setting up circuits of reverberatory activity that enables structural change in neurons to take place elsewhere in the brain. The discovery of **long-term potentiation** in hippocampal neurons has provided evidence broadly in line with this idea (see Box 8.1).

But why can HM apparently consolidate some types of knowledge into long-term storage and not others? Or, put another way, how can we best describe the nature of HM's memory deficit? One suggestion has been made by Cohen and Squire (1980) who proposed that HM's impairment is one of **declarative** but not **procedural** memory. This theory has its roots in the work of the British philosopher Gilbert Ryle who distinguished between memory arising from 'knowing that' and 'knowing how'. In short, declarative memory is knowledge which we normally use to think and talk about – that is, facts and information that can be brought ('declared') into consciousness. In contrast, procedural memory is largely non-conscious and only accessible through the performance of certain behaviours or actions (examples of procedural memory might include riding a bicycle or learning to type). Thus, HM's deficit would be one of declarative (conscious) memory with procedural (automatic) skills remaining intact. A slightly different idea is the distinction between **explicit** and **implicit** memory (Schacter 1987). Explicit memory is defined as memory which requires a subject to recollect a specific event (such as a word list or name of an object), whereas implicit memory occurs when a subject performs a task, or automatically 'remembers' information (e.g. how to do the Tower of Hanoi task) without being able to recall the learning event. In this respect, HM would appear to be capable of implicit, but not explicit, memory.

Box 8.1 LONG-TERM POTENTIATION

Some 50 years ago, George Hebb speculated that long-term memory involved permanent changes in the structure of neurons which were the result of electrical activity that 'reverberated' in neural circuits for some time after the learning event had occurred. Clearly, if such circuits exist then we would expect to find them (or at least part of them) in the hippocampus. Evidence supporting this idea has come from the discovery of long-term potentiation first shown in 1973 by Timothy Bliss and Terje Lomo working with rabbits. These investigators found that if they stimulated the perforant pathway (this is one of the main neural pathways entering the hippocampus) with a train of electrical impulses and then recorded from the hippocampal cells that received this input, these neurons demonstrated a form of 'memory'. In short, they showed increased electrical activity that persisted for up to 10 hours after the initial stimulation had occurred (it is now known that this effect can last for days or even weeks). Soon after this discovery, others found that long-term potentiation could also be produced in slices of hippocampal tissue kept alive in a saline bath. This was important as it enabled the neural basis of long-term potentiation to be studied outside the organism and in much greater detail (see Figure 8.8).

What causes long-term potentiation? It is now known that the first stage in the process involves the release of glutamate from the neurons of the perforant path, which crosses the synaptic gap and binds to an NMDA receptor located on the hippocampal cells. The activation of this receptor causes the entry of calcium ions into the postsynaptic cell which, in turn, sets into motion a series of chemical reactions (involving enzymes called protein kinases) within the neuron. The next stage is not well understood, although one idea is that the postsynaptic hippocampal cell then releases a substance (which some researchers think may be a 'gas' called nitric oxide) that feeds back onto the presynaptic cell, causing it to be structurally changed in such a way that it increases its release of glutamate in response to further stimulation (Figure 8.9).

But does long-term potentiation really underlie the neural basis of learning and memory? Some of the most convincing evidence that it does has come from Richard Morris and his colleagues who examined the effects of a drug (called AP5) that was known to disrupt long-term potentiation by blocking the effects of glutamate on the NMDA receptor (Morris *et al.* 1986). If long-term potentiation is necessary for memory, then clearly this drug should interfere with learning, and indeed this was found to be the case. When these researchers tested the effects of AP5 on the performance of the Morris water maze (see later in this chapter) they found that it impaired a rat's ability to learn the location of a hidden (submerged) platform, a skill that is known to require spatial memory and the involvement of the hippocampus. However, when the platform was made visible (e.g. it rose slightly above the surface of the water) the rat had no trouble swimming to it. Moreover, it did so without any sign of sensory or motor impairment. In other words, the deleterious effect of AP5 on water maze performance appeared to be due to its specific effect on learning and memory.

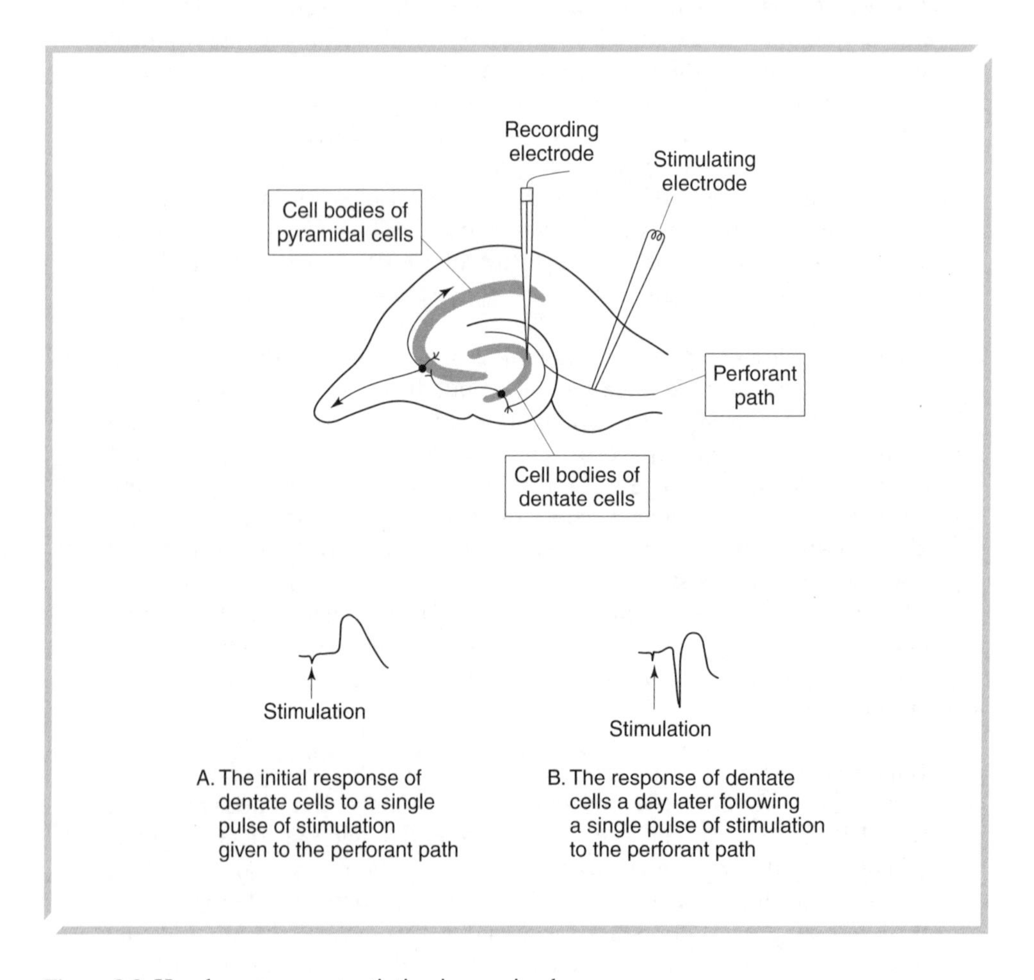

Figure 8.8 How long-term potentiation is examined.

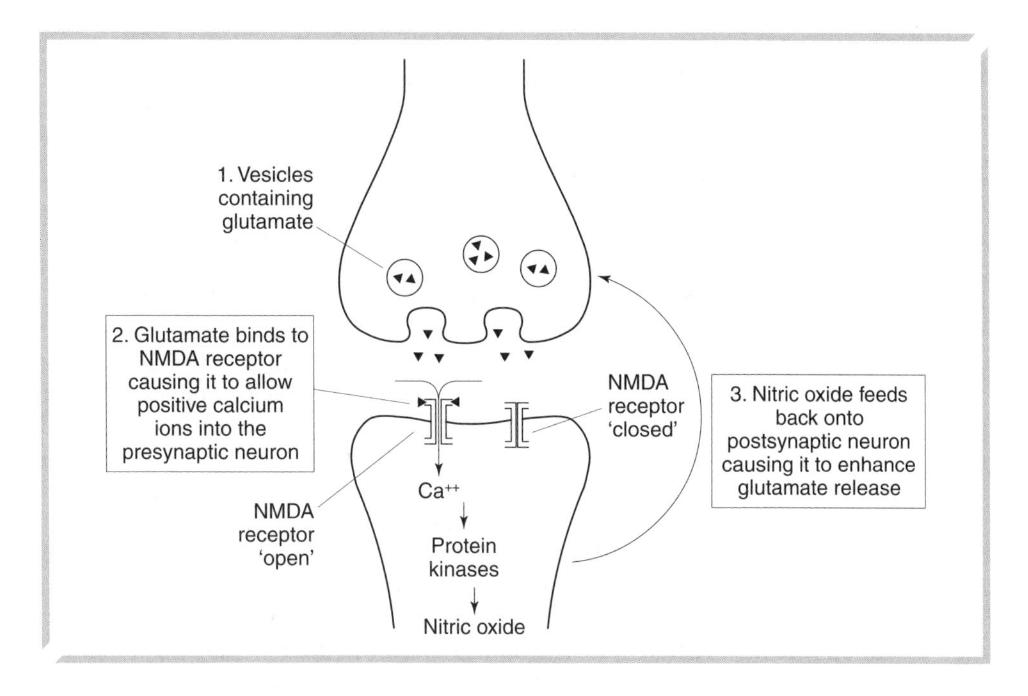

Figure 8.9 A hypothetical model of the chemical events underlying long-term potentiation.

Diencephalic amnesia

The medial temporal lobes are not the only area in the brain where damage produces memory impairment. In fact, the most common form of amnesia (providing by far the biggest source of amnesic patients for the psychologist to study) is **Korsakoff's syndrome**, named after the Russian physician Sergi Korsakoff who first described the condition in 1889. Korsakoff's syndrome is a memory disorder that is primarily found in chronic alcoholics and is associated with damage to the **diencephalon** (which includes the **thalamus** and **hypothalamus**) that is believed to occur as a result of thiamine (vitamin B1) deficiency due to a poor diet and long-term reliance on alcohol. The first signs of the disorder often appear as **Wernicke's encephalopathy** – characterised by confusion (in which the patient may suddenly not be able to recognise friends and surroundings), unsteadiness of balance, and poor co-ordination (**ataxia**). These symptoms can normally be reversed by a short hospitalisation (treated with thiamine and glucose injections) although, in the majority of cases, this is the start of a long irreversible illness that results in the deterioration of memory and personality. It is this second phase that is known as Korsakoff's syndrome.

One of the most striking features of Korsakoff's syndrome is a severe deficit in learning new information. For example, individuals with this disorder may require weeks or months of constant rehearsal and repetition to learn the names of their doctor and nurses, or even the location of their hospital beds. Although this type of declarative information can eventually be learnt (unlike HM) it nevertheless requires considerable effort. This has also been shown experimentally. For example, learning a list of paired associate words such as *man–hamster* in which the subject is required to recall the second word upon presentation of the first, may take the Korsakoff patient some 30 or 40 trials in comparison to only three or four for a normal subject (Butters 1984).

The patient with Korsakoff's syndrome may also show retrograde amnesia. In the majority of cases this is most pronounced for events occurring just prior to the onset of the illness, although the amnesia may sometimes cover much longer periods of time. For example, there are cases of Korsakoff patients who can recall in great detail their participation in the Second World War, yet are unable to recall the assassination of John Kennedy or the Apollo space missions. Indeed, there can be a tendency for these patients to be oblivious of the present and believe that they are actually living in the past (e.g. see the case of Mr G in Sacks 1985). Patients also tend to make up stories (or confabulate) if they have gaps in their memory. In fact, the Korsakoff patient may often provide a plausible answer to a question which, upon verification, is found to be totally false. This behaviour may partly be because the person is embarrassed at having memory loss, but also because he or she is genuinely confused. In addition, this problem is often exacerbated by the fact that these amnesiacs often have very little insight into their condition, and believe that there is nothing wrong with their memory! The characteristics of retrograde amnesia, confabulation, and lack of insight, help distinguish diencephalic amnesia from temporal lobe memory loss. Furthermore, there is some evidence that although people with diencephalic amnesia take a long time to learn new information, they nevertheless forget at normal rates, unlike those with damage to the medial temporal lobes who forget very rapidly (Huppert and Piercy 1979).

The neural basis of Korsakoff's syndrome

It has long been known (e.g. Gudden 1896) that Korsakoff's disease is associated with damage to the diencephalon, with the main area attracting the most attention being the **mammillary bodies** situated at the posterior end of the hypothalamus (Figure 8.10). For example, in 1928, Gamper examined the brains of 16 Korsakoff patients and found that all had degeneration of the mammillary bodies. Since then a large number of studies have confirmed this observation, including one by Adams *et al.* (1962) who undertook autopsies on 54 brains and found a significant correlation between mammillary damage and the severity of the memory deficit previously shown by the subjects. Despite this, it should be pointed out that the Korsakoff brain nearly always shows widespread damage which also involves the brainstem and other regions of the diencephalon. Indeed, the traditional view that mammillary body damage is responsible for Korsakoff's syndrome was seriously challenged in the early 1970s when a large-scale study (which examined over 80 Korsakoff brains) found five cases where mammillary body damage was not associated with memory decline (Victor *et al.* 1971). However, there was one structure where damage was always present, and this was another diencephalic region called the **dorsomedial thalamus**.

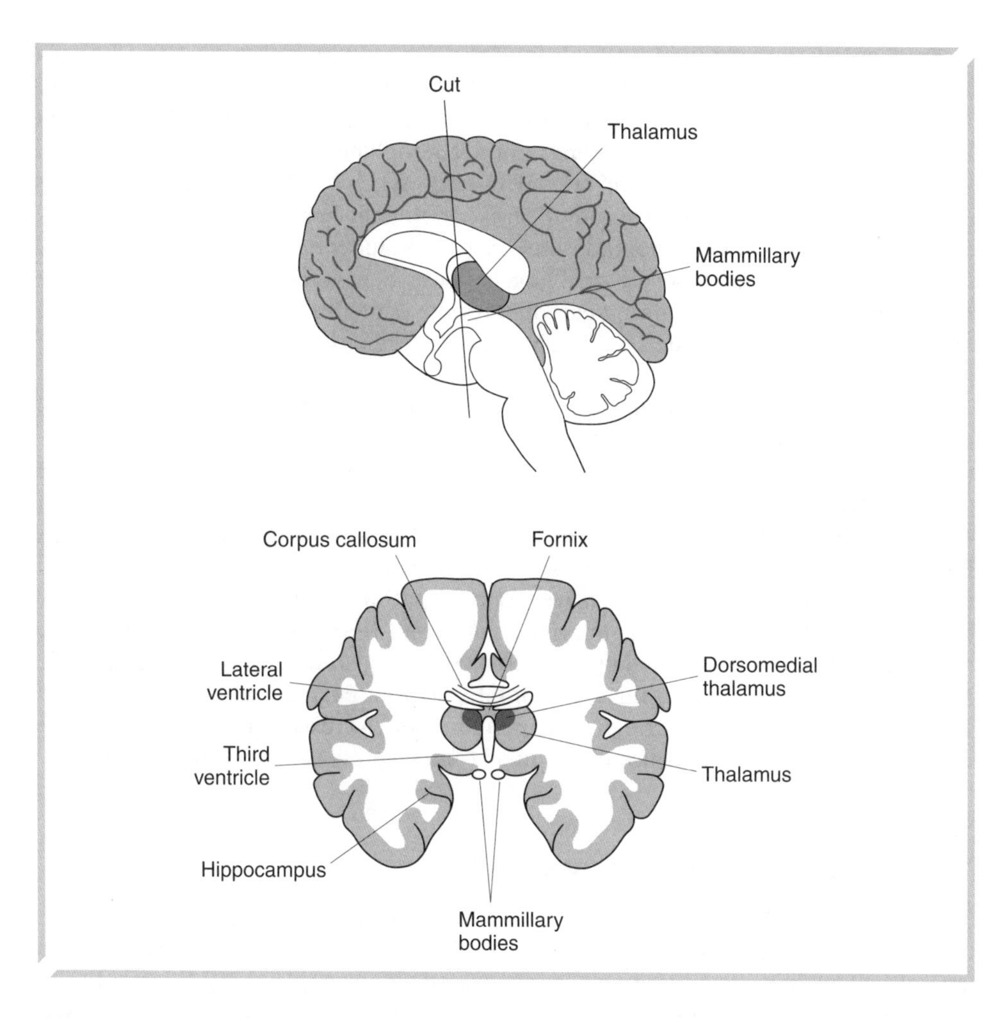

Figure 8.10 The location of the mammillary bodies and thalamus.

This finding has greatly complicated the neuroanatomical understanding of Korsakoff's syndrome. At first, the focus shifted from the mammillary bodies to the dorsomedial thalamus as the crucial site for the memory loss, and this idea was further supported by evidence showing that localised infarcts (or strokes) to the dorsomedial thalamus also caused amnesia. However, there have since been reports of Korsakoff's disease without significant damage to dorsomedial thalamus (Brion and Mikol 1978), and even cases where large bilateral damage to the thalamus has not produced anterograde amnesia (Markowitsch and Pritzel 1985). Thus, a more likely explanation is that some degree of damage to both the mammillary and dorsomedial thalamus needs to take place before diencephalic amnesia occurs. In other words, it is probably far too simple to assume that this disorder is the result of damage to just one structure or region.

Evidence supporting the involvement of the mammillary bodies and dorsomedial thalamus in amnesia has also come from the case of a patient known as NA who, at the age of 22, exhibited severe amnesia following a wound to the brain. The accident happened when NA was busy building a model aeroplane in the company of a friend who was playing with a fencing foil behind his back. When NA turned suddenly, he was stabbed through the right nostril with the foil entering the base of his brain. The initial effect of NA's injury was a retrograde amnesia (that lasted for a two-year period leading up to the injury) and a severe inability to learn new information. Although the retrograde amnesia largely disappeared (it is now limited to a two-week period) the anterograde amnesia persisted. In fact, NA can provide little information about his life since his accident in 1960.

In 1979 Squire and Moore performed a CAT scan on NA and found that the foil had terminated in the left dorsomedial thalamus. This first report indicated that the damage was highly localised with sparing of other brain structures, providing support for the view that the dorsomedial thalamus was critically involved in memory. More recent evidence using MRI scanning, however, has shown that the damage is not as localised as first believed. In addition to the dorsomedial thalamus, this scan has also revealed damage to the mammillary bodies, as well as to the pathway connecting the mammillary bodies to the anterior thalamus (Squire *et al.* 1989). In other words, damage to the mammillary bodies and the thalamus (both mediodorsal and anterior) could underlie NA's memory deficit. In a strange twist of fate, another person (called BJ) received a similar type of wound (and comparable memory deficit), except that in this case the weapon was a snooker cue which ended up in (and severely damaged) the mammillary bodies (Dusoir *et al.* 1990).

The Papez and Yakovlev circuits

As we have seen, there appear to be two separate regions of the brain where damage causes amnesia: the medial temporal lobes and the diencephalon. These two regions have also been shown to be anatomically connected. For example, in 1937, James Papez described a brain circuit that connected the limbic system with the cerebral cortex (see Chapter 5) and an important component of this system was a long arching pathway called the **fornix** which projected from the hippocampus to the mammillary bodies. One might expect, therefore, that this pathway would also be found to have a crucial involvement in memory. Surprisingly, damage that is confined to the fornix in humans often produces a mild memory impairment (or sometimes none at all) which appears to be inconsistent with its anatomical location (Parkin 1984). Thus, the role of the fornix in memory processing is at present very unclear.

Moreover, the Papez circuit does not project directly to the dorsomedial thalamus. Instead, the dorsomedial thalamus is part of a different system (sometimes known as the **Yakovlev circuit**) whose focal point appears to be the amygdala (see Chapter 5). Despite its close proximity to the hippocampus, the amygdala sends a major pathway to the dorsomedial thalamus which in turn projects to the frontal cortex. The circuit is then completed with the frontal cortex projecting back to the amygdala. Historically, this

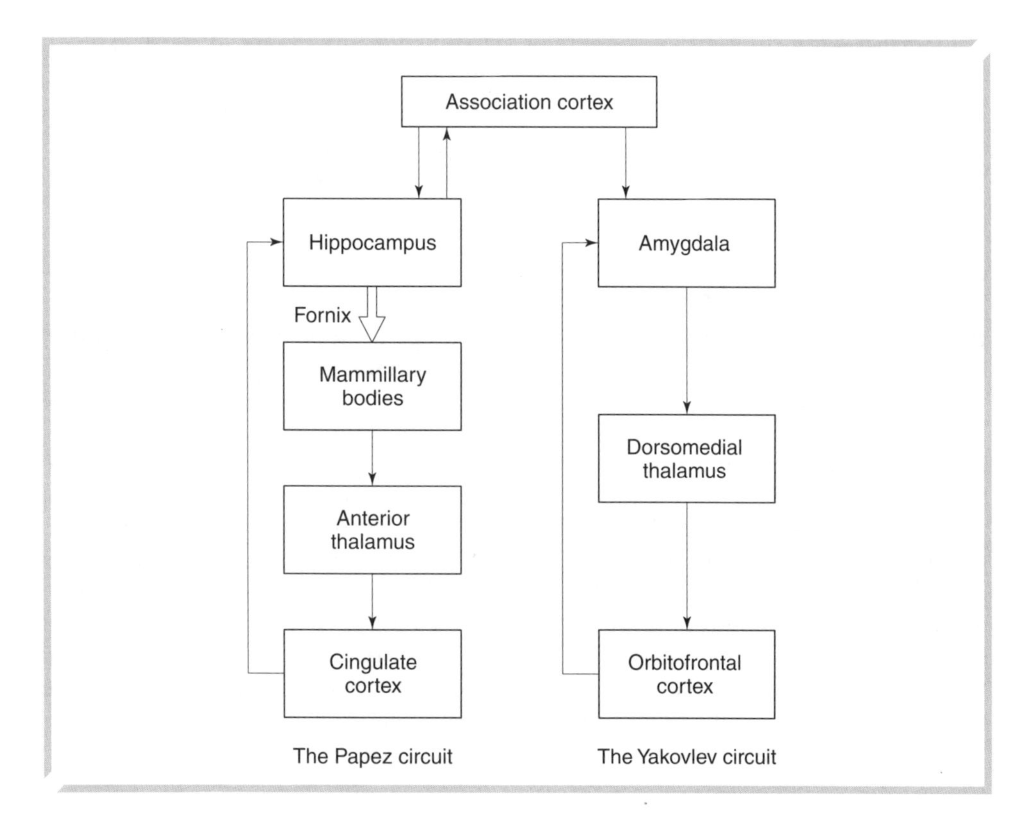

Figure 8.11 The Papez and Yakovlev circuits.

pathway has not attracted as much attention as the Papez circuit, perhaps because specific damage to the amygdala is not associated with amnesia (although in animals it has been shown to be important in learning about fearful events). Despite this, it should be remembered that HM had both the amygdala and hippocampus removed in his operation – which severed both the Papez and Yakovlev pathways. It may be, therefore, that damage to both circuits needs to occur before serious amnesia is produced (see Figure 8.11).

The evidence from animal studies

If the hippocampus is involved in memory, then it is reasonable to assume that its removal should produce memory deficits in animals as well as humans. Following Scoville and Milner's classic description of HM in 1957, a number of investigators began to examine this question. However, to many people's surprise, hippocampal damage did not always produce memory impairment in animals. In fact, hippocampal lesioned rats could perform a number of tasks including: (1) learning to press an operant lever for food; (2) learning a visual discrimination task in which they had to distinguish between a black and white goal box, one of which always led to food reward; and (3) avoiding an electric shock in a situation that required running to a 'safe' location (or box) whenever a warning tone was presented (Douglas 1967). Despite this, there were other tests where marked deficits were observed. Two such tasks were those that involved working memory and cognitive mapping.

Working memory

In their natural habitat, many animals have to forage for food which means that they have to find their way around their environment. Obviously, it helps if the animals can remember where they have just been, so they do not keep going back to the same location (many animals, including bees, are particularly adept at this skill). In 1976, David Olton designed a task which tested a similar type of memory in rats (Olton and Samuelson 1976). This was the radial arm maze, which consisted of a round platform with arms (containing food at their ends) that radiated out like the spokes of a wheel. To gain the maximum reward, the rat had to enter each arm once, without revisiting any of the previously entered arms. On first sight, this task would appear to be quite demanding since it requires the animal to keep track of where it has been, and where it still has got to go (or what Olton called 'working memory'). Nevertheless, Olton found that rats could perform this task very successfully – even when short delays were introduced between arms, or when the animals were forced down certain arms in order to abolish fixed sequences of responding (Olton *et al.* 1979).

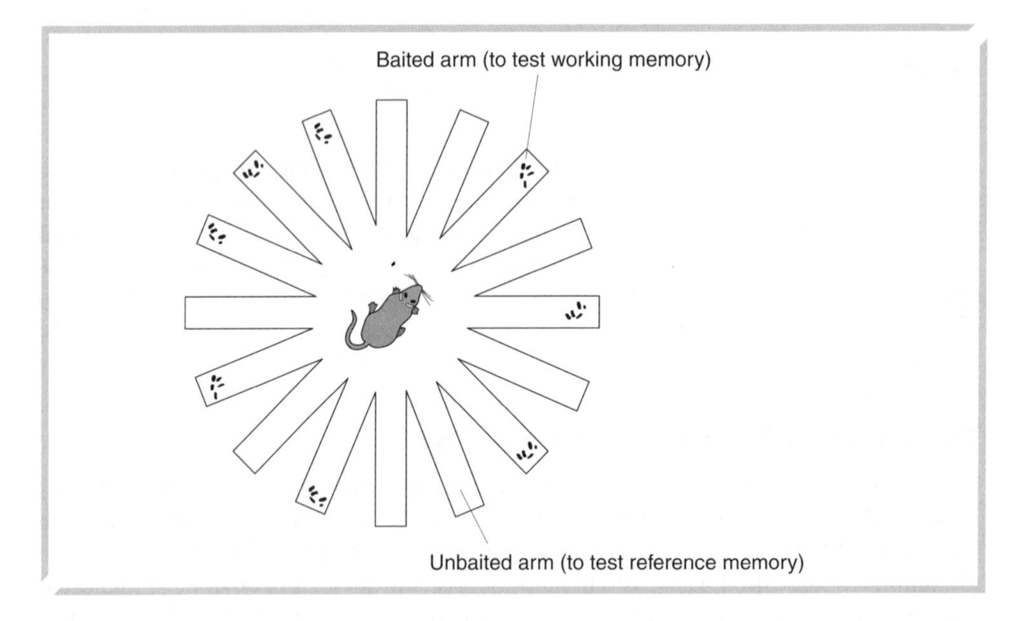

Figure 8.12 The radial arm maze (showing working and reference memory components).

This ability did not extend, however, to rats with hippocampal lesions who tended to retrace their paths and were apparently unable to keep track of where they had been (i.e. they appeared to have a deficit of working memory). However, there was a second explanation that could account for these findings: rather than having a deficit in working memory it was also possible that these animals were getting 'lost' because they were unable to form a cognitive map of their environment (this would be similar to us leaving our front door in the morning and not being able to find our way to work). To test whether this was a viable explanation, Olton and Papas (1979) constructed a 17-arm maze in which 9 of the arms always remained empty, and the other 8 arms always contained food (see Figure 8.12). This new task now needed the animal to learn two types of information. The first simply required the rat not to visit any of the empty arms (and since these remained unchanged from trial to trial, Olton argued that this skill depended on a form of long-term memory, or mental map, which he called 'reference memory'). The second component of the task, however, required the animal to find the food without revisiting any of the arms – that is, working memory.

When Olton tested normal rats on this maze he found that they soon learned to avoid the empty arms, while managing to retrieve food efficiently from the baited ones. That is, they were capable of both reference memory and working memory. The hippocampal lesioned animals also learned to avoid the non-baited arms; however, they still performed at chance levels, visiting the arms that contained food. In other words, the lesioned rats showed reference memory (which Olton believed was evidence of their ability to form a mental map of the radial maze), but were incapable of working memory.

Cognitive mapping

A different approach to understanding hippocampal function was undertaken by John O'Keefe and his colleagues at the University of London. Instead of examining the effects of hippocampal lesions, O'Keefe recorded the electrical activity of individual cells in the hippocampus as rats moved around their environment. His main finding was that some neurons only fired when the animal was in a certain location. These neurons would remain quiet until the animal reached a certain point when suddenly the neuron would begin to fire rapidly. As the animal moved away to a new location the neuron would stop firing. However, if the rat returned to the location at a later time the neuron would 'remember' the site and begin firing again. O'Keefe called these neurons **'place cells'**.

Further research showed that hippocampal place cells were dependent on the configuration of cues located outside the testing arena (extramaze cues) and not those within its confines. For example, O'Keefe and Conway (1978) trained rats to negotiate a T-maze in which one arm was always associated with food. The maze was surrounded by a black curtain which contained a cue on each of its four sides (a fan, a buzzer, a light and a square card). This curtain could be moved around the apparatus – although the cues always remained in the same place relative to each other. On all trials, the arm containing the food was always pointed towards the corner situated between the light and the card. To make sure that the rats learned the spatial location of the arm (and not a simple right or left turning response), the location of the starting position was changed from trial to trial.

Again, the results showed that the hippocampal place cells only fired when the animal was in a specific location in relation to the cues. If the curtain was moved around, shifting the configuration of the cues with it, the place cell still fired – providing the animal was in the same *relative* position to the cues. In other words, it was the animal's position relative to the external cues, and not the actual site in the maze, that was important. The importance of the external cues was further shown when they were removed. If any two cues were removed the place cells still continued to fire, but if more than two cues were removed, the place cells often stopped firing. The important factor, therefore, was the *spatial configuration* of the cues. According to O'Keefe and Nadel (1978) these findings showed that the function of the hippocampus was to provide the animal with a cognitive map that enabled it to find its way successfully around its environment.

Some of the strongest support for this theory has come from Richard Morris in 1982 who developed an ingenious test of spatial memory which required the animal to negotiate a water maze (Figure 8.13). The 'maze' was in fact a large circular tank of water,

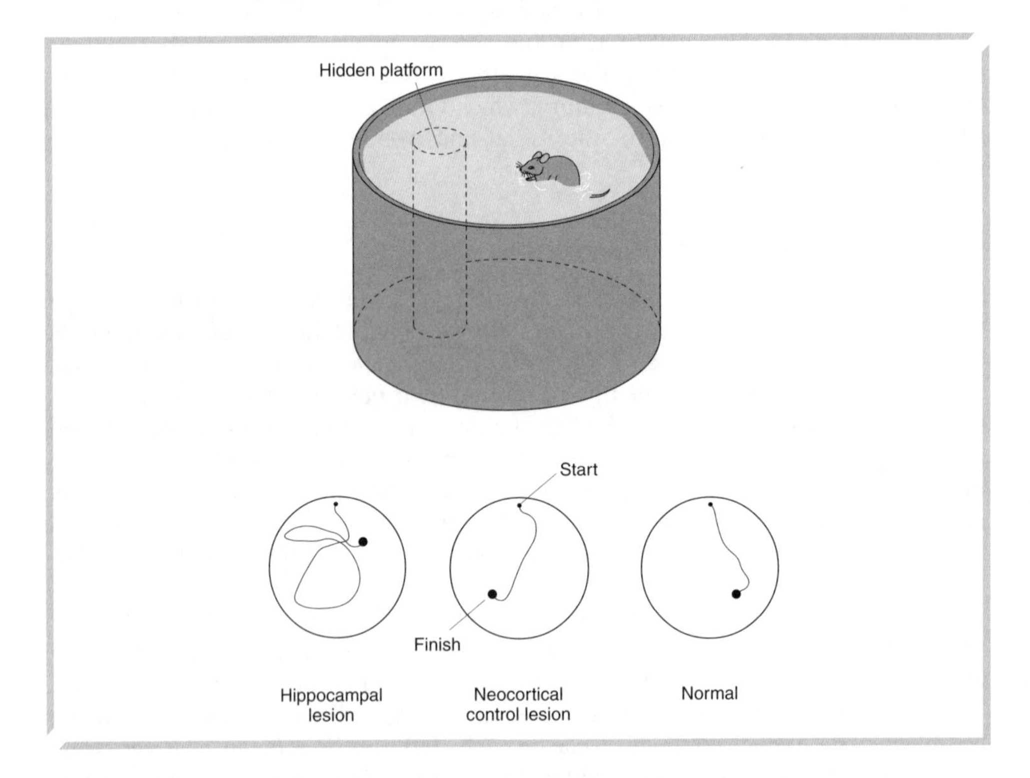

Figure 8.13 The Morris water maze. (*Source*: Examples of routes after training taken by rats in water maze taken from R. G. M. Morris *et al.*, *Nature* (1982), **297**, 681–3. Reprinted by permission.)

made opaque with the addition of milk, that contained a small escape platform hidden just below the surface. Rats were put into the water and allowed to swim around until they 'bumped' into the platform which they then inevitably climbed upon. Although the rats could not see the platform, Morris found that it took just a few trials for normal rats to learn to swim directly to it, despite being started in different locations. However, rats with hippocampal lesions were unable to learn this task, even after 40 days (and over 100 trials) of training. Since the platform cannot be directly observed, it must be that the animals are only able to learn the platform's location by determining its position in relation to the spatial configuration of extramaze cues around the water.

These results provide strong support for the cognitive map theory – although they are at odds with the work of Olton and Papas who showed that hippocampus lesioned rats have intact reference memory (which has also been shown to be dependent on learning the location of extramaze cues). In fact, the Morris water maze and the reference memory component of the radial maze appear to both require a spatial map of the environment, yet only one causes a problem for hippocampal lesioned animals. At present, the reason for this difference remains unclear.

Memory tasks involving primates

Primates provide an alternative way of examining the role of the hippocampus, and one that is likely to represent a closer approximation of human function, although this requires having to adopt a different set of experimental procedures by which to examine memory.

Because primates have good vision (like humans) the most commonly used tasks to test memory deficits are discrimination tasks, such as the **delayed non-matching to sample** procedure (Figure 8.14). In this situation, the monkey is presented with a tray containing two (or more) food wells, one of which is covered by a distinctive object (the sample) which the monkey has to remove to find a reward (such as a banana chip) underneath. Following this trial, the tray is removed for a set period of time, after which it is presented again with two test objects: the original sample and a new unfamiliar object. To obtain the reward on this next occasion, the monkey must now choose the unfamiliar object.

Surprisingly, when this type of task is given to primates with lesions confined to the hippocampus, their performance shows little impairment. For example, after a 10-minute delay on a non-matching to sample task, hippocampal lesioned monkeys were found to perform at 65–70 per cent accuracy, which was not a great deal less than the 80 per cent accuracy obtained with control animals (Zola-Morgan and Squire 1986). On first sight this finding is not easily reconciled with the human data, where the hippocampal deficit appears to be much more pronounced. The monkey's performance on the delayed non-matching to sample task following dorsomedial thalamic lesions, however, appears to be much closer to the human deficit. For example, this type of lesion in primates reduces accuracy to 62 per cent (which is close to chance at 50 per cent) after a 10-minute delay (Zola-Morgan and Squire 1985).

But why do hippocampal lesions produce such a small impairment on this type of

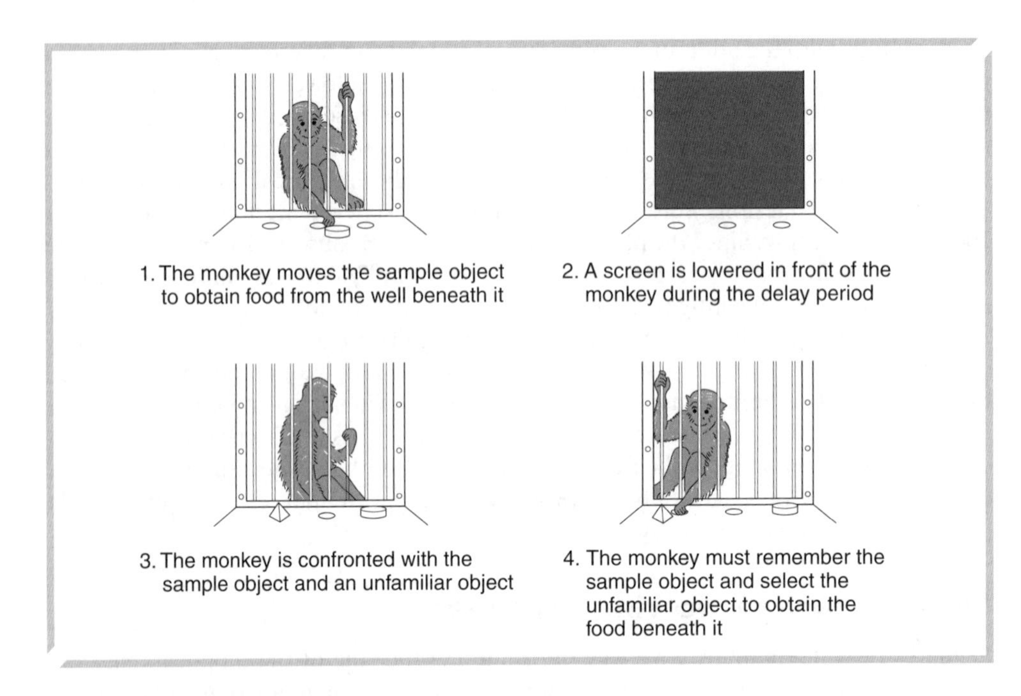

Figure 8.14 The delayed non-matching to sample task. (*Source*: From John P. J. Pinel, *Biopsychology*, 3rd edition. Copyright © 1997 by Allyn & Bacon. Reprinted by permission.)

task? (Or put another way, why is HM's amnesia so profound?) An experiment by Mishkin in 1978 has helped to clarify this issue. Mishkin made specific lesions to the hippocampus, or amygdala, in macaque monkeys and found that neither had much effect on the non-matching to sample task (both groups performed at about 90 per cent correct after a 2-minute delay). However, when he combined the two lesions together, a much more severe impairment was found, with performance falling to near chance (60 per cent) accuracy. This finding is particularly relevant because HM's operation also involved the removal of the amygdala and hippocampus (as well as the surrounding portions of the medial temporal lobe). Thus, the implication of Mishkin's work is that both the hippocampus and amygdala are necessary for memory processing. Indeed, as we have already seen, these two structures appear to be part of different memory circuits in the brain (the Papez and Yakovlev circuits). Thus, perhaps both circuits need to be damaged for severe amnesia to occur in monkeys and in humans.

Subsequent research has shown, however, that even this interpretation may not necessarily be the most accurate one. Mishkin's work has encouraged investigators to look at other types of temporal lobe damage; in particular, that made to the cortical tissue surrounding the hippocampus (which was also destroyed in HM's operation). These regions include the **perirhinal cortex** (this area also happened to be damaged by Mishkin's combined hippocampal–amygdala lesion), the **parahippocampal gyrus** and the **entorhinal cortex** (see Figure 8.15). In fact, all these areas have also been shown to

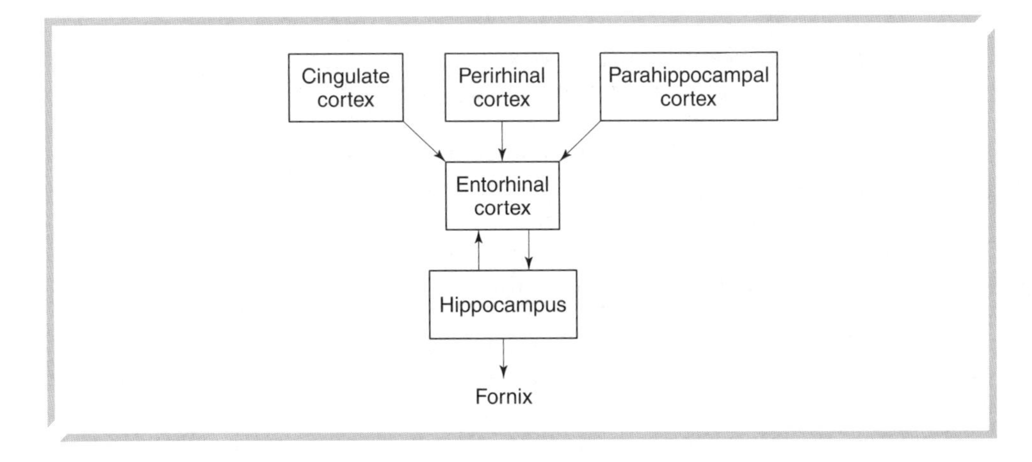

Figure 8.15 Cortical areas immediately adjacent to (and feeding into) the hippocampal formation.

be crucial for memory. For example, it was found that specific lesions made to the perirhinal cortex and parahippocampal gyrus (sparing the hippocampus and amygdala) produced a deficit on the non-matching to sample task which was nearly as severe as that for the combined hippocampal–amygdala lesion (Zola-Morgan *et al.* 1989). Thus, the medial temporal lobe contains several regions that collectively appear to be crucial for memory. Moreover, the hippocampus is known to project heavily back to the parahippocampal gyrus (via the **subiculum**), both of which then send information to the cerebral cortex. Thus, these two regions form part of neural circuits that connect the hippocampus with the cortex – and it may well be these pathways (rather than the Papez circuit) that are crucially involved in memory processing.

Box 8.2 ALZHEIMER'S DISEASE

The term *dementia* derives from the Latin for madness, although in current usage it refers more specifically to the rapid deterioration of intellectual functioning that arises as a result of a disease or brain dysfunction. There are more than 60 disorders that can cause dementia but by far the most common is Alzheimer's disease (first described by Alois Alzheimer in 1907). It has been estimated that approximately 5 per cent of the population over 65 suffer from this disorder and this figure rises to over 20 per cent in the over-80s (who also happens to be the fastest-growing age group in the population). This means that there are over half a million people with this disorder in the UK alone (Hughes 1991) and this figure is likely to increase in the future.

Moreover, complications arising from Alzheimer's disease may now be the fourth most common form of death in old people (Katzman 1976).

Although Alzheimer's disease initially manifests itself as a memory disorder it is soon followed by a deterioration of language skills, attention, social function and all aspects of cognition. By the later stages of the disorder, the patients require constant care and are unable to look after themselves. The disease can progress rapidly so that within five years or so, a healthy person can be transformed into what Dr Jonathan Miller has described as a 'corpse which the undertaker has forgotten to collect'. But there are other costs as well. For example, the economic burden of its care and treatment is enormous, and the psychological costs of caring for the disorder may be even greater (e.g. it has been estimated that already there are more women in society looking after elderly relatives than there are looking after children – Hart and Semple 1990). It is perhaps not surprising, therefore, that Alzheimer's disease has been called 'one of the most pervasive social health problems of our generation' (Royal College of Physicians 1981) and 'the disease of the century' (Thomas 1981).

A number of abnormalities are found in the brains of people with Alzheimer's disease including microscopic senile plaques (tiny round structures that contain a starch-like protein called amyloid) and neurofibrillary tangles (twisted tangles of fine filaments found within nerve cells). In addition, there is often marked degeneration of brain tissue resulting in enlarged ventricles. Although there is usually some degree of shrinkage with normal ageing (e.g. by the age of 80 the brain typically shrinks by about 15 per cent), in Alzheimer's disease this shrinkage can be 30 per cent or more, and in much younger individuals (this loss is most pronounced in the frontal and temporal lobes including the hippocampus). Despite this, there is great variation between individuals and brain atrophy by itself cannot be taken as proof of the disease. There is also widespread loss of many neurochemical substances, although the loss of acetylcholine is particularly marked. In fact, drugs which increase the amount of acetylcholine at the synapse, such as the AChE inhibitors (see Chapter 3), have provided one of the few medications that have some degree of benefit in treating the disorder.

What causes Alzheimer's disease? The frightening answer is that nobody really knows. Perhaps the strongest evidence has implicated genetic factors. Indeed, it is known that in a few cases an early onset form of Alzheimer's can be inherited through a mutated gene that is located on chromosome 21, although this form of the disease is very rare and is found in less than 5 per cent of cases. More recently, attention has shifted to a 'normal' gene (called the apolipoprotein or APO gene) situated on chromosome 19 that comes in three different forms or alleles (another example of an allele is the gene that controls eye colour). We inherit two APO genes (one from each parent) and it appears that the combination we receive has a significant bearing on at what age we are likely to develop Alzheimer's disease (see Table 8.1). Particularly unfortunate is the APO 4/4 combination which predisposes the carrier to a much greater risk of Alzheimers below the age of 70 years.

Despite this, other causes of Alzheimer's disease have also been suggested. For example, some investigators believe that it may be due to a transmissible viral agent such as the one responsible for causing Creutzfeldt–Jakob disease. Others have proposed that the disorder may have a toxic or environmental cause (e.g. drinking water with a high aluminium content). But perhaps most likely is that the disease will turn out to be due to a combination of genetic and environmental influences which will make any simple explanation of its aetiology difficult to formulate.

Table 8.1 Estimated mean age of Alzheimer's disease onset as a function of APOE allele inheritance

		Age of onset	
Genotype	% US population	Mean	Range
2/2	<1	?	?
2/3	11	>90	50 to 140
2/4	5	80 to 90	50 to >100
3/3	60	80 to 90	50 to >100
3/4	21	70 to 80	50 to >100
4/4	2	<70	50 to <100

Source: From Roses (1995), *Scientific American,* (Sept.).

Self-test questions

1. What is classical conditioning?
2. What did Lashley mean by *mass action* and *equipotentiality*?
3. In what ways has Lashley been criticised?
4. How did Donald Hebb explain the probable neural basis of memory?
5. What effect does rearing in enriched environments have on the structure of neurons?
6. Why has *Aplysia* been extensively used to examine learning?
7. How does habituation occur in *Aplysia*?
8. What is long-term potentiation?
9. How can one characterise the memory deficits of HM?

10. What sorts of learning and memory task can HM perform?
11. What is known about the neuroanatomical basis of Korsakoff's syndrome?
12. Briefly describe the Papez and Yakovlev circuits.
13. What is working memory?
14. How did John O'Keefe examine the functions of the hippocampus?
15. Explain how the Morris water maze has been used to examine spatial memory.
16. How does the delayed non-matching to sample task work?
17. What contribution has Mishkin made to our understanding of memory?

Key terms

Acetylcholine (p.233)
Acetylcholinesterase (AChE) (p.233)
Alzheimer's disease (p.255)
Amnesia (p.239)
Anterograde amnesia (p.239)
Aplysia (p.234)
Ataxia (p.245)
Classical conditioning (p.229)
Cognitive mapping (p.251)
Declarative memory (p.242)
Delayed non-matching to sample test (p.253)
Diencephalon (p.245)
Dorsomedial thalamus (p.246)
Engram (p.228)
Entorhinal cortex (p.254)
Equipotentiality (p.231)
Explicit memory (p.242)
Fornix (p.248)
Gill-withdrawal reflex (p.234)
Hebbian synapse (p.232)
Hippocampus (p.238)
Hypothalamus (p.245)
Implicit memory (p.242)
Korsakoff's syndrome (p.245)
Long-term potentiation (p.241)
Mammillary bodies (p.246)
Mass Action (p.231)
Medial temporal lobes (p.239)
Morris water maze (p.252)
Papez circuit (p.248)
Parahippocampal gyrus (p.254)
Perirhinal cortex (p.254)
Place cells (p.251)
Procedural memory (p.242)
Retrograde amnesia (p.239)
Subiculum (p.255)
Synaptic vesicles (p.236)
Thalamus (p.245)
Wernicke's encephalopathy (p.245)
Working memory (p.250)
Yakovlev circuit (p.248)

References

Adams, R. D. *et al.* (1962) Troubles de la memoire et de l'appretissage chez l'homme. In *Physiologie de l'hippocampe*. Paris: Centre National de la Recherche Scientifique.

Baily, C. H. and Chen, M. (1983) Morphological basis of long-term habituation and sensitisation in Aplysia. *Science*, **220**, 91–3.

Brion, S. and Mikol, J. (1978) Atteinte du noyau lateral dorsal du thalamus et syndrome de Korsakoff alcolique. *Journal of Neurological Science*, **38**, 249–61.

Butters, N. (1984) Alcoholic Korsakoff syndrome: An update. *Seminars in Neurology*, **4**, 226–44.

Castellucci, V. F. and Kandel, E. R. (1974) A quantal analysis of the synaptic depression underlying habituation of the gill-withdrawal reflex in Aplysia. *Proceedings of the National Academy of Science (USA)*, **71**, 5004–8.

Cohen, N. J. and Corkin, S. (1981) The amnesic patient HM: Learning and retention of a cognitive skill. *Society for Neuroscience Abstracts*, **7**, 235.

Cohen, N. J. and Squire, L. R. (1980) Preserved learning and retention of pattern-analysing skill in amnesia: Dissociation of knowing how and knowing that. *Science*, **210**, 207–10.

Corkin, S. (1984) Lasting consequences of bilateral medial temporal lobectomy: Clinical course and experimental findings. *Seminars in Neurology*, **4**, 249–59.

Douglas, R. J. (1967) The hippocampus and behavior. *Psychological Bulletin*, **67**, 416–42.

Dusoir, H. *et al.* (1990) The role of diencephalic pathology in human memory disorder: Evidence from a penetrating paranasal brain injury. *Brain*, **13**, 1695–1706.

Gudden, H. (1896) Klinische und anatomische beitrage zur kenntniss der multiplen alkoholneuritis nebst bemerkungen uber die regenerationsvorgange im peripheren nervensystem. *Arch. für Psychiat. und Nerven-krank-heiten*, **28**, 643–741.

Hart, S. and Semple, J. M. (1990) *Neuropsychology and the Dementias*. London: Taylor & Francis.

Hebb, D. O. (1949) *The Organisation of Behavior*. New York: Wiley.

Hughes, J. (1991) *An outline of modern psychiatry*. Chichester: Wiley.

Huppert, F. A. and Piercy, M. (1979) Normal and abnormal forgetting in organic amnesia: Effect of locus of lesion. *Cortex*, **15**, 385–90.

Kandel, E. R. (1979) Small systems of neurons. *Scientific American*, **241** (Sept.), 67–76.

Kandel, E. R. *et al.* (1995) *Essentials of Neural Science and Behavior*. Stamford: Appleton & Lange.

Katzman, R. (1976) The prevalence and malignancy of Alzheimer's disease: A major killer. *Archives of Neurology*, **33**, 217–18.

Milner, B. (1970) Memory and the medial temporal regions of the brain. In Pribram, D. H. and Broadbent, D. E. (eds) *Biology of Memory*. New York: Academic Press.

Milner, B. *et al.* (1968) Further analysis of the hippocampal amnesic syndrome: 14 year follow-up study of HM. *Neuropsychologia*, **6**, 317–38.

Mishkin, M. (1978) Memory in monkeys severely impaired by combined but not separate removal of the amygdala and hippocampus. *Nature*, **273**, 297–8.

Morris, R. G. *et al.* (1986) Selective impairment of learning and blockage of long term potentiation by an *N*-methyl-D-aspartate receptor anatonist AP5. *Nature*, **319**, 774–6.

O'Keefe, J. and Conway, D. H. (1978) Hippocampal place units in the freely moving rat: Why they fire when they fire. *Experimental Brain Research*, **31**, 573–90.

O'Keefe, J. and Nadel, L. (1978) *The Hippocampus as a Cognitive Map*. Oxford: Oxford University Press.

Olton, D. S. and Samuelson, R. J. (1976) Remembrance of places passed: Spatial memory in rats. *Journal of Experimental Psychology: Animal Behavior Processes*, **2**, 97–115.

Olton, D. S. and Papas, B. C. (1979) Spatial memory and hippocampal function. *Neuropsychologia*, **17**, 669–82.
Parkin, A. J. (1984) Amnesic syndrome: A lesion-specific disorder? *Cortex*, **20**, 479–508.
Prisko, L. (1963) Short term memory in cerebral damage. Unpublished PhD dissertation, McGill University.
Royal College of Physicians Committee on Geriatrics (1981) Organic mental impairment in the elderly. *Journal of the Royal College of Physicians*, **15**, 142–67.
Sacks, O. (1985) *The Man Who Mistook his Wife for a Hat*. London: Picador.
Schacter, D. L. (1987) Implicit memory: history and current status. *Journal of Experimental Psychology: Learning, Memory and Cognition*, **13**, 501–18.
Sidman, M. *et al.* (1968) Some additional quantitative observations of immediate memory in a patient with bilateral hippocampal lesions. *Neuropsychologia*, **6**, 245–54.
Squire, L. R. (1987) *Memory and the Brain*. Oxford: Oxford University Press.
Squire, L. R. *et al.* (1989) Description of brain injury in amnesic patient N.A. based on magnetic resonance imaging. *Experimental Neurology*, **105**, 23–5.
Thomas, L. (1981) The problem of dementia. *Discovery*, Aug., 34–6.
Turner, A. M. and Greenough, W. T. (1983) Synapses per neuron and synaptic dimensions in occipital cortex of rats reared in complex, social or isolation housing. *Acta Stereologica*, **2** (suppl.1), 239–44.
Turner, A. M. and Greenough, W. T. (1985) Differential rearing effects on rat visual cortex synapses. 1. Synaptic and neuronal density and synapses per neuron. *Brain Research*, **329**, 195–203.
Victor, M. *et al.* (1971) *The Wernicke–Korsakoff Syndrome*. Oxford: Blackwell.
Zola-Morgan, S. and Squire, L. R. (1985) Amnesia in monkeys following lesions of the mediodorsal nucleus of the thalamus. *Annals of Neurology*, **17**, 558–64.
Zola-Morgan, S. and Squire, L. R. (1986) Memory impairment in monkeys following lesions limited to the hippocampus. *Behavioural Neuroscience*, **100**, 155–60.
Zola-Morgan, S. *et al.* (1989) Lesions of the perirhinal and parahippocampal cortex that spare the amygdala and the hippocampal formation produce severe memory impairment. *Journal of Neuroscience*, **9**, 4355–70.

FURTHER READING

Cohen, N. J. and Eichenbaum, H. (1993) *Memory, Amnesia, and the Hippocampal System*. Cambridge, MA: MIT Press.
Dubai, Y. (1980) *The Neurobiology of Memory*. Oxford: Oxford University Press.
Hawkins, R. D. *et al.* (1987) Cell biological systems of learning in simple vertebrate and invertebrate systems. In Plum, F. (ed.) *Handbook of Physiology. 1. Higher Functions of the Nervous System*. Bethesda: American Physiological Society.
Lashley, K. S. (1950) In search of the Engram. *Symposium for the Society of Experimental Biology*, **4**, 454–82.
Markowitsch, H. J. and Pritzel, M. (1985) The neuropathology of amnesia. *Progress in Neurobiology*, **25**, 189–287.
Martinez, J. L. and Kesner, R. P. (eds) (1991) *Learning and Memory: A Biological View*. New York: Academic Press.

McGaugh, J. L. *et al.* (1995) *Brain and Memory: Modulation and Mediation of Neuroplasticity*. Oxford: Oxford University Press.
Morris, R. G. *et al.* (1982) Place navigation impaired in rats with hippocampal lesions. *Nature*, **297**, 681–3.
Ogden, J. A. and Corkin, S. (1991) Memories of H.M. In Abraham, W. C. *et al.* (eds) *Memory Mechanisms: A Tribute to G. V. Goddard*. Hillsdale, NJ: Lawrence Erlbaum.
Olton, D. S. *et al.* (1979) Hippocampus, space and memory. *The Behavioral and Brain Sciences*, **2**, 313–65.
Rose, S. (1992) *The Making of Memory: From Molecules to Mind*. London: Bantam Books.
Rosenzweig, M. R. *et al.* (1972) Brain changes in response to experience. *Scientific American*, Feb., 22–9.
Scoville, W. B. and Milner, B. (1957) Loss of recent memory after bilateral hippocampal lesions. *Journal of Neurology, Neurosurgery and Psychiatry*, **20**, 11–21.
Squire, L. R. and Butters, N. (1992) *Neuropsychology of Memory*. New York: Guilford Press.

Multiple choice questions

1. Lashley found that the memory trace (engram) for maze learning was stored in the:

(a) hippocampus
(b) visual cortex
(c) diffusely throughout the cerebral cortex
(d) nowhere – because his lesions had no effect on maze learning, he concluded that the engram did not exist

2. In classical conditioning, salivation is initially the ________________ and the buzzer becomes the ________________.

(a) unconditioned response, conditioned stimulus
(b) unconditioned stimulus, conditioned stimulus
(c) conditioned response, unconditioned stimulus
(d) unconditioned response, unconditioned stimulus

3. According to Donald Hebb the formation of memory involves:

(a) neural circuits called cell assemblies
(b) reverberatory activity
(c) structural change at the synapse
(d) all of the above

4. By rearing rats in enriched environments, Mark Rosenzweig found that his animals developed:

(a) a thicker cerebral cortex
(b) neurons with increased numbers of dendrites
(c) increased levels of AChE
(d) all of the above

5. In *Aplysia*, the habituation of the gill-withdrawal reflex is due to:

(a) the decline of action potential in the siphon's sensory neurons
(b) less transmitter being released by the siphon's sensory neurons onto motor neurons
(c) the motor neurons becoming 'fatigued' with continued activation
(d) the involvement of interneurons

6. HM's bilateral removal of the medial temporal lobes included the:

(a) hippocampus and mammillary bodies
(b) hippocampus and hypothalamus
(c) hippocampus only
(d) hippocampus, amygdala and adjacent cortex

7. Which of the following tasks can HM *not learn* to perform?

(a) mirror drawing
(b) Tower of Hanoi task
(c) delayed matching to sample of ellipses
(d) delayed matching of verbal material

8. According to Cohen and Squire (1980), HM has _______________ memory but not _______________ memory.

(a) procedural, declarative
(b) declarative, procedural
(c) short-term, long-term
(d) unconscious, conscious

9. In long-term potentiation, the experimenter typically stimulates the _______________ and records from the _________________.

(a) fornix, mammillary bodies
(b) fornix, granule cells of the hippocampal dentate gyrus
(c) perforant path, granule cells of the hippocampal gyrus
(d) perforant path, fornix

10. Korsakoff's disease is an example of _______________ amnesia.

(a) diencephalic
(b) temporal lobe
(c) frontal lobe
(d) Wernicke's encephalopathetic

11. The brain structures that have been most implicated in Korsakoff's disease are:

(a) hypothalamus and hippocampus

(b) amygdala and frontal cortex
(c) mammillary bodies and anterior thalamus
(d) mammillary bodies and dorsomedial thalamus

12. Which of the following structures is not usually considered to be part of the Papez circuit?

(a) amygdala
(b) hippocampus
(c) fornix
(d) mammillary bodies

13. David Olton's work has shown that hippocampal lesioned rats are impaired on tasks involving:

(a) spatial reference memory
(b) working memory
(c) (a) and (b) above
(d) inhibition of previously learned responses

14. According to O'Keefe and Nadel (1978), the role of the hippocampus is to provide the animal with:

(a) working memory
(b) long-term memory
(c) a cognitive map
(d) none of the above

15. Richard Morris, who examined spatial memory in hippocampal lesioned rats by using a water maze, found that they:

(a) were unable to learn the task even after 40 days of training
(b) could learn the task but only if enough cues were provided
(c) could learn the task but only if they were trained to find a visible platform first
(d) could learn the task eventually with visible platform training and plenty of cues

16. In the delayed non-matching to sample task, the monkey must choose on the second trial:

(a) the original object
(b) the new (unfamiliar) object
(c) the original food well regardless of what object is placed on it
(d) the food well that was not chosen before

17. Mishkin has demonstrated severe memory deficits in the delayed non-matching to sample task in monkeys with lesions of the ________________.

(a) hippocampus

(b) amygdala
(c) hippocampus and amygdala combined
(d) dorsomedial thalamus

18. Zola-Morgan has shown that lesions restricted to the perirhinal and parahippocampal gyrus in monkeys produce:

(a) little impairment on memory tasks
(b) a memory impairment similar to an amygdala–hippocampal lesion
(c) a memory deficit for *non-matching* but not *matching to sample* tasks
(d) a memory deficit for long delays but not for delays of 60 seconds or less

19. The second most common form of dementia in the UK is:

(a) Alzheimer's disease
(b) multi-infarct dementia
(c) Korsakoff's disease
(d) Creutzfeldt-Jakob disease

20. Pharmacological treatments for Alzheimer's disease (such as Tacrine and Physostigmine) work by increasing the levels of ________________ in the synapse.

(a) acetylcholine
(b) dopamine
(c) glutamate
(d) noradrenaline and serotonin

9 Language and cognition

IN THIS CHAPTER

- The main areas involved in the production and comprehension of language
- Different types of aphasia
- The Wernicke–Geschwind model of language
- Hemispheric differences and evidence from split-brain studies
- The development of lateralisation
- The causes of dyslexia
- Computerised scanning techniques and their application to understanding language

Introduction

Most animals communicate with each other, but humans are unique as they are the only ones to use an extremely complex, creative and powerful system of communication called language that enables them to express their thoughts and feelings using verbal and written information. And, this ability is remarkable in many ways. For example, during a simple conversation we are likely to speak around 180 words a minute from a vocabulary of between 60,000 to 120,000 words. This is an impressive figure, but even more important is the fact that we utilise an extensive knowledge of intricate linguistic rules including those that govern the sequencing of words and their form (grammar). In fact, this rule system provides us with the potential to make an infinite number of word sequences from a limited number of sounds, and without this ability we would only be able to produce (and understand) very simple forms of language. But, human language is much more than communication, it is also a system for representing knowledge and a vehicle for thought, that lies at the core of human cognition. It is hardly surprising, therefore, that language has been described as the greatest of all human achievements (Ornstein 1988) and the one species-typical behaviour that sets us apart from all other animals (Thompson 1993). Thus, by attempting to understand the biological basis of language, we are getting to the heart of what makes us (and our brain) truly unique.

Broca's area

Until recently, most of our knowledge about the biological basis of language has come from examining language impairments in patients who have suffered brain injury from strokes and accidents. This evidence first began to be systematically collected in the early part of the nineteenth century (particularly by French researchers), many of whom noted that damage to the frontal lobes was linked with language difficulties. For example, in 1836, Marc Dax described 40 patients who had speech problems due to frontal lobe injuries and later, in 1861, Simon Aubertin described the case of a man who had shot away part of his frontal cranium in a failed suicide attempt. Remarkably, Aubertin found that if he pressed a spatula against the exposed brain while the man was speaking, his speech was immediately halted (Finger 1994).

However, by far the most important discovery was made by French doctor Paul Broca who examined a patient (called Leborgne) who had been incapable of meaningful speech for 21 years. What made this patient unique, however, was that he was intelligent and capable of comprehending spoken and written language. Furthermore, he could also communicate with others using motor gestures. Yet, with one or two exceptions (such as being able to utter the word 'tan') he was unable to speak. When Leborgne died in 1861, Broca undertook an autopsy on his brain and found a single lesion located towards the back of the frontal lobes in the left hemisphere. This was an important finding because it provided the first clear evidence that certain functions (e.g. language) were highly localised to specific regions of the brain.

Following this discovery, Broca performed autopsies on eight other patients who had suffered similar types of language problem, and, in most cases, the language disability appeared to be linked with the same area of the frontal lobes in the left hemisphere. This region (now known as **Broca's area**) was found to be situated next to the part of the motor cortex that controlled the muscles of the vocal cord and mouth (Figure 9.1). In contrast, similar damage to the right frontal cortex appeared to have no effect on speech production or its understanding. In other words, language appeared to be localised not only to the frontal cortex, but also to the left hemisphere.

Broca's aphasia

It is now known that people who suffer damage to Broca's area show a language disturbance known as **Broca's aphasia** (aphasia refers to an impairment in language production or understanding that occurs as a result of brain damage). This form of aphasia

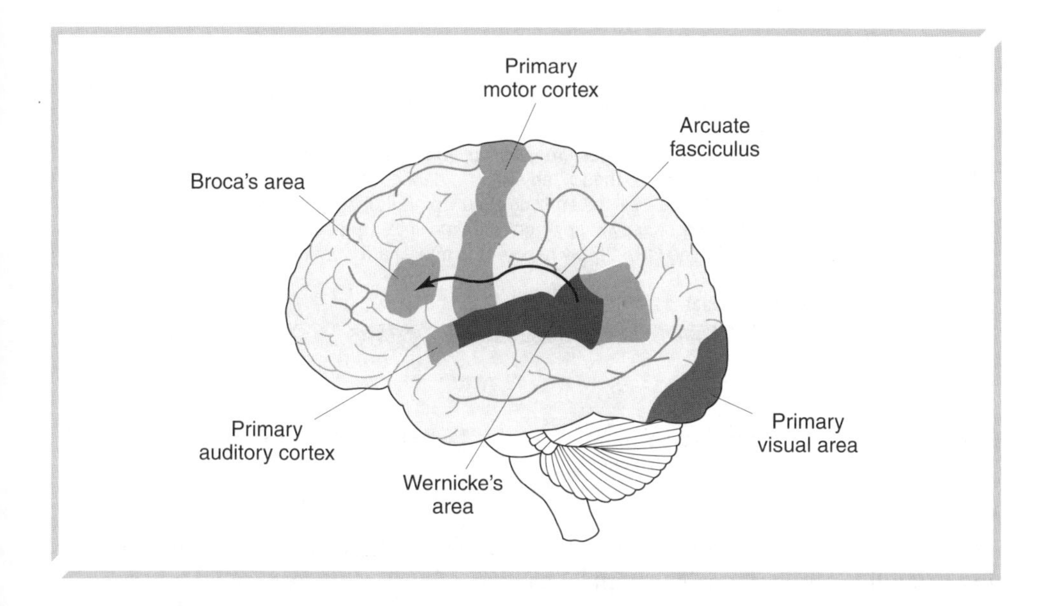

Figure 9.1 The location of the main brain areas involved in language.

is characterised by language that is slow, laboured, and without grammatical structure. Consequently, this speech often sounds as if it is being read from a telegram (being mainly composed of simple nouns, verbs and adjectives) and, even then, it typically lacks the intonation and inflection of normal language (see Figure 9.2).

Another problem associated with Broca's aphasia is a difficulty in finding the 'right word' (known as **anomia**) which often results in long pauses during speech. To make matters worse, the word that is chosen may sometimes be the 'wrong' one, or incorrect sounds may be substituted into it, which makes the Broca's aphasic's speech difficult to understand (despite this, the speakers 'know' what they are trying to say, and are normally aware of the errors they are making). Interestingly, simple 'automated' expressions such as 'hello' or emotional exclamations (such as swearing) are often spoken without difficulty, and in some cases a Broca's aphasic may even be able to sing old (well-learned) songs fluently and easily.

How then can we best characterise the deficit in Broca's aphasia? One clue comes from the fact that such individuals will often have difficulty in carrying out a simple command such as being asked to stick out their tongue (**oral apraxia**), yet they will typically have no problem licking their lips after eating a sugary doughnut. This observation suggests that the main deficit in Broca's aphasia is an inability to consciously produce the correct motor movements necessary for the articulation of speech (because of this, Broca's aphasia is sometimes known as expressive or **motor aphasia**). Although this explanation makes sense because Broca's area is also adjacent to the motor cortex it is nevertheless too simple since there may also be impaired language comprehension. For example, although Broca's patients may give the impression of having good

Asked to tell the story of Cinderella
(previously shown picture version of the story to facilitate recall)

Cinderella...yes...now...busy me (*gestures dusting, ironing etc.* ...)...la la la...happy...
no sad...two erm sss...sss...sisters...bad...bad sisters... dance...fff...fairy god dance swoosh
(*gestures magic wand*)...Cinderella...pr...pr...priz ch... no too hard (therapist: *'Prince Charming'*)...
Yes him...lovely...dancing...happy happy...oh no...time time...run shoe...Cinderella...
shoe...mine...mine OK... lovely happy...the end...hard work (*laughs*)

(underline indicates extra stress)

Figure 9.2 Non-fluent Broca's-type aphasia. (*Source*: Provided by Mandy Galling, Reg RCSLT, Guild Community Healthcare NHS Trust.)

comprehension of verbal speech, on closer inspection they often show difficulties in understanding 'grammatically complex' language (such as the command 'put the cup on top of the fork and place the knife inside the cup' – Bear *et al.* 1996). In addition, they may also have difficulty understanding written information, particularly if it is grammatically difficult.

Wernicke's area

In 1874, a 26-year-old German neurologist called Carl Wernicke described a very different type of aphasia, and one that was linked with damage to a region in the left hemisphere some distance from Broca's area. This region (now known as **Wernicke's area**) is located in the temporal lobe adjacent to the **primary auditory cortex**. Unlike Broca's aphasia, damage to Wernicke's area does not interfere with the rhythm and grammar of speech, and people are able to articulate quickly and fluently without difficulty. However, there is one major problem: their speech is largely devoid of meaning. Thus, although it may sound 'normal' and grammatically correct, the actual content is often meaningless. To a large degree this is because the language is made up of either inappropriate words (**paraphasias**) or ones that do not exist (**neologisms**). For example, in reply to the question 'Where do you work?' one Wernicke's aphasic was quoted as saying '*Before I was in the one here, I was in the other one. My sister had the department in the other one*' (Geschwind 1972). Alternatively, when Rochford (1974) asked a Wernicke's aphasic to name a picture of an anchor, the patient called it a '*martha argeneth*'; and when Kertesz (1979) asked a patient to name a toothbrush and a pen the patient responded with '*stoktery*' and '*minkt*' (McIlveen and Gross 1996).

Not only is speech meaningless, but damage to Wernicke's area also produces a profound deficit in language comprehension. While simple sentences and instructions may be understood, there is nearly always a marked inability to comprehend more complex forms of language. Thus, it is extremely difficult (if not impossible) to engage

Required to tell the therapist about trip to visit his daughter and a meal out

Claire?...yes...well...I was will...miner...mineral water...of my 'pitch' on stonework 'make' and 'ww' and 'wiker' of 'wenner'. December and London...on 'minter' of 'minder' and 'si' or 'risher'...I was 'madge'

(Targets very difficult to interpret. Items in quotation marks show broad phonological approximation)

Figure 9.3 Fluent Wernicke's-type aphasia. (*Source*: Provided by Mandy Galling, Reg RCSLT, Guild Community Healthcare NHS Trust.)

in meaningful conversation with Wernicke's aphasiacs. Furthermore, to make matters worse, they may be unaware that they have a speech or comprehension deficit! In other words, a person with Wernicke's aphasia may continue to talk gibberish, and act as if nothing is amiss (see Figure 9.3). Reading and writing are also similarly impaired. For example, there are Wernicke's aphasiacs who, if given a book, will go through the motions of reading it aloud only to produce utter nonsense (Springer and Deutsch 1989).

How can we then best characterise Wernicke's aphasia? One clue comes from its location next to the primary auditory cortex, which indicates that it is a problem associated with the translation of auditory information into words (indeed, Wernicke's aphasia is sometimes known as **receptive aphasia**). Also, because there is a marked deficit of comprehension, this indicates that Wernicke's area is also involved in translating words into their proper meanings (see also below).

Alexia and agraphia

In 1892, the French neurologist Jules Dejerine reported the cases of two patients who had yet another type of language deficit. Rather than suffering from aphasia, Dejerine found that his patients had great difficulty in reading (**alexia**) and writing (**agraphia**). One of his patients, for example, could speak and comprehend spoken language perfectly well – but was unable to read or write. When a brain autopsy was later undertaken, it revealed damage to a region called the **angular gyrus**, which was situated between Wernicke's area and the occipital (visual) cortex. Indeed, the angular gyrus appeared to be in an ideal position to receive visual input, and Dejerine concluded that it must somehow be involved in helping to connect written information with their sounds and meanings.

Dejerine's other patient was alexic (i.e. he was unable to read) but he could nevertheless still write. This deficit produced some seemingly odd patterns of behaviour. For example, although this patient could not read (i.e. comprehend) written words, he could copy the words correctly, and recognise their meaning as he wrote them out. Similarly, he was able to recognise the words when the individual letters were spoken out aloud to him (e.g. c-a-t). Perhaps even more remarkable, he even knew how to spell words that he could not read!

A clue to the underlying nature of the deficit came from the fact that this patient was also blind in his right visual field, which indicated that there was extensive damage to the left visual cortex (see Chapter 2). Indeed, this was confirmed at autopsy. However, more important to explaining the deficit was the finding that there was also damage to the posterior portion of the corpus callosum, which carries visual information between the two hemispheres. This meant that although the person could 'see' written information with his right intact visual cortex, he would have been unable to cross it over to the angular gyrus in the left hemisphere (where presumably 'reading' took place). Again, this finding supported the idea that the angular gyrus was a vital site for the identification and comprehension of written information.

But why was this person still able to copy out written information? The answer is probably because the connections between the intact right visual cortex and the motor areas that control hand movement were not disrupted. In other words, there was an alternative route from the right visual cortex for copying to take place that did not require the involvement of the left-sided angular gyrus.

The Wernicke–Geschwind model

As we have seen, Wernicke's and Broca's areas are involved in language comprehension and production, and the angular gyrus concerned with reading. But how are these regions connected and how do they interact with each other? The first person to offer a viable explanation was Carl Wernicke in the nineteenth century, and his ideas were to remain highly influential until they were elaborated further by Norman Geschwind in 1965. This new combined account is now widely known as the **Wernicke–Geschwind model**.

The basic idea is that when we hear spoken language, the initial message is passed from the auditory cortex to Wernicke's area where the sounds (words) are decoded and comprehended. A similar process is also believed to occur for reading, except in this case, the flow of information is passed from the visual cortex to the angular gyrus and then on to Wernicke's area. Thus, not only does Wernicke's area occupy a pivotal location (combining the streams of visual and auditory verbal information), but it is also the crucial site where comprehension takes place (i.e. verbal information is translated into thought). Wernicke's area is also hypothesised to play an important role in generating verbal responses, and for this to happen, thought processes have to be translated into a verbal code. This information is then passed to Broca's area which provides the articulation centre and contains the programmes for the complex co-ordination of the muscle movements necessary for speech. Thus, the neural code for the verbal response is believed to originate in Wernicke's area, and is then passed to Broca's area where it is transformed into language. Most of this processing is believed to take place in the left hemisphere – although information can also cross to the right hemisphere (and back) via the corpus callosum.

This theory, of course, implies that a pathway must exist between Wernicke's and Broca's areas. Although this connection had not been discovered by the end of the nineteenth century, Wernicke nevertheless had the foresight to predict the type of aphasia that would occur if this hypothetical pathway was destroyed. In short, he reasoned that it would not affect the comprehension of spoken or written information (because Wernicke's area would be intact), nor would it interfere with the production of language (since Broca's area would be intact). What then would be the deficit? According to Wernicke it would be highly specific: this type of aphasia would result in a person not being able to repeat words and sentences fluently.

In fact, Wernicke turned out to be largely correct in his prediction. For example, a pathway is now known to pass from Wernicke's area to Broca's area and is called the **arcuate fasciculus** (see Figure 9.4). Moreover, people with damage to this pathway have no difficulty in understanding language and are capable of producing fluent speech. Despite this, they suffer from a condition known as **conduction aphasia**, characterised by an impairment in repeating certain words and sentences. For example, although these patients may be able to repeat concrete words such as 'bicycle' and 'elephant', they are typically unable to repeat abstract words or non-words such as 'blaynge'. It has been suggested by Geschwind that this occurs because, upon hearing a concrete word, a

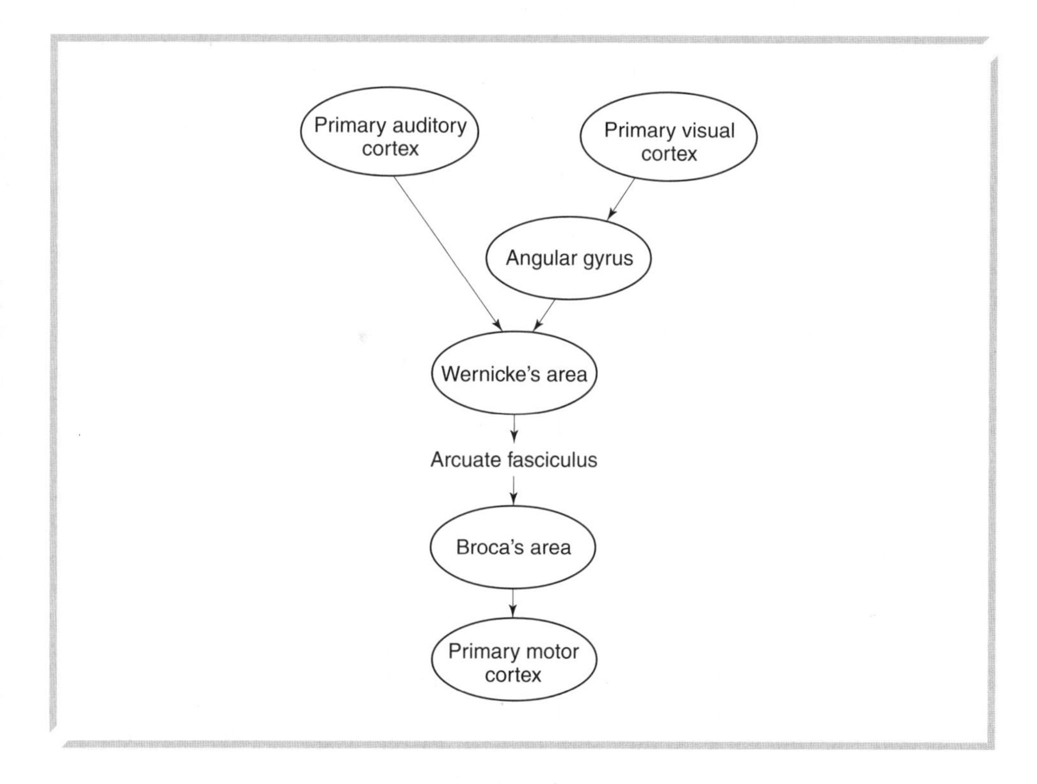

Figure 9.4 The Wernicke–Geschwind model of language processing.

visual image can be formed which is then able to pass to Broca's area via a different pathway to the arcuate fasciculus. In addition, patients with conduction aphasia often find it difficult to read out aloud (despite being able to read silently with good comprehension), and when given an object to name, they'll typically 'know' what it is (and what it is called), but be unable to put the correct name to it.

Problems with the Wernicke–Geschwind model

Although the basic tenets of the Wernicke–Geschwind model are generally accepted, it is probably only accurate up to a point. For example, in the 1950s, Wilder Penfield stimulated various regions of the cerebral cortex with electrical current in order to detect abnormal tissue in human patients that were about to undergo brain surgery for epilepsy (because the brain contains no pain receptors, subjects can remain fully conscious during this procedure). Penfield found that stimulation of the cortex could affect language in several ways. For example, it could induce vocalisations (e.g. a sustained utterance such as 'oh . . .'), interfere with the comprehension of language, or disrupt the production of speech. Despite this, the effects produced by stimulation did not always correspond with the brain regions predicted by the Wernicke–Geschwind model. For example, naming difficulties (i.e. 'That is a . . . I know. That is a . . .') or the misnaming of objects (e.g. saying 'camel' when meaning to say 'comb') were obtained from widespread regions of the left hemisphere that went beyond Broca's and Wernicke's speech zones (Kolb and Whishaw 1985). In addition, researchers have now found that the extent of the cortical language zones as identified by stimulation can vary considerably in size and location between individuals (Ojemann 1983). In other words, the language regions of the brain are not as clearly defined as the Wernicke–Geschwind model of language implies (and similar findings have also been found with modern scanning techniques – see below).

Another problem is that, until recently, the understanding of the neuroanatomical location of language was based largely on people who had suffered strokes or accidents. Unfortunately, this type of damage tends to be very diffuse with widespread bleeding and is rarely limited to one specific region. Thus, a stroke or a wound may well cause much more damage than first appears to be the case. This problem is highlighted by the paradoxical finding that long-lasting speech impairments rarely occur in patients who have precise surgical lesions made to their 'language' areas. For example, Penfield reported that the arcuate fasciculus could be removed without producing aphasia, and similar findings have also been found following surgical removal of Broca's area. Again, this indicates that the so-called 'language centres' may not be as strictly localised as first believed.

It has also been pointed out that the Wernicke–Geschwind model also fails to take into account the role of subcortical regions in language processing. For example, stimulation of the **pulvinar region** of the thalamus has been shown to arrest speech (Ojemann 1983) and it is known that damage to the **basal ganglia** (as occurs in Parkinson's disease) can result in language that sounds indistinct and without rhythm.

Box 9.1 CAN PRIMATES ACQUIRE LANGUAGE?

Communication is an important part of animal behaviour. For example, primates use a variety of sounds and gestures in social interaction to portray threat, intention, alarm, and so on – and highly sophisticated forms of communication are found in other species as well (whales and dolphins provide a fascinating example). But, for many researchers this is not the same as human language which is essentially infinite in its meaning (largely due to its grammar), and which is able to associate specific (and abstract) meanings with arbitrary sounds and symbols. Indeed, language is the thing that makes us uniquely human (or so the argument goes), and no other species comes close to emulating our ability to comprehend, use, and produce language.

But is language really unique to human beings? One problem with this theory is that other animals (including primates) cannot make our sounds. For example, they do not have the same fine control over their tongues, lips, and vocal cords, and are therefore unable to talk. Thus, if animals were able to learn or understand language they would not be able to tell us. With this possibility in mind, Beatrice and Roger Gardner during the 1960s set about teaching a female chimpanzee (called Washoe) a version of American sign language used by deaf people. The Gardners began when Washoe was about one year old – and within three years she had developed a vocabulary of over 130 signs (or 'words'). Moreover, she learned to combine the signs to make simple sentences, and to use 'words' in creative and novel ways (e.g. after learning the verb '*to open*' she would ask the investigators to 'open' the tap whenever she wanted a drink). Other researchers have confirmed these findings, and similar work has been undertaken with gorillas and orang-utans (Paterson and Linden 1981; Miles 1983).

However, the interpretation of these findings remains highly controversial. For example, some researchers have argued that these animals are not learning sign language *per se*, but rather they are only imitating the gestures made by their trainers. In support of this idea, they point out that primates often combine signs in illogical sequences and only occasionally join signs together in a meaningful way (which the trainer will inevitably then choose to reinforce). Others have argued that although primates might be able to communicate with language, there is little evidence to indicate that they can use it as a vehicle for thought. But there are also those who disagree. For example, some of the most compelling evidence for language in primates has come from Susan Savage-Rumbaugh and her colleagues who worked with a male pygmy chimpanzee called Kanzi. Apparently, this primate can understand about 150 English spoken words and can respond to complex and unfamiliar spoken commands such as 'throw your ball in the river' and 'go to the refrigerator and get out a tomato' (Savage-Rumbaugh 1990). Moreover, Kanzi can even use symbols to communicate past events, e.g. he pressed the symbols on a special keyboard to represent 'Matata bite' (Matata is a fellow monkey) to explain a cut that was on his hand.

These findings imply that language may not be a unique human ability after all – although to put this work into its correct perspective, it needs to be borne in mind that Kanzi's language skills are only equivalent to that of a 2-year-old human (Greenfield and Savage-Rumbaugh 1990). Thus, it still remains the case that no other species comes close to matching our ability to use and understand language. In other words, language is our natural medium for communication, although the same can clearly not be said of other animals.

The split-brain procedure

As we have seen, evidence linking the left hemisphere with language goes back to the early part of the nineteenth century. But, further support for this relationship was dramatically shown in the 1960s when the behaviour of patients that had received **commissurotomy** was closely examined. This operation, which involved the complete severing of the **corpus callosum** (the massive axon bundle containing over 200 million fibres that connects the two cerebral hemispheres), was performed in a small number of patients who suffered from severe epilepsy. In fact, commissurotomy had first been performed in the early 1940s to control the spread of epileptic seizures and, remarkably, this operation (which effectively split the brain into two) appeared to have little effect on behaviour – a situation which prompted Karl Lashley in 1950 to propose (tongue-in-cheek) that the main function of the corpus callosum was to stop the hemispheres sagging! (see Bogen 1979). Thus, the function of the corpus callosum was one of the great mysteries of physiological psychology.

In the 1960s, however, a much clearer picture of corpus callosum function began to emerge with the pioneering work of Roger Sperry and his associate Michael Gazzaniga. These researchers attempted to examine the functional role of the two hemispheres by delivering information individually to each cortex. However, this was not easy to do, because our main sensory system (vision) delivers information from each eye to both hemispheres (i.e. input from the right visual field of each eye goes to the left hemisphere, and input from the left goes to the right). To get around this problem, Sperry and Gazzaniga designed a task where they asked split-brain subjects to fixate on a point presented on a screen, following which they briefly flashed visual stimuli onto the right or left side of the screen (corresponding to the visual fields of the eyes). The exposure time was long enough for subjects to 'see' the stimulus, but brief enough to make sure

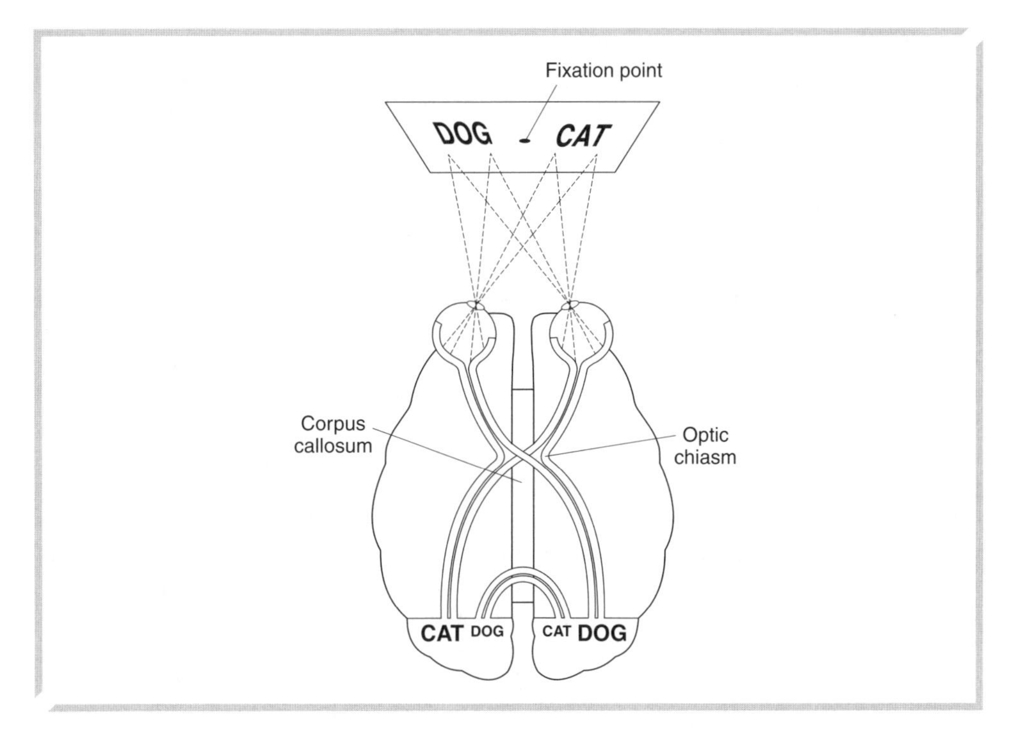

Figure 9.5 The presentation of visual stimuli to one hemisphere in split-brain subjects. (*Source*: From John P. J. Pinel, *Biopsychology*, 3rd edition. Copyright © 1997 by Allyn & Bacon. Reprinted by permission.)

that they did not have time to turn their eyes to it. In other words, this meant that stimuli presented to the left visual field passed to the right hemisphere, and stimuli in the right visual field went to the left hemisphere (Figure 9.5).

A second task developed by Sperry and Gazzaniga used split-brain patients who were blindfolded and asked to identify objects placed in either their right or left hands. In humans, the somesthetic pathways (which relay pressure, pain and touch information), unlike the visual system, completely cross from one side of the body to the opposite hemisphere of the brain. Thus, split-brain subjects who are blindfolded and asked to hold an object in their right hand will effectively be sending the information to their left hemisphere. With these two tasks, Sperry and Gazzaniga set out to examine the functions of the two hemispheres.

Language and the split-brain

It soon became clear using these new procedures that the left hemisphere was crucially involved in language. For example, when a written word was presented to the right visual field (so that it reached the left hemisphere) it was found that the split-brain patient had no trouble reading it out aloud or understanding its meaning. However, the same word presented to the right hemisphere elicited no verbal response. In fact, subjects often reported that they had seen nothing, or at best only detected a flash of light. Similarly, if patients were asked to name an object placed in their left hand (so that this information passed to the right hemisphere) they were often aware that something was in their hand, but unable to say what it was, unlike an object placed in their right hand which elicited a correct verbal response.

These results confirmed the dominance of the left hemisphere for language, and even implied that this side of the brain might be intimately connected with self-awareness since split-brain subjects appeared to be hardly aware of information presented to the right hemisphere. Despite this, the right hemisphere was not without its abilities. For example, when an object name was flashed to the right hemisphere (e.g. 'fork'), it was found that the left hand (controlled by the right hemisphere) could correctly select the target from a range of objects hidden behind a screen, although the subjects typically reported that they had not seen anything! And, despite correctly selecting the object, they could not describe what they had just picked up in their left hand. In fact, when different object names were flashed simultaneously to both hemispheres, patients would typically pick up the object chosen by their right hemisphere (or left hand), but name the object presented to the left hemisphere. Not surprisingly, subjects were astonished to find that they had misnamed the object when it was brought into full view.

These findings showed that the right hemisphere was able to understand simple object words, but could not name or produce any verbal response to accompany this recognition. This function was provided solely by the left hemisphere, which in these experiments was disconnected from the right cortex, and thus had no way of knowing what its other half was doing (which included recognising simple names and picking up the appropriate objects from the selection provided by the researchers).

Although it is now known that the right hemisphere has a very limited ability to read, and virtually no speech, this does not mean that it plays an unimportant role in human cognition. For example, when geometric patterns, drawings or faces are presented to the right hemisphere, the left hand is normally able to pick out the correct picture in a recognition test. Furthermore, a person's left hand (controlled by the right hemisphere) is much better at drawing pictures, learning finger mazes, completing jigsaws and arranging colour blocks to form a specific pattern. In short, the right hemisphere appears to show a superiority in visuo-spatial tasks, whereas the left hemisphere is much better dealing with language.

The right hemisphere and emotion

There is also evidence to show that the right hemisphere is predominantly involved in the processing of emotion. For example, studies have found that if a picture of a nude figure is presented to the right hemisphere, the split-brain subjects may report that they have not seen anything, while at the same time blushing and showing embarrassment (or humour), thus showing that recognition has taken place. The same degree of emotion, however, is not elicited when the stimulus is projected to the left hemisphere.

In fact, a difference between the two hemispheres in emotion had been suspected before researchers began to examine split-brain subjects seriously. For example, in the late 1930s, Goldstein reported that some patients with damage to their left hemisphere exhibited feelings of despair, hopelessness and anger – a set of responses which he called a **catastrophic–dysphoric reaction**. In contrast, those with right hemispheric damage tended to be placid and indifferent to their injury, even when it led to paralysis. Indeed, in one study that looked at the reactions of 150 people with unilateral brain injury, it was found that 62 per cent of those with left hemispheric damage showed the catastrophic reaction, compared to only 10 per cent with right-sided injuries. Alternatively, 38 per cent of subjects with damage of the right hemisphere were indifferent to their plight, whereas only 11 per cent of the left-sided group showed the same non-emotional response (Gainotti 1969). These results demonstrate that when the left cortex is damaged, the intact right hemisphere recognises the loss and responds with a strong emotional reaction. In contrast, this emotional reaction is nulled when damage (and loss of function) occurs to the right hemisphere.

It also appears that the right hemisphere is dominant when it comes to recognising the emotional tone of language. Speech is much more than just words, as shown by the fact that the tone of what we say may completely change its meaning (e.g. 'you look really nice today' can sound complimentary or sarcastic depending on the tone of the expression). Surprisingly, the ability to make these prosodic or tonal changes (prosody refers to the patterns of stress and intonation that are made during speech) is often impaired in people with damage to the right hemisphere. There is also evidence that the regions responsible for producing these deficits are the right-sided equivalent of the language centres in the left. For example, Elliot Ross has found that individuals with damage to the right-sided Broca's area often produce spoken language that is lacking in prosody, whereas those with damage to the right-sided equivalent of Wernicke's area are impaired in their ability to comprehend the prosodic nature of speech (Ross 1984).

The independence of the two hemispheres

The two cerebral hemispheres have their own specialised functions and are able to operate independently from each other (i.e. severing of the corpus callosum results in one brain effectively becoming split into two independent units). A number of further examples can also be used to illustrate this phenomenon. For instance, in one task where a split-brain patient was required to arrange a group of blocks to make a particular pattern with his right hand (i.e. testing the ability of his left hemisphere), it was found that the left hand (right hemisphere) persistently tried to take over the task so much that the experimenter actually had to wrestle with the left hand to stop it solving the problem. In other words, on a task which the left hemisphere finds difficult, it is the right hemisphere that attempts to take over proceedings. Michael Gazzaniga has also described the case of a patient who would sometimes pull his trousers down with one hand only to immediately pull them up with his other hand! Again, this provides compelling evidence that each of the two hemispheres, when disconnected, has a mind of its own. Indeed, as Roger Sperry has remarked, each hemisphere appears to have its own private sensations, perceptions, memories and ideas (Sperry 1974).

Of course, in normal circumstances, the right and left hemispheres are continually exchanging information through the corpus callosum to let the other know what it is thinking and doing. Thus, it is only when they are disconnected that they are forced to work independently at their own specialised skills. Interestingly, it also appears to be the case that consciousness is largely dependent on the language capabilities of the left hemisphere. This can be shown, for example, by the great surprise of split-brain patients when their left hand (controlled by the right hemisphere) does something unexpected (e.g. puts down an interesting book or makes a rude gesture). The left hemisphere does not appear to produce these types of unexpected responses, because the person is 'aware' or actively controlling his or her behaviour.

The Wada procedure

Another procedure that can be used to measure hemispheric function is the **Wada test**, named after its inventor Juan Wada in the late 1940s. This test was originally designed to help surgeons locate the main hemisphere for language prior to surgery so that they could avoid causing accidental aphasia (although language is normally dominant for the left hemisphere there can be exceptions as we shall see later). The Wada test involves injecting a short-acting anaesthetic (sodium amytal) into the carotid arteries (located at the side of the neck) that carry blood from the heart to the brain. Because there are separate right and left arteries, feeding their own respective hemispheres, it is a simple matter to selectively anaesthetise one side of the brain, thus causing its loss of function while the other hemisphere remains functionally intact. The effectiveness of the procedure can be quickly confirmed by paralysis of the opposite side of the body.

It is generally found that if sodium amytal is injected into the left (or dominant) hemisphere, then it produces a sudden and complete aphasia which lasts for around 5 minutes. Alternatively, if the anaesthesia is injected into the right (non-dominant) hemisphere, then language function remains relatively intact and the person will be able to converse and answer questions without difficulty. Indeed, in the vast majority of patients it is found that language is localised to the left hemisphere. However, this finding is not inevitable and, in a small number of patients, language may be confined instead to the right hemisphere, or be equally distributed across both cortices (mixed dominance).

One of the most interesting findings revealed by the Wada test is that the cerebral dominance of language has a tendency to be different in people who are either right or left handed. For example, Rasmussen and Milner (1977) have collected data from 212 patients, who have been examined with the Wada technique, and have found that 92 per cent of right-handed people had language that was strongly lateralised to the left hemisphere. However, in left-handed subjects this figure dropped to about 70 per cent. Of the rest, about 15 per cent of left handers were found to have language lateralised to the right hemisphere, and the remaining 15 per cent showed mixed dominance. Because it is known that around 90 per cent of people are right handed, a simple calculation shows that over 90 per cent of the population will have a left hemispheric dominance for language, with the remaining 10 per cent showing a right-sided specialisation or bias.

The development of lateralisation

Although the left hemisphere is normally dominant for the comprehension and production of language, it is also clear that the right hemisphere has the potential to take over this function in certain circumstances. For example, when the left hemisphere is damaged during infancy, it is generally found that near-normal language ability is attained by adulthood. An example of this was shown by Smith and Sugar (1975) who described the case of a 5-year-old boy, who had almost the whole of his left hemisphere removed to treat epilepsy. Prior to the operation, this boy was experiencing 10–12 seizures a day and was paralysed on his right side, which indicated widespread damage to the left hemisphere. Furthermore, although his verbal comprehension was normal, his speech production was poor (indicating that this function was also localised on the left). Following surgery, the boy's progress was monitored and, by the time he reached adulthood, he was found to have an above normal IQ, and superior language abilities. In other words, removal of the left hemisphere at an early age does not necessarily impair the development of language. However, this is in marked contrast to when damage occurs in adulthood (as in the case of stroke) which normally produces a drastic impairment in speech and writing, and one that rarely recovers to anywhere near its original level of function.

How then does lateralisation develop and when is it completed? According to some (e.g. Lenneberg 1967), damage to the left hemisphere produces little effect on language acquisition if it occurs before the age of 2 years, but causes increasing impairment after this age. According to Lenneberg this shows that both hemispheres are equipotent for language up to the age of 2 years, and only then does lateralisation slowly develop (normally in the left hemisphere) until it is completed in puberty. Further support for this idea has come from Eran Zaidel who has shown that most split-brain subjects have a degree of language ability in their right hemisphere which is approximately the same as that found in a 6-year-old child (Zaidel 1985). The most parsimonious explanation for this finding is that language becomes fully lateralised to the left hemisphere at around this time.

However, this theory has been undermined in recent years by the discovery that the structures of the two hemispheres, at least in most people, show innate anatomical differences. For example, in 1968, Norman Geschwind and Walter Levitsky drew attention to a region of the cerebral cortex called the **planum temporale** (this covers part of Wernicke's area along with some of the adjacent auditory cortex) that was normally much larger in the left hemisphere. For example, in adults, the left planum was on average 3.6 centimetres in length compared to 2.7 on the right, and was about one-third larger in area (and in some cases it was more than five times as large). Moreover, out of 100 brains examined at post-mortem, it was found that 65 had a larger planum temporale in the left hemisphere; 11 had it bigger in the right hemisphere; and the remaining 24 showed no difference (Geschwind and Levitsky 1968).

Importantly, a difference in the size of the planum temporale has also been found in the human foetus and it can be detected as early as the 31st week of gestation (Chi *et al.* 1977). In fact, it appears that the left planum temporale tends to be slightly more asymmetrical in infants than in adults, being some 57 per cent larger in the left hemisphere of infants and 50 per cent larger in adults. Thus, these findings show that the size of the planum temporale is not a developmental consequence of left hemisphere use for speech, but rather represents an innate predisposition for the two hemispheres to be different.

If this is the case, and assuming that the planum temporale is involved in language development, how then can we account for the fact that the right hemisphere is able to acquire language? Firstly, it needs to be remembered that language still has to be learned, and this process occurs at a time when the brain is especially plastic. Thus, if early developmental problems arise, the plasticity of the right hemisphere (which presumably is most pronounced in the first few years of life) has sufficient capacity to take over the control of language. Indeed, like many other types of neural development (such as that which occurs in the visual system) the acquisition of language appears to depend on innate capacities, that can be modified by experience for a limited period during maturation. Secondly, it must be pointed out that the significance of the planum temporale in language development still remains unclear. For example, as we have seen, a larger planum temporale in the left hemisphere only occurs in around 65 per cent of human brains, whereas the left hemispheric dominance of language is found in over 90 per cent. Moreover, it has also been found that higher apes tend to show a larger left-sided planum temporale, which casts further doubt on its presumed role in language.

Dyslexia

Although **dyslexia** ('dys' meaning *bad*, 'lexia' meaning *reading*) can be acquired through brain injury, in most cases it is a disorder of development that first manifests itself when the child begins to read. There are many types of dyslexia (with deficits ranging from mild to severe) and it has been estimated that 3 to 6 per cent of children may have reading problems that are severe enough to qualify for this label. However, despite popular belief, dyslexic children do not lack intelligence, they simply have difficulty reading. In some cases this may be due to an impairment in relating the characters of written language with the phonological sounds that they represent; and, in other instances, dyslexia may arise from difficulties in naming letters (letter blindness), reading words (word blindness) or reading sentences (sentence blindness). In addition, many dyslexics have problems with writing. For example, some children may try to write from right to left, or they confuse characters that are distinguished by their right–left orientation (such as *d*, *b*, *p* or *s*). In other words, a wide range of impairments accompanies dyslexia, and all imply a problem in brain function concerned with reading.

What causes dyslexia? One clue comes from the fact that reading difficulties are some 4–5 times more common in males than in females. Although the significance of this fact is not fully understood (however, see the work of Geschwind and Behan discussed later) it has been pointed out that males appear to have fewer fibres in the posterior parts of their corpus callosum (which connect the two visual association areas), and this may be a possible contributory factor in the development of the disorder. But what about the rest of the brain? Until recently, there appeared to be little sign of any abnormal difference in brain structure between dyslexic and normal subjects. That was until 1979, when Galaburda and Kemper showed that differences did exist (at least for some individuals). These researchers examined the brain of a young dyslexic man who had died in a fall, and found signs of abnormality in the planum temporale. As mentioned above, for most people the planum temporale is larger in the left hemisphere, but in this case it was the same size on both sides of the brain. Even more significant was the discovery that its neurons were immature, and the columnar organisation of its layers had not developed properly, a pattern that was similar to the type of brain structure known to occur in the sixth week of gestation when the last stages of neural migration take place in the cerebral cortex. In other words, it appeared that something had happened at this point in gestation to disrupt normal neural development.

Further post-mortem work confirmed these results in a number of other cases, as well as finding other types of damage (Galaburda *et al.* 1985, 1994). For example, abnormalities in the layering of cortical cells, excessive folding, and clusters of neurons in unusual locations have also been found in the frontal and temporal cortices, and these changes are much more common (and widespread) in the left than in the right hemisphere. In addition, the planum temporale appears consistently to be far less developed in the left hemisphere than normal (although this has been questioned by Schultz *et al.* 1994). Brain damage associated with dyslexia has also been found in subcortical sites, including smaller-than-normal neurons in the lateral geniculate nucleus and medial geniculate nucleus – areas that are involved in vision and audition respectively (Livingstone *et al.* 1991; Galaburda *et al.* 1994). Although it is still difficult to know the extent to which these changes are a consistent feature of dyslexia, it has nevertheless been claimed that no dyslexic brain, so far examined, has been found to be free of abnormality (Galaburda 1987).

What causes dyslexia?

Although dyslexia has a tendency to run in families, it does not appear to follow any clear pattern of inheritance. A more consistent finding is that dyslexia is more common in males, and occurs more frequently in people who are left-handed. This later finding was confirmed by Norman Geschwind and Peter Behan who looked at the distribution of dyslexia (along with other conditions) in a random sample of 500 left-handed subjects and 900 who were right-handed. The results showed that the incidence of dyslexia (and other learning disorders) was 10 times higher in the left-handed than in the right-handed group. A second unexpected finding also emerged from this study when it was found that left-handers had twice the rate of autoimmune disorders (such as allergies, arthritis and diabetes) than right-handers (Geschwind and Behan 1982).

Thus, by the early 1980s, it had been established that dyslexia was strongly sex-linked and associated with left-handedness and immune disorders. In addition, evidence was beginning to show abnormalities in the planum temporale. But how could all these seemingly discrepant findings be reconciled? Geschwind and Behan's theory was straightforward. They proposed that all these characteristics could be attributed to one factor:

an abnormally high level of the male sex hormone **testosterone** that occurred at a crucial juncture in foetal development.

To support their theory, Geschwind and Behan pointed out that during foetal growth the planum temporale normally starts to develop one to two weeks earlier on the right side of the brain, but is then overtaken in size by the later-developing left-sided planum. But, as we have seen, there is evidence that this switch does not take place successfully in dyslexics, because their planum temporale tends to be the same size on both sides of the brain. The important question is, therefore: Why? According to Geschwind and Behan, the likeliest explanation is that testosterone (which is known to be released during this period of gestation), if released in high enough amounts, will inhibit the development of the left hemisphere – leading to a smaller planum temporale forming in this side of the brain. This explanation would account for the fact that dyslexia is more frequent in males (i.e. they produce higher levels of testosterone), and explain why it is more likely in left-handers (i.e. their right hemisphere has become relatively more dominant). But, why is there an increased susceptibility to autoimmune diseases? According to Geschwind, the high level of testosterone which suppresses the development of the left hemisphere, also inhibits the formation of the immune system, in particular, by slowing down the development of the thymus gland.

Geschwind and Behan's theory is ambitious as it has attempted to take a complex disorder and explain it in terms of a single neurological problem (an undeveloped left hemisphere) and a single cause (high levels of testosterone at a certain point in development). Unfortunately, it is difficult at the present time to judge whether the theory is correct, particularly as it is difficult (if not impossible) to test experimentally. Nevertheless, it has generated much interest and, although controversial, it continues to provide an important focus (and talking point) for researchers interested in understanding the biological basis of dyslexia.

The development of brain-imaging techniques

Until recently, researchers interested in identifying brain areas involved in language were forced to rely largely on the post-mortem examination of patients who had previously experienced aphasia or language difficulties. This was far from ideal for a number of reasons, not least because the main source of patients was generally those who had suffered widespread brain damage as a result of stroke and head injury. Not only did this make identifying language regions difficult, but by the time the patient came to autopsy, some recovery of function had often taken place, which made it even more difficult to link the damage with behavioural deficits. Fortunately, researchers are no longer limited by this arrangement. Indeed, a revolution has taken place over the last two decades in the study of language with the development of non-invasive brain-imaging techniques that allow investigators to 'look' into a living brain in order to identify the location of damage, or even to observe the brain at work.

For most of this century the only way neurologists could visualise the brain in a living person was to make the major blood vessels visible through a procedure known as **cerebral angiography**. This technique involved injecting a radioactive dye into the carotid arteries (the same arteries that are used in the Wada procedure) and then observing the perfusion of the dye by taking X-ray photographs of the brain. The pictures produced by this technique (called angiograms) were useful in identifying vascular damage and the location of tumours, as shown by the displacement of blood vessels. This method works because X-ray photography is only effective when the internal structures of the body differ in the extent to which they absorb X-rays. Thus, if injected with a dye, the blood vessels and the surrounding brain tissue absorb the X-rays differently, thus allowing the blood vessels to stand out and be visualised.

Unfortunately, this technique was of little use in examining different brain regions because X-rays could only provide an outline of the main vascular pathways and not visualise the structural detail of the tissue surrounding them. However, in 1972, an electrical engineer called Godfrey Hounsfield, who was working for EMI, pioneered a system in which brain X-rays could be resolved by computers that performed a complex mathematical analysis of multiple photographs taken from many different angles. This technique, called **computerised axial tomography (CAT)**, involved passing a large number of narrow beam X-rays through the brain using a ray gun that moved around the person's head (see Figure 9.6). By the use of this type of multiple picture technique, it was found that the amount of radiation absorbed by the brain varied from region to region, and the amount of radiation picked up by the detectors could then be used by the computer to construct a three-dimensional image of the brain. Moreover, by adjusting the angles through which the X-rays were sent, the appearance of any slice (or plane) of the brain could be obtained. This technique produced clear X-ray pictures and, for the first time, the structure of the brain could be visualised in considerable detail (and in someone who was alive!).

Soon after this breakthrough, a second method of examining brain structure was developed through **magnetic resonance imaging (MRI)**, which produced a picture of even higher resolution than that provided by CAT. Magnetic resonance imaging does

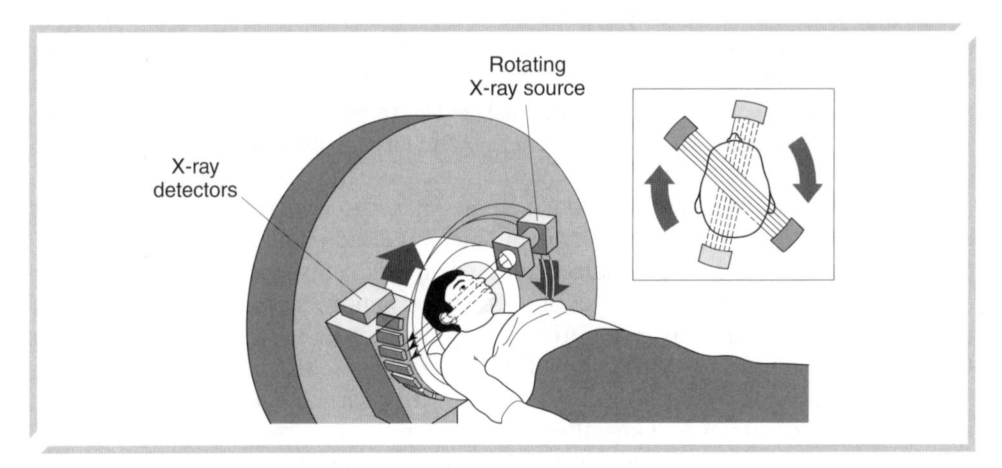

Figure 9.6 The basic procedure of computerised axial tomography. (*Source*: From D. Purves *et al.*, *Neuroscience*. Copyright © 1997 by Sinauer Associates Inc. Reprinted by permission.)

not rely on radiation to create its pictures, but uses radio-frequency waves. This type of imaging works on the basis that any atom with an odd electron (such as hydrogen) has an inherent rotation. Passing radio-frequency waves through tissue containing these atoms changes the direction of their rotation, making them spin in a different way. By measuring the energy that is created by this reverberation, it is then possible to get a computer to construct an image of the brain in much the same way as for CAT. Indeed, because grey matter (cell bodies), white matter (axons), cerebrospinal fluid and bone all differ in terms of their water content (and thus hydrogen), these tissues are easily distinguished by this type of imaging.

Both CAT and MRI scans have greatly facilitated the way in which researchers can judge the location and extent of brain damage. They are effective in identifying tumours and areas of damage produced by strokes; and they can identify enlarged ventricles which is generally an indication of brain atrophy and degeneration. Moreover, the resolution of CAT scans has been improved to such an extent that a relatively small change such as a shrinkage of a single gyrus can now be detected. Also, in the case of MRI it is possible to detect the loss of myelin around groups of axons which can be used to diagnose demyelinating diseases such as multiple sclerosis. Indeed, because of its sensitivity to myelin, MRI has been used to measure the difference in the size of the corpus callosum in people who are right or left handed. One study that used this technique has found that the corpus callosum is larger in people who are left-handers (Witelson 1985).

The measurement of human brain activity

Both CAT and MRI have been used extensively to identify regions of brain damage. But neither was designed to examine the brain 'at work' in its functional state. However, two techniques that have been developed to provide ongoing pictures of the brain while it engages in mental activity (or performs various tasks) are **regional blood flow (RBF)** and **positron emission tomography (PET)**. Both these procedures are based on the principle that the brain requires energy to function (in fact, the brain accounts for only 2 per cent of body weight yet consumes some 20 per cent of its energy), and that the regions of the brain most involved in a particular task will be those that use up the most energy. Thus, by monitoring the brain's use of energy, one has a window to its inner workings.

The earliest approach to this problem was to measure the rate of blood flow through the brain (based on the assumption that increased perfusion will reflect greater levels of oxygen flowing to that area, thus signifying increased metabolic and neural activity). One way of doing this is to get subjects to inhale a radioactive gas such as Xenon-133 (which does not react with the tissues of the body but simply 'flows' with the blood) and then detect the radioactivity given off with a gamma-ray camera. This technique was first developed in the early 1960s by Niels Lassen and his colleagues (e.g. see Lassen *et al.* 1978) who used a camera with 254 detectors, with each cell scanning a brain area of about 1 square centimetre. This information was processed by a computer and presented on a monitor (showing a diagram of the brain) which represented the different levels of blood flow (low to high) by a different colour (e.g. violet, blue, green, yellow, orange and red) over a short period of time (about 60 seconds).

This technique has been used as a diagnostic tool in the detection of tumours, strokes and abnormal brain activity (e.g. epilepsy). But, also importantly, it enabled psychologists (for the first time) to examine the brain when it was engaged in mental activity or various types of behaviour. For instance, it has been used to record the 'flow' of sensory information (e.g. visual input) in the brain, and to examine the patterns of activity in the motor regions that accompany voluntary movement (Lassen *et al.* 1978). It has also detected brain (or mental) abnormalities in people with psychological disorders (e.g. schizophrenics often show reduced blood flow to their prefrontal cortex). Also, as might be expected, it has been used to examine language. For example, one of the most interesting findings to emerge from the use of this technique is the similar activation of both right and left hemispheres in the performance of language tasks (e.g. Larsen *et al.* 1978).

However, two drawbacks of the regional blood flow technique, as described above, are the relatively short life of Xenon-133 (which only allows testing for about a minute or so) and its inability to measure blood flow in subcortical structures. A much more sophisticated technique that has overcome both these limitations is positron emission tomography (PET) first developed in the early 1970s (see also Box 9.2). Again, this technique works by measuring the level of metabolic activity in the brain, except, in this case, the radioactive substance can be anything that is able to emit positrons, (i.e. it must be able to be bound to a positron-emitting isotope) and this includes gases (such as oxygen) and chemical agents (such as glucose and water). The substance is then taken up into the brain (generally through inhalation or injection into the carotid arteries) where it starts to decay thus emitting positrons. For example, if 2-deoxyglucose is used, it will accumulate in the most active cells (or regions of the brain) where it then provides a source of radioactive particles (or positrons). A positron is, in fact, a short-lived particle which travels only a short distance before it collides with an electron. When this happens, the positron is turned into two gamma rays, which travel away from the impact exactly 180 degrees apart. These rays are picked up by gamma-ray detectors, and the site of the positron–electron collisions is reconstructed by the computer which then generates a continuous high-resolution three-dimensional colour picture of the regions where most decay (or brain activity) is taking place. This technique is increasingly being used in a wide variety of contexts including the detection of tumours, cerebrovascular disease, dementia and epilepsy, as well as the examination of the brain in cognition and behaviour.

Box 9.2 THE APPLICATION OF PET SCANNING TO UNDERSTANDING LANGUAGE

The application of modern scanning techniques to the study of higher mental function and language has already produced some unexpected findings. For example, in one study (see Posner and Raichle 1994, pp. 112–21) the amount of blood flowing through the cerebral cortex was measured using PET during the performance of several language-related tasks by college students. To measure brain activity, these investigators used intravenous injections of radioactive water since this affected the two hemispheres simultaneously, thus enabling the activity of each to be directly compared. Following this injection, subjects were given a series of tasks to perform. They were first asked to fixate on a small cross (+) shown on a computer monitor, and then to read (or listen via headphones) to simple nouns that were presented one by one. In the next condition, the subjects were asked to read the nouns aloud (or to recite them). Finally, subjects were given a task in which they had to provide an appropriate verb to go with the presented noun (e.g. *cake*: eat; *hammer*: hit).

The results from this study produced a very different pattern of cerebral activation to that which might have been predicted from the Wernicke–Geschwind model. For example, the passive viewing of the nouns increased activation in both halves of the occipital lobe (although admittedly most markedly on the left side) and not elsewhere in the cortex. More surprising, however, were the results from the verbal naming condition, which produced increased activity along the central fissures (which separate the frontal and parietal cortex) of both hemispheres – as well as producing marked activation of the cerebellum. Finally, it was found that the association of noun and verb task increased activity in several areas of the brain, including the left frontal cortex (just in front of Broca's area), the left posterior temporal lobe and, again, the cerebellum. The most surprising finding, however, was the non-participation of Wernicke's area in all of these reading tasks. Although Wernicke's area was activated when words were spoken to the subject, it was not active when words were read silently or aloud by the subject or when the generation of verbal responses was required. If this finding holds true, then it will undoubtedly require a major revision of the Wernicke–Geschwind model of language to account for these findings.

Self-test questions

1. Where in the brain is Broca's area located?
2. What are the effects of damage to Broca's area?
3. What are the probable functions of Wernicke's area?
4. Describe the main characteristics of Wernicke's aphasia.
5. What brain areas have been implicated in alexia and agraphia?
6. Briefly outline the main features of the Wernicke–Geschwind model of language processing.
7. What is conduction aphasia?

8. How did Roger Sperry test hemispheric function in split-brain subjects?
9. Summarise the main findings that have been derived from studies of split-brain patients.
10. What has the Wada test told us about the nature of handedness?
11. Where is the planum temporale located?
12. Briefly describe Geschwind's theory of developmental dyslexia.
13. What is the difference between computerised axial tomography and magnetic resonance imaging? In what ways have they been used?
14. How does regional blood flow work?
15. What is positron emission tomography? How has it been used to examine the cortical basis of language activity?

Key terms

Agraphia (p.269)
Alexia (p.269)
Angular gyrus (p.269)
Anomia (p.267)
Arcuate fasciculus (p.271)
Basal ganglia (p.272)
Broca's aphasia (p.266)
Broca's area (p.266)
Catastrophic–dysphoric reaction (p.277)
Cerebral angiography (p.282)
Commissurotomy (p.274)
Computerised axial tomography (CAT) (p.283)
Conduction aphasia (p.271)
Corpus callosum (p.274)
Dyslexia (p.280)
Magnetic resonance imaging (MRI) (p.283)
Motor aphasia (p.267)
Neologisms (p.268)
Oral apraxia (p.267)
Paraphasias (p.268)
Planum temporale (p.279)
Positron emission tomography (PET) (p.284)
Primary auditory cortex (p.268)
Pulvinar region (p.272)
Receptive aphasia (p.269)
Regional blood flow (RBF) (p.284)
Split-brain procedure (p.274)
Testosterone (p.282)
Wada test (p.278)
Wernicke–Geschwind model (p.270)
Wernicke's area (p.268)

References

Bear, M. F. *et al.* (1996) *Neuroscience: Exploring the Brain*. Baltimore: Williams & Wilkins.

Bogen, J. (1979) The callosal syndrome. In Heilman, K. M. and Valenstein, E. (eds) *Clinical Neuropsychology*. New York: Oxford University Press.

Chi, J. G. *et al.* (1977) Gyri development and the human brain. *Annals of Neurology*, **1**, 86–93.

Crow, T. J. (1982) Two syndromes in schizophrenia? *Trends in Neuroscience*, **5**, 352–4.

Finger, S. (1994) *Origins of Neuroscience*. New York: Oxford University Press.

Galaburda, A. M. (1987) Dyslexia. In Adelman, G. (ed.) *Encyclopedia of Neuroscience.* Boston: Birkhauser.

Galaburda, A. M. *et al.* (1985) Developmental dyslexia: Four consecutive patients with cortical abnormalities. *Annals of Neurology*, **18**, 222–33.

Galaburda, A. M. *et al.* (1994) Evidence for aberrant auditory anatomy in developmental dyslexia. *Proceedings of the National Academy of Sciences (USA)*, **91**, 8010–13.

Geschwind, N. (1965) Disconnexion syndromes in animals and man. *Brain*, **88**, 237–94.

Geschwind, N. (1972) Language and the brain. *Scientific American*, **226** (April), 76–83.

Geschwind, N. and Behan, P. (1982) Left handedness: Association with immune disease, migraine and developmental learning disorders. *Proceedings of the National Academy of Sciences (USA)*, **79**, 5097–100.

Geschwind, N. and Levitsky, W. (1968) Human brain: Left–right symmetries in temporal speech region. *Science,* **161**, 186–7.

Greenfield, P. M. and Savage-Rumbaugh, E. S. (1990) Grammatical combination in *Pan paniscus*: Processes of learning and invention in the evolution and development of language. In Parker, S. T. and Gibson, K. R. (eds) *Language and Intelligence in Monkeys and Apes.* New York: Cambridge University Press.

Kolb, B. and Whishaw, I. Q. (1985) *Fundamentals of Human Neuropsychology.* New York: Freeman.

Larsen, B. *et al.* (1978) Variations in regional cortical blood flow in the right and left hemispheres during autonomic speech. *Brain*, **101**, 193–209.

Lassen, N. A. *et al.* (1978) Brain function and blood flow. *Scientific American*, **239** (4), 50–9.

Lenneberg, E. H. (1967) *Biological Foundations of Language.* New York: Wiley.

Livingstone, M. S. *et al.* (1991) Physiological and anatomical evidence for a magnocellular defect in developmental dyslexia. *Proceedings of the National Academy of Sciences (USA)*, **88**, 7943–7.

McIlveen, R. and Gross, R. (1996) *Biopsychology.* London: Hodder & Stoughton.

Miles, H. L. (1983) Apes and language: The search for communicative competence. In de Luce, J. and Wilder, H. T. (eds) *Language in Primates: Perspectives and Implications.* New York: Springer-Verlag.

Ojemann, G. A. (ed.) (1975) The thalamus and language. *Brain and Language*, **2**, 1–120.

Ojemann, G. A. (1983) Brain organisation for language from the perspective of electrical stimulation mapping. *The Behavioral and Brain Sciences*, **2**, 189–230.

Ornstein, R. (1988) *Psychology.* San Diego: Harcourt, Brace & Jovanovich.

Paterson, F. G. and Linden, E. (1981) *The Education of Koko.* New York: Rhinehart & Winston.

Posner, M. I. and Raichle, M. E. (1994) *Images of Mind.* New York: Scientific American Library.

Rochford, G. (1974) Are jargon aphasics dysphasic? *British Journal of Disorders of Communication*, **9**, 35.

Ross, E. D. (1984) Right hemisphere's language, affective behavior and emotion. *Trends in Neuroscience*, **7**, 342–6.

Savage-Rumbaugh, E. S. (1990) Language acquisition in a nonhuman species: Implications for the innateness debate. *Developmental Psychobiology*, **23**, 599–620.
Schultz, R. T. *et al.* (1994) Brain morphology in normal and dyslexic children: The influence of sex and age. *Annals of Neurology*, **35**, 732–42.
Smith, A. and Sugar, O. (1975) Development of above normal language and intelligence 21 years after hemispherectomy. *Neurology*, **25**, 813–18.
Sperry, R. W. (1974) Lateral specialisation in the surgically separated hemispheres. In Schmidt, F. O. and Worden, F. G. (eds) *The Neurosciences: Third Study Program*. Cambridge, MA: MIT Press.
Springer, S. P. and Deutsch, G. (1989) *Left Brain, Right Brain*. New York: Freeman.
Thompson, R. F. (1993) *The Brain*. New York: Freeman.
Witelson, S. F. (1985) The brain connection: The corpus callosum is larger in left handers. *Science*, **229**, 665–8.
Zaidel, E. (1985) Language and the right hemisphere. In Benson, D. F. and Zaidel, E. (eds) *The Dual Brain: Hemispheric Specialization in Humans*. New York: Guilford Press.

FURTHER READING

Altmann, G. T. M. (1987) *The Ascent of Babel*. Oxford: Oxford University Press.
Gainotti, G. (1969) Réactions catastrophiques et manifestations d'indifférence au cours des atteintes cérébrales. *Neuropsychologia*, **7**, 195–204.
Gazzaniga, M. S. (1970) *The Bisected Brain*. New York: Appleton-Century.
Gazzaniga, M. S. (ed.) (1995) *The Cognitive Neurosciences*. Cambridge, MA: MIT Press.
Goldstein, K. (1939) *The Organism: A Holistic Approach to Biology Derived from Pathological Data in Man*. New York: American Books.
Kertesz, A. (1979) *Aphasia and Associated Disorders*. New York: Grune & Stratton.
Petersen, S. E. (1990) Activation of extrastriate and frontal cortical areas by visual words and word-like stimuli. *Science*, **249**, 1041–4.
Petersen, S. E. *et al.* (1988) Positron emission tomographic studies of the cortical anatomy of single word processing. *Nature*, **331**, 585–9.
Pinker, S. (1994) *The Language Instinct*. New York: William Morrow.
Plum, F. (ed.) (1988) *Language, Communication and the Brain*. New York: Raven Press.
Rasmussen, T. and Milner, B. (1977) The role of early left brain injury in determining lateralization of cerebral speech functions. *Annals of the New York Academy of Sciences*, **299**, 355–69.
Sperry, R. W. (1966) Brain bisection and consciousness. In Eccles, J. (ed.) *Brain and Conscious Experience*. New York: Springer-Verlag.

Multiple choice questions

1. Broca's area is located in the:

(a) anterior or prefrontal (front) part of the frontal cortex
(b) posterior (back) part of the frontal cortex
(c) motor cortex
(d) parietal lobes

2. Broca's aphasia is usually characterised by:

(a) slow, laborious and non-fluent ('telegraphic') speech
(b) anomia
(c) oral apraxia (difficulty in making voluntary oral motor movements)
(d) all of the above

3. Wernicke's area is located in the:

(a) frontal lobes
(b) temporal lobe (next to the primary auditory cortex)
(c) parietal lobes
(d) arcuate fasciculus

4. Wernicke's aphasia is usually characterised by:

(a) meaningless speech although sounding 'grammatically' correct
(b) normal comprehension
(c) slow, laborious and non-fluent ('telegraphic') speech
(d) paraphasias but not neologisms

5. What brain structure is believed to be mainly responsible for translating the visual form of a word into an auditory code?

(a) Broca's area
(b) Wernicke's area
(c) angular gyrus
(d) posterior portion of the corpus callosum

6. According to the Wernicke–Geschwind model, the ____________________ acts as the comprehension centre and ____________________ acts as the articulation centre.

(a) angular gyrus, Broca's area
(b) Broca's area, Wernicke's area
(c) Wernicke's area, prefrontal cortex
(d) Wernicke's area, Broca's area

7. Until relatively recently, most of the knowledge of brain areas involved in language has come from observations of people who have experienced:

(a) brain tumours
(b) brain infections
(c) cerebrovascular accidents
(d) gunshot wounds

8. Damage to the arcuate fasciculus has been shown to produce:

(a) receptive aphasia
(b) conduction aphasia
(c) motor aphasia
(d) alexia and/or agraphia

9. One reason why it is difficult (although not impossible) to present information to only one hemisphere in split-brain subjects is because:

(a) information can cross to each hemisphere through subcortical pathways
(b) information from each eye goes to both hemispheres
(c) information from each hand goes to both hemispheres
(d) all of the above

10. Sperry and Gazzaniga have shown that the right hemisphere is unable to:

(a) understand written information such as simple object words
(b) pick out the correct picture in a recognition task
(c) produce verbal (spoken) responses
(d) draw pictures

11. If objects are placed in the left hand of a split-brain patient who is blindfolded, he or she:

(a) is able to say what the object is
(b) is unaware that anything is happening
(c) is aware that something is in his or her hand but is unable to say what it is
(d) unconsciously tries to place the object in his or her right hand

12. The Wada procedure involves:

(a) hypnosis
(b) a contact lens that enables information to be presented to either the right or left visual field
(c) EEG recording of the corpus callosum
(d) selectively anaesthetising each hemisphere

13. The Wada procedure has shown that 70 per cent of people who are left-handed show ____________________ for language.

(a) right hemispheric dominance
(b) left hemispheric dominance
(c) mixed (equal) dominance
(d) mixed dominance but with more right hemispheric involvement

14. In the case of a 5-year-old boy who had his left hemisphere removed to treat epilepsy, it was found that as an adult he had:

(a) normal language comprehension but difficulties in producing speech
(b) retarded language comprehension and production (similar to a 6-year-old)
(c) superior language skills and a higher than normal IQ
(d) retarded language skills although a higher than normal IQ

15. Galaburda has found that in dyslexics, the ________________ tends to be poorly developed and more lateralised in the right hemisphere.

(a) Broca's area
(b) Wernicke's area
(c) angular gyrus
(d) planum temporale

16. Geschwind and Behan (1982) have shown that developmental forms of dyslexia tend to be more common in:

(a) males
(b) left-handers
(c) those with immune disorders
(d) all of the above

17. Geschwind has proposed that developmental dyslexia may be linked to:

(a) exposure to viral infections
(b) exposure to high levels of testosterone during foetal development
(c) early experience
(d) genetic causes

18. Which of the following techniques can be used to assess the structure and metabolic activity of the brain?

(a) angiography
(b) computerised axial tomography
(c) positron emission tomography
(d) all of the above

19. Which of the following techniques uses radio-frequency waves to generate pictures of the brain?

(a) computerised axial tomography
(b) magnetic resonance imaging
(c) positron emission tomography
(d) none – it is impossible to use radio waves to generate pictures of the brain!

20. The application of PET scanning to the investigation of language:

(a) has tended to confirm the importance of Wernicke's area in language comprehension
(b) has tended to produce results contrary to the predictions of the Wernicke–Geschwind model
(c) has tended to confirm the importance of the angular gyrus in reading
(d) has tended to confirm the relative unimportance of the right hemisphere for language

10 The biological basis of mental illness

IN THIS CHAPTER

- How antidepressant drugs work
- The catecholamine theory of depression
- The role of serotonin in depression
- How antipsychotic drugs work
- The causes of schizophrenia
- The dopaminergic theory of schizophrenia
- Types of brain damage found in schizophrenia
- New developments in schizophrenia

Introduction

The brain like any other organ of the body can malfunction in a number of ways. For example, it can be injured through accidents, develop tumours, or become infected, and all of these will impair its function. Although this may produce various forms of mental impairment, along with many other difficulties such as aphasia and paralysis, we would not normally describe these symptoms as mental illnesses. Rather, they are neurological disorders in which the dysfunction is directly linked to observable damage. In contrast, mental illnesses are conditions where the symptoms appear to be largely in the person's mood or thinking, and where there are *often* no discernible signs of structural brain damage (although some forms of mental illness may be associated with physical injury). This is not to say that there is nothing wrong with the brain in these instances (obviously, 'something' must be happening at some level of its functioning, perhaps involving synaptic or neurochemical changes), but whatever the problem is, it does not appear to entail irreversible tissue damage. Nonetheless, the symptoms of mental illness (which can include suicidal depression, mania, illogical and incoherent thought, hallucinations and anxiety) are very real and severely debilitating. Moreover, mental health problems are surprisingly common. For example, in Britain, about one person in eight will consult a doctor for psychological difficulties in any given year, and about 10 per cent of these patients will be referred to a psychiatrist (Gregory 1987, p. 470). This situation puts the onus on the biological psychologist to understand the neural basis of mental illness in order to help relieve its burden and to point ways forward for improved treatment.

Affective disorders: an introduction

It is a perfectly normal reaction from time to time to feel sad or 'depressed'. However, there are some people for whom **depression** is a much more serious problem. In such cases, the severity of depression may be extremely debilitating, and not linked to any life event or obvious 'cause'. Or, if there is an external factor at work, then the emotional response may be out of all proportion to the situation that caused it. It is difficult to say exactly at what point depression becomes a mental illness, although when it becomes so severe that the person continually feels suicidal and is unable to function properly, then the illness is clear for all to see. Moreover, the problem of depression occurs to some degree in almost every other psychiatric disorder.

Although, in everyday language, depression is generally viewed as a condition that is characterised by feelings of sadness or unhappiness, in most clinical cases there is much more to the disorder. In fact, there is often a constellation of symptoms which can be categorised under four main headings: emotional, cognitive, motivational and physical. For example, not only is the severely depressed person likely to feel sad and miserable (i.e. emotional symptoms), but he or she is also likely to have many negative or gloomy thoughts including low self-esteem and a sense of hopelessness or helplessness (i.e. cognitive symptoms). This is also likely to be accompanied by lethargy and varying degrees of psychomotor retardation where even the simplest chore may appear to be daunting (i.e. motivational symptoms) and, finally, there may be a number of physical problems including sleep disturbances and early morning awakening, loss of appetite, sexual difficulties, muscle weakness and various types of aches and pains (i.e. somatic symptoms). Clearly, when it is as severe as this, depression is beyond doubt an illness with loss of control over self, decline of effective functioning and disrupted interaction with the external world.

Depression is classified as an affective (mood) disorder although it is not the only one that is characterised by emotional extremes. For example, the opposite of depression can also occur (i.e. mania) which leads to heightened euphoria, exuberance and increased energy. In fact, most people who experience mania also suffer from bouts of depression (i.e. manic-depression) which can occur in a regular or cyclical pattern. Consequently, affective disorders are divided into two broad categories: **unipolar**

depression in which the person suffers exclusively from prolonged periods of sadness and despondency (although a very rare form of unipolar disorder involves just mania), and **bipolar depression** where the person undergoes alternating periods of depression and mania. As we shall see later, there is good evidence that these two disorders have a different biological basis.

Mood disorders are the most common form of mental illness. Indeed, it has been estimated that approximately 10 per cent of men and 20 per cent of women will suffer from at least one bout of unipolar depression in their life (and in many cases the depression will become recurrent). As these figures show, women are more likely to suffer from depression than men, although the reason why this occurs is controversial. Some researchers believe that these figures represent a biological difference in susceptibility to depression, whereas others argue that socialisation factors are more important (e.g. it may be that women are more inclined to seek help for their problems, or more likely to find themselves in life situations that give rise to depression). In contrast, bipolar illness is approximately 10 times less likely than unipolar depression and appears to occur in males and females equally (Goodwin and Jamison 1990).

The development of antidepressant drugs

Until the mid-1950s, the two main biological treatments for depression were electroconvulsive therapy (ECT) and, in extreme cases, brain surgery. Although ECT was often effective in treating depression (and is still used today in severe cases), it wasn't suitable for all types of affective disroder. Thus, there was a need to develop newer and more humane forms of therapy. The first breakthrough occurred in the early 1950s with the development of a drug called **iproniazid**. This drug was originally used (although not very successfully) as an antibacterial agent in the treatment of tuberculosis. However, it was discovered that iproniazid made a number of patients (many of whom were in a terminal condition) feel much happier and more optimistic. Thus, it appeared to exert an antidepressant effect. In 1956, the American psychiatrist Nathan Kline began testing iproniazid on hospitalised patients with various types of mental illness, and found that it significantly reduced depression (although it exacerbated schizophrenia). Within a year of this work (i.e. in 1957), iproniazid was being marketed as an antidepressant under the trade name of Marsilid, making it the first drug to be available for the treatment of depression.

The development of antidepressive drugs not only had a huge impact on the clinical treatment of depression, but they also provided researchers with a very important experimental tool by which to examine the biological nature of the illness. In short, if researchers could understand how iproniazid (and other antidepressant drugs) worked, then this knowledge might help to explain the neurochemical reasons why depression occurred in the first place. The first clue was provided in 1952 by Albert Zellar who found that iproniazid exerted its main biochemical effect by inhibiting an enzyme called **monoamine oxidase** (Zellar *et al.* 1952). This enzyme, located in nerve terminals and the synaptic cleft, was responsible for breaking down (and inactivating) the excess release of **monoamines** (i.e. neurotransmitters that contain a single amine in their chemical structure and which include **noradrenaline**, **dopamine** and **serotonin**). Thus, when monoamine oxidase was inhibited (by iproniazid) the net result was elevated levels of these neurotransmitters in the brain. The implication was clear: iproniazid appeared to be producing its antidepressant effect by increasing the level of monoamines in the brain, and presumably, in the process, correcting a deficit that had caused depression (see Figure 10.1).

Further evidence to support this theory came from the drug **reserpine**. This drug was first isolated from the Indian snakeroot plant (*Rauwolia serpentina*) in 1951 by the Ciba Drug Company and found to be effective in the treatment of hypertension. Unfortunately, reserpine also produced severe (and sometimes suicidal) depression in a significant number of patients. What was responsible for this mood-altering effect? In the early 1960s it was found that reserpine depleted the brain of **catecholamines** (neurotransmitters that contain a catechol nucleus in their chemical structure and which include the monoamines noradrenaline and dopamine) by making these transmitters 'leak out' from their protective vesicles in the nerve terminals (which then resulted in their being broken down by enzymes such as monoamine oxidase). Thus, reserpine produced almost exactly the opposite neurochemical effect to iproniazid (i.e. it depleted the brain of noradrenaline and dopamine), and by doing this it appeared to cause depression (see Figure 10.2).

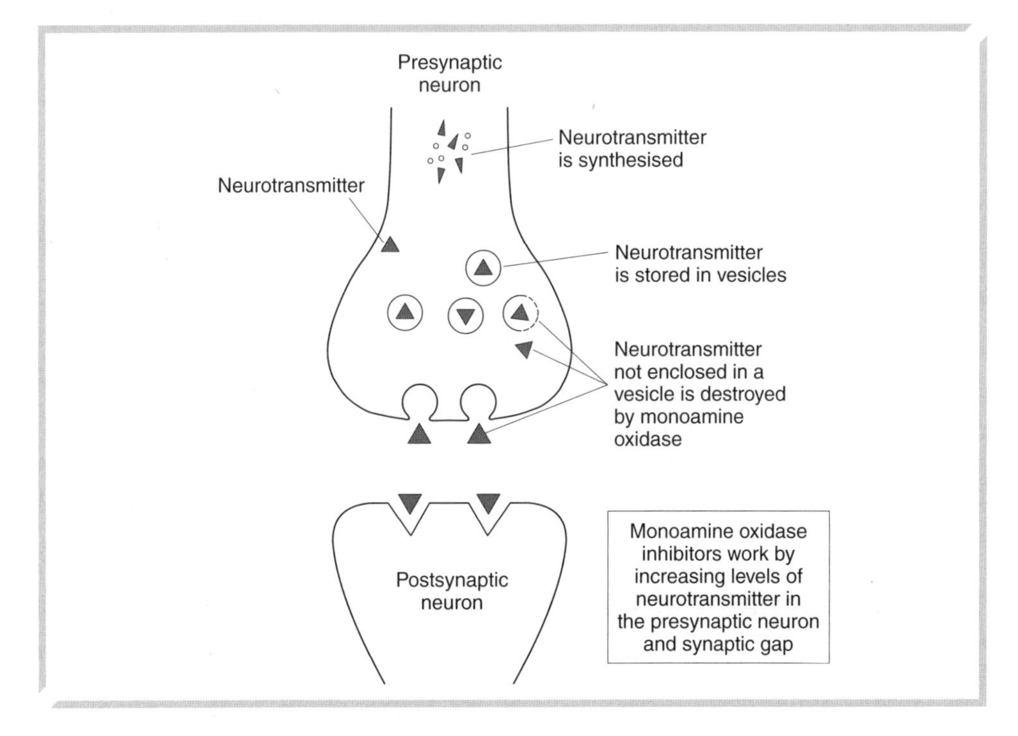

Figure 10.1 The mechanism by which monoamine oxidase inhibitors exert their pharmacological effects.

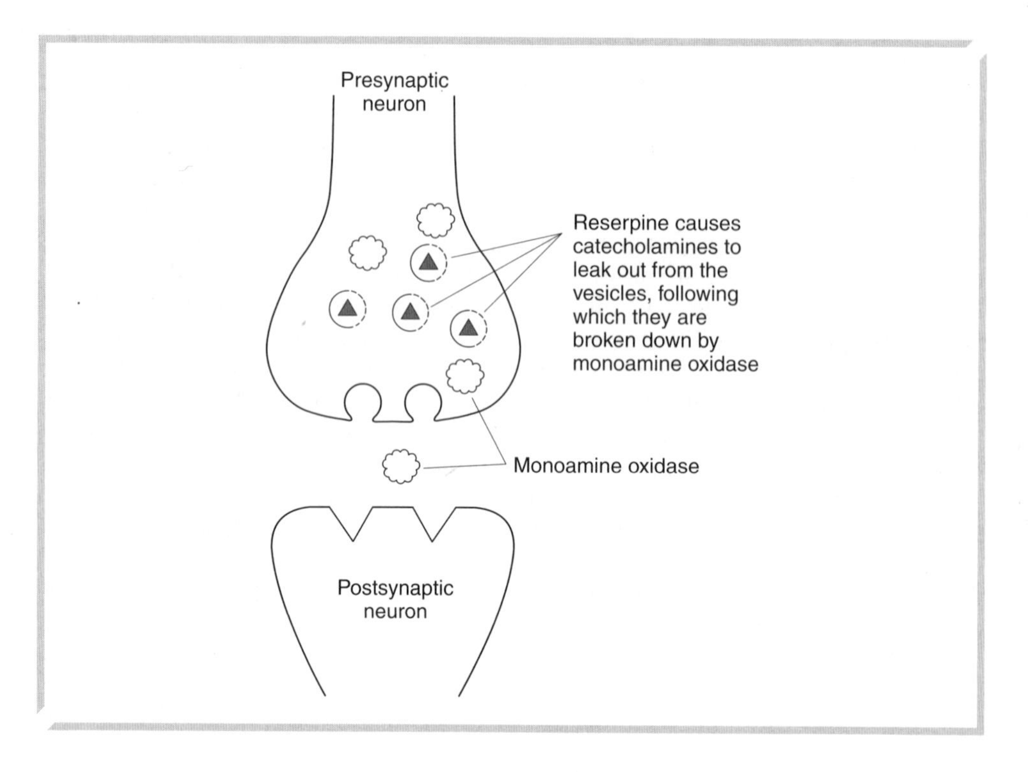

Figure 10.2 The mechanism by which reserpine exerts its pharmacological effects.

Although monoamine oxidase inhibitors (MAOIs) are still used in clinical practice today, they are normally only chosen when other treatments for depression have failed. One reason is that these drugs produce a number of side effects, many of which are caused by their interactions with various foodstuffs – e.g. cheese, wine, pickled fish and chocolate – which contain **tyramine**. Tyramine is a powerful elevator of blood pressure and is normally metabolised by the liver. However, MAOIs interfere with this metabolism and result in hypertensive effects that can prove fatal (or may produce severe headache, increased body temperature and intracranial bleeding). Thus, patients taking MAOIs have to be extremely careful with their choice of diet and avidly avoid certain foods.

The development of tricyclic antidepressants

The most frequently used types of drug for treating depression (or at least until recently) have been the **tricyclic antidepressants** (so called because their molecular structure contains a three-ring chain). The first tricyclic compound to be developed was **imipramine**, and similar to iproniazid the realisation that it was effective in treating depression was discovered by chance. Imipramine was originally developed by the

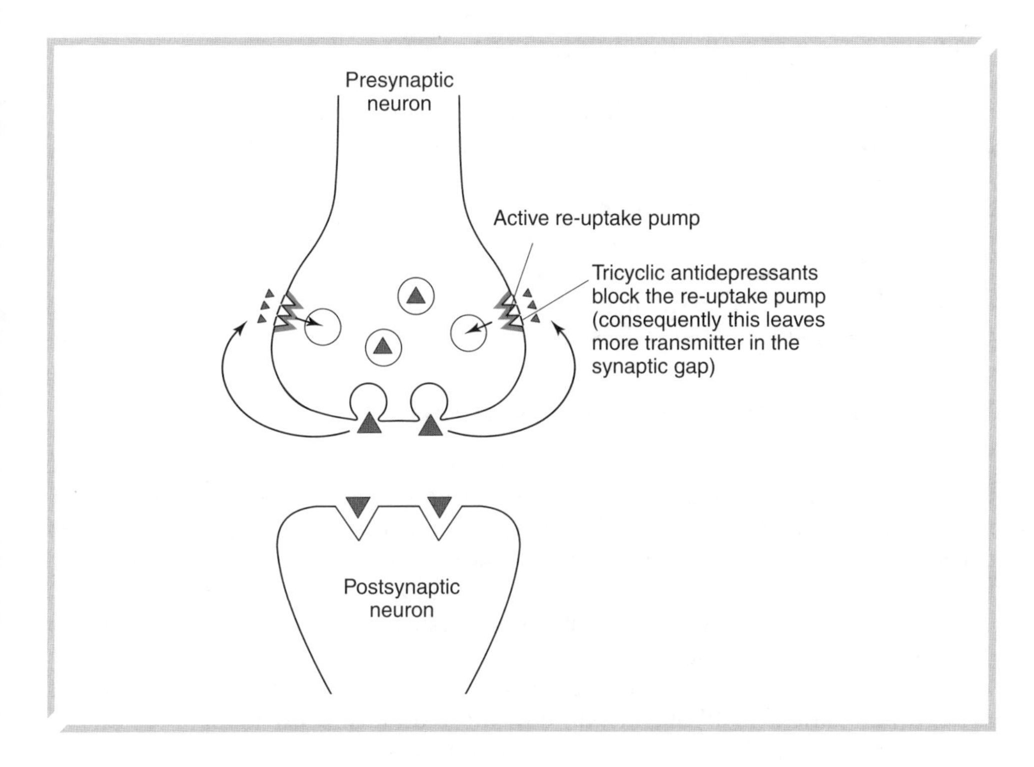

Figure 10.3 The mechanism by which the tricyclic antidepressants exert their pharmacological effects.

Geigy Drug Company as an antipsychotic substance to treat schizophrenia, but was found to be ineffective in its intended purpose. Instead, it was found to reduce depression (e.g. Kuhn 1958) and in the late 1950s imipramine was marketed under the trade name of Tofranil as an alternative antidepressant to Marsilid.

Although imipramine (and other tricyclic antidepressants) were found to elevate levels of monoamines in the brain, their pharmacological mode of action turned out to be very different to the MAOIs. In short, the tricyclic antidepressants prevented the re-uptake of monoamines. Re-uptake is the main method by which monoamines are removed from the synaptic cleft once they have been released by the presynaptic neuron. That is, the presynaptic neuron effectively pumps any excess transmitter back into its terminals, thus helping to regulate its amount in the synaptic cleft, as well as providing a way of 're-cycling' of transmitter back into the vesicles. The tricyclic antidepressants blocked this process (particularly in noradrenergic neurons) and, in doing so, increased the levels of noradrenaline in the synaptic cleft (see Figure 10.3).

Following the introduction of imipramine in 1958, more than 20 tricyclic antidepressants have been introduced into clinical practice in the UK, and most appear to exert similar beneficial effects on depression (Lader and Herrington 1990). Provided that they are given over a period of several weeks, they have been shown to be effective in reducing depression in around 70 per cent of patients compared to 35 per cent for placebo (Lickey and Gordon 1991). In addition, the tricyclic antidepressants are generally regarded as safer than the MAOIs, although they are not free of side effects. For example, they can cause death if taken in overdose (this is somewhat ironic since depressed people are the one group who might be expected to use these drugs for this purpose), and they may also produce cardiovascular problems including irregular racing heartbeats and hypotension (e.g. the person feels faint when suddenly standing up). In addition, they can result in psychomotor slowing, loss of concentration, muscle weakness, dry mouth and blurred vision.

The monoamine theory of depression

The discovery that reserpine produced depression, and that drugs which increased monoamines (either by inhibiting monoamine oxidase or by blocking the process of re-uptake) had antidepressant effects, led to the development of the **monoamine theory of depression** (sometimes called the catecholamine theory). One of the first proponents of this theory was Joseph Schildkraut who proposed in 1965 that depression was the result of reduced neurotransmission of catecholamines (particularly noradrenaline), and that mania was due to excess transmission.

One way of testing Schildkraut's theory was to measure the levels of catecholamines in depressed patients. Although it was difficult to do this by examining the levels of catecholamines in the brain (except in post-mortem cases – see below), it was possible, however, to look for biochemical abnormalities in the urine or cerebrospinal fluid of depressed patients. Indeed, if the catecholamine theory was correct then one would obviously expect to find a decrease in noradrenaline levels, or its major metabolites, in people with depression. However, this has not been found – or, at least, not consistently. For example, many researchers have attempted to examine noradrenergic function by measuring one of its metabolites called **MHPG** (3-methyl-4-hydroxy phenylglycol) which is known, in large part, to be derived from the brain. Contrary to the predictions of Schildkraut's theory, most evidence has found that there is great variability in levels of MHPG in depressed people – some patients show low levels, others have high levels, and yet others show normal levels.

Another way of testing the catecholamine theory is to conduct a post-mortem examination of brain tissue of people who have been severely depressed (not surprisingly, most studies have looked at this question in brains taken from people who have committed suicide). Again, this work has tended to show that there is no evidence of reduced levels of noradrenaline (or its metabolites) in patients who had been severely depressed (Brown *et al.* 1985).

Undoubtedly, one of the biggest problems with the catecholamine theory as formulated by Schildkraut is that it underestimates the importance of serotonin (which somewhat confusingly is not a catecholamine but an indolamine). For example, researchers looking at levels of serotonin, or rather its main metabolite 5-hydroxyindoleacetic acid (**5-HIAA**), in the cerebrospinal fluid of depressed patients have found that low levels of this chemical are often found in people who are most likely to commit suicide (Asberg *et al.* 1987). Moreover, several post-mortem studies have also shown decreased concentrations of serotonin (and its metabolites) in regions of the brain in depressed patients (Ashton 1992).

For this reason it is perhaps more meaningful to talk of the monoamine theory of depression (serotonin is both an indolamine and a monoamine) rather than the catecholamine theory. Indeed, it should not be forgotten that monoamine oxidase depletes the brain of both noradrenaline and serotonin (as well as dopamine) and that the tricyclic antidepressants block the uptake of both noradrenaline and serotonin in varying degrees. Thus, the catecholamine theory, as formulated by Schildkraut, appears to be too narrow to explain depression (although there is little doubt that it has had a major impact on stimulating research into its aetiology and treatment of depression). This is not to say that noradrenaline is unimportant in depression, rather that it is only one of the neurochemical factors that appear to be involved in this illness.

The problem of antidepressant time-lag

Perhaps the biggest problem with the original catecholamine theory of depression is that the blocking of re-uptake produced by tricyclic compounds is known to be immediate – yet it normally takes around 2–3 weeks before these drugs start to alleviate the symptoms of depression. This points to the distinct possibility that it is not the direct pharmacological action of the drug itself which is causing the antidepressant effect, but rather, the continual exposure of the drug is producing some form of secondary (longer-term) change to take place in the catecholamine neurons.

A number of theories have been proposed to explain the time-lag of tricyclic antidepressant action and perhaps the most convincing are the ones that see an important role for **autoreceptors** (see Figure 10.4). Autoreceptors are neurotransmitter receptors that are located not on postsynaptic neurons, but on presynaptic neurons. In other words, the neuron releasing the neurotransmitter has receptors for its own transmitter. This may at first appear to be nonsensical, although autoreceptors serve a very important function as they provide a mechanism for the presynaptic neuron to control the release of its own transmitter. In short, they monitor the amount of neurotransmitter in the synapse and help inform the presynaptic neuron to inhibit further release when levels become too high. Thus, autoreceptors essentially regulate the amount of neurotransmitter that is secreted into the synapse. One type of autoreceptor that is known to fulfil this role is the **alpha-2 receptor** found on the presynaptic terminals of noradrenergic neurons.

How then do autoreceptors explain the delayed therapeutic effect of tricyclic antidepressant action? To begin with, in the first days of antidepressant therapy, the autoreceptors might be expected to compensate for the initial uptake blockade by acting to reduce further release of noradrenaline (since there are already high levels of this neurotransmitter in the synapse). However, with repeated administration of tricyclic drugs over a 2–3-week period, this causes the alpha-2 autoreceptors to lose their inhibitory capacity, thus resulting in more noradrenaline being released. This may

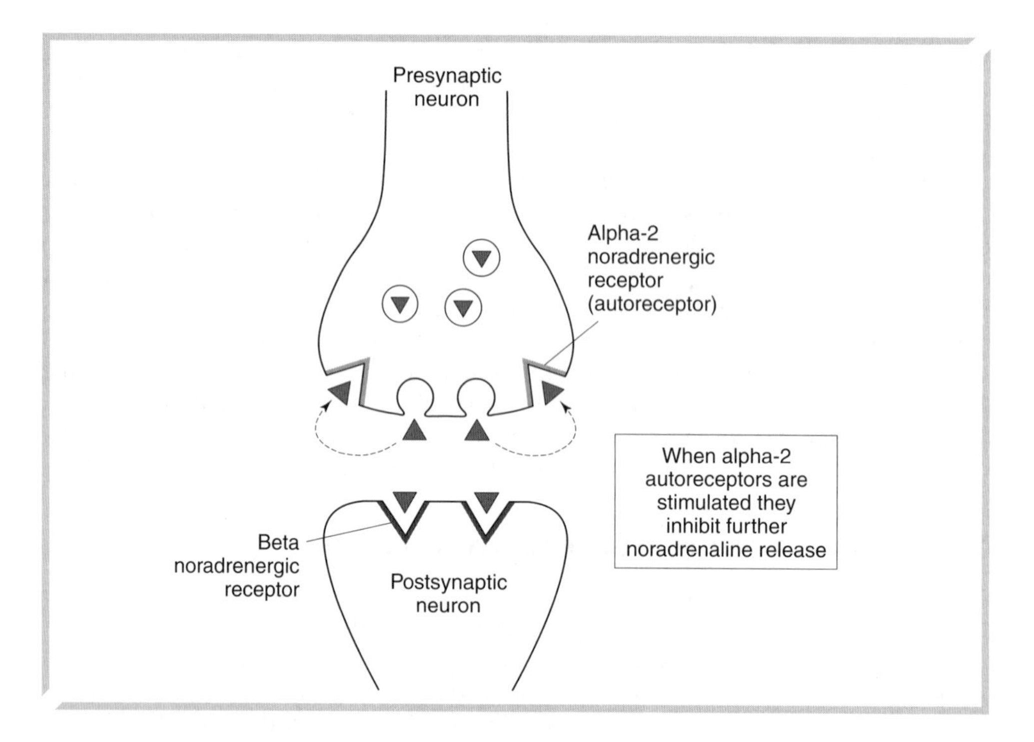

Figure 10.4 How autoreceptors affect presynaptic transmitter release.

happen in one of two ways: either the autoreceptors lose their sensitivity in response to the constant exposure of increased noradrenaline in the synapse, or the actual number of receptors become fewer (or **down-regulated**) in number. Whatever the mechanism, the effect is the same – the loss of inhibitory control of the autoreceptors causes the presynaptic neuron to gradually release more noradrenaline over a 2–3-week period.

But what about the receptors located on the postsynaptic neurons? These are, after all, the main target for the neurotransmitter, and we might expect changes in the chemical environment of the synapse (i.e. increased levels of noradrenaline) to affect these receptors as well. The main type of noradrenergic receptor found postsynaptically are **beta receptors** and, it appears that, like alpha autoreceptors, these also become down-regulated (and less sensitive) to increased exposure of noradrenaline. Thus, the tricyclic antidepressants may not only work on autoreceptors, but also by their eventual effect on beta receptors (see Figure 10.5). Indeed, until a few years ago, this explanation appeared to account so successfully for the time-lag of antidepressant therapy that some researchers believed that the desensitisation of beta receptors was a property shared by virtually all antidepressants (e.g. Wilner 1985, p. 256).

However, this explanation also greatly complicates the monoamine hypothesis of depression because it implies that it is not the synaptic levels of neurotransmitter (e.g.

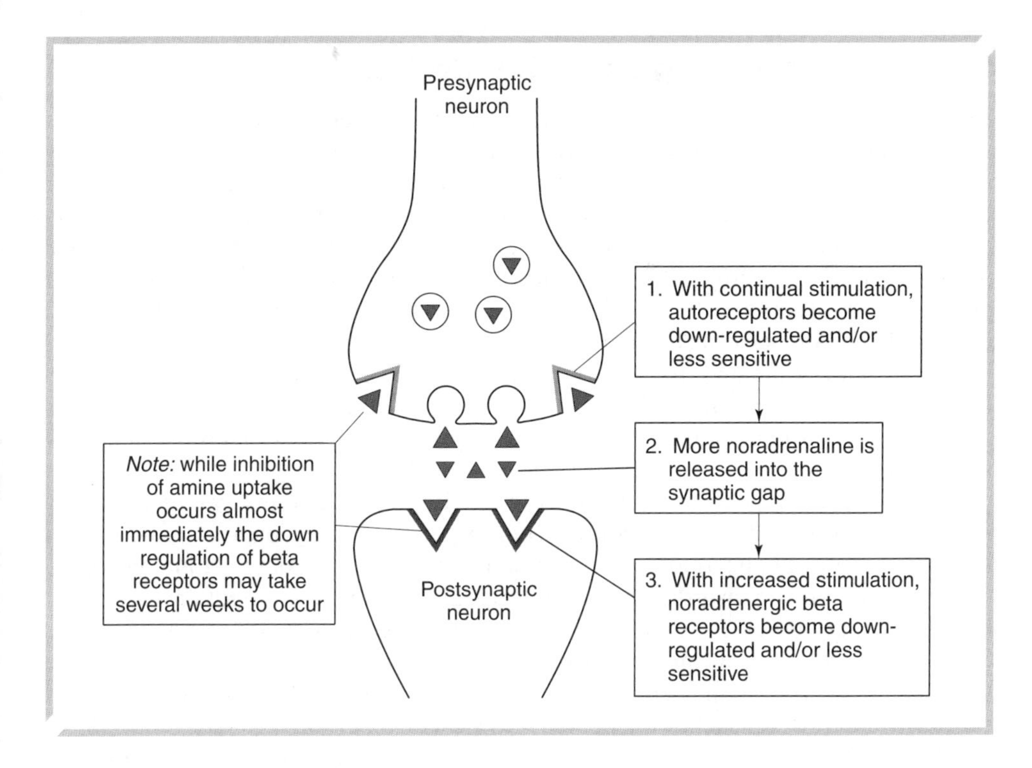

Figure 10.5 The time-lag from presynaptic uptake blockade to postsynaptic receptor down-regulation.

noradrenaline) that is the important factor in causing the illness, but rather it is the responsiveness of the receptors that is crucial. In fact, to complicate the picture even further, it is known that desensitisation of receptors occurs through a process known as phosphorylation (which involves alterations in the shape of membrane proteins), and phosphorylation is also known to alter ion channels, regulate enzymes, synthesise transmitters and control a diverse number of biological functions in the neuron. In other words, it is difficult to explain exactly how antidepressant drugs may exert their effects on neural function.

Furthermore, we now know that changing beta-receptor sensitivity (or down-regulation) is not a property shared by all antidepressants. Indeed, one new class of drugs that is now being widely used to treat depression comprises the selective serotonergic uptake blockers, which include **Fluoxetine (Prozac)**. These drugs, as their name suggests, produce their effect specifically on serotonergic systems, and have no direct action on beta receptors. In other words, noradrenergic beta down-regulation cannot explain why these new antidepressant compounds work (although it is plausible that they work in a similar way to other tricyclic drugs, except on serotonergic systems at both presynaptic and postsynaptic levels).

Selective serotonergic uptake blockers

As we have seen, one problem with the tricyclic antidepressants is that they are associated with a wide range of side effects and, because of this, there have been many attempts to find safer compounds by which to treat depression. Indeed, a large number of drugs have been developed over the years, and many of these 'second-generation antidepressants' are neither MAOIs nor tricyclics. Although many of these drugs have proved useful in treating depression, they nevertheless show a bewildering array of pharmacological actions which have made an understanding of depression all the more difficult. However, one drug to emerge from this group was Prozac. This drug (produced by Eli Lilly and Company) first appeared in the USA in 1987 and within a few months it was outselling every other antidepressant. Moreover, its pharmacological profile was relatively easy to understand: it blocked the uptake of just one neurotransmitter – serotonin.

Although Prozac is not superior to the tricyclic antidepressants in terms of its efficacy for treating depression, it is considerably safer (especially in overdose) and it has a much broader range of applications (i.e. it can be prescribed for anxiety, eating disorders, obsessive–compulsive disorder and alcoholism). Despite this, it is not totally free of side effects and may decrease sexual functioning and produce insomnia (there are also rare reports of aggression, self-mutilation and suicidal mania). Prozac also appears to have a stronger effect on making people 'feel good about themselves' and may be capable of turning a lethargic, low-achieving person into a cheerful, productive individual (Palfai and Jankiewicz 1997). Indeed, it may be that, in some cases, Prozac is being prescribed for reasons that are not legitimately 'medical' (i.e. to bolster productivity, make one feel more optimistic and to increase self-esteem).

Despite these controversies, the development of Prozac (and other selective serotonergic uptake blockers) makes a very strong case for the involvement of serotonin in the aetiology of depression, particularly as these drugs appear to have little direct effect on noradrenergic systems or their receptors. Does this mean, therefore, that noradrenaline is unimportant in depression after all? The answer to this question is almost certainly no. There is much evidence (as we have seen) to support the involvement of noradrenaline in depression (as there is with serotonin), and perhaps the best explanation is that both transmitters are involved in the causation of affective disorders. In fact, nearly 30 years ago, Birkmayer (Birkmayer and Linauer 1970) proposed that depression was the result of an imbalance in the activity of both noradrenergic and serotonergic systems, rather than being due to a dysfunction in just one system, and evidence is accumulating to support this position. For example, it is known that the locus coeruleus and raphe are anatomically connected and interact with each other (e.g. see Chapter 8) and that noradrenergic and serotonergic neurons often project to the same cells in the brain (e.g. many neurons contain both noradrenergic and serotonergic receptors). Thus, it may be that dysfunction in one system alters the functioning of the other, and, in much the same way, the stabilisation of one transmitter system (by antidepressants) may help stabilise the functioning of the other. In this respect, it is interesting to note that when serotonergic autoreceptors are destroyed (by a drug called

5,6-dihydroxytryptamine) the down-regulation of postsynaptic noradrenergic beta receptors by tricyclic antidepressant treatment does not occur (Brunello *et al.* 1982; Sulser 1989). Thus, clearly, noradrenergic and serotonergic systems are closely interrelated, and in ways that are still not fully understood.

Box 10.1 THE HYPOTHALAMIC–PITUITARY–ADRENAL AXIS AND DEPRESSION

Depression is often thought of as a mental disorder, but in many respects this is an oversimplification. For example, people suffering from severe depression often show a number of hormonal irregularities including elevated levels of the glucocorticoid cortisol. This hormone is released by the adrenal gland and is under the direct control of the hypothalamus and pituitary gland (this combined system is known as the hypothalamic–pituitary–adrenal axis – see Figure 10.6). In brief, the pituitary gland controls adrenal functioning by secreting adrenocorticotropic hormone (ACTH) into the bloodstream which, in turn, induces the adrenal cortex to release cortisol. This hormone then acts to mobilise the body's energy reserves into immediate use (as is necessary during times of acute or prolonged stress). High levels of cortisol also send a negative feedback message to the brain informing the pituitary gland (and hypothalamus) to turn off further secretion of ACTH.

It is perhaps not surprising that depressed persons show elevated cortisol levels since depression is obviously a very stressful condition. However, there appears to be more to increased cortisol secretion than this in depression, especially as it may be caused not so much by stress, but by a dysfunction of the hypothalamic–pituitary–adrenal axis. Evidence for this view has come from the dexamethasone test. Dexamethasone is a synthetic glucocorticoid and, if given to patients (normally at bedtime), it typically produces a suppression of ACTH from the pituitary gland, which then acts to inhibit cortisol release from the adrenal cortex (this is normally measured next morning). It appears that the dexamethasone 'fools' the hypothalamus into believing that there are high levels of circulating cortisol, which then responds by turning off the pituitary's secretion of ACTH. However, in a substantial proportion of individuals with clinical depression this does not occur. One possible explanation is that there is a decline in the numbers (or sensitivity) of hypothalamic glucocorticoid receptors that normally react to high or feedback levels of cortisol.

In fact, there is evidence to indicate that one of the reasons why antidepressants 'work' is because of their effects on correcting the functioning of the glucocorticoid receptors in the hypothalamus. For example, Reul *et al.* (1993, 1994) have shown that not only do antidepressants act to enhance noradrenergic and serotonergic activity, but they also increase the activity of genes involved in the formation of proteins that make up hypothalamic glucocorticoid receptors. For example, these researchers found that 5 weeks of treatment with desipramine (a tricyclic antidepressant) produced a 25 per cent increase in the number of glucocorticoid receptors in the hypothalamus. Moreover, the time course of this effect is similar to that which normally occurs in the clinical improvement of depression following antidepressant treatment (Barden *et al.* 1985). Thus, antidepressants not only correct activity in noradrenergic and serotonergic systems, but they also help to restore the normal functioning of the hypothalamic–pituitary–adrenal axis.

There are also other types of hormonal dysfunction in depression. For example, depressed patients tend to secrete more growth hormone than normal, and in some cases there can be underactive thyroid function. But, perhaps more importantly, depression is often associated with marked disruption of circadian rhythms with peaks of hormone release either occurring at the wrong time, or with reduced amplitude. This may not only result in many different circadian rhythms becoming desynchronised, but it can also produce behavioural effects. For example, many depressed people suffer from sleep disturbances including an early onset of REM sleep (which may occur after only 45 minutes of sleep) and early morning awakenings. To make matters worse, other circadian rhythms, such as temperature, may fall out of phase with the sleep patterns. For example, in healthy people, the lowest point in body temperature normally occurs at around 6 a.m., but in depressed people this may occur several hours earlier (often at the beginning of sleep). It is perhaps hardly surprising, therefore, that many people with depression often feel (or become) physically ill in addition to their mental anguish.

Bipolar illness and the discovery of lithium

A person who suffers from bipolar disorder alternates between periods of mania (from the Greek word for 'madness') and depression, generally passing through a period of normality on the way. During a manic episode an individual is excessively energetic. Patients are usually elated and self-confident, talk incessantly, flirt from one idea (or grandiose plan) to the next, and show a diminished need to sleep. If left untreated, the

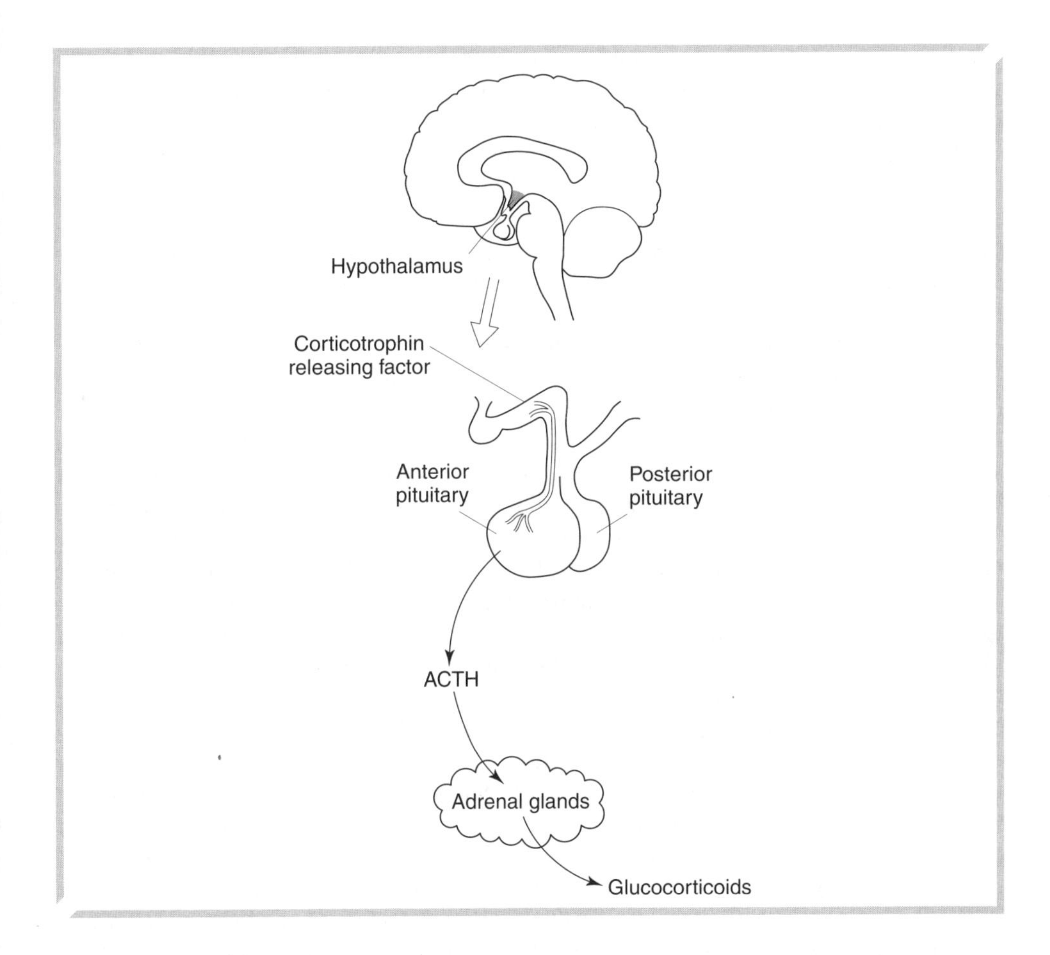

Figure 10.6 The hypothalamic–pituitary–adrenal axis.

mania may progress in severity, leading to the emergence of delusions and hallucinations. Although hypomania (a milder form of mania characterised mainly by hyperactivity) may be a relatively common personality trait, extreme (full blown) mania is almost unheard of as a unipolar condition. Thus, mania is a condition that almost exclusively is found with depression. Despite this, the cycles of depression and mania vary considerably from person to person. In some cases, episodes of depression and mania may alternate within 2–3-week periods, while in others the cycle may take place over a year or more. In fact, a few people follow such a regular cycle that one can predict their manic and depressive stages in advance, which is particularly useful if the patient needs to plan ahead (e.g. for family holidays, etc.)!

Considerable evidence shows that the biological basis of bipolar illness is different from unipolar depression. For example, not only is the incidence of bipolar illness (which is around 1 per cent) much less than that found in unipolar depression (5 per cent), but bipolar illness is also found equally in males and females. In addition, bipolar illness has a far stronger tendency to be inherited. For example, it is found in about 25 per cent of first-degree relatives of manic depressive parents; and the concordance rates for identical twins are about 70 per cent and 15 per cent for fraternal twins (the corresponding figures for unipolar depression are 40 per cent and 15 per cent). But, perhaps the strongest evidence showing that bipolar illness is different from unipolar depression is the fact that it is best treated with a drug called **lithium**, and not by standard antidepressants (such as the tricyclics) which tend to exacerbate the bipolar illness by precipitating mania.

Lithium was first used in the nineteenth century as a treatment for gout (to help 'dissolve' the build-up of uric acid in the joints) although its effectiveness in treating bipolar illness was not reported until 1949. The story begins in the mid-1940s when an Australian psychiatrist called John Cade hypothesised that mania might be due to a substance that builds up in the body fluids; and, if this was the case, Cade reasoned that it should be possible to induce mania in guinea pigs by injecting them with urine taken from manic patients. The problem with this idea, however, was that urine contained uric acid. Thus, to provide an adequate control group, Cade also injected animals with uric acid that had been dissolved with the help of lithium. To his great surprise he found that this combination made the animal extremely lethargic. In fact, the psychoactive ingredient turned out to be lithium, and when he administered it to his bipolar patients he obtained very dramatic results. In short, he had stumbled across one of the most effective substances in psychopharmacology for treating bipolar illness.

Following Cade's report the use of lithium quickly spread to Europe, particularly through the work of the Danish investigator Mogens Schou (although it took much longer to be accepted in the USA); and, the overwhelming evidence from a number of clinical trials showed that lithium improved manic depression and reduced the risk of relapse. Although the results of research studies vary it is probably fair to say that 80 per cent of bipolar patients respond positively to lithium. In fact, according to Lickey and Gordon (1991), without lithium the typical bipolar patient has one manic episode about every 14 months, whereas mania occurs approximately every 9 years if taking lithium medication. Of course, to provide this type of protection lithium has to be taken regularly, but providing the patient is carefully monitored there appears to be little risk of serious side effects.

Seasonal affective disorder

Some people also suffer from a form of depression known as **seasonal affective disorder**, in which they become depressed at a certain time each year (normally in winter), with their depression typically lifting in spring as the days get longer and brighter. As well as being associated with despondency and feelings of sadness, this disorder also has some unusual features including the need for increased sleep and carbohydrate cravings (the latter of which may lead to weight gain). Moreover, the depression may quickly remit within a couple of days if the sufferer goes to a sunny environment for a winter holiday. Obviously, for most of us, this is not a practical form of therapy, and consequently clinicians have resorted to using other methods of treating the disorder. One of the most successful is light therapy (which is effective in over 50 per cent of cases) – that is, if patients with seasonal affective disorder are exposed to light for a few hours each day (early morning treatment is probably best) their symptoms are often improved or relieved (Thompson and Silverstone 1989).

The reasons why this treatment works are controversial, but there is some evidence that it is linked to the hormone melatonin which is released from the pineal gland (see Chapter 8). Melatonin is released in highest amounts during the night and most people experience a 'melatonin surge' during the later part of the evening. However, there is some evidence that this surge is delayed in patients with seasonal affective disorder and, consequently, their melatonin rhythm is not synchronised properly with their patterns of sleep and waking. Thus, it has been suggested that light therapy works because it 're-sets' the melatonin rhythm to its normal time course (Lewy *et al.* 1989). Despite this, it has also been shown that oral administration of melatonin is not effective in treating seasonal affective disorder (as might be expected) and, consequently, it is probably the case that other biological mechanisms are also involved.

Schizophrenia

An introduction

Schizophrenia is one of the most common forms of mental illness (about 1 per cent of the population suffer from this condition and perhaps another 2 to 3 per cent show borderline symptomology), and it is also undoubtedly one of the most devastating and puzzling. The term schizophrenia was first introduced by Eugen Bleuler in 1911 who derived it from the Greek *schizio* meaning 'split' and *phreno* meaning 'mind'. By adopting this term, Bleuler was trying to emphasise the importance of fragmented thought processes that were 'split from reality' as one of the key features of the illness. However, in some respects the term schizophrenia is an unfortunate one because it is sometimes confused with a completely different (and rare) condition known as multiple personality syndrome, in which a person may exhibit two or more different personalities (like Dr Jekyll and Mr Hyde). A person with schizophrenia, however, does not have multiple personalities – but rather has a single personality that is overpowered by marked disturbances of mental function, feeling and behaviour that is 'out of step' with reality.

One of the most common features of schizophrenia is the occurrence of bizarre delusions. For example, schizophrenics may believe that they are being controlled by others (e.g. messages are being broadcast to them by radio), or that they are being persecuted in some way (e.g. someone is trying to poison them). In some cases the whole personality may become deluded, so that schizophrenics have feelings of grandeur (often believing that they are someone else such as Napoleon or Jesus), or thinking that they have a divine mission to fulfil. Delusions may also be supported by the presence of hallucinations – usually voices telling them what to do, although many other strange (and unpleasant) forms are possible. However, even without suffering from delusions and hallucinations, schizophrenics nearly always show incoherent and fragmented thought processes, which are also reflected in the nature of their speech, which can be incomprehensible and lacking in logic or continuity.

Schizophrenics are also likely to show abnormal emotional responses which may include increased excitability, reduced or blunted affect, or feelings that most normal people would consider inappropriate. And, this may also be linked to abnormal forms of behaviour – for example, schizophrenics may show signs of excitement or agitation (i.e. nervously pacing up and down and talking in repetitive rhymes) or, in other cases, may show catatonia (long periods without movement).

Despite this, the clinical picture of schizophrenia as just described is simple and stereotypical. In practice there are different types of schizophrenia, each with its own varied and complex set of symptoms. To help distinguish the symptoms of schizophrenia some theorists have divided them into two basic categories: positive and negative. Positive symptoms are those that seem to reflect overactive brain function such as hallucinations, delusions, confused thinking (in contrast to absence of thought) and odd emotions (as opposed to absence of emotions). Negative symptoms are those that seem to reflect under-aroused brain function and include poverty of thought or speech, blunted affect and social withdrawal. Some types of schizophrenia are predominantly characterised by positive symptoms, others by negative symptoms, and some by a mixture of the two (Crow 1980).

The genetics of schizophrenia

What evidence is there that schizophrenia has a biological cause? One source of evidence has come from studies that show that certain people have a genetic predisposition to becoming schizophrenic. One way this issue has been examined is to look at the rates of schizophrenia in identical and fraternal twins. Identical (or **monozygotic**) twins are twins that have been derived from the same fertilised egg and are therefore genetically identical, whereas fraternal (or **dizygotic**) twins develop from two different eggs (and thus two different sperms) and are genetically different. To be more precise, fraternal twins share 50 per cent of their genes with each other, and are no different (in a genetic sense) to any other brother or sister they may have.

The logic of comparing identical and fraternal twins is compelling. All things being equal, one would expect a trait that has a strong genetic cause to be more **concordant** (i.e. if one twin has the trait then so should the other) in a group of identical twins than in fraternal twins. Indeed, if a trait is always 100 per cent concordant (i.e. found in all twin pairs) then it can be considered to be a characteristic whose expression is not influenced (at least in any significant way) by environmental factors. However, most human behaviour is shaped by both genetic and environmental influences and thus it is unusual to find traits or behaviours that show perfect concordance. Twin studies of schizophrenia based on this logic have now been undertaken for over 50 years and nearly every report has shown that the concordance rate in schizophrenia is much higher in identical twins than in fraternal twins. In general, it appears that the concordance for identical twins is around 40–60 per cent, whereas the rate for non-identical twins is approximately 10–20 per cent (Gottesman and Shields 1982; Gottesman 1991). Since the prevalence of schizophrenia is around 1 per cent in the population as a whole, then this clearly indicates that there is a genetic factor at work in schizophrenia. Despite this, the genetic influence does not appear to be marked (e.g about 50 per cent), which suggests that the environment plays a crucial, if not equal, role in the development of the illness.

One problem with twin studies is that identical twins are nearly always brought up in the same environment and are treated alike by parents and friends. Ideally, it would be more meaningful, therefore, to examine identical twins who are reared apart in different homes. Of course, this type of situation rarely occurs. However, an alternative way of examining this type of situation is to look at the characteristics of people who were adopted when young but were born to schizophrenic parents. In short, if schizophrenia has a genetic basis then we would expect adoptees of psychotic parents to also show a higher incidence of schizophrenia. Indeed, this appears to be the case. For example, Kety *et al.* (1968) examined the records of all adopted children, born in Copenhagen between 1924 and 1947, who had been taken away from their parents at an early age. From this group, 33 adoptees were identified (as adults) who had been admitted to a psychiatric hospital suffering from schizophrenia. On closer examination it was found that 8.7 per cent of the biological parents, but only 1.9 per cent of the adoptive parents, had histories of mental illness including schizophrenia – thus highlighting the genetic link once again. Despite this, it remains the case that less than 10 per cent of the biological parents were schizophrenic, which shows that although there is a genetic predisposition at work, it does not appear to be particularly marked.

Environmental causes

What, then, are the possible environmental factors that could contribute to schizophrenia? There are many theories, but one consistent theme in the psychological literature is the importance of stress. For example, it has been pointed out that society's values are often contradictory and difficult to live with, and one way to escape the psychological conflict that they cause is to withdraw from the world and take 'refuge' in schizophrenia (in fact, some theorists such as Thomas Szasz have even argued that it is society which is sick, and not the schizophrenic). Others, such as R. D. Laing, have pointed to problems in the family (particularly difficulties relating to contradictory expectations and communication) as being important in causing schizophrenia. However, it is difficult to evaluate these theories. For example, in general, the incidence of schizophrenia is higher in lower social classes and large urban areas (where levels of stress might be expected to be higher). But, it could also be that schizophrenics have drifted down into these positions because they have been unable to hold down employment or relationships. Indeed, in partial support of this idea, the World Health Organisation have shown that schizophrenia is a worldwide disorder, found in all socioeconomic groups, and all types of society from industrial to the third world (Sartorius *et al.* 1986; Jablensky *et al.* 1992). Thus, it is probably too simple to lay the sole blame for schizophrenia on life's stresses – although there is little doubt that stress can affect the course of the illness, and contribute to the occurrence of schizophrenia in susceptible individuals.

More recently, evidence has focused on early exposure to virus infection as an important environmental cause of schizophrenia. For example, in the northern hemisphere there is a small but significant risk that people with schizophrenia will be born in the winter months (January, February and March). Moreover, this effect is more pronounced at higher latitudes and disappears in the tropics (Kalat 1992). But, why should this finding implicate viruses? The answer is that, in northern latitudes, viral epidemics are much more common in autumn – and for children born in winter, this period also corresponds to the second trimester of pregnancy, which is one of the most crucial times for brain development. Indeed, several studies have now shown a clear relationship between influenza epidemics that occurred during the second trimester of pregnancy and schizophrenia. For example, Sham *et al.* (1992) examined the outcome of pregnancies during several influenza outbreaks between 1939 and 1960 and found that there was a much greater likelihood of schizophrenia when an influenza outbreak occurred 5 months before birth. Although this may well be the most sensitive period, there is also some evidence to suggest that viral outbreaks occurring at any point in pregnancy may slightly increase the susceptibility to schizophrenia (Barr *et al.* 1990).

The fact that exposure to other types of viral agents (such as rubella or AIDS) can cause brain damage also lends further support to the influenza theory. Perhaps, the virus produces a toxin that harms the developing foetus at a critical stage, or it could be that the mother's immune system produces an antibody against the virus that also causes damage to the baby. But, whatever the explanation, there are still many unanswered questions concerning the viral theory. For example, schizophrenia does not normally appear until adulthood, so why should the illness take so long to develop if the triggering factor takes place prenatally? Even more difficult to answer is the fact that identical and fraternal twins are not always concordant for the illness. Indeed, it is not unusual for one twin to develop schizophrenia and for the other twin to be healthy. Clearly, this finding is awkward to explain in terms of early prenatal viral exposure.

Box 10.2 THE GENIAN QUADRUPLETS

The Genian quadruplets are four genetically identical women who were born in the early 1930s and who all developed schizophrenia in their early adulthood (the chances of this happening by chance have been estimated at 1 in 2 billion). Because they all share identical genes (this has been verified with blood tests) they provide an unique natural case study by which to assess the relative contributions of genetic inheritance and environment on the causation of schizophrenia. The sisters first came to the notice of the National Institute of Mental Health (NIMH) in the 1950s, where they were also extensively studied. To help provide the twins with anonymity, researchers at the NIMH invented the name 'Genian' (as a pseudonym for 'bad gene') – but they also named the sisters (from youngest to oldest) Nora, Iris, Myra and Hester, so their initials corresponded with those of the NIMH. The quads were originally described in a book by David Rosenthal (1963), and this research was extended 25 years later when the sisters were tested over several weeks on a variety of different tasks (the results being published in the journal *Psychiatry Research* in 1984).

Although all sisters were genetically identical, they nevertheless differed significantly in terms of their symptoms and severity of illness. For example, Nora at the age of 22 was the first to be hospitalised for schizophrenia although for much of her life she has been able to live in the community and hold down short-term clerical jobs. In contrast, Iris was first admitted to hospital seven months after Nora, and she has remained there, on and off, for more than 10 years. The next to be diagnosed was Hester (at the age of 24), who is regarded as the most severely ill of the four, and has spent much of her life (15 years) in hospital and under constant medication. The least affected, however, is Myra who probably would not have been diagnosed as schizophrenic until much later had she not participated in the NIMH study. For example, she worked steadily in clerical jobs and married at the age of 26 when she raised two children. In fact, Myra appears to have functioned normally until the age of 46 when, under stress, she became paranoid and delusional and was hospitalised for two months.

During the follow-up studies at the NIMH in 1981, all sisters underwent CAT scans of the brain. The results showed that there was little difference between the sisters and none showed ventricular enlargement. In other tests, all showed an elevated concentration of urine phenylethylamine (a possible hallucinogen) and there were significant differences when the sisters were taken off medication for a short period. For example, Nora and Hester quickly deteriorated, Iris maintained herself reasonably well, and Myra actually improved – so much so that she was taken off her medication when she left the NIMH. On another positive note, it also appears that the remaining three sisters who had taken antipsychotic medication for most of their previous 25 years had not suffered any further deterioration over this period. But, undoubtedly the most important (and the most puzzling) aspect of this study is the fact that all the sisters are so different in terms of their schizophrenic symptomology. Not only are they genetically identical, but, as far as researchers can tell, all have had a very similar upbringing in the same home together. In other words, there is no obvious environmental explanation for why the sisters have developed different forms of schizophrenia.

The biological basis of schizophrenia

As with the development of antidepressant drugs, the discovery of the first substances that were effective in the treatment of schizophrenia was somewhat fortuitous. In the 1940s the Rhône-Poulenc Drug Company were beginning to produce antihistamine compounds that could be used to treat allergies. However, one unexpected use for these drugs was the potentiation of anaesthesia – and in the late 1940s the French surgeon Henri Laborit began testing antihistamine compounds for this particular purpose. One unusual compound that he examined was **chlorpromazine**, which produced very marked sedation without any loss of consciousness. Since there was a genuine need at this time for a drug with this type of sedating effect, Laborit subsequently recommended it to his colleagues for testing on agitated patients. Although the initial results were disappointing, in 1951 two French psychiatrists, Jean Delay and Pierre Deniker, independently began administering chlorpromazine and found that it improved schizophrenia. Even more importantly, it appeared to reduce the symptoms of schizophrenia rather than simply causing sedation. For example, hallucinations and delusions disappeared with the patient showing more logical thought processes. In addition, they found that restless patients were often calmed down (and made more manageable) whereas catatonic patients were made more active, which enabled them to engage more effectively in psychotherapy.

In other words, chlorpromazine was a true antipsychotic drug, and after clinical trials it began to be used for this purpose in 1954 under the trade name **Thorazine** (thus making it the first drug to be approved specifically for treating a mental illness). In fact, within a few years of its introduction, it had proved so successful in treating schizophrenia (and psychotic behaviour) that the number of people resident in mental institutions began to show a marked decline. Moreover, it soon became clear that chlorpromazine was not the only drug with this type of effect. For example, it was found that chlorpromazine belonged to a class of drugs known as the **phenothiazines**, most of which also showed antischizophrenic properties. And, in the early 1960s another drug was discovered called **haloperidol** which, if anything, was even more effective in treating schizophrenia (haloperidol also belonged to a different class of antipsychotic drugs known as the **butyrophenomes**). Remarkably, both chlorpromazine and haloperidol have provided the mainstays of schizophrenia treatment for the last 30 or 40 years, and it is only relatively recently (within the last 10 years or so) that other types of drug have been developed that are comparable in efficacy.

Origins of the dopamine theory of schizophrenia

How then do chlorpromazine and haloperidol work to reduce the symptoms of schizophrenia? Beginning in the late 1950s evidence began to show that both drugs appeared to be exerting their main pharmacological effects by reducing dopamine activity in the brain. One of the first lines of evidence to support this theory came from the drug reserpine which (as we have seen above) is known to precipitate depression. But, it was also found to have similar effects to chlorpromazine in treating schizophrenia. Indeed, not only did reserpine and chlorpromazine cause sedation, but they both also produced Parkinson-like side effects such as rigidity and tremor, which were most apparent after high doses (or after several weeks of treatment). This suggested that chlorpromazine and reserpine were having similar effects on the brain. Moreover, since it was known that reserpine was depleting the brain of catecholamines (noradrenaline and dopamine), this indicated that chlorpromazine might be exerting a similar effect.

This view was reinforced in 1960 when it was found that Parkinson's disease was due to a deficiency of dopamine in the nigral–striatal pathway of the brain (see Chapter 3). Since both reserpine and chlorpromazine could effectively mimic the effects of Parkinson's disease, this was convincing evidence that they were also reducing dopamine activity. This finding also provided an important clue about the possible underlying biological cause of the illness. Put simply, if reserpine and chlorpromazine were reducing dopamine activity, this implied that schizophrenia was being caused by an excess (or overactivity) of this transmitter somewhere in the brain. This theory (although it comes in various guises) is known as the **dopamine theory of schizophrenia**.

Further support for this idea came from the drug **amphetamine** (see Figure 10.7). Injections of amphetamine (in high doses) can cause psychotic behaviour in many people, including hallucinations, delusions and agitated behaviour, that closely resembles schizophrenia (Connell 1958). Moreover, amphetamine exerts its pharmacolo-

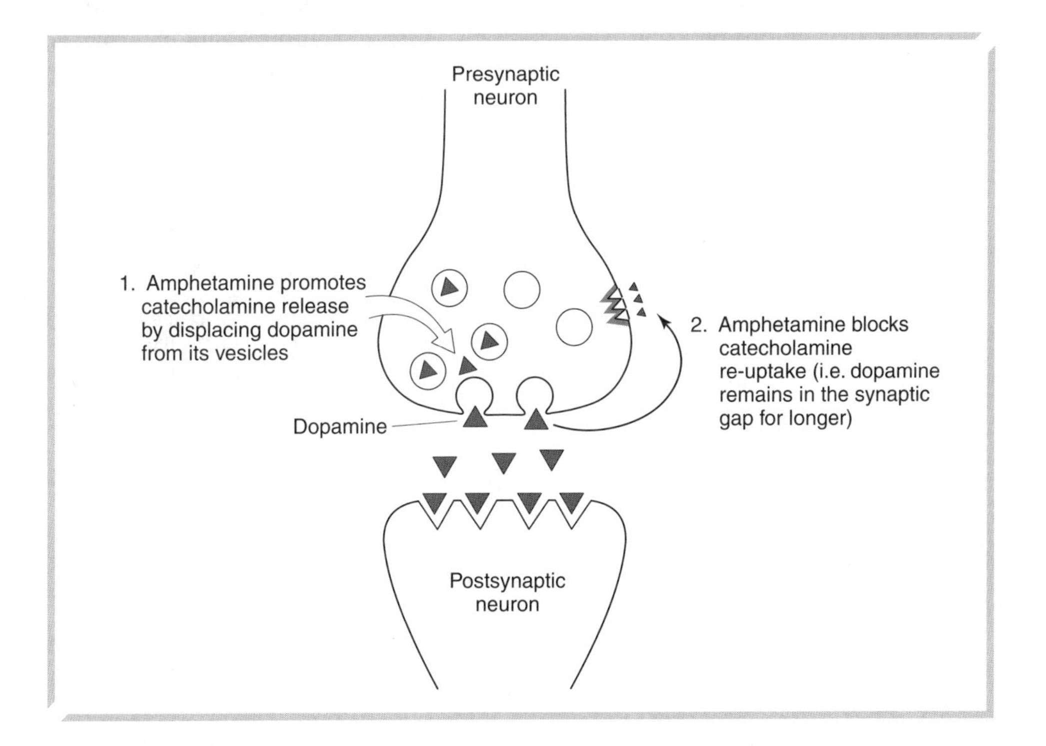

Figure 10.7 The mechanism by which amphetamine exerts its pharmacological effects.

gical effect by stimulating the release of catecholamines (particularly dopamine) from presynaptic nerve terminals (Leake 1958) (see Figure 10.7). Thus, by the early 1960s, strong evidence was beginning to link excess dopaminergic activity with the symptoms of schizophrenia.

How do antipsychotic drugs work?

As we have seen, both reserpine and chlorpromazine are effective in treating schizophrenia. Furthermore, since it was also known that reserpine caused the depletion of catecholamines in the brain (including dopamine) then, clearly, it was logical to suspect that chlorpromazine was having a similar mode of action. However, in 1963, Carlsson and Lindqvist showed this was not the case (see Figure 10.8). For example, when they injected rats with chlorpromazine (or haloperidol) they found that it did not deplete the brain of catecholamines and, if anything, the reverse was true, since the level of catecholamine **metabolites** (that is, the breakdown products of dopamine and noradrenaline) actually increased. Thus, this finding suggested that chlorpromazine was increasing the release of catecholamines, which were then being broken down into inert metabolites. In other words, reserpine and chlorpromazine appeared to be having different effects on the neurochemistry of the brain.

To account for these results, Carlsson and Lindqvist proposed a novel theory by suggesting that chlorpromazine was acting as a 'false' neurotransmitter. That is, chlorpromazine was attaching itself to the dopamine receptor – but instead of activating

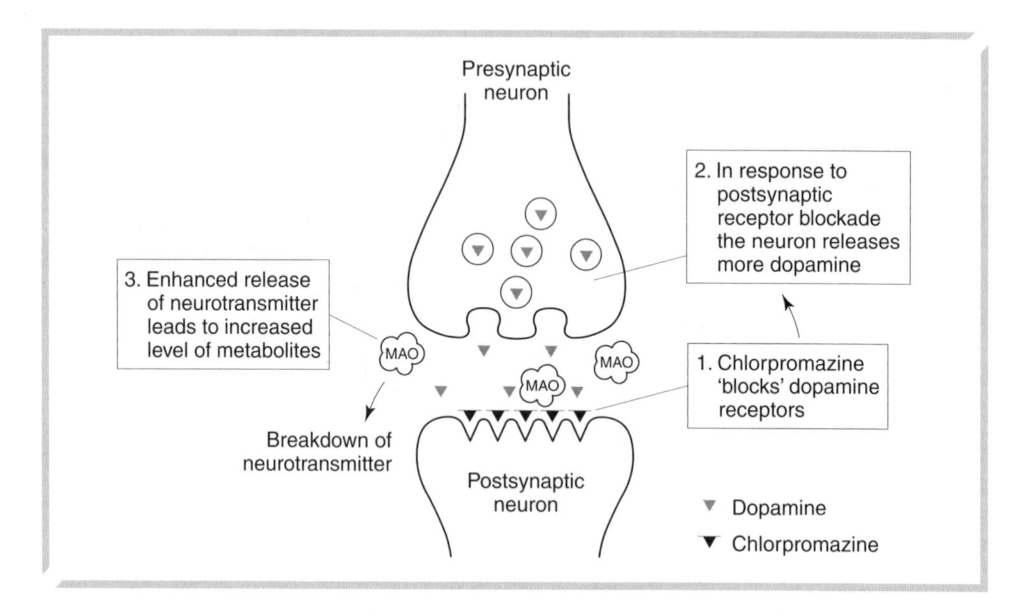

Figure 10.8 The Carlsson and Lindqvist (1963) theory of how chlorpromazine and haloperidol produce their pharmacological effects.

the receptor, the drug was *blocking* it. Thus, molecules of dopamine were unable to bind to their receptors and, in response to this blockade, the presynaptic neurons were increasing their release of dopamine further (this presumably occurred because the presynaptic neuron received a 'message' from the postsynaptic neuron informing it of the lack of dopamine stimulation). The net result of this receptor blockade was therefore an increased release of dopamine, which was then quickly broken down into metabolites as it remained trapped in the synaptic cleft (see Figure 10.8). Unfortunately, in the 1960s, there was no way of directly proving this theory and it remained largely hypothetical, although it nevertheless provided a convincing explanation for the action of chlorpromazine.

During the early 1970s, new research methods were brought to bear on the problem of identifying receptors in the brain, and one such technique, called **radioligand binding**, helped to show that Carlsson and Lindqvist were fundamentally correct. In this technique, a radioactive tracer is added to a neurochemical substance or drug that is known (or hypothesised) to bind selectively to certain receptors. This substance is then washed through specially prepared brain tissue (taken from brain regions believed to contain high numbers of the appropriate receptor), leaving behind tissue that emits a small amount of radioactivity. Because this emission is derived from the drug that is still bound to the tissue's receptors, the level of radioactivity thus allows an estimate of the number of receptors to be made. As might be expected, when this technique was used with dopamine, it was found to bind with high affinity to striatal tissue (the largest dopamine-containing area in the brain) which supported the idea that it was attaching itself to dopamine receptors (Cresse *et al.* 1976; Seeman *et al.* 1976).

Following the development of this technique, the effects of chlorpromazine and haloperidol on displacing radioactive dopamine were examined in a procedure known as **competitive binding**. This procedure rested on the assumption that if these two drugs blocked dopamine receptors, then it would follow that either would compete with radioactive dopamine if washed through the striatal tissue together. Consequently, less radioactivity should be emitted from the dopamine as less of it would manage to bind to its receptor. Indeed, this is what occurred when chlorpromazine was washed through striatal tissue with dopamine. In fact, not only did chlorpromazine block the effects of dopamine, but even more impressive was the finding that the potency of a wide range of antischizophrenic drugs correlated with their ability to compete with dopamine. In other words, the more effective a given drug was at treating schizophrenia, the better it was at stopping dopamine binding to its receptors (see Figure 10.9).

However, there was one notable exception to this rule, namely haloperidol, which also happened to be the most commonly used drug used to treat schizophrenia. Although haloperidol was one of the most potent antischizophrenic drugs in clinical studies, it appeared to be relatively weak at binding (and competing) with dopamine receptors. At the very least, its potency at binding to dopamine receptors did not appear to match its potency at treating schizophrenia. Despite this, haloperidol was clearly binding to striatal tissue and other dopaminergic areas in the brain, indicating that it was exerting an important receptor effect in these regions.

How could this puzzling finding be explained? The answer turned out to be that there

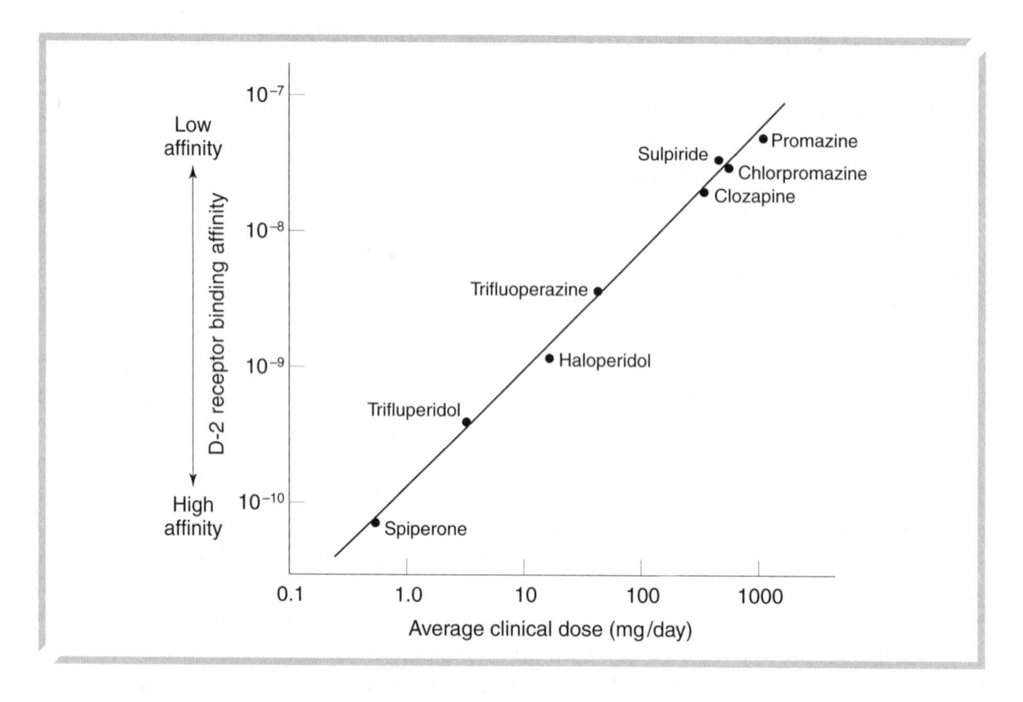

Figure 10.9 Graph showing the correlation between the clinical potencies of antipsychotic drugs and their ability to block the D-2 dopamine receptor.

was more than one dopaminergic receptor in the brain (Kebabian and Calne 1979). In fact, the brain (including the striatum) was shown to contain two types of dopamine receptor which were designated **D-1** and **D-2**. Importantly, it was also found that chlorpromazine bound with equal affinity to both D-1 and D-2 receptors, whereas haloperidol only bound to D-2 receptors. This was a crucial finding because it not only helped to explain the discrepant results obtained with competitive binding, but it also indicated that antipsychotic drugs worked specifically by blocking D-2 receptors. Extending this idea one step further, it also implicated the D-2 receptor as a possible causal factor in the aetiology of schizophrenia.

Problems with the dopamine theory

If chlorpromazine and haloperidol work by blocking dopamine receptors, then this would seem to imply that schizophrenia is caused through excess dopaminergic activity. Thus, one might predict that schizophrenics should have higher brain levels of dopamine than normal. However, in general, this has not been found. For example, there is little consistent evidence showing generalised increased levels of dopamine in the brains of schizophrenics at post-mortem (Deakin 1988), and most studies have not found increased levels of dopaminergic metabolites such as **homovanillic acid (HVA)** in the cerebrospinal fluid (Post *et al.* 1975). Although some studies have shown increased levels of dopamine in certain specific brain structures (such as the nucleus accumbens and caudate nucleus) these results have proved difficult to replicate. Interestingly, a finding that has been successfuly replicated, is the one showing higher dopamine levels in the left-sided amygdala compared to the right (Reynolds 1983). The significance of this finding, however, is far from clear.

In contrast to the largely negative results concerning levels of dopamine, a number of studies have found increased numbers of dopamine D-2 receptors in the brains of schizophrenic patients (Jaskiw and Kleinman 1988). Thus, rather than increased levels of dopamine being responsible for schizophrenia, it may be that heightened activity occurs at the receptor level. However, the problem with interpreting these findings is to know whether the increase in the number of receptors is actually part of the disease process itself, or whether it is simply an adaptive response to antipsychotic medication (which the vast majority of schizophrenic patients will have received). Although some studies have reported increased numbers of D-2 receptors in schizophrenic patients who had been drug-free for some time before their death (Owen *et al.* 1978), more recent studies, using PET scanning to count the number of dopamine receptors in medication-free subjects, have not confirmed these findings (Farde *et al.* 1990; Pilowsky *et al.* 1994).

Another problem with the dopamine hypothesis is that antipsychotic drugs normally block dopamine receptors very rapidly (within a day or two), although it generally takes several weeks for these drugs to exert their full clinical effect. In other words, it is not the blockade of dopaminergic receptors that provides the final mechanism by which these drugs work. Presumably, therefore, receptor blockade initiates a long-term change in the dopaminergic systems of the brain, that takes several weeks to reach its full effect. In fact, there is some evidence to suggest that whatever this crucial change is, it does not involve the dopamine receptors. For example, one expected effect of long-term antischizophrenic treatment would be to increase the sensitivity of dopamine receptors (or lead to their up-regulation) which, in turn, would be expected to cause a massive exacerbation of symptoms when the treatment was stopped. However, this type of withdrawal effect rarely occurs.

Evidence for brain damage

A number of studies have reported the existence of brain damage in schizophrenia (or at least in some people) with one of the most common findings being an enlargement of the lateral ventricles (which are situated in the two cerebral hemispheres). For example, Weinberger and Wyatt (1982) examined the CAT scans of 80 chronic schizophrenics and found that the relative size of the ventricles was more than twice the size compared to controls. Despite this, increased ventricle size is certainly not found in all cases, and it appears to be most highly correlated with negative symptomology including blunted affect, poverty of speech and loss of drive (Johnstone *et al.* 1978; Andreassen 1988). Moreover, these are the types of symptom that also tend to respond less favourably to antipsychotic medication (Weinberger *et al.* 1980).

These findings have led the British psychiatrist Timothy Crow to propose that there are two separate forms of schizophrenia which have their own symptoms, pathology and aetiology (Crow 1984). For example, type 1 schizophrenia is characterised by positive symptoms (including hallucinations and delusions) and, in Crow's view, is caused by dopaminergic dysfunction, whereas type 2 schizophrenia is marked by negative symptoms, and is seen as being caused by structural brain damage and neuron loss (particularly in the frontal lobes). Furthermore, these two types of schizophrenia also appear to respond differently to treatment. In short, type 1 schizophrenia seems to respond well to drug therapy with the long-term chances of recovery being good – whereas type 2 responds poorly to drug treatment and has a poor long-term prognosis (Crow 1984). Clearly, the implication of this classification is that schizophrenia is not a single disorder, but actually several different specific diseases that differ in important ways (see Table 10.1).

Despite this, many cases of schizophrenia do not fall neatly into Crow's classification system. For example, in one study that examined the progress of 52 schizophrenic patients that were hospitalised before the development of antipsychotic drugs, it was found that, over a 25-year period, positive symptoms (such as hallucinations and delusions) gradually changed into more pronounced negative symptoms such as social withdrawal and blunted affect (Pfohl and Winokur 1983). However, in other cases it does appear that these two types of schizophrenia can develop independently. For example, Andreassen (1985) reports that some patients with negative symptoms have no prior history of positive symptoms and they remain in this state for the rest of their lives. Similarly, there are many patients with positive symptoms who show few negative characteristics and have no signs of brain damage. Thus, although Crow's classification has probably helped to clarify the nature of schizophrenia, it nevertheless oversimplifies what is clearly a very complex illness.

Table 10.1 A summary of Crow's classification of schizophrenia (types 1 and 2)

Type 1 schizophrenia
Is characterised by positive symptoms including hallucinations, delusions and fragmented thought processes.
Often exhibits a fluctuating course with periods of remission.
Generally shows a good response to antipsychotic medication.
Is believed, in part, to be due to dopaminergic dysfunction (e.g. increased numbers of dopamine receptors).
Type 2 schizophrenia
Is characterised by negative symptoms including flattening of affect, poverty of speech and reduced motor activity.
Often exhibits a chronic course with little improvement.
Generally shows a poor response to antipsychotic medication.
Is believed, in part, to be due to neural loss (as supported by findings showing an increased likelihood of ventricular enlargement and reduced blood flow to the frontal lobes).

Side effects of antipsychotic drugs

Chlorpromazine and haloperidol are not without their limitations. For example, they are not very effective in treating the negative symptoms of schizophrenia, and are also associated with a wide range of side effects including tremor, postural rigidity, sudden cramps, and an unpleasant feeling of physical restlessness called **akathisia**. Furthermore, because many people with schizophrenia need to take medication for long periods of time, the continued use of these drugs can also have serious health effects. One such complication is **tardive dyskinesia**, which is associated with repetitive and involuntary movements, especially those involving the face, mouth, lips and tongue. For example, individuals with tardive dyskinesia may flick their tongue out some 30–40 times each minute (a problem which may be more socially debilitating than the schizophrenia itself). Tardive dyskinesia is particularly serious because, unlike other side effects, it does not always improve or disappear when the drugs are stopped. Unfortunately, it is common in certain groups of schizophrenic patients. For example, it has been estimated that tardive dyskinesia may occur in around 20 per cent of hospitalised patients with chronic schizophrenia who require long-term medication (Stoudemire 1998).

Although the biological basis of tardive dyskinesia is not well understood, it probably arises as a result of prolonged blockade of dopamine receptors which causes them to become supersensitive. Similarly, the other side effects of antipsychotic use (such as tremor, rigidity and akathisia) are also likely to occur because these drugs act on the striatum (which is hardly surprising as it is the largest dopaminergic area in the brain). Unfortunately, the striatum (which receives its dopamine input from the substantia nigra) is not believed to be the main dopamine pathway responsible for producing schizophrenia. In fact, much more likely to be involved are: the **mesolimbic pathway**, which projects to the nucleus accumbens, amygdala and hippocampus and is believed to play an important role in emotion, and the **mesofrontal pathway**, which projects to the frontal cortex and is believed to be involved in higher order cognition. However, chlorpromazine and haloperidol appear to be largely indiscriminate in their effects on all these dopamine systems. The main dopaminergic pathways to the brain can be seen in Figure 10.10 (see also Figure 1.18).

New drug developments in schizophrenia

Approximately 20 per cent of schizophenic patients respond poorly to chlorpromazine and haloperidol and, as we have seen, these drugs are also associated with a number of side effects. This has led researchers to search for new antipsychotic drugs that have a more selective action on treating the symptoms of schizophrenia. One such compound that has generated considerable interest is **clozapine**. This drug was first synthesised in 1958 as a tricyclic antidepressant, and used to treat schizophrenia in the early 1970s when it began to obtain 'myth status' (McKenna and Baily 1993). Unfortunately, it also produced fatal agranulocytosis (lack of white blood cells) in a few patients and was withdrawn from clinical practice. Despite this, it continued to be used experimentally,

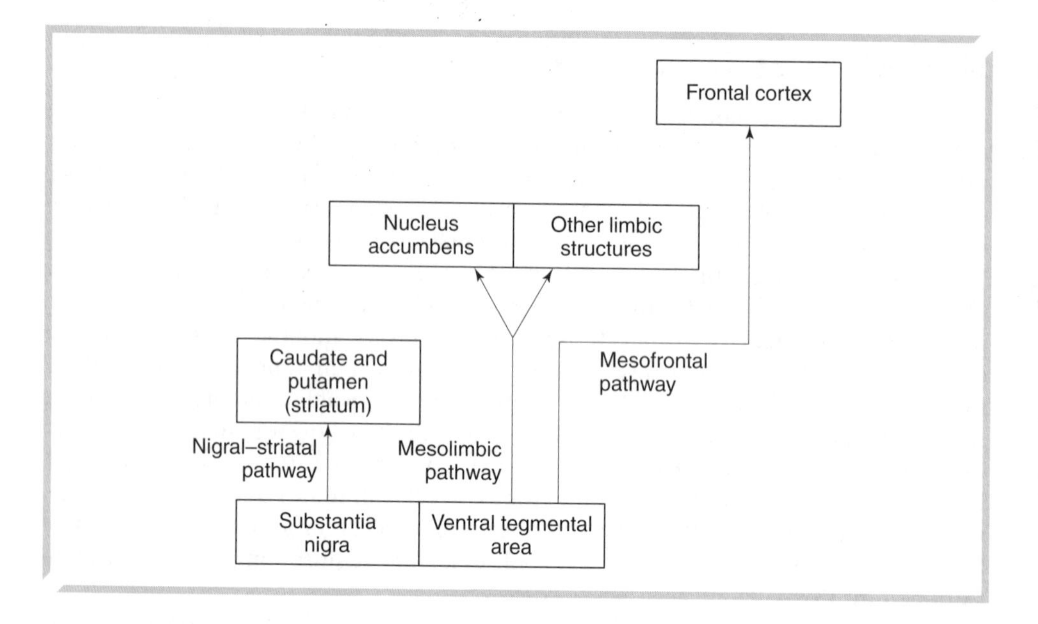

Figure 10.10 A reminder of the main dopaminergic pathways of the brain.

and in controlled studies was found to be at least as effective as haloperidol. But, perhaps more importantly, it also produced improvement in some 30–50 per cent of patients who did not respond to standard antipsychotic medication (Kane 1992). In some instances there were also documented cases of near total remission of symptoms after many years of chronic illness. Furthermore, clozapine not only improved both the positive and negative symptoms of schizophrenia, but was also associated with a very low incidence of extrapyramidal side effects and, in particular, a notable lack of tardive dyskinesia. Unfortunately, the problem of agranulocytosis remained and, because of this, clozapine is now restricted to closely monitored hospital patients who fail to respond to other medication. Nevertheless, there is little doubt that it has made a valuable contribution to treating such patients.

Clozapine has also attracted a great deal of interest from psychopharmacologists interested in understanding how it 'works' on the neurochemical systems of the brain. Surprisingly, it has been found to have little effect on dopaminergic D-2 receptors (its binding is short-lived) and has a greater blocking action on D-1 receptors. But, more importantly, clozapine is also a potent antagonist of 5-HT_2 receptors and increases serotonin release, and this action is believed to be the main mechanism through which clozapine exerts its effects (Sodhi *et al.* 1995). This is particularly interesting because certain hallucinogenic drugs such as lysergic acid diethylamide (LSD) are known to be agonists on 5-HT_2 receptors, and researchers have long been intrigued by a possible link between LSD hallucinations and schizophrenia. Another very interesting feature of clozapine is that it selectively blocks dopaminergic activity in the mesolimbic system, and has little effect on the nigral–striatal system. Indeed, this action probably explains why it produces so few extrapyramidal side effects. Not surprisingly, clozapine is currently acting as a prototype for newer antipsychotic compounds as well as opening up new areas concerning the biological basis of schizophrenia.

The last decade, or so, has also seen exciting advances taking place in the field of receptor pharmacology with the discovery of three more dopamine receptor subtypes (called **D-3**, **D-4** and **D-5**). The D-3 and D-4 receptors have generated considerable interest because they are structurally similar to the D-2 receptor. However, unlike the D-2 receptor, the D-3 and D-4 receptors appear to be found predominantly in the limbic system (particularly the nucleus accumbens and hippocampus) which is one of the main brain regions likely to be involved in schizophrenia (Seeman 1995). Perhaps, even more intriguing, is the finding that chlorpromazine is 10 times less effective in binding at D-4 receptors compared with D-2 or D-3, whereas clozapine is 10 times more potent at D-4 receptors than D-2 or D-3 (Feldman *et al.* 1997). Not only do these findings help to explain why clozapine has a much more selective effect on the mesolimbic system, but they also suggest that our understanding of how antipsychotic drugs work will probably have to undergo major revision in the coming years.

Self-test questions

1. What are the main differences between unipolar and bipolar depression?
2. What is monoamine oxidase?
3. Why does inhibition of monoamine oxidase have antidepressant effects?
4. Name two transmitters which are catecholamines.
5. What is meant by re-uptake?
6. How do tricyclic antidepressants work?
7. What are autoreceptors?
8. What arguments have been proposed to explain the time-lag of antidepressant therapy?
9. What drug is most commonly used to treat bipolar illness?
10. Describe the main characteristics of schizophrenia. What are positive and negative symptoms?
11. How was chlorpromazine first discovered?
12. How did Carlsson and Lindqvist explain the action of chlorpromazine?
13. What is the main pharmacological difference between chlorpromazine and haloperidol?
14. What are the main weaknesses of the dopamine theory of schizophrenia?
15. What evidence is there showing that there may be two different types of schizophrenia?
16. What is unique about the action of clozapine?
17. How many dopamine receptors are now believed to exist in the brain?

Key terms

Akathisia (p.321)
Alpha-2 receptors (p.301)
Amphetamine (p.315)
Autoreceptors (p.301)
Beta receptors (p.302)
Bipolar depression (p.296)
Butyrophenomes (p.314)
Catecholamines (p.297)
Chlorpromazine (p.314)
Clozapine (p.321)
Competitive binding (p.317)
Concordant (p.310)
D-1 & D-2 receptors (p.318)
D-3, D-4 & D-5 receptors (p.323)
Depression (p.295)
Dizygotic twins (p.310)
Dopamine (p.297)
Dopamine theory of schizophrenia (p.315)
Down-regulation (p.302)
5-HIAA (p.301)
Fluoxetine (Prozac) (p.303)
Haloperidol (p.314)
Homovanillic acid (HVA) (p.318)
Hypothalamic–pituitary–adrenal axis (p.305)
Imipramine (p.298)
Iproniazid (p.296)
Lithium (p.308)
Mesofrontal pathway (p.321)
Mesolimbic pathway (p.321)
Metabolites (p.316)
MHPG (p.300)
Monoamine oxidase (p.296)
Monoamine oxidase inhibitors (p.297)
Monoamine theory of depression (p.300)
Monoamines (p.296)
Monozygotic twins (p.310)
Noradrenaline (p.297)
Phenothiazines (p.314)
Radioligand binding (p.317)
Reserpine (p.297)
Schizophrenia (p.309)
Seasonal affective disorder (p.308)
Serotonin (p.297)
Tardive dyskinesia (p.321)
Thorazine (p.314)
Tricyclic antidepressants (p.298)
Tyramine (p.298)
Unipolar depression (p.295)

References

Andreassen, N. C. (1985) Positive vs negative schizophrenia: A critical evaluation. *Schizophrenia Bulletin*, **11**, 380–9.

Andreassen, N. C. (1988) Brain imaging: Applications in psychiatry. *Science*, **239**, 1381–8.

Asberg, M. *et al.* (1987) Psychobiology of suicide, impulsivity, and related phenomena. In Meltzer, H. M. (ed.) *Psychopharmacology. The Third Generation of Progress.* New York: Raven Press.

Ashton, H. (1992) *Brain Function and Psychotropic Drugs.* Oxford: Oxford University Press.

Barden, N. *et al.* (1985) Do antidepressants stabilise mood through actions on the hypothalamus–pituitary–adrenocortical system? *Trends in Neuroscience*, **18**, 6–11.

Barr, C. E. *et al.* (1990) Exposure to influenza epidemics during gestation and adult schizophrenia. *Archives of General Psychiatry*, **47**, 869–74.

Birkmayer, W. and Linauer, W. (1970) Storungen des Tyrosin und Tryptophan-metabolismus bei Depressionen. *Archive für Psychiatrie und Nervenkrankheiten*, **213**, 377–8.

Brunello, N. *et al.* (1982) Down regulation of β-adrenergic receptors following repeated injections of desmethylimipramine: Permissive role of serotonergic axons. *Neuropharmacology*, **21**, 1145–9.

Carlsson, A. and Lindqvist, M. (1963) Effect of chlorpromazine or haloperidol on the formation of 3-methoxytyramine and normetanephrine in mouse brain. *Acta Pharmacology and Toxicology*, **20**, 140–4.

Creese, I. *et al.* (1976) Dopamine receptor binding predicts clinical and pharmacological properties of antischizophrenic drugs. *Science*, **194**, 481–3.

Crow, T. J. (1980) Molecular pathology of schizophrenia: More than one disease process? *British Medical Journal*, **280**, 66–8.

Crow, T. J. (1984) The two-syndrome concept: Origins and current status. *Schizophrenia Bulletin*, **11**, 471–85.

Connell, P. H. (1958) *Amphetamine Psychosis.* London: Maudsley Monographs No. 5.

Deakin, J. F. W. (1988) The neurochemistry of schizophrenia. In Bebbington, P. and McGuffin, P. (eds) *Schizophrenia: The Major Issues.* Oxford: Heinemann.

Farde, L. *et al.* (1990) D2 dopamine receptors in neuroleptic free naive schizophrenic patients. *Archives of General Psychiatry*, **47**, 213–19.

Feldman, R. S. *et al.* (1997) *Principles of Neuropsychopharmacology*. Sunderland, MA: Sinauer.

Goodwin, F. K. and Jamison, K. R. (1990) *Manic Depressive Illness.* New York: Oxford University Press.

Gottesman, I. I. (1991) *Schizophrenia Genesis.* New York: Freeman.

Gottesman, I. I. and Shields, J. (1982) *Schizophrenia: The Epigenetic Puzzle.* Cambridge: Cambridge University Press.

Gregory, R. (ed.) (1987) *The Oxford Companion to the Mind.* Oxford: Oxford University Press.

Jablensky, A. *et al.* (1992) Schizophrenia: Manifestations, incidence and course in different cultures. A World Health Organisation 10 country study. *Psychological Medicine Monograph, Suppl. 20*.

Jaskiw, G. and Kleinman, J. (1988) Postmortem neurochemistry studies in schizophrenia. In Schulz, S. C. and Tamminga, C. A. (eds) *Schizophrenia: A Scientific Focus.* New York: Oxford University Press.

Johnstone, E. C. *et al.* (1978) The dementia of dementia praecox. *Acta Psychiatria Scandinavica*, **57**, 305–24.

Kalat, J. W. (1992) *Biological Psychology.* Pacific Grove: Brooks/Cole.

Kane, J. M. (1992) Clinical efficacy of clozapine in treatment-refractory schizophrenia: An overview. *British Journal of Psychiatry*, **160** (suppl. 17), 41–5.

Kebabian, J. W. and Calne, D. B. (1979) Multiple receptors for dopamine. *Nature*, **277**, 93–6.

Kety, S. S. *et al.* (1968) The types and prevalence of mental illness in the biological and adoptive families of adopted schizophrenics. In Rosenthal, D. and Kety, S. S. (eds) *The Transmission of Schizophrenia.* Elmsford: Pergamon Press.

Kuhn, R. (1958) The treatment of depressive states with G22355 (imipramine hydrochloride). *American Journal of Psychiatry*, **115**, 459–64.

Lader, M. and Herrington, R. (1990) *Biological Treatments in Psychiatry.* Oxford: Oxford University Press.

Leake, C. D. (1958) *The Amphetamines: Their Actions and their Uses.* Springfield, IL: Thomas.

Lewy, A. J. *et al.* (1989) Winter depression: The phase between sleep and other circadian rhythms may be critical. In Thompson, C. and Silverstone, T. (eds) *Seasonal Affective Disorder.* London: Clinical Neuroscience Publishers.

Lickey, M. E. and Gordon, B. (1991) *Medicine and Mental Illness.* New York: Freeman.

McKenna, P. J. and Bailey, P. E. (1993) The strange story of clozapine. *British Journal of Psychiatry*, **162**, 32–7.

Owen, F. *et al.* (1978) Increased dopamine receptor sensitivity in schizophrenia. *Lancet*, **ii**, 223–5.

Palfai, T. and Jankiewicz, H. (1997) *Drugs and Human Behaviour.* Madison, WI: Brown & Benchmark.

Pfohl, B. and Winokur, G. (1983) The micropsychopathology of hebephrenic/catatonic schizophrenia. *Journal of Nervous and Mental Disease*, **171**, 296–300.

Pilowsky, L. S. *et al.* (1994) D2 dopamine receptor binding in the basal ganglia of antipsychotic-free schizophrenic patients. *British Journal of Psychiatry*, **164**, 16–26.

Post, R. M. *et al.* (1975) Cerebrospinal fluid amine metabolites in acute schizophrenia. *Archives of General Psychiatry*, **32**, 1063–9.

Reul, J. M. H. M. *et al.* (1993) *Endocrinology*, **133**, 312–20.

Reul, J. M. H. M. *et al.* (1994) *Neuroendocrinology*, **60**, 509–19.

Reynolds, G. P. (1983) Increased concentrations and lateral asymmetry of amygdala dopamine in schizophrenia. *Nature*, **305**, 527–9.

Rosenthal, D. (1963) *The Genian Quadruplets.* New York: Basic Books.

Sartorius, N. *et al.* (1986) Early manifestations and first-contact incidence of schizophrenia in different cultures. *Psychological Medicine*, **16**, 909–28.

Schildkraut, J. J. (1965) The catecholamine hypothesis of affective disorders: A review of supporting evidence. *American Journal of Psychiatry*, **122**, 509–22.

Seeman, P. (1995) Dopamine receptors and psychosis. *Scientific American: Science and Medicine*, Sept., 28–37.

Seeman, P. *et al.* (1976) Antipsychotic drug doses and neuroleptic/dopamine receptors. *Nature*, **261**, 717–19.

Sham, P. C. *et al.* (1992) Schizophrenia following pre-natal exposure to influenza epidemics between 1939 and 1960. *British Journal of Psychiatry*, **160**, 461–6.

Sodhi, M. S. *et al.* (1995) Association between clozapine response and allelic variation in the 5-HT_{2c} gene. *NeuroReport*, **7**, 169–72.

Stoudemire, A. (1998) *Clinical Psychiatry for Medical Students.* Philadelphia: Lippincott-Raven.

Sulser, F. (1989) New perspectives on the molecular pharmacology of affective disorders. *European Archives of Psychiatry and Neurological Science*, **238**, 231–9.

Thompson, C. and Silverstone, T. (1989) *Seasonal Affective Disorder*. London: CNS (Clinical Neurosciences) Publications.

Weinberger, D. R. and Wyatt, R. J. (1982) Brain morphology in schizophrenia: *In vivo* studies. In Henn, F. A. and Nasrallah, H. A. (eds) *Schizophrenia as a Brain Disease.* New York: Oxford University Press.

Weinberger, D. R. *et al.* (1980) Cerebral ventricular enlargement in chronic schizophrenia: An association with poor response to treatment. *Archives of General Psychiatry*, **37**, 11–13.

Wilner, P. (1985) *Depression: A Psychobiological Synthesis.* New York: Wiley.

Zellar, E. A. *et al.* (1952) Influence of isonicotinic acid hydrazide (INH) and 1-isonicotinyl-2-isopropyl hydrazine (IIH) on bacterial and mammalian enzymes. *Experimentia*, **8**, 349–50.

FURTHER READING

Barondes, S. H. (1993) *Molecules and Mental Illness*. New York: Scientific American Library.

Bebbington, P. and McGuffin, P. (eds) (1988) *Schizophrenia: The Major Issues*. Oxford: Heinemann.

Bloom, F. E. and Kupfer, D. J. (eds) (1995) *Psychopharmacology: The Fourth Generation of Progress.* New York: Raven Press.

Cheetham, S.C. *et al.* (1991) Post-mortem studies of neurotransmitter biochemistry in depression and suicide. In Horton, R. and Katona, C. (eds) *Biological Aspects of Affective Disorders.* London: Academic Press.

Horton, R. and Katona, C. (eds) (1991) *Biological Aspects of Affective Disorders*. London: Academic Press.

Snyder, S. H. (1986) *Drugs and the Brain*. New York: Scientific American Library.

Multiple choice questions

1. Which of the following is not an example of an affective disorder?

(a) depression
(b) mania
(c) bipolar disorder
(d) schizophrenia

2. Iproniazid (Marsilid) works by:

(a) increasing the uptake of noradrenaline
(b) increasing the uptake of serotonin
(c) inhibiting monoamine oxidase
(d) all of the above

3. The enzyme which normally acts to break down excess amounts of catecholamines is:

(a) adenylate cyclase
(b) cAMP
(c) monoamine oxidase
(d) adenosine triphosphate

4. Reserpine depletes the brain of:

(a) catecholamines
(b) monoamine oxidase
(c) tyramine
(d) acetylcholine

5. Most tricyclic antidepressants work by directly:

(a) stimulating noradrenergic receptors
(b) stimulating presynaptic autoreceptors
(c) blocking the re-uptake of noradrenaline
(d) inhibiting monoamine oxidase

6. Schildkraut (1965) believed that depression was primarily due to a decrease in levels of ________________ and that mania was due to an increase in levels of __________________.

(a) noradrenaline, dopamine
(b) noradrenaline, noradrenaline
(c) serotonin, dopamine
(d) monoamine oxidase, noradrenaline

7. In post-mortem studies low levels of ____________________ have been found in the brains of people who have committed suicide.

(a) noradrenaline
(b) MHPG (a metabolite of noradrenaline)
(c) 5-HIAA (a metabolite of serotonin)
(d) all of the above

8. Over the long term, treatment with traditional tricyclic antidepressants has been postulated to cause:

(a) synaptic increases in the level of noradrenaline
(b) down-regulation of noradrenergic autoreceptors
(c) desensitisation of postsynaptic noradrenergic beta receptors
(d) all of the above

9. Which of the following is a selective serotonergic uptake blocker?

(a) reserpine
(b) imipramine
(c) iproniazid
(d) fluoxetine

10. Lithium appears to exert its main neurochemical effects by directly:

(a) acting on second messenger systems
(b) blocking re-uptake of noradrenaline
(c) stimulating noradrenergic autoreceptors
(d) blocking noradrenergic beta receptors

11. Which of the following is not a positive symptom of schizophrenia?

(a) delusions
(b) hallucinations
(c) fragmented and overactive thinking
(d) blunted affect

12. The concordance rate for schizophrenia in identical twins has been shown to be around:

(a) 100 per cent
(b) 50 per cent
(c) 10 per cent
(d) zero

13. In the northern hemisphere there is a small but significant risk that people with schizophrenia will be born in:

(a) winter
(b) spring
(c) summer
(d) autumn

14. Which of the following would be likely to exacerbate the symptoms of schizophrenia?

(a) chlorpromazine
(b) haloperidol
(c) reserpine
(d) amphetamine

15. When Carlsson and Lindqvist (1963) treated rats with chlorpromazine they found that:

(a) dopamine levels in the brain were depleted (similar to reserpine)
(b) dopamine levels were unchanged, but levels of DA metabolites were increased
(c) there was no change in dopamine or levels of its metabolites
(d) dopamine levels were significantly increased

16. Chlorpromazine has been shown to block:

(a) both dopaminergic D-1 and D-2 receptors
(b) dopaminergic D-1 receptors
(c) dopaminergic D-2 receptors
(d) the release of dopamine

17. A number of studies (although not all) have found increased numbers of _____ receptors in the brains of schizophrenics.

(a) D-1
(b) D-2
(c) both D-1 and D-2
(d) abnormal

18. According to Tim Crow, type 2 schizophrenia is characterised by:

(a) negative symptoms
(b) poor long-term prognosis
(c) poor response to antipsychotic medication
(d) all of the above

19. Which of the following is not a dopaminergic pathway in the brain?

(a) nigral–striatal pathway
(b) mesolimbic pathway (to the nucleus accumbens)
(c) mesofrontal pathway (to the frontal cortex)
(d) perforant pathway (to the hippocampus)

20. Clozapine is currently attracting a great deal of interest because as well as working on D-4 receptors it also shows affinity for blocking _______________ receptors.

(a) noradrenergic
(b) serotonergic
(c) cholinergic
(d) benzodiazepine

11 Drugs and addiction

IN THIS CHAPTER

- The neural basis of reinforcement
- The role of dopamine in reward
- The role of opiate systems in the brain
- The concept of addiction
- Biological and psychological factors in drug tolerance and withdrawal
- The pharmacological effects of commonly used 'abused' drugs

Introduction

Put in simple terms, a drug is any chemical that alters biological function. However, the effects of drugs on biological systems are far from simple, and this is particularly true with regard to psychoactive substances that act on the brain and can influence a person's mood, cognition or behaviour. In the previous chapter we saw how drugs could be used to treat various forms of mental illness, but of course drugs can also be used for other purposes, and not least for their intoxicating and pleasurable properties. Indeed, human beings have been taking psychoactive agents for thousands of years (records show that opium was used 4,000 years ago and the use of alcohol may go back over 10,000 years) and there are few places in the world where drugs have not been used for their mind-altering qualities. Man, it has been said, is a drug-taking animal (Leonard

1992) and one only has to imagine life without alcohol, nicotine and caffeine to realise the truth of this statement. Yet, drugs are not without their risks, and there are many substances where the perceived costs of use, either to the well-being of the individual or to society, are deemed too great for them to be freely (or legally) available. One of the most serious risks is drug addiction, widely seen as one of the biggest difficulties facing our society today. Not surprisingly, this problem (along with the fact that there has been a significant increase in illegal drug use over the last 30 years) has led to unprecedented efforts to understand how drugs produce their effects and influence behaviour. But, there is much more to this subject than first meets the eye. By understanding why people become addicted to drugs, one is also essentially examining the neural basis of pleasure, which is arguably the most important determinant of behaviour for us all.

The discovery of rewarding brain stimulation

Considerable evidence (and common sense) tells us that the biological basis for drug abuse must lie to a large extent with the reward systems of the brain. However, the discovery that the brain contains specific areas and pathways that mediate reward was not made until 1954 when James Olds, and his research student Peter Milner, decided to test the unrelated issue of whether electrical stimulation of the reticular formation could facilitate arousal and learning. Firstly, Olds and Milner looked at the effects of stimulation when a rat was placed in a large open box. To their surprise they found that if they stimulated the animal when it was located in one of the corners, it would either remain there, or quickly return if moved away. In other words, the rat appeared to find the stimulation pleasurable. This discovery was important because it suggested for the first time that the brain might contain specific sites that were involved in reward or pleasure. Olds and Milner were also to receive a second surprise. When they examined the location of the electrode placements after their test, they found that they had not stimulated the reticular formation after all, but a different region of the brain closely linked with the hypothalamus called the septal area. Thus, they had discovered the rewarding effects of brain stimulation by chance! In fact, had their electrode placements been correctly positioned they probably would not have discovered the effect as stimulation of the reticular formation is often found to be aversive to the animal.

But was the electrical stimulation really acting as a reward? There was some degree of doubt since the stimulation also caused the rat to look around and sniff the air, raising the possibility that the procedure might instead be provoking curiosity or exploration. To examine this further, Olds and Milner trained hungry rats to negotiate a T maze which required them to make either a right or left turn for food reward. The task was designed, however, so that the choice of goal arms had different consequences for the animal. In one of the arms, Olds and Milner gave the rat brain stimulation before the food was reached, while in the other arm, the animal was allowed to eat the food unperturbed. The important question was: What arm would the rat choose if given a free choice (i.e. would it choose stimulation or food)? The results showed that the rat always chose the arm where it received stimulation, and, more importantly, it actually stopped at the stimulation point ignoring the food that was only inches away! In other

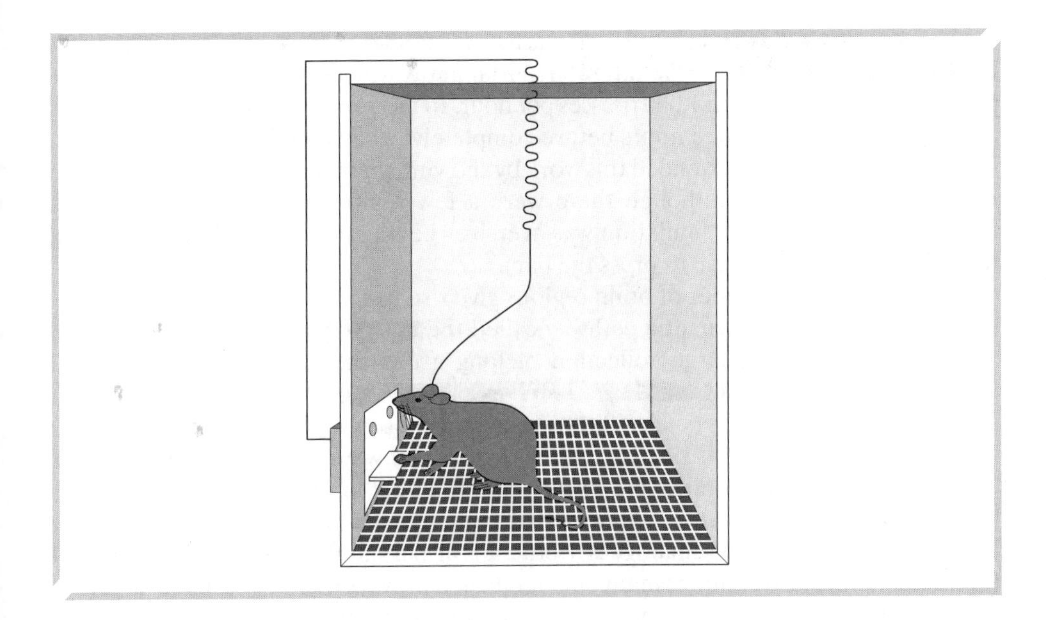

Figure 11.1 Experimental set-up for intracranial self-stimulation.

words, despite being hungry the animal would wait for the brain stimulation. Thus, there seemed to be little doubt that the electrical stimulation was highly rewarding.

Following this discovery, Olds and Milner developed a simpler and even more efficient procedure of testing and recording the effects of brain stimulation (see Figure 11.1). In short, they used an operant situation in which every bar press (or combination of bar presses) made by the animal triggered a train of electrical impulses to its brain via a lead which emerged through the ceiling of the chamber. The animal required little training to perform the task (i.e. it simply had to learn to press the lever) and, moreover, it had full control over the stimulation it received. In turn, the experimenters could estimate the extent of the reward by recording the number of bar presses that the rat was prepared to make to obtain stimulation. With this technique, Olds and Milner (1954) effectively opened up a new field of research that allowed the reward systems of the brain to come under close scrutiny.

The medial forebrain bundle

One of the first things that researchers sought to discover about self-stimulation was the nature of the brain sites from which it could be elicited. Indeed, it was soon found that sites capable of supporting self-stimulation were not confined to the septal area, but were found throughout the brain. In particular, Olds and Milner found that high rates of self-stimulation could be obtained from the **septum**, **amygdala** and anterior **hypothalamus** (in the region of 500 bar presses per hour), whereas more moderate levels of responding (200 bar presses per hour) were obtained from nearby structures including the **hippocampus, cingulate gyrus** and **nucleus accumbens**. However, by far the most impressive region of all was the **lateral hypothalamus** which sometimes produced bar pressing rates of more than 1,000 presses per hour. In fact, one rat made 2,000 responses per hour for 24 consecutive hours before completely exhausting himself (Olds 1958). Other investigators also extended this work by showing that many other sites could give rise to self-stimulation, although there were a few regions (including some of the 'reward' centres) where stimulation was aversive (i.e. the animal would try to escape from the situation or refuse to press the bar).

Although a large number of brain regions give rise to self-stimulation, most contribute to a massive multisynaptic pathway called the **medial forebrain bundle** (Figure 11.2) which contains a large collection of long axons that connect brainstem and midbrain regions (such as **ventral tegmental area** and **periaqueductal grey region**) with a variety of forebrain areas (such as **limbic system, striatum** and **neocortex**). In fact, the medial forebrain bundle is one of the few major pathways of the brain that passes between its higher (forebrain) and lower (midbrain and brainstem) regions, and has been likened to an interstate highway that connects the two coasts of a continent (Graham 1990). While this analogy is useful, it is also a simplification since the medial forebrain bundle also contains many smaller axon pathways that help connect adjacent regions (such as the neural link between the lateral hypothalamus and the septal area). Thus, the medial forebrain bundle is not only an important interstate route, but it is also an extremely complex road system (containing in the region of 50 different fibre systems) that allows communication over a large area.

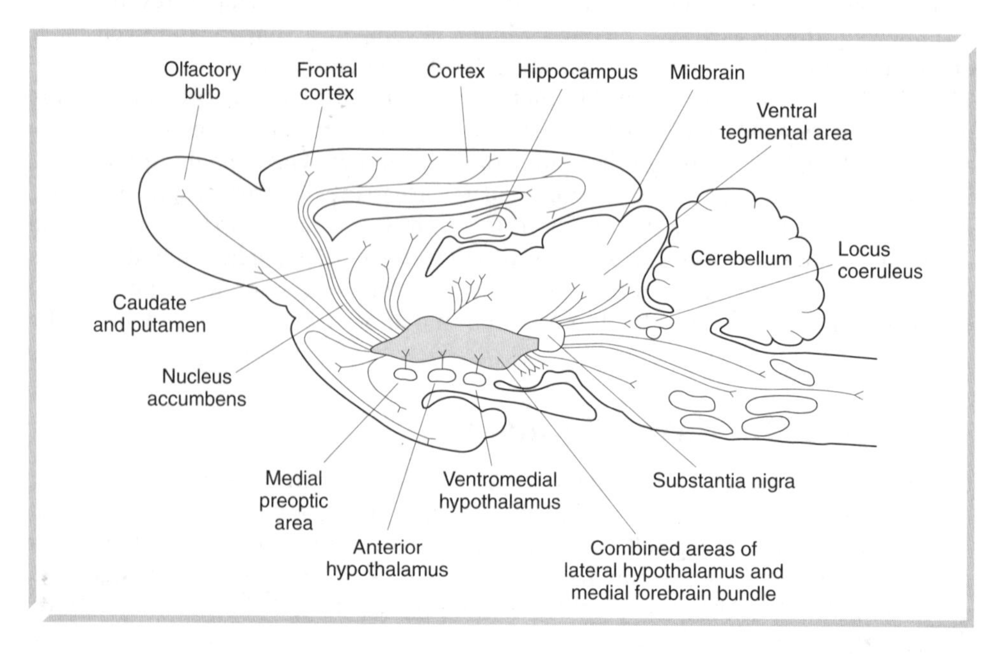

Figure 11.2 The medial forebrain bundle.

Although it would be wrong to assume that the medial forebrain bundle is only involved in reward and reinforcement (e.g. it has a wide range of functions as shown by the fact that the nigral–striatal pathway forms part of this system), it nevertheless remains that this system sends branches to practically every area from which self-stimulation can be obtained. Thus, on first sight at least, the medial forebrain bundle would appear to play a very important role in reward. Moreover, situated right at the heart of the medial forebrain bundle is the lateral hypothalamus which, as we have seen above, gives rise to exceptionally high levels of self-stimulation. Indeed, this fact led to one of the first theories of medial forebrain function by Olds and Olds (1963) who proposed that this system acted to collect information about reinforcement from a wide range of brain sites (governing such activities as eating, drinking, aggression, sexual behaviour and sleep), and to channel this information to the lateral hypothalamus which provided the most important rewarding (and drive-reducing) event in reinforcement. Thus, the medial forebrain bundle was seen as the brain's reward system with the lateral hypothalamus providing the most important terminus (and reward site) for its many converging pathways. However, as we shall see below, this theory is now known to be incorrect.

Problems with the medial forebrain bundle hypothesis

If the medial forebrain bundle is the critical structure underlying reward, then it follows that damage to this system should abolish the effects of self-stimulation. In 1966, Valenstein and Campbell attempted to examine this question by looking at the effects of septal self-stimulation in animals that had most of their medial forebrain bundle lesioned. In fact, they managed to destroy over 90 per cent of its cell bodies and axons, which also included the complete destruction of the lateral hypothalamus. Despite this, lesioned animals still continued to show high rates of self-stimulation when the electrodes were placed into the septal area. Thus, it appeared that the lateral hypothalamus (nor indeed any portion of the medial forebrain bundle) was not essential for septal self-stimulation to occur. This suggested that other pathways lying outside the medial forebrain bundle were also involved in reward.

Further support for this idea has come from research showing that self-stimulation can also be evoked by a number of brain structures that do not appear to contribute to the medial forebrain bundle. These regions include the **cerebellum**, **thalamus** and numerous sites in the basal ganglia and cerebral cortex. Indeed, another brain area which also gives rise to particularly high rates of self-stimulation and yet appears to be largely independent of the medial forebrain bundle (although there are anatomical connections between the two) is the **medial frontal cortex**. For example, lesions of the medial forebrain bundle do not disrupt medial frontal cortex stimulation, and it has also been shown that self-stimulation of the frontal cortex produces a pattern of neural activity (as shown by the uptake of **2-deoxyglucose**) in the brain that is very different to that obtained with medial forebrain stimulation (Yadin *et al.* 1983). Thus, the medial forebrain bundle is not the only reward system in the brain.

Box 11.1 THE EFFECTS OF SELF-STIMULATION IN HUMANS

Although most of the research examining self-stimulation has been undertaken on animals, there are instances where this procedure has also been performed with humans (e.g. some researchers have experimented with this technique as a form of treatment for especially severe forms of schizophrenia and depression, or as therapy for intractable pain). Indeed, because the brain contains no pain or touch receptors, electrodes can be positioned into an awake patient without discomfort (providing the scalp is anaesthetised beforehand). And, similar to animal research, these studies have shown that humans have their own reward systems which can give rise to high rates of self-stimulation.

One of the first studies to use this technique was undertaken by Heath (1954) who examined 23 schizophrenic patients and found that electrical stimulation of the septal region produced alertness, euphoria and a feeling of pleasure. In a further study, two patients were given the opportunity to self-stimulate themselves by pressing a button which delivered short trains of electrical stimulation to their brain. The results showed that self-stimulation of the amygdala, caudate nucleus and tegmental area elicited rates of 224–488 presses per hour. Further, not only did these two patients report that the self-stimulation 'felt good' and was pleasurable, but when made to the septal region (which also included the nucleus accumbens) it elicited sexual thoughts – with one patient reporting that the stimulation was building to a sexual orgasm! In another study, the strength of brain stimulation was shown by a patient who ignored an attractive tray of food while self-stimulating, even though he had not eaten for 7 hours (Heath 1964).

Not all brain regions, however, give rise to pleasurable sensations. For example, emotional feelings such as euphoria, pleasure and sexual excitement are rarely evoked by electrical stimulation of the surface of the cerebral cortex (Penfield and Jasper 1954). Instead, cortical stimulation typically produces sensory and motor changes as well as memory 'flashbacks'. In this respect, it is also interesting to note that Penfield found that repeated stimulation at the same cortical site often produced different 'memories', and that the removal of this tissue failed to destroy the memory for the experiences that had been elicited (Penfield 1958). In other words, it would appear that our memories are not stored in any one particular place.

The role of noradrenaline in reward

As well as examining the neuroanatomical basis of reward in the brain, researchers have also looked at the role of its various chemical pathways. This approach first began in the early 1960s when investigators began to map out **catecholaminergic** (**noradrenaline** and **dopamine**) **pathways** in the brain using **histofluorescence techniques** (see Chapter 1). One of the striking features to emerge from this work was the discovery that catecholaminergic pathways closely followed the distribution of sites that gave rise to self-stimulation. In fact, almost every catecholaminergic pathway that passed from the midbrain to forebrain was found to travel in the medial forebrain bundle, indicating that they were importantly involved in reinforcement. This view was supported when it was found that drugs that increased activity in catecholaminergic systems (such as amphetamine), or those that had **agonist** actions (e.g. which mimic the effects of noradrenaline and dopamine), increased the rate of responding to rewarding brain stimulation. In contrast, drugs which depleted the brain of catecholamines (such as reserpine), or those with **antagonist** actions at receptors (such as chlorpromazine) had the opposite effect (Stein 1962).

But what type of catecholamine was more important in reward – noradrenaline or dopamine? Although this was an important question, it was not easy to answer with traditional lesioning approaches because many of the regions that elicited self-stimulation received integrated projections from both systems. In addition, many of the drugs that were initially used to examine catecholaminergic function (such as amphetamine and reserpine) affected both noradrenaline and dopamine. Thus, the first attempts (in the early 1960s) to understand the role of catecholamines in reward were frustrated by these problems.

One way of examining whether catecholamines are involved in reinforcement is to measure their levels following self-stimulation. In short, if rewarding brain stimulation is dependent upon the release of catecholamines, then it follows that levels of noradrenaline and dopamine should increase following this procedure. This hypothesis was examined by Stein and Wise (1969) who extracted noradrenaline from a number of brain sites that were known to elicit self-stimulation. In order to do this, these researchers implanted **push–pull cannulae** (essentially double-barrelled tubes) into the brain, through which fluid was introduced ('pushed') to pick up various neurochemicals in the vicinity of the cannula tip – and then withdrawn ('pulled') for collection and chemical analysis (see Figure 11.3). Using this technique, Stein and Wise found that when they stimulated the medial forebrain bundle (at a site which they knew to be rewarding for the animal), a marked increase of noradrenaline was obtained from the lateral hypothalamus and amygdala. In other words, this appeared to show that noradrenaline was the crucial neurotransmitter in reward.

Stein and Wise (1971) also provided further evidence to support the noradrenaline hypothesis. The formation of noradrenaline in neuron terminals is known to involve a number of chemical steps, one of which requires the formation of dopamine, that is converted into noradrenaline by the enzyme dopamine-β-hydroxylase. When Stein and Wise injected their animals with a drug called disulphiram which inhibited

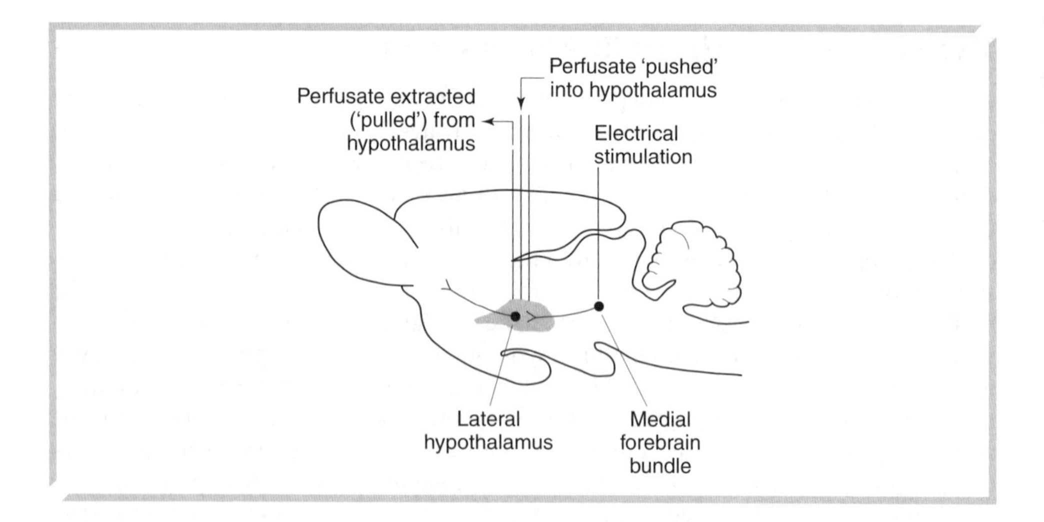

Figure 11.3 The push–pull experimental set-up used by Stein and Wise.

dopamine-*β*-hydroxylase activity (thereby reducing the release of noradrenaline, but not dopamine) they found that this inhibited self-stimulation. Moreover, this behaviour was quickly reinstated following the administration of noradrenaline. Thus, this appeared to show that noradrenaline, not dopamine, was the catecholaminergic mediator of reward.

However, not all evidence supported this interpretation. For example, lesions of the dorsal bundle (the pathway that arises from the locus coeruleus and provides the most important noradrenergic input to the medial forebrain bundle) were found to have little effect on self-stimulatory behaviour (Clavier and Routtenberg 1975). In addition, the interpretation of the above study by Stein and Wise (1971) was questioned when it was found that disulfiram-treated animals, if aroused by the handling of an experimenter, would respond by a burst of bar pressing if placed in an operant chamber. This finding suggested to some researchers (e.g. Roll 1970) that disulfiram caused sedation, and that noradrenaline mediated arousal rather than reward. Indeed, the development of two drugs (called FLA-63 and U-14625) which had a similar action to disulfiram (but with fewer side effects) were found to have little effect on self-stimulation despite substantially depleting the brain of noradrenaline (Olds and Forbes 1981). In addition, the arousal theory of noradrenergic function is further supported by its involvement in sleep (see Chapter 6), and by the fact that noradrenaline pathways are widely distributed throughout the brain, and not just at its reward sites.

The role of dopamine in reward

Although many of the substances that were initially used to examine the role of catecholamines in reward had effects on both noradrenaline and dopaminergic systems, during the early 1970s a number of drugs were developed (including pimozide and spiroperidol) that were highly selective in blocking dopamine (but not noradrenergic) receptors. And, importantly, these agents were also found to be effective in reducing self-stimulation from a number of brain sites including the lateral hypothalamus, septal area, nucleus accumbens and ventral tegmental area (Wauquier 1976). The involvement of dopamine in reward and pleasurable sensations was further supported when it was found that the feelings of euphoria produced by amphetamine in humans could be eliminated by dopaminergic (although not noradrenergic) antagonists (Wise and Bozarth 1984).

Unlike noradrenaline, dopamine neurons are not as widely distributed in the brain, and are largely confined to pathways that project from areas of the midbrain (substantia nigra and ventral tegmental area) to certain regions of the forebrain (striatum, limbic system and frontal cortex). In fact, all of these areas give rise to high rates of self-stimulation, which lends further support to the theory that dopamine is crucially involved in reward. Despite this, there is a serious methodological difficulty with the dopamine theory and that is: drugs that inhibit self-stimulation (e.g. dopamine antagonists) are also known to depress motor activity. In other words, it may be that dopaminergic antagonists inhibit self-stimulation not by reducing the sensation of reward, but because the animal has difficulty moving or making the appropriate response (e.g. lever pressing).

It has proved surprisingly difficult to completely rule out this explanation as a cause of behaviour in self-stimulation experiments, although there is now good evidence to show that the motor depressant effects of dopaminergic drugs do not explain all aspects of reduced responding. For example, Rolls (1975) has pointed out that injections of the dopaminergic antagonist spiroperidol (at a dose of 0.05 mg/kg) has little effect on reducing self-stimulation from electrodes placed in the ventral tegmental area, whereas the same dose significantly reduces the response produced by nucleus accumbens stimulation. Clearly, if spiroperidol simply acted to suppress movement then these two different effects should not occur.

Another way of examining dopaminergic involvement in reward is to use **lesioning** approaches. One pathway that has attracted considerable attention is the **mesolimbic system** that arises from the ventral tegmental area and which projects to limbic regions such as the nucleus accumbens, septum and amygdala, all of which are known to give rise to very high rates of self-stimulation. When Philips and Fibiger (1978) looked at the effects of tegmental stimulation in rats that had received chemical lesions of mesolimbic pathway, they found that self-stimulation was attenuated. In other words, the mesolimbic neurons probably provide the main pathway for mediating the effects of ventral tegmental stimulation.

Finally, there is yet another way researchers can examine the role of dopamine in reward. In short, if it is involved in mediating reinforcement, then levels of dopamine in the brain should increase following self-stimulation. Unfortunately, dopamine is quickly broken down after its release making it difficult to measure, and consequently researchers have to use other means to assess its activity. One of the most frequently used techniques is to measure the ratio of DOPAC (one of dopamine's main breakdown products) with dopamine. In short, as the ratio of DOPAC to dopamine increases, the greater the presumed release (or turnover) of dopamine. In support of the dopamine theory of reward, it has been found that the DOPAC ratio increases significantly in both the nucleus accumbens (part of the mesolimbic pathway) and frontal cortex following bouts of self-stimulation using electrodes placed in the ventral tegmental area (Fibiger and Philips 1987).

Chemical self-stimulation

Some of the most dramatic evidence implicating dopamine in reward has come from experiments where animals have been allowed to inject themselves with chemical agents. Instead of using electrical stimulation, animals can also be made to work (e.g. by pressing a lever) to turn on a pump that injects a drug directly into their veins (or brain) by means of a flexible plastic tube (Weeks 1962). This procedure has, in fact, proved to be very useful for examining the addictive potential of drugs as many of the substances that animals self-administer are also those that are abused by humans. One class of drugs that give rise to particularly high rates of self-injection are those that increase dopaminergic activity, including amphetamine (which acts to release dopamine from its nerve terminals) and cocaine (which among its many effects is a highly selective uptake blocker for dopamine).

Cocaine, in particular, has a marked effect in this type of paradigm. Not only do animals typically learn to self-administer cocaine more readily than any other drug, but they are also prepared to work harder for it. For example, in one study involving monkeys (reported by McKim 1991) the rewarding property of cocaine was compared with a number of other drugs by using a progressive ratio procedure in which the animals had to increase their bar presses by 50 every time they received a reinforcement. In other words, the task is effectively designed so that the monkey has to progressively work harder for each reward until the demand becomes so great that the responding stops. And, presumably, the more reinforcing a drug is, the more responses it will make. In fact, it was found that in 4 out of 6 monkeys, cocaine was the most reinforcing drug tested, and one monkey was even prepared to press the lever 6,400 times to obtain a cocaine reinforcement.

In another study (Deneau *et al.* 1969), monkeys were allowed unlimited access to cocaine 24 hours a day – a situation that resulted in such a high rate of self-administration that many suffered from convulsions and died within 30 days. To avoid this problem, the researchers restricted the maximum intake of cocaine to 1 dose (1.0 mg/kg) per hour. Although this schedule stopped the fatal overdosing, the animals nevertheless self-administered the drug around the clock until exhaustion occurred (typically some 2–5 days into the experiment), following which the drug taking started again. Thus, the monkeys' behaviour showed a great deal of fluctuation with sessions of high cocaine intake along with periods of abstinence. Interestingly, a similar type of pattern often occurs with humans, showing that this procedure has relevance for understanding our own drug-taking behaviour.

Cocaine not only blocks the re-uptake of dopamine, but also inhibits the uptake of noradrenaline and serotonin. In addition, it acts as a local anaesthetic and appears to increase catecholamine receptivity sensitivity. Thus, we must be cautious about assuming that cocaine exerts its rewarding effect by selectively working on dopamine systems. Nevertheless, considerable evidence indicates that dopamine is the most important neurotransmitter underlying the reinforcing actions of cocaine. For example, a number of other highly specific dopaminergic drugs can be used to elicit self-stimulation, and to substitute for cocaine in this procedure (Wise 1987). Conversely, drugs that selectively block dopaminergic receptors (particularly D-2) abolish the rewarding properties of cocaine in animals (Kuhar *et al.* 1991). This effect also appears to apply to humans. For example, pretreatment with the D-2 antagonist haloperidol has been shown to reduce the 'high' produced by intravenous cocaine, although it does not appear to stop the 'rush' that immediately follows the injection (Sherer *et al.* 1989). It has also been found that haloperidol reduces craving in addicts when they are exposed to cues that are normally associated with cocaine administration (Berger *et al.* 1996). Thus, enhanced dopaminergic activity appears to explain at least some of the pleasurable sensations of cocaine, and the cravings associated with its use.

The neuroanatomy of dopaminergic reinforcement

If cocaine exerts its rewarding effect by its action on blocking the re-uptake of dopamine (thus increasing the amount of dopamine in the synapse), then clearly this event must be taking place at some point within the dopamine pathways of the brain. But where exactly? The answer appears to be surprisingly simple: it is a part of the mesolimbic dopamine pathway called the nucleus accumbens. Evidence in support of this theory has come from work which shows that infusion of dopaminergic blocking drugs into the nucleus accumbens, not only reduces reward produced by medial forebrain bundle stimulation (Stellar and Corbett 1989), but also that caused by intravenous self-administration of cocaine (Philips and Broekkamp 1980). The same effect, however, is not obtained with similar injections into the frontal cortex (the mesofrontal pathway) or caudate nucleus (the nigral–striatal pathway), showing that it is the nucleus accumbens which provides the crucial site for cocaine's rewarding effects. Also lending further support to this theory is research showing that cocaine self-administration is attenuated by lesions of the nucleus accumbens (Roberts *et al.* 1977) and ventral tegmental area (Roberts and Koob 1982) – but not prefrontal cortex (Martin-Iverson *et al.* 1986).

It might come as a surprise, therefore, to find that animals do not work (e.g. bar press) to obtain cocaine infusion into the nucleus accumbens (although they will do so for amphetamine and other dopaminergic agonists). One possible explanation is that direct injections of cocaine into the nucleus accumbens produce a local anaesthetic effect – although to confuse the issue, rats will self-administer cocaine into the medial prefrontal cortex (Goeders and Smith 1983). Thus, clearly there are other dopamine pathways involved in reward (and cocaine has an effect on them), although it probably is the case that the nucleus accumbens provides the most important site for producing cocaine's pleasurable (and reinforcing) effects. Further support for this idea has come from studies that have measured dopamine levels in various brain sites (using **micro-dialysis**) following intravenous injections of cocaine. For example, it has been shown that moderate doses of cocaine (1 mg/kg) produce an increase of dopamine in the nucleus accumbens, whereas higher doses (2 mg/kg) produce an increase in the prefrontal cortex – but still to a much lesser degree than that found in the accumbens (Fibiger *et al.* 1992).

The reward circuits of the brain revisited

The above evidence suggests that one reason why stimulation of the medial forebrain bundle is reinforcing is because it increases activity in dopamine pathways that originate in the ventral tegmental area. However, as we saw earlier, stimulation of the lateral hypothalamus and septal area also produces reward. How then does this fit into the picture of the medial forebrain bundle previously described? Part of the answer seems to be that the lateral hypothalamus (and other medial forebrain structures) also mediate reward through their effect on dopaminergic systems. For example, Stellar and Corbett (1989) injected a dopamine antagonist into 56 different sites throughout the brain, and found that only one area, the nucleus accumbens, had any effect on reducing the rewarding effects of lateral hypothalamic stimulation. Conversely, injections of amphetamine into the nucleus accumbens have been shown to enhance self-stimulation of the hypothalamus (Spencer and Stellar 1986). Also, importantly, there are reports of lateral hypothalamic stimulation producing an increased release of dopamine in the nucleus accumbens (Stellar 1990).

How then does the lateral hypothalamus (and the many fibre systems that travel through this region of the brain) affect dopaminergic functioning? The answer appears to be through a pathway that projects down into the ventral tegmental area (see Figure 11.4). For example, Bielajew and Shizgal (1986) inhibited neuronal activity in the ventral

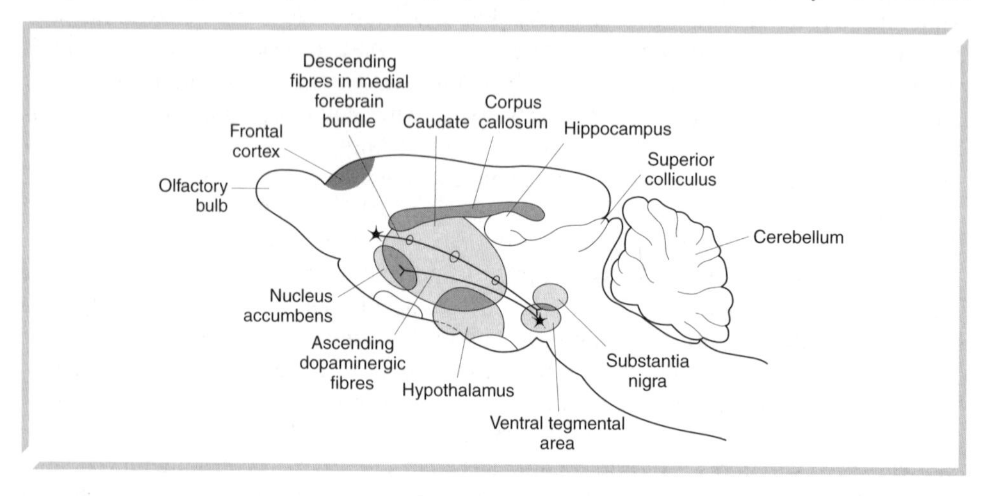

Figure 11.4 Diagram showing how descending fibres of the medial forebrain bundle are able to influence ascending dopaminergic systems which have their cell bodies in the ventral tegmental area. (*Source*: From R. B. Graham, *Physiological Psychology*. Copyright © 1990 by Wadsworth Inc. Reprinted by permission.)

tegmental area by means of an electrode that used hyperpolarising (negative) current, and found that this blocked the effects of lateral hypothalamic self-stimulation. The simplest interpretation of this finding is that fibres travelling 'downwards' through the medial forebrain bundle (including those from the lateral hypothalamus) synapse in the ventral tegmental area which, in turn, exerts an excitatory effect on the ascending dopamine pathways – thereby causing increased dopamine release in forebrain regions such as the nucleus accumbens.

These results suggest that the dopamine pathways arising from the ventral tegmental area provide the final common pathway for reward in the brain (Wise 1980). If this hypothesis is correct, then clearly all rewarding stimuli should activate the tegmental dopamine systems, although this does not appear to be the case. For example, although lesioning of the nucleus accumbens abolishes the rewarding effects of cocaine, it has no effect on operant responding for food reward (Roberts *et al.* 1977). Even more problematical is the finding that huge lesions of the forebrain that destroy most of the dopamine terminals of the nucleus accumbens, septum, striatum and frontal cortex, have relatively little effect on reducing lateral hypothalamic stimulation (Colle and Wise 1987; Stellar 1990). There is also other evidence: for example, studies that have looked at the uptake of radioactive 2-deoxyglucose in brain neurons following lateral hypothalamic stimulation, have not found increased metabolic activity in the nucleus accumbens, although increased activity was seen in other regions (Gallistel 1986).

Perhaps the safest conclusion to draw from this research is that dopamine and the nucleus accumbens have important roles to play in reward produced by medial forebrain bundle stimulation, although dopamine is not the only neurotransmitter, and the accumbens not the only brain site, involved in producing this effect. And, although the nucleus accumbens appears to be crucial for producing the rewarding effects of cocaine, there are undoubtedly other brain regions lying outside the medial forebrain bundle that are also involved in reward processes.

The opiates and reward

The '**opiates**' refer to any substance, natural or synthetic, that has properties similar to opium (which includes morphine and heroin) and they are the classic example of an addictive class of drugs. For example, heroin may cause such dependence, both mentally and physically, that the user's life revolves around obtaining the drug. Moreover, to maintain the habit, the addict may turn to crime to obtain funds to buy the drug which, in turn, exerts a massive toll on society. Indeed, it has been estimated that there are over 100,000 heroin addicts in the UK (ISDD 1992) and that at least £15 million worth of goods are stolen every day to fund illegal usage (Tyler 1986). But why do users take the drug in the first place? One reason is that opiate substances can be 'rewarding' and produce feelings of pleasure (e.g. injections of heroin often produce a 'rush' which is sometimes described as 'orgasmic' by its users). Thus, we might predict that opiates should have important effects on dopamine and the reward systems of the brain.

Almost nothing was known about how opiates worked until the early 1970s when natural (or 'endogenous') opiate substances were discovered in the brain by Hans

Kosterlitz and his colleagues in Aberdeen (Hughes *et al.* 1975). This had been preceded by the discovery that the brain also contained receptors for these substances (Pert and Snyder 1973) which implied that they served a neurotransmitter (or neuromodulatory) type of role. When the locations of these opiate receptors were mapped out, it was found that particularly high amounts were found in the limbic system, ventral tegmental area and nucleus accumbens – that is, areas closely linked with the dopaminergic reward systems. In other words, this suggested that opiate drugs might produce their pleasurable effects by acting on dopamine systems.

Indeed, support for this theory has come from experiments showing that animals will quickly learn to lever press at high rates to obtain infusions of morphine into the ventral tegmental area, although this effect is not reliably obtained from other brain areas (Bozarth 1986). In fact, it is now clear that morphine acts to inhibit **GABA** neurons in the ventral tegmental area and, by doing this, they release dopaminergic neurons from their usual inhibition – and one consequence of this effect is an increase of dopamine release in the nucleus accumbens (Bozarth 1987). Further support for the involvement of dopamine in opiate use has come from findings showing that the injection of drugs that block opiate receptors (e.g. **naloxone**) into the ventral tegmental area, or nucleus accumbens, stops the rewarding effects of intravenous heroin in experimental animals (Vaccarino *et al.* 1985). Moreover, this effect is probably dependent on an intact nucleus accumbens as lesions of this structure also abolish the rewarding effects of heroin (Bozarth and Wise 1986).

Despite this, it appears that opiates are fairly specific in their effects on the reward systems of the brain since drugs that block opiate receptors, unlike dopaminergic antagonists, do not inhibit the rewarding effects of medial forebrain bundle stimulation (Wise and Bozarth 1984). This suggests that information from the medial forebrain bundle can reach the ventral tegmental area, and nucleus accumbens, without involving an opiate receptor (see Figure 11.5). Perhaps, opiate-containing neurons project into the ventral tegmental area from structures elsewhere, or maybe opiate-containing **interneurons** exist within the ventral tegmental area.

Although most of the evidence suggests that the dopaminergic link between the ventral tegmental area and the nucleus accumbens underlies the rewarding effects of opiates, there is still some degree of doubt over this conclusion. For example, Pettit *et al.* (1984) trained rats to self-administer cocaine and heroin on alternate days and then they lesioned the nucleus accumbens. Although this lesion completely abolished cocaine self-stimulation, it had little effect on heroin self-administration. Why this should happen is not clear, although it is relevant to note that cessation of morphine infusion into the ventral tegmental area does not result in withdrawal symptoms (such as shaking and hypothermia), whereas this does occur when animals stop receiving opiate injections into the periaqueductal grey area (Bozarth and Wise 1984). Indeed, as we shall see below, withdrawal symptoms (or rather their avoidance) have often been viewed as important in the maintenance of drug misuse in humans, and this may partially explain the results obtained above. At the very least this shows that addiction is too complex a state to be explained in terms of a single pathway or neurotransmitter.

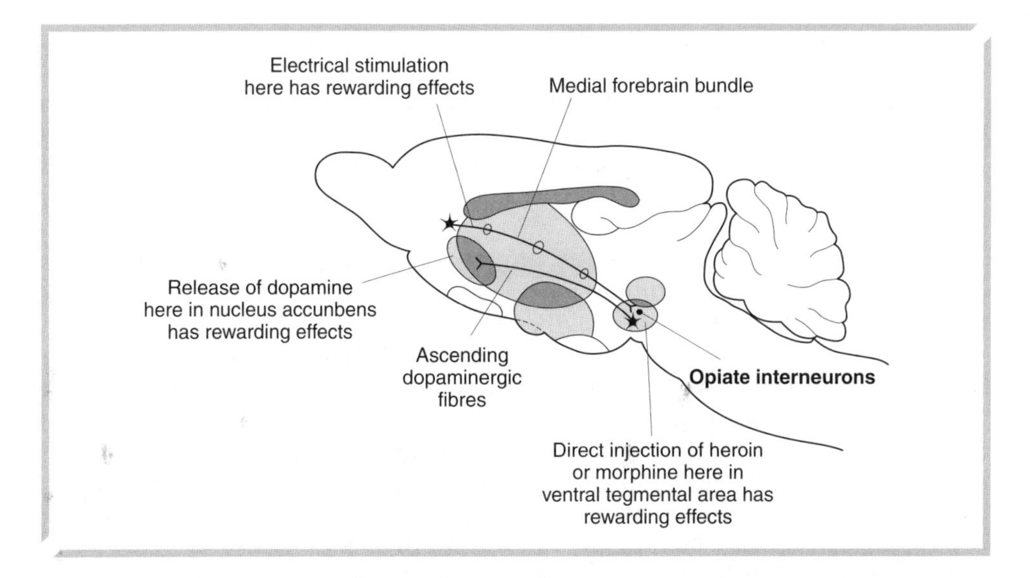

Figure 11.5 The role of opiate-containing interneurons in the ventral tegmental area.

What is meant by addiction?

The term 'addiction' first began to be associated with drug use in the late nineteenth century when the temperance and anti-opium movements started to use it as a replacement for words such as 'intemperance' and 'inebriety'. Around the same time alcohol and opiate misuse also began to be viewed as a medical problem, and not just simply as a moral issue or weakness of character, as had previously been the case. In this new 'enlightened' climate, addiction was quickly seen as an illness (or disease) over which the person had little control. Indeed, since three of the main problems associated with alcohol and opiate misuse were tolerance, withdrawal and craving (see below), it is perhaps not surprising that these were taken as the defining features of addiction (and have remained so). Nevertheless, these three aspects of drug use remain highly controversial – not because they do not occur, but because the medical view of addiction implies that they are all inevitable consequences of taking particular drugs which force us to behave in certain ways. In fact, no drug (not even heroin) has this type of power, and contrary to what one might expect (or have been told), the most important causes of addictive behaviour are psychological in nature and not biological.

Drug tolerance

Drug tolerance occurs when decreased sensitivity to a substance develops as a result of its continuous use. For example, many of us will remember the intoxicating effects of our first alcoholic drink as an adolescent, although it was probably not much later that increased consumption was needed to produce the same effect. In other words, tolerance occurs when a drug produces less of an effect than it did previously (or, put another way, it requires a higher dose to repeat the initial effect). This process is also seen at work in addiction. For example, it is not unusual for heroin addicts to increase their consumption tenfold (or more) over several months of regular use, and to reach a level of use that would kill a new (non-tolerant) individual several times over. Similarly, an alcoholic is often able to drink prodigious amounts of alcohol without becoming sick, somnolent or inebriated.

Obviously, there must be a biological component to drug tolerance. Indeed, when a drug is administered over a period of time, a number of adaptive physiological changes take place in the body. For example, the rate at which the drug is broken down (or metabolised) may be increased. This is called **metabolic tolerance** and is known to occur with alcohol consumption, when the liver increases its production of certain enzymes (such as alcohol dehydrogenase) to speed up its metabolism of alcohol. Another form of tolerance is **functional tolerance** which involves changes in the function of cells. For example, it may be that the neuron's receptors become less sensitive over time to the effects of a given drug, or that the properties of its membrane change in some way, or that they release less neurotransmitter. In fact, all these types of neural adaption are believed to play a role in the tolerance that occurs with heroin and alcohol.

Despite this, it may come as a surprise to find that biological factors do not fully account for tolerance, and that learning plays a vital (if not the most important) role in drug adaption. Indeed, this has been shown for several drugs, including alcohol. For example, in one study (Wenger *et al.* 1981), rats were given alcohol injections and placed on a moving treadmill which required them to maintain motor co-ordination. The results showed that the rats quickly became tolerant to the effects of alcohol on subsequent days of testing. However, when another group of rats were given exactly the same treadmill experience, but this time were given alcohol after each trial, it was found that they showed no tolerance to the disruptive effects of alcohol when they were switched to a trial where injections were given *before* the treadmill task. Because both groups of rats were given exactly the same amount of training and alcohol, it must have been the learning experience with the alcohol that was the crucial factor in the development of this form of tolerance.

Another important factor contributing to tolerance is the environment in which the drug is taken. Again, the effects of alcohol provide an example of how this can occur. In one experiment (Le *et al.* 1979) the effect of alcohol on producing hypothermia was examined in a number of rats that were given alcohol in one testing room and saline (salt water) in another. As expected, the administration of alcohol produced a decrease in body temperature, which became less severe over subsequent days with repeated injections (i.e. the rats became tolerant to this effect of alcohol). However, when the animals were given alcohol in the room in which they had previously been given saline, the alcohol produced its inital (non-tolerant) hypothermic effect. In other words, the tolerance was only associated with one particular testing room (see Figure 11.6). Moreover, the researchers also demonstrated another interesting effect: when saline was given to the animals in the 'alcohol' room they showed an increase in body temperature, or what is known as **conditioned compensatory response** (see also below).

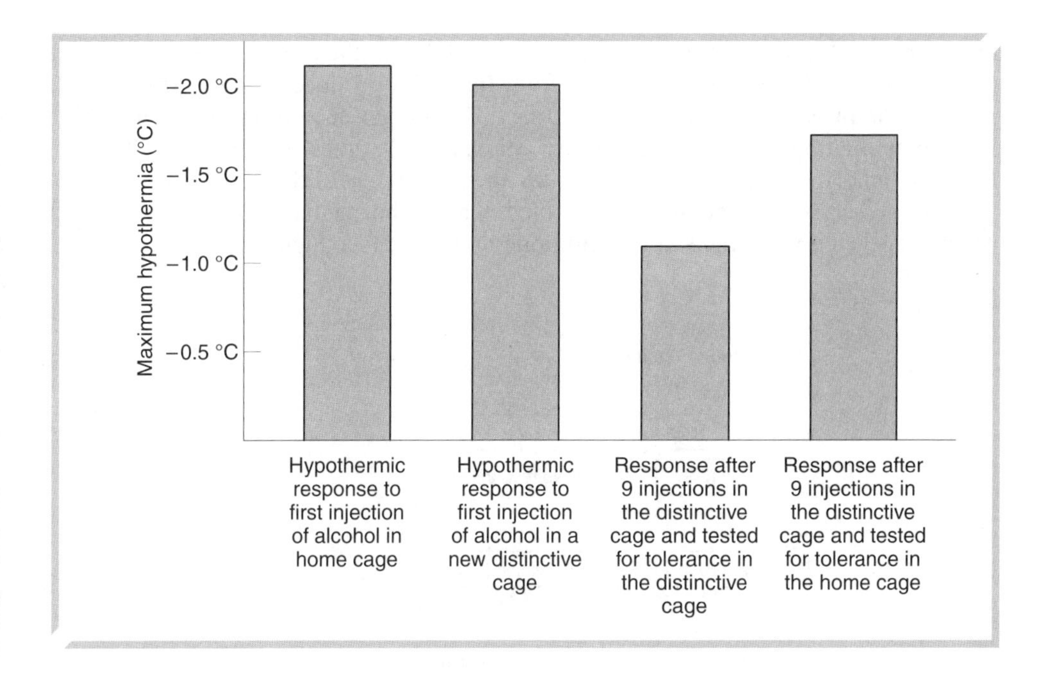

Figure 11.6 The situational specificity of tolerance to the hypothermic effects of alcohol. (*Source*: Adapted from A. D. Le *et al.*, *Science* (1979), **206**, 1109–10.)

It is clear, therefore, that situational factors and learning play an important role in the development of drug tolerance. But how can such an effect be explained? One of the most interesting theories has been proposed by Shepard Siegel who believes that the process comes about through a form of Pavlovian conditioning. Pavlov was originally a physiologist who won a Nobel Prize in 1904 for his work on digestion, and part of this work involved giving dogs food to elicit salivation. In Pavlovian terminology, the food could be viewed as the unconditioned stimulus (UCS), and salivation as the 'unlearnt' or unconditioned response (UCR). However, Pavlov also discovered that when he repeatedly paired the food (UCS) with the sound of a bell (the conditioned stimulus or CS), after several trials the bell alone would elicit salivation (the conditioned response or CR). In other words, the animal had learned that the bell was associated with food, and as a result it produced salivation in anticipation of being fed. This discovery was to have a great impact on the development of psychology since it offered a mechanistic theory of learning that fitted in well with the prevailing views of the time (e.g. Watson 1913).

According to Siegel, the development of drug tolerance comes about through a similar process – although it also differs in crucial respects to Pavlov's formulation. In short, Siegel sees the various environmental cues that regularly accompany the use of the drug (e.g. pubs, washrooms, needles, etc.) as conditioned stimuli (CSs) which elicit conditioned responses (CRs). But, what types of CRs are produced by these drug-related stimuli? In Pavlov's experiment the CR was the same as the original UR (i.e. salivation). Does this mean, therefore, that CRs produced by the drug stimuli produce the intoxicating effects of the drug? The answer according to Siegel is 'No'. Instead of eliciting feelings of drug intoxication, Siegel argues that drug stimuli (CSs) have the opposite effect, and they act to 'weaken' the effect of the drug on the person. That is, the CSs reduce the drug's probable impact rather than enhance it – a reaction which Siegel calls a compensatory conditioned response (see Figure 11.7).

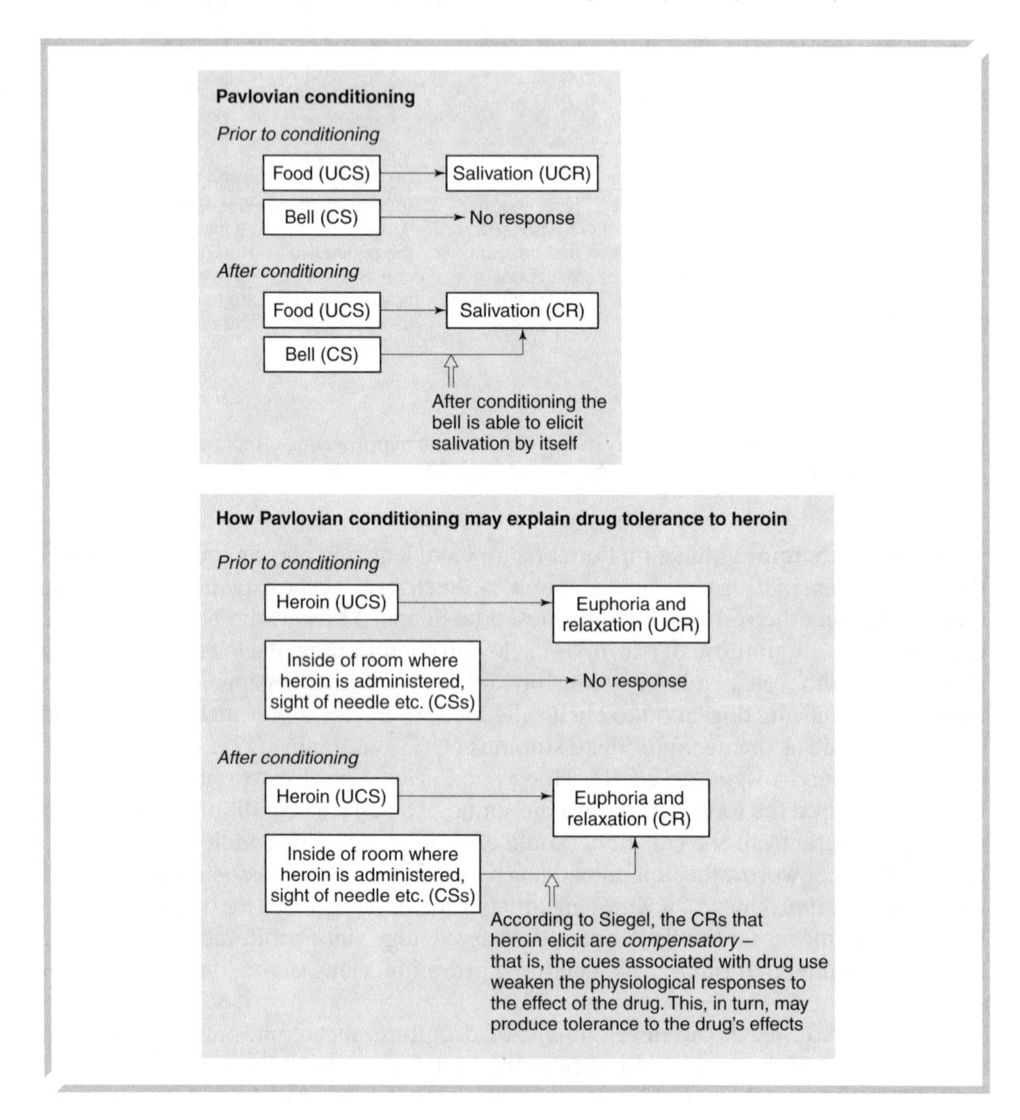

Figure 11.7 The differences between conditioned responses in Pavlovian conditioning and conditioned compensatory responses shown by Siegel.

Although at first this idea may not sound very plausible, it nevertheless helps to explain why tolerance occurs in certain environments that are associated with drug use. And it can also explain why drug administration in novel environments causes a reversal of tolerance (i.e. the compensatory conditioned responses no longer act to reduce the impact of the drug). Not only does this theory account for the findings obtained by Le *et al.* (1979) concerning the hypothermic effects of alcohol (discussed above), but it may also help to explain some puzzling aspects of human drug-taking behaviour (see Box 11.2). Thus, rather than being due to biological adaption, the evidence indicates that drug tolerance is essentially a type of learned behaviour.

Box 11.2 THE STRANGE CASE OF HEROIN OVERDOSES

Each year approximately 1 per cent of heroin addicts die from a heroin overdose, and in many cases the underlying cause of death is unclear. Many fatalities, of course, result from a pharmacological overdose, a lethal cocktail of drugs, or from heroin that has been adulterated (e.g. with quinine). However, there are also instances where these explanations do not account for the death of the heroin user. Indeed, many addicts die following a dose that would not be expected to be fatal from their previous drug experience – and there are even cases of fatal overdoses following self-administration of a quantity of heroin that had been well tolerated the preceding day.

One possible explanation is that tolerance to heroin is dependent upon the situation in which it is taken. That is, if heroin is repeatedly administered in the same environment, this will result in compensatory conditioned responses being formed to the situational cues that help produce tolerance – but, if taken in a new situation, these responses no longer occur, resulting in the previously obtained tolerance being 'lost'. To test this hypothesis, Siegel *et al.* (1982) administered increasing doses of heroin to rats over a period of 30 days, and then on the final day of testing, injected the animals with a high dose of heroin, either in their normal injection room or in a new distinctive environment. The results showed that 96 per cent of the animals died when given heroin in the novel situation, but only 64 per cent died when administered the same dose of heroin in their usual injection room.

But what about humans? To examine this question, Siegel (1984) interviewed 10 former heroin addicts from a methadone facility in New York whose medical records showed previous hospitalisation for a heroin overdose. These self-reports revealed that unusual circumstances had surrounded the overdose in seven of the survivors, which included two instances where heroin administration had taken place in locations where the addicts had never injected before. Despite this, these results must be viewed with a certain degree of caution. Not all researchers have replicated these findings, and other investigators have shown that compensatory conditioned responses do not account for all types of tolerance (e.g. see Gouldie and Griffiths 1984). Also common sense also tells us to be sceptical. For example, if we drink regularly in the same bar (say over a period of several weeks) and then find a new location, Siegel's theory would suggest that this is likely to prove a very intoxicating experience. For what it is worth, it is the impression of the author that this does not happen!

Drug dependence and withdrawal

The term 'dependence' is often used to refer to a state where the discontinuation of a drug causes withdrawal symptoms. This typically occurs when drug use is suddenly terminated after a long period of time, leading to unpleasant physiological reactions (which are often opposite to the effects produced by the drug) and psychological distress. In fact, some of the most severe withdrawal symptoms are seen following long-term alcohol and opiate use. For example, alcoholics may experience seizures, frightening hallucinations (delirium tremors), shaking and anxiety, whereas heroin addicts can suffer from general feelings of illness, pain and hypothermia. Moreover, the occurrence of such withdrawal problems has traditionally been seen by many as a powerful reason for the continuation of drug taking – especially as the symptoms are normally quickly relieved by the re-administration of the drug. Although this theory is now known to be far too simplistic (see below), it nevertheless remains that the ability to cause withdrawal symptoms is generally regarded as one of the most important defining features of an addicting drug, and the presence of physical dependence an important characteristic of an addict.

It is often assumed that the continued presence of a drug such as heroin or alcohol produces compensatory changes in the nervous system (similar to those that produce biological tolerance) which become withdrawal symptoms when the drug is suddenly discontinued. However, as with tolerance, there is also considerable evidence that the environment and psychological factors play an equally, if not more important, role in producing withdrawal. For example, it is not unusual for a 'clean' and drug-free heroin user to experience strong withdrawal symptoms (such as sweating, nausea and lacrimation) when placed back in an environment where drugs had previously been used or obtained.

Further evidence showing the importance of the social setting on drug taking has come from studies during the Vietnam War. For example, during the late 1960s and early 1970s it was estimated that at least 35 per cent of enlisted men were trying heroin while in Vietnam, and that half of these users were becoming addicted to it (Robins

1979). In response to these findings, the US army hastily set up treatment centres in Vietnam – although they were generally regarded as a 'total failure' (Zinberg 1984). Not surprisingly, when the full extent of this drug use was realised, it raised widespread fears in the USA that the addicted servicemen would bring their drug problems home with them. In fact, these fears did not materialise, and it was found that only 12 per cent of users were dependent on heroin some three years after returning to the USA. Clearly, it was the abhorrent social setting of Vietnam which led men who would not normally have considered using heroin to take it – and when this situation was alleviated by returning home, their drug craving was soon eliminated.

Although many people equate addiction with the spiral of drug taking and subsequent withdrawal, which leads to further drug use and so on, this conception is now known to be largely inaccurate. For instance, heroin withdrawal (which is often assumed to provide the classic example) has been described as one of the most misunderstood aspects of drug use (McKim 1991). In short, the withdrawal symptoms are often not as severe as many people believe, and typically involve flu-like symptoms with muscle tiredness, a runny nose and watery eyes. In heavy users there may also be restlessness and agitation – but very rarely as severe as that portrayed in films and in the media. Moreover, heroin withdrawal proceeds in predictable stages. It starts 6–12 hours after the last administration of the drug, peaks at 26–72 hours and, for the most part, is over within a week (McKim 1991). Clearly, if addiction was simply the result of physical withdrawal effects then it could easily be treated by hospitalising addicts for a few days until their symptoms had subsided. However, this form of treatment is not normally effective.

Although addicts sometimes take drugs to alleviate their withdrawal symptoms, this is rarely the primary motivating factor for their drug use. Rather, it is more often the case that people compulsively take drugs for personal reasons which results in psychological dependence on a substance. Perhaps the drug can make individuals feel more able to cope with their life, reduce anxiety, or increase confidence, and without this crutch they may feel unable to cope. In many cases, this type of psychological explanation provides a more accurate description of the reason why people become addicted to drugs (including heroin and alcohol) than simply the avoidance of withdrawal symptoms.

Other commonly abused drugs

Prior to our discussion of addiction, we had examined the effects of psychostimulants (such as amphetamine and cocaine), and opiates (such as heroin), on the reward systems of the brain, and in particular their effects on dopamine and the nucleus accumbens. But what about other drugs that have a reputation for being misused? Do they also have an effect on the reward systems of the brain, or do we have to find alternative explanations to account for their addictive potential? The answer to this question is not straightforward as different classes of drugs tend to have contrasting and varied pharmacological effects. Despite this, as we shall see, a case can be made for all the drugs discussed below to have at least some effect on dopamine systems (caffeine is perhaps the exception), which may help explain why they have a tendency to be misused.

Alcohol

It has been estimated that approximately 75 per cent of the population drink alcohol at least occasionally, and that 25 per cent of men and 15 per cent of women regularly drink more than is considered 'safe' (Hughes 1991). Although the term 'alcoholism' has no strict definition, a general feature is a *loss of control* of drinking accompanied by serious personal dysfunction or disability (Stoudemire 1998). Moreover, alcoholism is surprisingly common, with approximately 7–10 per cent of adults suffering this disorder in any one year (Gelder *et al.* 1996). But this is just the tip of the iceberg. For example, it has been estimated that around 80 per cent of people in prison have committed their offence while under the influence of alcohol (this is particularly true for violent crime), and that 50 per cent of drivers killed on the road have been drinking. In addition, there are around 100,000 arrests each year for drunkenness. Thus, although many people enjoy alcohol and use it responsibly, it is nevertheless a problem drug (Royal College of Psychiatrists 1986).

A large number of different types of alcohol are known to the chemist, although the form we normally drink (in diluted form) is **ethanol**. This is a very small molecule, soluble in both water and fat, which quickly becomes distributed throughout the body, including the brain where its net effect is to depress neural firing. Unlike most other psychoactive substances, alcohol does not bind to receptors or uptake mechanisms directly, but exerts its main effect by dissolving in the outer membrane of cells. This increases the fluidity of the membrane which, in turn, alters the function of the various structures embedded in this layer, including receptors, ion channels and various enzymes. Thus, by acting on the membrane in this relatively non-specific manner, alcohol is able to influence the functioning of the cell in many different ways.

Some of the structures, located in the membrane, that are particularly affected by alcohol are the ion channels which allow the transport of positively and negatively charged particles in and out of the neuron. For example, alcohol has been shown to decrease the influx of calcium into nerve endings which reduces neurotransmitter release, and to decrease the flow of sodium into the dendrites and cell body thereby inhibiting neural excitability (Ashton 1992). Moreover, alcohol also appears to exert an important effect on certain receptors that are closely linked with ion channels. For example, alcohol enhances the effects of GABA at its receptor thereby increasing the flow of negative chloride ions into the cell (this is believed to be an important mechanism by which alcohol causes neural inhibition). Among its many other effects, alcohol also activates the enzyme adenylate cyclase (involved in second messenger functions) and inhibits monoamine oxidase (an enzyme which is involved in the destruction of monoamine neurotransmitters).

If this wasn't complex enough, there is also evidence that it might not be alcohol *per se* that produces the most important psychoactive effects, but rather its metabolites. For example, alcohol is metabolised by the liver to produce acetaldehyde, which has been found to interact with catecholamines (especially dopamine) in the brain to form opiate-like substances called **tetrahydroisoquinolines** (TIQs). In fact, not only do TIQs act on opiate receptors, but they also appear to stimulate the release of dopamine from nerve endings (Hoffman and Cubeddu 1982). Despite this, the role of the TIQs in producing the psychoactive effects of alcohol remains highly controversial (Blum and Payne 1991).

Although alcohol acts throughout the brain, some sites are probably more important than others. One of the most sensitive regions to alcohol appears to be the reticular formation. For example, in low doses, alcohol appears to excite the reticular formation which, in turn, releases the cerebral cortex from its normal inhibition, resulting in increased euphoria and a deterioration of discrimination and judgement. However, as the dose of alcohol is increased, reticular activity becomes inhibited, and ataxia, slurred speech, stupor and eventually unconsciousness take over. But why should people consume alcohol in the first place? Interestingly, low doses of alcohol have been shown to increase the firing rate of neurons in the ventral tegmental area and to stimulate the release of dopamine in the nucleus accumbens (Feldman *et al.* 1997). Thus, alcohol has an effect on the reward systems of the brain that, to some extent at least, is similar to the effects of the stimulants and opiates – and this may help to explain why it has a tendency to be abused.

Nicotine

Nicotine is arguably one of the most addictive substances of all. It has been estimated that around 35 per cent of the population smoke in the UK, and although this figure has declined in recent years, it is nevertheless clear that smoking is on the increase in many countries, especially those of the third world. Unlike alcohol, the actions of nicotine on neurons are reasonably well understood as it acts on a specific type of cholinergic receptor that is sensitive to nicotine. However, because this nicotinic receptor is found in both the somatic and autonomic nervous systems, as well as throughout the brain, the biological effects of nicotine (or smoking) are extremely complex. For example, nicotinic receptors are found at the neuromuscular junction (where the effects of smoking can decrease both muscle tone and the strength of skeletal reflexes), and in the sympathetic nervous system (where nicotine increases heart rate and blood pressure, and causes a constriction of blood vessels in the skin). But nicotine probably has its greatest effect on the brain. For example, nicotine receptors are particularly abundant in the cerebral cortex, especially on the terminals of the ascending fibres that project from the reticular formation (indeed, this is probably one important reason why nicotine increases cortical arousal and stimulates EEG activity which makes the person feel more alert). In addition, high numbers of nicotinic receptors are also found in the ventral tegmental area, nucleus accumbens, striatum and substantia nigra.

It appears that nicotinic receptors are found predominantly on presynaptic nerve terminals where they act to enhance the release of a wide range of neurotransmitters. In particular, they are located on the endings of catecholaminergic neurons, especially those projecting to the cortex and limbic system. Although there are undoubtedly many reasons why people enjoy nicotine (e.g. to increase concentration or make the person feel more relaxed), it has nevertheless been shown that 90 per cent of chronic smokers find their habit highly pleasurable. Thus, we might expect to find that nicotine has an important effect on the reward systems of the brain. Indeed, this has been shown to be the case. For example, nicotine increases the release of dopamine in the nucleus accumbens at plasma concentrations that are similar to those found in smokers – although it appears that the amount of dopamine is less than that which occurs with cocaine or heroin (Di Chiara and Imperato 1988; Benwell 1990). In addition, it has been found that lesions of the nucleus accumbens reduce (although not abolish completely) the effects of nicotine self-stimulation in rats (Singer *et al.* 1982; Wise 1996a, b). Thus, increased stimulation of dopamine in the brain may provide one reason why smoking is so enjoyable (and difficult to give up).

Cannabis

According to Ernest Abel in his book *Marihuana: The First Twelve Thousand Years* (1980), of all the plants man has ever grown, none has been praised and denounced as often as marijuana (otherwise known as the hemp plant or *Cannabis sativa*). This plant, which grows as a weed and is cultivated all over the world, has been used for cloth and paper for centuries and was the most important source of rope until the development of synthetic fibres. The plant has also had innumerable other uses, but the one that concerns the legal authorities is its use as a psychoactive agent. In fact, cannabis is by far the most widely abused illegal drug in the UK, accounting for some 80 per cent of all drug convictions and 90 per cent of all seizures by HM Customs and Excise. Moreover, surveys show that around 20–30 per cent of all adults have tried cannabis at least once, with around 1.5 million people using it on a regular basis (General Household Survey 1988) – and this is despite the fact that cannabis is rated as a class B substance under the Misuse of Drugs Act (1971) with possession liable to result in a criminal conviction.

There are many psychoactive ingredients in cannabis (the marijuana plant contains around 460 such compounds) but the most important is a substance called **delta-9-tetrahydrocannabinol (THC)**. This substance is highly lipid (fat) soluble and rapidly enters the brain after it has been smoked. In small doses, THC results in a change in mood characterised by a sense of relaxation and well-being, often accompanied by loquaciousness and fits of giggling. In addition, the perception of visual and auditory stimuli is typically enhanced, and time perception is altered so that time appears to pass more slowly. Cannabis also impairs short-term memory, and this is often seen when users find it difficult to follow a long conversation. Larger doses of cannabis (especially if ingested by eating) can induce hallucinations, delusions and feelings of paranoia. In this situation, thinking may also become extremely disorganised and euphoria becomes replaced by anxiety, which can reach panic proportions.

Similar to alcohol, THC (in large doses) has the ability to dissolve in the fatty part of the neural membrane thus producing a number of non-specific effects. However, unlike alcohol, a receptor also exists for THC in the brain – and an endogenous cannabinoid substance for this receptor called **anadamide**, derived from the Sanskrit word for bliss, has also been discovered (the exact function of this substance is unknown although it may be involved in regulating neurotransmitter release). Thus, in low doses, THC probably produces most of its psychoactive effects by acting on cannabinoid receptors, and because these are found throughout the brain, it is clear that cannabis must produce a wide range of neurochemical effects. Nevertheless, one of its actions is to stimulate the release of dopamine. For example, Chen *et al.* (1990) injected rats with low doses of THC and found that this caused the release of dopamine in the nucleus accumbens and medial frontal cortex. Interestingly, THC's effect on the nucleus accumbens was blocked by injections of the opiate antagonist naloxone, indicating that THC may be producing its dopaminergic effect through the release of opioids. It is also relevant to note that very small traces of cannabinoids have been found in chocolate and may be one reason why this food is so popular (di Tomaso *et al.* 1996).

Caffeine

Caffeine belongs to a class of drugs known as the methylxanthines and is found in some of our most popular beverages and foods, including coffee, tea, fizzy drinks and chocolate. More than 80 per cent of the world's population, regardless of age, gender and culture, consumes caffeine daily, which makes it by far the most popular drug in the world. It has been estimated that the world uses 120,000 tons of caffeine per annum, with people in the UK consuming around 165 mg per person on a daily basis (made up of 118 mg from tea, 32 mg from coffee and 15 mg from other sources – Max 1986). Although widely perceived as harmless, it has nevertheless been argued that at ordinary levels of habitual use, caffeine is a risk factor for cardiovascular disease, poses a threat to foetal growth, interacts adversely with common therapeutic drugs, and can lead to dependence and withdrawal symptoms (James 1997). In other words, caffeine fulfils a number of criteria as a drug of abuse.

Why, then, do we drink caffeine-containing drinks? One reason is that caffeine is a stimulant. For example, a cup of coffee (which contains approximately 100–150 mg of caffeine) increases arousal, reduces fatigue and depresses sleep. Caffeine also has a reputation for enhancing vigilance and performance on cognitive tasks – and it increases heart rate, respiration, and the tension of skeletal muscles which helps in the undertaking of physical work. At higher doses caffeine can also produce feelings of tension and anxiety, and these feelings are sometimes produced (along with headache) if regular caffeine use is suddenly stopped. Although this type of withdrawal is normally only seen in heavy users, it can sometimes occur in individuals who consume as little as 100 mg of caffeine per day. Indeed, some researchers now believe that relief from withdrawal symptoms is a major factor in chronic coffee drinking, particularly with regard to the first cup in the morning.

The means by which caffeine exerts its stimulatory effects is still not fully understood. One effect of caffeine is as a phosphodiesterase inhibitor. Phosphodiesterase is an enzyme that controls the level of the second messenger cAMP in certain cells (especially those using noradrenaline in the autonomic nervous system) and this inhibition is known to cause cardiac stimulation and bronchodilation. However, very high doses of caffeine are needed to inhibit phosphodiesterase, and it is now accepted that caffeine is more likely to exert its biological effects by blocking **adenosine** receptors. Adenosine acts presynaptically on neurons in the body and the brain to inhibit the release of a wide range of neurotransmitters including acetylcholine, serotonin and the catecholamines. Thus, by blocking adenosine receptors, caffeine produces stimulatory effects (including the release of dopamine, noradrenaline and serotonin). Despite this, the reason for the popularity of caffeine from a pharmacological perspective is not clear. For example, it might be predicted that caffeine's effects on dopamine might provide an explanation for its use. However, there is much inconsistent data regarding this hypothesis. For example, although it has been found that the stimulatory effects of caffeine in animals are blocked by dopaminergic antagonists, it has also been shown that caffeine antagonises amphetamine-induced locomotor activity (Corrodi *et al.* 1972) and raises the threshold for electrical self-stimulation of the medial forebrain bundle (Mumford *et al.* 1988). In other words, alternative explanations probably have to be sought to explain caffeine's stimulant effects.

Self-test questions

1. What did Olds and Milner (1954) first discover?
2. Describe the main characteristics of the medial forebrain bundle.
3. According to Olds, what structure in the medial forebrain provided the most important site for reinforcement?
4. How did Stein and Wise (1969) implicate noradrenaline in reinforcing self-stimulation?
5. What evidence implicates dopamine in reinforcement?
6. Describe the main dopamine pathways in the brain.
7. How is it possible to get animals to self-administer drugs?
8. Describe some of the ways that cocaine is known to act on the brain.
9. In what ways do opiate substances affect dopamine functioning?
10. How does the medial forebrain bundle interact with the nucleus accumbens?
11. What is meant by drug tolerance and withdrawal?
12. How have psychological factors been implicated in drug tolerance?
13. Describe some of the pharmacological effects of alcohol.
14. Explain how nicotine may work on the reward systems of the brain.
15. What is the active psychoactive substance in cannabis?
16. How does caffeine produce its stimulatory effects?

Key terms

Addiction (p.345)
Adenosine (p.355)
Agonist (p.337)
Amygdala (p.333)
Anadamide (p.354)
Antagonist (p.337)
Caffeine (p.355)
Catecholaminergic pathways (p.337)
Cerebellum (p.335)
Cingulate gyrus (p.334)
Conditioned compensatory response (p.346)
Delta-9-tetrahydrocannabinol (p.354)
2-deoxyglucose (p.335)
Dopamine (p.337)
Drug dependence (p.350)

References

Abel, E. L. (1980) *Marihuana: The First Twelve Thousand Years.* New York: Plenum Press.

Ashton, H. (1992) *Brain Function and Psychotropic Drugs.* Oxford: Oxford University Press.

Benwell, R. B. (1990) The comparative effects of nicotine with other substances: A focus on brain dopamine systems. In Warburton, D. M. (ed.) *Addiction Controversies.* Chur: Harwood Academic Publishers.

Berger, S. P. *et al.* (1996) Haloperidol antagonism of cue-elicited cocaine craving. *Lancet*, **347**, 504–8.

Bielajew, C. and Shizgal, P. (1986) Evidence implicating descending fibers in self-stimulation of the medial forebrain bundle. *Journal of Neuroscience*, **6**, 919–29.

Blum, K. and Payne, J. E. (1991) *Alcohol and the Addictive Brain.* New York: The Free Press.

Bozarth, M. A. (1986) Neural basis of psychomotor stimulant and opiate reward: Evidence suggesting the involvement of a common dopaminergic system. *Behavioral Brain Research*, **22**, 107–16.

Bozarth, M. A. (1987) Ventral tegmental reward system. In Engel, J. and Oreland, L. (eds) *Brain Reward Systems and Abuse.* New York: Raven Press.

Bozarth, M. A. and Wise, R. A. (1984) Anatomically distinct opiate receptor fields mediate reward and physical dependence. *Science*, **244**, 516–17.

Bozarth, M. A. and Wise, R. A. (1986) Involvement of the ventral tegmental dopaminergic system in opioid and psychomotor stimulant reinforcement. In Harris, L. S. (ed.) *Problems of Drug Dependence 1985.* Washington, DC: US Government Printing Office.

Chen, J. *et al.* (1990) Tetrahydrocannabinol produces naloxone-blockade enhancement of presynaptic basal dopamine efflux in nucleus accumbens of conscious, freely moving rats as measured by intracerebral microdialysis. *Psychopharmacology*, **102**, 156–62.

Clavier, R. M. and Routtenberg, A. (1975) Brainstem self-stimulation attenuated by lesions of the medial forebrain bundle but not by lesions of locus coeruleus or the caudal ventral norepinephrine bundle. *Brain Research*, **101**, 251–71.

Colle, L. M. and Wise, R. A. (1987) Opposite effects of unilateral forebrain ablations on ipsilateral and contralateral hypothalamic self-stimulation. *Brain Research*, **407**, 285–93.

Corrodi, H. *et al.* (1972) Effects of caffeine on central monoamine neurons. *Journal of Pharmacy and Pharmacology*, **24**, 155–8.

Deneau, G. *et al.* (1969) Self-administration of psychoactive substances by the monkey. *Psychopharmacologia*, **16**, 30–48.

Di Chiara, G. and Imperto, A. (1988) Drugs abused by humans preferentially increase synaptic dopamine concentrations in the mesolimbic system of freely moving rats. *Proceedings of the National Academy of Sciences*, **85**, 5274–84.

Di Tomaso, E *et al.* (1996) Brain cannabinoids in chocolate. *Nature*, **382**, 677–8.

Feldman, R. S. *et al.* (1997) *Principles of Neuropsychopharmacology*. Sunderland, MA: Sinauer.

Fibiger, H. C. and Philips, A. G. (1987) Role of catecholamine transmitters in brain reward systems: Implications for the neurobiology of affect. In Engel, J. and Oreland, L. (eds) *Brain Reward Systems and Abuse.* New York: Raven Press.

Fibiger, H. C. *et al.* (1992) The neurobiology of cocaine-induced reinforcement. In Ciba Foundation Symposium 166. *Cocaine: Scientific and Social Dimensions.* Chichester: Wiley.

Gallistel, C. R. (1986) The role of the dopaminergic projections in MFB self-stimulation. *Behavioral Brain Research*, **20**, 313–21.

Gelder, M. *et al.* (1996) *Oxford Textbook of Psychiatry.* Oxford: Oxford University Press.

General Household Survey (1988) Quoted in *National Audit of Drug Misuse in Britain* (1992). London: ISDD.

Graham, R. B. (1990) *Physiological Psychology.* Belmont: Wadsworth.

Goeders, N. E. and Smith, J. E. (1983) Cortical dopaminergic involvement in cocaine reinforcement. *Science*, **221**, 773–5.

Gouldie, A. J. and Griffiths, J. W. (1984) Environmental specificity of tolerance (letter to the Editor). *Trends in Neurosciences*, **7**, 310–11.

Heath, R. G. (1954) *Studies in Schizophrenia: A Multidisciplinary Approach to Mind–Brain Relationships.* Cambridge, MA: Harvard University Press.

Heath, R. G. (1964) *The Role of Pleasure in Behavior.* New York: Hoeber.

Hoffman, I. S. and Cubeddu, L. X. (1982) Presynaptic effects of tetrahydropapaveroline on striatal dopaminergic neurons. *Journal of Pharmacology and Experimental Therapeutics*, **220**, 16–22.

Hughes, J. (1991) *An Outline of Modern Psychiatry.* Chichester: Wiley.

Hughes, J. T. *et al.* (1975) Identification of two related pentapeptides from the brain with potent opiate agonist activity. *Nature*, **258**, 577–9.

James, J. E. (1997) *Understanding Caffeine.* London: Sage.

Kuhar, M. J. *et al.* (1991) The dopamine hypothesis of the reinforcing properties of cocaine. *Trends in Neurosciences*, **14**, 299–302.
Le, A. D. *et al.* (1979) Conditioned tolerance to the hypothermic effect of alcohol. *Science*, **206**, 1109.
Leonard, B. E. (1992) *Fundamentals of Psychopharmacology.* Chichester: Wiley.
McKim, W. A. (1991) *Drugs and Behaviour.* Englewood Cliffs, NJ: Prentice Hall.
Martin-Iverson, M. T. *et al.* (1986) 6-hydroxydopamine lesions of the medial prefrontal cortex fail to influence intravenous self-administration of cocaine. *Psychopharmacology*, **88**, 310–14.
Max, B. (1986) This and that: Please the patient and pass the coffee. *Trends in Pharmacological Sciences*, 12–13.
Mumford, G. K. *et al.* (1988) Caffeine elevates reinforcement threshold for electrical brain stimulation: Tolerance and withdrawal changes. *Brain Research*, **459**, 163–7.
Olds, J. (1958) Satiation effects in self-stimulation of the brain. *Journal of Comparative and Physiological Psychology*, **51**, 675–8.
Olds, J. and Milner, P. (1954) Positive reinforcement produced by electrical stimulation of septal area and other regions of the rat brain. *Journal of Comparative and Physiological Psychology*, **47**, 419–27.
Olds, M. E. and Forbes, J. L. (1981) The central basis of motivation: Intracranial self-stimulation studies. *Annual Review of Psychology*, **32**, 523–74.
Olds, M. E. and Olds, J. (1963) Approach-avoidance analysis of rat diencephalon. *Journal of Comparative Neurology*, **120**, 259–95.
Penfield, W. (1958) *The Excitable Cortex in Conscious Man.* Springfield, IL: Thomas.
Penfield, W. and Jasper, H. (1954) *Epilepsy and the Functional Anatomy of the Human Brain.* Boston: Little Brown.
Pert, C. B. and Snyder, S. H. (1973) Properties of opiate-receptor binding in rat brain. *Proceedings of the National Academy of Sciences*, **70**, 2243–7.
Pettit, H. O. *et al.* (1984) Destruction of dopamine in the nucleus accumbens selectively attenuates cocaine but not heroin self-administration in rats. *Psychopharmacology*, **84**, 167–73.
Philips, A. G. and Broekkamp, C. L. E. (1980) Inhibition of intravenous cocaine self-administration by rats after micro-injection of spiroperidol into the nucleus accumbens. *Society for Neuroscience Abstracts*, **6**, 105.
Philips, A. G. and Fibiger, H. C. (1978) The role of dopamine in maintaining intracranial self-stimulation in the ventral tegmentum, nucleus accumbens and medial prefrontal cortex. *Canadian Journal of Psychology*, **32**, 58–66.
Roberts, D. C. S. and Koob, G. (1982) Disruption of cocaine self-administration following 6-hydroxydopamine lesions of the ventral tegmental area in rats. *Pharmacology, Biochemistry and Behavior*, **17**, 901–4.
Roberts, D. C. S. *et al.* (1977) On the role of the ascending catecholaminergic systems in intravenous self-administration of cocaine. *Pharmacology, Biochemistry and Behavior*, **6**, 615–20.
Robins, L. N. (1979) Vietnam veterans three years after Vietnam. In Brill, L. and Winick, C. (eds) *Yearbook of Substance Abuse.* New York: Human Science Press.

Rolls, E. T. (1975) *The Brain and Reward.* Oxford: Pergamon Press.

Roll, S. K. (1970) Intracranial self-stimulation and wakefulness: Effects of manipulating ambient catecholamines. *Science*, **168**, 1370–2.

Royal College of Psychiatrists (1986) *Alcohol: Our Favourite Drug.* London: Tavistock.

Sherer, M. A. *et al.* (1989) Effects of intravenous cocaine are partially attenuated by haloperidol. *Psychiatry Research*, **27**, 117–25.

Siegel, S. (1984) Pavlovian conditioning and heroin overdoses: Reports by overdose victims. *Bulletin of the Psychonomic Society*, **22**, 428–30.

Siegel, S. *et al.* (1982) Heroin 'overdose' death: Contribution of drug-associated environmental cues. *Science*, **216**, 436–7.

Singer, G. *et al.* (1982) Effect of dopaminergic nucleus accumbens lesions on the acquisition of schedule induced self-injection of nicotine in the rat. *Pharmacology, Biochemistry and Behavior*, **17**, 579–81.

Spencer, D. and Stellar, J. R. (1986) Accumbens infusion of amphetamine increases and picrotoxin decreases reward from hypothalamic stimulation. *Society for Neuroscience Abstracts*, **12**, 1142.

Stein, L. (1962) Effects and interaction of imipramine, chlorpromazine, reserpine and amphetamine on self-stimulation. *Recent Advances in Biological Psychiatry*, **4**, 288–308.

Stein, L. and Wise, C. D. (1969) Release of norepinephrine from hypothalamus and amygdala by rewarding medial forebrain bundle stimulation and amphetamine. *Journal of Comparative and Physiological Psychology*, **67**, 189–98.

Stein, L. and Wise, C. D. (1971) Possible etiology of schizophrenia: Progressive damage to the noradrenergic reward system by 6-hydroxydopamine. *Science*, **171**, 1032–6.

Stellar, J. R. (1990) Investigating the neural circuitry of brain stimulation reward. *Progress in Psychobiology and Physiological Psychology*, **14**, 235–94.

Stellar, J. R. and Corbett, D. (1989) Effects of regional neuroleptic infusion suggest a role for nucleus accumbens in lateral hypothalamus self-stimulation. *Brain Research*, **477**, 126–43.

Stoudemire, A. (1998) *Clinical Psychiatry for Medical Students.* Philadelphia: Lippincott-Raven.

Tyler, A. (1986) *Street Drugs.* London: Hodder & Stoughton.

Vaccarino, F. J. *et al.* (1985) Blockade of nucleus accumbens opiate receptors attenuates intravenous heroin reward in the rat. *Psychopharmacology*, **86**, 37–42.

Valenstein, E. S. and Campbell, J. F. (1966) Medial forebrain bundle–lateral hypothalamic area and reinforcing brain stimulation. *American Journal of Physiology*, **210**, 270–4.

Watson, J. B. (1913) Psychology as the behaviorist views it. *Psychological Review*, **20**, 158–77.

Wauquier, A. (1976) The influence of psychoactive drugs on brain self-stimulation in rats: A review. In Wauquier, A. and Rolls, E. T. (eds) *Brain Stimulation Reward.* New York: Elsevier.

Weeks, J. R. (1962) Experimental morphine addiction: Method for autonomic intravenous injections in unrestrained rats. *Science*, **138**, 143–4.

Wenger, J. R. *et al.* (1981) Ethanol tolerance in the rat is learned. *Science*, **213**, 575–6.
Wise, R. A. (1980) Action of drugs of abuse on brain reward systems. *Pharmacology, Biochemistry and Behavior*, **13**, 213–23.
Wise, R. A. (1996a) Neurobiology of addiction. *Current Opinion in Neurobiology*, **6**, 243–51.
Wise, R. A. (1996b) Addictive drugs and brain stimulation reward. *Annual Review of Neuroscience*, **19**, 319–40.
Wise, R. A. and Bozarth, M. A. (1984) Brain reward circuitry: four circuit elements 'wired' in apparent series. *Brain Research Bulletin*, **12**, 203–8.
Yadin, E. *et al.* (1983) Unilaterally activated systems in rats self-stimulating at sites in the medial forebrain bundle, medial prefrontal cortex or locus coeruleus. *Brain Research*, **266**, 39–50.
Zinberg, N. E. (1984) *Drug, Set, and Setting.* New Haven: Yale University Press.

FURTHER READING

Goldstein, A. (1993) *Biology of Addiction: From Biology to Drug Policy*. New York: Freeman.
Liebman, J. M. and Cooper, S. J. (eds) (1989) *The Neuropharmacological Basis of Reward*. Oxford: Oxford University Press.
Siegel, S. (1976) Morphine analgesic tolerance: Its situation specificity supports a Pavlovian conditioning model. *Science*, **193**, 323–5.
Spencer, D. and Corbett, J. R. (1986) Accumbens infusion of amphetamine increases and picrotoxin decreases reward from hypothalamic stimulation. *Society for Neuroscience Abstracts*, **12**, 1142.
Stellar, J. R. and Stellar, E. (1985) *The Neurobiology of Motivation and Reward*. New York: Springer-Verlag.
Wise, R. A. (1987) The role of reward pathways in the development of drug dependence. *Pharmacology and Therapeutics*, **35**, 227–63.

Multiple choice questions

1. Olds and Milner found that the area of the brain that gave rise to the highest rates of self-stimulation was the:

(a) amygdala
(b) septum
(c) lateral hypothalamus
(d) reticular formation

2. The medial forebrain bundle is a large fibre tract that connects the ___________ with the ____________.

(a) cerebral cortex, reticular formation
(b) forebrain, midbrain and upper brainstem
(c) hippocampus, lateral hypothalamus
(d) lateral hypothalamus, ventral tegmental area

3. Large lesions of the medial forebrain bundle:

(a) abolish self-stimulation when electrodes are placed in the septal area
(b) abolish self-stimulation when electrodes are placed in the medial frontal cortex
(c) none of the above
(d) both of the above

4. Stein and Wise (1969) found that rewarding stimulation of the medial forebrain bundle caused the release of:

(a) noradrenaline
(b) dopamine
(c) serotonin
(d) all of the above

5. The effects of amphetamine-induced euphoria in humans can be eliminated by the administration of:

(a) noradrenergic antagonists
(b) dopaminergic antagonists
(c) serotonergic antagonists
(d) it cannot be done (without lesioning the brain)

6. Fibiger and Philips (1987) have shown that levels of the dopaminergic metabolite DOPAC increase in the ____________ and ____________ following stimulation of the ventral tegmental area.

(a) lateral hypothalamus, septum
(b) striatum, nucleus accumbens
(c) lateral hypothalamus, striatum
(d) frontal cortex, nucleus accumbens

7. The main pharmacological action of cocaine is to:

(a) block postsynaptic dopamine (D-2) receptors
(b) block the re-uptake of dopamine
(c) block alpha-2 noradrenergic receptors
(d) block ion channels for calcium

8. Medial forebrain self-stimulation and the intravenous self-administration of cocaine can be blocked by injection of dopaminergic antagonists into the:

(a) lateral hypothalamus
(b) striatum
(c) nucleus accumbens
(d) frontal cortex

9. Which of the following structures is not generally accepted as part of the mesolimbic dopaminergic system?

(a) nucleus accumbens
(b) amygdala
(c) ventral tegmental area
(d) hypothalamus

10. It appears that fibres travelling 'down' in the medial forebrain bundle synapse in the _______________ which, in turn, exerts an excitatory effect on ascending dopaminergic pathways.

(a) periaqueductal grey area
(b) substantia nigra
(c) locus coeruleus
(d) ventral tegmental area

11. Which of the following drugs is known to block opiate receptors?

(a) disulphiram
(b) naloxone
(c) spiroperidol
(d) GABA

12. Animals will quickly learn to lever press at high rates to obtain infusion of morphine into the:

(a) ventral tegmental area
(b) septal area
(c) substantia nigra
(d) lateral hypothalamus

13. Drug tolerance occurs when:

(a) decreased sensitivity to a substance develops as a result of its continuous use
(b) a drug produces less of an effect than it did previously
(c) it requires a higher dose to repeat the initial drug effect
(d) all of the above

14. According to Siegel, drug tolerance comes about through the process of:

(a) habituation
(b) instrumental conditioning
(c) Pavlovian conditioning
(d) metabolic changes in the body

15. When Siegel *et al.* (1982) gave rats a high dose of morphine in a testing room in which they had not been previously given injections they found that it:

(a) decreased the likelihood of a fatal overdose
(b) increased the likelihood of a fatal overdose
(c) had no effect on overdose fatalities compared to control (same room) rats
(d) none of the above (because he injected methadone – not morphine!)

16. Alcohol produces its main pharmacological effects by:

(a) dissolving in the outer (fatty) membrane of neurons
(b) blocking GABA receptors
(c) binding to dopamine receptors
(d) all of the above

17. Nicotine exerts its pharmacological effect by acting on ____________ receptors.

(a) cholinergic
(b) dopaminergic
(c) GABAergic
(d) all of the above

18. The main psychoactive ingredient in cannabis is:

(a) methaqualone
(b) anadamide
(c) delta-9-tetrahydrocannabinol (THC)
(d) naloxone

19. Caffeine is believed to produce its main pharmacological effect by:

(a) stimulating cAMP
(b) blocking adenosine receptors
(c) inhibiting phosphodiesterase
(d) increasing dopamine release

20. The formation of opiate-like substances called tetrahydroisoquinolines (TIQs) is associated with what drug?

(a) heroin
(b) cannabis
(c) cocaine
(d) alcohol

12 Genes and behaviour

IN THIS CHAPTER

- Darwin's theory of evolution
- The biological basis of inheritance
- How genes produce proteins
- The effects of nature and nurture on behaviour
- Behavioural genetic approaches to understanding alcoholism
- Recombinant DNA and the use of transgenic animals

Introduction

A fundamental assumption of biological psychology is that the structure of the brain (e.g. its anatomy, physiology, neurochemistry, etc.) and its function (e.g. the combined activity of its neurons) ultimately produce behaviour. Although we have concentrated on examining the brain's function throughout much of this book, we should not forget that the architects of the brain's structure are its genes. For example, we have evolved over millions of years and during this time Homo Sapiens have developed 23 pairs of chromosomes that contain around 100,000 genes, that provide the genetic blueprint by which our body (and brain) is made. Thus, we all have a brain (and body) that is distinctly human and this is the main reason why we behave differently from other animals. But, of course, this is not the whole story because we also have our own individual traits and behaviours. What then causes this individual variation? In short, there are two main reasons: (1) we inherit an unique pattern of genes (or more accurately **alleles**) that is different from that of everyone else, unless we have an identical twin, and (2) we are all subject to different environmental influences. In fact, from the moment of our birth (perhaps even from our conception) these two factors continually interact – our genetic inheritance predisposing us towards and setting limits for certain behaviours, and our environment determining their expression. Indeed, no psychological (or physiological) characteristic emerges full-blown from our genetic blueprint without environmental influence. Not surprisingly, the question of how these factors interact, and the relative importance of each to a wide range of behaviours (such as intelligence, alcoholism or homosexuality) continue to fascinate psychologists and cause considerable controversy. Such questions are also increasingly of relevance to the biological psychologist who is interested in how genes work and how they affect neural development and function.

Darwin and the theory of evolution

The era of 'modern' biology is often said to have begun with Charles Darwin's book *On the Origin of Species by Means of Natural Selection*, first published in 1859. Darwin was just 22 years old when he sailed, almost by chance, from England on HMS *Beagle* in 1831. The primary mission of the voyage was to chart the South American coastline although Darwin's task as the ship's naturalist was to collect new specimens of fauna and flora. During his journey, Darwin was impressed by the great diversity of life he came across. For example, on the Galapagos Islands he noticed that there were 14 different types of finch which all shared very similar features, yet each bird had a beak that was uniquely adapted to its own particular habitat (and the food source it contained). It was as if all these birds had arisen from a common ancestor, but had become slightly modified to allow them to adapt more effectively into their own ecological niche.

This may sound like a perfectly reasonable theory today, but in the nineteenth century it was in direct contradiction to the teachings of the Bible that held that all species, including man, had been formed by the divine hand of God, and had remained unaltered since the time of creation. Darwin's theory was blasphemous as it contradicted long-held and dogmatic religious views. Indeed, he knew that his theory would be highly controversial and partly because of this Darwin spent more than 20 years compiling evidence and working on his ideas before daring to publish them (and even then he was prompted by the fact that a young naturalist called Alfred Wallace had independently formulated a similar theory). Nonetheless, despite this delay, the impact of his work was highly sensational as it completely changed humanity's concept of itself in the world. And, just as importantly, it also became widely accepted as one of the great unifying theories of biology.

The suggestion that living things change with time, which is the fundamental notion of evolution, did not originate with Darwin, but he was the first to provide a plausible mechanism by which it could occur. The theory he developed was called **natural**

selection and was based on two simple concepts: competition and variation. The first concept derived from Darwin's observation that all living creatures appear to provide more offspring than are needed to replace their parents. Yet, it was also clear to Darwin that animal populations remain relatively stable and do not expand beyond certain limits. Thus, the consequence of increased numbers of offspring and limited resources must be that all creatures are thrown into competition with each other.

The second component of natural selection is that all individuals of a species show great variation in terms of their biological characteristics. For example, as humans we all look similar, but each person is different in terms of physique, strength, intelligence, etc. The consequence of this variability is that some individuals will be much better suited to their competitive environment than others. In turn, the individuals that are best suited will be the ones most likely to reproduce, thereby passing their 'desirable' genes on to their offspring so that the species is continued. This became Darwin's principle of selection for which Herbert Spencer coined the term the 'survival of the fittest' (although it would have been more accurate to call it 'reproduction of the fittest'). However, Darwin's most important insight into natural selection was that over the course of many generations the selection process would cause great changes in the form to develop. For example, because ancestral giraffes had a liking for feeding in tall trees, natural selection would favour the development of long necks. Following this argument to its logical conclusion, it was possible to predict that the ultimate development of natural selection would eventually be the origin of a new species.

Although Darwin described the process of evolution in great detail, he did not explain how inheritance worked. Genes had not been discovered in the nineteenth century, and the lack of knowledge concerning the mechanisms of inheritance was the main obstacle to his theory. Ironically the answers to this problem had been formulated in 1865 by Gregor Mendel, a young Augustine monk living in Bohemia, but the work had not been fully appreciated at the time and was forgotten until it was rediscovered around 1890. Mendel's work provided the precise rules of genetic inheritance that Darwin's theory needed to explain how natural selection worked. Sadly Darwin died in 1882 and never knew of Mendel's research or the true legacy of his ideas to biology.

The work of Gregor Mendel

The concept that transmissible units were responsible for producing the organism's inheritable characteristics was first proposed by Gregor Mendel in 1865. Prior to this time, scientists had believed that inheritance was a blending process in which the 'bloods' of the parents were mixed together in their offspring. However, Mendel disproved this theory in a series of experiments involving the common garden pea plant that took place over an eight-year period. The choice of this plant turned out to be a fortunate one. Firstly, not only were peas simple to breed (e.g. pea plants carry both male and female organs and it is easy to fertilise any female flower with pollen taken from any male), but it was also possible to cross different plants or self-fertilise the same one, which meant that a variety of breeding experiments could be undertaken. Secondly, the traits that Mendel decided to examine, such as the size of the plant (e.g.

tall versus dwarf), the colour of its seed (yellow versus green), the seed texture (smooth versus wrinkled), and so on, were dichotomous, meaning that plants had either one trait or the other (i.e. there was no in-between). Thus, Mendel avoided many of the complexities associated with animal breeding where inherited characteristics (such as size) were not dichotomous. But, most important of all, by using dichotomous traits it was easy to count how many times they occurred in the offspring of selectively bred plants. Although the ratios that this technique provided were simple, they nevertheless enabled Mendel to develop a scientific explanation of his results.

In one of his studies, Mendel crossed tall plants (that were 5 to 6 feet in height) with dwarf plants (that were about 1 foot in height). The results showed that all the offspring (called the F1 or first filial generation) were tall. In other words, the dwarf plants had disappeared from the new generation. However, when Mendel self-fertilised the tall F1 plants to produce the F2 generation a different set of results were obtained. Although about three-quarters of the F2 offspring turned out to be tall, the rest were dwarf plants. In other words, whatever was responsible for causing shortness had not been lost in the F1 generation after all, rather it had simply been suppressed by the dominant taller plants. Mendel also obtained similar results with other traits. For example: smooth seeds were dominant over wrinkled; yellow seeds were dominant over green; and red flowers were dominant over white. Furthermore, in this type of experiment, the F1 generation always showed only one type of trait, whereas the F2 generation always gave rise to the two traits in the ratio of 3:1. Clearly, the consistency of these results implied that some fundamental law of inheritance was at work (see Figure 12.1).

How could these findings be explained? To provide an answer, Mendel proposed that each individual plant contained two 'factors' which controlled each trait, but only one of these factors was passed on to the offspring from each parent (these units were later called genes by Johannsen in 1909). Thus, each parent carried two 'genes', but transmitted only one to their offspring. But why should some pea plants be tall and others short? To answer this, Mendel suggested that the factors controlling size in pea plants came in more than one form – or what are known today as alleles (an example of an allele in humans is the gene that produces eye colour). In other words, although there was only one gene controlling size, this gene came in different forms, which meant that plant size could be expressed as either tallness or shortness. But if this was the case

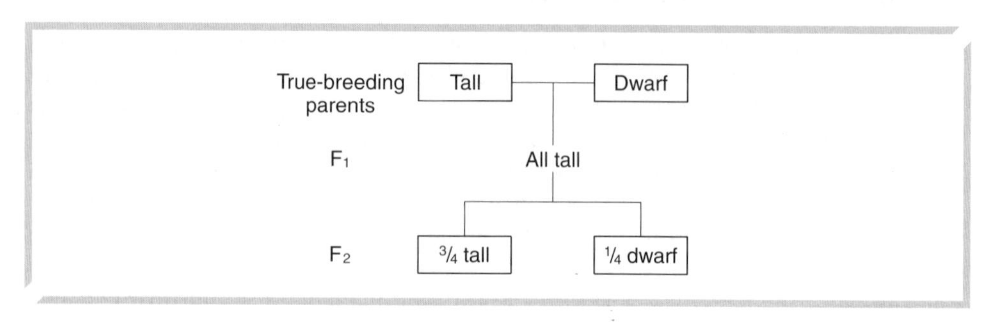

Figure 12.1 The effects of crossing true-breeding pea plants with smooth and wrinkled seeds.

then why were all pea plants in the F1 generation tall? Mendel's explanation was that the alleles could also be **dominant** or **recessive**. In other words, when two different alleles were combined together, the allele for tallness would always dominate over the dwarf allele.

These explanations also neatly explained the results that Mendel obtained in his experiments. For example, assuming that Mendel started off his experiments by crossing true-breeding (or **homozygous**) tall plants (containing the genes TT) with homozygous dwarf plants (containing dd genes), then all the plants in the F1 generation were tall because they all contained the allele combination Td (which is also known as a **heterozygous** gene combination). Moreover, because the T allele is always dominant over the d allele, all these plants will be tall.

But why does the F2 generation also show a mixture of traits in the ratio of 3:1? To help see what happens, refer to Figure 12.2. In short, it can be seen that when the heterozygous F1 hybrids (all containing the allele combination of Td) are crossed together, this throws up a different assortment of allele combinations. That is, if each plant can only pass one allele to its progeny, and if this is done in a random fashion, then such a cross will be predicted to produce three types of plants – TT, Td and dd – and in the proportions 1:2:1. Since T is the dominant allele, then TT and Td combinations will become tall plants, but the dd plant will become a dwarf. In other words, as a result of breeding F1 hybrids, one would expect to obtain three tall plants and one dwarf in the F2 generation.

It should be pointed out that all the traits that Mendel studied were caused by a single gene, whereas a great deal of evidence shows that the vast majority of human traits (although not all – see below) are controlled by many different genes. Furthermore, not all alleles operate in a dominant or recessive fashion. For example, many alleles are additive, meaning that they each contribute something to the offspring, whereas other

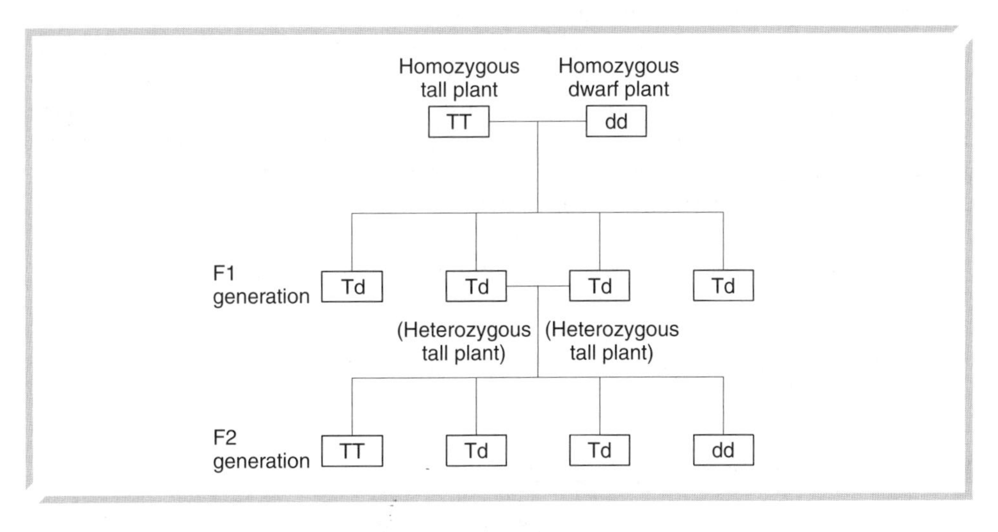

Figure 12.2 The effects of dominant and recessive alleles on the crossing of pea plants.

genes may have interactive effects with each other (or they may even cancel each other out). And, to complicate matters further, the environment may also have a powerful effect on the way that genes are expressed. Nonetheless, Mendel had shown how inheritance worked, and although his work was to lay undiscovered for over 30 years it was to be proved fundamentally correct.

The chromosomal basis of inheritance

The results of Mendel's work were published in 1866, and his paper sent to academic institutions and learned societies throughout the world (a copy of his paper even went to Darwin's office), but, incredibly, his findings were ignored and forgotten for many years. Despite this, other important breakthroughs were taking place in biology at around this time that were also to support Mendel's conception of genetic inheritance. For example, in 1875 Oskar Hertwig observed the process of fertilisation (in sea urchin eggs) which involved the fusing together of the **gametes** (sperm and the egg) and, in 1879, Walther Flemming discovered tiny rod-like structures within the nucleus of the cell that were made of a material called chromatin (which were later to be called **chromosomes**). Importantly, it was also shown that chromosomes existed in pairs, which was consistent with Mendel's hypothesis of two separate factors being involved in the process of genetic transmission. This idea was further supported in 1883 when Edouard van Beneden saw the chromosomes from sperm and egg mingle together during fertilisation. He also noticed that although the cells of the body contained pairs of chromosomes, the egg and sperm were an exception as they only contained half the normal number of chromosomes. However, when the chromosomes came together in the process of fertilisation, they joined up to make the normal paired complement. This again was in accordance with Mendelian theory that implied that pairs of genes came together in fertilisation to produce new progeny.

Finally, in 1900, the importance of Mendel's work was brought to the attention of the scientific community when three scientists (de Vries, Correns and Tschernmak), after discovering the basic 3:1 hybrid ratios for themselves, independently tracked down the original paper. And, in 1903, the American geneticist Walter Sutton proposed that Mendel's factors (or genes) were located on chromosomes, with their inheritance coming about through the transmission of chromosomes into the fertilised egg. In short, the notion that traits were somehow transmitted along 'bloodlines' had been shattered. Instead, it was clear that traits were transmitted by indivisible genetic particles that somehow maintained their identity while being shuffled into fresh combinations in new offspring. And, again, as had been inferred by Darwin, it was apparent that biological organisms, including human beings, were governed by the same laws that apply to the rest of the universe.

DNA: the basis of heredity

What do genes look like? To answer this question we must first look at the structure of the chromosomes themselves. Chromosomes are long rod-like type structures comprising a protein matrix that holds in place a very special chemical that is coiled up and tightly packed called **deoxyribonucleic acid (DNA)**. Although DNA had been identified by Miescher in 1869 (he had called it nuclein) and was suspected of being involved in genetic transmission, it was not until 1953 – when James Watson and Francis Crick worked out the structure of this molecule – that the secret of how DNA provided the genetic basis of transmission was finally solved. For this momentous discovery, which also effectively initiated a brand-new field of scientific inquiry now known as molecular genetics, Watson and Crick (along with Maurice Wilkins) were to win the Nobel Prize in 1962.

DNA is a large molecule made up of two chains (composed of phosphate and a sugar called deoxyribose) that wind around each other in the shape of the double helix (Figure 12.3). Holding the two strands together as they swivel around each other are pairs of simple molecules (like rungs of a ladder) known as **bases**. DNA contains only 4 types of base (adenine, guanine, cytosine and thymine), and because these are held together with weak bonds, the two strands making up the DNA are easily able to unzip and separate into two units. The bases also have another important characteristic in that they are very selective in who they form bonds with. In fact, adenine can only bond with thymine, and cytosine with guanine. Consequently when the two strands of DNA unwind and separate, each of the individual 'exposed' bases can only act as a magnet for its own special or complementary base. If the exposed bases are successful in attracting new partners then the result will be the construction of a brand-new strand that is identical to the old one. In this way, one molecule is able to transform itself into two. Thus, the DNA molecule has the remarkable property of being able to duplicate itself – a vital prerequisite for transmitting genetic information to new cells.

DNA, however, does much more than simply replicate – it also contains the genes by which proteins and enzymes are made that are essential for creating (and maintaining) various life forms. In short, genes are made up of base sequences that lie between the two spiralling long chains that provide DNA with its distinctive shape. As we have seen, the alphabetic is very simple and composed of only four bases (which we can label A, T, G and C). Despite this small number of bases, however, there are astronomical numbers of bases on each stretch of DNA (or chromosome) making the content of the overall message incredibly complex. For example, it has been estimated that the human genome (i.e. the total complement of all 23 pairs of chromosomes) contains over 3,000 million base pairs, which breaks down into approximately 6.5 million base pairs (or paired letters) for each individual chromosome. To put this figure into perspective, the 1969 edition of the *Encyclopaedia Britannica* (which also coincidentally consists of 23 volumes) contains only 200 million letters; or, put another way, enough information to fill approximately three chromosomes. Remarkably, to enable over 3,000 million base pairs to exist together, each individual cell of the body contains about 6 feet of DNA crammed into a nucleus that is 0.005 mm in diameter. Put simply, this would appear to be the amount of information needed to build a human being from scratch and to maintain it through life.

Returning to our original question set out at the beginning of this section: genes are essentially stretches of DNA that contain long strings of bases. It has been estimated

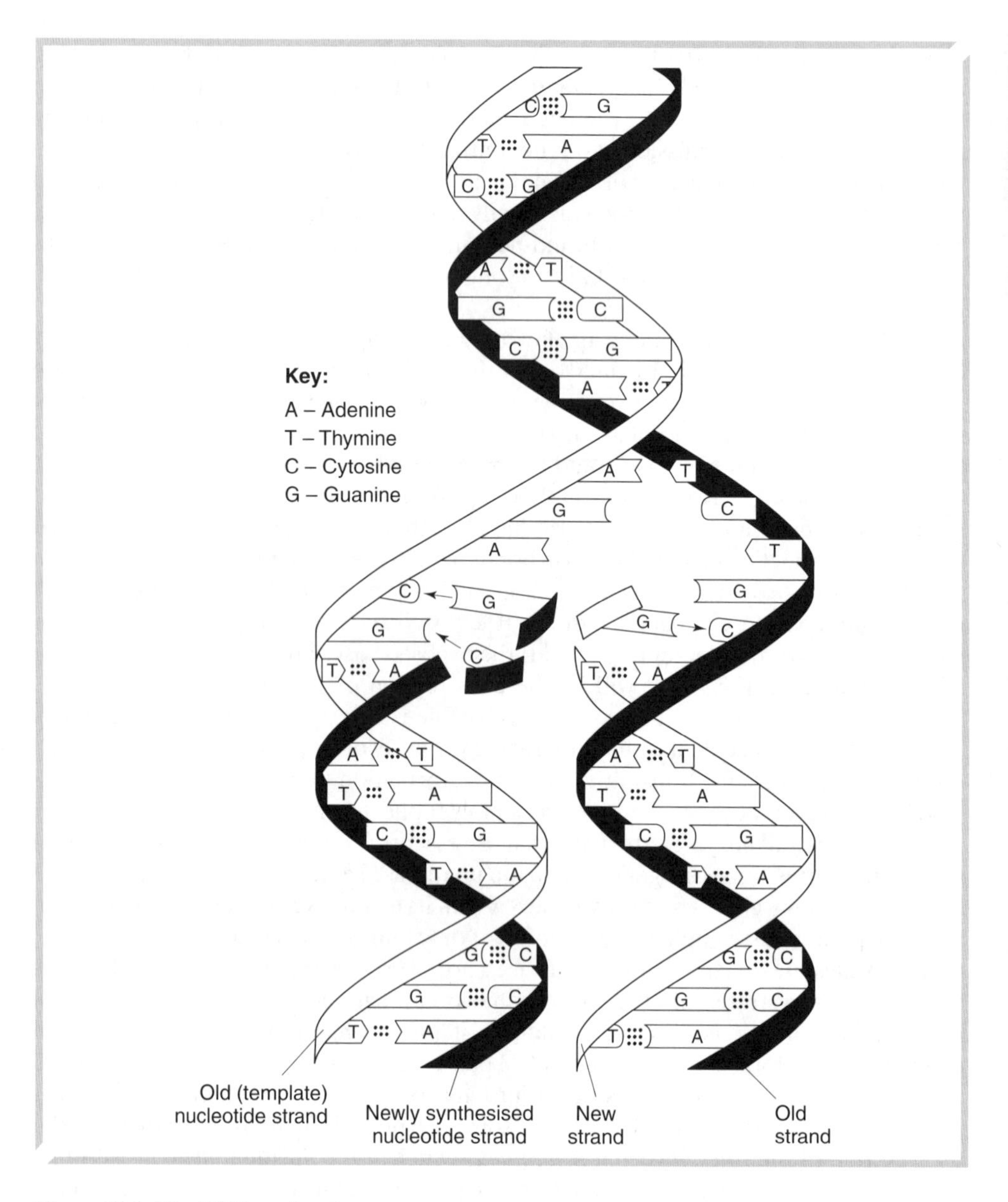

Figure 12.3 The DNA molecule.

that our chromosomes contain around 100,000 genes (maybe a few less) with most specifying the code for making just one protein (see next section). Moreover, these 'working' stretches of DNA come in many different sizes, with the smallest gene consisting of around 500 bases and the largest containing well over 2 million. But how do the bases provide the blueprint for making proteins? The answer is that the overall

Table 12.1 The codons (consecutive triple bases of DNA) by which amino acids are made

Amino acid*	DNA code
Alanine	CGA, CGG, CGT, CGC
Arginine	GCA, GCG, GCT, GCC, TCT, TCC
Asparagine	TTA, TTG
Aspartic acid	CTA, CTG
Cysteine	ACA, ACG
Glutamic acid	CTT, CTC
Glutamine	GTT, GTC
Glycine	CCA, CCG, CCT, CCC
Histidine	GTA, GTG
Isoleucine	TAA, TAG, TAT
Leucine	AAT, AAC, GAA, GAG, GAT, GAC
Lysine	TTT, TTC
Methionine	TAC
Phenylalanine	AAA, AAG
Proline	GGA, GGG, GGT, GGC
Serine	AGA, AGG, AGT, AGC, TCA, TCG
Threonine	TGA, TGG, TGT, TGC
Tryptophan	ACC
Tyrosine	ATA, ATG
Valine	CAA, CAG, CAT, CAC
(Stop signals)	ATT, ATC, ACT

*The 20 amino acids are organic molecules that are linked together by peptide bonds to form polypeptides, which are the building blocks of enzymes and other proteins. The particular combination of amino acids determines the shape and function of the polypeptide.
Source: From Plomin *et al.* (1990) *Behavioral Genetics*.

blueprint of the gene is made up of smaller units (or codes) that are used to make **amino acids** (the building blocks of proteins). In fact, despite the great complexity of our genes, they are only capable of making 20 types of amino acid – although from this limited pool a large variety of proteins can be constructed. Moreover, the creation of each amino acid is derived simply from a code for just three consecutive DNA bases (such as CGA or TGG) otherwise known as **codons** (Table 12.1). In short, a single gene is basically a long sequence of codons that code for all the amino acids necessary to assemble a specific protein.

Protein synthesis

The coded instructions for making **proteins** (genes) are stored on chromosomes locked in the cell's nucleus. However, protein manufacture does not take place in the nucleus, but in the cell's cytoplasm. Thus, genetic information must pass out of the nucleus into the cytoplasm. But how does this occur? The answer lies with another type of nucleic acid called **ribonucleic acid (RNA)**. There are several types of RNA, but the one with responsibility for transporting the DNA's instructions into the cytoplasm is called **messenger RNA (mRNA)**. This molecule then takes part in a fundamental process that underlies all protein manufacture and which can be described simply as follows: DNA is transcribed into mRNA which is then translated into protein.

Although RNA is a close cousin to DNA in terms of its chemistry, the most important difference between the two molecules is that RNA is much smaller and exists only as a single strand. This enables RNA to move freely in and out of the nucleus, as well as providing a template by which to copy transcripts of the much larger DNA molecule. Once a copy of the DNA's message has been transcribed onto the mRNA, it then leaves the nucleus and enters the cytoplasm where it seeks out a special structure called a **ribosome**, which is the site where the assembly of the protein will take place. Ribosomes are ball-like structures made up of protein and another type of RNA called **ribosomal RNA (rRNA)**. It appears that the rRNA helps to position the mRNA, and once it is pinned down it exposes the mRNA's codons (3 base sequences) one at a time. As this happens, the exposed bases become immediately hooked-up with complementary bases that are brought to the ribosome by yet another type of RNA called **transfer RNA (tRNA)**. Once the codon has been filled up (thus creating an amino acid), a peptide bond is created that links the newly formed amino acid with the next one in the chain. Following this, the next codon is exposed and this process continues until all the bases in the mRNA transcript have been filled. When all the transcripts have been completed and joined together, a protein is made (see Figure 12.4).

The construction of a protein is an incredibly efficient process. It has been estimated that amino acids are incorporated into the growing polypeptide chains at a rate of about 100 per second, and that it takes less than a minute to make an average protein. Furthermore, our cells are continually processing proteins and it has been estimated that more than 1 million peptide bonds are made *every second* in an average mammalian cell. This high rate of synthesis is needed because the human body contains tens of thousands of different proteins that are continually being broken down and replaced every day.

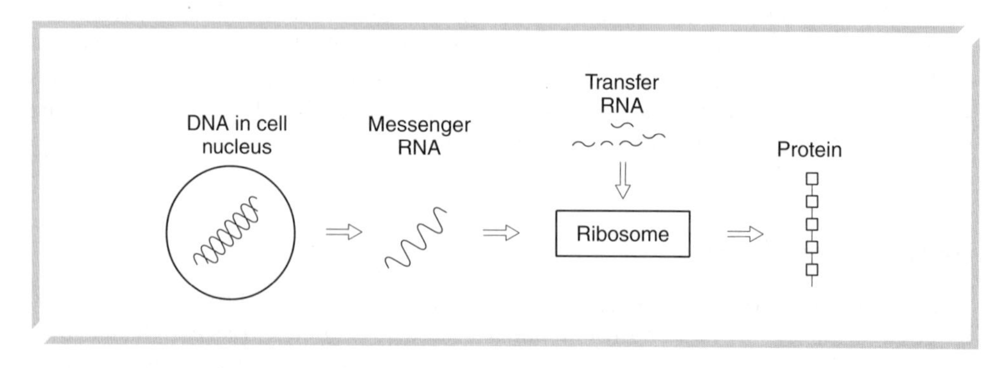

Figure 12.4 The stages of protein synthesis.

Box 12.1 THE HUMAN GENOME PROJECT

The ultimate aim of the human genome project is simple: it is to determine the complete sequence of the 3,000 million base pairs that make up the human genome (i.e. our 23 pairs of chromosomes) and to identify among these bases the 100,000, or so, genes that uniquely define us as human beings. The notion of the human genome project had its beginnings in the United States in the mid-1980s, and was put into practice in 1990 as an internationally organised research effort involving hundreds of laboratories around the world. In addition to mapping the human genome, the project also involves the complete mapping of the genome of several other organisms that are also important to genetic research including the bacterium (*Escherichia coli*), the yeast (*Saccharomyces cerevisiae*), the nematode (*Caenorhabditis elegans*), the fruit fly (*Drosophila melanogaster*) and the laboratory mouse (*Mus musculus*). Part of the reason for this extended work lies with the fact that many species share similar genes with our own. For example, genes involved in human cancer have been found to be similar to certain genes in worms where they can be more easily studied. Furthermore, comparing genes between species also helps researchers to understand how genes have evolved, thus allowing further insight into their function.

The mapping of the human genome, however, is an arduous and mammoth task. As we have seen above, our DNA is made up of only 4 bases (A,C,G and T) that are arranged in pairs. And, it is the aim of the human genome project to list these bases in their correct sequence. The work on the project has already resulted in a rough map of nearly all of our chromosomes, and it is estimated that the human genome should be finished before the year 2006 (Roberts 1993). The reward will be, in effect, to fill the equivalent of 13 sets of the *Encyclopaedia Britannica* with rows upon rows of letters representing our 4 bases. In terms of bedtime reading it would undoubtedly be the most boring book ever written (not that it will ever be published in this format), but as a potential set of instructions for understanding the biological nature of human beings it will have no equal. It is certain that this knowledge, and its many ramifications, will dominate human biology and medicine over the next millennium.

Why then are researchers going to such trouble to map the human genome? There are several good reasons. For example, sequencing the structure of genes will enable their identification, and this should allow doctors to identify the most important genes that contribute to disease. Indeed, it is feasible that in 20 years' time one will be able to take DNA from a newborn infant and analyse 50 or more genes that are known to predispose humans to common diseases such as heart disease, cancer and dementia. From this information, a lifestyle and medical regime could be drawn up that will help the individual minimise their chances of disease, and maximise their chances of a long, healthy life. Despite this, being able to simply identify genes tells us very little about their function and, in the long term, another advantage of the human genome project will be in helping to determine what proteins they make, when they act, and what functions they serve. This is a huge task and the human genome project is only the starting point for this much more complex and enlightening journey. But, the rewards are likely to be great: in short, the understanding of how genes create the body, how they control and maintain it throughout life, and how they lead to its demise through disease and ageing. Moreover, the psychologist will undoubtedly gain a far greater appreciation of how genes act to produce behaviour, which may well revolutionise our understanding of nature and nurture.

The importance of proteins

As we have seen, genes are the blueprints from which proteins are constructed, and if we are to understand why genes are so important then we have to understand proteins. Proteins (the word is derived from the Greek *proteios* meaning 'of primary importance') are vital constituents of all living things from bacteria to humans, and without these unique chemicals life as we know it could not exist. Proteins are large molecules (although they still cannot be seen with an electron microscope) which consist of chains of much simpler subunits (amino acids) that become twisted and folded to form highly complex three-dimensional shapes. Proteins make up more than 50 per cent of the dry weight of cells and are crucial in almost everything they do. In fact, we contain around 60,000 different types of protein each with its own unique function. For example, some proteins are used to make ion channels or receptors, whereas others form structures that are found inside the cell. Other proteins provide connective tissue and muscle, while others act as carriers that are responsible for transporting chemical substances around the body (e.g. red blood cells). And yet others form neurochemicals, hormones and antibodies. But the most important function of proteins is their role as enzymes that act as catalysts in the chemical reactions upon which life depends. It is a simple truth that life is chemistry and in this respect there is hardly a cellular chemical reaction that does not require the presence of an enzyme. In fact, the vast majority of the proteins that are made by our genes are enzymes which are continually at work within our cells every second of our lives.

It can be difficult for a psychologist interested in behaviour to scale down to the molecular level to understand the size of proteins. To give some idea of the scale we are talking about: one of the smallest objects to the naked eye is a grain of salt which is about half a millimetre or 500 microns (500 millionths of a metre) in size. The cell body of an average animal cell is much smaller (about 30 microns in diameter), and yet this is huge compared to a protein which may be no more than a few nanometres in length (a nanometre is a thousand-millionth of a metre). It is therefore remarkable to contemplate that each protein will carry out some vital function in the body, such as helping to build and operate the nervous system, which in turn may ultimately shape behaviour.

Single genes and behaviour

In the simplest scenario, one gene controls the expression of one protein, and that one protein controls the expression of a particular trait. In fact, this is essentially the type of inheritance that Mendel studied with his pea plants. But, this type of 'single trait inheritance' is not only confined to peas. For example, there are over 4,000 genetic conditions that are known to affect humans which are caused by a single mutated gene (with about 10 per cent of these disorders resulting in mental retardation). Moreover, in many of these instances, if one inherits the mutated gene then one will develop the disorder – with other genes and environmental factors having little impact on its expression.

Huntington's disease

One such single genetic disorder (which we came across in Chapter 3) is **Huntington's disease** (Figure 12.5) which leads to degeneration of the brain (particularly of the striatum) and is characterised by involuntary dance-like movements that get progressively worse as the disease progresses. Huntington's disease is an example of **autosomal dominant inheritance**, which means that if one is unfortunate enough to inherit just one copy of the mutated gene (from either parent), that gene will become dominant and produce the faulty protein that causes the disease. The chances of inheriting Huntington's disease if one parent carries the mutated gene is 50 per cent,

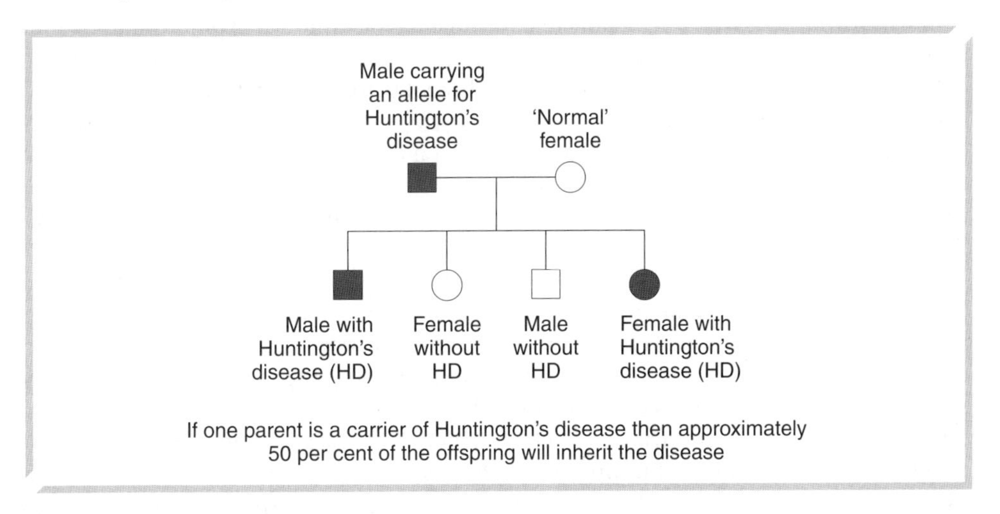

Figure 12.5 The inheritance of Huntington's disease.

and this can be explained by using knowledge of Mendel's laws (see also Figure 12.2). For example, if we assume that the carrier parent has one dominant allele (H) and one recessive normal allele (h), and that the other (unaffected) parent has two normal hh alleles, then it can be seen that there are 4 possible combinations of paired alleles that can result in the offspring. In short, the offspring will always inherit a normal h allele from the unaffected parent, but will have a 50 per cent chance of inheriting the H allele from the carrier parent. This means that 50 per cent of the possible gene combinations in the offspring will carry the dominant (mutated) gene.

In 1983, the gene for Huntington's disease was narrowed down to a small part of chromosome 4 (Gusella *et al.* 1983), which allowed the condition to be detected with a high degree of accuracy, and 10 years later the gene was actually isolated and analysed (MacDonald *et al.* 1993). Interestingly, the cause of the mutation was found to lie with a triple repeat of the bases CAG. Normal chromosomes contain between 11 and 34 copies of this base repeat, but the Huntington's gene was found to contain more than 40 copies. Moreover, it was found that the onset of the disease was correlated with the number of repeats that the gene contained. For example, early onset of Huntington's disease was associated with genes that contained around 60 repeats, whereas later onset (after 65 years) was associated with genes that contained 40 copies of the triple repeat. It also appears that this particular triplet is unstable and can increase in subsequent generations. This phenomenon might explain a non-Mendelian process called 'genetic anticipation' in which symptoms appear at earlier ages and with greater severity in subsequent generations (Plomin *et al.* 1997).

Phenylketonuria

Another single genetic defect is **phenylketonuria** which affects about one person in every 10,000. Individuals with this condition do not produce a liver enzyme called phenylalanine hydroxylase, which is responsible for turning the amino acid phenylalanine into a slightly different amino acid called tyrosine. The result is that phenylalanine builds up in the liver and passes into the bloodstream where it can enter the developing brain and causes considerable damage. In particular, excess phenylalanine (and its toxic by-products) in early development reduces brain weight, produces a deficiency of myelin and causes fewer dendrites to be formed. The consequence is a very severe mental retardation with victims seldom learning to speak and often exhibiting an IQ of less than 20 (Hay 1985).

Mendel's laws also help to explain the inheritance of phenylketonuria. Unlike Huntington's disease, phenylketonuria is due to an allele that is recessive. In other words, for offspring to be affected, they must inherit two copies of the allele. Those who only inherit one copy of the allele are totally unaffected by the disorder, although they remain carriers and can pass it on to their offspring. Remarkably, about one person in 50 carries the phenylketonuria gene, which means that about one in 2,500 couples (50 times 50) have the potential to produce a child with phenylketonuria. However, even assuming that both parents are carriers, it nevertheless follows that they only have a 25 per cent chance of producing a child with this disorder. To understand why, we can again

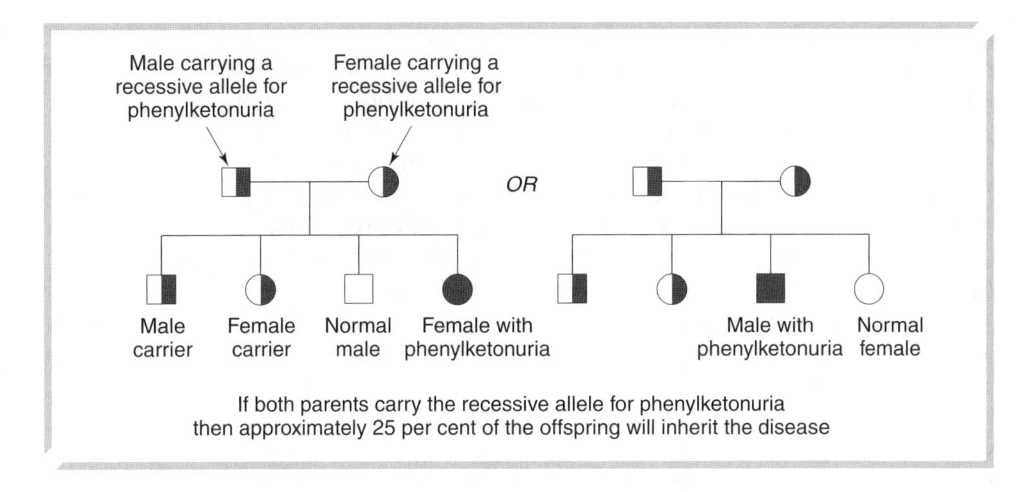

Figure 12.6 The inheritance of phenylketonuria.

refer to Mendelian laws of inheritance (see Figure 12.6). For example, if each parent carries one mutant allele (P) and one normal allele (p) it can be seen that the only combination that will produce phenylketonuria (e.g. PP) will occur with a 1 in 4 probability.

Fortunately, phenylketonuria can be detected soon after birth by a simple blood test which has now become standard practice in hospitals. But, even more important is the fact that something can be done about a positive diagnosis. Phenylalanine is one of the 10 essential amino acids that the body cannot manufacture for itself, and consequently all of the body's supply of this substance must come from the diet. Thus, by restricting its dietary intake, the build-up of phenylalanine (and its metabolic products) can be prevented. Indeed, by following such a diet, many individuals develop normally and show IQs of over 100 (providing the diet is initiated early enough in life). This example again shows that some human traits can result from complex and subtle interactions between genes and the environment.

Multiple genes and behaviour

As we have just seen, one feature of single genetic inheritance is that traits are dichotomous (that is, one either inherits the gene and exhibits the trait, or doesn't, there is no in between). However, the vast majority of human traits are the result of many different genes and do not follow this simple pattern of inheritance. Instead, polygenic traits show a continuous range of variation, and this can be illustrated using the example of human height. If our height was due to a single gene, then only three different heights would be possible. In short, everyone who was homozygous for the 'height' gene would be tall, everyone who lacked the gene would be short, and all those who were heterozygous would be the same intermediate height (Steen 1996). The fact that there is a great variation in human height (which may vary from under 2 feet to well over 8 feet) shows that it is determined by many different genes (e.g. such as the ones that code for growth hormone or control the rate of calcium deposition in the bones). Yet, despite this, environmental factors also play an important role in determining height. For example, the absence of sunlight can result in inadequate synthesis of vitamin D which may slow down bone growth, and poor nutrition in childhood may also have a similar effect. In fact, the combined effect of genetic and environmental influences working in a given population will generally result in a trait that shows continuous variation in the form of a normal distribution or bell-shaped curve (Singer 1985).

Height is a relatively simple trait, but the simplest human behaviour is undoubtedly many times more complex. In fact, behaviour can be regarded as the most complex and subtle of all human traits, and not only are there likely to be a multitude of genetic influences at work, but environmental factors are also extremely important. This can be shown, for instance, by the almost endless variety of ways in which humans behave. And, to complicate matters further, many aspects of human behaviour do not remain the same for long periods of time (e.g. most of us do not behave the same way as we did 10 years ago). In short, human behaviour is highly complex and changeable.

Nevertheless, it is certain that genes must have a bearing on our behaviour. But how can we show this to be the case? Mendel was fortunate in choosing pea plants that had simple dichotomous characteristics. But, of course, this approach will not work for human behaviour (although it works for certain genetic disorders). How then can we analyse the effects of genetic inheritance on animal and human behaviour? There are in fact a number of methods that can be used, including twin studies (to examine human behaviour) and experimental breeding approaches (to examine animal behaviour). And, it is to these methods we now turn.

Twin and adoption studies

There are two types of twins: **monozygotic**, who derive from one egg, and **dizygotic**, who derive from two separate eggs. In brief, monozygotic twins develop from the same egg which, after being fertilised, splits into two at a very early stage of development and results in two genetically identical individuals – while dizygotic twins arise when two eggs (rather than the usual one) are released at ovulation and are fertilised by different sperms. In this latter instance, the genetic relationship between the dizygotic twins is the same as that of other brothers and sisters – that is, they share 50 per cent of their genes. This situation neatly provides geneticists with a kind of natural experiment in which the behavioural resemblance of identical twins (whose genetic relatedness is 1.0) can be compared with the resemblance of dizygotic twins (whose genetic relatedness is 0.5). In other words, if heredity affects a given trait or behaviour, then identical twins should show a greater resemblance for that trait compared to fraternal twins.

One measure used by geneticists to express the relative influence of heredity and environment on behaviour is **concordance**. In short, twins are said to be concordant for a trait if both of them express it (or if neither does), and discordant if only one of the pair shows the trait in question. Thus, if concordance rates (which can range from 0 to 100) are significantly higher for identical twins than for fraternal twins, then this is evidence that genetic influences play an important role in the expression of that particular behaviour. This can be illustrated with the example of Huntington's disease. As we have seen, this disorder is inherited from a single gene and the concordance rate for identical twins must be 100 per cent (1.0), whereas the concordance for fraternal twins must be 50 per cent (0.5). But what about other disorders? As mentioned in the previous chapter, the concordance rate for schizophrenia has been shown to be around 50 per cent for monozygotic twins and 15 per cent for dizygotic (Gottesman 1991). It is interesting to compare this with, say, bipolar illness which shows a concordance rate of 69 per cent for monozygotic twins and 13 per cent for dizygotic twins (Rush *et al.* 1991). In other words, these results indicate that genetics plays a more important role in the causation of bipolar illness than schizophrenia – a finding that has also been confirmed by others.

Despite this, there are several problems associated with twin studies. For example, identical twins tend to share very similar environments, and this might provide another reason why they show very similar patterns of behaviour. Moreover, this type of influence may operate in many different ways. For example, if identical twins were to experience a more similar environment than fraternal twins (perhaps because family and friends treat them as a 'pair') then this would clearly inflate estimates of genetic influence. Alternatively, if parents attempted to treat their identical twins differently, then this would produce the opposite effect. Thus, we must be very cautious about using concordance rates to assess the heritability of a given behaviour.

A much better solution to this problem would be to study twins who were separated early in life and then reared apart in different types of environment. Of course, this is much more difficult to do because the separation of twins in this way is a rare event, and it also requires considerable detective skills (and luck) by researchers to find such groups of subjects. Nevertheless, a number of attempts have been made, and the most comprehensive of all is the Minnesota Study of Twins Reared Apart conducted by Thomas Bouchard and his colleagues (e.g. Bouchard *et al.* 1990). These researchers (which include psychologists, psychiatrists and medical doctors) have now managed to find 59 pairs of identical twins, and 47 pairs of fraternal twins, who were separated and reared apart from an early age. Moreover, each pair have been brought to the University of Minnesota where they undergo 6 days of intensive testing (which lasts approximately 50 hours) during which time they answer around 15,000 questions (including a full medical history) and take part in innumerable tests (including those for IQ, personality, spatial abilities, mathematics, memory and so on).

The crucial question, therefore, is to what extent would identical twins reared apart be different to those brought up together and raised in the same environment? One way that Bouchard *et al.* (1990) examined this question was to look at intelligence as measured by the Weschler Adult Intelligent Scale. The results of this test showed that the average correlation for twins reared apart was 0.70, whereas the correlation for those reared together was 0.85. In other words, the high correlation coefficients showed that genetic factors appeared to be the main contributing factor to the differences between the subjects on their intelligence scores. And a similar finding has also been reported with personality (Bouchard 1994).

From these findings Bouchard has estimated the heritability of intelligence to be around 0.70; that is, most of the variation in the twins' intelligence in this particular study is due to genetic variation. However, these results do not prove that IQ is 70 per cent genetic. For example, if the twins had been separately adopted by European royalty and African bushmen, then the resulting heritability estimates would probably have been much lower. Thus, we cannot put an exact figure on the relative estimates of genetic and environmental influences. In fact, it is even misleading to think of them as separate influences. For example, we normally think of genes acting to promote psychological differences between individuals – but there is also evidence to show that people with similar genetic endowments tend to seek out similar environments and experiences. For example, individuals whose genetic inheritance promotes aggression, are likely to become involved in aggressive activities (e.g. football or competitive fighting), with these experiences also contributing further to the development of aggressive tendencies (Pinel 1997). Since such individuals are likely to seek outlets for their aggressive tendencies (regardless of the environment in which they are reared) then clearly one will never be able to arrive at an undisputed estimate of aggression heritability.

Box 12.2 ONE CASE OF IDENTICAL TWINS

It is clear that many identical twins exhibit similar behaviour patterns when reared together. But what about identical twins reared apart? Do they share the same interests and lifestyle behaviours? Or does the environment cause them to become significantly different? Although it is difficult to generalise, in certain cases the similarities have been shown to be remarkable. For example, Thomas Bouchard has come across a pair of twins that were separated at birth (both, incidentally, named James by their adoptive parents) and who were reunited at the age of 39 years. In terms of physical appearance the two men looked quite different, having distinct hair styles and clothes. But in terms of lifestyle and previous history the resemblances were uncanny. For example, both drove Chevrolets and enjoyed stock car racing. Both had a background in police work and had worked part-time as deputy sheriffs. Both chain smoked and enjoyed taking holidays in Florida. Each had built a workshop in the basement of his house in which one built miniature picnic tables and the other miniature rocking chairs. The coincidences even extended to their wives, children and choice of pet. For example, each had been married twice with both of their first wives being called Linda, and both of their second wives being called Betty. The twins also gave identical names to their sons (James Alan and James Allan respectively) and both had dogs named Toy. As perhaps might be predicted, both had similar medical histories, with each twin having identical pulse and blood pressure as well as haemorrhoids! Their sleep patterns were also very similar, and both had inexplicably put on 10 pounds at the same time earlier in their lives.

Bouchard and his colleagues have also collected many other twin histories that show surprising coincidences. Despite this, we must be careful to view these findings in their correct perspective. For example, both twins were raised in similar socio-economic backgrounds which would have allowed them to develop their interests in very similar ways. And, this particular case is undoubtedly exceptional in the number of minor coincidences that it has produced. Indeed, not all identical twins show such a high degree of similarity in life pattern or interests. For example, in the 1950s, Franz Kallmann collected the life histories of over 1,700 pairs of twins (not separated) and found a difference of 36 months between the time of death of identical twin pairs, and 74 months for fraternal twins. These findings suggest that considerable differences must also arise between identical twins over the span of an average life.

Inbred strain lines

Attempts to produce different genetic strains of animals by **inbreeding** (i.e. brother–sister mating over several generations) has provided further evidence of the influence of genetic inheritance on behaviour. Inbreeding is an important technique in genetic analysis because inbred lines lose much of their genetic variation, thereby making all members of an inbred strain genetically similar. The reason why this occurs is that it increases the chances of producing matching (or homozygous) alleles. And, once two identical alleles have come together in an inbreeding stock, they are not easily bred out of successive generations unless new genetic material is introduced. In fact, typically after 20 successive brother–sister matings all members of an inbred strain are as genetically alike as they are likely to get. Despite this, each strain will have its own unique combination of homozygous genes which, of course, means that they will be genetically different to other inbred strains.

Inbreeding has, for example, been used to examine the effects of genetic inheritance on longevity. In one study, Pearl and Parker (1922) inbred fruit flies through many generations to produce five different strains of fly each with its own individual average longevity. Their ages ranged from 14 days in the shortest-lived strain to 49 days in the longest-lived strain. Furthermore, once each strain was developed, the flies continued to produce generation after generation of offspring, each with its own average life span typical of that strain. Thus, these findings clearly show the importance of genetic make-up on longevity. However, despite this, the ages of all the strains obtained by Pearl and Parker were shorter than those found in normally bred fruit flies, showing that inbreeding is not an advantageous strategy for longevity. One reason for this situation is that many harmful genes are often 'hidden' in 'normal' strains because they are normally recessive, but with inbreeding they often find themselves matched with identical genes which makes them become dominant.

Similar principles also apply to humans with regards to intelligence. For example, it is known that children of marriages between first cousins generally show a lower IQ than for controls. In fact, it has also been shown that the risk of mental retardation is more than three times greater for children of a marriage between first cousins than for unrelated controls. And, the reason is the same as for the fruit flies described above – that is, inbreeding increases the chance of harmful recessive genes (which most of us carry) becoming unmasked and homozygous.

Selection studies

Another way of studying the heritability of behavioural traits in animals is by **selective breeding**. Indeed, as farmers have known for thousands of years, if a trait is inheritable then it can be obtained by selective breeding. For example, wild cattle and sheep have long legs for speed and large horns for defence, yet domestic cattle and sheep look very different with their short legs and horns accompanied by larger bodies. Similarly, dogs have been bred for a number of behavioural characteristics such as to herd (sheep dogs), retrieve (labradors), and hunt (terriers). And, in much the same way, researchers have bred special strains of animals in the laboratory to examine certain behaviours. The rationale is straightforward: if a trait is influenced by genetic factors then it should be possible to change it through selective breeding.

A classic example of selective breeding is the study by Robert Tryon (1940) who selected for maze-learning ability in rats. Tryon began his study by examining the performance of a large number of rats, obtained from a variety of sources, to run through a complex 17-choice maze for food reward. Following training, Tryon then mated together the males and females that had performed most effectively (i.e. had made fewer mistakes or wrong turns) to create a group of maze-bright rats. Similarly, he mated together the males and females that had made the most errors to produce a group of maze-dull animals. When the offspring derived from these two groups matured, they were tested again in the maze, with the best 'maze bright' and worst 'maze dull' rats being selected again for breeding purposes. In fact, Tryon carried on this artificial selection procedure for 21 generations, and descendants of these animals are still available today for researchers interested in rodent learning ability.

The results of this study showed that Tryon's selection strategy produced two strains of rats that differed significantly in their ability to learn the maze. In fact, after just seven generations, the two groups were so different in their performance that the distribution of the error scores no longer overlapped (Figure 12.7). And, at this point, the two groups continued to maintain their behavioural differences over subsequent generations.

Another important study that examined the performance of maze-bright and maze-dull rats was reported by Cooper and Zubek in 1958 who examined the effects of rearing on these groups of animals. These researchers reared their bright and dull rats in one of three environments: (1) a standard laboratory cage as used by Tryon, (2) an enriched environment consisting of a large cage that contained toys, tunnels and ramps, and (3) an impoverished environment consisting of a small grey wire-mesh cage without any extra objects. The results of this study showed that when the maze-bright rats reached

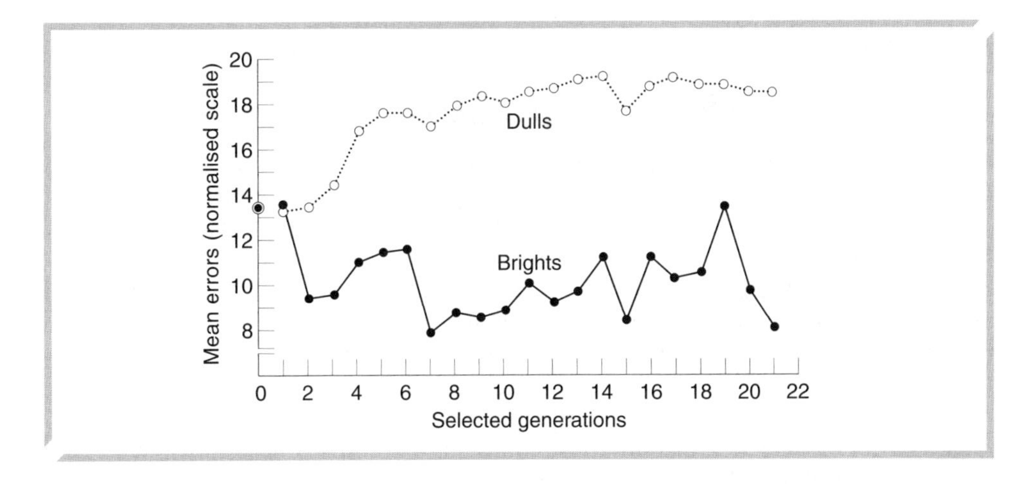

Figure 12.7 Graph showing the results of Tryon's selective breeding for maze-bright and maze-dull rats.

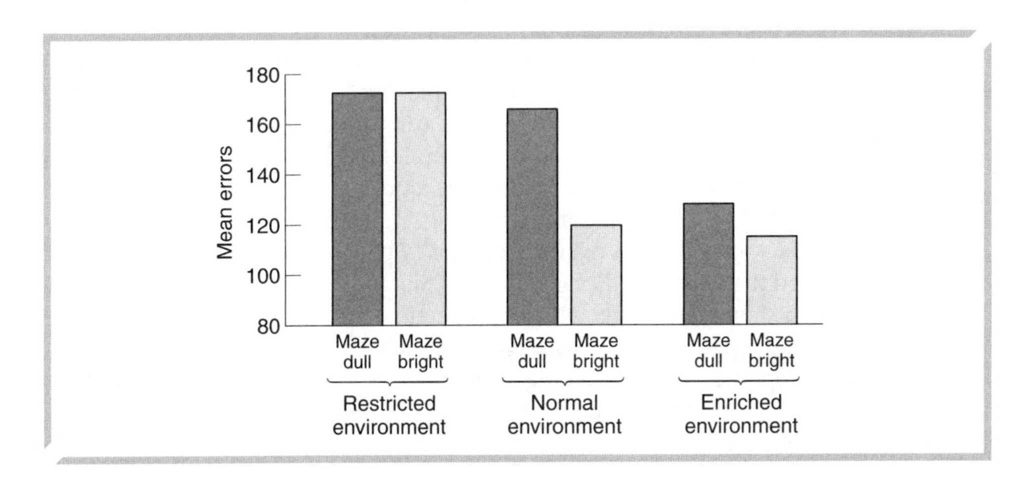

Figure 12.8 The effects of enriched and impoverished rearing on maze-bright and maze-dull rats.

maturity they made almost the same amount of errors as the maze-dull animals reared in the enriched environment (see Figure 12.8). Thus, by changing the environmental conditions in which the rats were reared, the effects of the genetic difference between the bright and dull rats were virtually eliminated. This is an excellent example of how a genetic predisposition can be influenced by environmental conditions.

Alcoholism

Selective breeding for alcohol preference

Artificial selection studies using rats and mice have helped to show that a genetic basis may also exist for alcoholism. For example, one of the earliest studies to show that certain strains of mice exhibit a marked preference for alcohol was reported by McClearn and Rogers in 1959. These researchers allowed mice a choice between drinking from a bottle that contained water and one that contained a 10 per cent alcohol solution, and found that a particular strain of mice (called C57BL) gradually began to drink most of their daily consumption from the alcohol bottle. However, other strains of mice (e.g. DBA/2) strongly avoided drinking alcohol. Indeed, by selectively breeding animals that drink the most alcohol, it is possible to develop strains that show even greater differences in their alcohol consumption. For example, one strain of rats called the P (preference for alcohol) line, have been shown to consume up to five times as much alcohol than the NP (no preference for alcohol) strain (Lumeng *et al.* 1977, 1993). Moreover, not only are the alcohol-preferring rats more tolerant to the effects of alcohol, and show signs of withdrawal when it is no longer available, but they also contain lower levels of dopamine and serotonin in their brains. This finding also supports the role of genes in alcoholism.

As well as preference for alcohol, researchers have also selectively bred animals that exhibit a different sensitivity to alcohol. For example, McClearn and Kakihana (1981) made the assumption that animals that sleep more after drinking alcohol must be more sensitive to its effects compared to those that sleep less. Consequently, these investigators injected mice with alcohol and measured the amount of time they spent sleeping. Following this, they began to mate together the short-sleeping mice – as well as the long-sleeping mice (in fact, they did this over a period of 17 generations). These two lines of mice are now called the Colorado Long and Short Sleep lines and they show considerable differences in their sleep time following injections of alcohol. For example, the long-sleep animals sleep for about an average of 2 hours following an alcohol injection, while the short-sleep mice show an average sleeping time of 10 minutes! In fact, there is no overlap in sleeping times between the short-sleep and long-sleep strains which indicates that a large number of genes are involved in producing this behaviour (Plomin *et al.* 1997).

The genetic basis of alcoholism in humans

In terms of alcohol preference, humans are not fundamentally dissimilar to the rats and mice described above. For example, approximately 90 per cent of the population drink alcohol at least occasionally, yet half of all the alcohol drunk is consumed by only 10 per cent of the population (Cloninger 1987). But why does such wide variability exist in human populations? One obvious explanation is that some people are more genetically predisposed to drinking alcohol than others. In fact, the idea that human drinking behaviour is inherited has a long history. For example, Aristotle declared that drunken women 'bring forth children like themselves' and Plutarch wrote that 'one drunkard begets another' (Goodwin 1980). But, it is also the case that humans have not been selectively bred for their alcohol preference (unlike experimental animals) and it is possible that alcoholism is predominantly a learned behaviour which arises as a result of environmental experience. An understanding of this issue has more than just theoretical significance because it is likely to provide greater insight into alcoholism, and point ways forward to more effective intervention and treatment.

Studies of twins have provided one source of evidence for a genetic factor in alcoholism. One of the largest studies to examine this issue was undertaken in Sweden by Kaij (1960) who compared 1,974 male twin pairs, where one of the pair was known to have an alcohol problem (e.g. they had been convicted of drunkenness or involved in an alcohol-related misdemeanour). The results showed that the concordance rate of identical twins for alcoholism was 54 per cent compared to 28 per cent for the fraternal twins. Although this difference was significant it was not particularly marked (especially when considering that most of the twins had been raised in similar environments) which suggested that learning also had a very important role to play in producing alcohol-related behaviour. A similar conclusion has also been reached in a more recent report (Pickens *et al.* 1991) that examined alcoholism in males and females. The results of this study showed that the concordance rate for identical male twin pairs was 76 per cent compared to 61 per cent for the fraternal twins, and the corresponding figures for female twins were 36 per cent and 25 per cent. Perhaps more importantly, according to these researchers (who undertook further statistical tests on this data), the results indicated that alcoholism was 36 per cent inheritable for men and only 26 per cent inheritable for women. In other words, the environment appeared to exert a strong influence in causing alcohol abuse and this was more marked for females.

Of course, the main problem with twin studies (as mentioned earlier) is that the twins tend to be reared in very similar environments. One way of overcoming this type of problem is to follow children, born to alcoholic parents, who have then been placed (adopted) into new homes by alcoholic or non-alcoholic parents. Thus, any differences in the incidence of alcoholism can be attributed to the environment since all of the children will have a similar genetic heritage (e.g. at least one parent who was alcoholic). One study of this sort was undertaken by Goodwin *et al.* (1973) in Denmark. These investigators followed children of alcoholics who were adopted at, or shortly after, birth and were raised by 'normal' (non-alcoholic) adoptive parents. The results showed that alcoholism was four times more likely in adopted-out sons of alcoholic fathers compared to adopted-out sons of non-alcoholic fathers. In other words, genetic inheritance appeared to exert an important effect on subsequent alcohol-related behaviour.

A Swedish study conducted by Michael Bohman has extended and confirmed these findings. This study was based on a much larger sample of people who were born to single women between 1930 and 1949 and were adopted at an early age (1,125 men and 1,199 women). Furthermore, extensive information about alcohol abuse, mental illness and medical problems was available for most of these adoptees, and for their biological and adoptive parents. Again, the results of this study showed that genetic factors appeared to play an important role in alcoholism. For example, Bohman found that adopted sons of alcoholic parents were three times more likely to become alcoholic than adopted sons of non-alcoholic fathers. In addition, adopted sons of alcoholic mothers were twice as likely to become alcoholic than those born to non-alcoholic mothers (Bohman 1978).

Are there different types of alcoholism?

One criticism that has been made of studies which have attempted to examine the genetic basis of alcoholism is that they assume that there is only one form of the disorder. However, there is considerable evidence to suggest that different types of alcoholism exist. For example, E.M. Jellinek who did much to promote the idea that alcoholism was an illness, and who wrote an highly influential book *The Disease Concept of Alcoholism* (1960), believed there were five different types of alcoholism. In particular, he emphasised the distinction between individuals who had persistent alcohol-seeking behaviours ('an inability to abstain entirely') and others who could abstain from alcohol for long periods but were unable to stop drinking binges once they had started ('loss of control'). Similarly, the American Psychiatric Association has defined two types of alcoholism: one where the person is psychologically dependent on alcohol and engages in intermittent heavy consumption, and one where both physical and psychological dependence occur with increased tolerance and physical withdrawal symptoms resulting when drinking ceases.

One attempt to examine different types of alcoholism from a genetic perspective was undertaken by Robert Cloninger who was invited by Michael Bohman to re-examine the data of his Swedish adoption study described above (e.g. see Bishop and Waldholz 1990). When Cloninger and Bohman started to look at the severity of alcoholism in male adoptees, they found that the more severe the alcoholism (as shown by the number of criminal offences made under the influence of alcohol intoxication), the greater the chance that the adoptee had an alcoholic parent. However, as they examined this relationship further, Cloninger and Bohman began to realise that a number of other features also distinguished 'severe' alcoholics from those who had more moderate problems. In fact, the data showed two completely different types of alcoholism, each with its own distinguishing personality characteristics and types of genetic inheritance. In short, the less severe form was associated with binge drinking (type 1), while the more severe form of alcoholic behaviour was characterised by heavy and persistent drinking (type 2).

The most common form of alcoholism according to Cloninger is type 1. This has a late onset (it normally occurs after the age of 25) and is found in both males and females. Although individuals with this form of alcoholism may not drink for long periods of time, once they start they cannot control or stop their drinking behaviour. In terms of personality they also tend to be anxious, inhibited, cautious, shy and emotionally sensitive. This form of alcoholism tends to be relatively mild (it often goes untreated), and it appears to require both a genetic predisposition (there is often an alcoholic parent) and a triggering influence in the environment. In short, it is not strongly genetic and depends heavily on environmental factors. In contrast, type 2 alcoholism is much more severe. It is associated with persistent drinking along with antisocial tendencies that include a lifelong history of fighting, lying, impulsiveness and lack of remorse for social acts. Moreover, it is only found in males and typically occurs before the age of 25 years. It also appears to be strongly genetic, with the environment playing little part in its expression. For example, the risk of alcoholism in these adoptees is nine times that of sons of all other fathers. Moreover, drinking and antisocial behaviour emerged in young adulthood – regardless of the type of environment in which the adoptee is reared.

It remains to be seen whether Cloninger's classification will stand the test of time. The theory has not received universal support and it appears that some alcoholics do not fit neatly into either category. Nevertheless, there has also been support for certain aspects of the theory (e.g. Hesselbrock 1985), and there is little doubt that this work represents a valuable contribution to our understanding of the interaction between genetics and environment.

Is there a gene for alcoholism?

Clearly, if alcoholism has a genetic basis then it should be possible to identify the individual genes that contribute to this behaviour. Several years ago a group of researchers led by Kenneth Blum generated considerable excitement when they claimed to have discovered such a gene (Blum *et al.* 1990). These investigators studied the brains of 70 deceased individuals, half of whom had been alcoholics. A sample of frontal cortex was

Table 12.2 Characteristics of type 1 and type 2 alcoholism as formulated by Cloninger

Type 1 ('binge type')
Has a late onset (typically after the age of 25) and is characterised by binges or loss of control (once the person starts they can't stop) punctuated by periods of abstinence
The personality is often characterised by anxiety, shyness and inhibition. In addition, there may be guilt and fear over their dependence leading to depression
Can occur in both males and females and does not appear to have a strong genetic basis
Has been suggested that these persons are physiologically over-aroused and that alcohol serves as a depressant which acts to decrease anxiety and arousal
Type 2 ('persistent type')
Has an early onset (before the age of 25) and is characterised by persistent moderate to heavy drinking without periods of abstinence
The personality is generally characterised by impulsiveness and lack of anxiety. In addition, there is often antisocial behaviour with evidence of other forms of drug taking and/or criminality
Occurs predominantly in males and appears to be strongly inherited from the father
Has been suggested that these persons are physiologically under-aroused and that alcohol serves as a stimulant which acts to increase arousal

taken from each cadaver and tested against nine DNA probes, each of which had been proposed as a possible alcoholism gene from previous research. Out of these nine probes, only one corresponded to DNA found in the brain tissue, and this matched the gene that was responsible for producing the dopamine D-2 receptor. Moreover, this gene (which is located on chromosome 11) occurs in two different forms (alleles). The majority of us have a form known as the A-2 allele, but some have the less common A-1 version, and it was the A-1 allele that was found in the tissue taken from the alcoholics' brains. In fact, this gene was present in 69 per cent of the alcoholics' brains, but absent in 80 per cent of the non-alcoholics.

The significance of this finding was immediately obvious, especially in light of the fact that dopaminergic systems of the brain have been shown to play an important role in reinforcement and in the pleasurable effects of such drugs as cocaine, nicotine, alcohol and heroin (see Chapter 11). Indeed, Blum and his colleagues proposed that the A-2 allele might help to cause alcoholism by directing the manufacture of defective dopamine receptors on the surface of brain cells. This would then result in these cells not being able to get enough dopamine, thereby causing craving for substances (such as alcohol) that helped to stimulate the release of this neurotransmitter (Blum *et al.* 1991). The discovery of the A-1 gene was also important from another perspective as it raised the possibility that a test could be developed to screen for alcoholism in the general population.

Unfortunately, the initial excitement has been tempered by evidence showing that the A-1 allele is also found in the brains of individuals suffering from a wide range of mental problems including **attentional deficit disorder**, **autism** and **Tourette's syndrome** (Comings *et al.* 1991). Furthermore, it appears that the original estimate of the A-1 allele frequency reported by Blum *et al.* (1990) may have been rather high. For example, Noble (1993) has reviewed nine studies that have compared a total of 491 alcoholics with a total of 495 controls, and has shown that the A-1 allele existed in 43 per cent of the alcoholics' brains and in 25.7 per cent of control subjects. Although these are positive findings, the fact that the A-1 allele is not found in the majority of alcoholics clearly implies that it is not the primary cause of alcoholism (in fact, even in alcoholics that are judged as 'severe' the frequency of the A-1 allele only increases to 56 per cent).

Serotonin and alcoholism

Another neurotransmitter (and presumably a different genetic influence) to be implicated in alcoholism is serotonin. One of the first studies to suggest this link was provided by Takahashi *et al.* (1974) who examined 30 alcoholics and found that those with the most severe withdrawal symptoms had lower levels of **5-HIAA** (a metabolite of serotonin) in their cerebrospinal fluid (CSF). This finding was extended by Ballenger *et al.* (1979) who also measured 5-HIAA levels, but this time either within 48 hours of the last drink or after 4 weeks of supervised abstinence. Unexpectedly, the results showed that the 5-HIAA levels were relatively normal at 48 hours, but were significantly depressed at 4 weeks. This finding suggested that some types of alcoholic (especially those with severe withdrawal symptoms) had naturally low levels of serotonin, which became elevated when they consumed alcohol. And, the obvious implication was that a deficit in serotonin might be responsible for driving the alcoholic to seek and consume alcohol in order to restore the levels of this neurotransmitter in the brain.

Since this study, a growing literature has confirmed that serotonergic abnormalities exist in some alcoholics – particularly those with male-limited (or type 2) alcoholism (Roy *et al.* 1987). However, this relationship is not as straightforward as it first appears because low CSF levels of 5-HIAA have also been found to be linked with a variety of impulsive behaviours including aggression, animal torture, suicide and arson. In addition, low levels of 5-HIAA are also associated with depression and suicide (especially that which is violent and impulsive in nature). Thus, most researchers now believe that low levels of 5-HIAA are more closely linked with impulsiveness and aggression than with alcoholism *per se*. This is also supported by evidence showing that many alcoholics have normal or even high levels of 5-HIAA (Roy and Linnoila 1989). Despite this, it probably remains that low serotonergic function is a contributory factor for alcoholism in at least some individuals.

If serotonin is involved in the craving for alcohol then one would also expect to find this relationship in animals. Indeed, there is considerable evidence to support this supposition. For example, low levels of 5-HIAA in rats are associated with an enhanced preference for alcohol, whereas drug-induced stimulation of serotonergic systems (e.g. by selective serotonergic uptake inhibitors) decreases alcohol consumption (Sellars *et al.* 1992). Moreover, reduced alcohol intake can also be induced by injections of serotonergic agonists (such as buspirone) into the nucleus accumbens. Importantly, these findings also imply that serotonergic drugs may have uses for treating alcoholism in humans and, in general, this has shown to be the case with drugs such as **fluoxetine** (Prozac) being well tolerated by alcoholics and reducing drinking in some individuals. Unfortunately, the magnitude of the decrease is not particularly marked. For example, in heavy drinkers, 60 mg of fluoxetine per day (that is, three times the dose generally used to treat depression) decreased daily mean alcohol intake from 8.7 drinks during a baseline period to 6.9 drinks during a 4-week trial (Kranzler and Anton 1994). And, in individuals who have been diagnosed as alcoholics the effectiveness of these drugs is even less marked. Nonetheless, such drugs are likely to play an increasingly important role in the treatment of alcoholism, especially if accompanying psychotherapy (Gallant 1993).

Recombinant DNA and genetic engineering

So far we have looked at methods which, in one way or another, have been used to discover genes (or genetic influences) that help determine behaviour. However, in recent years more direct ways of examining the function of genes have been developed. One technique is that of genetic engineering, which involves taking genes from one organism, cloning them (i.e. making multiple copies) and implanting them into another. In fact, genetic engineering is already taking place on a large scale. It is being used in farming to increase crop yields and to make plants more resistant to disease. And, animals have been given genetically engineered products to make them grow bigger, or to increase meat and milk yields. In addition, genetically engineered cells have been commercially used to mass-produce hormones, antibodies and vaccines, with a large-scale biotechnology industry developing to take advantage of these developments. Genetically engineered cells have even been introduced into human beings to correct certain genetic diseases.

The beginning of genetic engineering, or more accurately the start of DNA recombinant technology (recombinant DNA is that which is constructed outside the living cell by splicing two or more pieces of DNA from different sources to provide a novel combination of genes not normally found in nature) took place in the late 1960s when scientists discovered a class of enzymes (called **restriction enzymes**) that severed DNA at a specific base sequence and with great precision. These enzymes were first found in bacteria who used them to disable the DNA of invading viruses – but researchers soon realised that they could also be used in the laboratory as 'molecular scissors' to cut DNA. In short, DNA could be extracted from a living organism, isolated, put into a test tube with restriction enzymes and, a little later, lots of DNA fragments would be obtained that were all neatly snipped at the same place. In fact, within a decade of their discovery, geneticists had discovered over 300 enzymes taken from a variety of bacteria that enabled them to cut DNA at many different places. For instance, a restriction enzyme might cut through a specific genetic sequence such as CCGTA by always severing it between the G and the T.

By themselves, lots of DNA snippets floating around in a test tube have little use. However, a couple of years after the first restriction enzymes were found (*circa* 1969) geneticists also discovered that some of these enzymes also produced DNA fragments that had so-called 'sticky ends' which allowed the snippets of DNA to be joined together. Incredibly, for this to occur, the DNA didn't even have to come from the same genome; that is, it was possible to join bits of DNA together from different organisms – or, in effect, to implant new genes into foreign DNA. But, again, this recombination was taking place *in vitro* – that is, outside the cell (or in the confines of the test tube). However, in 1972 this changed when a way of introducing new DNA into living cells was discovered. This was first achieved by Paul Berg who managed to take genes from a bacterium and implant them into the DNA of a virus. A year later came an even more astonishing feat. This time, Herbert Boyer and Stanley Cohen took DNA from a toad and placed it inside the DNA of a bacterium. In fact, every time the bacteria divided, the 'foreign' DNA was also copied and it passed into the new bacteria. Thus, the new foreign gene had not only been incorporated into a new host, but it was also there to stay for all future generations.

The technique of artificially inserting genes into rapidly dividing organisms (such as bacteria) was to have a huge impact on research because, for the first time, it allowed a means of cloning large numbers of identical genes. Thus, bacteria could be likened to factories that were able to make endless copies of their implanted genes. Indeed, because bacteria are able to divide every 20 minutes, a single gene placed into a bacterial host can be multiplied many times over in a short space of time (remarkably, if given adequate nutrition, bacteria could in theory provide a mass greater than that of our planet in less than 2 days!). Thus, bacteria provided the assembly lines by which

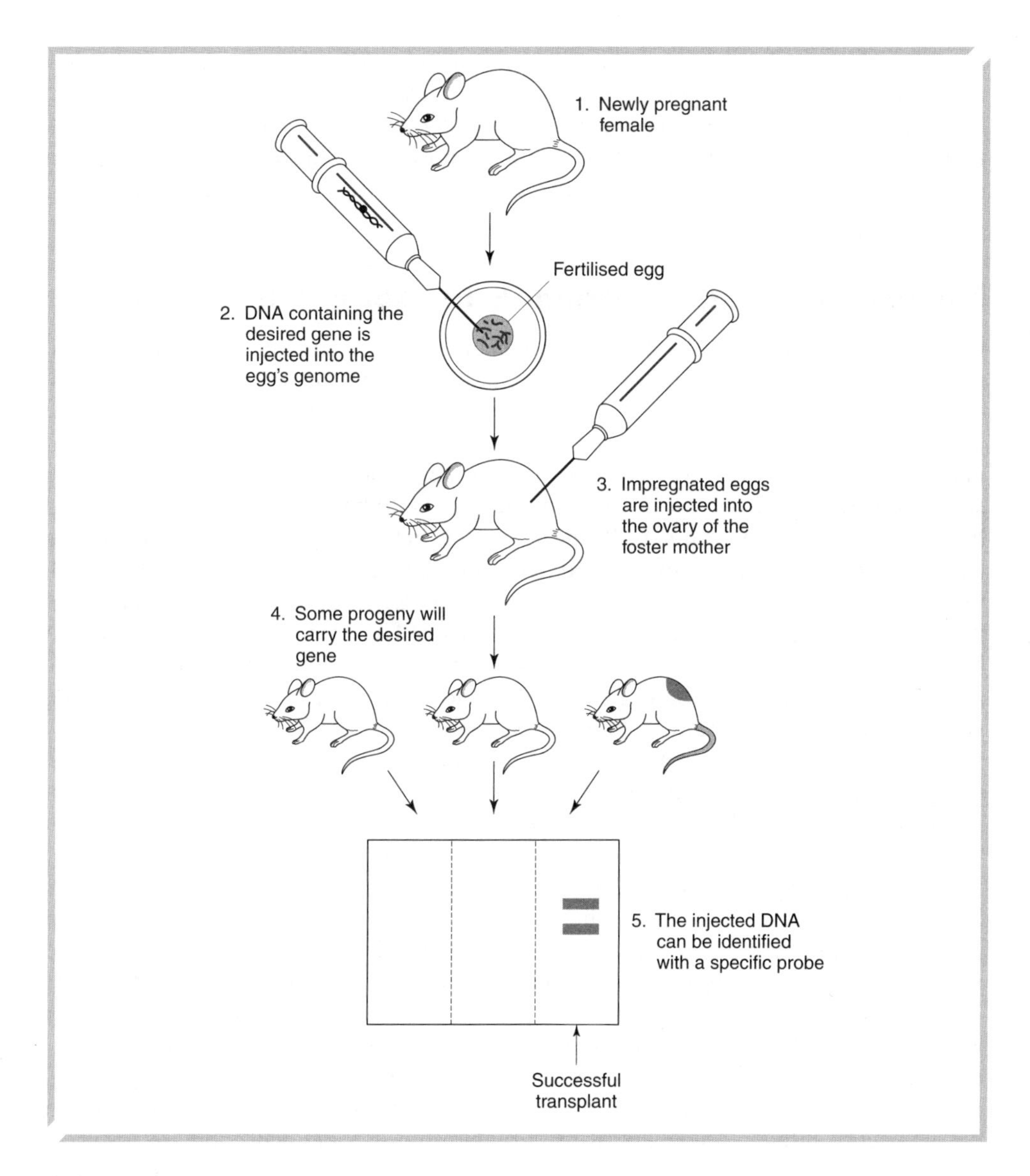

Figure 12.9 The production of transgenic animals.

recombinant genes could be made. This new technique revolutionised the study of molecular biology because for the first time it allowed large amounts of new DNA to be produced. Not only did this enable investigators to work out with relative ease the sequences of bases making up genes (which was important because it helped them predict the type of protein it made), but it also allowed them to place these cloned genes back into various organisms to see what their proteins (or genes) might do. For example, this can be done by injecting the purified DNA into the egg (just after fertilisation) using a very fine pipette under direct vision. Consequently, every cell in the body that develops from this embryonic egg will then carry the new gene. Organisms that have been manipulated in this way are known as **transgenic animals** and, in particular, have been used extensively to examine a wide range of genetic disorders (see Figure 12.9).

The use of transgenic animals to examine behaviour

One way in which recombinant DNA has been used to examine behaviour is in the production of transgenic animals that have had a certain gene 'knocked out' – that is, completely inactivated. The logic of this approach is compelling. For example, if a gene was taken away that caused a mouse to have a malformed cerebellum, then one would know that this gene was involved in neural cerebellar development. And because we share over 99 per cent of our genes with mice, it would be likely that this gene would have a similar function in humans (Capecchi 1994). In theory, producing **knockout mice** (the most common type of animal used in this procedure) is relatively straightforward. One first implants a base sequence into the developing egg (or early embryo) that aligns itself next to the gene in question and inactivates it. The animals are then reared and bred together to produce inbred strains where the knocked-out genes become homozygous. In fact, by using this approach it is possible to engineer transgenic mice carrying virtually any desired alteration of the genome (Capecchi 1994).

Knockout mice have recently been used to help explain why drugs such as cocaine and amphetamine cause addiction. For example, Giros *et al.* (1996) have produced a strain of mice in which the gene responsible for the uptake of dopamine has been 'knocked out' (the uptake process normally acts to remove excess dopamine from the synapse; see Chapter 11). Not only did this manipulation cause the mice to be extremely hyperactive, but it was also found that they were unaffected by the administration of cocaine and amphetamine – a finding which suggested that these two drugs produce their main effects by acting on this particular 'transporter' protein. Also of great interest was the discovery that these mice actually produce less dopamine than normal. In other words, the knockout of the dopamine uptake protein results in a general down-regulation of the entire dopamine system. These findings may also have practical relevance. For example, the use of these knockout mice may help pharmacologists to develop more effective blockers of the uptake pump (which will increase levels of dopamine) that can be used to treat illnesses such as Parkinson's disease. Alternatively, it may be possible to design drugs that stop cocaine and amphetamine affecting the transporter protein, thus providing an effective treatment for stimulant abuse.

Knockout mice have also been used to examine alcohol-related behaviour. For example, it has been shown that mutant mice lacking the serotonergic 1B receptor (5-HT_{1B}) drink twice as much alcohol as normal, and will voluntarily ingest solutions containing up to 20 per cent alcohol. In addition, they are less sensitive to the effects of alcohol as measured by ataxia (Crabbe *et al.* 1996). Interestingly, mice lacking the 5-HT_{1B} receptor also show a marked increase in aggressive behaviour (Sandou *et al.*

1994) which indicates that this receptor may be particularly linked with type 2 alcoholism. Another type of gene, this time linked with increased alcohol sensitivity, has been reported by Miyakawa *et al.* (1997). These researchers examined mice that were mutant for a gene which produces an enzyme called Fyn kinase – an enzyme that had previously been shown to influence learning and memory by its effect on influencing neuronal excitability. However, Miyakawa and colleagues found that when this enzyme was missing in mutant mice they were also much more sensitive to the effects of alcohol (e.g. when injected with a high dose they would take twice as long to right themselves compared to normal). These findings lend further support to the idea that a wide range of genes underlies alcohol-related behaviour, and there is little doubt that many more genes will be found in the future using similar knockout mice and DNA recombinant technology.

Self-test questions

1. What two main concepts is Darwin's theory of natural selection based on?
2. Briefly describe how Mendel's work has contributed to our understanding of genetic inheritance.
3. What is an allele?
4. What is the difference between a homozygous and heterozygous gene combination?
5. Describe the structure of the DNA molecule.
6. What is the difference between a gene and a codon?
7. How many types of RNA are there? How do they combine to make a protein?
8. Why are proteins important?
9. If both parents carry the gene for phenylketonuria, what are the chances of the offspring inheriting the disorder?
10. What is the difference between a monozygotic and dizygotic twin? Why are comparisons of these twins important in genetic research?
11. Why are inbred strains of animals important in genetic research?
12. Describe how selective breeding experiments have been used in alcohol research.
13. Describe Cloninger's two main types of alcoholic.
14. What is the A-1 allele?
15. How has serotonin been implicated in alcoholism?
16. What is recombinant DNA?
17. Briefly describe some of the ways transgenic animals have been used in behavioural research.

Key terms

Alcoholism (p.385)
Alleles (p.366)
Amino acids (p.373)
Attentional deficit disorder (p.390)
Autism (p.390)
Autosomal dominant inheritance (p.377)
Bases (p.371)
Chromosomes (p.370)

Codons (p.373)
Concordance (p.380)
Deoxyribonucleic acid (DNA) (p.371)
Dizygotic twins (p.380)
Dominant gene (p.369)
Fluoxetine (p.391)
Gametes (p.370)
Genetic engineering (p.391)
Heterozygous genes (p.369)
5-HIAA (p.390)
Homozygous genes (p.369)
Human genome project (p.375)
Huntington's disease (p.377)
Inbreeding (p.383)
Knockout mice (p.393)
Messenger RNA (mRNA) (p.374)
Monozygotic twins (p.380)
Natural selection (p.366)
Phenylketonuria (p.378)
Proteins (p.373)
Recessive gene (p.369)
Recombinant DNA (p.391)
Restriction enzymes (p.392)
Ribonucleic acid (RNA) (p.374)
Ribosomal RNA (rRNA) (p.374)
Ribosome (p.374)
Selective breeding (p.384)
Tourette's syndrome (p.390)
Transfer RNA (tRNA) (p.374)
Transgenic animals (p.393)

References

Ballenger, J. C. *et al.* (1979) Alcohol and central serotonin metabolism in man. *Archives of General Psychiatry*, **36**, 224–7.

Bishop, J. E. and Waldholz, M. (1990) *Genome.* New York: Simon & Schuster.

Blum, K. *et al.* (1990) Allele association of human dopamine D2 receptor gene in alcoholism. *Journal of American Medical Association*, **263**, 2055–60.

Blum, K. *et al.* (1991) Association of the A1 allele of the D2 dopamine receptor gene with severe alcoholism. *Alcohol*, **8**, 409–16.

Bohman, M. (1978) Some genetic aspects of alcoholism and criminality. *Archives of General Psychiatry*, **35**, 269–76.

Bouchard, T. J. Jr (1994) Genes, environment and personality. *Science*, **264**, 1700–1.

Bouchard, T. J. Jr *et al.* (1990) Sources of human psychological differences: The Minnesota study of twins reared apart. *Science*, **250**, 223–8.

Capecchi, M. R. (1994) Targeted gene replacement. *Scientific American*, March, 52–9.

Cloninger, C. R. (1987) Neurogenetic adaptive mechanisms in alcoholism. *Science*, **236**, 410–16.

Comings, D. E. *et al.* (1991) Dopamine D2 receptor locus as a modifying gene in neuropsychiatric disorders. *Journal of the American Medical Association*, Oct., 1793–1800.

Cooper, R. M. and Zubek, J. P. (1958) Effects of enriched and restricted early environments on the learning ability of bright and dull rats. *Canadian Journal of Psychology*, **12**, 159–64.

Crabbe, J. C. *et al.* (1996) Elevated alcohol consumption in null mutant mice lacking 5-HT_{1B} serotonin receptors. *Nature Genetics*, **14**, 98–101.

Gallant, D. (1993) Amethystic agents and adjunct behavioral therapy and psychotherapy. *Alcoholism: Clinical and Experimental Research*, **17**, 197–8.

Giros, B. *et al.* (1996) Hyperlocomotion and indifference to cocaine and amphetamine in mice lacking the dopamine receptor. *Nature*, **379**, 606–12.

Goodwin, D. W. (1980) Genetic factors in alcoholism. In Mello, N. K. (ed.) *Advances in Substance Abuse*, vol. 1. Greenwich: JAL Press.

Goodwin, D.W. *et al.* (1973) Alcohol problems in adoptees raised apart from alcoholic biologic parents. *Archives of General Psychiatry*, **28**, 238–43.

Gottesman, I. I. (1991) *Schizophrenia Genesis.* New York: Freeman.

Gusella, J. F. *et al.* (1983) A polymorphic DNA marker genetically linked to Huntington's disease. *Nature*, **306**, 234–8.

Hay, D. A. (1985) *Essentials of Behaviour Genetics.* Melbourne: Blackwell.

Hesselbrock, M. N. (1995) Genetic determinants of alcoholic subtypes. In Begleter, H. and Kissin, B. (eds) *The Genetics of Alcoholism.* Oxford: Oxford University Press.

Jellinek, E. M. (1960) *The Disease Concept of Alcoholism.* New Haven, CT: Hillhouse.

Kaij, L. (1960) *Studies on the Etiology and Sequals of Abuse of Alcohol.* University of Lund: Department of Psychiatry.

Lumeng, L. *et al.* (1977) New strains of rats with alcohol preference and non-preference. In Thurman, J. R. *et al.* (eds) *Alcohol and Aldehyde Metabolizing Systems.* New York: Academic Press.

Lumeng, L. *et al.* (1993) Genetic influences on alcohol preference in animals. In Begleter, H. and Kissin, B. (eds) *The Genetics of Alcoholism.* Oxford: Oxford University Press.

Kranzler, H. R. and Anton, R. F. (1994) *Journal of Consulting and Clinical Psychology*, **62**, 1116–26.

MacDonald, M. E. *et al.* (1993) A novel gene containing a trinucleotide repeat that is expanded and unstable on Huntington's disease chromosomes. *Cell*, **72**, 971–83.

McClearn, G. E. and Kakihana, R. (1981) Selective breeding for ethanol sensitivity: SS and LS mice. In McClearn, G. E. *et al.* (eds) *The Development of Animal Models as Pharmacogenetic Tools.* Washington: NIAAA Monograph.

McClearn, G. E. and Rodgers, D. A. (1959) Differences in alcohol preference among inbred strains of mice. *Quarterly Journal of Studies on Alcohol*, **52**, 62–7.

Miyakawa, T. *et al.* (1997) Fyn-kinase as a determinant of ethanol sensitivity: Relation to NMDA-receptor function. *Science*, **278**, 698–701.

Noble, E. P. (1993) The D2 dopamine receptor gene: A review of association studies in alcoholism. *Behavioral Genetics*, **23**, 119–29.

Pearl, R. and Parker, S. L. (1922) Experimental studies on the duration of life. II. Hereditary differences in duration of life in live-breed strains of Drosophila. *American Naturalist*, **56**, 5–19.

Pickens, R. W. *et al.* (1991) Heterogeneity in the inheritance of alcoholism: A study of male and female twins. *Archives of General Psychiatry*, **48**, 19–28.

Pinel, J. P. J. (1997) *Biopsychology* (3rd edn). Boston: Allyn & Bacon.

Plomin, R. *et al.* (1997) *Behavioral Genetics* (3rd edn). New York: Freeman.

Roberts, L. (1993) Taking stock of the genome project. *Science*, **262**, 20–2.

Roy, A. and Linnoila, M. (1989) CSF studies on alcoholism and related disorders. *Progress in Neuropsychopharmacology and Biological Psychiatry*, **13**, 505–11.

Roy, A. *et al.* (1987) Serotonin and alcoholism. *Substance Abuse*, **8**, 21–7.
Sandou, F. *et al.* (1994) Enhanced aggressive behaviour in mice lacking 5-HT_{1B} receptor. *Science*, **265**, 1875–8.
Sellars, E. M. *et al.* (1992) 5-HT and alcohol abuse. *Trends in Pharmacological Sciences*, **13**, 69–75.
Singer, S. (1985) *Human Genetics.* New York: Freeman.
Steen, R. G. (1996) *DNA and Destiny: Nature and Nurture in Human Behaviour.* New York: Plenum Press.
Takahashi, S. *et al.* (1974) CSF monoamine metabolites in alcoholism: A comparative study with depression. *Psychiatria Neurologica Japan*, **28**, 347–54.
Tryon, R. C. (1940) Genetic differences in maze-learning ability in rats. *Yearbook of the National Society of Studies in Education*, **39** (1), 111–19.

FURTHER READING

Blum, K. and Payne, J. E. (1991) *Alcohol and the Addictive Brain*. New York: The Free Press.
Bodner, W. and McKie, R. (1994) *The Book of Man*. London: Abacus.
Gershon, E.S. and Cloninger, C. R. (1994) *New Genetic Approaches to Mental Disorders.* Washington, DC: American Psychiatric Press.
Holden, C. (1994) A cautionary genetic tale. The sobering story of D_2. *Science*, **264**, 1696–7.
Rush, A. J. *et al.* (1991) Neurological basis for psychiatric disorders. In Rosenberg, R. N. (ed.) *Comprehensive Neurology.* New York: Raven Press.

Multiple choice questions

1. The term 'survival of the fittest' was coined by:

(a) Charles Darwin
(b) Herbert Spencer
(c) Gregor Mendel
(d) William James

2. When Mendel crossed true-breeding 'dominant' tall pea plants with true-breeding 'recessive' dwarf plants the F1 (first generation) always produced:

(a) all tall plants
(b) all dwarf plants
(c) three tall plants for every one dwarf plant
(d) plants that were intermediate in size

3. When a pea plant contains two different genes (alleles) for height it is said to be a _______________ combination.

(a) homozygous
(b) heterozygous

(c) recessive
(d) dominant

4. Each sperm and each egg contains:

(a) the full set of 23 paired chromosomes
(b) different things (sperm contains chromosomes and the egg contains DNA)
(c) 23 individual chromosomes
(d) no chromosomes (they are formed after fertilisation)

5. Which of the following is not a base in DNA?

(a) adenine (A)
(b) guanine (G)
(c) cytosine (C)
(d) ribose (R)

6. A codon (specific 3 base sequences of DNA) is a code for making:

(a) amino acids
(b) proteins
(c) carbohydrates
(d) RNA

7. Which of the following is not a legitimate form of RNA?

(a) messenger
(b) transfer
(c) merger
(d) ribosomal

8. The genetic fault in Huntington's disease is due to:

(a) an extra copy of a gene on chromosome 4
(b) a gene which has triple repeats of the bases CAG
(c) a missing gene located on chromosome 4
(d) none of the above – the gene has not yet been discovered (although it is known to reside on chromosome 4)

9. If *one* parent carries the gene for Huntington's disease, what are the chances of them producing a child with this disorder?

(a) 100 per cent
(b) 99.9 per cent
(c) 50 per cent
(d) 25 per cent

10. If *both* parents carry the gene for phenylketonuria, what are the chances of them producing a child with this disorder?

(a) 25 per cent
(b) 50 per cent
(c) 75 per cent
(d) 100 per cent

11. Inbreeding is an important technique in genetic analysis because:

(a) it increases the chances of producing homozygous alleles
(b) it results in members of the inbred strain becoming genetically similar
(c) an almost 'true' inbred strain can be produced after 20 successive brother–sister matings
(d) all of the above

12. Cooper and Zubek (1958) found that they could impair the relative performance of maze-bright rats by:

(a) feeding them with diets that were deficient in acetylcholine
(b) testing them in a maze that was different to the one used to test previous generations
(c) not testing them until they had reached maturity
(d) rearing them in an impoverished environment

13. McClearn and Kakihana (1981) selectively bred different strains of rats that varied in their sensitivity to alcohol by measuring:

(a) alcohol preference when given the choice of two drinking bottles
(b) sleeping duration
(c) ataxia (motor co-ordination)
(d) body temperature

14. According to Robert Cloninger, type 1 alcoholism is:

(a) characterised by binge drinking
(b) often found in individuals who are anxious and emotionally sensitive
(c) found in both males and females
(d) all of the above

15. The discovery of the A-1 allele in the brains of alcoholics by Blum *et al.* (1990) implicated ____________ receptors in the aetiology of alcoholism:

(a) noradrenaline
(b) serotonin
(c) dopamine
(d) acetylcholine

16. Ballenger *et al.* (1979) found depressed levels of the serotonergic metabolite 5-HIAA in the CSF of alcoholics who had just stopped drinking:

(a) at both 48 hours and 4 weeks
(b) only at 48 hours
(c) only at 4 weeks
(d) none of the above

17. In animal studies, reduced alcohol intake can be produced by injections of serotonergic agonists (such as buspirone) into the:

(a) nucleus accumbens
(b) hypothalamus
(c) hippocampus
(d) frontal cortex

18. Restriction enzymes can be used to:

(a) stop the transcription of DNA into mRNA
(b) 'snip' DNA at certain known base sequences
(c) join up bits of DNA
(d) 'snip' amino acids at certain known codons

19. A strain of mice that have the gene for their dopamine uptake transporter 'knocked out' as shown by Giros *et al.* (1996):

(a) are very sensitive to the effects of amphetamine and cocaine
(b) show a marked up-regulation of their dopaminergic systems
(c) show increased hyperactivity
(d) all of the above

20. Mice that have had the gene for the serotonergic 5-HT$_{1B}$ 'knocked out':

(a) are more aggressive
(b) drink twice as much alcohol as normal
(c) are insensitive to the effects of alcohol
(d) (a) and (b) above

ANSWERS TO MULTIPLE CHOICE QUESTIONS

	Ch1	Ch2	Ch3	Ch4	Ch5	Ch6	Ch7	Ch8	Ch9	Ch10	Ch11	Ch12
1	d	c	c	b	a	c	d	c	b	d	c	b
2	d	b	d	c	c	c	a	a	d	c	b	a
3	b	a	d	d	d	b	d	d	b	c	c	b
4	b	a	c	a	a	c	a	d	a	a	a	c
5	c	b	a	d	c	b	d	b	c	c	b	d
6	a	d	a	a	d	d	a	d	d	b	d	a
7	d	d	a	d	a	a	c	c	c	c	b	c
8	b	c	c	c	c	a	b	a	b	d	c	b
9	b	c	d	a	d	c	d	c	b	d	d	c
10	b	c	b	b	b	d	c	a	c	a	d	a
11	d	a	c	d	d	d	c	d	c	d	b	d
12	d	c	d	c	d	d	d	a	d	b	a	d
13	b	b	c	d	b	b	c	b	b	a	d	b
14	c	b	d	b	c	a	a	c	c	d	c	d
15	a	d	b	a	b	d	c	a	d	b	b	c
16	d	d	c	d	c	c	c	b	d	a	a	c
17	a	a	b	a	c	c	d	c	b	b	a	a
18	b	c	d	d	d	d	c	b	c	d	c	b
19	a	a	b	c	d	b	b	b	b	d	b	c
20	d	a	c	a	c	c	c	a	b	b	d	d

AUTHOR INDEX

SUBJECT INDEX